PHENOMENOLOGY

Joseph J. Kockelmans was born in The Netherlands in 1923. After receiving his Ph.D. in 1952 he studied mathematics and physics for five years, followed by three years of advanced study in contemporary philosophy. Dr. Kockelmans was professor of philosophy at the Agricultural University of Wageningen (The Netherlands) before coming to the United States. He has since taught philosophy at the New School for Social Research and is currently teaching at the University of Pittsburgh.

Dr. Kockelmans has published two books and several articles in the realm of philosophy of science; one of the books, a study on the special theory of relativity, was awarded the gold medal of *Teylers Tweede Genootschap* in 1956. His most recent publications are in the area of contemporary continental European philosophy and include, in addition to many articles, two books on Heidegger's philosophy, one on Husserl's philosophy, and one on Husserl's phenomenological psychology.

PHENOMENOLOGY

The Philosophy of Edmund Husserl
and Its Interpretation

EDITED BY

JOSEPH J. KOCKELMANS

Anchor Books
DOUBLEDAY & COMPANY, INC.
Garden City, New York

THE ANCHOR BOOKS EDITION
IS THE FIRST PUBLICATION OF
PHENOMENOLOGY
THE PHILOSOPHY OF EDMUND HUSSERL
AND ITS INTERPRETATION
ANCHOR BOOKS EDITION: 1967

LIBRARY OF CONGRESS CATALOG CARD NUMBER 67–21704
COPYRIGHT © 1967 BY JOSEPH J. KOCKELMANS
ALL RIGHTS RESERVED
PRINTED IN THE UNITED STATES OF AMERICA

PREFACE

What the reader is about to encounter in the pages of this anthology is not, as it might seem initially, a collection of essays written by various phenomenologists on a variety of typically phenomenological topics. Instead, the material that appears here was chosen for the contribution it could make toward the answering of one vital question: What is phenomenology? Some may wonder if indeed an entire anthology is required to provide an answer to what appears a not-too-difficult question, especially since some authors have already undertaken with considerable success the task of exploring and explaining the work of Edmund Husserl and the phenomenological movement for which he is radically responsible. However, the truth is that despite the existence of some excellent attempts to delineate just what phenomenology is, and in just what realms of investigation its application has proved fruitful, many all-important questions have remained unanswered. And without these answers, phenomenology's full meaning continues to be elusive.

What phenomenology is, and in what areas of inquiry it has exercised an important influence, are questions so intricate and comprehensive in nature that no one-volume anthology such as this can provide the final word on the subject. However, the present collection can make a substantial contribution toward this end, especially by its deliberate one-sidedness: the editor has, in the main, limited the discussion to papers that deal with Husserl's conception of phenomenology as he developed it between 1907 and 1931 and as he explained it in his own major publications, *Ideas, Formal and Transcendental Logic,* and *Cartesian Meditations.* To compensate, minimally, for this one-sidedness, a few selections are included that deal with some of the major ideas of Husserl's *Logical Investigations* (1900–1), and some of the important topics that came to the fore in his later philosophy and are substantially contained in manuscripts written between 1925 and 1938.

To illustrate the further development of Husserl's conception of phenomenology, I have elected to present here the insights of representatives of the so-called existential-phenomenological movement. Because of its actual influence on the contemporary scene, the ideas of that movement are in my opinion of greater importance than those of Scheler, Pfänder, Geiger, Ingarden, and Conrad-Martius, nonetheless important phenomenologists also. In the area of French existential phenomenology, the choices have been limited to the work of the two leading phenomenologists, Sartre and Merleau-Ponty, thereby excluding the contributions to phenomenology of Marcel, Ricoeur, and Levinas, among others. In an attempt to render the views of Sartre and Merleau-Ponty more understandable, I have included selections dealing with Heidegger's position within the phenomenological movement as a whole, but in doing so have once again chosen only what seemed absolutely necessary to achieve the goal of the anthology. For simplicity's sake, I have grouped these selections under the heading "existential-phenomenology," although such a label is not adequate insofar as Heidegger's philosophy as a whole is concerned. Lastly, I have included certain selections on Heidegger's hermeneutic phenomenology because his monumental work *Being and Time,* as well as his mostly implicit criticism of Husserl's phenomenology, has so deeply influenced the points of view adopted by Sartre and Merleau-Ponty.

As a final word in this brief attempt to provide a frame of reference for approaching the anthology, the reader may wish to know that in dealing with the adaptation of phenomenology to realms of investigation outside philosophy, I have not mentioned Husserl's studies on mathematics, logic, and the physical sciences, nor Becker's and Geiger's phenomenological inquiries in the field of mathematics, nor my own investigations concerning the relationship between phenomenology and physical science, nor Buytendijk's contribution to the biological sciences, nor, finally, the very important studies on psychiatry and on religion made by such eminent scholars as Jaspers, Minkowski, Binswanger, Straus, Boss, Scheler, and Tillich. I have preferred to focus attention upon the sciences of man in general, choosing psychology in particular as a paradigm.

It goes without saying that many outstanding studies which would have been appropriate have not been included. In some instances length was the prohibitive factor; in others it was not possible to secure permission for reprint. Nevertheless, I believe that this anthology, intended as a first introduction to the effort to answer the question, what is phenomenology?, gives a clear idea of what is going on within the most important trends of the phenomenological movement.

The material contained in this anthology was drawn from a wide variety of sources so that the reader will find a certain variety in spelling and style, as well as in the quotation of literature in the footnotes. In view of the copyrights of the material used I have reprinted each selection exactly and without changes except for the correction of typographical errors and some obvious mistakes, and changes in the numbering of the footnotes where this appeared to be necessary.

Grateful acknowledgment is made to the publishers, authors, and translators represented here for their generosity in granting permission to reprint selections from copyright material and for their kind cooperation throughout the work. The author is especially indebted to Mrs. Kay Scheuer, Philosophy Editor of Anchor Books, for her support and enthusiasm for this project, and for her unremitting cooperation in bringing it to this final form.

Joseph J. Kockelmans, Ph.D.

Department of Philosophy
University of Pittsburgh
October 25, 1966

CONTENTS

PART I

THE PHENOMENOLOGY OF EDMUND HUSSERL

INTRODUCTION

1. *Biographical Note*

Edmund Gustav Albrecht Husserl was born on the eighth of April 1859, in Prossnitz, a village in Czechoslovakian Moravia, which at that time was part of the Austrian Empire. He went to elementary school there, then to the *Realgymnasium* in Vienna and later to the *Staatsgymnasium* in Olmütz. Between 1876 and 1878 he studied mathematics, physics, and astronomy at the University of Leipzig. It is known, however, that he also made it a point to attend the lectures in philosophy given by Wilhelm Wundt. When, in 1878, he transferred to the Friedrich Wilhelm University of Berlin, Husserl continued to study mathematics under Kronecker, Kummer, and the famous Weierstrass, but the interest in philosophy which had been stimulated by Wundt was kept alive through the inspiring lectures of Friedrich Paulsen.

Although Husserl found himself increasingly drawn to philosophy, he nevertheless transferred to the University of Vienna in 1881 for the purpose of finishing his mathematical education. Studying under Königsberger, he received his Ph.D. in 1883 for a dissertation entitled *Beiträge zur Theorie der Variationsrechnung* (Contributions to the Theory of the Calculus of Variations), which dealt with an important chapter of modern differential calculus.

In the winter of 1882–83 Husserl received an invitation from Weierstrass to return to Berlin and become his assistant. Husserl was pleased and honored by the offer but received it without great enthusiasm, for he had decided to devote himself entirely to philosophy. He felt that he would have much more opportunity to do so at the University of Vienna than at the Friedrich Wilhelm University of Berlin. When Weierstrass subsequently became ill and it seemed that he would be away from his work indefinitely, Husserl's conflict was resolved, and he left for Vienna to complete his philosophical education. From 1884 to 1886 he attended the lectures of

Franz Brentano. He was particularly impressed by the way Brentano acquainted his students with the philosophies of Hume and J. Stuart Mill, and by Brentano's personal investigations into important psychological, ethical, and logical problems. It was Brentano who first brought Bolzano's *Wissenschaftslehre* (Theory of Science) to Husserl's attention. Not until later, however, after he had studied Lotze's *Logik,* did Husserl begin to realize the genuine importance of Bolzano's theory.

Following Brentano's advice, Husserl, in 1886, went to the University of Halle, became an assistant under Stumpf, and thereby availed himself of an outstanding opportunity to obtain a thorough grounding in psychology. A year later he became Privat-dozent on the philosophy faculty there. In 1891, while in residence at Halle, Husserl published his first book, *Philosophie der Arithmetik* (Philosophy of Arithmetic), which was in fact the *Habilitationsschrift* he had completed under Stumpf's direction. The book was criticized by Frege, among others, and it was particularly his critique that prompted Husserl to abandon the "psychologism" he had defended in it. Subsequently, in the first part of his *Logische Untersuchungen* (Logical Investigations), viz. *Prolegomena to Pure Logic* (1900), he even explicitly rejected any form of "psychologism" in the realm of logic and mathematics. This latter work was well received by many philosophers and logicians and established Husserl irrevocably as a philosopher.

In 1900 Husserl received an invitation to join the philosophy faculty at the University of Göttingen, and he was later appointed an *extraordinarius professor* in philosophy, a position in which he functioned actively for the following sixteen years. During that time he produced some of his most important works, although only a few of his writings were published then. Among them were: *Vorlesungen über Phänomenologie* (Lectures on Phenomenology) (1904–5), *Vorlesungen zur Phänomenologie des inneren Zeitbewusstseins* (Lectures on Phenomenology of Inner Time Consciousness) (1905–10), *Die Idee der Phänomenologie* (The Idea of Phenomenology) (1906–7), his famous *Logos* article, *Philosophie als strenge Wissenschaft* (Philosophy as Rigorous Science) (1911), and the first volume of his main work, *Ideen* (Ideas) (1913). From these dates it is clear that Husserl's new philosophy, to which he always referred by the term "phenomenology," was gradually taking shape between 1904 and 1907, and that it received its relatively final form in 1913. It is worthy of note here that these writings also reflect the increasing influence of Descartes and Kant, whose works Husserl was studying over the course of the same years.

Husserl received a full professorship at Freiburg im Breisgau in 1916, and there he remained until 1928, when he applied for retirement. The twelve years were fruitful ones. Husserl wrote the last two volumes of his *Ideas* (1912 ff.), *Erste Philosophie* (First Philosophy) (1923 ff.), *Phänomenologische Psychologie* (Phenomenological Psychology) (1925 ff.), and *Formale und transzendentale Logik* (Formal and Transcendental Logic) (1928), though only the last of these was published during his lifetime, appearing in 1929.

Between 1929 and 1938 Husserl worked at a tremendous pace, producing several major works, of which he published only his *Cartesianische Meditationen* (Cartesian Meditations) (1931) in a French version, and the first part of his book *Krisis* (Crisis) (1936). Two years after the publication of *Krisis*, Husserl died of pleurisy after months of suffering.

It is possible to trace different stages of development in Husserl's thought, and this has in fact been done by Fink, Spiegelberg, and others. For my part I should like to suggest four periods as the main stages in Husserl's gradually evolving and developing conception of phenomenology: 1) the pre-phenomenological period, culminating in the ideas formulated in the first volume of *Logical Investigations* (1887–1900); 2) the period of phenomenology as a limited epistemological enterprise (1901–6); 3) the period of pure phenomenology as the universal foundation of philosophy and science, which took shape around 1906–7 and soon led not only to the formulation of a new kind of transcendentalism, but also to a completely new type of idealism (1913) whose increasing radicalization was the main theme of Husserl's thought in Freiburg (1906–28); 4) a last period in which the life-world idea gradually emerged and began to occupy a more central place in his phenomenology (1928–38). Although I agree with Spiegelberg that it is not necessary to delineate this last period from the third one, I have done so nevertheless, despite the difficulty of determining its precise beginning. My reason is that many of the contemporary commentators on Husserl's work[1] seem to presuppose such a period, as will become evident in one of the following readings.

The essays and articles in Part I are concerned almost exclusively with the third period. My article concerning transcendental idealism is intended not as a personal study, but rather as a brief survey of some highly important essays on Husserl's "idealism."

Although I am convinced personally that Merleau-Ponty, De Waelhens, Brand, and others transcend Husserl's own ideas in their interpretations of his later manuscripts (by interpreting too strenuously from a Heideggerian point of view), I have nevertheless included an essay by Gerd Brand because I believe that this interpretation of Husserl's last writings, although historically improbable, is at least not impossible. Furthermore, it seems to me that Brand's essay serves as an excellent transition to the reinterpretations of Husserl's phenomenology by Heidegger, Sartre, and Merleau-Ponty.

2. *The Husserl-Archives*

The Husserl-Archives was founded by Dr. Herman L. Van Breda at Louvain (Belgium) in 1939. It contains not only Husserl's manuscripts, but his philosophical library, letters, and numerous transcriptions in longhand of manuscripts previously written in shorthand form. Among the some eight thousand works housed at Louvain are many publications dedicated to Husserl by renowned philosophers and scientists. Also, at Louvain are the unpublished manuscripts left untouched after Husserl's death and now being transcribed; they comprise approximately forty thousand pages of shorthand set down by Husserl in the Gabelberg system. And in addition to an extensive collection of letters and diaries there are more

---

[1] Merleau-Ponty, De Waelhens, Brand, and others.

than seven thousand pages of longhand transcriptions of Husserl's original shorthand manuscripts that his assistants Edith Stein, Ludwig Landgrebe, and Eugen Fink worked out before 1938. Since 1939 the task of transcribing these manuscripts has been continued by Fink, Landgrebe, Strasser, Walter and Marly Biemel, and Rudolf Boehm.

To date, more than 60 per cent of the manuscripts have been typed in fivefold. Copies of such manuscripts are forwarded to the four cooperating centers: Paris, Freiburg im Breisgau, Cologne, and Buffalo. At these locations the texts are studied further and, in consultation with the Archives at Louvain, prepared for publication. By 1962 nine volumes, totaling some four thousand pages, had been published in the *Husserliana* series.

Since 1958 there has been a supplement to these publications entitled *Phaenomenologica*, consisting of philosophical studies written by scholars who think in the phenomenological vein. In 1964 this series had reached eighteen volumes.

Since its inception the Husserl-Archives has organized three international congresses for phenomenology: Brussels (1951), Krefeld (1956), and Royaumont (1957).

3. *Selective Bibliography*

MAJOR WORKS

Philosophie der Arithmetik. Psychologische und logische Untersuchungen. Erster Band (Halle a.S.: C. Pfeffer, 1891).

Logische Untersuchungen. 3 vols. (Halle a.S.: Max Niemeyer, 1921–22). The first edition in 2 vols. was published in 1900 and 1901; the second edition in 3 vols. in 1913.

Die Idee der Phänomenologie. Fünf Vorlesungen (1907). Herausgegeben und eingeleitet von Walter Biemel (Husserliana, Band II) (The Hague: Martinus Nijhoff, 1950).

  The Idea of Phenomenology. Trans. William P. Alston and George Nakhnikian (The Hague: Martinus Nijhoff, 1964).

"Philosophie als strenge Wissenschaft," *Logos*, 1 (1910–11), pp. 289–341.

  "Philosophy as Rigorous Science," in Quentin Lauer, *Edmund Husserl: Phenomenology and the Crisis of Philosophy* (New York: Harper & Row, 1965), pp. 69–147.

Ideen zu einer reinen Phänomenologie und phänomenologischen Philosophie. Erstes Buch: *Allgemeine Einführung in die reine Phänomenologie.* Herausgegeben von Walter Biemel (Husserliana, Band III). (The Hague: Martinus Nijhoff, 1950).

Ideas. General Introduction to Pure Phenomenology. Trans. W. R. Boyce Gibson (London: George Allen and Unwin Ltd., 1931).

Zweites Buch: *Phänomenologische Untersuchungen zur Konstitution.* Herausgegeben von Marly Biemel (Husserliana, Band IV) (The Hague: Martinus Nijhoff, 1952).

Drittes Buch: *Die Phänomenologie und die Fundamente der Wissenschaften.* Herausgegeben von Marly Biemel (Husserliana, Band V) (The Hague: Martinus Nijhoff, 1952).

Erste Philosophie. Erster Teil: *Kritische Ideengeschichte* (1923–24). Herausgegeben von Rudolf Boehm (Husserliana, Band VII) (The Hague: Martinus Nijhoff, 1956).

Zweiter Teil: *Theorie der phänomenologischen Reduktion* (1923–24). Herausgegeben von Rudolf Boehm (Husserliana, Band VIII) (The Hague: Martinus Nijhoff, 1959).

Phänomenologische Psychologie (1925). Herausgegeben von Walter Biemel (Husserliana, Band IX) (The Hague: Martinus Nijhoff, 1962).

"Phenomenology," in *Encyclopædia Britannica,* 14th edition (London: 1927), Vol. 17, pp. 699–702.

Formale und transzendentale Logik. Versuch einer Kritik der logischen Vernunft (Halle a.S.: Max Nijmeyer, 1929).

Cartesianische Meditationen und Pariser Vorträge. Herausgegeben und eingeleitet von Prof. S. Strasser (Husserliana, Band I) (The Hague: Martinus Nijhoff, 1950).

Cartesian Meditations. An Introduction to Phenomenology. Trans. Dorion Cairns (The Hague: Martinus Nijhoff, 1960). Originally published in French in 1931. Trans. J. Peiffer and E. Levinas.

Die Krisis der europäischen Wissenschaften und die transzendentale Phänomenologie. Eine Einleitung in die phänomenologische Philosophie. Herausgegeben von Walter Biemel (Husserliana, Band VI) (The Hague: Martinus Nijhoff, 1954).

Erfahrung und Urteil. Untersuchungen zur Genealogie der Logik. Redigiert und herausgegeben von Ludwig Landgrebe (Hamburg: Claassen, 1939).

STUDIES IN ENGLISH

M. Farber, *The Foundation of Phenomenology. Edmund Husserl and the Quest for a Rigorous Science of Philosophy* (Cambridge: Harvard University Press, 1943).

——, ed., *Philosophical Essays in Memory of Edmund Husserl* (Cambridge: Harvard University Press, 1940).

Joseph J. Kockelmans, *A First Introduction to Husserl's Phenomenology* (Pittsburgh: Duquesne University Press, 1967).

——, *The Phenomenological Psychology of Edmund Husserl* (Pittsburgh: Duquesne University Press, 1967).

Quentin Lauer, S.J., *The Triumph of Subjectivity* (New York: Fordham University Press, 1958).

——, *Edmund Husserl: Phenomenology and the Crisis of Philosophy* (New York: Harper & Row, 1965).

Andrew D. Osborn, *The Philosophy of Edmund Husserl in its Development from his Mathematical Interest to his First Conception of Phenomenology in Logical Investigations* (New York: International Press, 1934).

Robert Sokolowski, *The Formation of Husserl's Concept of Constitution* (The Hague: Martinus Nijhoff, 1964).

Herbert Spiegelberg, *The Phenomenological Movement. A Historical Introduction*, 2 vols. (The Hague: Martinus Nijhoff, 1960), Vol. I, pp. 73–167.

E. Parl Welch, *The Philosophy of Edmund Husserl. The Origin and Development of his Phenomenology* (New York: Columbia University Press, 1965).

I. WHAT IS PHENOMENOLOGY?

Some Fundamental Themes
of Husserl's Phenomenology*

JOSEPH J. KOCKELMANS

Hegel's Phenomenology. Anyone familiar with the situation knows that as soon as he uses the term "phenomenology" he enters a sphere of ambiguity. The term was used as early as 1765 in philosophical writings, and Kant occasionally had recourse to it also. Nevertheless, it was only with Hegel that a well-defined technical meaning became attached to it.[1] For Hegel phenomenology was not knowledge of the Absolute-in-and-for-itself, in the spirit of Fichte or Schelling, but in his *Phenomenology of Mind* he wanted solely to consider knowledge as it appears to consciousness. In this book Hegel wanted to ascend from this self-criticizing phenomenal knowing to the knowledge of the Absolute, which itself must be called an absolute knowledge. Thus, phenomenology for Hegel is the science describing the development which natural phenomenal consciousness undergoes by way of science and philosophy toward the absolute knowledge of the Absolute.[2] The object of his investigations, then, was phenomenal knowing.[3]

Although this knowing cannot be considered to be the science *par excellence*, nevertheless, it must be conceived as the origin of the road which natural consciousness takes in order to arrive at true and authentic knowledge. Differently expressed, phenomenal knowing must be viewed in principle as

* From Joseph J. Kockelmans, *Phenomenology and Physical Science*, translated by Henry J. Koren, Duquesne University Press, Pittsburgh, Pa., 1966, pp. 30–40. Reprinted with permission of the publishers.

[1] I. Bocheński, *Die Zeitgenössischen Denkmethoden*, München, 1954, p. 22.

[2] J. Hyppolite, *Genèse et structure de la phénoménologie de l'esprit*, vol. I, Paris, 1946, p. 10.

[3] G. Hegel, *Phänomenologie des Geistes*, ed. J. Hoffmeister, Hamburg, 1952, p. 66.

the starting point from which the individual mind, through various stages and together with other individual minds, ascends to *the* Mind, who knows in full self-experience what He is in Himself. In this sense Hegel's phenomenology itself is not yet science of the Absolute but only the approach leading from phenomenal knowing to an absolute knowledge of Absolute Mind.[4]

Husserl and Descartes. When we speak today of phenomenology, we no longer understand this expression in the sense of Hegel, even though it remains true that the phenomenological writings of contemporary authors bear an Hegelian imprint. Anyone who wants to arrive at a clear understanding of the essence and aim of phenomenology cannot avoid studying the background of this movement as painted by Hegel in his *Phenomenology of Mind.*[5] Despite its actuality, the phenomenological movement is also, at least in part, a historical phenomenon.

Nonetheless, when contemporaries speak about phenomenology, the name that arises spontaneously is that of Edmund Husserl. Yet it is not easy to express Husserl's idea of phenomenology. The reason lies in the fact that hitherto only a relatively small part of his writings have been published, and most of these publications are more concerned with picturing an ideal program than with its execution. Moreover, the phenomenological analyses which Husserl has actually made seem to eliminate that ideal program and its implied self-interpretation, although Husserl himself does not seem to have realized this.

According to the grandiose program which Husserl drew up for his philosophical life and which he described extensively in his *Ideas* and his *Cartesian Meditations,* he viewed his own work as a radicalization of Descartes' demand that all philosophical knowledge be founded in an absolutely certain insight, raised above every possibility of doubt. But in many

---

[4] Hegel, *ibid.,* pp. 66 f.

[5] A. de Waelhens, "Phénoménologie husserlienne et phénoménologie hégélienne," *Revue philosophique de Louvain,* vol. 52 (1954), pp. 234–249.

points his numerous and extensive analyses appear to contradict his endeavor to think radically about the modern problematics of the subject.[6] In these analyses this problem reveals
itself as a pseudoproblem, so that Husserl's standpoint in this
matter comes very close to that of Heidegger and Merleau-
Ponty.[7]

Philosophy as a Rigorous Science. Later we will revert to
this point. For the present we wish to emphasize that by means
of his phenomenology Husserl wanted to arrive at "philosophy
as a rigorous science."[8] Explaining this standpoint, Husserl
stressed that, since its beginning in Greece, philosophy has
always aspired to be an all-encompassing, intellectually justified knowledge of all that is.[9] For this reason philosophy is
not a matter of feeling or of a more or less fanciful building
of systems according to subjective views. Every cultural period and every system has endeavored to realize this essential
aim of philosophy in its own way, but Husserl seriously wanted
to attain the goal by means of his phenomenology.[10] Through
a rigorously critical and systematic investigation, Husserl's
phenomenological philosophy wanted to attain absolutely valid
knowledge of things.[11]

[6] L. Landgrebe, *Philosophie der Gegenwart,* Bonn, 1952, pp. 31–
40.

[7] M. Merleau-Ponty, *Phenomenology of Perception,* pp. 60, 243,
365, 376.

[8] E. Husserl, "Philosophie als strenge Wissenschaft," *Logos,* vol.
1 (1910–11), pp. 289–341.

[9] Husserl, *Ideen zu einer reinen Phänomenologie und phänomenologischen Philosophie,* 3 vols., The Hague, 1950–52; *Nachwort,*
vol. 3, pp. 138–139; *Die Krisis der europäischen Wissenschaften und
die transzendentale Phänomenologie. Eine Einleitung in die Phänomenologie,* The Hague, 1954, p. 66.

[10] Husserl, "Entwurf einer 'Vorrede' zu den 'Logischen Untersuchungen,'" *Tijdschrift voor Philosophie,* vol. 1 (1939), pp. 117
and 132; E. Fink, "Die phänomenologische Philosophie Edmund
Husserls in der gegenwärtigen Kritik," *Kantstudien,* vol. 38 (1933),
p. 340.

[11] Husserl, *Ideen, Nachwort,* vol. 3, pp. 138–141. For this whole
question see also H. Boelaars, "Husserls reducties en haar betekenis
voor het thomisme," *Tijdschrift voor Philosophie,* vol. 6 (1944),
pp. 334–335.

Accordingly, by virtue of its essential aim, philosophy wants to be a "rigorous science." One should keep in mind, of course, that the scientific character of philosophy differs entirely from that of the sciences of nature and of the mind.[12] Unlike philosophy, these sciences usually have at their disposal an elaborate apparatus of refined methods. Thus a superficial spectator can easily get the impression that philosophy is less scientific. On closer inspection, however, it appears that all non-philosophical sciences start from a complex of presuppositions which are not clarified in these sciences themselves.[13] Philosophy, on the other hand, does not want to leave anything unsolved; it wants to reduce everything to primary "presuppositions" which do not need to be clarified because they are immediately evident and cannot even be clarified. It is only in this sense that philosophy as the "science of ultimate grounds" is a rigorous science.[14]

The Natural Attitude. Thus we see that, according to Husserl, we must make a clear distinction between philosophy and non-philosophical sciences. The latter flow from the "natural attitude," while the former are born from an entirely different attitude of mind, a philosophical attitude. In the natural attitude man's perception and thinking are wholly turned toward things, which are given to us as unquestionably obvious and, depending on our standpoint, appear now in this way and now in that. Among all our acts that refer to things perception is the most original. What perception offers to us we express in judgments, first in singular judgments, and then in universal judgments. From these judgments we proceed through induction and deduction to new knowledge. "In this way natural knowledge makes progress. Constantly more encompassing, it lays hold of hitherto obviously existing and given reality whose extent and content, elements, relationships and laws are to be

[12] E. Fink, "Das Problem der Phänomenologie Edmund Husserls," *Revue internationale de philosophie*, vol. 1 (1938–39), pp. 240–242.

[13] Husserl, *Ideen*, vol. 1, pp. 57–59 and 136–137.

[14] Husserl, "Philosophie als strenge Wissenschaft," *Logos*, vol. 1, p. 340; *Ideen, Nachwort*, vol. 3, pp. 159–162.

more and more investigated."[15] In this way the various sciences of the natural attitude have arisen. Because of the success they have attained in the course of the centuries, those who assume the natural attitude feel no need to ask any question concerning the possibility of knowledge and science or concerning their proper meaning.[16]

Moreover, in the natural attitude one tacitly assumes that we are in a world through which our mind can roam at will and in which we can consider any part we want, without changing the objective nature of what we consider. According to this view, the object-pole of our knowing is an objectively existing, fully explainable world that can be expressed in exact, objective laws. This "objective" world exists wholly in itself and possesses a rationality that can be fully understood. The subject, on the other hand, is pure consciousness; it is fully transparent to itself and faces that rational world, which it can know objectively as it is in itself.

This idea of a single, objective, absolute, autonomous and real world implies also that each of the different sciences has to occupy itself with a part of reality. Otherwise it would not be possible to explain the differences of these sciences because, in this view, there is no reason at all to defend a difference in method. Hence it stands to reason that all sciences together have to constitute a single objective synthesis. An essential difference between philosophy and the other sciences is not even possible.[17]

Husserl protests against such views. "Philosophy," he says, "lies in an entirely different dimension. It needs entirely new starting points and an entirely new method, which is in principle different from those of any 'natural' science."[18] "A philosophy [can] not naively begin at once, like the positive sciences do, which base themselves on the presupposed foun-

---

[15] Husserl, *Die Idee der Phänomenologie,* The Hague, 1950, p. 18.

[16] Husserl, *ibid.,* pp. 17–19.

[17] Husserl, *Die Krisis . . . ,* pp. 18–20.

[18] Husserl, *Die Idee . . . ,* p. 24.

dation of experience of the world as something that is pre-given as obviously existing."[19] "Its aim as philosophy implies a radicalism of foundation, a reduction to absolute presuppositionlessness, a fundamental method through which the philosopher at the beginning secures an absolute foundation for himself."[20]

The Original Intuition. Husserl seeks the ultimate foundation of all our rational assertions in an immediate vision, i.e., an original intuition of the things themselves concerning which we want to make a statement. His call, "Back to the things themselves," then, means that we must return to the immediate, original data of our consciousness. That which manifests itself there in "bodily presence" is apodictically evident. It does not need any further foundation, but is true and certain.[21]

Accordingly, Husserl does not see the ultimate root, the radical and absolute starting point of philosophy, in any single basic concept, in any single fundamental principle, in one simple *cogito*, but in an entire field of original experiences.[22] His philosophy is a phenomenology precisely because it has as its starting point a field of primordial phenomena. Within this field Husserl does not want any induction or deduction but solely intuition on the basis of a very exact analysis and description.[23] None of the methods used by the other sciences can be of value here, because they have to presuppose something in addition to what is actually given, while in the field of primordial phenomena presuppositions are simply inconceivable. The fundamental principle, then, applying to this field is "that every originarily giving intuition is a legitimate

[19] Husserl, *Ideen, Nachwort,* vol. 3, p. 160.

[20] Husserl, *ibid.,* p. 160.

[21] Husserl, *Ideen,* vol. 1, pp. 42–44, 50–53; *Die Idee . . . ,* pp. 29–32.

[22] Husserl, "Philosophie als strenge Wissenschaft," *Logos,* vol. 1, p. 341; *Die Krisis . . . ,* p. 104; *Cartesianische Meditationen und Pariser Vorträge,* The Hague, p. 69 (see also pp. 57–72).

[23] Husserl, "Philosophie als strenge Wissenschaft," *Logos,* vol. 1, p. 341.

source of knowledge, that everything which presents itself to us originally in 'intuition,' so to speak in its bodily presence, has to be taken simply as what it presents itself to be, but only within the limits in which it presents itself."[24]

Intuition, however, implies that subject and object are present to each other on the same level. Hence the intuition of the "origins and beginnings" demands that we first try to arrive at the "lowest field of work," in which these foundations are immediately present to our knowing "I." Husserl thinks that his "reductions" can lead us to this field.[25] By reduction he means in general that methodic procedure by which one places oneself in the "transcendental sphere," the sphere in which we can perceive things as they are in themselves, independently of any prejudice. In other words, it is a change of attitude, by virtue of which we learn to see the things we previously thought to perceive, in a different way, i.e., in an original and radical way. We penetrate deeper into things and learn to see the more profound "layers" behind what we first thought to see.[26]

Eidetic Reduction. Husserl distinguishes a twofold reduction: the "eidetic reduction" and the complex of reductive phases which he labels the "phenomenological reduction."[27] The eidetic reduction leads us from the realm of facts to that of general essences, and the phenomenological reduction makes us pass from the world of realities to that of their ultimate presuppositions.[28] The eidetic reduction, then, is the methodic procedure through which we raise our knowledge from the level of facts to the sphere of "ideas." By essence or idea Husserl means here not the "empirical generalities" which provide us with types encountered in experience, but

---

[24] Husserl, *Ideen*, vol. 1, p. 52.

[25] Husserl, *ibid.*, pp. 118–119, 136–149; Fink, "Die phänomenologische Philosophie . . . ," *Kantstudien*, vol. 38, p. 370.

[26] Boelaars, *art. cit.* in footnote 11, pp. 338–339; Husserl, *Ideen*, vol. 1, p. 5 and *Nachwort*, vol. 3, p. 141.

[27] Husserl, *Ideen*, vol. 1, p. 6.

[28] Husserl, *ibid.*

"pure generalities," which put before our mind pure possibilities whose validity is independent of experience.[29]

In the eidetic reduction one proceeds as follows:[30] as a rule, we start with an arbitrarily perceived or fancied individual sample of this or that kind of things. With the aid of memory, modifications in perception, and especially acts of phantasy, we carefully investigate what changes can be made in the sample without making it cease to be the thing it is. Through the most arbitrary changes, which wholly disregard reality as it is and which therefore are best made in our phantasy, the immutable and necessary complex of characteristics without which the thing cannot be conceived manifest themselves. This "invariant"[31] arises automatically and passively because the objects of the different acts partly overlap, but this "pre-constituted" and still imperfect identical content must still be seized in an "actively intuiting grasp."[32] Through this grasp, the absolutely immutable and unique *eidos* which governs all individuals of this species stands before our mind.

Phenomenological Reductions. In addition to these eidetic reductions, Husserl admits also a complex of phenomenological reductions. They are sometimes divided as follows:

1. The phenomenological reduction in the strict sense, which is also called the "bracketing of being."

2. The reduction of the cultural world to the world of our immediate experience (*Lebenswelt*).

3. The transcendental reduction which is to lead us from the phenomenal worldly "I" to transcendental subjectivity.[33]

In the following pages we will speak only about the reduction leading us from the cultural world to the *Lebenswelt* because, in our opinion, it would be difficult to interpret the

[29] Husserl, *ibid.*

[30] Husserl, "Philosophie als strenge Wissenschaft," *Logos,* vol. 1, p. 315; *Formale und transzendentale Logik,* Halle a.d.S., 1929, pp. 218–221; *Erfahrung und Urteil,* Hamburg, 1954, pp. 409–426.

[31] Husserl, *Formale und transzendentale Logik,* p. 219.

[32] Husserl, *Erfahrung und Urteil,* p. 414.

[33] Boelaars, *art. cit.* in footnote 11, pp. 345–362.

other two in a non-idealistic way.[34] Unsurprisingly, these two do not occur in the works of Heidegger and Merleau-Ponty.[35]

To continue, when Husserl wants to explain what the phenomenological reduction is in general and how one can best come to realize its necessity, he begins with an explanation of the concept "intentionality." His teacher Franz Brentano, who was not unfamiliar with Aristotelian philosophy, had introduced this concept into modern psychology. In Aristotelian philosophy the term "intention" indicates the orientation of the mind to its object and, in harmony with this orientation, this object begins to exist in an intentional way in the mind. For Brentano this feature of directedness became *the* characteristic of all psychical activities. Although Husserl did not follow Brentano in his psychological views, the fact that all consciousness is intentional, that all consciousness is consciousness-of-something, became for him the core of his new philosophy.[36]

Every act of consciousness, in order to be an act, demands a certain object because every conscious act intends something. Every act is "characterized by what the medieval scholastics called the intentional . . . inexistence of an object."[37] If, then, an act of a certain structure is present, then by that very fact a certain object is also present; moreover, the character of this object is co-determined by the character of the

---

[34] Cf. Kockelmans, "Realisme—Idealisme en Husserls phaenomenologie," *Tijdschrift voor Philosophie*, vol. 20, pp. 395–442 (especially 430–441).

[35] L. Landgrebe, *Phänomenologie und Metaphysik*, Hamburg, 1949, pp. 83–100; W. Biemel, "Husserls Encyclopaedia Britannica Artikel und Heideggers Anmerkungen dazu," *Tijdschrift voor Philosophie*, vol. 12 (1950), pp. 246–280; Merleau-Ponty, *Phenomenology of Perception*, pp. xi–xiv, 60, 243, 365.

[36] Landgrebe, *op. cit.*, pp. 59–69; Boelaars, "De intentionaliteit der kennis bij Edmund Husserl," *Bijdragen*, vol. 3 (1940), pp. 111–161 and 221–264; A. Diemer, *Edmund Husserl. Versuch einer systematischen Darstellung seiner Phänomenologie*, Meisenheim a.Gl., 1956, pp. 45–71.

[37] Husserl, *Logische Untersuchungen*, Halle a.d.S., 1913, vol. 2, pp. 366–367; F. Brentano, *Psychologie vom empirischen Standpunkt*, Leipzig, 1924, vol. 1, p. 124.

act in which the object appears.[38] The character, therefore, of the known object depends on the character of the act by which it is grasped. The large majority, however, of the intentional acts made by an adult civilized human being are not original acts but derived acts. But if it is universally true that the character of the object is co-determined by the character of the act in which it appears, then it follows that "any kind of being has a way of giving itself that is exclusively its own."[39]

Accordingly, if we want to arrive at the sphere in which things appear to us primordially, we have to find a way to lead us from what manifests itself actually in the derived acts to the original objects of our most primordial acts. For the intentional activity of the adult, civilized man is, generally speaking, extremely complex and, correspondingly, that which is constituted by his tending, i.e., meaning, is built up of a manifold of layers of meaning. As a consequence of this, the total meaning can and has to be analyzed in its various components of meaning, each of which is an intentionality. Husserl, now, speaks of "intentional analysis" in reference to the method used when we go back in our questioning from our derivative cognitive acts and their correlates to the original lived experiences (*Erlebnisse*), in which any being whatsoever primordially appears as itself in its immediate givenness.[40]

The dominant tradition of positive science, in which we have been educated, has imposed on us certain prejudices regarding the supposed original object of experience. It claims that this object is the object as it manifests itself through the exact description and determination of the sciences. In fact, however, the object of positive science is an abstraction and an artificial structure in reference to the world of our original experience. If, then, we want to discover the truly original

---

[38] Husserl, *Logische Untersuchungen,* vol. 2, p. 372; Boelaars, *art. cit.* in footnote 36, pp. 158–161.

[39] Landgrebe, *Phänomenologie und Metaphysik,* p. 85.

[40] Husserl, *Cartesianische Meditationen,* pp. 66–91; *Die Krisis . . . ,* pp. 116–118 and 173–176; Landgrebe, *op. cit.,* pp. 42–49 and 94–97; P. Ricoeur, "Méthodes et tâches d'une phénoménologie de la volonté," *Problèmes actuels de la phénoménologie,* Paris, 1952, pp. 115–123.

structures of the objects in the various domains of being in order to use them as guide lines in the investigation of the corresponding acts of consciousness, we have to abandon the prejudices of the positive sciences and must try to reach reality as it is immediately given in primordial experience. In other words, we have to return to the world as it manifests itself in primordial experience, we must endeavor to find a "natural" world, the world of immediate experience (*Lebenswelt*).[41] It is the task of the phenomenological reduction to lead us back from the cultural world of the sciences to the primordial world of life. This reduction will have to be used in conjunction with the above-mentioned intentional analyses.

Intentionality. As we have indicated, intentionality is the characteristic property of our consciousness, always directing this consciousness to that which it itself is not. This description needs to be rendered more precise. For one could imagine that, according to Husserl, this intentionality would force consciousness to adapt itself passively to whatever it encounters outside itself in the real world. But that is not what Husserl means. When he says that consciousness essentially tends to that which it is not, he wants to say that it belongs to the essence of our consciousness to form a meaning and consequently to constitute its own objects.

Intentionality, then, does not consist in an external object entering somehow into a relationship with consciousness nor in a relationship arising between two psychical contents in our consciousness. Intentionality has nothing to do with relations between "real" objects, but is essentially an act that gives meaning. Thus the object of any act is an inseparable aspect of the meaning phenomenon itself. In Husserl's philosophy the object appears as essentially determined by the structure of thinking itself; this thinking itself first gives meaning to the object and then continues to orient itself to the pole of identity which it itself has already created. When Husserl speaks of transcendence, he does not begin with the reality of the object but always with the meaning of the object. Hence the inten-

41 Merleau-Ponty, *La structure du comportement,* Paris, 1949, p. 235; *Phenomenology of Perception,* pp. 407, 430.

tional analyses ultimately always become constitutive analyses, i.e., analyses which do not indicate how meaning is found in the primordial experiences, but which want to explain how the meaning of things is primordially constituted in and through consciousness.[42]

This is not all. Hitherto we have limited ourselves to intentionality in function of a theory concerning meaning. Now, however, we must proceed to a more fundamental consideration and endeavor to determine what a consciousness is which itself is essentially intentional. Here there is no longer question of the intentionality of a simple and determined act (*Akt-Intentionalität*) but of the essence itself of consciousness (*fungierende Intentionalität*).[43] The development of this idea, however, probably leads beyond Husserl into the thought of Heidegger.

In any case, if we want to discover what the essence of intentionality, and consequently of our consciousness, really is, we must try to discover our own real presence to ourselves and our presence to things and the world, which is inseparably connected with this self-presence. Certainly, all consciousness is consciousness-of-something, consciousness of the world and of the things of the world. But of even greater importance seems to be the idea that in every concrete, conscious act the unity of the world appears to be already constituted before this unity is explicitly posited as such in a cognitive act of identification. In that case, the cognitive relationship to the world is evidently no longer, in the proper sense of the term, the most primary relationship between man and world; knowledge itself is then a founded relationship and its necessary orientation to the other-than-itself then appears to be a datum

---

[42] Husserl, *Ideen,* vol. 1, pp. 134–136, 212–215, 363–380; *Cartesianische Meditationen,* pp. 17–34; *Die Krisis . . . ,* pp. 114–116, 146–151, 170–173, 182–193, 207–214; G. Berger, *Le cogito dans la philosophie de Husserl,* Paris, 1941, pp. 92–117, 129–131; A. de Waelhens, "L'idée phénoménologique de l'intentionnalité," in D. M. de Petter, "Het tweede internationaal colloquium over de phenomenologie," *Tijdschrift voor Philosophie,* vol. 18, pp. 727–731; G. Brand, *Welt, Ich und Zeit,* pp. 34–41; Diemer, *op. cit.* in footnote 36, pp. 55–71 and *passim.*

[43] Brand, *op. cit.,* pp. 22–25.

no longer characteristic of knowledge alone. In that case, the constitution of an object in knowledge must be considered rather as a tendency pertaining to knowledge only in a typically derivative sense. But then it also becomes evident that consciousness itself cannot be anything other than openness, directedness to the other, and denial of self-foundation. In this way consciousness appears to be not pure interiority, but should be understood as a going-out-of-itself, as ek-sistence. And explicit acts of cognition are only a mode of our human existence based on our being-in-the-world.[44]

[44] de Waelhens, *loc. cit.* in footnote 42.

II. HUSSERL AND PHILOSOPHIC RADICALISM

The Ideal of a Presuppositionless Philosophy*

MARVIN FARBER

I. The Ideal of Presuppositionlessness

The claim of presuppositionlessness has been made at various times, and has been held up as an ideal. In the words of Shadworth Hodgson,[1] "The philosophical problem is to find the means of philosophizing without making assumptions." The attempt to achieve a presuppositionless beginning of philosophy occurred in various ways. One way was to base philosophy upon one ultimate principle. But it is only by a process of self-deception that the philosopher can suppose that he has thereby dispensed with all assumptions. It is sufficient to recall Hegel's notion of the aseity of spirit as an example of the tradition. But Hegel's use of the dialectic method was certainly not presuppositionless. In fact, the principle of presuppositionlessness has been called the greatest presupposition.

The principle of the aseity of spirit is at the basis of idealism. In his discussion of absolute idealism, Feuerbach pointed out that this really amounted to the restoration of a divine being to a post of honor. The materialist, of one type or another, endeavors to account for spirit either analytically, causally, or historically. The idealist is compelled to argue for the absoluteness of spirit, which is as little accounted for as is the

---

* From Marvin Farber, "The Ideal of a Presuppositionless Philosophy," in Marvin Farber, ed., *Philosophical Essays in Memory of Edmund Husserl* (Cambridge, Mass.: Harvard University Press, 1940), pp. 44–64. Reprinted by permission of the publishers. Copyright 1940 by the President and Fellows of Harvard College.

[1] In a letter to William James, in 1882. Cf. R. B. Perry, *The Thought and Character of William James* (Boston, 1935), 1, 623.

impersonal God of modern religion. This is a "substantive" assumption. It may take the form of an absolute consciousness, a transcendental ego, or an all-embracing mind. Leibniz accounted for his spiritual monads by an act of divine creation; and the divine being was provided by bad logic. The cognitive predicament which has been used to support idealism does not account for spirit. It is rather a way of rendering plausible the necessity of the substantive assumption, which is to be taken as absolute.

Empiricism also aimed at presuppositionlessness, using particular facts and observations as the source of knowledge. It was effective as a weapon against authoritarian beliefs and rationalistic dogmas. But the strict application of the method of empiricism, which would mean restriction to what is given in sensory experience, would be inadequate for purposes both of science and philosophy. That it actually does make use of assumptions is well known. These include the recognition of principles transcending actual and even possible experience, and involving the use of conceptual devices.

Husserl chose an alternative to psychological atomism. He adopted the descriptive method, but made it more complete by attempting to do full justice to the essential structure of experience and its objects; and he sought to clarify all principles and to "constitute" all things on the basis of "pure consciousness," a realm purged of all beliefs in transcendent existence. There were to be no presuppositions, at least in the ordinary sense of the term. Radicalism of method was the aim of Husserl's phenomenological investigations from their beginning. His original studies in the theory of knowledge were made to conform to the ideal of presuppositionlessness, which was derived from the earlier philosophical writings of the 1880's, his immediate philosophical background. It is proposed in this paper to consider the meaning of this ideal, which requires the distinction of the various meanings of "presupposition"; the meaning such an ideal may have for logic and the theory of knowledge; and finally the question of the foundation of phenomenology itself.

II. The Meaning of "Presupposition"

The term "presupposition" is highly ambiguous. Literally it means "posited as holding or as existing in advance." Because of its many uses the term must be interpreted in a twofold manner, having regard to existence as well as to thought. In its broadest meaning it refers to any kind of supposition or assumption,[2] such as a material or ideal domain, a realm of existence, a process of experience, or a system of knowledge. It may also be taken to refer to formal principles, either in the sense of arbitrary assumptions or of necessary logical principles.

The following classification of types of presupposition will be helpful. (a) There are material presuppositions, which are either physical in their reference, or relate to domains of abstract things. In the world of experience, for example, the continuity of existence in time, the independence of existence with regard to cognition, causal uniformity, and infinite extension in a *macro* as well as in a *micro* respect, are generally considered to be basic presuppositions. (b) Mention is often made of cognitive presuppositions, such as the reliability of perception and memory, and the validity of knowledge. These should not be treated as assumptions, however, but as results to be achieved. Our ability to know reality truly does not have to be assumed if all known evidence overwhelmingly verifies it. (c) There are formal assumptions in special systems. The postulational method is a practical matter, and is employed because of human limitations and purposes. In the nature of the case the systems of knowledge could not be dealt with actually as simple wholes. The distinction between assumptions and deductions is a response to the problem of the statement of knowledge, which admits of alternatives, and of the deductive demonstration of propositions. No one set of propositions could be singled out as the necessary foundation of a system. This is different from (d) the principles of logic, which are peculiarly fundamental and which do not admit of alterna-

[2] Cf. Husserl, *Ideas*, p. 455.

tives, although they may be defined in different ways. Thus they may be taken to apply to the infinite system of all conceivable propositions, or only to those which may be verified or constructed. For a completely formal or "realistic" logic, they apply to the entire structure of knowledge and are requirements which are imposed upon any systems or parts of knowledge. The question of just which principles are to serve as postulates of logic is not different from the case of the special systems mentioned in (c), for the system of logic has the properties of a special system. It merely happens that its structure as a system is determined by its own laws. There are equivalent alternative postulate sets for logic; but these are to be distinguished from alternative versions of logical principles, such as the principle of the excluded middle, with regard to their range of application, as illustrated by intuitionism and formalism. The cherished "gilt-edged" principles of the traditional logic, the "laws of thought," may appear as theorems in the system of logic. They are no more necessary than any other logical principles. That is not to imply, however, that all sets of logical propositions are on the same level as far as deductive power is concerned. In this sense, "logically prior" may be taken to mean "deductively more powerful."[3]

Other possible meanings of the term "presupposition" should be mentioned for completeness. These include motivation, influences, significance for society and history, as well as beliefs. According to Brentano,[4] for example, the term "presuppositionless" meant "free from prejudice" or from prejudgments. The requirement that the cultural sciences should proceed presuppositionlessly was understood to mean freedom from world-view assumptions.[5] Motives, as one kind of presupposition, were eliminated by Husserl in his use of the

[3] Cf. C. I. Lewis' discussion of presuppositions in *Mind and the World-Order*, pp. 200 ff., 415 ff.

[4] In his anonymous article, "Über Voraussetzungslose Forschung" (1901), which deals with freedom of thought and investigation. Cf. F. Brentano, *Die Vier Phasen der Philosophie und ihr augenblicklicher Stand* (Leipzig, 1926), pp. 137–144.

[5] Cf. E. Spranger, "Der Sinn der Voraussetzungslosigkeit in den Geisteswissenschaften," *Sitzungsberichte der Preussischen Akademie der Wissenschaften* (Berlin, 1929), pp. 2–30.

phenomenological method;[6] or at least only phenomenological motives were allowed. There were to be no motives derived from the natural world, or from any non-phenomenological realm, any more than there were to be prejudgments. The attempt to dispense with presuppositions in all meanings of the term requires the disregard, or the suspension, of all traditional formal and non-formal assumptions. It must lead to a mind divested not only of all bodiliness, but also of all real and ideal conditions of experience and thought. It would seem that solipsism is the unavoidable beginning. If one's quest for ultimate understanding leads him to such a basis, he must be prepared to pass beyond solipsism. The phenomenological method undertakes to meet this problem.

III. The Conception of a Presuppositionless Theory of Knowledge

The need for the clarification of logic by the theory of knowledge was urged by Husserl at the beginning of the century, a task which led him to examine the fundamental ideas of the theory of knowledge as well, and to set up the ideal of a philosophical beginning without presuppositions. As he expressed it later, this meant that pure logic was to be "bracketed" along with everything else. The method of reflective analysis, as developed by him, was intended to make possible a final foundation of logic and philosophy.

The requirement that the theory of knowledge be free from presuppositions was prominent in the literature of Husserl's older contemporaries. In his essay on the theory of knowledge as a presuppositionless science, Volkelt[7] pointed out that all sciences except epistemology presuppose the possibility of knowledge. In his view, epistemology must precede all other

---

[6] Cf. E. Fink, "Die phänomenologische Philosophie Edmund Husserls in der gegenwärtigen Kritik," *Kant-Studien* (Berlin, 1933).

[7] In 1881 Volkelt expressed the ideal of presuppositionlessness in "Die Aufgabe und die Fundamentalschwierigkeit der Erkenntnistheorie als einer voraussetzungslosen Wissenschaft," a paper published in the *Philosophische Monatshefte*, XVII, 513–541. Cf. also Volkelt's *Erfahrung und Denken* (Hamburg and Leipzig, 1886); *Gewissheit und Wahrheit* (München, 1918).

sciences, and may not make logical, psychological, or meta-physical assumptions. In order to make an indubitable beginning and to avoid circularity, he began with his own consciousness. Since he restricted himself to that which is absolutely self-evident, there could be no talk of other minds, or of general propositions which are ordinarily assumed as principles. Volkelt's indubitable sphere of consciousness proved to be devoid of promise, for he declared that nothing of regularity or law or connection could be discovered in it. He was unable to give a satisfactory answer to the question as to how the epistemologist is to get out of the sphere of his own consciousness. His program for epistemology was intended to make clear the extent of knowing and the degrees of certainty.

As expressed in his *Certainty and Truth,* the requirement of presuppositionlessness means that the theory of knowledge be begun by means of a proposition to which immediate certainty is attached without restriction, and which is therefore self-evident. Even logic may not form the basis of epistemology. Propositions derived from logic or psychology must be gained by means of epistemology. They must either be certain in themselves, or possess certainty by virtue of being inferences from other already established propositions, which ultimately are known to be self-evident. Thus knowledge belonging to other sciences can be brought within the framework of epistemology. Volkelt's proposal to dispense with the assumption of the independent validity of mathematics and science clearly shows his conception of the radical ideal of critically examining all knowledge and belief. The truth of science is presupposed in the investigation of the "transcendental" basis of scientific knowledge, and hence such a theory of knowledge cannot be fundamental. The "transcendental presupposition" was made by Kant, Windelband, and others. As distinguished from them, Volkelt attempted to make epistemology presuppositionless, in accordance with its definition as the science of the validity of knowledge, or of the possibility of knowledge. To assume the validity of knowledge for being would reduce the entire undertaking to a comedy, as he stated it. Volkelt's "epistemological epoché" corresponds to Husserl's phenomenological suspension of judgment and belief, but his belief that he had fulfilled by epistemology what Husserl requires for phenomenology can only be justified if one mistakes the will for the deed. Recognition of the general programmatic nature of a presuppositionless theory of knowledge designed to serve as a "first philosophy" is not equivalent to the rigorous formulation of the necessary method. Volkelt's type of analysis failed to offer even a remote equivalent of the elaborate and painstaking descriptive analyses which make up the real content of phenomenology.

It will be sufficient, finally, to mention Schuppe's and Rehmke's views as illustrations of the pre-phenomenological treatment of the problem. Schuppe[8] agreed with Volkelt in regarding epistemology as the fundamental science. He interpreted "presuppositionlessness" as meaning that only those presuppositions are made without which the undertaking itself would be devoid of meaning and content. These include a conscious being, the doubt of the epistemologist, a concept of truth and error, and the required activity of thought. Schuppe had also tried to follow the line of Descartes' method of doubt, but was no more successful than Volkelt in finding a way which leads to something outside of the thinking consciousness. He did no more than pose the problem.

By the presuppositionlessness of a science Rehmke[9] understood the requirement that no determinations concerning its particular subject-matter are to be accepted in advance of its investigation. That would be to make prejudgments. Only the fundamental science of philosophy is completely free from prejudgments. Historical science, for example, assumes "consciousness simply" or "man simply" as determinately given. Rehmke emphasized the difference between presuppositionlessness and prejudgmentlessness. For science, only the latter concept applies, for a presuppositionless science would be impossible. That holds also for the fundamental science, which

[8] W. Schuppe, "Zur 'voraussetzungslosen' Erkenntnistheorie," *Philosophische Monatshefte*, XVIII (1882), 375–386.

[9] Johannes Rehmke, *Philosophie als Grundwissenschaft* (Leipzig, 1910), pp. 40 ff. Cf. also his *Anmerkungen zur Grundwissenschaft* (Leipzig, 1913).

presupposes "givenness simply" and nothing further. Apart from that, it places everything in question.

A survey of the relevant literature shows that there is a vast difference between the general aim to achieve a philosophy as a fundamental science and the actual elaboration of a method to realize it. The time was ripe to provide the latter.

IV. Formal Reasoning and the Reflexive Predicament

The problem of the "founding" of logic was of central importance for Husserl, and provided the initial motivation for the development of a universal phenomenological method. It will therefore be well to consider first the question of the self-sufficiency of formal reasoning.

In the usual case, there are characteristic concepts and postulates which distinguish a special system of knowledge. The ideal of deduction is the construction of all knowledge homogeneously, which means in terms of one basis. Basic conceptual unity has been achieved in principle in formal science; the fundamental concepts of logic have been shown to be adequate for the construction of mathematical concepts. The former, however, stand in need of further investigation.

The attempt to determine the fundamental principles of logic involves the question of the circularity of formal reasoning. The latter is circular for the same reason that all terms cannot be defined; i.e., universal demonstration is as impossible as universal definition, *as a matter of presentation*. It is impossible to prove all propositions, for there must always be an assumed basis for demonstration. This restriction refers exclusively to the medium of reasoning and not to the particular nature of the propositions. It cannot be said that any particular significant proposition is incapable of proof, even though it is true that all propositions are not thus capable of proof, at least within deduction. In a well-founded system, significant propositions, or propositions which are proper to the given system, are essentially either true or false. There is no inherent reason why they may not be proved to be one or the other. The question of our finite, human ability to prove or disprove propositions does not enter into the problem of circularity.

That concerns the foundation of the principles of logic. Assumptions must be made in all reasoning, including reasoning in logic itself. The attempt to demonstrate any of the principles of logic requires the use of premises, and either a part of logic is involved therewith, or another and perhaps larger system of propositions. The essence of the method of deduction is really in question here.

The aim of formal reasoning is to operate with purely formal structures as far as possible. The sharp delimitation of formal logic is necessary for the development of the science. All philosophical or non-formal considerations must therefore be eliminated. Husserl's judgment that the traditional logic is grounded in the world of mundane existence does not hold for symbolic logic, which is kept as free from all non-formal elements as possible. But it does presuppose a possible world for its realization. The importance and significance of epistemological, psychological, and ontological questions pertaining to logic cannot be denied, for logic is admittedly not a self-sufficient discipline. Deductive reasoning involves cognitive operations, if not actually, then possibly, "as though" such processes were carried out. This applies not only to such operations as substitution and inference, but also to the process of idealization, which provides the ideal objects and relations of logic. It is becoming increasingly clear that logic requires the preparatory analysis of meaning and the concept of reality. The reference to something objective presents a problem for which the analysis of meaning and symbolism is necessary. The fundamental principles of knowledge which govern truth and meaning apply to all systems, either as wholes or to their constituent propositions. The crucial question for a presuppositionless philosophy, as far as deduction is concerned, is that of the possibility of examining the grounds and processes of knowledge in such a way that the fundamental concepts and principles are evident, as a prelogical undertaking. In short, there are presuppositions of logic which concern its cognitive aspects, endow it with the element and criteria of meaning, thus constituting its subject-matter, and provide for its reference to an objective realm.

The self-foundation of formal logic must be supplemented

by another dimension of investigation. The phenomenological treatment of logic has the function of clarifying its basic ideas, and also of providing its very elements by means of the descriptive analysis of such concepts as judgment and meaning. The concepts of the understanding, and hence all of the ideas used on the higher level of formal reasoning, are traced to their "origin" in pre-predicative experience.[10] This procedure is designated "genetic," not in an empirical, factual, or historical sense, but in the sense of the intentional reference of all ideas or principles to their "original" evidences—in the last analysis, to the direct evidence of individuals. The element of historical time is simply irrelevant to such analysis. Husserl regarded the domain of the logical as being much greater than in the traditional logic. Logical "contribution" was found by him to be present on all levels of experience, and not only on the comparatively high level on which the traditional logic begins in its analysis. But he held that it is on the lower levels that the concealed presuppositions are to be found, on the basis of which the evidences of the logician on a higher level are to be understood.

The logocentric predicament is incurred, as Sheffer has pointed out,[11] because of the necessity of presupposing and employing logic in order to give an account of logic. This difficulty is met by attempting to make explicit that which is assumed to be valid, and by a kind of formal epoché, which makes it possible to distinguish sharply between the study of formal structure and its interpretation in terms of any kind of objectivity, and also between both of these and the study of the conditions that make considerations of notation and interpretation significant and valid. Even if the logocentric predicament could be avoided by means of a purely intuitive method, another predicament would take its place on the epistemological level. In order to investigate cognition, it is necessary to make use of knowledge. This is sufficiently justified in the course of the investigation, but it must nevertheless be regarded as an assumption for the initial purpose of episte-

[10] In the language of Husserl's *Erfahrung und Urteil*, edited by L. Landgrebe (Prague, 1939).

[11] Cf. *Isis*, VIII (1926), 226 ff.

mological analysis. That is unavoidable because of the essentially reflexive character of philosophic inquiry. Corresponding to the formal epoché, in which abstraction is made from all concrete, sensory meanings, but more sweeping in its extent, is the epistemological epoché, which suspends all logical, psychological, and ontological principles. That is necessary for the thoroughgoing descriptive analysis of cognition. The degree of clarification is greatly increased thereby, for lower levels of cognition may be investigated by means of "genetic" analyses. As in the case of the logocentric predicament, there is no insurmountable difficulty, as long as all tentatively assumed elements are made explicit.

V. The Program of Phenomenology

There was recognition of the ideal of presuppositionlessness as applied to logic and the theory of knowledge in the *Logical Investigations*,[12] and with regard to philosophy as a whole in the *Logos* essay, "Philosophy as a Rigorous Science." The mechanism for this ideal was first provided by the method of phenomenological reduction, which was systematically presented in the *Ideas* and *Cartesian Meditations*.

The phenomenological studies in the *Logical Investigations* were preparatory in character. From Husserl's statement that a scientific investigation in the theory of knowledge must satisfy the requirement of presuppositionlessness, it can be inferred that this ideal was recognized as the acid test of a truly critical philosophy. In his view this meant the strict exclusion of all assertions which could not be completely realized phenomenologically, i.e., in terms of intuitive experience alone, and subject to well-defined conditions. The "theory" to be achieved is simply the reflective and evident understanding of the nature of thinking and knowing in general. Acts of thought may refer to transcendent or even to non-existent and impossible objects. But the meaning of such experiences is clarified purely on the basis of the experience. The question regarding the justification of the assumption of "psychical" and "physi-

---

[12] *Logische Untersuchungen* (Halle, 1901), II, 19 ff.

cal" realities that are transcendent of consciousness is not proper to the pure theory of knowledge. The question of the existence and nature of the "external world" is metaphysical. It is true that epistemology, as the general explanation of the ideal essence and valid meaning of thought, considers the question of the possibility of knowing "real" objects or things, which are essentially transcendent to the experiences by which they are known, and the nature of the norms of such knowledge. But it is not concerned with the empirical question, whether human beings can actually gain such knowledge on the basis of the factual data given to them.

As Husserl regarded it, epistemology is really not a theory at all; it is not a science in the pregnant sense of a unity of theoretical explanation. Its aim is not the construction of deductive theories. This is shown by the most general theory of knowledge which Husserl described in the *Prolegomena*[13] as the philosophical supplement to the pure mathesis, which comprises all *a priori* categorial knowledge in the form of systematic theories. The "formal" theory of knowledge, which explains this theory of theories, is prior to all empirical theory; hence it is prior to all explanatory real science, to physical science and psychology, and also to metaphysics. It aims, not to explain the factual occurrence in objective nature in a psychological or psychophysical sense, but rather to clarify the idea of knowledge with respect to its constitutive elements and laws. It is interested in understanding the ideal meaning of the connections of experience, in which the objectivity of knowledge is documented, and seeks to bring the pure forms and laws of knowledge to clarity and distinctness by recourse to adequately fulfilled intuition. This clarification occurs within the framework of a phenomenology of knowledge which is concerned with the essential structures of the "pure" experiences and their meanings. There is no assertion concerning real existence, and hence no use can be made of premises drawn from metaphysical or natural science, especially psychology. It is this metaphysical, natural scientific, psychological presuppositionlessness, and no other kind, which Husserl proposed to realize at this time. If reference was made to actual languages and the merely communicative meaning of some of their forms of expression, he did not overstep the limits of his inquiry, for the analyses presented would retain their meaning and epistemological value regardless of whether there are actually languages and intercourse between people, or whether there are people and a world of nature. The analyses would hold even if everything existed only in the imagination, or as a possibility. The only premises recognized by Husserl are those which meet the requirement of an adequate phenomenological justification, which means fulfillment through evidence in the strictest sense of the term.

The conception of philosophy advanced in his *Logos* essay, in which philosophy is portrayed as a discipline that provides the sciences with a new dimension and a final completion, indicates the universal scope of Husserl's analysis. He emphasized the importance of the radical criticism of the naturalistic philosophy, urging a positive critique of its foundations and methods. The term "radical" is a popular one in phenomenology. Negatively it spells freedom from assumptions or beliefs of any kind, and positively it signifies the insightful establishment of all elements of knowledge. In Husserl's view, the natural sciences are "naïve" with respect to their points of departure.[14] For them, nature is "simply there," and things *are* in infinite space and time; they are "pre-given." The same holds for things from the standpoint of psychology. Every psychological judgment posits physical nature as existent, whether explicitly or not. It follows that if physical natural science cannot be philosophy, then neither can psychology, which is based upon it. The "naïveté" with which nature is regarded as given for natural science is "immortal" in it, as Husserl expressed it. He recognized the fact that natural science is very critical in its way, which is satisfactory as long as we remain in natural science and think with its attitude. But, he contended, a different critique of experience is both possible and necessary, a critique which places all experience in question and, along with it, experiential-scientific thinking.

[14] *Logos*, I, 298.

The proposed critique requires that all scientific and pre-scientific assertions concerning nature, or all statements which imply that things are posited as existent in space, time, causal connection, etc., must be eliminated on principle. This procedure was extended to include the elimination of the existence of the investigator himself, of his psychical faculties, and the like.

The clarification of consciousness and of all forms of objectivity is undertaken by phenomenology, and its procedure is supposed to be radical in the sense that no existence is assumed. This is made possible by essential intuition, in which an essence is grasped without positing any existence. Essences can be "seen" just as immediately as tones can be heard; for example, the essence "tone," or the essences "thing-appearance," "visible thing," "judgment," etc. Pure phenomenology was defined by Husserl (in the *Logos* essay) as a science which investigates essences alone, and not as concerned with the investigation of existence, or with "self-observation." The knowledge of essences and of essential relations was held to provide all that is necessary for the clarification of empirical knowledge and of all knowledge. Such knowledge was regarded as being prior to empirical knowledge, in the sense that the essential knowledge of the psychical is presupposed by all psychological knowledge.

If the procedure is to be thoroughly radical, no "pre-givenness" may be allowed; nothing is to be handed down for a beginning.[15] Inasmuch as philosophy is defined as being essentially the science of true beginnings or origins, the science of the radical must be required to be radical in its procedure in every respect. The method of philosophy is in short a method of direct intuition. The phenomenological grasping of essences opens up an endless field for work, and provides knowledge without any indirect symbolism and mathematical methods, without the apparatus of inference and proof. This appears to be the most rigorous type of knowledge.

Husserl's motives were thus given a vigorous expression, and this early account has the advantage of clearly formulating the

[15] *Logos,* I, 340.

general program which his later work has extended and deepened. The *Ideas* presented a much more detailed account of this program, and introduced the method and technique of phenomenological reduction. Characteristic of the work is the orientation with respect to Descartes, in particular the method of doubt. In Descartes' hands the method was nugatory. As employed in phenomenology, it is of aid in determining the ultimate grounds of knowledge, and also in providing a universal plane of experience and knowledge.

The phenomenological method is not only a possible method for the theory of knowledge, but is one which necessarily must be developed and carried through consciously for the understanding of the nature and structure of knowledge. In fact, it has been tacitly assumed and used in part in the past. It is to Husserl's credit that he was able to elaborate it systematically as a descriptive method applied to pure experience, i.e., independent of the thesis or belief in spatio-temporal "natural existence," but including that realm in its scope. It would be a misunderstanding of the method to expect it to derive existence by means of a device which abstracts from existence. The positive program of phenomenology is devoted to the task of the "constitution" of the world of nature and culture. Interpreted properly as a method of construction, in accordance with the descriptive ideal of phenomenology, the procedure is a legitimate part of the theory of science or of knowledge. Husserl spoke[16] of the "constitution of objectivity as referred to its subjective source" as one phase of his inquiry. This indicates the importance of determining the scope of constitutive phenomenology. Does it comprise reality, or possible reality, throughout; or is it concerned merely with the constitution of objectivity in this relationship to subjectivity, which is of course a possible and defensible theme? The latter is alone meaningful for phenomenology. Care should be taken not to interpret constitution as a creative activity in a metaphysical sense, if the method is to be kept free from dogma. This is not to suggest that there is no creative element in experience. The

[16] *Ideas*, p. 234.

examination of the creative performances of the understanding, for example, is also a matter for accurate descriptive analysis.[17]

VI. The Foundation of Phenomenology

The question as to whether anything is assumed in phenomenology must now be considered. Take, for example, Husserl's statement,[18] that "the stream of experience cannot begin and end." The same could be said of consciousness, in his view. The consciousness or experience of individual beings begins and ends. Which consciousness or stream of experience may be meant? It can only be an absolute process, the phenomenological status of which must then be established. And what shall be said of the permanent, objective validity of essential insight, or of the uniformity of the constitutive process itself, the fixed, temporal structure of consciousness, the validity of memory, and the egos of various types of construction? These must be justified by phenomenological analysis.

The bulk of Husserl's discussions of method shows that he does not acknowledge the use of assumed elements and constructions. They have no place in a philosophy conceived as a rigorous science with a final foundation.[19] No alleged self-evident elements may function as an unquestioned ground of knowledge in a science which is charged with final self-responsibility. Of course, something may not be unquestioned, and may nevertheless be assumed, at least provisionally. Husserl's ideal of philosophy was held to be realizable in an infinite historical process. The radical reflection which is required examines systematically "the ultimate thinkable presuppositions" of knowledge. The reflective inquiry leads first to the "universal subjective being and life" which is presup-

[17] Cf. *Erfahrung und Urteil*, part II.

[18] *Ideas*, p. 236.

[19] Cf. Husserl, "Nachwort zu meinen Ideen zu einer reinen Phänomenologie," *Jahrbuch für Philosophie und phänomenologische Forschung*, XI (1930), 549–570. This is Husserl's introduction to the English edition of the *Ideas*, plus a preface of about three pages, to which reference is made here.

posed as pre-scientific in all theorizing, and then proceeds to the "transcendental subjectivity," which is regarded as the primal source of all endowment of meaning and verification of being. Husserl called attention to the new meaning of the expression "transcendental subjectivity" the retention of which was an unhappy circumstance. This rigorous science of philosophy was held to be a universal and absolutely founding discipline, and there was no question about its being advanced as something essentially new. Husserl warned against transcendental anthropologism and psychologism as dangers besetting those who fail to reach the real ground of philosophy by means of the phenomenological reduction. If the procedure is thoroughgoing, no elements of an empirical or *a priori* anthropology are retained.

In the continuation of his description of the phenomenological method[20] Husserl distinguished between ordinary presuppositions of a positive kind and that which is presupposed implicitly in all presupposing and in all questioning and answering. The latter was held to exist necessarily, and to continue to exist, and was not acknowledged to be an assumption. It was regarded rather as the first thing to be freely and expressly posited, and that "with a self-evidence which precedes all conceivable instances of self-evidence, and is contained implicitly in them all."

That the repeated declarations concerning the presuppositionless ideal of philosophy did not refer to assumptions in every sense of the term is thus shown by Husserl's last published writings. The absolute basis which philosophy secures for itself was declared by Husserl to constitute the totality of presuppositions that can be taken for granted.[21] This was stated more pointedly in an article on phenomenology,[22] in which he wrote that the transcendental problem derives the means of its solution from an existence-stratum which it presupposes and sets beyond the reach of its inquiry. This realm

[20] Cf. the author's preface to the English edition of the *Ideas*.

[21] *Ideas*, p. 28. Cf. also Fink, "Das Problem der Phänomenologie Edmund Husserls," *Revue internationale de Philosophie*, vol. I (1939).

[22] *Encyclopædia Britannica*, 14th ed., XVII, 701 f.

was described as the bare subjectivity of consciousness in general. All knowledge was to be founded upon this basis by referring everything to the "transcendental origin." Husserl's idealistic position was clearly indicated by his thesis that all objective existence is essentially "relative," owing its nature to a unity of intention which is established according to transcendental laws.

VII. Significance of the Ideal

The problem of presuppositions derives its prominence from the idealistic argument concerning the priority of thought to being. It is due to the cognitive approach to philosophy, i.e., beginning with the knower and his objects, which has its historical explanation. That is one line of development leading to transcendental idealism, with its *a priori* construction of thought-forms, and to transcendental phenomenology, which is designed to be the self-clarifying, constitutive basis of all knowledge. Another line of development proceeds from the "logic of the world" to abstractions or logical forms and their deductive arrangement, which gives rise to the question of the circularity of logic and the status of its fundamental principles. These were conceived by Husserl to hold unconditionally, in accordance with the "logical absolutism" of the *Logical Investigations,* a position which was given a transcendental foundation by his later logical studies. We are referred therewith to the self-foundation of phenomenology as a theory of knowledge.

It has been seen that what Husserl calls the genetic method is different from what is ordinarily understood as the naturalistic genetic method. The latter operates within the space-time framework of the actual world. For it, things have a history, and the temporal order is essential. Thus the mental development of a particular individual is traced back to the earliest formation of abstractions, or there is interest in the development from the first blurred confusion of experience to distinct ideas and the discrimination of the elements of experience. For the phenomenological genetic method, all actual, historical individuals are of no interest as such; abstraction is made from the real temporal order. An idealized meaning, for example, is traced back essentially to a simpler experience which it presupposes. Ultimately this means the experience of individuals. This is similar to the way in which remembrance as such refers back to an original perception.

This method is presuppositionless in a way that formal logic is not and cannot be, for formal logic operates on the "higher" level of idealizations. If everything is to be placed in question and understood by recourse to primitive experience, the idealizations of logic must be accounted for. The phenomenological method, with its technique of reduction and essential analysis, is the most radical of all methods, if used correctly. The intentional analysis of the cognitive process, when restricted to cognition and its correlates as such, may well be the most critical possible beginning for philosophy.

In logic one operates with proposition-meanings and structures which represent past products of intellectual activity. There are two possible ways to go back to their "origin": first, to go back to their actual historical origination in the minds of particular thinkers; and second, to proceed from the actual matters of fact merely in order to "remake" or "constitute" them by going back to their perceptual, judgmental basis, and showing how they arise essentially. It is the latter procedure which is adopted by phenomenology. The exclusive consideration of essential structures and relations is the first step; and the phenomenological reduction makes possible the final elucidation of all elements of knowledge and experience by enabling us to get back of and to the bottom of all presuppositions. Because this means the reduction to the conscious life of an individual knower to begin with, as the basis for all later constitutive activity, and because the perception of individuals is the starting-point, this method makes possible a truly descriptive philosophy.

What is assumed at this point? Not the spatio-temporal world; none of the scientific theories which are used to interpret the world of existence; no independent or continuous existence; no other human beings; not one's own bodily existence or empirically conditioned ego; not the ideal science of pure logic, or any of the idealizations of theoretical knowledge: in short, nothing is assumed, and as a beginning there is only the self-validating cognitive experience itself. "The world" is, to be sure, "pre-given." But that region of pre-givenness, whose acknowledgment rules out the onesidedness of subjective idealism, plays no role in the constitutive method itself. It is used as a guiding-thread, or as a clue, just as the traditional logic is used. They are provisional presuppositions. When constituted "originally" they are no longer presuppositions. As far as individual knowers are concerned, the constitutive process represents an infinite task.

In his *Experience and Judgment,* Husserl stated that the being of the world is not achieved through a judgmental activity, but is the presupposition of all judging. If one apprehends an object, he discerns it as having been there previously, even if he were not attending to it. Thus all existence that affects us does so on the ground of the world; it is given to us as supposed existence, and the activity of knowledge aims to test whether it is truly such as it is supposed. The world as an existent world was regarded by Husserl as being the universal passive pre-givenness of all judgmental activity, of all theoretical interest that may enter in. As Husserl maintained, however, the concept of a presupposition receives a new meaning in the radicalism of transcendental phenomenology. "The world," which was the basis of all previous philosophies, is always there for it as a domain that is already valid, just as it is in everyday life. But it is not an explicit premise. In phenomenology, an epoché is performed upon this fixed, posited being. The pre-given world is finally regarded as constituted by transcendental subjectivity. To attain to this one must proceed from the "original life-world" to the subjective "contributions" from which the latter arises. In this sense transcendental logic investigates the participation of the logical contributions of consciousness in the construction of the world.

The examination of all assumptions, including its own, is made possible by the phenomenological method, which in its complete form includes reference to historical and cultural meanings, to which may be added the inspection of the method itself with regard to its place in history and culture. There need be no narrowness; nothing need be inaccessible to a truly descriptive method. The method of intentional analysis has the additional advantage of extending the field for description. The thoroughgoing justification of this method is not accomplished at one stroke, but must be achieved progressively. That is the task of the critical self-justification of all knowledge upon the basis of the self-givenness of the objects of experience.

The ideal of presuppositionlessness that is illustrated by Husserl's actual procedure in his investigations, including his logical as well as epistemological writings in all periods of his development, requires that there be no unexamined assumptions of any kind; that there be no metaphysical or existential assumptions unless there is a special reason for explicitly positing them; and that there be no prejudgments. It properly means the explicit examination and constitutive analysis of all elements of the structure of knowledge and reality. In contributing toward that end, Husserl has made one of the most striking advances in recent philosophy.

III. PHENOMENOLOGICAL REDUCTION

Husserl's Transcendental-Phenomenological Reduction*

RICHARD SCHMITT

Philosophers before, as well as since, Husserl have spoken of a philosophic discipline called "phenomenology" which describes its objects instead of constructing explanations. Husserl's phenomenology differs from all the others in the conditions which any inquiry must fulfill in order to deserve being called "phenomenological." Phenomenology, according to him, can begin only after the "transcendental-phenomenological reduction" has been performed by the beginning phenomenologist. Descriptions not preceded by this "reduction" are not phenomenological. Anyone who wants to understand the claims made by Husserl for his "Transcendental Phenomenology" and, even more, anyone who wants to employ the phenomenological method must first understand and practice the transcendental-phenomenological reduction. But such understanding is difficult to achieve; Husserl's own descriptions are quite perplexing and the commentators differ widely in their interpretations of these descriptions. I shall try to clarify this initial phase of phenomenology by showing that Husserl's characterizations of the transcendental-phenomenological reduction are, in fact, suggestions for a phenomenological description of reflection as opposed to straightforward, nonreflective thinking. This will provide only a partial explication of the transcendental-phenomenological reduction. How phenomenological reflection differs from other kinds, as (for

* From Richard Schmitt, "Husserl's Transcendental-Phenomenological Reduction," in *Philosophy and Phenomenological Research*, 20 (1959–1960), pp. 238–245. Reprinted with permission of the author and the editors.

instance) scientific reflection, must be treated in a separate paper.

We must begin by rehearsing, once again, Husserl's descriptions of the transcendental-phenomenological reduction. There are a number of different ways of approaching the reduction. One may follow Descartes on his road of total doubt. Alternatively one may examine one of the traditional philosophic disciplines, e.g., logic, in an attempt to uncover the aims implicit in its development.[1] By either way one is led to question what had previously seemed self-evident. On the Cartesian road we are led to question all presuppositions of human experience; in logic the presuppositions of judging, of validity and truth become questionable. We begin, then, by questioning what we had previously taken for granted, or by wondering at what seems most familiar.[2] This involves a change of attitude (*Einstellung*);[3] we must look at the world with "new eyes." What exactly is this new attitude which I adopt as I perform the transcendental-phenomenological reduction? Here Husserl provides a variety of phrases designed to exhibit this new attitude to the reader: I no longer attach any validity to the "natural belief in the existence of what I experience";[4] I "invalidate," "inhibit," "disqualify," all commitments (*Stellungnahmen*) with reference to experienced objects; I "bracket the objective world."[5] This last is one of the best-known phrases used in this connection. Husserl draws his metaphor from mathematics where we place an expression in brackets and put a + or − sign in front of it. By thus bracketing the objective world we "give it a different value."[6] In

[1] *Formale und Transcendentale Logik*, Halle, 1929, p. 6 ff. This work will be referred to as *Formale*.

[2] *Die Krisis der Europäischen Wissenschaften und die Transcendentale Phänomenologie*, ed. Walter Biemel, Husserliana Vol. VI, The Hague, 1954, p. 80. This work will be referred to as *Krisis*.

[3] *Ideen zu einer reinen Phänomenologie und phänomenologischen Philosophie*, ed. Walter Biemel, Husserliana Vol. III, The Hague, 1950, p. 61. This work will be referred to as *Ideen I*.

[4] *Cartesianische Meditationen*, ed. S. Strasser, Husserliana Vol. I, The Hague, 1950, p. 59. This work will be referred to as *Cart*.

[5] *Op. cit.*, p. 60.

[6] *Ideen I*, p. 174.

performing the reduction, the phenomenologist establishes himself as "disinterested spectator"[7] and changes his practical aims.[8] The result of this change of attitude is a change in my experience. Previously experienced reality now becomes "mere phenomenon." This Kantian term is here used in a new sense; any object of experience becomes "phenomenon" for the observer who recognizes the object's claim to reality, but reserves decision on the validity of that claim. In the "natural," preanalytic and prephenomenological attitude—sometimes Husserl also calls it the "naive" attitude, but not in any pejorative sense—we generally believe that objects perceived are real; we believe that we live in a real world. This belief is "put out of action," suspended, we make no use of it.[9] We are left with a world-as-phenomenon, a world which claims to be; but we refuse, for the time being, to pass on the validity of these claims.[10]

A further result of this movement is the discovery of the transcendental ego. I suddenly recognize that it is I who must decide whether the claims to reality of the objects of experience in particular, and of the world as a whole in general, are valid claims. I discover that whatever has sense and validity, has sense and validity for me.[11] I thus discover the "absolute being of the transcendental ego."[12] "Absolute being (Seiendes) is in the form of an intentional life which, whatever else it may be aware of in itself, is at the same time awareness of itself."[13] The "I" which transforms the world into mere phenomenon is, in so doing, aware of itself as transforming the world and cannot be subjected to the same transformation. But apart from its "modes of relatedness" and its "modes of behavior," this "I" is completely devoid of any content which could be studied or explicated. It is completely indescribable, being no more than a pure ego.[14]

[7] Cart., p. 73.
[8] Krisis, p. 399.
[9] Ideen I, p. 65.
[10] Cart., pp. 58–61.
[11] Op. cit., p. 65.
[12] Ideen I, p. 72.
[13] Formale, p. 241.
[14] Ideen I, p. 195, and Cart. p. 99.

Husserl insists that the transcendental-phenomenological reduction in no way limits experience. The phenomenologist
does not turn away either from the whole of experienced reality and actuality or from certain areas of it; he only suspends
judgment concerning the reality or validity of what is experienced. The world before the transcendental-phenomenological
reduction and the world which I have transformed into "mere
phenomenon" do not differ in content, but in the way in which
I am related to each of them.[15]

We are now in a position to understand Husserl's choice of
terminology better. The transcendental-phenomenological reduction is called "transcendental" because it uncovers the ego
for which everything has meaning and existence. It is called
"phenomenological" because it transforms the world into
mere phenomenon. It is called "reduction" because it leads us
back (Lat. *reducere*) to the source of the meaning and existence of the experienced world, in so far as it is experienced,[16]
by uncovering intentionality. Husserl also uses the term
"epoché." At first it appears as a synonym for "reduction."
In his last writings he differentiates between the two terms:
the change of attitude, i.e., the suspension of all natural belief
in the objects of experience is called the "epoché"; it, in turn,
is the precondition for reducing the natural world to a world
of phenomena.[17] The term "transcendental-phenomenological
reduction" covers both the *epoché* and the reduction in the
narrower sense of Husserl's last writings.

Throughout his writings of the middle and late period Husserl insisted that phenomenology is a reflective enterprise.[18]
It seems reasonable therefore to interpret the transcendental-
phenomenological reduction as a phenomenological description of the transition from a nonreflective to a reflective attitude, albeit a reflective attitude of a particular kind. If
phenomenology is a reflective enterprise, it does not follow
that all reflection is, therefore, phenomenological. But, before
we can distinguish phenomenological from other kinds of re-

[15] *Cart.*, pp. 59–60.
[16] *Cart.*, p. 65.
[17] *Krisis*, p. 155.
[18] Cf. *Ideen I*, p. 177; *Cart.*, p. 59; *Krisis*, p. 457.

flection, we must first turn to the more general question: what distinguishes reflection from nonreflective thinking? (henceforth to be referred to merely as "thinking").

Traditionally the distinction between thinking and reflection rested on the distinction between what was inside the mind and what was outside of it. According to John Locke, ". . . . the mind . . . . when it turns its view inward upon itself and observes its own actions about the ideas it has, takes from hence other ideas . . . ."[19] and these ideas are ideas of reflection. Hume draws the distinction in a very similar way.[20] The traditional distinction is intimately tied up with the doctrine that the mind has an "inside" and since this view is no longer popular, the difference between thinking and reflection bears re-examination.

A more serious objection against this concept of reflection as "the mind thinking about itself" is, that there is much thinking about oneself which is anything but reflective, but is, on the contrary, often only a means to escape the necessity for reflection. This kind of nonreflective and evasive thinking about oneself is found in brooding about one's own feelings and emotions, self-pity, nursing feelings of resentment or a sense of injury and, in extreme cases, a hysterical exaggeration of emotions.[21] Take a child who has been punished for disobedience. He will retreat to his room in anger, turning over and over in his mind how he has been wronged, and how unjustly he has been dealt with. This child thinks, and he thinks about his own "mind" and the "ideas therein," about his own loneliness and unhappiness, and how no one loves him. But, so far, he does not reflect. He does not ask himself whether his punishment may not, perhaps, be partially justified, whether it is really true that he is being punished merely out of sheer malice and ill will on his parents' part. Caught up in his own anger and misery the child has not been able to "stand

---

[19] John Locke, *An Essay Concerning Human Understanding*, Bk. II, ch. vi, par. 1.

[20] David Hume, *A Treatise on Human Nature*, Part I, Bk. I, Sec. II.

[21] Cf. Max Scheler, "Die Idole der Selbsterkenntnis" in *Vom Umsturz der Werte*, Vol. II, Leipzig, 1923, p. 61.

back" and survey the situation calmly and with some detachment. In his anger he loses his "sense of proportion" and his "proper perspective." Reflection, on the other hand, involves just this critical detachment. Once the child begins to reflect, after the first violent emotion is spent, he will, to be sure, still think about himself but not merely about himself, his own suffering, and the sins of others against him. He will, instead, think about himself in relation to the other persons involved. He will review the events, try to see them from his parents' point of view, how his behavior may have embarrassed or hurt them. Thus taking "the other's point of view" will, at the same time, lead the child to think about himself in a different light. He will no longer merely interest himself in his own unhappiness—that is put aside for the moment—but will think about what he actually did do. Thus the scope of reflection about oneself is considerably wider than that of thinking about oneself, since it includes facts about one's relations to others and about oneself which had before remained unnoticed or had appeared irrelevant.

This difference between thinking and reflection does not only hold where one's person is the object; it also applies "outside" the mind. A political reformer (for instance) is firmly committed to his view of the world: he sees and experiences society rent by class dissensions. Yet he is not content to mouth tired political catch phrases. He thinks about this world in which he finds himself, and everywhere he discovers new evidence for his diagnoses of society's ills. Much thought also goes into the application of his proposed remedies. To be a successful revolutionary a man must think but he need not, and perhaps should not, reflect. If the reformer were to reflect he would have to temper his revolutionary zeal, detach himself from his aims and his habitual attitude toward the world, and question what had seemed self-evident before. He would have to raise the question whether the world which he had taken to be immediately experienced is not at least in part the embodiment of his own wishes and the product of his imagination. Here again reflection requires detachment and widens the scope of inquiry.

These examples show that the difference between thinking

and reflection does not lie in the respective objects of these
activities since any object can be the object of thinking as well
as of reflection. The examples have also provided us with
material for showing where the difference between thought
and reflection does lie. Besides, we shall find that Husserl's
description of the transcendental-phenomenological reduction
provides us with all the terms and distinctions needed for the
analysis of these two examples.

(a.) The person who thinks is "interested" in the objects of
his thought; they attract him.[22] We saw this very clearly in
our two examples: the child was overwhelmed by his anger
and sense of injury; the reformer was "caught up" in his world
which was waiting to be reformed. (b.) To be interested or to
be attracted by an object brings with it that the object which
is attracting me is accepted as it presents itself; it "imposes"
itself on the observer.[23] For the child his anger and hurt are
indubitably real. He would reject emphatically any suggestion
that "things are really not so bad." The man who is, in this
sense, attracted by or interested in the world or in himself accepts the world and himself "at face value." This attitude Husserl calls *"natuerlicher Seinsglaube"*[24] the unquestioning acceptance of the existence of what is experienced. (c.) In order
to begin to reflect one must perform the *epoché*, i.e., one must
suspend this interest, become disinterested.[25] Thus, the child
begins to reflect only after his commitment to the existing
experience is weakened, if he stands back and takes up a
"neutral attitude."[26] This involves cancelling or suspending
the earlier acceptance of experience, placing oneself, as Husserl puts it sometimes, "above" the natural world, where by
"natural" he means "prereflective."[27]

(d.) The *epoché* thus renders questionable what previously
had been taken as certain and self-evident. This does not mean

[22] *Erfahrung und Urteil*, ed. by Ludwig Landgrebe, Hamburg,
1949, p. 80. This work will be referred to as *Erfahrung*.
[23] *Ibid.*
[24] *Cart.*, p. 59.
[25] *Op. cit.*, p. 73.
[26] *Ideen I*, p. 264 ff.
[27] *Krisis*, p. 395.

that experience as a whole is rejected. To question something is not to deny it. The child does not suddenly say, "Oh, I'm not really angry"; the reformer does not deny that the world is riddled with injustices, but experience ceases to be unambiguous and the door is opened to questions. The certainty once possessed by experience now becomes a mere claim. World as well as psychological self become, in Husserl's language, "mere phenomenon." We are beginning to take up a properly reflective attitude, one of detachment and questioning. Here the *epoché* ends and we are entering the phase which Husserl calls the reduction.

For this new attitude, what was once a clear datum becomes a complex experience in need of clarification; what seemed actual becomes mere possibility,[28] and this transformation has several important implications:

(e.) What had, at one time, seemed to be a fact of immediate experience now looks as if it might have been merely an interpretation and, possibly, a false one. Maybe his father's severity was not a manifestation of ill will or sheer arbitrariness. Perhaps the poverty of the workers is not merely a result of exploitation and the greed of employers. Only in the reflective attitude do we begin to separate what is really given in experience, what close and attentive scrutiny reveals to be "really there" from what was merely added to this experience by the observer, as interpretation or anticipation. We distinguish here, Husserl says, between what is "self-given" (*selbstgegeben*),[29] what is given "in the flesh" (*leibhaft*),[30] and what is merely associated opinion (*Mitmeinung*).[31] It is here, in reflection, that the distinction between true belief and knowledge is first drawn.

(f.) On the other hand, interested thought is selective. As long as I accept the world of natural experience unquestioningly, certain facts of the situation are either not noticed at all or are put aside as unimportant. But now, in reflection, the facts which had previously seemed self-evident have become

[28] *Cart.*, p. 66.
[29] *Formale*, p. 251.
[30] *Ideen I*, p. 52.
[31] *Cart.*, p. 82.

questionable, and thus facts which they had overshadowed
before or which, in relation to them, had seemed insignificant
now come to light and must be examined carefully. The scope
of relevant subject matter is widened considerably as soon as
we make the transition from thinking to reflection. The angry
child goes beyond his own anger and reflects about this anger
in relation to his own conduct and that of his parents. The
reformer considers facts previously ignored or unnoticed; he
must, among other things, face up to his own preconceptions.
These new facts had previously been "anonymous"; now they
lose this anonymity.[32] Concepts or feelings which had been
merely "at the back of my mind," as well as objects which I
had seen or heard without noticing them are now brought out
into the open.

(g.) Reflection must describe these new facts rather than
explain them.[33] Explanations are in order where we know
what the world or my present condition is like, and we want to
find out why they are in this state. But as we turn from thinking to reflection we relinquish former certainties. Accordingly,
there is nothing definite that would require or even be capable
of an explanation. Instead, there are facts, only casually observed before or perhaps not observed at all, which need to
be examined or re-examined in order to separate what is evidently given in our experience from what is merely associated
opinion or outright fiction. Once the revolutionary questions
his former world-view the facts lose the ready-made significance which his previous theories had given them. The once
intelligible world is replaced by disjointed experiences which
refuse to fit into any kind of pattern, and his first task is to
pay close attention to actual observation to find what his society is really like, what in his former experience was genuine
fact, and what merely supposition and interpretation.

(h.) Throughout the unfolding of these two transformations, the *epoché* and the reduction, repeated reference was
made to the reflecting self. These must now be rendered more
explicit. As the subject takes up a more detached attitude, his

32 *Cart.*, p. 84.
33 *Ideen I*, pp. 171–174.

experience takes on a different complexion, and this is true whether the object is myself or the world. Thus, it appears, that the content of experience is dependent on myself as subject; experience presents to me its claim to validity: I must certify this claim. I can withdraw my confidence or belief from the object, thereby transforming it from a valid experience into a mere phenomenon. In this sense I, as a subject, am the source of the validity of experience,[34] but this, at the same time, transforms the meaning of the experience. Once the validity of present experience is put in question, one looks at the world with "new eyes" and the world looks different to one. In this sense the subject is not only the source of validity of experience, but also of its significance (*Sinn*).[35]

(i.) As the scope of awareness widens, the self as subject falls under notice: the reformer begins to ask how much his own wishes, desires, needs, prejudices shaped his experience of the world. The child wonders whether his actions have merited the punishment inflicted. Reflection, thus, is always expanding in two directions: The world is examined in relation to myself when I try to distinguish those aspects of experience which are genuinely evident from those which I merely assume or suppose to be the case. The subject is examined in relation to the world when I inquire into the beliefs, feelings, desires, etc., which shaped the experiences about which I am now reflecting. Husserl distinguishes these two directions of reflection as the "noetic" and the "noematic" aspects of the intentional relation; the former refers to the subject-in-relation-to-the-object, the latter to the object-in-relation-to-the-subject.[36] These two aspects of the intentional relation are strictly correlative;[37] they determine each other and each can only be understood in the light of the other. There is no object unless it is object for some subject,[38] and no subject unless it has a world as its object.[39]

[34] *Cart.*, p. 65.
[35] *Ibid.*
[36] *Ideen I*, p. 218 ff., and *Cart.* p. 74.
[37] *Formale*, p. 231.
[38] *Ideen I*, p. 110 ff.
[39] *Cart.*, p. 99.

(j.) Noetic analysis only reveals the ego in so far as it has become the object of a reflective act; the ego which reflects here, as in all reflection, remains irrevocably anonymous. We are aware of its presence but it has no content, it cannot be described.[40] Reflection, then, takes a subjective turn in three different ways: The object of thinking is revealed as object-for-a-subject, as object whose validity and significance flows from this subject. The subject is seen as being the subject-of-this-object, the subject which, in Husserl's language, "constitutes" the object. At the same time the ego which reflects but eludes all descriptive grasp makes itself felt.

We have now shown that the transcendental-phenomenological reduction shows all the common features of the transition from thinking to reflection. It remains for another paper to show the distinguishing marks of phenomenological reflection which sets it apart from reflection in everyday life or in the sciences.

The Thesis of the Natural Standpoint and Its Suspension*

EDMUND HUSSERL

The Word of the Natural Standpoint: I and My World About Me

Our first outlook upon life is that of natural human beings, imagining, judging, feeling, willing, *"from the natural standpoint."* Let us make clear to ourselves what this means in the form of simple meditations which we can best carry on in the first person.

[40] *Ideen I*, p. 195.

* From Edmund Husserl, *Ideas: General Introduction to Phenomenology,* translated by W. R. Boyce Gibson (London: George Allen & Unwin Ltd., 1931), Vol. I, secs. 27–32. Reprinted with permission of the publishers.

I am aware of a world, spread out in space endlessly, and in time becoming and become, without end. I am aware of it, that means, first of all, I discover it immediately, intuitively, I experience it. Through sight, touch, hearing, etc., in the different ways of sensory perception, corporeal things somehow spatially distributed are *for me simply there*, in verbal or figurative sense "present," whether or not I pay them special attention by busying myself with them, considering, thinking, feeling, willing. Animal beings also, perhaps men, are immediately there for me; I look up, I see them, I hear them coming towards me, I grasp them by the hand; speaking with them, I understand immediately what they are sensing and thinking, the feelings that stir them, what they wish or will. They too are present as realities in my field of intuition, even when I pay them no attention. But it is not necessary that they and other objects likewise should be present precisely in my *field of perception*. For me real objects are there, definite, more or less familiar, agreeing with what is actually perceived without being themselves perceived or even intuitively present. I can let my attention wander from the writing-table I have just seen and observed, through the unseen portions of the room behind my back to the verandah, into the garden, to the children in the summer-house, and so forth, to all the objects concerning which I precisely "know" that they are there and yonder in my immediate co-perceived surroundings—a knowledge which has nothing of conceptual thinking in it, and first changes into clear intuiting with the bestowing of attention, and even then only partially and for the most part very imperfectly.

But not even with the added reach of this intuitively clear or dark, distinct or indistinct *co-present* margin, which forms a continuous ring around the actual field of perception, does that world exhaust itself which in every waking moment is in some conscious measure "present" before me. It reaches rather in a fixed order of being the limitless beyond. What is actually perceived, and what is more or less clearly co-present and determinate (to some extent at least), is partly pervaded, partly girt about with a *dimly apprehended depth or fringe of indeterminate reality*. I can pierce it with rays from the illuminating focus of attention with varying success. Determining representations, dim at first, then livelier, fetch me something out, a chain of such recollections takes shape, the circle of determinacy extends ever farther, and eventually so far that the connexion with the actual field of perception as the *immediate* environment is established. But in general the issue is a different one: an empty mist of dim indeterminacy gets studded over with intuitive possibilities or presumptions, and only the "form" of the world as "world" is foretokened. Moreover, the zone of indeterminacy is infinite. The misty horizon that can never be completely outlined remains necessarily there.

As it is with the world in its ordered being as a spatial present—the aspect I have so far been considering—so likewise is it with the world in respect to its *ordered being in the succession of time*. This world now present to me, and in every waking "now" obviously so, has its temporal horizon, infinite in both direction, its known and unknown, its intimately alive and its unalive past and future. Moving freely within the moment of experience which brings what is present into my intuitional grasp, I can follow up these connexions of the reality which immediately surrounds me. I can shift my standpoint in space and time, look this way and that, turn temporally forwards and backwards; I can provide for myself constantly new and more or less clear and meaningful perceptions and representations, and images also more or less clear, in which I make intuitable to myself whatever can possibly exist really or supposedly in the steadfast order of space and time.

In this way, when consciously awake, I find myself at all times, and without my ever being able to change this, set in relation to a world which, through its constant changes, remains one and ever the same. It is continually "present" for me, and I myself am a member of it. Therefore this world is not there for me as a mere *world of facts and affairs,* but, with the same immediacy, as a *world of values,* a *world of goods,* a *practical world.* Without further effort on my part I find the things before me furnished not only with the qualities that befit their positive nature, but with value-characters such as beautiful or ugly, agreeable or disagreeable, pleasant or unpleasant, and so forth. Things in their immediacy stand there as objects to be used, the "table" with its "books," the "glass to drink from," the "vase," the "piano," and so forth. These values and practicalities, they too belong to *the constitution of the "actually present" objects as such,* irrespective of my turning or not turning to consider them or indeed any other objects. The same considerations apply of course just as well to the men and beasts in my surroundings as to "mere things." They are my "friends" or my "foes," my "servants" or "superiors," "strangers" or "relatives," and so forth.

The "Cogito." My Natural World-about-me and the Ideal Worlds-about-me

It is then to this world, *the world in which I find myself and which is also my world-about-me,* that the complex forms of my manifold and shifting *spontaneities* of consciousness stand related: observing in the interests of research the bringing of meaning into conceptual form through description; comparing and distinguishing, collecting and counting, presupposing and inferring, the theorizing activity of consciousness, in short, in its different forms and stages. Related to it likewise are the diverse acts and states of sentiment and disapproval, joy and sorrow, desire and aversion, hope and fear, decision and action. All these, together with the sheer acts of the Ego, in which I become acquainted with the world as *immediately* given me, through spontaneous tendencies to turn towards it and to grasp it, are included under the one Cartesian expression: *Cogito.* In the natural urge of life I live continually in *this fundamental form of all "wakeful" living,* whether in addition I do or do not assert the *cogito,* and whether I am or am not "reflectively" concerned with the Ego and the *cogitare.* If I am so concerned, a new *cogito* has become livingly active, which for its part is not reflected upon, and so not objective for me.

I am present to myself continually as someone who perceives, represents, thinks, feels, desires, and so forth; and *for the most part* herein I find myself related in present experience to the fact-world which is constantly about me. But I am not always so related, not every *cogito* in which I live has for its *cogitatum* things, men, objects or contents of one kind or another. Perhaps I am busied with pure numbers and the laws they symbolize: nothing of this sort is present in the world about me, this world of "real fact." And yet the world of numbers also is there for me, as the field of objects with which I am arithmetically busied; while I am thus occupied some numbers or constructions of a numerical kind will be at the focus of vision, girt by an arithmetical horizon partly defined, partly not; but obviously this being-there-for-me, like the being there at all, is something very different from this. *The arithmetical world is there for me only when and so long as I occupy the arithmetical standpoint.* But the *natural* world, the world in the ordinary sense of the word, is *constantly there for me,* so long as I live naturally and look in its direction. I am then at the *"natural standpoint,"* which is just another way of stating the same thing. And there is no need to modify these conclusions when I proceed to appropriate to myself the arithmetical world, and other similar "worlds," by adopting the corresponding standpoint. The natural world *still remains "present,"* I am at the natural standpoint after as well as before, and in this respect *undisturbed by the adoption of new standpoints.* If my *cogito* is active *only* in the worlds proper to the new standpoints, the natural world remains unconsidered; it is now the background for my consciousness as act, but it is *not the encircling sphere within which an arithmetical world finds its true and proper place.* The two worlds are present together but *disconnected,* apart, that is, from their relation to the Ego, in virtue of which I can freely direct my glance or my acts to the one or to the other.

The "Other" Ego-subject and the Intersubjective Natural World-about-me

Whatever holds good for me personally, also holds good, as I know, for all other men whom I find present in my world-about-me. Experiencing them as men, I understand and take them as Ego-subjects, units like myself, and related to their natural surroundings. But this in such wise that I apprehend the world-about-them and the world-about-me objectively as one and the same world, which differs in each case only through affecting consciousness differently. Each has his place whence he sees the things that are present, and each enjoys accordingly different appearances of the things. For each, again, the fields of perception and memory actually present are different, quite apart from the fact that even that which is here intersubjectively known in common is known in different ways, is differently apprehended, shows different grades of clearness, and so forth. Despite all this, we come to understandings with our neighbours, and set up in common an objective spatio-temporal fact-world as *the world about us that is there for us all, and to which we ourselves none the less belong.*

The General Thesis of the Natural Standpoint

That which we have submitted towards the characterization of what is given to us from the natural standpoint, and thereby of the natural standpoint itself, was a piece of pure description *prior to all "theory."* In these studies we stand bodily aloof from all theories, and by "theories" we here mean anticipatory ideas of every kind. Only as facts of our environment, not as agencies for uniting facts validly together, do theories concern us at all. But we do not set ourselves the task of continuing the pure description and raising it to a systematically inclusive and exhaustive characterization of the data, in their full length and breadth, discoverable from the natural standpoint (or from any standpoint, we might add, that can be knit up with the same in a common consent). A task such as this can and must—as scientific—be undertaken, and it is one of extraordinary importance, although so far scarcely noticed. Here it is not ours to attempt. For us who are striving towards the entrance-gate of phenomenology all the necessary work in this direction has already been carried out; the few features pertaining to the natural standpoint which we need are of a quite general character, and have already figured in our descriptions, and been sufficiently *and fully clarified.* We even made a special point of securing this full measure of clearness.

We emphasize a most important point once again in the sentences that follow: I find continually present and standing over against me the one spatio-temporal fact-world to which I myself belong, as do all other men found in it and related in the same way to it. This "fact-world," as the world already tells us, I find to *be out there,* and also *take it just as it gives itself to me as something that exists out there.* All doubting and rejecting of the data of the natural world leaves standing the *general thesis of the natural standpoint.* "The" world is as fact-world always there; at the most it is at odd points "other" than I supposed, this or that under such names as "illusion," "hallucination," and the like, must be struck *out of it,* so to speak; but the "it" remains ever, in the sense of the general thesis, a world that has its being out there. To know it more comprehensively, more trustworthily, more perfectly than the naïve lore of experience is able to do, and to solve all the problems of scientific knowledge which offer themselves upon its ground, that is the goal of the *sciences of the natural standpoint.*

Radical Alteration of the Natural Thesis "Disconnexion," "Bracketing"

Instead now of remaining at this standpoint, we propose to alter it radically. Our aim must be to convince ourselves of the possibility of this alteration on grounds of principle.

The General Thesis according to which the real world about me is at all times known not merely in a general way as something apprehended, but as a fact-world *that has its being out there,* does *not* consist of course *in an act proper,* in an articulated judgment *about existence.* It is and remains something all the time the standpoint is adopted, that is, it endures persistently during the whole course of our life of natural endeavour. What has been at any time perceived clearly, or obscurely made present, in short everything out of the world of nature through experience and prior to any thinking, bears in its totality and in all its articulated sections the character "present" "out there," a character which can function essentially as the ground of support for an explicit (predicative) existential judgment which is in agreement with the character it is grounded upon. If we express that same judgment, we know quite well that in so doing we have simply put into the form of a statement and grasped as a predication what already lay somehow in the original experience, or lay there as the character of something "present to one's hand."

We can treat the potential and unexpressed thesis exactly as we do the thesis of the explicit judgment. A procedure of this sort, *possible at any time,* is, for instance, *the attempt to doubt everything* which Descartes, with an entirely different end in view, with the purpose of setting up an absolutely indubitable sphere of Being, undertook to carry through. We link on here, but add directly and emphatically that this attempt to doubt everything should serve us *only as a device of method,* helping us to stress certain points which by its means, as though secluded in its essence, must be brought clearly to light.

The attempt to doubt everything has its place in the realm of our *perfect freedom.* We can *attempt to doubt* anything and everything, however convinced we may be concerning what we doubt, even though the evidence which seals our assurance is completely adequate.

Let us consider what is essentially involved in an act of this kind. He who attempts to doubt is attempting to doubt "Being" of some form or other, or it may be Being expanded into such predicative forms as "It is," "It is this or thus," and the like. The attempt does not affect the form of Being itself. He who doubts, for instance, whether an object, whose Being he does not doubt, is constituted in such and such a way doubts *the way it is constituted.* We can obviously transfer this way of speaking from the doubting to the *attempt* at doubting. It is clear that we cannot doubt the Being of anything, and in the same act of consciousness (under the unifying form of simultaneity) bring what is substantive to this Being under the terms of the Natural Thesis, and so confer upon it the character of "being actually there" (*vorhanden*). Or to put the same in another way: we cannot at once doubt and hold for certain one and the same quality of Being. It is likewise clear that the *attempt* to doubt any object of awareness in respect of it *being actually there necessarily conditions a certain suspension* (*Aufhebung*) *of the thesis;* and it is precisely this that interests us. It is not a transformation of the thesis into its antithesis, of positive into negative; it is also not a transformation into presumption, suggestion, indecision, doubt (in one or another sense of the word); each shifting indeed is not at our free pleasure. *Rather is it something quite unique. We do not abandon the thesis we have adopted, we make no change in our conviction,* which remains in itself what it is so long as we do not introduce new motives of judgment, which we precisely refrain from doing. And yet the thesis undergoes a modification—whilst remaining in itself what it is, *we set it as it were* "*out of action,*" we "*disconnect it,*" "*bracket it.*" It still remains there like the bracketed in the bracket, like the disconnected outside the connexional system. We can also say: The thesis is experience as lived (*Erlebnis*), *but we make* "*no use*" *of it,* and by that, of course, we do not indicate privation (as when we say of the ignorant that he makes no use of a certain thesis); in this case rather, as with all parallel expressions, we are dealing with indicators that point to a definite but *unique form of consciousness,* which clamps on to the original simple thesis (whether it actually or even predicatively *posits* existence or not), and transvalues it in a quite peculiar way. *This transvaluing is a concern of our full freedom, and is opposed to all cognitive attitudes* that would set themselves up as co-ordinate with the *thesis,* and yet within the unity of "simultaneity" remain incompatible with it, as indeed it is in general with all attitudes whatsoever in the strict sense of the word.

In *the attempt to doubt* applied to a thesis which, as we presuppose, is certain and tenaciously held, the "disconnexion" takes place in and with a modification of the antithesis, namely with the "*supposition*" (*Ansetzung*) *of Non-Being,* which is thus the partial basis of the attempt to doubt. With Descartes this is so markedly the case that one can say that his universal attempt at doubt is just an attempt at universal denial. We disregard this possibility here, we are not interested in every analytical component of the attempt to doubt, nor therefore in its exact and completely sufficing analysis. *We extract only the phenomenon of "bracketing" or "disconnection,"* which is obviously not limited to that of the attempt to doubt, although it can be detached from it with special ease, but can appear *in other contexts also,* and with no less ease *independently.* In relation to every thesis and wholly uncoerced we can use this peculiar ἐποχή, (*epokhe*—abstention), *a certain refraining from judgment which is compatible with the unshaken and unshakable because self-evidencing conviction of Truth.* The thesis is "put out of action," bracketed, it passes off into the modified status of a "bracketed thesis," and the judgment *simpliciter* into *"bracketed judgment."*

Naturally one should not simply identify this consciousness with that of "mere supposal," that nymphs, for instance, are dancing in a ring; for thereby *no disconnecting* of a living conviction that goes on living takes place, although from another side the close relation of the two forms of consciousness lies clear. Again, we are not concerned here with supposal in the sense of *"assuming"* or *taking for granted,* which in the equivocal speech of current usage may also be expressed in the words: "I suppose (I make the assumption) that it is so and so."

Let us add further that nothing hinders us *from speaking bracketing correlatively* also, in respect of *an objectivity to be posited,* what ever be the region or category to which it belongs. What is meant in this case is that *every thesis related to this objectivity* must be *disconnected* and changed into its bracketed counterpart. On closer view, moreover, the "bracketing" image is from the outset better suited to the sphere of the object, just as the expression "to put out of action" better suits the sphere of the Act or of Consciousness.

The Phenomenological ἐποχή

We can now let the universal ἐποχή, (*epokhe*—abstention) in the sharply defined and novel sense we have given to it step into the place of the Cartesian attempt at universal doubt. But on good grounds we *limit* the universality of this ἐποχή. For were it as inclusive as it is in general capable of being, then

since every thesis and every judgment can be modified freely
to any extent, and every objectivity that we can judge or
criticize can be bracketed, no field would be left over for unmodified judgments, to say nothing of a science. But our design
is just to discover a new scientific domain, such as might be
won precisely *through the method of bracketing,* though only
through a definitely limited form of it.

The limiting consideration can be indicated in a word.

*We put out of action the general thesis which belongs to
the essence of the natural standpoint,* we place in brackets
whatever it includes respecting the nature of Being: *this entire
natural world therefore* which is continually "there for us,"
"present to our hand," and will ever remain there, is a "fact-
world" of which we continue to be conscious, even though it
pleases us to put it in brackets.

If I do this, as I am fully free to do, I do *not* then *deny*
this "world," as though I were a sophist, *I do not doubt that
it is there* as though I were a sceptic; but I use the "phenomenological" ἐποχή, which *completely bars me from using any
judgment that concerns spatio-temporal existence (Dasein).*

Thus *all sciences which relate to this natural world,* though
they stand never so firm to me, though they fill me with wondering admiration, though I am far from any thought of objecting to them in the least degree, *I disconnect them all, I
make absolutely no use of their standards, I do not appropriate
a single one of the propositions that enter into their systems,
even though their evidential value is perfect, I take none of
them, no one of them serves me for a foundation*—so long,
that is, as it is understood, in the way these sciences themselves
understand it, as a truth *concerning the realities* of this world.
I may accept it only after I have placed it in the bracket. That
means: only in the modified consciousness of the judgment as
it appears in disconnexion, and *not as it figures within the
science as its proposition, a proposition which claims to be
valid and whose validity I recognize and make use of.*

The ἐποχή here in question will not be confined with that
which positivism demands, and against which, as we were compelled to admit, it is itself an offender. We are not concerned
at present with removing the preconceptions which trouble the

pure positivity (*Sachlichkeit*) of research, with the constituting of a science "free from theory" and "free from metaphysics" by bringing all the grounding back to the immediate data, nor with the means of reaching such ends, concerning whose value there is indeed no question. What *we* demand lies along another line. The whole world as placed within the nature-setting and presented in experience as real, taken completely "free from all theory," just as it is in reality experienced, and made clearly manifest in and through the linkings of our experiences, has now no validity for us, it must be set in brackets, untested indeed but also uncontested. Similarly all theories and sciences, positivistic or otherwise, which relate to this world, however good they may be, succumb to the same fate.

IV. ESSENCES AND EIDETIC REDUCTION

Introduction

The following selections require a short introduction. In the foregoing studies it has already been stressed several times that from the very beginning Husserl characterized his phenomenology as a study of the general essence of consciousness and of its various structures. Phenomenology is not interested in "factual facts" but in the essences of the immediately given phenomena. Husserl uses the term "essence" to indicate that which in the intimate self-being of an individual thing or entity tells us "what it is." Every such essence can be expressed by a concept.

In the natural attitude all knowledge begins with experience and remains within the realm of experience. In this attitude the cognitive acts, which are all ultimately based upon primordial experiences, posit reality in *individual* form; they posit it as having a spatio-temporal existence, as something existing here and at this particular point in time, as having this particular duration, as having a real content whose essence could just as well be present in any other point of time. They posit it, moreover, as something which is present now at this particular place and in this particular physical shape, although the same real thing, so far as its essence is concerned, could just as well be present in any other place and in any other form or shape.

Every empirical and individual experience, however, can be transformed into an essential insight by means of a special process which Husserl calls "ideation." The object of such an ideation is the corresponding essence or *eidos*. This *eidos* is in turn a new kind of object: just as the datum of individual or empirical experience is an individual object, so the datum of essential intuition is an essence or *eidos*. Consequently, essential insight is a new kind of intuition which is to be carefully distinguished from the intuition which as primordial object-giving act is the source of all our knowledge in the realm of the natural attitude.

In Husserl's view essential intuition is based upon an individual intuition, although it does not necessarily presuppose any apprehension of an individual's reality. In other words, no essential intuition is possible when the ego cannot freely direct its glance to an individual counterpart, while, conversely, no individual intuition is possible unless there is a free possibility of carrying out an act of ideation. All this, however, does not alter the fact that the two kinds of intuition are fundamentally different.[1]

The first description of the process of ideation can be found in Husserl's *Logische Untersuchungen*.[2] This first tentative description of the ideation or *Wesensschau* that from the very beginning occupied a central place in phenomenology caused a great misunderstanding. Husserl, therefore, tried to correct and clarify this method in his article "*Philosophie als strenge Wissenschaft*."[3] Further elaborations and clarifications of this method are found in *Ideen*[4] and in *Phänomenologische Psychologie*.[5] The point of view reached in these latter publications is later maintained in *Cartesianische Meditationen*[6] and in *Formale und transzendentale Logik*[7] where Husserl tried to define the position and function of the eidetic reduction in its relationship to other phenomenological procedures. The most exhaustive of Husserl's descriptions of the "eidetic reduction" appeared only much later in *Erfahrung und Urteil*,[8] which was published posthumously by Ludwig Landgrebe in 1939.

It is of some importance to notice that in the beginning, Husserl seemed to adopt the point of view that ideation takes place on the basis of the particular experience of an individual of a certain class. Later we see an increasingly important role assigned to the imagination, until ultimately Husserl saw

[1] Edmund Husserl, *Ideen*, Vol. I, secs. 1–4.
[2] Edmund Husserl, *Logische Untersuchungen*, Vol. III, pp. 235–36.
[3] Edmund Husserl, *Phil. str. W.*, pp. 315–19.
[4] Edmund Husserl, *Ideen*, Vol. I, pp. 12–17, 159–63.
[5] Edmund Husserl, *Phän. Psych.*, pp. 72–87.
[6] Edmund Husserl, *Cart. Med.*, pp. 103–6.
[7] Edmund Husserl, *F. t. L.*, pp. 218–19.
[8] Edmund Husserl, *Erf. u. Urt.*, pp. 394–98, 409–43.

the imagination as the essential factor in the revealing of the essences of things. It is also important to remark that Husserl's investigations concerning essences brought him to the conclusion that, in the realm of essences, it is necessary to make a distinction between *eidē* and *pure essences*. In the selection taken from Levinas' *Théorie de l'intuition dans la phénoménologie de Husserl* both points are clearly explained.

The selections from Husserl's *Ideen* are taken from a chapter which is completely devoted to methodological considerations. After a short section explaining the importance of methodological considerations for phenomenology, Husserl deals briefly with the phenomenological reduction. Then he goes on to say that in view of the fact that phenomenology is nothing but a theory of essences developed within the realm of pure intuition, it is of vital importance to express the intuitively given data in an unambiguous terminology. Although the phenomenological terminology is mostly derived from our everyday language, its "technical" meaning must be carefully determined on the basis of the analyses through which the intuition of the primordial data are to be prepared. Then he proceeds in sections 67–75 to explain his view on a "descriptive eidetic of essences." Sections 72–74 are omitted here because the most significant insights contained in them are dealt with in the Levinas essay which follows.

Intuition of Essences*

EMMANUEL LEVINAS

Introductory Note

[Chapter VI of Levinas' book *Théorie de l'intuition dans la phénoménologie de Husserl*, entitled *Intuition of Essences*, begins with the remark that Husserl is often accused of having defended a form of logicism or a certain Platonic realism. In Levinas' view it was the first volume of *Logische Untersuchungen* in particular which earned Husserl this "bad" reputation.

In explaining his own view of the issue, Levinas points out that the first volume of *Logische Untersuchungen* did indeed try to show that it is impossible to identify the laws of logic with psychological laws. It is, however, of the greatest importance to realize that the psychology that Husserl opposed is a naturalistic psychology which, as a science of facts, is unable to account for the "ideal" laws of logic. It is clear for Husserl that since logical laws are intrinsically *a priori*, logic itself must be completely independent of psychology, which will never be able to yield more than *a posteriori* truths.

In the second *Investigation* Husserl resumes this thesis and tries to establish that in general it is impossible to reduce ideas to facts or to reduce essences to concrete individual things. This *Investigation* is intended as a careful and radical criticism of the conceptualist and nominalist theories of nineteenth-century English empiricism. Finally, in the third and fourth *Investigations* Husserl occupies himself with the ideal laws

* From Emmanuel Levinas, *Théorie de l'intuition dans la phénoménologie de Husserl*, Librairie Philosophique J. Vrin, Paris, 1963, pp. 152–74. Reprinted by permission of the publishers. The present excerpt was translated into English expressly for this edition by Joseph J. Kockelmans.

that in his view are founded ultimately in universal essences. It is in this context that Husserl introduces his well-known distinction between essential and empirical generalities.

Clearly, if one reads the second, third, and fourth *Investigations* somewhat superficially and, in addition, isolates them from the two *Investigations* which follow them, it would indeed seem that Husserl's doctrine consists essentially either in a certain logicism or in a kind of Platonic realism. However, it is Levinas' view that if stress is put rather upon the final two *Investigations,* it is immediately manifest that Husserl defends neither logicism nor Platonism, but develops instead a new form of transcendental idealism, which he was to explain more systematically in the first volume of his *Ideas* and later in the *Cartesian Meditations.*

For though Husserl maintains in his last two *Investigations* the thesis developed in the first four essays, it is nevertheless quite clear at this point that he is deeply aware of the necessary relation between the object of logic and the subjectivity which thinks and obeys its laws. In a manuscript prepared after 1920 Husserl writes that the main problem discussed in the *Logische Untersuchungen* necessarily follows from the fact that hidden lived experiences are connected even with every ideal entity. These experiences must be in harmony with their corresponding fully determined productions. How, then, must they manifest themselves in order that the subject is able to be conscious of these ideal entities as objects in an, at least ultimately, evident act of knowledge? For even ideal entities are given to us only in and through experiences, albeit experiences of a very special kind. No philosophical logic, therefore, can deny them. In order to explain how the ideality of logical objects can be combined with a necessary relationship between these objects and the thinking subject, Husserl appeals to his view of intentionality. According to this idea the structures of the subjective act parallel those of its objective correlate. This parallelism constitutes the basis for subsequent investigations in which both these aspects of any "complete phenomenon" must be described in connection with each other.

But if Husserl does not defend a kind of logicism or Platonism as far as these essences are concerned, what then was his view on the ontological status of these essences? This is what Levinas hopes to determine in the following selection.]

What meaning then is to be attributed to the existence of essences? As we have already shown, the essence exists in another way than an individual object. It does not occupy any place in space. It is not individualized in time, so that it neither comes into being nor perishes.[1] It is in precisely this that its ideality consists. And this ideality of the essence and the general, far from being negligible and undetermined, admits subdivisions and descriptive differences:[2] the generality of the type "an A" is different from that of "all A's" or that of "A in general." It is by reflecting upon one's ideative life and by paying attention to its intrinsic meaning that one can, so to speak, put one's finger not only on the ideality of the essences but also on this or that particular form of ideality.

The ideality characteristic of the essence and of the general in all its forms—which Husserl's analyses carefully distinguish and which we can only mention in passing here—is from this point of view not a real predicate or a determination (that is to say the property of an object as having extension, for instance), but it consists, first of all, in another mode-of-Being; it reveals to us a new dimension of Being. The ideality of the object does not mean that it exists first and is to be characterized later by an indifference in regard to space and time. The indifference and the rest constitutes the mode-of-Being itself of the ideal, namely its mode of presenting itself in consciousness, of constituting itself there, as Husserl expresses it. As Hering so aptly remarks: ". . . It is not as "general," but as idea that [the general] is not of this world."[3]

One therefore understands the very principle of the criticism which Husserl, in his second *Investigation*, directs against English empiricism in its attempt to reduce the ideality of essences to a property of the individual object. When Locke

[1] Edmund Husserl, *Logische Untersuchungen*, 3 vols. (Halle a.S.: Max Niemeyer, 1921–22), Vol. II, pp. 124 and 155.

[2] *Ibid.*, Vol. II, pp. 147, 187, 223.

[3] Hering, *Phénoménologie et philosophie religieuse* (Paris: Alcan, 1925), p. 46.

wanted to explain the general by means of an undetermined
individual, he was already in error from the very start, even
disregarding the impossibility of such a reduction by neglect-
ing the ideal mode-of-Being of the general object.[4] We would
commit the same fundamental mistake if we were to try to
identify the essence with a characteristic trait or a moment of
the individual object that has been isolated by an effort of
one's attention. The genus "red" is not the red of the individual
object which is brought into relief; for this, too, remains something individual, whereas the genus is ideal.[5] Furthermore, it
is for the same reason that the theory of generic images must
also be rejected. The generic image is vague and changing, but
nonetheless remains an individual image. The essence is not
necessarily unprecise but can in its own way be well determined. The ideality is not the indeterminateness of the object,
but rather characterizes its mode-of-Being.

There are, then, both the right to be and the specific mode-
of-Being characteristic of the ideal. We can now understand
what is meant by the intuition of the ideal, the intuition of
essences or *eidē*—the eidetic intuition, the famous *Wesensschau*
of Husserl.

Just as does the individual object, so does the ideal being or
essence admit the distinction between true and false. Essences
are not fictions about which we may affirm whatever we
wish.[6] In geometry, for instance, we can distinguish between
a true geometrical thought and a false one;[7] we can have concepts of essences which are "merely meant," but which do not
exist, such as the concept of a regular decahedron.

In the domain of essences we can distinguish thus between
the "merely significative" thought and the act which immediately directs itself toward the essence and which, so to speak,
possesses it in the original.

For the realm of essences as well as for the realm of forms,
the act of primordial intuition is identified in *Logische Untersuchungen* with the act of perception, insofar as it is char-

---

[4] Edmund Husserl, *op. cit.,* Untersuchung II, Vol. II, pp. 106–224.
[5] *Ibid.,* pp. 106–7.
[6] *Ibid.,* pp. 124–25.
[7] Edmund Husserl, *Ideen,* Vol. I, p. 52; *Phil. str. W.,* p. 316.

acteristic of the essence of the act of perception to possess a parallel imaginative activity. Husserl broadens the notion of imagination and admits a "categorical imagination"[8] and even gives examples of it.[9]

However, in the *Vorlesungen zur Phänomenologie des inneren Zeitbewusstseins,* written between 1905 and 1910, Husserl denies that in regard to ideal objects there is a viable distinction between the perceived and the imagined.[10] Parallelism between perception and imagination is due to the *temporal* character of certain objects.[11] The concept "intuition" is more general and does not presuppose that parallelism. What holds true for the sensible intuition *as such* does not hold true for the *eidetic* intuition. Here, as everywhere else, intuition is that mode of life in which the object intended by it, is not only "meant" but also primordially given.[12] In order to possess the character of intuition, knowledge which grasps the ideal must not be a simple operation as is the sensible perception;[13] it is adequately characterized by the fact that it has its object given before itself.[14]

We have already met the intuition of the ideal in the form of the categorical intuition. But these categories were merely formal objects. One must distinguish them from material essences (*sachhaltige*) which constitute another type of ideal object. Such would be, for instance, the essences of red, triangle,[15] man, and so on, or in the realm of consciousness, the essences of memory, intentionality, and the like. We have shown how the intuition of formal categories comes about with the help of an intuition of the sensible object, and how

8 Edmund Husserl, *L. U.,* Vol. III, p. 144.

9 *Ibid.,* pp. 163–64.

10 Edmund Husserl, *Zur Phänomenologie des inneren Zeitbewusstseins,* p. 448.

11 But Husserl always maintains that intuition is analogous to perception inasfar as it presents the essence "in person" and is susceptible of truth (*Ideen,* Vol. I, p. 52).

12 Edmund Husserl, *Ideen,* Vol. I, pp. 14–15; *Phil. str. W.,* p. 318.

13 E. Levinas, *Théorie de l'intuition,* pp. 125–26.

14 *Ibid.,* Chap. VII.

15 Space is not something formal as the category "object-in-general." One must distinguish between formal mathematics (*mathesis universalis*) and material mathematics (such as geometry).

the sensible object in a way cooperates in the constitution of
the *Sachverhalt*. But the act of *ideation* which leads us to
the intuition of the material essence has a different structure.
True, I must take my starting point in the individual object—
the red of this fabric which is, for instance, now before me
—but I do not focus attention upon the individual object, but
on the red in general, of which the individual red is but an
example. I completely abandon the intention which directs itself toward the sensible object in order to think an ideal object. This latter thought can, therefore, very well be an intuition, for the ideal object, considered in its exemplar, can
be given to us "in person."

> We do not think it in a "merely significative" manner
> as in the case that we simply understand the general
> names, but we grasp it, we intuit it. And it is surely legit-
> imate to talk here about the intuition . . . of the gen-
> eral.[16]

But although it is true that the individual object does not
take part in the constitution of the ideal object as is the case
for the categorical intuition,[17] the relation to the individual
object is nevertheless not a contingent relation, and the individual object which functions as an example, is a necessary
term in this relation. In the same way as in the intuition
of the *Sachverhalt*, the sensible objects which take part in
its constitution are indispensable in that they afford a foundation to the "categorical synthesis," so is the individual object
an indispensable basis for the perception of the essence. The
mode-of-Being characteristic of the ideal object refers us in
a certain manner to the individual object and implies a relationship to it. But the existence of the individual object does
not play the part of a premise in the knowledge of the eidetic.
The latter is independent of the "effectiveness" of the individual object.[18]

Another problem directly connected with the existence of

---

16 Edmund Husserl, *L. U.*, Vol. III, pp. 162–63.

17 *Ibid.*, p. 162.

18 Edmund Husserl, *Ideen*, Vol. I, pp. 17, 21, and 74; *Phil. str. W.*,
p. 316.

the ideal and the intuition of essences is that of our *a priori* knowledge. What meaning can the very concept of *a priori* knowledge possess in the intuitionist theory of truth? Does the theory of intuition not reduce all truths to truths of fact, because in it truth seems to justify itself through experience, although it remains true that experience must be understood in a manner broader than sensible experience.

Let me say at once that the *a priori* has its place within the intuition of ideal objects and in the judgments which are founded upon these objects.[19] Indeed the *eidetic intuition* possesses a privileged position. Therefore let me dwell longer upon this point.

We have already mentioned that the domain of the general encompasses objects of different types of generalities. Thus, for example, an intuition of generality accompanies the word, even when it indicates an individual object. This generality, which is wholly specific and characteristic of every expression, gives to the word the character of *"concept,"* and one must distinguish it from the general *object* in the strict sense,[20] such as "white," "man in general," and so on. Once it is expressed, the object possesses two generalities of different character: that of the expression, and its own generality. But inside the realm of general objects in the proper sense, one must still introduce another distinction, that which separates the general objects-in-general from the *pure essences*.

In the *Logische Untersuchungen* this distinction is not made, and in the *Ideen* it is not made explicitly. Nevertheless it is of vital importance. For from the *Logische Untersuchungen* on, Husserl identified *a priori* knowledge with the intuition of *pure essences*. Now as long as the distinction between general objects and pure essences is not made, one can disagree with Husserl by stating the intuition of pure essences is no more than an hypostasis of empirical experience, because there are general objects which have a merely inductive

[19] See for instance *Phil. str. W.*, p. 322.
[20] Edmund Husserl, *Ideen*, Vol. I, pp. 304–5, 307, 233; *L. U.*, Vol. II, pp. 102–3. For this distinction between concept and essence see also: *Ideen*, Vol. I, pp. 28–29.

origin.[21] We might confront Husserl with the following objection: If you have the concept of "swan in general," you would say that "every swan is white," thereby aspiring to a truth founded upon the intuition of the essence "swan"; but your concept "swan" stems merely from induction, and so your claimed intuition of the essence of swan might therefore be false; and, in fact, there are black swans. If, therefore, there is no difference between "ideal objects" and "pure essences," then the truths which the intuition of essences reveals to us, are either simple tautologies (the essence of the white swan implies whiteness), or they contain truths attained through induction.

However, to consider this objection a valid one would be to accuse Husserl of an absurdity, or, formulated in a better way, of a philosophical naïveté which could never have entered his mind. True, one must admit that the distinction is not made in an explicit way in Husserl's published works,[22] and that the characteristic traits by which the intuition of pure essences differs from the intuition of other general objects are missing. The description of the eidetic intuition as we have summarized it briefly scarcely transcends the very general phenomenon of the intuition of an ideal entity. How can what is grasped by the intuition of the ideal, as a consequence of the inner structure of the intuition be a pure essence? We are not able to explain the problem with the texts which we presently have at our disposal. And so one can understand the very remarkable efforts of Husserl's disciples in this regard.[23] It is particularly to Hering that honor is due for having posed the problem and for having distinguished the empirical essence from the apriorio one in the way indicated.

[21] See Kynast, *Das Problem der Phänomenologie* (1917) and *Intuitive Erkenntnis* (1919).

[22] From what we believe we know about it, the unpublished writings try to justify this distinction.

[23] In particular see the works of Hering: "Idee, Wesen, Wesenheit," in *Jahrbuch für Philosophie und phänomenologische Forschung*, Vol. IV, pp. 495 ff.; also: Hering, *Phénoménologie et philosophie religieuse*, p. 52. See also: Hans Lipps, *Untersuchungen zur Phänomenologie der Erkenntnis*, 2 vols., Bonn, 1927–28; Roman Ingarden, "Essentiale Fragen," in *Jahrbuch*, Vol. VI.

But though the distinction is not elaborated in Husserl's works, it is nonetheless made in an implicit way. What he understands by essence—the foundation of the *a priori* laws—is not purely and simply identical with "general idea." This is what he says on pp. 12–13 of the *Ideen* when attempting to characterize the essence:

> An individual object is not simply and quite generally an individual, a "this-here," something unique; but being constituted thus-and-thus "in itself" it has its own proper mode-of-Being, its own supply of essential predicables which must qualify it, which must belong to it, if other secondary and relative determinations are to qualify it also.

In characterizing the essence of the object, Husserl does not limit himself to talking about its ideality, he does not exclusively oppose it to the individual, the "this-here"; in his view it is not sufficient to raise the individual object, with all its determinations, to generality, to the realm of the ideal in order to make an essence out of it.[24] In the determinations of the object there is a hierarchy, and the first ones are required in order for the others to be possible. The essence of the object thus is its necessary structure:[25] what makes it into what it is, that which before each empirical characteristic trait of the object makes it possible and understandable, in short—its principle.

Thus for a sound, for instance, to have a determined intensity, a definite timbre, such and such pitch, it must possess timbre, intensity, and pitch in general—an ensemble of characteristics which evoke each other mutually and necessarily and which constitute the necessary structure of the sound.

But what is the meaning of this characteristic of necessity

[24] It is in the light of this concept of essence that one must interpret the passages where the essence seems to be identical with the "what" made into an idea (*Ideen*, Vol. I, p. 13). This "making something into an idea" must be understood as transition to the necessary constitution.

[25] Edmund Husserl, *Ideen*, Vol. I, pp. 12–13.

proper to the structure of the object? What is the meaning of this characteristic of necessity which is inherent in the laws founded upon essences? This question directly concerns that of the part played by intuition. In fact, if it is true that the act of intuition is always an act of reason, what then is the meaning of the necessity characteristic of the laws founded upon essences? Do we not again encounter in the following form the as yet absolutely unsolved problem concerning the nature of reason: how are we to understand and explain the necessity of truths founded upon essences? Are we not led again to look for the *reason* of this necessity itself? Do we not have to see the fundamental act of reason in the discursive procedure by means of which reason has deduced the necessity of the essence?

In order to answer this question we must go back to the elaboration of the concept of eidetic necessity in the third and fourth *Investigations*. We will see, on the one hand, that the necessity owes nothing to deduction because deduction itself is merely a particular case of the necessity of the essence which is the primordial phenomenon and the paradigm of rational necessity. On the other hand, we will be able to characterize the necessity in a positive way.

At the very beginning of the third *Investigation* Husserl makes a distinction between *"dependent* contents" and *"independent* contents." In order to exist *dependent contents* need *other contents;*[26] for instance, the color which cannot be unless extended. A house and a tree, on the contrary, are independent contents because they need not be completed by other objects in order to exist.

What is the meaning of this dependence? Notice first that "independent content" does not mean "a content which cannot be represented without other contents": the dependence is a characteristic trait of the content itself. The fact of being dependent or its opposite is not a subjective necessity of an "I cannot imagine it differently," but an objective and ideal necessity of an "it cannot be otherwise."[27]

[26] *Ibid.*, p. 35.
[27] Edmund Husserl, *L. U.*, Vol. II, p. 238.

But if this dependence is necessarily inherent in the nature of the respective objects, then the necessity—in virtue of which the color, for example, is not conceivable without extension, or without the colored material object—is therefore not purely empirical; it is not the result of induction as is the necessity of the laws of nature.[28] It is not founded upon an empirical observation (at a certain moment in time, for instance, a color appears to us as extended), but upon the genus, upon the essence itself of color.

In order not to be empirical, this characteristic of necessity, proper to dependence, does not have to be logical either. Logic is a science of the form "object-in-general."[29] The necessity of truth which is logically deduced has its foundation in the laws of logic but, precisely for that reason, it does not encroach on the material content of the objects. Thus the laws of "dependence" express "material laws." Therefore we run into a necessity here which is independent of all logic,[30] and all deduction, and is founded upon "the essential peculiarity of the contents in their specificity . . ."[31] The genera and species which can serve as such a foundation constitute the world of essences. In intuiting them we are able to know the necessities which they impose by reason of their very nature, without being obliged to go back again to premises and without having to justify them through a deduction.

Therefore the intuition of material essences such as "house, tree, color, sound, space, sensation, sentiment"[32] makes it possible for us to have necessary and at the same time material cognitions. This direct vision of the necessary structure of the essence is for Husserl the first phenomenon of our intellection.[33] Moreover, when in this way we identify the intuitive act with the act of reason, when we affirm their indifference in regard to logic and deduction, then far from under-

---

[28] *Ibid.*, Vol. II, p. 234.

[29] E. Levinas, *Théorie de l'intuition*, p. 21 and passim.

[30] Edmund Husserl, *Ideen*, Vol. I, p. 38.

[31] Edmund Husserl, *L. U.*, Vol. II, pp. 251–52.

[32] *Ibid.*, p. 252.

[33] "If in asking why [a statement is justified] we ascribe no value to the 'I see that it is so,' we fall into absurdity." (*Ideen*, Vol. I, p. 44.)

mining the possibility of necessary cognitions, we give ourselves the means of extending them to an infinite realm of
the matter of knowledge.

But there is still more. The necessity of the laws of deduction themselves is founded upon the intuition of essences.
For the necessity of the conclusion of a syllogism is founded
upon the formal essence of its premises in which it is grasped
as evident. Every "chain" of the deduction is an intuition
of essences, albeit in this case an intuition of *formal* essences.
The role of the deduction consists in reducing a certain truth
which is not evident by itself to an intuition which is evident
by itself, by means of a series of terms evident in themselves.[34]
It is evidence which is the rational element of knowledge and
not the deduction—an act by means of which certain truths
are reduced to the evidence of their principles; and deduction is not the characteristic trait of each rational cognition,
but only of well-defined realms of objects. When the truths
can be deduced from a *finite* number of principles, their domain is called by Husserl a "mathematical or determined multiplicity": such are the objects of geometry and the world of
logical forms, the objects of the *mathesis universalis*.[35] Consequently, it is clear that making analytic or synthetic logic
into the model of all intelligibility means, in the final analysis,
to conceive of science as fashioned after the model of mathematics, and to start from too narrow a concept of reason.
In Hamelin's view the essential function of reason is to construct the real according to a rule. Husserl's attitude is exactly
the opposite. It is not a dialectic construction which makes the
laws of essences intelligible, but it is from the intelligibility
of an essential relationship that the dialectic construction borrows its own intelligibility.

It is now possible to characterize in a positive way the necessity of eidetic laws and the privileged position of the *a
priori*. In this respect the passage in the third *Investigation*,
about which we have already spoken, affords us further clarification.

---

[34] Edmund Husserl, *Ideen*, Vol. I, pp. 346–48, 21–22.
[35] For these problems see *Ideen*, Vol. I, pp. 163–71, 22–23, and
passim.

The "independent content"—which Husserl calls *concrete* in contradistinction to the dependent content which is called *abstract*[36]—is indifferent in regard to other contents and does not require such and such determined complements, necessary to make it concrete. Some properties of the independent object can be separated from it, and this separability from the concomitant contents gives these contents the ability to vary absolutely freely. It means that

. . . we are able to maintain this content as identical in our representation while the other contents which are connected with it or, more generally, are given with it, vary without limits (in a contingent way *without being fixed by a law which is founded upon the essence of that content*[37]); in other words the content remains intact, notwithstanding the destruction (*Aufhebung*) of the ensemble of concomitant contents, whatever this ensemble may be.[38]

In this way, for instance, we are able in our imagination, to vary the form of a material object without limits; we can also imagine it in different places and at different times.—In this case our imagination is absolutely free, nothing stops it, the object remains concrete, that is to say, it can exist "in itself." But if we want to vary the material object, so far as to deprive it completely of its form, then the concrete characteristic of the object, its possibility to exist, gets lost. Now it is the essence of the independent object which determines the limits within which the contents of the object can vary. A variation which exceeds this limit imposed by the essence would strip the object from its concrete character, its independence, that is to say its possibility to exist. In this way the essence of the object seems to express the conditions which must be realized for the existence of the object to be possible. The predicates of the object may vary without jeopardizing the possibility of the object; it is only the *essential* predicates which do not tolerate a variation. And what is more,

[36] *Ibid.*, pp. 35–36.
[37] Italics by E. Levinas.
[38] Edmund Husserl, *L. U.*, Vol. II, p. 235.

it is precisely their constancy which allows the variation of
the other predicates: each variation, indeed, presupposes
something constant which makes it possible. In this way we
come again upon the definition of essence which we have already formulated, according to which essence is constituted
by an ensemble of predicates which the object must mate-
rialize for the other predicates ever to be able to belong to it.
Without identifying the essence of the object with its quiddity,
this definition shows that it is not a question of elevating all
the characteristics of an individual object into generality, but
that only *some* of them play this privileged part: they form
the condition of the very possibility of the object.

With this the privileged position of eidetic truth comes to
light. Our knowledge of essences is not only knowledge of
an ideal world placed side by side with the empirical world.
The eidetic sciences investigate a new dimension of Being:
the very conditions of its existence, the structure of the object
without which it cannot be. It is in this sense that the knowledge of these sciences is a knowledge *a priori,* because the
sciences know what is presupposed by all other knowledge.
And it is without a doubt because the necessity of the laws
of essences is a necessity of the very conditions of the existence of beings, that Husserl calls these sciences *ontologies.*
Knowledge *a priori* is not distinguished from knowledge *a
posteriori* solely by the mere fact that it is necessary and
"apodictic";[39] in addition it shows an *ontological dignity.*

We understand from all of this the meaning, the place, and
the role of the sciences *a priori* in regard to the sciences of
nature and the sciences of fact in general. Indeed, the discovery of the material *a priori* does not mean the reduction
of all empirical truths to aprioric truths for which Kant has
sometimes been challenged; Kant had not solved Hume's dilemma, for by making a rational deduction of causality in
general, Kant does not deduce each particular case of causality. Now a law of nature is the result of the intuition of
individual facts. That is why it remains contingent and its
necessity is merely probable. This characteristic of a law of

---

[39] Husserl introduces this term in *Ideen,* Vol. I, p. 337.

nature belongs to its essence. The contingency of the empirical fact is not conditioned by our being finite nor by our being ignorant; it belongs essentially to the very essence of the "fact."[40] A law of nature is essentially found by induction.[41] Husserl's philosophy therefore refuses to reduce the laws found by induction to laws *a priori*;[42] it would be a falsification of the meaning of the fact if one were to reduce it to a law *a priori*. If the essence is the principle of the object, then in this case, "principle" does not mean the highest premise from which one can logically derive the contingent properties of the object (was that not the preoccupation of Leibniz and even of Hamelin?). "Principle" means here "that which makes the existence of the object possible": a structure without which it would be inconceivable.

As a result of this, an irreducible difference asserts itself between the *a priori* and the *a posteriori* and the proper parts which each of them play in the sciences. Between causality in general, understood as the essential structure of being, and the contingent causal relationship of the empirical being, there must be a hiatus;[43] they move on two different levels. Extreme naturalism pursued by psychologism will be criticized by Husserl not only because it conceives of consciousness as modeled on nature, but because it does not see the part which the *a priori* plays in our knowledge of nature itself.[44]

The body of the aprioric sciences—whatever be the form under which they offer themselves—is therefore not a miracle of necessity in a world of universal contingency. The necessity of the aprioric sciences has an ontological character. It is inherent in the very meaning of being as being, and the laws which bear the mark of this necessity define the meaning of the respective beings.[45] Once being is defined by the ontological sciences, the sciences of fact are able to ask reasonable questions in regard to their subject matter. Then and

[40] *Ibid.*, pp. 12–13.
[41] Edmund Husserl, *L. U.*, Vol. I, p. 61.
[42] *Ibid.*, pp. 255–57; *Ideen*, Vol. I, pp. 20–21, 138–39.
[43] Edmund Husserl, *Phil. str. W.*, p. 318.
[44] *Ibid.*, pp. 308–9.
[45] Edmund Husserl, *Ideen*, Vol. I, pp. 37–38.

then only is it possible to "perform" experiences.[46] By itself induction is able to yield necessities-of-induction only; it never gives ontological necessities.[47] And in order to pose problems to induction, in order to know what type of experience is required for a given domain of objects, one must start by distinguishing its ontological meaning.[48] In Husserl's view what has made the great progress of modern physics possible is the fact that Galileo noticed that the ontology of nature is to be found in the geometry and mathematics developed in antiquity.[49] The great mistake of all other sciences —as of psychology, for instance—consists in this, that they have seen in this ontology of nature the ontology proper to all regions of the given, or that they have rejected all forms of ontology. What imposes itself upon us, therefore, albeit only in order to contribute to the progress of the sciences, is that we have to establish the ontologies of all regions of objects.[50]

From this it becomes understandable that philosophy is absolutely independent from the sciences. It is in quite another domain of experience, and with a completely different method, that philosophy must work. Upon that depends not only the progress of the sciences but even their rationality: if the sciences, indeed, want to reach an absolute rationality,[51] if they want to avoid the crises in which the meaning itself of what they study becomes obliterated,[52] then ontology must first have explored the intimate and aprioric structure of their objects and clarify the *essential* categories which constitute it. Furthermore, it is also necessary [. . .] that the existence of the objects of the sciences, and the manner in which they offer themselves to consciousness, be equally elucidated.

In such discussions of the theory of essences the primordial role of the concrete becomes manifest and—as we have said in passing—this is to be identified with what materializes

---

[46] Edmund Husserl, *Phil. str. W.*, p. 310.

[47] *Ibid.*, pp. 306–7, 320 (*Ideen,* Vol. I, pp. 193–94).

[48] *Ibid.*, pp. 307–8.

[49] *Ibid.*, p. 308 (*Ideen,* Vol. I, p. 25).

[50] *Ideen,* Vol. I, p. 25.

[51] *Ibid.; Phil. str. W.*, p. 321 and passim.

[52] *Phil. str. W.*, pp. 306–7.

the conditions of existence.[53] The delimitation of being is also
to be made with the help of the concept of the concrete. The
ideal world of essences shows a hierarchy of genera and
species;[54] and the laws which find their principles in their essences govern the corresponding domain of the temporal being which individualizes these essences. In this way the classification of essences is at the same time the delimitation of
the different realms of the real. But it is not with the help
of the highest material genera that we achieve the classification of beings.[55] For the highest genera can be just as well
the genera in which only an abstract element of the object
(a dependent element) is grasped, as with, for example, a
color.[56] As a matter of fact, the different domains of beings
are to be determined from a concrete individual, as for instance, "material object," "consciousness," "animality." The
concept of the *region* of being is defined by the highest genera taken as a whole; the last specifications of these genera,
by supplementing each other, make a concrete individuality
possible.[57] This ensemble of highest genera constitutes the
"regional essence"—such as the essence "nature." This is constituted with the help of genera such as "color," "extension,"
"time," "causality," "materiality," and so on, which are necessarily connected with each other[58] by a necessity which
is the necessity characteristic of the possible existence of an
empirical object of nature. In addition to this region there
are also others, such as "animality," "humanity," "society,"
and so on; to all these, there corresponds *concrete* individua-
tions.

The highest genera whose ensemble constitutes the *region*,
are called material categories. It is in these categories that
all the laws *a priori*, which (in the Kantian terminology) are

[53] For this subject see the penetrating remarks made by A. Gurwitsch in *"La philosophie phénoménologique en Allemagne,"* Revue
de Métaphysique et de Morale, 1928, no. 4.
[54] Edmund Husserl, *Ideen,* Vol. I, pp. 13–14, 34–35.
[55] The text which seems to say this (*Ideen,* Vol. I, pp. 12–13) is
specified on the pp. 37–38 of the same book.
[56] Edmund Husserl, *Ideen,* Vol. I, pp. 36–37.
[57] *Ibid.,* pp. 37–38, 165–66.
[58] *Ibid.,* pp. 165–66.

called synthetic *a priori*,[59] find their foundation; these stand
in opposition to the laws whose principle is found in the pure
form of the object-in-general and which have a universal value
independent of the material essences of the different regions.
Husserl calls them analytic.[60]

But the concept "category" is not, as in Kant, derived from
our judgments: the categories are the structures of the beings,
and not of our knowledge. Therefore, in drawing up the table
of categories, Husserl did not appeal to traditional logic, nor
to the logic of the modern sciences of nature (as is done by
the Neo-Kantians), but to the different regions of the concrete
beings themselves.

The ensemble of the aprioric cognitions which each region renders possible, constitutes what Husserl calls "regional
ontologies."[61] At present these ontologies are still *desiderata*
only.[62] Their realization especially appealed to Husserl's first
disciples who were bound up with the period of the *Logische
Untersuchungen*. The first volumes of Husserl's *Jahrbuch* are
filled up with aprioric investigations, with ontologies of society, nature, and so on. But—let us notice it once again—
these investigations do not have to be deductive in order to
be aprioric. The eidetic sciences must be established with the
help of an eidetic intuition; they are descriptive sciences. By
taking our starting point in the concretely given (that is,
either perceived or imagined)[63] world, for example, we are
led to its essence and can describe its necessary structure.

In the language of phenomenology this attitude which consists in considering the world of objects, but in so doing
ignores the individual existence in order to dwell exclusively
upon the essence, is called eidetic reduction.[64] The world of
individual realities, not only in consciousness but also in nature, must be subjected to it. This is the first step toward the
phenomenological attitude.

[59] *Ibid.*, pp. 37–38.
[60] *Ibid.*, p. 28.
[61] *Ibid.*, pp. 37–38, 166.
[62] *Ibid.*, p. 39.
[63] *Ibid.*, p. 16.
[64] *Ibid.*, p. 6. See also: *Phil. str. W.*, p. 318.

But does the eidetic reduction finally lead to a distortion of the concrete real, as Bergson's critical remarks about conceptual thought would have us believe? Does the intuition which consists in placing us immediately in the world of individual beings lose contact with the concrete aspect of this world by becoming *eidetic* intuition? Does the eidetic reduction not "freeze" this mobile and changing world with its unprecise outlines into a fixed and dead reality? True, it has been shown that there is no contradiction between our intellect as the power to grasp the ideal and the abstract, and intuition as the immediate perception of the concrete; but does this contradiction not manifest itself again in that the ideal is always fixed and defined, whereas the infinitely flexible and mobile intuition takes pains to espouse the sinuosity of the concrete?

We may safely put aside these objections. As early as in the *Logische Untersuchungen,* Husserl distinguishes between the idea in the Kantian sense of the term and the idea in the Platonic sense,[65] which is indicated in the *Ideen* with the new term "eidos."[66] The "eidē" are the essences of the individual objects which surround us, considered in their concrete aspects. They do not possess the exactness nor the perfect determination of geometrical concepts; a certain vagueness is inherent in them, a vagueness for which the scientist is not responsible.[67] This inexactness, this indetermination belongs to the very essence of certain objects.

The spatial figure of the tree, exactly taken as it is present in the corresponding perception, that is to say as a moment of the intentional object, is not a geometric formation; neither is it ideal nor exact in the sense of exact geometry. In the same way an intuited color is not an ideal color.[68]

If we try to express the inexact data of perception in an exact manner, then we cause them to lose their concrete and

[65] Edmund Husserl, *L. U.,* Vol. II, p. 245.
[66] *Ideen,* Vol. I, pp. 8–9.
[67] *Ibid.,* p. 169.
[68] *L. U.,* Vol. II, p. 245.

living aspects.[69] Notions such as "great" and "small,"
"roundish" and "oblique," "warm" and "cold," "heavy" and
"light" taken in their approximative and vague nature—these
are the characteristics of the concrete world of our perception, and not the exact notions of geometry and science such
as "straight line" and "circle," "temperature" and "gravita-
tion."[70] It is by these concepts first of all that the essence
of the world is determined: the world of exact scientific concepts is—as we have shown[71]—a derivative.

Botany and zoology are examples of empirical sciences
which work with the help of vague concepts which are inexact because of the nature of their objects.

> The most perfect geometry and its most practical appli-
> cation cannot help the scientist who attempts to develop
> a descriptive science of nature to express precisely (in
> exact geometrical concepts) that which in so plain, so
> understandable, and so entirely suitable a way he ex-
> presses in the words: notched, grooved, lens-shaped,
> umbrella-like, and so forth—concepts which are essen-
> tially and not accidentally inexact and are, therefore, also
> unmathematical.[72]

In addition to the inexact, merely empirical concepts, one
can speak about inexact apriorioc essences which express the
essence of the individual world.

> The essences grasped in intuitive data by means of an
> act of direct ideation are inexact essences.[73]

They express the object of the intuition in its complete concrete aspect.

> If it behoves us to bring to suitable conceptual expres-
> sion the intuitable corporeal data in their intuitively given

[69] *Ideen*, Vol. I, pp. 171–72.
[70] We take the liberty of copying these examples from an unpublished manuscript of Husserl, but we accept the complete responsibility for them.
[71] E. Levinas, *Théorie de l'intuition*, Chap. I.
[72] Edmund Husserl, *Ideen*, Vol. I, pp. 170–71.
[73] *L. U.*, Vol. II, p. 245.

essential characters, we must indeed take them as we find them. And we do not find them otherwise than in flux. . . .[74]

It is thus the world of perception which becomes the object of an eidetic science. Space, time, colors, sounds, and so on, can be studied in their essences. But this descriptive science of space is not geometry which always studies an idealized space. Space, taken just as it is immediately given in our concrete life, is not geometrical. It can be described with the help of morphological concepts.[75] In regard to this last point we will limit ourselves to a simple remark. [. . .]

Husserl's essential idea is his affirmation of the primacy of inexact morphologic essences over exact mathematical essences. And this primacy can easily be explained because the exact essences are merely idealizations of inexact essences. The different shades of red (inexact essences belonging to a certain genus) show the different degrees of an ideal red which they approach more or less. This ideal red, after which they strive in one way or another, is not the genus "red." In regard to this latter it is an ideal limit. The genus "red" remains an asymptote in regard to the ideal red. It is this ideality of a completely different type which Husserl indicates by "idea in the Kantian sense of the term."[76] That idea has its origin from the comparison of a series of "eidē" in which there is disclosed a gradation toward a goal which is continually approached but never reached, in other words toward an ideal; and so there is a certain primacy of the "eidos" over the "idea."[77]

Husserl's distinction, as well as the opposition between the morphological essences as a result of an act of ideation and the exact essences as products of idealization, permits us to escape from the dilemma described by Bergson. Intuition can

[74] *Ideen,* Vol. I, p. 170.

[75] Husserl uses this term to indicate the "inexact essences."

[76] This is a reminiscence of the determination of the concept "idea" by Kant in the *Critique of Pure Reason* (B, 370–75). See: Edmund Husserl, *Ideen,* Vol. I, p. 170.

[77] *Ideen,* Vol. I, pp. 166–67, 170–71. For applications of this conception of "idea" see: *Ideen,* Vol. I, pp. 201–3, 350–51.

be ideative without falsifying for that reason the meaning of
the concrete real, as Bergson supposes. Although the inexact
essences are the fundaments of the necessary laws, such as
the mathematical essences, they express nevertheless all of the
mobility, continuity, and vagueness that there is in the real.
The essence which is criticized by Bergson is a geometrical
idea; it is not the result of *ideation* which grasps the essence
of the thing in all the vagueness which is characteristic of
it, but of idealization which pushes the data that are concretely given concerning things, up to the last and ideal limits.
The geometrical concepts, just as the other scientific concepts,
are the result of this idealization of the concrete, but they
are not the only concepts possible,[78] in the same way as the
mathematical essences, which proceed by deduction from a
finite number of axioms, are not the only objects of eidetic
sciences.[79] Moreover they derive their origin and their meaning from the concrete world. We do not cease translating
these idealized essences into the language of the concrete
world in order to understand them.[80] Therefore we must not
consider the inexact aspect of the concrete world as provisional and insufficient; on the contrary, this description always
serves as fundament for our scientific knowledge in that it is
a source of principles; that is, a philosophic science. In order
to respect the intrinsic meaning of our life we must attribute
a primacy to the Being of the world of perception in all its
inexactness.[81]

But here we might still reproach Husserl for his intellectual-
ism. If he has come to such a profound idea, namely that
in the ontological order the world of science is later than the
concrete and vague world of perception and depends upon
it, then he was probably still in error in taking this concrete
world primarily as a world of perceived objects. Is our first
attitude in the presence of the real the attitude of theoretic

[78] *Ibid.*, pp. 164–65.
[79] *Ibid.*, pp. 173–74.
[80] We owe this idea to a conversation with Husserl, but we accept the complete responsibility of it.
[81] *Ideen*, Vol. I, pp. 123–25.

contemplation? Does the world not manifest itself in its very Being as a center of action, as a field of activity or concern, to speak the language of Martin Heidegger?

On Eidetic Reduction*

EDMUND HUSSERL

Method of Clarification. The "Nearness" and "Remoteness" of Given Data

Of greater interest to us are certain considerations of method which, instead of relating to the verbal expression, relate to the essence and the essential connexions which they once fixated and now express. If the glance of inquiry is turned towards experiences, these will generally be presented with a certain *emptiness* of content and *vague* sense of *distance* which prevents their being employed in reaching conclusive results, whether singular or eidetic. The matter would stand otherwise if, interested not so much in the experiences for their own sake as in the manner of their presentation, we wished to study the essential nature of emptiness and vagueness themselves, for these on their side are not vague but are presented with fullest clearness. But if that itself which is vaguely known, the unclear floating image, shall we say, of memory or fancy, produces its own essence, that which it produces can only be something imperfect; i.e., where the *single intuitions* which underlie our apprehension of the essence are on a lower plane of clearness, so *also* are the *apprehensions of the essence*, and correlatively the *object apprehended* has an *"unclear"* meaning, it has its disorderly mixtures, its lack of proper distinctions both within and without. It is impossible or "only

* From Edmund Husserl, *Ideas: General Introduction to Phenomenology,* translated by W. R. Royce Gibson (London: George Allen and Unwin Ltd., 1931), Vol. I, secs. 67–71, 75. Reprinted by permission of the publishers.

roughly" possible to decide whether what is apprehended now here and now there is the same (the same Being) or something different; it cannot be determined what components are really present, and what the components which already show themselves in vague relief, and give but a wavering indication of their own presence, "properly are."

We must then *bring* to the normal distance, *to complete clearness*, what at any time floats before us shifting and unclear and more or less far removed, intuitionally, so that our intuitions of the essence may be given a corresponding value in which the intended essences and essential relations are given to the fullest possible advantage.

Apprehension of the essence has accordingly its own *grades of clearness*, just as in the case of the particular which floats before our gaze. But for every essence, just as for the corresponding phase of its individual counterpart, there exists, so to speak, an *absolute nearness,* in which its givenness is in respect of this graded series absolute, i.e., *pure* self-givenness. The objective element does not only meet one's gaze as "itself" in general, and we are not only aware of it as "given," but it confronts us as a self given *in its purity, wholly and entirely as it is in itself.* So far as a vestige of unclearness remains over, so far too does a factor of obscurity enter into the "self-"given phase, which therefore does not pass within the circle of light reserved for that which is given pure. In the case of *full unclearness,* the polar opposite of full clearness, the phase of givenness, is not reached at all, consciousness is "obscure," *intuits no longer,* in the strict sense it no longer "gives objects" at all. We must accordingly state the matter as follows:

Dator consciousness in the pregnant sense of the term and the *intuitable* over against the *unintuitable,* the *clear* over against the *obscure,* these are parallel oppositions. Similarly: *Grades of givenness, of intuitability, of clearness.* The zero-limit is obscurity, the unity-limit is full clearness, intuitability, givenness.

But givenness in this connexion is not to be understood as primordial givenness, therefore not as givenness of the perceptual type. We do not identify the *"self-given"* with the "*primordially given*," with the "embodied." Understood in a strict sense, "given" and "self-given" may be used indifferently for each other, and the use of the super-sufficient expression should serve only to exclude *givenness in that wider sense* in which it is said of everything presented that it is given in presentation (though maybe emptily).

Our distinctions apply further, as is forthwith apparent, to *intuitions of any and every kind,* including *empty* presentations; therefore, too, *without restriction in respect of the objects referred to,* although we are here interested only in the ways in which experiences are given and in their phenomenological constituents (real [*reellen*] and intentional).

But with reference to future analyses we must also take care that what is most essential to the matter is retained, whether the glance of the pure Ego searches through the whole of the relevant conscious experience, or, to put it more clearly, whether the pure Ego "*turns towards*" a "given matter" and eventually "*grasps*" it, or does not do so. Thus, for instance, "given percept-wise," instead of being tantamount to "perceived" in the strict and normal sense of the apprehensions of this given object as it is, may mean no more than "ready to be perceived"; likewise "given fancy-wise" need not mean so much as "grasped through a movement of fancy," and so generally, and indeed with respect also to all grades of clearness or obscurity. We may refer thus in advance to the "readiness," which at a later stage we will discuss more closely, but let it be also noted that under the heading "givenness," where no contrary indication is added or obviously implied by the context, we *understand as an included factor the being apprehended,* and, where the givenness of the essence is concerned, the being apprehended primordially.

Genuine and Counterfeit Grades of Clearness.
The Essence of Normal Clarifying

But we must continue our descriptions. If we speak of grades of givenness or clearness, we must distinguish between *genuinely* graded increases of clearness, to which one should also add *graded increases in obscurity,* and *ungenuine in-*

creases of clearness, namely, *enlargements extensive in kind of the scope of the clearness*, with an accompanying rise, maybe, in its intensity.

A phase already given, already really intuited, can be given with greater or lesser clearness—a tone or a colour, for instance. Let us exclude all apprehensions which reach beyond the intuitively given. We have then to deal with serial gradations that develop within the framework in which the intuitable can really be intuited; intuitability as such under the rubic clearness admits of continuous differences of the intensive type, the intensities starting from zero, but closing at the upper end with a fixed limiting value. To this, one might say, the lower grades, in a certain sense, point forward; when we look at a flower in some mode of imperfect clearness, we "mean" the colour as it is "in itself," and this is precisely that which is given when the clearness is perfect. And yet we must not allow ourselves to be led astray by the metaphor of "pointing"—as though one thing were a sign for another— and one should be just as chary of speaking here (we recall what we have already noted once before)[1] of exhibiting the clear "in itself" through the unclear: as the property of a thing, maybe, "exhibits" in intuition through sensory phases, namely, through perspective appearances. *The graded differences of clearness are proper throughout to the mode of being given.*

It is quite otherwise when an apprehension that reaches *beyond* what is intuitively given weaves empty apprehensions into the real intuitive apprehension, for now, by degrees as it were, an increasing amount of what is emptily presented can become intuitable, or of what is already intuitable emptily presented. Thus the procedure of *making clear to oneself* consists here in two interconnected sets of processes: *rendering intuitable*, and *enhancing the clearness of what is already intuitable*.

In these words we have described *the essential nature of the normal process of making something clear*. For as a rule no pure intuitions are present, and there are no pure empty pres-

[1] Cf. *supra*, § 44.

entations passing over into pure intuitions; it is the *impure intuitions* which, as intermediate grades maybe, play the chief part, bringing their objective matter on certain sides or in certain phases intuitively before us, and on other sides or in other phases yielding mere empty presentations.

The Method of Apprehending Essences with Perfect Clearness

Perfectly clear apprehension has this advantage, that in virtue of its own essential nature it permits us with absolute certainty to identify and distinguish, to relate and make explicit, enables us, briefly, to carry out "with insight" all "logical" acts. Under this class come the *acts of apprehending the essence,* to whose objective correlates, as already stated above, the distinctions of clearness, now more familiar to us, are transferred, just as on the other side the methodological knowledge we have just gained is transferred to the objective of securing that the essence shall be perfectly presented.

Thus in general the method which is *a basic part of the method of eidetic science generally* is one of going forward step by step. The particular intuitions which minister to the apprehension of the essence may be already sufficiently clear to render possible a completely clear grasp of some essential generality, and yet not so adequate as to satisfy the main intention; there is a lack of clearness as regards the closer definitions of the interwoven essences; thus we need to scrutinize our illustrative instances more closely or to contrive others that are better suited, in which the pertinent single features left confused and obscure stand out and can then be transformed into data of the clearest kind.

We can always bring the data nearer to us even in *the zone of obscure apprehension.* What is obscurely presented comes closer to us in its own peculiar way, eventually knocking at the door of intuition, though it need not for that reason pass over the threshold (and perhaps cannot do so "on account of psychological resistances").

We have further to consider that *what is given to us at the moment has a determinable margin, not yet determinate,* and possessing its own way of effecting the transition through a process of "*unfolding*," of separating out into series of presentations at first; it may be passing once more into obscurity, then emerging once again in the presentational sphere, until the object referred to (*das Intendierte*) passes into the brightly lit circle of perfect presentation.

Further, we would draw attention to the point that it would be *going too far to say that all self-evident apprehension of the essence demands that the subsumed particulars in their concrete fullness should be fully clear*. It is quite sufficient when grasping essential differences of the most general kind, as those between colour and sound, perception and will, that the exemplifying instances should show a lower grade of clearness. It is as though the most general character, the genus (colour in general, sound in general), were *fully* given, but not as yet the difference. That's a shocking way of putting it, but I could not see how to avoid it. Let the reader figure the situation for himself in vivid intuition.

The Role of Perception in the Method for Clarifying the Essence. The Privileged Position of Free Fancy

Let us, as a further step, accentuate some of the specially important features of the method of apprehending essence.

It belongs to the general and essential nature of immediate, intuitive essence-apprehension (and the point is one that we have already stressed)[2] that it can be carried out on the basis of *the mere present framing* of particular illustrations. But such presenting under the form of fancy, for instance, can, as we have just been showing, be so perfectly clear as to enable us to see and apprehend perfectly the essential nature of things. In general, *perception* with its primordial dator quality, and external perception, of course, in particular, has advantages of its own as compared with all forms of representation. And this, moreover not merely as the empirical act whereby we fix the content of an objective experience—such fixing does not at present concern us—but as the basis

2 Cf. § 4.

for firmly establishing the essential being of things on phenomenological lines. Outer perception has its perfect clearness in respect of all objective phases which reach their mode of givenness really within it and on primordial lines. But it also offers, with the eventual assistance of the reflexion directed back upon it, clear and steady details for general analyses of a phenomenological kind, directed towards essences, and even, on closer inspection, for analyses of acts as well. Anger reflected upon may dissipate, quickly modifying its content. It is also not always available like perception, not producible at pleasure with the help of convenient experimental apparatus. To study it reflectively in its primordiality would be to study an anger in process of dissipation, which has its own meaning, no doubt, but perhaps not that which was to be studied. Outer perception, on the contrary, so much more accessible as it is, does not "dissipate" under reflexion, and we are able, without special trouble in fixing the conditions of clearness and keeping within the limits of primordiality, to study in general its essential nature, and that also of its own components and essential correlates. If one says that perceptions also have their differences of clearness (in relation, namely, to the cases of perception), e.g., in the dark, in fog, and so forth, we will not let ourselves be drawn into further discussion as to whether these differences are quite so similar to those already referred to as they are here assumed to be. Let it suffice that perception is not ordinarily conditioned by fog, and that clear perception, as it is needed, is always at our disposal.

Now if for purposes of method the advantages of primordiality were very marked, we should have to consider where and how and to what extent it could be realized in the different types of experience; which of these types come specially near in this respect to the pre-eminently privileged domain of sensory perception, and many similar questions. But as it is we can disregard all this. There are reasons why, in phenomenology as in all eidetic sciences, representations, or, to speak more accurately, *free fancies*, assume *a privileged position over against perceptions,* and that *even in the phe-*

*nomenology of perception itself, excepting of course that of
the sensory data.*

The geometer when he thinks geometrically operates with
imagery vastly more than he does with percepts of figures or
models; and this is true also of the "pure" geometer, who
dispenses with the methods of algebra. In fancy it is true he
must toil to secure clear intuitions, and from this labour the
drawing and the model sets him free. But in actual drawing
and modelling he is restricted; in fancy he has perfect freedom in the arbitrary recasting of the figures he has imagined,
in running over continuous series of possible shapes, in the
production therefore of an infinite number of new creations;
a freedom which opens up to him for the first time an entry
into the spacious realms of essential possibility with their infinite horizons of essential knowledge. The drawings therefore
follow normally *after* the constructions of fancy and the pure
eidetic thought built upon these as a basis, and serve chiefly
to fix stages in the process already previously gone through,
thereby making it easier to bring it back to consciousness
once again. Even where the thinker "meditates" over the
figure, the new processes of thought which link themselves
on to it have fancy-processes as their sensory basis, and it is
the results of this work of fancy which fix the new lines on
the figure.

Keeping to the most general considerations, the position for
the phenomenologist, who has to deal with experiences as
reduced and with the correlates which essentially belong to
them, is substantially the same. There is also an infinite number of essential forms of the phenomenological kind. The
worker in phenomenology, as in other fields, can make only
a limited use of the help supplied through the primordial order
of givenness. He has indeed at his disposal as primordial data
all the main types of perception and representation. He has
them as perceptual illustrations for a phenomenology of
perception, of fancy, of memory, and so forth. For the most
part he has likewise at his disposal in the sphere of the primordial examples for judgments, supposals, feelings, volitions.
But naturally not for all possible special forms, just as little
as the geometer depends on drawings and models for the infi-

nite variety of his corporeal types. Here too at all events the freedom of research in the region of the essence necessarily demands that one should operate with the help of fancy.

It is naturally important, on the other hand (once again as in geometry, which has recently and not idly been attaching great value to collections of models and the like), to make rich use of fancy in that service of perfect clearness which we are here demanding, to use it in the free transformation of the data of fancy, but previously also to fructify it through the richest and best observations possible in primordial intuition; noting, of course, that this fructifying does not imply that experience as such can be the ground of validity. We can draw extraordinary profit from what history has to offer us, and in still richer measure from the gifts of art and particularly of poetry. These are indeed fruits of imagination, but in respect of the originality of the new formations, of the abundance of detailed features, and the systematic continuity of the motive forces involved, they greatly excel the performances of our own fancy, and moreover, given the understanding grasp, pass through the suggestive power of the media of artistic presentation with quite special ease into perfectly clear fancies.

Hence, if anyone loves a paradox, he can really say, and say with strict truth if he will allow for the ambiguity, that the *element* which *makes up the life of phenomenology as of all eidetical science* is "fiction," that fiction is the source whence the knowledge of "eternal truths" draws its sustenance.[3]

The Problem of the Possibility of a Descriptive Eidetic of Experiences

In the preceding pages we have repeatedly described phenomenology quite frankly as a descriptive science. A fundamental question of method is again raised, and with it a doubt which checks us as we press eagerly forward into the

[3] A sentence which should be particularly appropriate as a quotation for bringing ridicule from the naturalistic side on the eidetic way of knowledge!

new territory. *Is it right to set phenomenology the aims of pure description? A descriptive eidetic:* is that not *something altogether perverse?*

The motives to such questioning are sufficiently familiar to all of us. He who, like ourselves, is feeling his way, so to speak, in a new eidetic, asking what researches are here possible, what points to start from, what methods to adopt, glances involuntarily towards the old, highly developed eidetic disciplines, towards the mathematical therefore, and in particular towards geometry and arithmetic. But we notice at once that in our own case these disciplines cannot be appealed to for guidance, that the conditions in their case are essentially different. There is indeed some danger here that the novice who has not yet come across any bit of genuine phenomenological essence-analysis may be misled as to the possibility of a phenomenology. Since the mathematical disciplines are the only ones at the present time which could effectively represent the idea of a scientific eidetic, the thought at first does not suggest itself that there may be still other types of eidetic disciplines, non-mathematical in character, and in their whole theoretical cast radically different from the type already known. Hence, if someone has allowed himself, on the strength of general considerations, to be won over to the demand for a phenomenological eidetic, the attempt, doomed to miscarry from the outset, to establish such a thing as a mathematics of phenomena, may mislead him into abandoning the very idea of a phenomenology. But that again would be perverse.

So let us in the most general way make clear to ourselves *the distinctive uniqueness of the mathematical disciplines in opposition to that of a theory of experiences in their essential aspect,* and at the same time be clear as to the precise aims and methods which should in principle be unsuited for the sphere of experience.

Phenomenology as Descriptive Theory of the Essence of Pure Experiences

As concerns Phenomenology, it aims at being a *descriptive* theory of the essence of pure transcendental experiences from the phenomenological standpoint, and like every descriptive discipline, neither idealizing nor working at the substructure of things, it has its own justification. Whatever there may be in "reduced" experiences to grasp eidetically in pure intuition, whether as a real portion of such experience or as intentional correlate, that is its province, and is a vast source of absolute knowledge for it.

Still, let us see more clearly to what extent really scientific descriptions can be set up on the phenomenological field, with its infinite number of eidetic concreta, and to what services they can be put.

It is part of the peculiarity of consciousness generally to be continually fluctuating in different dimensions, so that there can be no talk of fixing any eidetic concreta or any of the phases which enter immediately into their constitution with conceptual exactness. Let us take, for instance, an experience of the genus "imagery of a thing" as it is given us either in phenomenologically immanent perception or in some other (of course reduced) intuition. The phenomenologically particular object (the eidetic singularity) is then just this imagery of the thing in the whole wealth of its concreteness, precisely as it participates in the flow of experience, with the precise determinacy or indeterminacy with which it lets its thing appear, now in this aspect, now in that, and with just that distinctness or mistiness, that fluctuating clearness and intermittent obscurity, and so forth, which is peculiar to it. It is *only the individual* element which phenomenology ignores, whilst it raises the whole essential content in its concrete fullness into eidetic consciousness, and takes it as an ideally selfsame essence, which like every essence could particularize itself not only *hic et nunc* but in numberless instances. We can see at once that a conceptual and terminological *fixation* of this and every similar flowing *concretum* is not to be thought of, and that this applies to each of its immediate and no less flowing parts and abstract aspects.

If now there is no question of an unambiguous determination of *eidetic singularities* in our realm of description, it is quite otherwise with the essences at a *higher specific level*. These are susceptible of stable distinction, unbroken self-identity, and strict conceptual apprehension, likewise of being analyzed into component essences, and accordingly they may very properly be made subject to the conditions of a comprehensive scientific description.

Thus we describe and determine with *rigorous* conceptual precision the generic essence of perception generally or of subordinate species such as the perception of physical thinghood, of animal natures, and the like; likewise of memory, empathy, will, and so forth, in their generality. But the highest generalities stand foremost: experience in general, *cogitatio* in general, and these make it possible to give comprehensive descriptions of the essential nature of things. Moreover, it belongs to the very nature of a general apprehension of essences and of general analysis and description that there is no corresponding dependence of what is done at higher grades on what is done at the lower. In point of method we cannot insist, for instance, on a systematic inductive procedure, on a gradual ascent, rung by rung, up the step-ladder of generality.

We now note a further consequence. It follows from what we have said that all deductive theorizing is excluded from phenomenology. *Mediate inferences* are not positively denied it; but seeing that all its knowledge is descriptive and must be purely adjusted to immanent requirements, it follows that inferences, unintuitable ways and means of every description, have only the methodological meaning of leading us toward the facts which it is the function of an ensuing direct essential insight to set before us as given. Analogies which press upon us may, prior to real intuition, supply us with conjectures as to the essential relations of things, and from these may be drawn inferences that lead us farther forward; but in the end the conjectures must be redeemed by the real vision of the essential connexions. So long as this is not done we have no result that we can call phenomenological.

The pressing question whether within the eidetic domain of reduced phenomena (in the domain as a whole or in some one or other of its subdivisions) an idealizing procedure may be adopted *side by side with* the descriptive, substituting for the intuitable data pure and rigorously conceived ideals, which might then indeed serve as the fundamental nexus for a mathesis of experiences and as a counterpart to *descriptive* phenomenology, is indeed not settled by the foregoing considerations.

Much as the studies we have just completed must leave open to inquiry, they have considerably furthered our quest, and not only through bringing into our field of view a series of important problems. We are now quite clear that for the grounding of phenomenology there is nothing to be gained from mere analogies. It is only a misleading prejudice to suppose that the historical methods of the *a priori* sciences, which are *exact* ideal sciences throughout, must be accepted without question as the pattern for every new method of science, and especially for our transcendental phenomenology—as though all eidetic sciences must show one type of method only, that of "exactness." Transcendental phenomenology as descriptive science of Essential Being belongs in fact to *a main class of eidetic science wholly other* than that to which the mathematical sciences belong.

V. INTENTIONALITY, CONSTITUTION, AND INTENTIONAL ANALYSIS

*On the Intentionality of Consciousness**

ARON GURWITSCH

The intentionality of consciousness may be defined as a relation which all, or at least certain, acts bear to an object. In this manner, Brentano introduced the notion into contemporary philosophy. Seeking to account for the difference between what he calls "physical phenomena" and what he calls "psychical phenomena," Brentano found, among other characteristics, that the latter are distinguished by a relation to, or a direction toward, an object.[1] This directedness of "psychical phenomena" is interpreted by Brentano as their containing within themselves an "immanent" object-like entity. Although Husserl takes over Brentano's notion of intentionality, he raises some objections against this interpretation.[2] His examination of Brentano's conception of intentionality finally leads him to abandon it completely; but he agrees with Brentano in acknowledging the existence of a highly important class of mental facts—for which Husserl reserves the title of acts[3]—which have the peculiarity of presenting the subject

---

* From Aron Gurwitsch, "On the Intentionality of Consciousness," in Martin Farber, ed., *Philosophical Essays in Memory of Edmund Husserl* (Cambridge, Mass.: Harvard University Press, 1940), pp. 65–83. Reprinted with permission of the publishers. Copyright 1940 by the President and Fellows of Harvard College.

[1] F. Brentano, *Psychologie vom empirischen Standpunkt* (ed. by O. Kraus, Leipzig, 1924), Book II, ch. I, par. 5.

[2] *Logische Untersuchungen*, II, v, sec. 9–11; *Ideas*, sec. 90. Lack of space forbids us to summarize Husserl's criticism of Brentano's doctrine; some essential differences between Brentano's and Husserl's conceptions are emphasized by L. Landgrebe, "Husserl's Phänomenologie und die Motive zu ihrer Umbildung," in *Revue internationale de Philosophie*, vol. I.

[3] *Log. Unt.*, II, 378.

with an object. Experiencing an act, the subject is aware of an object, so that the act may be characterized, as Husserl does, as a *consciousness of* an object whether real or ideal, whether existent or imaginary.

This peculiarity, however, ought not to be considered as a real quality or as a real property of acts, such, for example, as intensity, which is held by many psychologists to be a real property common to all sense data. In fact, to ascribe to an act, under the heading of intentionality, a real quality which makes it transcend itself to seize an object belonging, as is the case in the perception of a real thing, to a universe external to the sphere of consciousness, to which the act, though endowed with the transcending quality, remains tied nevertheless—this would be to bestow on the act a magic or at least mysterious power. Conscious acts confront us with objects; experiencing such an act, the subject is aware of an object, and he is so owing to the reference the act bears in itself to the object. The objectivating function of consciousness is, however, a problem rather than a simple datum, which one could content himself to take notice of. In fact, the objectivating function involves a whole complex set of problems. Out of these we choose the most elementary, but, as we think, at the same time the most fundamental one. *To be aware of an object means that, in the present experience, one is aware of the object as being the same as that which one was aware of in the past experience, and as the same as that which one may expect to be aware of in a future experience, as the same as that which, generally speaking, one may be aware of in an indefinite number of presentative acts.* Identity in this sense is, no doubt, constitutive of objectivity (*Gegenständlichkeit*). But, even if considered on the most elementary level, the identity of objects, inasmuch as it is a conscious fact—and it is only for this reason that we have any knowledge of it and may talk of it—turns out to be an insoluble problem for the traditional conception of consciousness. We shall go on to show, if possible, that the treatment of this problem leads to a new conception of consciousness that is radically opposed to the traditional one.

I. The Problem of Identity as Stated by Hume

Let us consider the problem of identity in its most accentuated form, as stated by Hume concerning perceptible things.

Following Locke[4] and Berkeley,[5] Hume asserts "that our ideas of bodies are nothing but collections formed by the mind of the ideas of the several distinct sensible qualities, of which objects are composed, and which we find to have a constant union with each other."[6] Now the "sensible qualities" in question are identified, by Hume as well as by his predecessors, with the sensations which are produced in the mind when a perceptual act is experienced; these "sensible qualities" are taken for real elements, of which the perceptual experience is composed; consequently they pass for real elements of consciousness itself, i.e., for elements existing within consciousness. Hence the object, being composed of the same data which figure in the perceptual experience, turns out to be a real element of this experience, and to coincide with it; at any rate, the object itself is also conceived to exist within consciousness, and to be a content of it. This thesis is indeed defended by Hume. "Those very sensations, which enter by the eye or ear, are . . . the true objects . . . there is only a single existence, which I shall call indifferently *object* or *perception* . . . understanding by both of them what any common man means by a hat, or shoe, or stone, or any other impression conveyed to him by his senses."[7] This thesis is presented by Hume not as a result of philosophical inquiry, but as the opinion of the "vulgar," i.e., the opinion of all of us, when, without philosophizing, we adopt the natural attitude and are concerned with any things we find in our surroundings.

Then a problem must arise. Taking up again the observation of a thing we have already observed some time ago, as,

[4] Cf. Locke, *An Essay Concerning Human Understanding,* Book II, chap. XXIII, especially sec. 6 and 14.

[5] Cf. Berkeley, *A Treatise Concerning the Principles of Human Knowledge* in *Works,* ed. by A. C. Fraser (Oxford, 1901), I, 258.

[6] Hume, *A Treatise of Human Nature,* ed. by T. H. Green and T. H. Grose (London, 1890), I, 505–506.

[7] *Ibid.,* I, 491.

for example, shutting and opening our eyes alternately, we are provided with a set of sense data. The latter may resemble one another to a very high degree, but yet they remain distinct from one another and do not fuse, in any manner whatever, into a single one. We can enumerate these multiple sense data by means of the perceptual acts which we experience successively, and to which the data belong respectively. Nevertheless we believe—we do so as "vulgar ones"—that we are in the presence not of a set of objects, however much they resemble one another, but of one single object appearing as identically the same in every one of the successive experiences. In the very face of the multiplicity of sense data, the identity of the object and our belief in it must be accounted for, without forgetting that the object is conceived as a complex composed of sense data. In these terms Hume stated the problem,[8] and the solution he adduced for it is well known.[9] Because of the resemblance among the sense data, the mind passes so smoothly and so easily from one to another that it is scarcely aware of the transition. This resemblance puts the mind in a state similar to that in which it is when it surveys, without interruption, an unchangeable object for some time; this latter state gives rise to the idea of identity.[10] Thus, on account of the double resemblance, the mind mistakes similarity for identity. Whereas there is in fact only a succession of sense data, of which none, when it has disappeared, can be brought into existence again, the imagination misleads us to believe that such data, having ceased to appear, i.e., to exist, can return as the same when the interrupted observation is taken up again. The belief in the singleness of the perceived object rests on confounding resembling, but yet distinct, sense data with identical ones.[11]

[8] *Ibid.*, I, 493: "The very image, which is present to the senses, is with us the real body; and 'tis to these interrupted images we ascribe a perfect identity."

[9] *Ibid.*, I, 491–494.

[10] We shall come back later to the identity of an object observed uninterruptedly for some time.

[11] Cf. Hume, *op. cit.*, p. 535.

The mere presence to the mind of sensuous data composing an object is not sufficient for giving rise to the idea of its identity. Hume is perfectly right in emphasizing that the notion of identity needs that of time.[12] This means, in the case under discussion, that the object perceived now, after opening the eyes again, is held to be the same as that which appeared before shutting the eyes. Perceiving the object, the mind must recall previous perceptions; the impressions which are now present to the mind must be attended with ideas, which, although resembling the former at all points, differ from them, according to Hume's doctrine, with respect to force and vividness. In order to conceive identity, the mind must confront itself with a plurality of items. But as soon as it has done so, it must overlook not only the differences as to intensity, but also, and chiefly, the fact that it has presented to itself a plurality of items. Since identity consists in the illusion of holding the resembling, but distinct, items to be a single one, the function of the imagination in producing this illusion is such as to abolish the condition that is indispensable to put the imagination into function.[13] This illusion therefore can subsist only as long as the subject is inattentive to what really happens in his mind. The contradiction, however, between the experienced succession of sense data and the irresistible propensity created by imagination to mistake them for a single and identical one is too striking to be overlooked. To disentangle itself from this contradiction, the imagination devises the further fiction of a "continued existence"

[12] *Ibid.*, pp. 489–490.

[13] In the excellent analysis which J. Laporte ("Le scepticisme de Hume," in the *Revue philosophique de la France et de l'Étranger*, cxv, 1933, pp. 92–101) gives of the passages of the *Treatise* referred to here, he emphasizes the stress Hume laid on the "operation" of the mind in producing the illusion of identity. Laporte's analysis, however, renders the more obvious the contradiction upon which we insist. The operation of the mind does not consist in making something out of the materials for which this operation is employed, as is the case when objects are united into an ensemble, when they are numbered, when a perceived matter of fact enters into a judgment and undergoes categorial formation, and so on. Here, on the contrary, the operation, as it were, has to make disappear, before the mind, the materials necessary to set it going.

ascribed to the "broken and interrupted appearances."[14] But this new fiction cannot help Hume, since only in case the identity of the object, perceived after the interruption of that perceived before it, has been established may the question be raised as to the existence of the object during the interruption.

The case is the same with the identity of an object observed for some time without interruption.[15] Under these circumstances, identity means "*invariableness* and *uninterruptedness* of any object, through a supposed variation of time." Variation of time implies succession and change, if not in the object in question, which is supposed to be permanent and unaltered, then in the coexistent objects. Nevertheless, the unchangeable object is imagined to participate in these changes,[16] without suffering, in itself, any modification whatsoever. Again: on the one hand, succession and variation of time must not only happen in fact, but also be experienced by consciousness, for otherwise there would be only a single permanent object, and the mind would be provided with the idea, not of identity, but of unity. On the other hand, the transition from one moment to another, which constitutes duration and variation of time, must scarcely be felt, no other perception or idea must be brought in play, in order that the disposition of the mind might be such as to continue surveying one permanent, unchangeable, identical object.[17] Variation of time must be felt, but not enough to produce any alteration in the mind's activity. Once more the operation of imagination is in contradiction to the very condition of this operation.

If Hume's explanation of identity is untenable, it is not because identity is held to be a "fiction," i.e., a creation of imagination. Had Hume contented himself to assert that identity is no matter of sensibility, but is due to another mental

[14] Hume, *op. cit.,* pp. 494–497. We must neglect here to examine Hume's account of continuous existence.

[15] *Ibid.,* pp. 489–490.

[16] It will be shown later that the "participation" of an object which stands before consciousness for some time, and which during this time is given as permanent and identical, in those changes which constitute its presence-time and its duration is not a "fiction" but an immediately experienced fact.

[17] Hume, *op. cit.,* p. 492.

faculty, namely, imagination, he would have advanced a two-factor theory of perception. Such a theory is, no doubt, open to criticism, but it cannot be rejected as inconsistent, the main objection which, it seems, is to be made against Hume's theory. His task is to account for the fact that the perceiving subject, experiencing these impressions and by means of them, is aware of something identical, despite impressions being "internal and perishing existences,"[18] subject to variation of time, so that none of them when once passed can ever return. But there is no room in Hume's doctrine both for *identity* and for *temporality*. It is highly significant that Hume talks of our tending to "disguise, as much as possible, the interruption,"[19] to "remove the seeming interruption by feigning a continued being."[20] If we could sacrifice either identity or temporality, we would get rid of the irreconcilable contradiction in which these principles stand to each other; but we cannot, because of the irresistible tendency created by the imagination to ascribe identity to resembling perceptions on the one hand, and because, on the other hand, the interruptions of these perceptions are too striking to be overlooked.[21] *Identity and temporality turn out then, for Hume, not only to be opposed to, but even to exclude each other.* These principles stand in a perpetual struggle with each other. As long as we are inattentive enough, we may believe in identity, although in reality there is merely a succession of resembling items. Philosophical reflection comes to show the falsehood of this belief, without, however, being able to shake it seriously.[22] According as we adopt the attitude of practical life or the philosophical one, we waver from instinctive and natural opinion to "studied reflections," without ever gaining a conclusive solution of the problem.[23] Thus Hume fails to account for a very simple fact, familiar to the "vulgar" in their everyday lives, the fact formulated by saying: The thing I see now, I saw some time ago, and to-

18 *Ibid.*, p. 483.
19 *Ibid.*, p. 488.
20 *Ibid.*, p. 496.
21 *Ibid.*, p. 494.
22 Cf., *ibid.*, pp. 497–498 and pp. 501–505.
23 *Ibid.*, pp. 535–536.

morrow I shall take up its observation. In a case like this, identity as well as temporality stand before the subject's mind, whether his attention bears upon the one or upon the other.

The ultimate reason for Hume's failure is to be sought, I submit, in his general conception of consciousness: ". . . the true idea of the human mind, is to consider it as a system of different perceptions or different existences, which . . . mutually produce, destroy, influence, and modify each other. . . . One thought chases another, and draws after it a third, by which it is expelled in its turn."[24] *Consciousness is then conceived as a unidimensional sphere of being, whose fundamental structure consists only and exclusively in temporality.* What constitutes the mind "are the successive perceptions only," the mind being "nothing but a bundle or collection of different perceptions which succeed each other with an inconceivable rapidity, and are in a perpetual flux and movement."[25] Hume expressly likens consciousness to a theatre, but it is, so to speak, a theatre without a stage; in modern terminology, one could compare consciousness with a perpetual succession of kinematographic pictures.

Whatever differences may exist among the different kinds of perceptions, "primary qualities," "secondary qualities," passions, affections, and so on, in so far as they are perceptions, i.e., contents of consciousness, they must be taken to be on the same footing and to have the same manner of existence.[26] That is to say, all of them are real events happening in the stream of consciousness; they appear and disappear, and every one of them has its place in this stream with relation to other events belonging to the same stream. Nothing can ever be found in consciousness but such an event, one picture among others which precede or succeed it, and which in their succession constitute the conscious life.[27] Being aware of an object is reduced to the mere presence in consciousness of a

[24] *Ibid.*, pp. 541–542.

[25] *Ibid.*, pp. 534–535.

[26] Cf., *ibid.*, pp. 480, 482–483.

[27] Cf., *ibid.*, p. 487: ". . . nothing is ever really present to the mind, besides its own perceptions."

real content.[28] Hence the identification mentioned above of sensible qualities with sensations, through which the former appear, both designated, as a rule, by the same terms, as color, smoothness, ruggedness, and so on.[29] After all, the object as composed of real contents of consciousness must itself become a real element in the conscious stream. For consciousness conceived in this way there can indeed exist nothing identical.[30]

Though formulated by Hume in the most explicit manner, this conception of consciousness as a unidimensional sphere constituted by the mere succession of real events was already effective with Locke and with Berkeley and—as far as I can see—it has been embraced more or less explicitly by all philosophers up to the present day. With regard to the problem under discussion, it makes no great difference whether the perceptions are considered, with Hume,[31] as distinguishable and separable from one another, or whether, like James[32] and Bergson,[33] one lays stress upon the continuity of the stream of consciousness and upon the interpenetration of the mental states, so that demarcations may no longer be drawn to separate them from one another. This conception constitutes the ultimate sense of what Husserl calls *psychologism*.[34] What is true for perceptible objects belonging to the real world holds good also for mathematical entities, for significations, propositions, and for all kinds of products of logical thinking.

[28] Cf., *ibid.*, p. 483: ". . . every thing which appears to the mind is nothing but a perception, and is interrupted, and dependent on the mind."

[29] See Husserl's criticism of this confusion in *Log. Unt.*, II, v, sec. 2, and *Ideas*, sec. 41.

[30] It is worth noting that even the identity of objects undergoing a real change, by the addition or diminution of parts, is explained by Hume (*op. cit.*, pp. 537–538) in some cases by inattention. The essential condition of ascribing identity in such cases is that the changes be insignificant enough not to strike the mind.

[31] *Ibid.*, p. 495.

[32] W. James, *The Principles of Psychology* (London, 1908), I, 237–243.

[33] H. Bergson, *Essai sur les données immédiates de la conscience* (Paris, 1932), chap. II.

[34] Cf. *Formale und transzendentale Logik* (Halle, 1929), sec. 56–58, 62, 65.

Reduced to the real elements and contents which constitute the acts of awareness of them, none of these objects can ever be apprehended as the same, in an indefinite number of acts. Since objectivity is to be defined by this sameness of the object as opposed to the multiple acts, whether they be experienced by one person or by different persons, on the basis of the conception of consciousness under discussion there can be no objects at all, of any kind whatever.

II. Husserl's Noesis-Noema Doctrine

The preceding discussion leaves us with the problem of how identical and identifiable objects may exist for, and stand before, a consciousness whose acts perpetually succeed one another; every one of these acts, in addition to their succeeding one another, incessantly undergoes temporal variations. For what is meant by James's "stream of thought" and by Bergson's *"durée"* does express an experienced reality, of which we may become conscious at any moment, if we are attentive to what happens in our conscious lives.

A solution has been given to this problem by Husserl by means of his theory of intentionality; and as far as I know it is the only one that exists. Lack of space prevents me from studying the growth of this theory throughout Husserl's writings. When in the *Logical Investigations* he tackled intentionality for the first time, Husserl was not yet dealing with the problem we have emphasized. His theory of intentionality gradually got a reference to this problem, and, though this reference did not become manifest until the *Formal and Transcendental Logic,* it seems to us that the form in which intentionality is advanced in the *Ideas,* chiefly in the *noesis-noema doctrine,* already constitutes an answer to our problem. Taking the noesis-noema doctrine into consideration from this point of view, we shall proceed beyond what was explicitly formulated by Husserl himself.

When an object is perceived there is, on the one hand, the act with its elements, whatever they may be; the act as a real event in psychical life, happening at a certain moment of phenomenal time, appearing, lasting, disappearing, and, when it has disappeared, never returning. On the other hand, there is what, in this concrete act, stands before the perceiving subject's mind.[35] Let the thing perceived be a tree. This tree, at any rate, presents itself in a well-determined manner: it shows itself from this side rather than from that; it stands straight before the observer or occupies a rather lateral position; it is near the perceiving subject or removed from him at a considerable distance, and so on;[36] finally it offers itself with a certain prospect, e.g., as giving shade, or, when the subject perceiving the tree recalls to his mind his past life, the tree perceived appears in the light of this or that scene of his youth. What has been described by these allusions is the *noema of perception,* namely, the object such, exactly such and only such, as the perceiving subject is aware of it, as he intends it in this concrete experienced mental state. It is with respect to the noema that the given perception is not only a perception of this determined object, but also that it is such an awareness of the object rather than another; that is to say that the subject experiencing the act in question, the *noesis,* finds himself confronted with a certain object appearing from such a side, in the orientation it has, in a certain aspect, and so on. Hence the noema may also be designated as the perceptual sense.

The noema is to be distinguished from the real object.[37] The latter, the tree for instance, as a real thing appears now in this determined manner; but it may offer itself from a different side, at another distance, in a different orientation and aspect; and it does so in fact when the subject goes around it. It shows itself in a multiplicity of perceptions, through all of which the same real tree presents itself; but the "perceived tree as such" varies according to the standpoint, the orientation, the attitude, etc., of the perceiving subject, as when for instance he looks at the tree from above, or at another time perceives it while in the garden. Indeed, a real thing may not present itself as such except by means of a series of perceptions

[35] *Ideas,* sec. 88.
[36] Cf. *Méditations Cartésiennes,* p. 34.
[37] *Ideas,* sec. 89–90.

succeeding one another.[38] These perceptions enter into a synthesis of identification with one another, and it is by, and in, this synthesis and the parallel synthesis among the corresponding noemata, that what appears successively constitutes itself, for consciousness, into this real thing which it is, one and identical as opposed to the multiple perceptions and also to the multiple noemata.[39] Hence problems arise as to the relation of the act and its noema to the real thing perceived through the act, and further as to the relations the noemata uniting themselves by the synthesis of identification bear to one another;[40] at any rate it is obvious that the real object ought not to be confounded with a single noema.

On the other hand, the noema is distinct from the act in the sense that it does not constitute a part, an element, a factor of the act, and does not really exist within consciousness, as the act does.[41] When, looking at a thing, we alternately shut and open our eyes again, without any change in the position of our body or in the direction of the glance, we experience a number of perceptual acts, all different from one another. Through every one of these acts, however, not only does the same object offer itself, but it appears also in the same aspect and orientation, from the same side, at the same distance, and so on. The tree presents itself now in exactly the same manner as it did a moment ago, as it did yesterday, as it is expected to do tomorrow. The "perceived tree as such" is identically the same, notwithstanding the variety of the acts to which it corresponds. *In the noema,* then, *we have something identical* which, for this very reason, ought not to be mistaken for an element of the corresponding act. Were it such an element, it would appear and disappear with the act, and it would be tied up, as the act is, to the place the latter occupies in phenomenal time.

The noema, as distinct from the real object as well as from the act, turns out to be an unreal or ideal entity which belongs to the same sphere as meanings or significations. This is

[38] *Ibid.,* sec. 42, 44, 143.
[39] *Ibid.,* sec. 41, 86, 135, 145, 150, and *Méd. Cart.,* sec. 17–18.
[40] *Ideas,* sec. 98 and 128–131.
[41] *Ibid.,* sec. 97.

the sphere of sense (*Sinn*).[42] The unreality of entities belonging to this sphere lies, first of all, in their atemporality, i.e., in a certain independence of the concrete act by which they are actualized, in the sense that every one of them may correspond, as identically the same, to another act, and even to an indefinite number of acts. Noemata are not to be found in perceptual life alone. There is a noema corresponding to every act of memory, expectation, representation, imagination, thinking, judging, volition, and so on.[43] In all these cases, the object, matter of fact, etc., in itself, toward which the subject directs himself through the act, is to be distinguished from the object such, exactly such, as the subject has it in view, as, through the act, the object stands before the subject's mind. As to judging, the difference is between *objects about which* and *that which is judged as such*.[44] It is worth noting that somehow James[45] anticipated Husserl's notion of the noema of thinking and judging.

Husserl's noesis-noema doctrine, which we must content ourselves with summarizing briefly, far from being a constructive or explanatory theory, is rather a simply descriptive statement of an objectivating mental state, i.e., of a mental state through which the experiencing subject is confronted with an object. Every mental state of this kind must then be accounted for in terms of identity as well as of temporality. The traditional conception of consciousness, in which emphasis is placed upon temporality, the succession of acts and the variations each act undergoes by its duration, is truly not false, since the fact emphasized is a real fact of consciousness. But this conception is incomplete and unilateral. No mental state is to be conceived only and exclusively as a real and temporal event in the stream of consciousness, without any reference to a sense. This reference is overlooked in the traditional conception. *Identity is to be acknowledged as a fact irreducible to any other; it turns out to be a fact of consciousness, no less authentic and no less fundamental than tem-*

[42] *Ibid.*, sec. 133.
[43] *Ibid.*, sec. 91 and 93–95.
[44] *Logik*, sec. 42, 44–45, 48.
[45] James, *op. cit.*, I, 275–276.

porality is. Thus we are led to a duality. And it must be stressed that this duality holds good even for the most elementary level of consciousness, where the question concerns the repeated appearance of an object in the same manner of presentation, without there being a need for going on to consider the appearance of an object, one time in perception, another time in memory, representation, etc., and, still more, to take into consideration the successive presentations of an object, appearing as identically the same, from various sides and in the most different aspects.

III. Temporality and Identity

Before setting off the general conception of consciousness implied in and following from the noesis-noema doctrine, let us look at the nature of this duality and at the relation between the terms composing it.

That identity is a fundamental fact in conscious life does not signify a permanent explicit awareness of it. In all perceiving, thinking, judging, and so on, in all theoretical and practical life, we make use of the identity of the objects we deal with; when perceiving a thing, for instance, we take it for the same as that perceived some time ago, or when thinking of a proposition, we hold it to be the same as the one which we demonstrated yesterday, and then go on to verify this demonstration (the same as that performed yesterday), or to reason further upon the basis of this proposition. So we may behave and so we do behave, without necessarily grasping identity in an explicit way, although all of our behavior is constantly guided by it. The object with which we are concerned is our theme, and our only one; as a rule, the identity of this object does not constitute a secondary theme accompanying the former. But, of course, identity may be rendered explicit to the subject's mind and may be taken as a theme. How then does it become so? In what way do we get an original awareness of identity?

A perceived object offers itself in a certain manner of presentation. Experiencing such a perception, we are free to remember past perceptions and to look forward to future perceptions, so that to all these mental states, past as well as

future ones, there corresponds the same noema as that corresponding to the present experienced perception. Thus we
become aware in an original way of the noema and of its
identity, as distinct from and opposed to the multiple acts to
which it corresponds. It is of no importance, if the past experiences are recalled with a more or less exact temporal determination, and also if the moment at which the future acts
are expected to happen may be foreseen with some exactness.
It is not even necessary that the acts taken into consideration
be recalled perceptions, i.e., appear as having been present at
a past moment, and that the experiences considered as future
be really expected to happen. For the present purpose, it will
be quite sufficient to conceive acts as possible or potential,
and such as to differ from one another and also from the present perception, but as to actualize the same noema. Acts
through which the same object appears and offers itself in the
same manner of presentation can differ from one another
only as to the moments in conscious time at which each of
them takes place. At any rate, *we may not render identity of
the noema explicit and ascertain it by an original experience
unless we also become aware of the temporality of consciousness.*

Noematic identity may be brought up to explicitness, even
without taking into consideration acts different from the present experienced one, on the condition that there be reflection
upon the duration of the latter. Duration consists in, and manifests itself for consciousness by, an incessant transformation
of every "actual now" into a "having just been an actual
now." When time is elapsing, the present moment does not
sink into past, so that it could not be recalled again to the
mind, except by reproduction; on the contrary, the present
moment, ceasing to be present, is yet retained in "primary
memory"[46] and takes the form of "having just been present."
At once that which has just been present, relative to the actual
now, when this is transformed in the manner mentioned, un-

---

[46] As to the difference between "primary memory" (retention)
and "secondary memory" (reproduction), see Husserl, *Vorlesungen
zur Phänomenologie des inneren Zeitbewusstseins* (Halle, 1928),
par. 19.

dergoes a transformation in its turn, passing into a "retention of a retention"; it is then removed still more from the occasional actual now, until it disappears from immediate memory, no longer being retained.[47] Thus reflecting on what really happens in consciousness, at every moment we find a continuous variation and transformation: a continuous passing of the present phase into a retained one, and of a phase given in a retention of any degree into a retention of a higher degree, a continuous iteration of this transformation.[48] Upon these incessant variations is based the stream-character of consciousness,[49] which, owing to their continuity, is experienced as a unidimensional order. What is concerned by these transformations is, however, not the object perceived, or its manner of presentation, but only its temporal orientation, its temporal modes of appearance.[50] In other words: what is concerned is the act rather than its noema, the fact that a perceived object as such stands before consciousness rather than the perceived object as such itself. Looking at the stream elapsing, we become explicitly aware of the fact that the perceived object as such has already appeared for a long time, or that it has just begun to appear, and—if we also allow for protentions—that we expect it to continue appearing, or that we foresee interruption of its appearance, and so on. Once more, *explicit awareness of identity requires that of temporality* and, in the case just analyzed, even of *intrinsic temporality*. Hume was then perfectly right in referring to temporality when he sought to account for identity.

On the other hand, were there nothing identical standing before consciousness, awareness of temporality would no longer be possible. With this hypothesis, retentional modifications could no longer be variations in the temporal orientations of something which may successively assume different temporal orientations. The very reality of conscious life, when an act is an enduring one, is a phase of present actuality most intimately connected with a whole continuity of phases re-

[47] *Ibid.*, sec. 8 and 10.
[48] *Ibid.*, sec. 39 and Supplement I.
[49] *Ibid.*, sec. 36 and pp. 466–467.
[50] *Ibid.*, sec. 30–31 and Supplement IV.

tained (in retentions of various degrees), all these phases being related to one another, and the phase of present actuality constituting a limit of this continuity.[51] With our hypothesis, however, instead of this continuity of phases there could be only a set of punctiform act-impulses among which one would bear the character of actual presence, whereas the others would be provided with characters different from one another as well as from that of the former. All these act-impulses, though simultaneously given, would still remain in isolation from one another; at any rate, they would lack the intrinsic relationship to connect them into a unitary act; for the unity of an enduring act is possible only with regard to something identical whose appearance may assume different temporal phases.[52] Conscious life being in incessant variation, at every moment one set of such act-impulses would be displaced by another one, without any intrinsic reference between them; for such a reference supposes the same to pass from one temporal phase into another. At every moment, then, the unity and the continuity of conscious life would be broken off. Since experienced time consists but in the progressive removal either of a certain phase of an act or of the act in its entirety from the actual now, in such a way that what is being removed appears as having been, a moment ago, nearer to the actual now than it is at present—a consciousness for which the hypothesis under discussion would be valid could not become aware of time. Consequently for such a consciousness time would not exist at all.[53]

It is then by way of the very same reflection that the subject, in an original way, ascertains the identity of the object offering itself in a certain manner of presentation, of the noema, as well as the temporality of the noema's appearance, the duration of its appearance and all changes the duration carries with itself. Temporality and identity are, no doubt, poles opposed to each other. As against Hume, however, *they are poles which do not exclude but require each other. Tem-*

[51] *Ibid.*, par. 16. For the sake of brevity we confine the discussion to the intrinsic temporality of an enduring act.
[52] *Ibid.*, Supplement XI.
[53] *Ibid.*, pp. 376–377.

*porality and identity are related to each other like the terms
of a correlation.* This is indeed the nature of the duality to
which Husserl's noesis-noema doctrine leads.

IV. The Correlation-Conception of Consciousness

To each act there corresponds a noema, namely, an object
such, exactly and only such, as the subject is aware of it and
has it in view, when he is experiencing the act in question.
Consciousness is not to be mistaken for a mere unidimensional
sphere composed of acts, as real psychical events, which co-
exist with and succeed one another. Rather it ought to be
considered as a *correlation, or correspondence, or parallelism
between the plane of acts, psychical events, noeses, and a second plane which is that of sense (noemata).* This correlation
is such that to each act its noema corresponds, but the same
noema may correspond to an indefinite number of acts. It is
then not a one-to-one correspondence.

The noetico-noematic correlation is what has to be meant
by the term intentionality. In this light, the formula "consciousness *of* something" is to be understood:[54] a conscious act
is an act of awareness, presenting the subject who experiences
it with a sense, an ideal atemporal unity, identical, i.e., identifiable. It is not by virtue of favorable circumstances calling for
an explanation and for a reduction to more elementary facts,
but owing to what constitutes the nature of consciousness itself, that an experienced act bears a reference to a sense. Consciousness is to be defined by its bearing reference to a sphere
of sense, so that *to experience an act is the same thing as to
actualize a sense.* Hence every fact of consciousness must be
treated in terms of the relation *cogito-cogitatum qua cogitatum,*[55] and no mental state may be accounted for, except
with regard to the objective sense (*gegenständlicher Sinn*),
of which the experiencing subject becomes aware through
this act.[56]

Intentionality means the objectivating function of conscious-

[54] *Méd. Cart.*, p. 28.
[55] *Ibid.*, pp. 30–31, and *Logik*, p. 120.
[56] *Ideas,* preface, sec. 6.

ness. In its most elementary form, this function consists in confronting the subject with senses, ideal unities, to which, as identical ones, he is free to revert an indefinite number of times. No sooner than this elementary structure of the objectivating function has been established, problems may be tackled as to higher structures of intentionality, concerning for instance syntheses by means of which particular perceptual senses are united into systems which are the real perceptual things, concerning categorial forms bestowed upon the perceptual data in thinking,[57] dealing with syntactical operations by which, in apophantics, more and more complicated meanings and significations are constructed from out of simpler ones,[58] and so on. All structures of intentionality rest upon the noetico-noematic correlation which, for this reason, is the most elementary structure. But it is, at the same time, also the most fundamental and the most universal one, since every sense-entity, of whatever kind and of whatever degree of complication, is an identical and identifiable unity, to which the subject may come back again and again. Thus the noetico-noematic parallelism enters into all forms of mental activity; and it is to it that one is led by the basic problems of logic.[59]

The objectivating function belongs to an act, but not as taken in itself and as isolated from other mental states. On the contrary, this function is possessed by an act even when the latter has the distinctive character of evidence or self-presentation, on account of its being inserted into the whole of the experiencing life and only with regard to this whole.[60] Objectivity is identifiableness, i.e., the possibility of reverting again and again to what, through the present experienced act, is offered to consciousness, and the possibility of so doing whether in the same or in any other mode of awareness.[61] This holds good for real as well as ideal objects.[62] It holds good also for "inner perception." When a present experi-

---

[57] *Log. Unt.*, II, VI, chap. VI.
[58] *Ibid.*, II, IV, sec. 13, and *Logik*, sec. 13.
[59] *Logik*, sec. 73.
[60] *Ibid.*, pp. 142–143.
[61] *Ibid.*, p. 139.
[62] *Ibid.*, sec. 61–62.

enced mental state is grasped by an act of reflection and is
thus made the object of this act of inner perception, the latter
possesses the character of evidence, since the apprehended
act is offered directly, immediately, and bodily, not by memory or in any symbolic manner. Nevertheless, it is not on this
account that the act of inner perception is objectivating; it is
so only because what appears through it, although its self-
presentation never can be actualized again, may yet be recalled later, and may be so an indefinite number of times.[63]
Objectivity and identity have then no sense, unless with regard
to a multiplicity of acts, that is to say, with reference to the
temporality of conscious life. These analyses of Husserl's concerning objectivity, by which he has cleared up the ultimate
meaning of his struggle against psychologism,[64] throw a
new light upon the here advanced correlation-conception of
consciousness.

Though never formulated by Husserl in quite explicit terms,
this conception seems to be at the root of a large part of his
theories, and, when his work is considered in its growth, this
conception reveals itself, I submit, to be one of the teleological
goals toward which phenomenology is tending.

Intentional and Constitutive Analyses*

JOSEPH J. KOCKELMANS

For a good understanding of phenomenology as a *method*
[. . .] it seems necessary to dwell somewhat longer on what
we have called "intentional" and "constitutive analyses." With
Paul Ricoeur we think that most existential phenomenologists,

[63] *Ibid.*, pp. 140–141 and sec. 107 b.

[64] *Ibid.*, sec. 56–57, 65, 67.

* From Joseph J. Kockelmans, *Phenomenology and Physical
Science,* translated by Henry J. Koren (Pittsburgh, Pa.: Duquesne
University Press, 1966), pp. 40–47. Reprinted by permission of
the publishers.

138 PHENOMENOLOGY

theoretically at least, underestimate the importance of these analyses within a phenomenological philosophy. "If in every problem," he says, "we go straight to the 'existential project' and the 'movement of existence' which carries along all authentically human behavior, we run the risk of disregarding the specific character of the problems, of drowning the contours of the various functions in a kind of indistinct existential monism, which ultimately would induce us to repeat the same exegesis of 'existence' with respect to the imagination, the emotions, laughter, gestures, sexuality, speech, etc."[1]

Summary. To explain more accurately the importance of these analyses, let us first summarize as concisely and as clearly as possible the various points discussed above. The aim of phenomenology as a method is to provide philosophy with an absolute and radical starting point. Following Descartes, Husserl sees this starting point in an *ego cogito,* but for him every *cogito* is essentially the *cogito* of a *cogitatum.* Against Descartes, therefore, Husserl maintains that not only the fact of the *cogito* is an absolute and indubitable datum but that the *cogitatum* also is such a datum, provided this *cogitatum* is taken as it immediately appears in the *cogito.* The absolute and radical starting point of philosophy, therefore, lies not in a single certain thesis (Descartes' *ego cogito*) but in an indefinite number of "theses," provided these theses are taken precisely as they manifest themselves immediately and intuitively in an indubitably certain cogitation.[2]

The last-named requirement demands that the phenomenologist try to attain the proper sphere before he begins to analyze and describe the content of his *cogito cogitatum.* The method of reduction is to lead him to this sphere. It makes him pass from the realm of derivative acts, marked by our culture and especially by the influence of the sciences, to that of acts which make things present to us "bodily" in an original fashion, in an experience that is characteristic for each type of being. Once

[1] P. Ricoeur, *"Méthodes et tâches d'une phénoménologie de la volonté," Problèmes Actuels de la Phénoménologie* (Paris: 1952), pp. 115–116.
[2] Husserl, *Die Idee der Phänomenologie,* pp. 29–32; *Cartesianische Meditationen,* p. 11.

he has arrived in the proper sphere, he can begin to analyze
and describe accurately whatever manifests itself primordially
there to him. This analysis and description have to be noetico-
noematic, i.e., in this description and analysis attention must
be paid to both the noetic and the noematic aspects of the
whole "given," in other words, to both the act in which the
cogitatum is given and to this *cogitatum* itself which originally
appears in this act.[3]

For, if one admits that all consciousness is consciousness-
of-something, it is evident that nothing can be said about
consciousness unless attention is paid to that of which one became conscious in the various acts. On the other hand, it is
obvious that in this way the question about the essence of any
being is reduced to that of the modes of consciousness in
which the being had to manifest itself *originally* as "this" or
"that." The essence of things, therefore, can be determined
only by returning in an intentional analysis to the acts of our
consciousness in which any being constitutes itself *originally*
as "this" or "that." This assertion appears a necessary consequence flowing from the application of the idea of intentionality to human knowledge.

Because all this is of the greatest importance for a correct
understanding of intentional analysis, we will dwell a little
longer on it. But for the sake of clarity, we will no longer
speak about acts of consciousness in an abstract way, but will
pay attention to the most important of these acts, the act of
perception.[4]

Profiles.   When one analyzes a particular act of perception
carefully, it becomes at once evident that each act of perception seizes the perceived object only in a certain respect. Expressed in a correlated way, any perceptible thing is always
perceived from a determined standpoint, a well-defined viewpoint. Standing in front of the house, I effectively perceive
only the facade. The sides and the rear are hidden to me. I
can, of course, change my standpoint and place myself in a

---

[3] Husserl, *Ideen,* vol. 1, pp. 218–221.
[4] In this matter we follow the broad lines suggested by A. Gurwitsch, *The Field of Consciousness,* Pittsburgh, 1964, pp. 202–305.

different position with respect to the house. If I do so, I still perceive the same house, but now only in a different respect. No matter how I place myself, I always perceive this house in a determined respect. The perceived gives itself in and through the act of perception only by means of profiles (*Abschattungen*) which are correlated to a determined attitude and standpoint of the perceiver.[5]

Moreover, this determined standpoint, with respect to the house, refers intrinsically to other possible standpoints, just as the effectively perceived aspects refer intrinsically to other possible perceptible aspects. While I perceive the facade of the house, I am aware that I could also perceive the other sides by simply changing my standpoint. For each perceptible object it is true that its perception can take place only in a quasi-infinite series of profiles, corresponding to a quasi-infinite number of possible standpoints.[6]

Noesis—Noema. Let us assume now that I perceive this particular house from the street in front of it so that I can effectively see only its facade. If, subsequently, I want to learn more about this house's exterior appearance, then the only possibility is to have recourse to ever-new "partial perceptions," each of which will manifest separately a certain aspect of this house. What is typical here is the fact that in any such case we will always experience the manifold of profiles as profiles of this particular house. And in a correlate way we experience the manifold of partial perceptions as perceptions of a single thing.

Thus, the perceived thing clearly does not exhaust itself in any one of its individual profiles, but that which is intended in each of the concrete acts, without, however, being effectively and as such perceived in any particular act whatsoever remains the same in all cases. In this particular act of perception or *noesis* this house effectively manifests itself always in this

[5] Husserl, *Ideen*, vol. 1, pp. 91–95; *Erfahrung und Urteil*, pp. 26–27. For the "theory of profiles" see especially C. Graumann, *Grundlagen einer Phänomenologie und Psychologie der Perspektivität*, Berlin, 1960.

[6] Husserl, *Ideen*, vol. 1, pp. 100–104; W. Luijpen, *Existential Phenomenology*, Pittsburgh, 6th impr., 1966, pp. 97 f.

particular profile when this particular standpoint is assumed; but, nonetheless, each concrete act intends more than this particular profile and aims at the house as a whole. This intended total meaning which is clearly constituted as the perceptional meaning in every particular act of perception of this house, precisely insofar as it manifests itself in this act, is called *noema*. This noema explains why every individual act of perception refers to other, possible perceptions of this same house. These perceptions are destined to complement and strengthen the first perception; and, by virtue of them, this first perception is able to appear as a phase of a possible total process.[7] Let us clarify this point somewhat more extensively.

The Process of Perception as Fulfillment (*Erfüllung*). When different acts of perception are concerned with the same house, we experience all these acts as referring to one and the same thing and, therefore, these distinct acts are in harmony and agreement, although that which is effectively perceived as such differs in all these cases. Despite the fact, however, that the profiles of the separate acts are different, it is clear that these acts cannot be in agreement if the profiles in question do not harmonize in one way or another. Consequently, the fusion of the different individual acts of perception concerning one and the same thing into a total process of perception presupposes, of necessity, that the corresponding profiles fit into a "connected whole." Because the corresponding profiles organize themselves into a single, connected whole, the acts of perception can appear as phases of a total process.[8]

Thus, the unification of the individual acts does not depend on the temporal relationships existing between them. It does not even appear necessary that the acts succeed one another without interruption. In other words, the unification in question does not refer to the acts themselves as psychical events

[7] Husserl, *Ideen*, vol. 1, pp. 91–98, 241–249; *Cartesianische Meditationen*, pp. 77–79; Gurwitsch, *op. cit.*, pp. 202–204.

[8] Husserl, *Ideen*, vol. 1, pp. 363–368; *Cartesianische Meditationen*, pp. 87–89; Gurwitsch, *op. cit.*, pp. 204–210.

occurring in a phenomenal time, but only to their intentional
correlates, i.e., the noemata corresponding to them. Consequently, because the different partial perceptive representations of one and the same material thing constitute a single
noematic system, we can explain that the one-sidedness of
each individual act is at the same time both experienced and
overcome.

The one-sidedness of each particular act of perception of
one and the same thing is overcome in the total process of
perception only if the different profiles contained in the noematic system successively actualize themselves in and through
the corresponding acts in such a way that the thing appears in
a manifold of different but harmonious explicit aspects. For in
this way each particular perceptive act in which the thing
manifests itself only in a particular aspect implies references
to other partial acts in which the thing manifests itself in constantly different but harmonious aspects. Viewed *noematically*, these references are essential features of the perceptive
noema in question; and *noetically* considered, they appear as
anticipations of new acts destined to complement this particular actual perception. Thus, it is not the temporal succession of the acts that overcomes the one-sidedness of each particular act, but the fact that they confirm, complement and
perfect one another. Accordingly, the process of perception,
noetically viewed, is a process of fulfillment (*Erfüllung*).[9]

Internal Horizon. Above we have said that in the perceptive
noema, i.e., in the thing as it manifests itself to us in and
through a given act of perception, by way of a particular profile, a distinction has to be made between that which effectively
manifests itself now and is given as such and, on the other
hand, the "rest." When we perceive a house, we effectively
see only one side of it. Nevertheless, our actual perception
has a greater content than what is effectively seen, for aspects
that are not effectively perceived always play a role in the
noema. Without such factors we would merely see a not-too-
sharply-defined surface having a certain color but not the

9 Husserl, *Ideen*, vol. 1, 333–353; Gurwitsch, *op. cit.*, pp. 210–
213.

facade of a house. In other words, that which is effectively perceived always appears in the light of data that are not effectively perceived. The complex, now, of the effectively and non-effectively perceived aspects constitutes the perceptive meaning in question.

To express the matter differently, every perceptive noema contains a rigidly defined core which is immediately given in experience and which, moreover, refers to not-immediately given aspects. The whole of the not-immediately given factors, Husserl calls the "internal horizon" of the perceptive noema.[10] We may add that the noematic core refers to the structures of the internal horizon, to a greater or a lesser extent, in proportion to the familiarity we already have with the perceived object. For this reason the internal horizon can be unfolded on the basis of what is here and now effectively perceived, provided this explicitation adheres rigidly to the limits set by that which is effectively perceived.[11]

External Horizon. Finally, we should keep in mind that whatever appears to man in his various acts of perception always manifests itself within a certain context. Every perceived thing or noema, Husserl says, has not only an internal horizon but also its external horizon,[12] for every perceptible object appears to us as a certain figure against a certain background. The house, which I experience as a unit through a quasi-infinite series of profiles, appears really as a house only against the horizon of the street, the park, the square, or the garden in which it stands. A house that is not found in the certain surroundings of which it is a part could never be a real house and could never be perceived as a house. When I direct my attention to this particular house in this street, then this house detaches itself from the background of meanings, but this horizon remains constitutive of the perceived real thing. If I direct my gaze to another house or to the car in front of it, the first house enters again into the horizon and cedes its privileged position to the other object of perception.

[10] Husserl, *ibid.,* pp. 100–101; *Erfahrung und Urteil,* pp. 26–37; Gurwitsch, *op. cit.,* pp. 228–238.
[11] Gurwitsch, *op. cit.,* pp. 238–245.
[12] Husserl, *Ideen,* vol. 1, p. 58; *Erfahrung und Urteil,* p. 28.

Thema and Thematic Field.   The same idea can be expressed in a different way. The house is the thema of my perceptive act, and as such it is surrounded by a thematic field consisting of other themata. Something similar applies to other cognitive acts. If, for instance, in logic one makes a certain proposition the object of his study, the thema of a certain complex of explicit acts, then this thema also is surrounded by a thematic field consisting of other propositions and theses which flow from the first or from which the first has been deduced. In general, one can say that the thema of a particular act is that on which the subject at a given moment centers his attention. The corresponding thematic field is the complex surrounding the thema in this act, the total context in which this thema manifests itself in this particular act.

It is to be noted that the thematic field is not simply identical with the field of perception. For the field of consciousness, the field of perception, the external horizon encompasses the totality of everything which in any way whatsoever is co-present in consciousness to a given thema. Therefore, it would be better to make a distinction in the external horizon between those data that are immediately related to the perceived thing (the noema or thema), which together constitute the thematic field; and, on the other hand, those elements which have nothing to do with the thema here and now considered and which therefore could be called the "margin."

The thematic field is very important for a correct view of the thema, for the thema refers to the thematic field, and the field gives to the thema a certain color and shading or at least co-determines its complete concrete meaning.[13] Thus, the structure of figure–horizon, which A. Rubin discovered in his study about the perception of sketches and figures,[14] and which Merleau-Ponty extended to the entire domain of perception,[15] may be conceived as a general structure of consciousness. The figure–horizon structure is nothing but a special case of the general structure of thema–thematic field.

[13] Gurwitsch, *op. cit.*, pp. 318–335.
[14] A. Rubin, *Visuell wahrgenommene Figuren,* København, 1921.
[15] Merleau-Ponty, *Phenomenology of Perception,* pp. 3 f., 33–36, 67–72, 280–298, 312–317.

Function and Importance of the Intentional Analysis. After these brief explanations it should no longer be too difficult to understand the importance of the intentional analyses. The original function and importance of this method lies in its unveiling the implicit aspects contained in the actual states of our consciousness. Generally speaking, it is the method of bringing forward meanings and making them explicit, the method of disengaging constituent elements which are implicitly contained in certain actually given meanings.[16] Its application to perception is based on an accurate analysis of that which is here and now given immediately but only implicitly in concrete perception.

If, then, we want to disclose the "meaning of a perception," we must try to make explicit the internal horizon together with the thematic field. This process has both a noetic and a noematic aspect. Noetically considered, this method demands that the thematic field be described as a deciphering of the anticipations of possible new and still potential perceptions. This particular perception, therefore, must be considered in relation to the whole "system" of acts which in one way or another are connected with this concrete perception and which could actuate its virtual content. Noematically considered, the intentional analysis endeavors to make explicit in consciousness all meanings which were only implicitly indicated in the effectively given datum. In fulfilling this function, it takes into account all the essential influences exercised by the internal horizon and the thematic field.[17]

In the preceding pages we have spoken about the act of perception. But any other act in which the subject tends to something can also be subjected to such an analysis, for instance, all cognitive acts based on perception, all affective acts, and strivings. In all these cases the aim is to show, through analysis and description, what this act really is in itself and which object is primordially constituted in this act. Because philosophy is not interested in the concrete as such, the em-

[16] Husserl, *Cartesianische Meditationen*, pp. 83–86.
[17] Gurwitsch, *op. cit.*, pp. 292–295.

phasis in these analyses will always fall on the essential structures. The guiding principle for such an analysis is most properly borrowed from the noematic aspect of the total datum. For this reason these analyses are sometimes called "noematic reflections." By carefully "peeling off" the intentionalities which cover and cross one another in the noema, viewed in its connection with the intentional acts aiming at it, we must try to arrive at a radical insight into the total datum.

A philosopher who wants to perform an intentional analysis and is solely or at least primarily interested in the epistemological problems of the empirical sciences has, of course, to rely on the derived acts which actually constitute the science in question. Although it would be possible to apply such an analysis immediately to these derived acts, it will, generally speaking, be better if he limits himself to the experiences that are primordial to the science in question. A concrete example may serve to clarify this point. When we ask ourselves what physical science really is and what is meant by nature, as it is considered by physical science, we are faced with the fact that physical science presents itself as a deductive theory or as a complex of deductive theories. Through the syntactic and semantic analyses of contemporary logic it is possible to isolate those acts which occupy a fundamental place in the deductive system. This procedure has the added advantage that the generally complex mathematical formalism in which the scientific theses concerning nature are formulated need not be made part of the intentional analysis. Later we will have an opportunity to revert to this point.[18]

[18] Ricoeur, *art. cit.* in footnote 1, pp. 114–117; Husserl, *Ideen,* vol. 2, pp. 1–11. See also our work *Tijd en ruimte,* Haarlem, 1958, pp. 66–69 and the literature quoted there.

Some Results of Husserl's Investigations*

DORION CAIRNS

According to those in a position to know, the bulk of Husserl's philosophy lies not in his published works but in his literary remains. Therefore, so long as the latter remain inaccessible, any statement of what is "most noteworthy in Husserl's thought" must be provisional.

If phenomenological investigation has penetrated beneath all usual presuppositions, a community of experience on the deeper level must be established before its results can be properly understood. Nearly every new reference to phenomenology is new evidence that such a community remains practically non-existent. The attempt to extend it now, with seven hundred words, would be futile. Preferring grave inadequacy to absolute unintelligibility, I therefore leave out the heart of Husserl's thought—the very part that, he maintained, can alone make genuine philosophy possible—and enumerate only results that can be superficially understood, as contributions to psychology and philosophy in the usual sense:

1. Differentiation between the real determinations of the stream of consciousness and what pertains to its intentional correlate.

2. Analysis of the general structure of the conscious act and its intentional correlate: the object as it is posited with its objective sense and in its manner of givenness.

3. Analysis of the horizon of acts predelineated by the given act, especially the horizon of acts intending the object as identical.

4. Distinction between various kinds and modes of positing

* From Dorion Cairns, "Some Results of Husserl's Investigations," *The Journal of Philosophy*, 36 (1939), pp. 236–239. Reprinted with permission of the author and the editors.

and between various manners of givenness, original or reproductive, direct or indirect.

5. Analysis of evidence as a manner of givenness; distinction between types of evidence, adequate, inadequate, apodictic; evidence of clarity or fullness and evidence of distinctness; fictive selfgivenness as evidence of possibility.

6. Conception of synthesis; fulfillment as a synthesis of identification between the more and the less evident.

7. Differentiation between individual objects and essences.

8. Analysis of sense-perception and of the general nature of the world of sensually perceivable objects.

9. Conception and realization of the idea of constitutive analysis.

10. Analysis of the passive self-constitution of the stream of consciousness with its temporal phases and simultaneous complexity.

11. Analysis of the passive constitution of objects transcendent of the stream of consciousness, particularly the constitution of the sensually experienced world through founding objective strata.

12. Analysis of the passive constitution of other minds and the world as intersubjective.

13. Description of spontaneity in general: ego-stimulation, attention, action.

14. Analysis of secondary passivity, the habitual retention of the products of active constitution.

15. Conception of the ego as subject-pole; analysis of the constitution of the ego's habitual character through spontaneity.

16. Analysis of categorial objects (e.g., facts) as constituted in synthetical acts founded ultimately in non-syntactical acts (e.g., of sense-perception).

17. Clarification of the relation between the reflectively intended categorial sense and the straightforwardly intended categorial object.

18. Description of syntheses of fulfillment of acts in which categorial objects are intended.

19. Distinction between formalization and generalization; correlatively, between formal and material essences.

20. Clarification of the idea of logic and of the relations of mathematics and logistic to formal logic and formal ontology.

21. Conception and realization of the idea of material ontologies.

22. Analysis of axiotic and practical acts and objects; development of formal and material *a priori* theories of value and practice.

23. Analysis of the relation of expression to objective sense.

24. Analysis of the relation of the world of physical science to the world as given in direct experience.

25. Rudimentary constitutive analyses of the social and cultural worlds.

26. Clarification of the sense of Occidental science and philosophy since the Renaissance.

27. Clarification of the nature of phenomenology and its relation to other sciences.

VI. EVIDENCE

On Evidence*

QUENTIN LAUER

After what has [. . .] been said, it might well seem superfluous to add a section on the Husserlian conception of evidence. But since it is possible to characterize Husserl's entire philosophical endeavor, particularly in its epistemological overtones, as a quest for the kind of evidence that will make knowledge "scientific," there is no better point of view from which to assess the advances made over the years in Husserl's thought about the nature of phenomenology itself. No philosophy, it is true, can be indifferent to the evidences available to it in the employment of its method, but it is not common to find the very concept of evidence assuming such importance as it does in transcendental phenomenology. If, however, a philosophy is to be conceived as a strict science never to be satisfied with a cognition whose objective validity is less than unimpeachable, it must devote considerable attention to just what meaning evidence is going to have for it. This is particularly true of transcendental phenomenology, where the motivating force behind the identification of absolute being and phenomenal being is the desire to attain to a being given in such a way that the impossibility of it being otherwise imposes itself on consciousness.

One need not, after all, be a phenomenologist in order to recognize (as did Hume, for instance) that an act of consciousness—be it perception, imagination, memory, or desire—is given in itself and as itself in such a manner that the subject of the act cannot doubt the being of the act. This is pre-

---

* From Quentin Lauer, "Introduction: Structure of the Ideal," in Edmund Husserl, *Phenomenology and the Crisis of Philosophy*, translated by Quentin Lauer (New York: Harper & Row, 1965), pp. 58–66. Reprinted by permission of the publishers. English translation copyright © 1965 by Quentin Lauer.

cisely the significance that Husserl sees in the Cartesian *cogito*, which to him revealed not the existence of a substantial subject—an invalid inference from the *cogito*—but revealed only itself and whatever is contained in it. What neither Descartes nor Hume saw, says Husserl, is that in the *cogito* the *cogitatum* is given with the same immediacy and certainty as is the *cogito* itself. Had either seen this, he would have discovered the essential intentionality of consciousness, and the step to transcendental phenomenology would have been inevitable. According to this theory, the being of an object as *cogitatum* is its veritable being, which is but another way of saying that in the intentionality of consciousness an object is "absolutely" given, provided that the act in which it is given is rational.

When one sees things thus, one *is* a phenomenologist, having deliberately chosen to center one's attention on phenomenal being because of its givenness. It is for this reason, according to Husserl, that being and consequently truth are functions of evidence. To be is to be given to consciousness; to be absolutely is to be given absolutely to consciousness, to be present to consciousness in such a way as to manifest the impossibility of being given otherwise. Though one must avoid the temptation to oversimplify—the phenomenological process is an extremely elaborate one—one can say that absolute givenness and hence absolute being are available to a careful reflection on the acts of consciousness. In the act itself is revealed the manner in which the intentional object of the act is given, which is to say that the act contains its own evidence, its own guarantee of givenness. The reasoning process is supremely logical: if the only being that can be absolute is the being that can be absolutely given, and if the only being that can be absolutely given is phenomenal being, then only phenomenal being can be absolute being. Of course, the first supposition, that absolute being is what is absolutely given, could be disputed, but since in this situation it is but a definition of what is meant by "absolute being," the dispute cannot get very far. Transcendental phenomenology wants a being absolute in this sense, and it chooses phenomenal being as the only being that can fulfill the requirements.

It is readily apparent that a philosophy that remains at this level is little more than a phenomenism, à la Hume. In it an absolute certainty has been secured, but it is found to be an empty certainty, for being in any significant sense still eludes one. It is in order to escape this trap of phenomenism that Husserl gradually elaborated his theory of evidence. He saw as clearly as anyone that no new theory was required in order to show that cognition gains in certainty in proportion as it is more immanent. He saw equally clearly, however, that a new theory was necessary in order to show that the certainty thus obtained is not empty, a theory that would effectively unite immanence and genuine objectivity. If Husserl could show that his own theory united absolute certainty with a genuinely objective knowledge of a real world, his task would be accomplished. This, then, is the double movement of Husserl's philosophy, which reveals itself in the gradual unfolding of a theory of evidence, a movement in the direction of ever greater certainty and a movement toward more assured objectivity. He seeks to assure objectivity in cognition by insisting on the essential necessity that manifests itself in immanent analysis of conscious acts. The essential is the ideal, and the locus of the ideal is in the acts of consciousness wherein it is constituted. Thus the essential necessity of objectivity is contained in the necessity according to which objectivity is constituted in the various acts of consciousness. A subjective necessity that is logical rather than psychological is by that very fact a guarantee of objectivity.

Returning to *Logische Untersuchungen,* we find there the foundations for a theory of evidence in the notion of intuitive "fulfillment" of the intention of meaning, an intention by itself "empty." Language functions in communication because the meaning given to it by the one who uses it is the meaning grasped by the one who understands it. The intention of meaning is the effective link between a conscious subject and the "state of affairs" expressed in language. For both parties in a communication, however, the conscious relationship can be an illusion if it is no more than an intention of meaning. What rescues it from illusion is the verification furnished by an intuition, wherein an object or "state of affairs" is not simply "intended" but rendered, so to speak, "bodily present" or "present-in-itself" to the consciousness that intends it. When the object intended and the object given in an intuition are identical, and the conscious subject is aware of the identification, the object, or better still, the proposition, is evident, its intention has been fulfilled.[1]

Up to this point the newness of Husserl's theory of verification might justifiably be questioned; it differs but slightly from that of Kant, of the empiricists, or of the positivists. Yet there is something definitely new in the theory, which, we must remember, is not clearly formulated as a theory until *Ideen I*. The novelty lies in Husserl's insistence that intuition, in the full sense of the term, is the presence to consciousness of an essence, with all that that implies by way of necessity and universal validity. Phenomenological intuition is essential intuition,[2] which is to say an intellectual intuition, the impossibility of which Kant had so vigorously asserted. It is plain to see, then, that such an intuition must be something more than the simple view contained in perception or imaginative representation, even though these latter acts are the examples from which the notion of intuition is derived. For Husserl intuition means more than empirical contact with an object. On the other hand, it is not some sort of mystical penetration into a world of essences inaccessible to merely rational thought. The whole secret of the phenomenological method, as conceived by Husserl, is that it is a laborious process wherein objects are brought to "self-givenness" in intuition. The phenomenological techniques elaborated over a long period of years and culminating in the intentional constitution whereby experience itself is rationalized, are but the implementation of the original determination to accept as evident only what pre-

[1] "The vital experience of the agreement between the intending and the self-present which it intends, between the actual sense of the expression and the self-given content, is evidence, and the idea of this agreement is truth" (*Log. Unt.*, I, 190–191).

[2] Spiegelberg, I, 11, goes so far as to define phenomenology (in the sense that it is common to the whole "movement") as an "intuitive method for obtaining insights into essential structures."

sents itself to consciousness with the same immediacy as does the *cogito*.[3]

There is no need here to describe once more the techniques devised by Husserl to effect the essential intuition demanded by the ideal of evidence as he sees it. If essences are to present themselves immediately to consciousness, they can do so only as ideal, since immediacy to consciousness and ideality are inseparable. Thus the technique of ideation, which plays such a large part in *Logische Untersuchungen,* must be completed by the techniques of *epoché* and "reduction," if it is to be more than a process of very imperfect induction. An essence that would somehow be in-itself, standing behind the appearances present to consciousness, could only be conjectured, it could never be evident. On the other hand, an essence constructed by the mind on the basis of the appearances present to it would be no more than a subjective projection— an ideal, it is true, but without guarantee of objectivity. Only in appearances stripped of all that is foreign to their appearing can essences legitimately be found. Thus the *epoché* is necessary in order to strip objectivity of all that is not phenomenal. Our everyday way of looking at things may clothe them with attributes our philosophical thinking cannot justify, but we must have the courage to eliminate such attributions from our consideration. This done, we must then "reduce" the phenomenal residue to its positive content and find there the essential richness we seek. With nothing but phenomena to go on, we can find by noetico-noematic analysis all the objectivity available to us in a reflection on the acts of consciousness themselves. The apparent negativity of these techniques may seem to offer only very impoverished results, but we must be willing to sacrifice the dross of conjecture for the pure gold of essential knowledge.

To speak of essential knowledge, however, is to speak of

---

[3] The similarity with Descartes here is striking. Descartes sought in the *cogito* the model for all certain knowledge. Thus he determined to accord the same evidence to whatever presented itself with the same clarity and distinctness as did the "I am." Husserl will adopt the same model for evidence, though he will seriously question that the Cartesian "I am" is part of the evidence.

what is necessarily so, and to speak of what is necessarily so
is to speak of reason, the faculty of necessity. What reason
genuinely sees to be necessary, is necessary—in one way or another this is the presupposition of all rationalism. However,
the condition for the sort of necessity seen by reason is that
reason suffer no interference from what is not reason. One
way to assure noninterference is to eliminate the very possibility of interference—and this Husserl has done in his *epochē*
and reductions. More than that, one must hand over everything to reason, and this Husserl does with the development
of "intentional constitution." Whatever is an object of consciousness, to the extent that it is an object of consciousness,
has its source in consciousness itself and is constituted as an
object, according to the "mode" of constitution which is necessity. The object so constituted is an object of reason. This is
at one and the same time thoroughly consistent rationalism
and thoroughly consistent transcendental phenomenology.
Notwithstanding the fact of logic to the contrary, the ultimate
rationalist and phenomenologist explanation of knowledge
must be, "I see it that way."[4] Logic or phenomenological
method may be the means of assuring that I see correctly, but
the ultimate court of appeal is still seeing—what I see to be rationally necessary, I see to be absolutely true. This sort of
seeing, however, is possible only if in the context it leaves
nothing unseen, and this is possible only if what is seen is
constituted as seen in reason.

In all this there is a certain inevitability. Given the original
purpose of securing apodictic certitude in matters philosophical, without which philosophy would not be "science," whatever makes for uncertainty must be eliminated from philosophical consideration. But where there is not merely question
of postulatory definition, as in mathematics, or of proposi-
tional functions, as in logic, there is ultimately only one source
of apodictic certainty, and that is seeing. Philosophy, then, is

---

[4] The objection has often been raised that different phenomenologists can come up with contradictory "essential intuitions,"
with no criterion for choosing between them. Husserl answers quite
simply that one genuine essential intuition cannot contradict another (cf. *Log. Unt.*, I, 191; II, Part 2, 127).

either a seeing, or it is no science at all. Furthermore, if all
that is not seen is eliminated from consideration, only what is
constituted in consciousness is left (unless, of course, reason is
to be considered as a finite participation in universal reason,
and of this Husserl would have no part). The structure of
reality is to be looked for in reason, since only there is it revealed. But Husserl could not be satisfied with a parallelism
of reason and reality, that would after all still be a mystery
and could not itself be rationalized. Only a reality whose
source is reason is a reality with nothing of the irrational
about it; its being and its intelligibility are constituted in
reason.

Yet along with the inevitability of this there goes also a certain opportunism. Phenomenology began as a quest for objectivity, but what it has done is to define objectivity in terms
of what it has found. There can be no question, as Kant saw
so well, that by suppressing transcendence, the source of all
doubt, one can arrive at an absolutely certain cognition. This
phenomenology has done. Then, by a detailed analysis of this
certain cognition it has arrived at a unique and unifying
"sense" in the multiple modes manifested by the objective
relation immanent in this certain cognition. Finally, it has defined objectivity as this unified sense it has found, without
even questioning whether it has sacrificed reality in the process, whether perhaps uncertainty is the price one must pay for
a genuine contact with reality. By eliminating the factual, it is
true, one may arrive at the essential, but philosophically
speaking, the price may be more than we can afford, if the
essential must be identified with the hypothetical.[5]

There is nevertheless a remarkable consistency to this way
of thinking. Taking as its point of departure the conviction
that a strictly scientific knowledge of being should be accessible to man (a somewhat sentimental conviction, since such a
knowledge is conceived as necessary if man's dignity is to be
safeguarded), it rejects successively a transcendent objective
essence and a subjective psychological necessity of thinking as

---

[5] A Hegelian might well say that Husserl has made the mistake
of stopping at essential intuition instead of seeing it as merely a
"moment" in a larger process.

explanations of objectively valid cognition. Once granted that Husserl's scientific ideal in philosophy is possible, the only alternative left is an objectivity based on an essential necessity revealed in cognition itself, insofar as this latter is an act proceeding from pure phenomenological consciousness. Such an essential necessity (be it ever so hypothetical) is the only objectivity available to such a way of thinking. Consciousness being what it is, only the act of consciousness can be absolutely given. If, then, objectivity is to be given, it must be given in the act of consciousness; but the only objectivity given in consciousness is the ideal term of its intentional orientation. The only objective analysis that phenomenology can consistently accept is the immanent analysis of intentionality, and the only possible source of this intentionality is consciousness itself—or, in the final analysis, transcendental subjectivity. This latter, however, is meaningless if it is not constitutive of its own cognition, both in its formal and its material aspects. Husserl has succeeded in thoroughly rationalizing cognition, even down to its experiential bases. Whatever escapes this rationalization is conjecture, not knowledge.

If Husserl's phenomenology has done nothing else, it has drawn attention in a very striking way to the unquestionably subjective elements in all "rational" knowledge, especially the rational knowledge of "essences." Who can question that facts have about them a definite impenetrability? It has become almost axiomatic in our positivistically oriented culture to look askance at essences, as being simply unknowable. The conclusion we can draw from Husserl would seem to be exactly the reverse: only essences are knowable at all. We know to the extent that we grasp essences. Beyond this we opine.

Phenomenology of Reason*

EDMUND HUSSERL

When we speak of objects *simpliciter,* we mean as a rule real objects that truly are and belong to this or that category of Being. Whatever we assert then concerning objects—provided we speak reasonably—we must submit, whether as meant or spoken, to *"logical grounding," "proof" (Ausweisen),* to showing in an immediate or mediate way. Basically, in the realm of logic, i.e., in that of statement, *"that which truly or really (wirklich) is" and "that which is rationally demonstrable" (Ausweisbar) are intrinsically correlated;* and so for all doxic modalities ontical or positional. Of course the possibility of a rational demonstration *(Ausweisung)* which stand here in question is not to be understood as empirical but as ideal, as an essential possibility.

The First Basic Form of Rational Consciousness: the Primordial Dator "Vision"

If we now ask what is meant by a rational setting forth *(Ausweisung),* i.e., wherein the *rational consciousness* consists, we find at once the intuitive representing of examples and the beginnings of essential analysis carried out upon them the source of several distinctions:

We have *in the first place* the distinction between positional experiences in which what is set down acquires *primordial givenness,* and those in which it does *not* acquire such givenness; between *"perceiving," "seeing" acts, that is—understood in a broad sense—*and *non-"perceiving" acts.*

* From Edmund Husserl, *Ideas: General Introduction to Phenomenology,* translated by W. R. Boyce Gibson (London: George Allen & Unwin Ltd., 1931), Vol. I, secs. 136–138. Reprinted by permission of the publishers.

Thus a recollective consciousness, for example that of a landscape, is not given in a primordial sense; the landscape is not perceived as though we were really seeing it. In stating this we have not wished to say that the recollective consciousness has no independent right of its own, but just that this is not one of "seeing." Phenomenology presents an analogue of this opposition for *all types of positional* experiences. We can, for instance, predicate in a "blind" way that $2 + 1 = 1 + 2$; we can, however, carry out the same judgment with insight. The positive fact (*Sachverhalt*), the synthetic objectivity which corresponds to the synthesis of judgment, is then primordially given, grasped in a primordial way. It is this no longer *after* the living fulfilment of the insight, for the latter passes off at once into the obscurity of a retentional modification. The latter may indeed have a rational advantage over any other dim or confused consciousness of the same noematic meaning, over an "unthinking" reproduction, for instance, of something once previously learnt and perhaps with insight; but it is no longer a consciousness primordially given.

These distinctions do not concern the pure meaning and position, for this is the same for both members of every such pair of examples, and may also be consciously and intuitively grasped as identical every time. The distinction concerns *the way in which the mere meaning or position*, which as a mere abstractum requires a plus in the way of supplementing phases in the full development (*Konkretion*) of the noema of consciousness, is or is not filled out.

Fullness of meaning is not the only requisite; we are also concerned with the mode (*Wie*) of the filling out. One mode of experiencing the meaning is the *"intuitive,"* whereby we are made aware of the "meant object as such" through direct mental vision, and as a particularly outstanding case we have that wherein the mode of direct vision is the primordial *object-giving* mode. The meaning in the perception of the landscape is perceptively filled out, and we become aware of the perceived object with its colours, forms, and so forth (so far as they "fall within perception") in the mode of the "embodied." We find similar distinctions in all act-spheres. The situation has again its two aspects in the parallelistic sense, a noetic and a noematic. In the noematic setting we find the character of embodiment (as the primordial state of being filled out) blent with pure meaning, and *the meaning stamped with this character now functions as the foundation of the noematic character of positionality,* or, which here means the same thing, the ontical character. The parallel holds good of the noetic setting also.

A specific character of rationality pertains, however, to that of positionality as its own, as a *distinction* which is *then and only then essential* to it when it is a positing grounded not merely in meaning generally but in a filled out, primordial dator meaning.

Here and in every kind of rational consciousness the phrase "belonging to" receives the meaning of "being its own." For instance: To the corporeal appearing of a thing there *belongs* in all cases positionality. It is not only one with this appearing in a general way (as a mere general fact, shall we say, which is here unquestioned); it is one with it in a unique sense, it is *"motivated"* by it, and still again not merely in a general way but *"rationally motivated."* And this means that the positing has its *original ground of legitimacy* in the primordial givenness. In other forms of givenness the ground of legitimacy need not exactly be wanting; what is, however, lacking is the prerogative of the *original* ground which plays its outstanding part in the relative appreciation of the grounds of legitimacy.

The positing of the essence or essential relationships "primordially" given in our *vision of Essential Being* likewise "belongs" to its positing "material," to the "meaning" in its mode of givenness. It is reasonable and, as believing certitude, originally motivated positing; it has the specific character of *"that which understands"* (*der "einsehenden"*). If the positing is a *"blind"* one, if the meanings of the words are determined on the basis of a dim act-background of which we are only confusedly aware, the rational character of the insight is necessarily lacking; with such mode of givenness (if we are still to use this word here) of the significant fact (*Sachverhaltes*), or, alternatively, with such noematic accompaniment of the nucleus of meaning, the character of reason is *essentially incompatible.* On the other hand, this does not exclude a secondary rational character, as the example of the imperfect reproduction of essential cognitions shows.

Insight, *self-evidence* generally, is thus an entirely distinctive occurrence; at its "centre" it is the *unity of a rational positing with that which essentially motivates it,* the whole situation here indicated being intelligible in terms of the noema as well as of the noesis. The reference to motivation fits excellently the relation between the (noetic) positing (*Setzen*) and the noematic meaning posited (*Satz*) *in its mode of intuitional saturation* (*Erfülltheit*). The expression "*self-evident posited meaning*" in its noematic rendering is immediately intelligible.

The twofold meaning of the word self-evidence in its application now to noetic characters, or full acts (e.g., self-evidence of judging), now to noematic positions (e.g., self-evident logical judgment, self-evident stated meaning), is a case of the general and necessary ambiguities of the expressions related to the phases of correlation between noesis and noema. The phenomenological indication of the source they spring from renders them harmless, and even permits us to recognize their indispensability.

We have yet to note that the expression "*fulfilment*" (*Erfüllung*) has still another ambiguity which lies in a quite other direction: at one time it is "*fulfilment of intention*," as a character which the actual thesis takes on through the special mode of meaning; at another it is precisely the peculiarity of this mode itself or the peculiar property of the meaning in question, to conceal "rich resources" which motivate in accordance with reason.

Self-Evidence and Insight. "Primordial" and "Pure" Assertoric and Apodeictic Self-Evidence

The pairs of examples made use of above illustrate at the same time a *second* and a *third* essential difference. That which we ordinarily call self-evidence and *insight* (or *seeing into*) is a positional doxic and also *adequate* dator consciousness which "excludes Otherness"; the thesis is motivated in a quite exceptional way through the adequacy of the given material, and is in the highest sense an act of reason. The arithmetical example illustrates that for us. In the example of the landscape we have indeed a seeing, but not the experience-of-self-evidence (*Evidenz*) in the ordinary pregnant meaning of the word, a "seeing into." When the contrasted examples are looked into more closely, we are struck by a *double difference:* in the one example we are treating of the *essence,* in the other of the *individual;* in the second place the primordial givenness in the eidetic example is *adequate;* in the example from the sphere of experience it is *inadequate.* Both differences which intercross under certain circumstances will prove of importance in respect to the type of insight (*Evidenz*) involved.

So far as the first difference is concerned, we may state on phenomenological grounds that the so to speak *"assertoric" seeing of an individual,* for instance, the "awareness" of a thing or of some individual state of things, is in its rational character essentially distinguished from an *"apodeictic" seeing, from the in-seeing of an essence or an essential relationship;* but also likewise from the modification of this in-seeing, which may take place through a mixing of the two, namely, in the case of the application of an insight to something assertorically seen, and generally in the *knowledge of the necessity of* a posited particular being so-and-so.

Evidential Vision (*Evidenz*) and Insight, in the ordinary meaningful (*prägnanter*) sense, are taken as meaning the same thing, namely, apodeictic in-seeing. We propose in our terminology to separate the two words. We are in real need of a more general word which shall include in its meaning assertoric seeing and apodeictic in-seeing. We should consider it as a phenomenological finding of great importance that they both really belong to *one* generic essence, and that, understood in a still more general way, *Rational Consciousness in general designates a summum genus of thetic modalities,* in which the "seeing," used in its very widest sense, and as bearing on primordial givenness, constitutes a well-defined class. In giving a name to the summum genus one has the option either of extending the meaning of the word "seeing" (as we did just now, but going very much farther) or of

widening the meaning of the words "in-seeing" and "evidential vision" (*Evidenz*). It might be most suitable to choose the
word: *evidential vision* to stand for the most general concept;
the expression *primordial evidential vision* would then be available for representing every rational thesis characterized by a
relation of motivation in respect of the primordiality of what
is primordially given. We should then have to decide further
between the *assertoric* and *apodeictic forms of evidential vision,* and to leave to the word *insight* the special task of des-
ignating this *apodeictic character.* Proceeding still farther, we
would set up as opposites *pure* insight and *impure* insight (the
latter including the cognition of the necessity of an element of
fact, the Being of which does not need to be self-evident), and
likewise, and in a quite general way, we would draw a contrast between *pure and impure evidential vision.*

Further differences arise as our inquiry deepens, differences
concerning the bases of motivation and affecting the character of the evidential vision; for example, the difference between *purely formal* ("analytic," "logical") and *material*
(synthetic-*a priori*) evidential vision. But at this point we
should not go beyond the briefest indications.

Adequate and Inadequate Self-Evidence

Let us now turn back to the second of the two differences
indicated above, which is closely connected with that between
adequate and inadequate givenness, and gives us occasion at
the same time to describe an outstanding type of "impure"
evidential vision. The positing act (*Setzung*) grounded in the
corporeal appearance of the *Thing* is indeed rational, but the
appearance is never more than a one-sided "imperfect" appearance; not only are we conscious in corporeal form of
the very object that is in process of appearing, but of the thing
itself *simpliciter,* the whole in its collective though only one-
sidedly intuitional and in addition variously undetermined
meaning. But of course that which "verily" appears must not
be separated from the Thing as though it were itself a separate
thing; its correlate of meaning constitutes a *dependent* part
within the full meaning of the Thing, a part which can have

unity of meaning and independence only within a whole which *necessarily* conceals in itself components of emptiness and of indeterminacy.

In principle a thing in the real world, a Being in this sense, can within the finite limits of appearance appear only *"inadequately."* Essentially connected therewith is the fact that *not rational positing which rests on an appearance that presents itself so inadequately* can be *"definitive,"* "invincible"; that no such positing in its particularity is equivalent to the downright assertion that "the Thing is real," but only to the assertion "It is real" on the supposition that the advance of experience does not bring in its train "stronger rational motives" which exhibit the original positing as one that must be "cancelled" in the further connexion. Moreover, the positing is rationally motivated only through the appearance (the imperfectly fulfilled perceptual meaning) in and for itself, considered in its particularized detail.

The phenomenology of Reason in the sphere of the types of Being which can on principle be only inadequately given (the sphere of *transcendents* in the sense of realities (*Realitäten*) has therefore to study the different occurrences within this sphere which have been indicated *a priori* and in advance. It has to make clear how the inadequate consciousness of givenness, the partial appearing, is related to one and the same determinable X, whilst continuously advancing towards ever-fresh appearances which are continuously passing over into one another, and also to indicate the essential possibilities which here present themselves; how, on the one hand, a sequence of experiences is possible here and constantly motivated on rational lines through the rational placements [*positings*] that are continuously at one's disposal, namely, the course of experience in which the empty places of the appearances that have preceded get filled again, the indeterminacies more closely determined, moving forward all the time towards *a thoroughgoing harmonious filling out, with the steadily increasing rational power that goes with this.* On the other hand, we have to make clear the opposite possibilities, the *cases of the fusions or polythetic syntheses where there is disagreement or determination otherwise* of that X which we are constantly aware of as one and the same—otherwise, that is, than in harmony with the original bestowal of meaning. We have to show, moreover, how positional components of the earlier course of perception suffer *cancellation* together with their meaning; how under certain circumstances the whole perception *explodes,* so to speak, and breaks up into *"conflicting apprehensions of the Thing,"* into *suppositions* concerning the thing; how the theses of these suppositions annul one another, and in such annulling are modified in a peculiar way; or how the one thesis, remaining unmodified, "conditions" the cancelling of the "contrary thesis"; and other contingencies of the same kind.

As further and closer objects of study we may note the peculiar modifications which the original positings of Reason suffer owing to the fact that in the course of harmonious filling out they undergo a *positive phenomenological enhancement* with respect to their *motivating "power,"* that they increase steadily in *"weight,"* that they thus constantly and essentially possess weight, but one that differs *gradually.* The other possibilities also call for analysis, in respect of such points as how the weight of positings suffers from *"countermotives,"* how in *doubt* they mutually *"balance"* one another, how one placement in rivalry with another of "greater" weight is *"outweighed," "abandoned,"* and so forth.

In addition, of course, the circumstances which are essentially determinative of the changes in the positional characters in the sense in which they belong to the *positional content* should be subjected to a comprehensive analysis on essential lines (e.g., the circumstances accompanying the "conflict" or the "rivalry" of appearances). For here, as everywhere, in the phenomenological sphere, there are no contingencies, no mere matter-of-fact connexions (*Faktizitäten*); all is essentially and definitely motivated.

In a similar way the *inquiry into the essential nature of all kinds of rational acts in their immediacy* should be carried through in connexion with a general phenomenology of the noetic and noematic given material.

To every region and category of supposed objects corresponds phenomenologically not only a *basic kind of meaning or position*, but also a *basic kind of primordial dator-consciousness* of such meaning, and, pertaining to it, a *basic type of primordial self-evidence*, essentially motivated through a primitive givenness that conforms to the basic divisions just referred to.

Every such self-evidence, the word being understood in the extended sense we have given to it, is either *adequate*, incapable in principle of being either "strengthened" or "weakened," thus *without the graded differences of a weight;* or it is *inadequate*, and therewith *capable of increase and decrease*. Whether in any given context the former or the latter kind of self-evidence is possible depends on its generic type; it is thus prefashioned, *a priori*, and to demand the perfection which self-evidence possesses in one content (e.g., that of essential relations) in other contexts which essentially exclude it is simply absurd.

We have still this remark to make, that we were obliged to transfer the original meaning of the concepts "adequate" and "inadequate," which relates to the mode of presentation, to the essential peculiarities of the rational positings themselves, grounded on them. We were enabled to do so by the very fact of their connexion. It is one of those unavoidable equivocations due to transference, which lose their power to harm so soon as one recognizes them as equivocal, and has clearly and consciously distinguished the derived from the original.

VII. INTERSUBJECTIVITY

The Other Explained Intentionally*

QUENTIN LAUER

[The following selection is a brief survey of the fifth meditation of Husserl's *Cartesianische Meditationen*. Husserl explained already in the fourth meditation that as far as their
full meaning is concerned, objects as well as the subject itself
must be constituted by the subject as transcendental. For the
meaning of the concept of constitution see pp. 121–43 of this
anthology; what is said there mainly for objects holds good
also for the subject, albeit in an analogous way.]

Fifth Meditation: up to the present Husserl has been content
to explain the universally a priori laws of cognition and hence
of being on the level of a reflection wherein the subject requires no other equipment than its own subjectivity. The laws
of *all* subjectivity are discoverable in the transcendental *ego*,[1]
since an intuition of their validity establishes them as essential
and hence infallible. Still, even while examining the problematic of the *Logical Investigations* one could have seen that a
purely solipsistic explanation of intentional constitution would
ultimately prove inadequate. In that early work, the starting
point of the investigations is to be found in an analysis of discourse. If there are "empty" or "unfulfilled" intentions, the
reason is that concepts have somehow been communicated
through discourse, and these concepts have not been critically
examined. Now, if communication constitutes a phenomenological problem, the solution cannot be confined to a solipsistic

* From Quentin Lauer, *The Triumph of Subjectivity: An Introduction to Transcendental Phenomenology* (New York: Fordham
University Press, 1958), Chap. 8. Reprinted by permission of the
publishers.
[1] No possible subject can be *essentially* different from the *ego*
discovered in an essential intuition.

justification of the concepts which figure in discourse. If there is communication at all, no matter what its explanation be, there must be a plurality of subjects who communicate. Incidentally, if a phenomenologist writes a book, he does so in order to communicate his own convictions to others, nor can he as a consistent phenomenologist be satisfied with the naïve assumption that there are other subjects who will understand what he seeks to communicate.

If, then, we assume with Husserl that there can be no explanation of being in any form outside of intentional constitution, the problem becomes infinitely more complicated, just at the moment when a solution seems imminent. The constitution of objectivity has been explained; the concomitant constitution of one's own subjectivity has been explained too. What has not been explained is the presence (or even possibility) of other subjects, which, if they are to be significant, must be constituted, but which would seem to resist any attempt at a constitutive explanation. The *essential* laws of subjective constitution have already been discovered; if a subject is constituted in any other way, either its constitution is not valid and the result is zero (at least scientifically), or the laws which have been discovered are not essential. Both of these conclusions are inadmissible: the first because it would destroy the universality of phenomenological science; the second because it would destroy the scientific character of universal phenomenology.

If we reject both conclusions, then we must face the dilemma of a constitution which is not objective, since its term is a subject, nor can this constitution be subjective, since, as we have been made to believe up to the present, subjective constitution is self-constitution, whereas what we are seeking is some sort of constitution of one subject by *another*. We have, it is true, been told in the Fourth Meditation of an objective constitution of a subject, but this had to be subsequent to its subjective constitution. We have not been told of an objective constitution whose direct form is a subject. The self is constituted in and with its experiences, but since I cannot constitute another's experiences, how can I constitute another's subjectivity? And, if I cannot do this, how can another *be for me?*

Is there a third kind of constitution, which is neither objective nor subjective, or is there a synthesis of objective and subjective constitution wherein is constituted an object, which is at the same time a subject? The Fourth Meditation contains a hint as to the answer in its insistence that the constituted subject can be concretized by being objectified—by reflection we can grasp our own subjectivity as an object. It remains to find a means of grasping some element of the objective world as a subject.

Although, as we said before, Husserl prefers to lay down the rules of intentional constitution and leave the details of concrete application to others, this is one concrete application which he cannot bypass. His own notion of universally valid objectivity makes it imperative that his universal subject be not abstract but concrete; and a concrete universal subject means nothing if it does not mean a concrete multiplicity of subjects. Now, if there are many subjects, many conclusions follow which have not yet been so much as suggested: (1) Each subject must be self constituted, else it can have no significance in a phenomenological framework. (2) Each subject must be constituted as such (either individually or collectively) in each other subject, or the result will be a completely monadological universe, where communication is impossible. (3) The constitution of the other must correspond to the other's self-constitution, else it will be invalid; and my constitution of self must correspond to others' constitution of me,[2] else I will be myself and not myself. (4) Each must constitute a world of objectivity which is in some sense identical with the world constituted by the others, or there will be no common ground for communication. (5) The world which each one constitutes must be a world comprising oneself and others, else the unity of the world will be destroyed, as Sartre has destroyed it by making the self ultimately the "néant."

Husserl was certainly not unaware of all these problems involved in his theory of intentional constitution. It is for this reason that he spent so much time during the last years of his

[2] This, obviously, admits of degrees; no one need know me as I know myself. Still, one constitution cannot contradict another.

life trying to evolve a consistent theory of intersubjective constitution. It is doubtful whether he himself was convinced that the theory as he was able to evolve it answered all the questions which can be legitimately asked, but there is no doubt that he saw no reason in the intersubjective problematic for abandoning the completely constitutive explanation of all being for which he had opted. Having once and for all rejected any possibility of a causal explanation of cognition, the only consistent thing to do was to reject with equal vigor any causal explanation of intersubjective communication. Thus, though in many places Husserl gives evidence of having conceived this theory of intersubjectivity as an additional guarantee for the validity of subjective constitution, it is difficult to see how the theory as actually evolved does any more than explain how the fundamental theory of constitution can be extended to the presence of other subjects in the cognitive field, without thereby adding anything to the already-developed theory. The theory of intersubjectivity is, as it were, a particular application of intentional constitution, an application which could not be avoided, as were most other applications, since the central concept of objective validity demands an objectivity recognized as binding on *all possible* subjects; and the very admission that other subjects are possible demands that the theory account for the constitution of such subjects—even if only as possible.[3] Thus, it is impossible to escape the impression that the numerous pages consecrated by Husserl, in both his published and unpublished works, to intersubjective constitution add no explanation whatever to the problem of objectivity.[4] Rather, intersubjective constitution is but an extension of the theory of objective constitution, concerned with an object which is constituted both as an object and as a subject. It is difficult to see how it could be more than this with-

[3] Admittedly, it is difficult to conceive what possibility can mean in that which is *merely* possible. Can there be a possibility without reference to actuality? Nicolai Hartmann has instituted a detailed critique of "logical possibility" in *Möglichkeit und Wirklichkeit* (2nd ed.; Berlin: de Gruyter, 1949).

[4] The best known are the Fifth Cartesian Meditation and *Ideen II.* In the latter Husserl is concerned with laying the groundwork for a genuine essential psychology.

out entering into the existential problematic, which Husserl never effectively does. It is for this reason that we have devoted a separate chapter to the Fifth Cartesian Meditation, since it seems to be conceived as a particular application of what has been developed in the first four Meditations.

Understood in this way the problem is traceable to a certain paradox inherent in the very notion of intentional constitution, particularly when viewed as a constitution of the *ego*, as it is in the Fourth Meditation. Such an *ego* must be at one and the same time *constitutive* and *constituted*. We ourselves can be *in the world* only to the extent that we are for ourselves *objects* in the world, since the world has been defined as the totality of objects for a subject. Now it is clear that the self-constitution described in the Fourth Meditation is not the constitution of an object; it is the progressive constitution of a "pure" subject, in and through a series of objective references to an objectively constituted world. On the other hand, it is clear both from the Fourth Meditation and from the psychological studies of *Ideas II* that the transcendental *ego* both *can* and *should* be objectified. The important thing to remember is that when the *ego* is objectified, its constitution does not enjoy the same priority as does subjective constitution; it is preceded by the world in general, constituted as a sum total of objectivity. By a sort of paradox it is also preceded, according to Husserl, by the constitution of the other subject, as the first example of object which is also subject.[5] If we could look upon this as a recognition on the part of Husserl that a subject is not fully constituted as subject except in a community of subjects, we might consider the whole thing a modification of his general theory. Thus, it could be said that the other subject is genuinely *given with* the proper subject, precisely because it is essential to a subject that it not be given in isolation. This seems to be the position of phenomenologists like Scheler and Heidegger, but it is too Hegelian in tone to have been acceptable to Husserl.[6]

Now, the problem of the other, known as a subject, is not confined to phenomenology. Every philosophy must recognize among its field of objects one object which is like none of the others; it is presented not only as known by the knower but also as knowing the knower.[7] The difficulty is that to be subject means to have experiences; to be experienced as subject is to be experienced as having experiences. Somehow, then, the experiences of others must form part of my intentional life, without at the same time being my experiences. Consequently, Husserl is obliged to find an intentional category comprising some sort of experience of others' experiences. This one can do somehow, he says, by "empathy" (*Einfühlung*).[8] In empathy Husserl finds the key to a constituted world which will be objectively valid for all subjects—actual or possible. What he has done, however, is to realize that such a solution demands a kind of intentional experience which has for its object the experiences of others. Since such an intentional experience is necessary, he postulates it and calls it "empathy." Still, this procedure is not as arbitrary as it might seem: Husserl does not pretend in his explanation that empathy is a known phenomenon, whose essence he has intuited; rather it is a sort of tentative explanation of what he is convinced will be ultimately explained intentionally—though the explanation may have to come from more detailed investigations.[9] As Eugen Fink puts it, Husserl has no intention of interpreting empathy but merely of using it as an "explicitation of the

[7] More than anyone else, perhaps, Hegel has exploited this recognition in a series of dialectics leading up to consciousness of self; cf. *Phänomenologie des Geistes,* ed. Lasson (Hamburg: Meiner, 1948), pp. 133–71. J.-P. Sartre has pushed the same thing to a pathological extreme; cf. *L'être et le néant,* pp. 310–68, 431–503; *Huis clos; infra,* chap. ix, p. 178.

[8] Unfortunately this notion seems to have been contrived in order to fill a need. Much, of course, has been said about it in contemporary psychology and esthetic theory, but from them Husserl has borrowed little more than the name. As for a phenomenological analysis of empathy, it seems to be confined to saying what it *must* be if it is to fulfill the function for which Husserl needs it.

[9] Cf. *Philosophie als strenge Wissenschaft,* p. 322, n. 1.

reduction,"[10] whereby the first contact with other subjects on the naïve level is raised to the transcendental level. Once more the naïve object—which is here a subject—acts as "transcendental guide" for the phenomenological investigation.

To get back to the argument of the Fifth Meditation, we can, simply by placing ourselves at the point to which the Fourth Meditation has brought us, distinguish three elements absolutely *given* to pure consciousness. They are: (1) my animated body (*Leib*), infallibly perceived as a material object; (2) my soul (*Seele*), as the psychological subject of objectifying operations; (3) the body of the other (*Körper*), not considered as either animated or inanimate, but simply as an object resembling my own body.[11] The point, then, is to show that, by virtue of the principle of "association,"[12] there is given with these objects something else whose indubitability is the same as theirs. In order to show this, it is necessary, in accord with the already established phenomenological procedure, to analyze not only the given objects but also their manner of being given. If the proper subject, which is unquestionably *given* in any experience, is objectified, it is given in another way. All that is now needed is that this other mode of givenness should involve (not by causal inference) other subjects.

It is possible, by a sort of abstraction, to separate from the sum total of constituted nature a part which has sense for me and for me alone. This is my (animated) body (*Leib*), the

[10] "Die phänomenologische Philosophie Ed. Husserls," p. 368. The concept has been put to good use in the realm of esthetics by Theodor Lipps, *Aesthetik*, I (Leipzig: Voss, 1914), pp. 96–223, and by Max Scheler, *Wesen und Formen der Sympathie* (5th ed.; Frankfurt am Main: Schulte-Bulmke, 1948), pp. 259–65, in the realm of psychology.

[11] Husserl has, in fact, said little or nothing of these three *objects* in the Fourth Meditation. He is presupposing them as belonging to the stage reached there; they are explained in *Ideen II*.

[12] It will be seen that this principle of association has been imperceptibly modified. It is not so much the calling up of a constituted objectivity through its connection with another, as it is the original but not direct constitution of an independent objectivity, the evidence for which is contained in the evidence of other objectivities.

only real object in the world which is not simply a body
(*Körper*). Thus, the experience of one's own body is unique
in the whole field of experience, a fact which is, of course,
recognized by all philosophers. The body is given immediately
as animated by a soul, and by the same token the soul is immediately given in the same evidence.[18] Herein, then, the
ego can, so to speak, constitute itself as a "body-soul" com-
posite, which is the psycho-physical *ego*. As such it is a transcendental subject, and, since it has been objectively constituted, it is an objective subject. Now, just as the subjective
grasp of the subject is at the same time an objective grasp of
the world, constituted in the subject, so the world is contained
by "association" in the objective grasp of the transcendental
subject. Only on this "secondary" level of subjectivity, where
the subject is grasped as an object, is it possible to distinguish
that which is proper to the subject from that which is "foreign"—impossible on the level of the *pure* transcendental *ego*,
since there all objectivity is equally objectivity constituted in
the *ego*. On the *secondary* level, however, where the individual *ego* is distinguished from the transcendental *ego* as such,
objectivities can be distinguished as constituted in this and/or
that subject. And here, for the first time, it is possible to grasp
what is experience for others. Thus, by distinguishing within
the generality of the transcendental *ego* between what is foreign and what is proper, one has an intuition of one's own
individual subjectivity, which when grasped in the sort of constant identity which characterizes an object becomes a *personal*
subject.

Once the individuation of the proper personal *ego* within
the pure transcendental *ego* has been accomplished, the *possibility* of other individual subjects has been seen, as particular
participations of the universally valid idea of subjectivity.
And, just as phenomenological interpretation of the world is a
constitution of the evidence in which the world is given, so
too a phenomenological interpretation of the other will be a
constitution of the evidence in which the other is given, or, it

---

[18] Since the epochē and reductions are still operative, the "soul"
is not given as substantial, merely as a center of reference for
"psychic" operations.

will be constitution of a world in which there are other subjects. Thus, the evidence of self as an individual will be the same evidence in which other individuals are given. The world is first given as the objective correlate, so to speak, of a transcendental *we,* but the very first differentiation of subjects within this *we* gives both self and others. In this, however, there is a certain convergence of evidence: the proper subject is first given vaguely as subject in general and then objectified as individual; the other is first given as a sort of object in general and then subjectified as individual. What is primarily given, then, is the world and with it pure transcendental subjectivity. With this, by a sort of association, is given the differentiation of multiple subjects, which is to say that the *meaning* of multiple subjects has been constituted.

Still, since the other represented in this way has no other determination than that of being a subject and of not being myself,[14] it is as yet a subject demanding positive determination. The first determination is purely objective: the body (*Körper*) of the other is perceived as an object. By an associative transfer, however, it is grasped as an animated body (*Leib*). It is by its *behavior* that the other's body is perceived as similar to one's own body. And so, although the other is presented as an intentional modification of my own field of perception, of my own *ego,* it is at the same time presented as an *ego,* that is, having its own correlative world. It is possible to take the simple determinations of "here" and "there" as corporeal characteristics and to realize through them a distinction between *this body here* and *that body there,* which is ultimately a distinction between two subjects. I can comprehend the other as a subject having the experiences I *would* have if I were *there.*[15] This, of course, demands that the subject have already had a series of experiences in which the

---

[14] Remarkably similar to the beginning of the Fichtean dialectic of *ego* and *non-ego.*

[15] There is a peculiar oversimplification here, based on the conviction that the first intuition of subjectivity so gives the essence of experience that a multiplication of subjects cannot significantly modify this "essence."

same object is recognized as the same from "here" and from "there."

Once another subject is recognized, however vaguely, as having experiences similar to one's own of a world which is also one's own world, the step to a recognition of the world as object of a *common* constitution is not a long one, though, what a "common constitution" can mean must remain vague. What is more, this raises a further difficulty with regard to the constitution of the other subjectivity. As subjectivity it must certainly be self-constituted, and as individual subject it must be objectively constituted. Now, for me it is constituted as "there," whereas for itself it is constituted as "here"; which is to say, it is not constituted in both cases as absolutely identical, since "here" and "there" are modes of corporeity sufficient to distinguish bodies and, hence, subjects. Husserl's answer is that corporeal nature is commonly constituted with two distinct modalities whereby there are two subjects. This may seem insignificant, but it is enough to indicate that common constitution stops at a certain generality; particularization involves a differentiation introduced by individual subjects. It may be that two subjects experience things (or *some* things) in exactly the same way, but there is no way of *knowing* that this agreement is anything but general. Thus, the world is commonly constituted, but the result is a common world with different modalities, so that the one world is for different subjects both the same and different. The sameness is discoverable in the a priori *laws* of intentional constitution, which are determined on the level of pure transcendental subjectivity, prior to any distinction of multiple subjects. All of which makes one wonder if other subjects are genuinely *given* or whether what is given is merely that any other possible subject must correspond to the essence of subjectivity.

The theory of intersubjectivity, however, does permit Husserl to approach a subjective community not too far removed from the one Hegel presents in his *Phenomenology of Spirit*. This, perhaps, is the real significance of the theory. In self-constitution it is first the pure transcendental subject which is constituted as the correlative of all objectivity. Only thereafter is the subject constituted as a recognizable object. With the other subject the process is precisely the reverse—first objectivity, then subjectivity. And, just as there is a sort of correspondence in the constitution of the self and of the other as individual subjects, so there is a correspondence between the subjective and the intersubjective constitution of the pure transcendental subjectivity. Had Husserl been able to develop this last point more completely and more consistently he might have attained to a concrete community of consciousness, whose history would be a *total* history, because a history of "Spirit," as it is for Hegel.

On the objective side this theory does introduce an important distinction which appears only late in Husserl's writings. The concrete individual subject, as we have seen, is limited by the world therein constituted. This world Husserl calls *Umwelt*, corresponding to the individual *personal* subject. Besides this, it is now possible to recognize a *personality* of a higher order, a *social* unity, having as its correspondent a "community" world, which Husserl calls the *Kulturwelt*.[16] In this, then, is discovered an intersubjective a priori, which cannot contradict but can expand the subjective a priori. Though Husserl himself does not develop the theme, one can see in it the possibility of some sort of intersubjective verification of subjective insights. Were this more thoroughly developed it might silence some of the objections which continue to find Husserl's whole methodology too arbitrary.[17] Husserl himself is convinced that this intersubjective a priori excludes any arbitrariness in constitution, making it resemble a "discovery" far more than a "creation," and by the same token making it profoundly *metaphysical*.[18]

The importance of the theory, then, is not so much in the actual explanation which is given as in the realization that

[16] Cf. *Cartesianische Meditationen*, pp. 168–77; *Ideen II*, secs. 50–51.

[17] One can find hints of this sort of "social" development, from different points of view, in the works of Gabriel Marcel and Maurice Merleau-Ponty; there are also hints of it in Max Scheler's remarkable *Wesen und Formen der Sympathie*, and in his sociological works.

[18] *Cartesianische Meditationen*, pp. 166–68; cf. *ibid.*, pp. 108, 113.

some sort of explanation is necessary, if transcendental phenomenology is to be a complete theory of cognition. Husserl has, in fact, remained remarkably faithful to the Kantian intuition, according to which a critique of objectivity must be essentially a critique whose aim is to establish the validity of the cognition in which objectivity is given. He also remained faithful to his own fundamental intuition, according to which cognition is not objective because it is valid, but rather is valid because objective. Now, though such an intuition demanded a new concept of objectivity evolved in the course of the transcendental analysis, it brought Husserl to the conviction that no cognition could with reason be called objective—and hence valid—unless it be a cognition effectively the same for all possible subjects. There is even a certain negative advantage to be gained from the vagueness attaching to the theory of intersubjectivity; from it we see that the most important element in the whole of transcendental phenomenology, the element of objective validity in knowledge, is not to be secured by some cut and dried technique (or techniques) which needs but good will in order to be carried out successfully. In *Ideas I* he had said that the all-embracing problem of phenomenology is intentionality,[19] but his remaining writings show that intentionality is to yield a solution to the problems of philosophy only at the cost of painstaking analysis from every side.

It would certainly be saying a great deal to say that the theory of intersubjectivity has, precisely from the point of view of theory, contributed concrete results notably superior to those already obtained on the level of *pure* transcendental subjectivity.[20] Still, if we remember that the general aim of phenomenology is to establish a method whereby that which was already given in consciousness prior to the application of the method should be adequately constituted—and thus verified, validated, made evident—we can recognize in this last, undeveloped theory a positive contribution in the form of an explanation of subjects as well as of objects, which is of con-

[19] *Ideen I*, p. 357.
[20] Although Husserl does say it; cf. *Nachwort zu meinen Ideen*, pp. 14–15.

siderable importance (as Husserl recognized in *Ideas II*), if positive psychology is to be established on a firm basis. "Other" subjects present no less a problem in any conceivable philosophy than they do in transcendental phenomenology; the only difference being that a philosophy which does not pretend to be "scientific" need not be so embarrassed at not finding a "solution." There is, nevertheless, even some justification in Husserl's contention that there is here an approach to the problematic of *existence*. In explicitating the "sense" of the other, which is already contained implicitly in the very concept of an objectivity which must be equally valid for all possible subjects, the theory of intersubjectivity recognizes that the other must be a "real" subject, if objectivity itself is to have any "sense" at all. Science, after all, can have no recognizable validity if its contents are verifiable only for one subject, even though that subject be convinced that it is the representative of subjectivity as such. If nothing else, it should be possible to show how knowledge could be communicable to others, on the mere supposition that there are others. Further, if the "science" of philosophy is to be the task of a community of scholars imbued with the same ideal and employing the same method, as we read in *Philosophy as a Strict Science*, then this community of scholars must be more than a vague generalization.

It might, of course, be objected that Husserl has maneuvered himself into an untenable position by his insistence that philosophy be nothing less than a strict science, but that is a criticism which applies to the ideal, not to the consistency with which Husserl has tried to realize the ideal. Like every other philosopher, Husserl was a child of his times, and his times would be satisfied with nothing less than scientific verifiability for every proposition which is to be recognized as meaningful.[21] In Husserl, then, we see a heroic effort to re-establish metaphysics according to the canons set up by science. It may well be doubted that he was wholly successful; it is indisputable that his researches have opened up new vistas of pos-

[21] Cf. *Philosophie als strenge Wissenschaft,* pp. 340–41.

sibility, which have been and are being exploited by philosophers whose ultimate orientations are extremely diverse. It is
precisely Husserl's faithfulness to an original ideal, expressed
in the consistent effort to explain all of philosophy in terms of
the phenomenal analysis which has provided the initiative for
a new approach to being, which will strive to avoid mere
verbal analysis and to grasp reality in the way it is present to
consciousness in itself and not through symbols of itself.

Husserl himself would be the last to say that he had evolved
during his career a complete philosophy, or even to say that
his method has been completely formulated. More than once
he expressed dissatisfaction with the formulation of that
method. Of two things, however, he never ceased to be convinced: first of all, that philosophy as he conceived it could
develop only in accord with the scientific ideal he had conceived from the beginning; and secondly, that no development which in any way contradicted the *essential laws* of intentional constitution, of which he would recognize no doubt,
could possibly be admitted as genuinely philosophical. Modifications which spring from a deeper penetration into original intuitions could be admitted—and the theory of intersubjectivity he sees in this light—but changes which would imply
that the original intuitions might not be essential could not
be admitted. Within Husserl's own writings phenomenology
undergoes considerable development, but it is always a recti-
linear development, all of it implied in the first of all phenomenological intuitions, which is that wherein consciousness is
seen as essentially "intentional" in its operation. If one is
compelled to read not only all Husserl's published works but
also all his manuscripts, the constant "return to beginnings"
can prove extremely annoying; it is unquestionably repetitious,
and it leaves precisely the most burning questions unanswered,
but it bears eloquent testimony to his heroic efforts to make of
phenomenology an instrument of precision for the resolution
of perennial philosophical problems. For the actual fruitfulness of this method we cannot look to Husserl's own works;
we must look to those who have, to a greater or less extent,
drawn much of their inspiration from Husserl.

In one sense it is true to say that *The Crisis of European Sciences,* the last of Husserl's works,[22] only one third of which was published during his lifetime,[23] adds nothing doctrinal to what has already been presented in his major published works. In another sense, however, it does add something new, in that it situates historically and describes phenomenologically the "rationalism" for which Husserl had been pleading since 1900. In it the theme of *Philosophy as a Strict Science* is renewed, but it is presented in a more consciously historical —or, at least, "teleological" framework.[24] The forms of rationalism, from Plato to Logical Positivism, have varied considerably, though the ideal, according to Husserl, has remained substantially the same. What he attempts to show in this "last will and testament" is that forms of rationalism have succeeded—and superseded—each other down through the ages, and that particular forms have proved, in the light of those which succeed them, to be inadequate.[25] Phenomenology, then, is a historic form of rationalism. It supersedes all others, precisely because it has been able to rationalize our *experience* of the world. Thus, the whole of history can be interpreted as a teleological process aiming at the ultimate rationality of

[22] For an excellent summary and critique of the *Krisis,* cf. Aron Gurwitsch, "The Last Work of Edmund Husserl," *Philosophy and Phenomenological Research,* XVI, 3 (March, 1956), XVII, 3 (March, 1957).

[23] The first Part was published in *Philosophia,* I (Prague, 1936).

[24] This is a teleology proper to consciousness and conscious-being. An analysis of the act of consciousness shows that all its elements are oriented toward a goal, which is knowledge (cf. Ms. F I 17, pp. 154–55). The fundamental principle in the teleology of consciousness is intentionality, which is a tendency to give oneself an *object,* in the full sense of the term (cf. *Formale und transzendentale Logik,* p. 232). During the period which saw the writing of *Krisis,* Husserl sees a "historical" teleology in philosophy itself: "The entire development of philosophy as a preparatory stage for science" (*Brief an den VIII. internationalen Kongress der Philosophie in Prag,* Sept., 1934, p. 13). It is the only way one can speak of a "sense" of history in Husserl's thought.

[25] Cf. Gurwitsch, *art. cit.,* II (1957), p. 397. It is characteristic of Husserl that he is better at criticising the defects of historical positions than he is at evaluating their positive contributions.

transcendental phenomenology.[26] No new elements of that
rationality are here introduced, but it is situated as a sort of
final stage in the process of safeguarding the primacy of
rationality in man's historical destiny.[27] To transform the
ideal of rationality in the light of modern scientific advances
has proved a necessity, but the greatest tragedy for Western
culture would be to interpret the transformation of the ideal
as an abandonment of the ideal. As Gurwitsch says so well
in summary: "Surrender to the anti-rationalistic and anti-
intellectualistic tendencies, a surrender urged upon us from
many quarters, is nothing short of self-betrayal of Western
man and betrayal of the teleological destiny and idea of man
at large. This destiny is none other than the autonomy of
reason which actualizes itself in a historical process; viz.,
through the historical transformations of the idea of rationalism."[28]

Thus, the *Krisis* does not serve as a modification of Husserl's fundamental position. Rather, it confirms that fundamental position and, by situating it "historically" in the process toward ultimate rationality, marks the transition to those
developments in phenomenology which another world of experience renders possible. In this last sense Husserl has in
the *Krisis* given the "green light" to developments which, in
his earlier days, he might well have considered infidelities to
the ideal of transcendental phenomenology.

[26] In "Die Ursprung der Geometrie," p. 220, Husserl gives a
definition of history which leaves it in the sphere of immanence,
in the sphere of "essences" and not in that of "existence." He
says: "History, as we understand it, is no other than the vital
movement of a formation and a sedimentation of sense, the one
with and *in* the other." This, of course, supposes the intersubjective
ego as a sort of concrete universal spirit, a notion which is not too
comprehensible in the framework of a theory of *transcendental*
intersubjectivity.

[27] Husserl does not feel that philosophy has reached its goal with
him, but rather that he has contributed the point of view which
will enable it to reach that goal: much remains to be done, but it
can be done only in a framework of transcendental phenomenology,
which framework has already been outlined.

[28] Gurwitsch, *art. cit.*, II, p. 396.

VIII. TRANSCENDENTAL IDEALISM

Husserl's Transcendental Idealism*

JOSEPH J. KOCKELMANS

Those who have read the foregoing selections dealing with
Husserl's phenomenological philosophy will have received the
impression many times that Husserl's phenomenology, taken
from a metaphysical point of view, represents a certain form
of idealism. In approaching the conclusion of these investigations, therefore, it is appropriate to focus attention upon
this important theme and explicitly to ask the question: To
what extent may Husserl's phenomenology be called idealistic? And further, What in the final analysis is the meaning of
this kind of idealism? As a prelude to the answer of these
closely connected questions it seems in order to describe
briefly how Husserl himself understood his own phenomenology at the end of his long career.

Genuine Phenomenological Philosophy
as Transcendental Idealism

In his *Cartesian Meditations,* in the first sections of the
Fourth Meditation, Husserl tried to show that all the problems of phenomenology can be reduced to the universal problem concerning the static and genetic constitution of the objects of possible consciousness.[1] In Section 40 he concluded
that phenomenology is to be characterized as a *transcendental*
theory of knowledge. In order to explain his view further
he compared it with the traditional epistemological theories.
In doing so he briefly indicated that the fundamental problem
of traditional epistemology had always been the question of

* This selection is an English summary of my article *"Realisme—
Idealisme en Husserl's phaenomenologie," Tijdschrift voor Philosophie* 20 (1958), 395–442.
[1] Edmund Husserl, *Cart. Med.,* pp. 99–114 (65–81).

how knowledge, which comes about wholly within the immanence of consciousness, can acquire objective significance for a world outside consciousness.[2]

Husserl goes on to state, in Section 41, that the whole traditional epistemological difficulty is a quasi-problem. Descartes' discussion of it involves an inconsistency because he did not understand the genuine meaning of the phenomenological reduction to the pure ego. And in post-Cartesian philosophy the situation became even worse when philosophers tried to formulate and answer the question before performing any reduction whatsoever. In Husserl's view it is evident that he who remains within the realm of the natural attitude cannot ask any "transcendental" questions; as natural man, he cannot seriously ask himself the question of how he can get outside his "island of consciousness" and how what manifests itself in his consciousness can acquire objective significance. For when I apperceive myself as a natural man, I have already apperceived the spatio-temporal world and conceived of myself as in space where I already have a world-outside-me. Transcendental questions can be asked only within the phenomenological attitude, which is to be opened up by the phenomenological reduction.[3]

As soon as I undertake to perform such a reduction and attempt, as a pure ego involved in systematic self-investigation, to uncover my own field of consciousness, then it becomes clear to me that all that is, for this pure ego, is constituted as that which it is in myself, and that every kind of Being has its own particular form of constitution. When I try to understand the real meaning of this insight, I must come to the conclusion that transcendence, in whatever form it may manifest itself to me, is an immanent characteristic constituted within the sphere of the pure ego itself. Stated in another way, every possible sense and every imaginable being, whether it manifests itself as immanent or transcendent, falls within the domain of my transcendental subjectivity which ultimately constitutes all sense and Being. Once I under-

[2] *Ibid.*, pp. 114–16 (81–83).
[3] *Ibid.*, p. 116 (83).

stand this, I see also that every attempt to conceive the universe of true Being as something lying outside the universe of *possible* consciousness is nonsensical because true Being and consciousness belong together essentially and inseparably, being concretely one in the only absolute concretion of transcendental subjectivity. But if it is true that transcendental subjectivity *is* the universe of all possible sense and Being, then an "outside of consciousness" is certainly nonsense. As Berkeley has shown, this is true not only for my *de facto* ego and what manifests itself in fact and thanks to my own constitution as existing for me, but also for this ego as an example of the *eidos* "ego," that is to say, for the transcendental ego.

Thus it becomes evident that a genuine epistemology cannot operate any longer with inconsistent inferences leading from a supposed immanence to a supposed transcendence, which as "Being in itself" is obviously essentially unknowable and, therefore, completely meaningless. Epistemology appears to be meaningful only as a transcendental phenomenology which tries to clarify in a systematic way our cognitive achievements as essentially intentional achievements, constituting their intended objects, and which thus tries to show that every kind of Being, real or ideal, becomes understandable only as a product of transcendental subjectivity.[4]

From this point of view transcendental phenomenology is clearly and *eo ipso* transcendental idealism, but in a fundamentally new sense. For it is not a "psychological idealism" which tries to derive a meaningful world from meaningless sense-data, nor is it a Kantian idealism that still maintains, although as a limited idea only, the reality of the world of "beings in themselves." On the contrary, we have here a kind of idealism which is nothing more than a consequently performed self-explication in the form of a systematic, egological science as it has just been specified.[5]

[4] *Ibid.*, pp. 116–18 (83–85).
[5] *Ibid.*, pp. 118–21 (86–88).

Different Interpretations of the Meaning of Husserl's Transcendental Idealism

Although Section 41 of Husserl's *Cartesian Meditations* seems to be clear, and although many arguments can be presented for the thesis that exactly the same view is found in his publications since 1906, yet for over thirty years scholars have been unable to agree in their interpretations of it. Some interpreters hold that Husserl's phenomenology is "realistic" in its very essence;[6] others see his work as a whole as one or other form of "idealism," the exact nature of which they cannot, however, determine or agree upon.[7] And in recent years an "existentialistic" interpretation of Husserl's phenomenology has been presented; here it is argued that Husserl transcends the classical opposition between realism and idealism.[8]

The noteworthy aspect of this situation is that none of the solutions so far advocated has been satisfactory, and the discussion goes on. Moreover, every solution refers to an extensive series of clear texts which in themselves seem to be convincing; but when quotations presented by the opposing views are taken into account, the persuasiveness of the texts evaporates. There can be no doubt that Husserl recognized the problem and that he thought he had given a clear and convincing answer to it. But notwithstanding this, the situation remains, and in order to cope with it several authors have searched for additional considerations. Still, despite the core of truth which their efforts certainly contain, the fundamental ambiguity in Husserl's texts persists.

[6] For the most important historians who have defended this view, see H. Boelaars, *"De intentionaliteit der kennis bij Edmund Husserl,"* in *Bijdragen,* 3 (1940), 111–61, 221–64, pp. 112–21.

[7] For this point of view see the publications of Gaston Berger, Ludwig Landgrebe, Alphonse De Waelhens, Paul Ricoeur, Pierre Thévenaz, Max Müller, Stephan Strasser, Eugen Fink, Walter Biemel, Jean Wahl, Aron Gurwitsch, Roman Ingarden, and Quentin Lauer.

[8] This view is defended by Maurice Merleau-Ponty, Alphonse De Waelhens (in some of his more recent publications), Gerd Brand, and others.

Before proposing an attempt at a solution to this difficult problem, I want to deal briefly with the ambiguity that without a doubt is present in Husserl's works, and explain briefly why I think that supplementary considerations proposed by several authors, though valuable, are nonetheless finally inadequate.

Ambiguity in Husserl's Texts

Everyone[9] who advocates an idealistic interpretation of Husserl's phenomenology has to concede that the arguments for a realistic interpretation are not offered without reason. Therefore almost every "idealist" admits that in Husserl's work, series of texts are found which can be interpreted either in an empiristic-realistic way, or in an existentialistic manner, and which in any case seem to resist an "idealistic" interpretation. Some years ago Jean Wahl composed a whole anthology of such quotations,[10] a few points of which we wish to underline here.

Husserl often argues explicitly that phenomenology in the first place deals with "things themselves," with Being as such. In our contact with things experience occupies an important place. Although Husserl often posits that all reality consists in a meaning for consciousness only, he argues also that every meaning is founded on an act of seeing; thus, according to him, intuition seems to be the original approach to Being. Elsewhere Husserl proposes meaning as a form which has to "inform" a non-intentional matter. Sometimes it seems that meaning transcends itself and intends an object which must give the final mark of reality to that meaning and which, thus, has to give "reason" to consciousness. In Husserl's doc-

[9] The following is a very brief survey of my article *"Realisme— Idealisme en Husserls phaenomenologie," Tijdschrift voor Philosophie* 20 (1958), 395–442. For a more complete version of this article see my book: *A First Introduction to Husserl's Phenomenology* (Pittsburgh, Pa.: Duquesne University Press, 1967), Chapter XI.

[10] Jean Wahl, *"Note sur quelques aspects empiristes de la pensée de Husserl,"* in *Phénoménologie—Existence* (Paris: Arthaud, 1947), pp. 107–35.

trine of evidence, which plays an important role in his phenomenology, evidence itself is defined finally in terms of a
"bodily presence" of the intended objects. Also, his idea of
fulfillment, which is closely connected with his conception of
evidence, is probably to be interpreted in a realistic way. In
many places Husserl calls intentionality the center of phenomenology; that, however, is often to be understood as
Being-in-the-world, while the subject then seems to appear as
an openness to the world. The relation between *noesis* and
noema seems to require an existentialistic context, too. Elsewhere Husserl writes that it is important to notice explicitly
that the world really exists, and that the task of phenomenology consists precisely in determining the final meaning of that
undeniable reality.[11]

On the other side of the picture, every "realist" and "existentialist" has to concede that there are many texts in Husserl's works that resist a non-idealistic interpretation. It seems
to be true that for Husserl sense or meaning is more important than Being. For him Being is Being-object. In his view
only sense and meaning exist; every being is only a sense for,
in, and through consciousness. In this way phenomenology
seems to be a study of pure consciousness, since there is
nothing "outside" consciousness. Husserl often argues that a
complete reflection is possible. Although in several places an
original giving experience seems to be assigned primordial
importance, elsewhere it is said to be the affirmation of a
being which is based on consciousness itself. In many instances
it is impossible that intentionality be conceived as an ontological relationship; it turns out to be the experience of meaning rather than an original Being-in-the-world: consciousness
then is no longer proposed as an openness to the world. Otherwise, Husserl never speaks of *Dasein,* of encounter, openness, etc., but always of consciousness and subjectivity.
Furthermore, it seems that in Husserl's phenomenology immanence prevails over transcendence; encounter is not the
primary datum, but consciousness itself. Transcendence is even

11 *Ibid.* See also: P. Ricoeur, *"Etudes sur les Méditations Cartésiennes," Revue Philosophique de Louvain,* 52 (1954), 75–109,
pp. 95–96.

defined in terms of immanence, and existence in terms of reason. Only transcendental consciousness is absolute; the world depends upon an actual consciousness, both in regard to its Being and to its meaning. Husserl's ideas about reduction and constitution often are understandable only in an idealistic interpretation. Phenomenological reduction is represented frequently as "bracketing of Being," a view that seems to be based on idealistic prejudices. However, his considerations about the transcendental reduction in particular seem to be incompatible with an existentialistic interpretation of intentionality. Many "idealist" authors find it of great importance that Heidegger and Merleau-Ponty considered Husserl's doctrine to be an inadmissible form of idealism; an essential difference exists between the phenomenology of Husserl and that of the "existentialists."[12]

Supplementary Considerations— Valuable but Inadequate

Obviously the ambiguity that exists in Husserl's work gives no satisfaction. In order to escape it, several authors have searched for supplementary considerations. Some have tried to solve the problems by admitting an evolution in Husserl's phenomenology in this respect. For instance, Boelaars and several older commentators on Husserl's work argue that Husserl proceeded from a point of view that antecedes the alternative realism-idealism through a critical period to his later transcendental idealism.[13] Yet, if we do not consider the unpublished manuscripts, we may posit that such a solution to our problem is very improbable, for the problem persists in all that Husserl wrote between 1907 and 1938. Since 1940, therefore, this interpretation has been generally rejected. We must agree with Landgrebe, Fink, Berger, and Ricoeur and admit that such a process of growth in Husserl's thinking between 1907 and 1938 is inadmissible; the solution to our

[12] L. Landgrebe, *Phänomenologie und Metaphysik* (Hamburg: Schröder, 1949), pp. 83–100; P. Ricoeur, *l.c.*, pp. 77–78, 92–94, 96–100, 107–9.

[13] H. Boelaars, *l.c.*, pp. 112–21, 158–61, 238–40, 254–59.

problem is to be found elsewhere.[14] There is, however, no
further agreement among these authors.

It is Berger's opinion that the solution lies in the fact that
the series of incompatible texts are incompatible only when
they are considered from the natural attitude. If we really
want to understand Husserl's view, we must try to attain the
transcendental sphere. The ambiguity in Husserl's texts is explained by the fact that even in the transcendental sphere we
must use a language which is proper to our natural attitude.
However, this ambiguity, and with it all the problems, will
disappear immediately if we are sufficiently conscious of the
fundamental analogy of the words to be used in phenomenology; phenomenology will then prove to be a philosophy of
creative intuition. Although there seems to be a certain truth
in Berger's consideration, it is not completely satisfactory
since, as Berger explicitly concedes, he cannot give a convincing explication of Husserl's conception of the relation between constitution and intuition.[15]

Landgrebe and Ricoeur attempt to find a solution by distinguishing between analyses and the most profound intention
with which these analyses are written. Husserl is an idealist
in regard to his intention, but an "existentialist" with respect
to his analyses, thereby refuting his basic intention.[16]

Other authors maintain that Husserl will analyze only in
opposition to all "free-floating constructions and accidental
findings."[17] He will evade all metaphysical prejudices in order to describe the things which manifest themselves to us
and only insofar as they manifest themselves. Now it is evi-

[14] G. Berger, *Le cogito dans la philosophie de Husserl* (Paris:
Aubier, 1941), pp. 12–15; E. Fink, *"Die phänomenologische Philosophie Edmund Husserls in der gegenwärtigen Kritik,"* Kantstudien, 38 (1933), 319–83; *"Das Problem der Phänomenologie
Edmund Husserls,"* Revue Internationale de Philosophie, 1 (1938–
39), 226–70.

[15] G. Berger, *op. cit.,* pp. 100–17; P. Ricoeur, *l.c.,* pp. 96–100.

[16] L. Landgrebe, *Philosophie der Gegenwart* (Bonn: Athenäum
Verlag, 1952), pp. 31–40. *"Seinsregionen und regionale Ontologien
in Husserls Phänomenologie,"* Studium Generale, 9 (1956), 315–
24, p. 316.

[17] M. Heidegger, *Sein und Zeit*, p. 27 (52).

dent that the problem of the opposition between realism and idealism is a theoretical problem that cannot be solved by means of analyses alone. On the other hand, it is also evident that the point of view that Husserl assumes in this way cannot be maintained in a consequent manner since, as Fink pithily expresses it, it is impossible to say anything whatsoever about the phenomenality of phenomena by means of analyses alone; still, it is absolutely necessary that one have some point of view in regard to this question, since otherwise the series of analyses is not founded. Thus, although Husserl explicitly rejects a metaphysical *a priori*, nonetheless, he implicitly accepts a metaphysical standpoint. It is not surprising then that this *a priori* view is not always the same, simply because it is always implicitly present only. Whatever the case may be, Husserl conceives this *a priori* viewpoint sometimes in a realistic way, at other times in an idealistic way, insofar as the nature and the object of the analyses require it.[18]

In addition Fink points out that in the work of every philosopher a distinction is to be made between thematical and operational concepts. What is striking in Husserl's philosophy is that the most fundamental concepts and conceptions are operational concepts only, with which he works without explicitly defining them. It follows immediately then that we shall not find an answer for our problem in his philosophy, although he himself undoubtedly (probably implicitly) had one solution or another.[19]

It is De Waelhens' opinion that after 1906 Husserl was thinking against an existentialistic background. De Waelhens thinks that the opposition between realism and idealism was radically transcended in Husserl's philosophy. However, it seems to be understandable and admissible that in such a view it is always possible, and even necessary, to use a realistic terminology as well as an idealistic.[20]

[18] E. Fink, *"L'analyse intentionelle,"* in *Problèmes Actuels de la Phénoménologie* (Paris: Desclée de Brouwer, 1952), pp. 68–70.
[19] E. Fink, *"Operative Begriffe in Husserls Phänomenologie,"* in *Husserl* (Paris: Minuit, 1959), pp. 321–37.
[20] A. De Waelhens, *"L'idée phénoménologique de l'intentionnalité,"* in *Husserl et la pensée moderne* (The Hague: Martinus Nijhoff, 1959), pp. 116–27.

Finally, other authors maintain that the ambiguity we are discussing is fundamental and even essential to Husserl's philosophy; though Husserl was certainly aware of it and aware of the necessity of resolving it, he was nevertheless unable to choose between transcendental idealism and an existential solution.[21]

Different Attitudes. Husserl's Idealism

Despite the element of truth that all these considerations contain, none of them seems to be satisfactory because the ambiguity is maintained as fundamental *in Husserl's texts*. It is certain that in Husserl's works written between 1906 and 1938 texts can be found which demand an idealistic interpretation, and that others require a realistic or existential interpretation. On the other hand, however, the authors cited who without exception admit the ambiguity in Husserl's texts, nonetheless share the opinion that his work is to be interpreted in either an idealistic or existentialistic way. It is not clear to me how the generally admitted ambiguity in the texts can be squared with a judgment, held with certainty, as to the final characterization of Husserl's view. And it is unacceptable to me also that a great philosopher, as Husserl certainly was, did not find a clear solution to one of the most important problems of modern philosophy.

Therefore I propose that philosophers pay special attention to the fact that Husserl does not always think and write with the same mental attitude. We should distinguish three attitudes and correlatively with them, three spheres: "the natural attitude," in which Husserl advocates an empirical realism inasmuch as he makes a pre-given objective world prevail over consciousness, which in the last resort is passive in respect to the world;[22] the "phenomenological sphere," for which Husserl endorses a point of view that could be called "existential," to the extent that in the phenomenological sphere

[21] P. Ricoeur, *l.c.*, pp. 108–9.
[22] Edmund Husserl, *Ideen*, Vol. I, pp. 57–63.

consciousness and world are perfectly correlative;[23] and the "transcendental sphere," for which Husserl favors a transcendental idealism because consciousness as a transcendental subjectivity appears there as the only absolute reality, while the world proves to be no more than a product-of-achievement for, in, and through this consciousness.[24] Because in Husserl's eyes this last sphere is the most fundamental one, his phenomenology ought to be characterized as transcendental idealism.

The advantages of this interpretation are that the "other" series of texts no longer appear as heterodox, and that no further essential development in Husserl's work need be assumed. The ambiguity continues to inhere in accidental points of Husserl's work, but now it may be accounted for by the fact that he avoids theory as much as he can, and in addition sometimes slides imperceptibly from one sphere to another.

Thus interpreted, Husserl's phenomenology as a whole is not acceptable. His analyses of the second sphere, however, are of lasting importance if his idea of intentionality is interpreted in an ontological way and if the phenomenological reduction is understood merely as a reduction of the world of culture to the original *Lebenswelt*.

[23] Edmund Husserl, *Ideen*, Vol. II, pp. 1–297. See also P. Ricoeur, "*Analyses et problèmes dans 'Ideen II' de Husserl,*" in *Phénoménologie–Existence*, pp. 23–76.

[24] See for instance: Edmund Husserl, *Ideen*, Vol. I, secs. 32, 44, 46, 47, 49, 55, 81; *Ideen*, Vol. II, pp. 297–302; *Ideen*, Vol. III, pp. 149–55.

IX. LIFE-WORLD AND WORLD-EXPERIENCING LIFE

Introduction

Preliminary study of Husserl's manuscripts, and the posthumous publication of the previously unpublished part of his last work, *Krisis,* as well as of other unpublished writings, have revealed many fertile ideas. Among these, in the opinion of many interested scholars, the idea of the life-world (*Lebenswelt*) is the most important. During Husserl's lifetime only a few of his friends and followers were acquainted with his investigations of the life-world, and actually Husserl did not carefully formulate these ideas until he was preparing the final draft of the second part of *Krisis,* the book he was working on at the time of his death. Nevertheless, that the concept of the life-world must have preoccupied him for at least the last fifteen years of his life becomes apparent, for example, in his posthumously published *Phänomenologische Psychologie,* which, written between 1925 and 1928, contains penetrating analyses of the "world of our immediate experience" as we "live" it before every theoretical, and in particular, every scientific reflection. Husserl's ideas along these lines were first made known by Ludwig Landgrebe in an article published in 1940. Then in 1945 Merleau-Ponty used these ideas, with which he had become acquainted while studying Husserl's manuscripts in Louvain, as one of the central issues of *Phénoménologie de la perception.* Following the publication in 1950 of the relevant Husserlian manuscripts on this subject, the life-world concept became and remains the subject of many publications and discussions.

In the *Phenomenology of Perception* Merleau-Ponty gives the impression that Husserl's original studies of the transcendental subjectivity were later replaced by his ideas of the life-world. However, most of the scholars who are well acquainted with Husserl's philosophy feel that there is no truth to this contention. In their opinion his investigation of the life-world is but one of the four different approaches Husserl uses to reveal the constitutive activity of transcendental subjectivity. There is no doubt, in their view, that the life-world is not the deepest layer to which phenomenology can penetrate. They hold that on the contrary Husserl always maintained that the life-world itself is also constituted, and that a careful explanation of its original constitution should reveal the most radical anonymous achievements of the transcendental ego. It is my personal conviction that this view is essentially correct, and that it is convincingly substantiated in Sections 39–55 and 71–72 of Husserl's *Krisis* as well as in other texts written about the same time.

However, there are several well-known authorities on Husserl's philosophy who believe that Merleau-Ponty's interpretation of Husserl's life-world concept, if not identical to Husserl's own final view on the subject, is at least very close to it. A. De Waelhens in Belgium and G. Brand in Germany have been the most important proponents of this position. Although, as I have indicated, the interpretation is not very plausible historically, it nevertheless remains possible that Husserl's ideas were developing in the direction of the insights defended by Heidegger in *Sein und Zeit*. Whatever the case may be, it is of some importance to include here a discussion of this interpretation of Husserl's last ideas, not only because it sheds a completely different light upon some of the basic concepts of his phenomenology as a whole, but also because it can serve as an introduction to ideas developed later by the so-called existential phenomenologists. Before going on to it, a few orienting remarks may be helpful.

Husserl claims in his last book that a study of the history of our culture since the time of Galileo reveals a gradual replacing of the world of our common, immediate, lived experience (*Lebenswelt*) by an objectively true and valid world of the sciences. It is this world that in the opinion of most scientists passes for reality in the strict sense of the term. In Husserl's view, it is not difficult to show that such a view is completely untenable. First of all, it is obviously impossible to consider any objective entity of the sciences without recourse to our immediate experience of the objects and relationships out of which the entity in question arose. The life-world, on the other hand, manifests itself actually or virtually in any perceptual experience whatsoever and reappears in all acts that are derived from that experience. It also becomes clear that the scientific universe is but a network of inter-locking ideal constructs. These constructs are but the theoretico-logical "substruction" of the immediately given things and relationships. Our conception and understanding of the network are of the same nature as the ideas of the mathematical sciences. The construction of the universe of the sciences includes certain typical procedures in which idealization and abstraction occupy a central position, and abstraction and idealization clearly point to something that is prior to these activities. It is in this sense that the sciences rest on a foundation; and this foundation can be nothing other than the life-world, the world of the immediate evidence of our lived experience. When we speak here of "evidence" we refer to the immediate "bodily presence" of the thing, to the immediate self-presentation of the object in question. The whole of theoretical truth, including the logical and mathematical truth of the positive sciences, finds its ultimate justification and validity in the type of evidence that concerns events and occurrences of the life-world. Husserl withdraws the privileged position from the evidences ruling objective scientific theory and accords it to the evidences governing in the life-world. This means that the theoretical scientific world must find its foundation in the life-world rather than the life-world finding its ultimate justification in scientific theory.

Underlying the mental activities that construct the objective world of the sciences are the acts through which the life-world appears to us as always present, as pre-given, and as prior to and independent of any scientific theory. Husserl calls the totality of all these acts immediately referring to the life-world "our world-experiencing life." In further developing this idea he comes to the conclusion that on that original level consciousness as world-experiencing life manifests itself as anonymously functioning intentionality. It is precisely the implications of this idea which constitute the subject-matter of Gerd Brand's essay.

Intentionality, Reduction, and Intentional Analysis in Husserl's Later Manuscripts*

GERD BRAND

Functioning Intentionality

[. . .] Husserl calls intentionality that essential characteristic of consciousness owing to which it is always "consciousness-of." At first sight this seems to mean only that consciousness is never without an object "of" which it is conscious; that there never is an empty consciousness, thinking without thought, judging without something to be judged, a feeling without something felt; in other words that intentionality is the formal expression of the subject's essential property of always having an object confronting itself. [In this view] consciousness as intentionality would be essentially consciousness of objects.

Upon closer investigation, however, one must notice that this consciousness, which seems to be such a simple consciousness of an object, is at the same time consciousness of modes of consciousness that are implied in the meaning of its object. It is true that these modes transcend the effectively perceived object, but it is also true that they are, as its implicit unity of meaning, precisely what make the perception of this object possible. Intentionality, therefore, is not a static consciousness-of, but a dynamic process through which consciousness continuously transcends itself. Intentionality is not just *being*, but,

* From Gerd Brand, *Welt, Ich, und Zeit*, Martinus Nijhoff (The Hague: 1955), pp. 22–41. Reprinted by permission of the publishers. Translated into English expressly for this volume by Joseph J. Kockelmans.

rather, *functioning*. That is why Husserl calls it "functioning intentionality."[1]

In each experience, intentionality functions simultaneously as implicit pro-ject (*Vor-wurf*) and as retro-spect (*Rück-schau*). "At the starting point," Husserl says, "the first ray originates and darts out as having the character of a beginning, and possesses a pre-horizon (*Vorhorizont*) which refers to things to be achieved later . . ."[2] But as pro-ject intentionality is nonetheless already completely saturated with legacies from earlier perceptions, which are, as it were, "sedimented" in the actual perception. Consciousness is not a *tabula rasa* on which time and again new signs manifest themselves; on the contrary, while consciousness forges ahead continually transcending the horizons, it already has consciousness behind it as well. The object is grasped in the pro-ject of its possible explanations together with the history sedimented in it.

We cannot, therefore, speak simply of "consciousness-of" as consciousness of compact unities, the meaning of which emerges only at the moment one speaks of intentionality; such a view is the result of a simplifying achievement. While the object is grasped in its "whence" and "whither," consciousness-of-it turns out to be the merging of many multiplicities of consciousness whose explication, in the last analysis, leads to the life of consciousness in its totality.

As the living potentiality of the implications of consciousness' intentionality is usually concealed, because the totality which is obtrusive and is grasped first, does not, so to speak, give its explaining elements (*Explikate*) a chance to get a word in.

In the explication of an object alternately new moments which, at first, obtrude themselves, have their say and are given a hearing. In the first, straightforward grasp of the whole these moments are already present in it;

[1] *Cf.* Eugen Fink, *"Das Problem der Phänomenologie Husserls,"* *Revue internationale de Philosophie,* 1 (1939), 226–70, p. 226.
[2] Edmund Husserl, Ms. C 3 III, p. 19.

but at first the whole forced itself upon us, preponderating over them and, perhaps even, necessarily dominating them.[3]

Initially the concrete real thing is merely straightforwardly self-given, grasped through *one* ray of consciousness; grasped already as what it is, but in such a way that its quiddities are still wrapped up, not yet unfolded. "This 'implicit' mode of being given is a mode which is universally found even in every experience whatever."[4]

We have already become acquainted with this mode of being given—which, although implicit, nonetheless gives meaning as such—in the inner horizon which is characteristic of every experience. Having specified this, we must note that in our first grasp [of a thing] the horizon is already co-perceived, but as "anonymous" only, as Husserl expresses it.[5] Its anonymity means that as horizon it does not let itself be known immediately, and that in its functioning as meaning-implication of the straightforwardly grasped object it is, at first, even unknowable. The horizon lets itself be known only when, by explaining the being, we enter the horizon and in this way deliver it from its anonymity.

For Husserl, intentionality is functioning but is at the same time anonymous, and anonymous on two different levels. When in the natural attitude we are dealing with objects, then the functioning intentionality is completely anonymous—that is to say, it is functioning but unknown. When we uncover it, we deliver it from the state in which its functioning was unknown. When this uncovering becomes a genuine explanation, intentionality is continuously further delivered from the anonymity characteristic of it as functioning, but it nonetheless remains anonymous. Functioning intentionality always transcends itself, and transcends that part of itself which is already explained and therefore already delivered from anonymity, in the direction of the world in whose anonymity (as familiar foreign domain) it maintains itself.

[3] Ms. C 10, p. 14.
[4] Ms. A VII 9, p. 42.
[5] *Cf.* Ms. C 11 V, pp. 11–15.

The fact that every experience has its inner horizon, a fact which functions in the perception of the given, *is* intentionality itself, which functions in this perception. The moment we recognize that the anonymous ego-like "doing"—that pro-ject and retro-spect in the perception of the particular—leads us through its multiple gradual implications toward the totality of our consciousness as world-experiencing life, we recognize also that functioning intentionality is nothing but world-experiencing, which in every simple experience functions anonymously while giving it meaning and Being. World-experiencing life is anonymously functioning intentionality.

Reduction

[. . . The foregoing explanation necessarily presupposed that the phenomenological reduction was already performed.] For phenomenological reduction is nothing but the discovery of the functioning intentionality through which we have come to a primordial intuition of Being (*Seinssehen*)—primordial because it is the "ground" which no longer refers to anything else and upon which the concrete being, with which we deal in our straightforward life of the natural attitude, is already founded, insofar as it has any meaning at all. Reduction means discovering the functioning intentionality in the complete transparency of the discovering. We must now perform this movement once more in order to become explicitly conscious of its structure.

Let us take as our starting point our natural life, oriented toward the world, in which we experience mundane things, are occupied with this or that thing, and in which we eventually also assume a reflexive attitude; and let us notice that in that natural life we always experience beings exclusively, never ourselves as the ego that functions in its possessing of the world (*Welthabe*). The functioning of the functioning intentionality is such that provisionally and usually it is concealed (*verdeckt*).

"In the functioning itself, a concrete thing as being in the world is always the theme of my activities (thanks to the continuous consciousness of world which always belongs to the functioning as such); however, the whole of this achieving and ultimately functioning doing (which I continually carry out in the performance of my consciousness of world and my 'living-the-world') is precisely anonymous and continuously un-thematic; and all this happens without any performance of a special activity which has reference to it, and which makes it into a doing which is for me, and which is specifically so immediately and perceptually."[6]

Indeed, what we experience is not opinions, meanings, references, insights; on the contrary, what we experience is being, something objective; and among these objectivities that we experience, we do not come across our functioning intentionality. "I experience things, I do not experience 'meaning of Being' (*Seinssinn*), things as meaning."[7] We experience what manifests itself but not its own appearing.

However, we must now note further, that although it is true that in experiencing things "only," we do not experience them *as* meaning, we nevertheless experience them yet in *their* meaning. Whenever we experience an object, we experience it as *what* it is; and this object is *what* it is in the "whence" and "whither" of the functioning intentionality. In all this, however, the functioning intentionality itself remains anonymous, it does not let itself be known as that which it actually is, as giving meaning and ground.

Whenever a being is grasped, intentionality is functioning, since the being has meaning. How does this intentionality become uncovered in its functioning and delivered from its anonymity? That a being has meaning signifies that we understand it. This understanding can be made the subject matter of our investigation by thematizing the being itself. This is why Husserl says: "Being as such has its most original exis-

---

[6] Ms. K III 6, p. 37; see also: *Ibid.*, p. 52 ff.; Edmund Husserl, "*Phänomenologie und Anthropologie,*" *Philosophy and Phenomenological Research*, 2 (1941–42), 1–14, p. 12.

[7] Ms. K III 6, p. 54.

tential meaning as 'theme.' "⁸ And in so doing we are no longer simply occupied with being only, but we make that being into our theme. For Husserl "theme" means planning to explicate something. Because being has meaning and thus is already a possible theme, being itself, even taken in the way in which it is given in the simplest experience, always implies the demand of realizing this possibility, of delivering its meaning-horizon from anonymity. The simple fact of making a being into a theme—the unfolding of its horizon—is not yet identical with the discovery of our functioning intentionality. Our functioning intentionality reveals itself only when the process of making a being into a theme strives for definitiveness, when we penetrate deeper and deeper into it, are led from horizon to horizon, and go forward in a radical way until we reach the roots and discover the being in its complete reference and in the totality of its references. That is why Husserl posits that functioning intentionality manifests itself to a radical and universal questioning of the horizons; ". . . only when I question the horizons in a *universal* and systematic way, too, do I come across the discovery of a consciousness-of-world as ultimately founding, and shall I discover that I always have already presupposed it. . . ."⁹

That a being has meaning means that it *is* as datum, as "intention," of the anonymously functioning intentionality, and in no sense that a meaningless being is "besouled" by the functioning intentionality. There is no meaningless being just as there is no objectless meaning. That a being has meaning means that it is objective, given, intuitable, but also that as such it *is* only on the basis of our functioning intentionality which gives it its ground. This intentionality itself, however, is no longer something objective, but the continuously functioning, continuously self-transcending understanding in which the ego always *is* as world-experiencing life, in the actual movement of itself as self-alienation.

Thus, we do not have on one side simple being-at-hand and on the other an ego that bestows meaning upon it, on one

⁸ Ms. A V 5, p. 147.
⁹ Ms. K III 6, p. 56.

side the *"hylē"* and on the other its conceiving view. On the contrary, what *is* is being in its meaning; what is object, is object in the tension of its property of having horizons only on the basis of the functioning intentionality as possessing the world and as always transcending the object.[10]

"Meaning" is not something that takes place in "consciousness" the moment I know an object. A being is not exclusively object; it itself has meaning. Concerning meaning one does not ask: What subjective conditions belong to it when a being of such and such a kind is given to us? Rather one must ask: In what horizon (that is, in what possibilities that the explanation is going to open up) is the given itself a given of such and such a kind?

We cannot separate the object from its horizon, the ego from the world, the subject from the object; nor can we ask ourselves how it is possible that they are so closely connected, because in that case, too, we relinquish the principle of all principles, that is, the principle of the original intuition, and posit an object on one side and a subject on the other. For Husserl all speaking about subject and object, ego and world, can draw its meaning only from, and must be measured by, the originality of the functioning intentionality, which was brought to the fore here.

As we have seen, in the "natural" attitude the functioning intentionality is concealed (*verdeckt*). True, it is a conscious datum and makes things conscious, but it is, for that reason alone, not yet perceived and understood. In that attitude it cannot even be brought to light since, strictly speaking, in that attitude we never really ask in a radical way about the meaning of a being, or the truth of a being. The questioning characteristic of the natural attitude moves within the realm

---

[10] It may be interesting to note here not only that Husserl has changed his earlier view concerning this question, but also that he was aware of this change, something that very seldom occurs in his writings, because most of the time he focused attention exclusively upon the work at hand. "Is it not true that my original view of the immanent sphere with its immanent data, which finally 'turn into conceptions' solely through the passive achievements of association, is a residue of the old psychology and its sensualistic empiricism?" (Ms. B I II, 8).

of certain Being-structures which in that attitude are considered to be self-evident—that is to say, not questionable—and it
tries merely to understand their interrelationships, by time
and again inserting [into the already known] what becomes
problematic, and thus explaining it.

The philosophical attitude, on the contrary, is characterized for Husserl by the search for *complete* justification;
what was self-evident to the natural attitude now becomes
problematic, that is, questionable. That is why, driven by the
tension between what is self-given and what is co-intended,
Husserl discovers, by this radical questioning, the functioning
intentionality, the ego as world-experiencing life; in other
words, that is how Husserl is able to show the dimensions in
which, for him, a being can be questioned in its own Being.

> "The theoretical task and idea [of philosophy] . . .
> have reference to the life which originates in a universal
> overview of its possibilities as given in experience, and
> more specifically in the fundamental distinction between
> genuine self-givenness and that which is co-intended in
> and through horizons. Instead of following his experi-
> ences in their naïve harmony as they appear in the con-
> tingent and traditional course of his life, which constitutes
> his apperceptions, [the philosopher] tries to encompass
> the universality of the existing world, in such a way that,
> instead of taking as ground the world naïvely pre-given
> to him, he grasps it as 'intention' (*Meinung*) and treats it
> as problematic. Then, in the attitude of the *epoché*
> (which, in the present undertaking, is prerequisite to the
> achievement of a critical verification of the world) he
> questions the achievement and range of the naïve self-
> presentation of the world . . ."[11]

In the dimension opened up by the reduction, beings become questionable. In this dimension a being is no longer the
objective; it is that by which the world announces itself.
True being is not being-object; there is, therefore, no truth
of one being. That is why Husserl says: "A true being is

[11] Ms. K III 6, pp. 137–38.

definitive only in the totality (*Allheit*) of all genuine being."[12]

In the beginning of this explanation it was remarked that reduction has a double character, that it is both positive and negative at the same time, as going-back-to and refraining-from, as reduction and *epochē* or bracketing. We must ask now the following question: When we perform the act of going-back-to the functioning intentionality, to our world-experiencing life, what then is it from which we refrain, what is it that we "put between brackets"? That, too, is already indicated: We perform the bracketing of the "natural world," in which we live, and which we have before us as a ready-made structured product without ever having justified for ourselves its "constitution," or having discovered its character of possessing the horizons which are its ground.

The "world" of our natural attitude is in a certain sense a many-leveled, immanently moved, and complex anticipated judgment [pre-judice (Vor-Urteil)], the foundation and implied co-intentions of which remain concealed for us in that attitude.

A prejudice is not recognized as prejudice as long as we remain caught in it, but only after it is conquered, that is, after its provisionalness is discovered. Reduction is the discovery of the pre-judice of the natural world; and it enables us at the same time to refrain from this prejudice.

Thus we can and will now refrain from accepting every value that is brought to light in naïve activities; we no longer accept the world that is pre-given to us simply in the way we have previously done. We want to thematize it in its mundaneness, we want to see how functioning intentionality functions and, therefore, gives it ground; we want to see what consciousness-of-world looks like, we want to try explicitly to grasp our world-experiencing life.

"I do not make judgments about the world, but about my primordial living being and about the world only inso-far as it is intended and is operative therein as such. I do not simply accept the pre-given world in its Being and So-Being, but I thematize the pre-givenness of the

[12] Ms. K III 2, p. 119.

world and of this concrete world *as* Being and So-Being, exactly in the flowing modes in which consists this Being, pre-given-to-me, having this or that meaning for me, and verifying itself in this or that way. In other words, world is for me a continuous-living pre-judice and is, in a certain sense, the totality of all my prejudices in my natural life. I practice radical presuppositionlessness when I question the primordial dwelling place of all my judgments, the ones which I have acquired myself as well as the ones I have accepted from tradition, and also when I question all the self-evident [conceptions] that, because of their implicitness, are at first hidden from me although they nonetheless determine me in my views . . ."[13]

To assume the philosophical attitude of phenomenological reduction in its going-back-upon and its refraining-from, therefore, is a self-reflection in which the ego unfolds itself in its self-alienation, as world-experiencing life; that is to say, the ego explains how it itself is and at the same time how the world is. Be it understood, however, that the ego's life that is to be unfolded is not our human life, not our life as "man" of the natural attitude. For we [have decided to] refrain from just the attitude in which "I as man" is a being which is encountered in the world among other beings, which recognizes the world, constitutes it, and has consciousness of it. Our usual manner of taking ourselves as "human beings" is one of those prejudices within the all-encompassing prejudice of the "natural" world that is never made explicit. Our "being a man" is itself an event in the natural world; that is why we cannot hope to find the ultimate philosophical foundation in its "life of consciousness."[14] However, we are not yet able to say very much about what this ego that we have taken possession of through the phenomenological reduction is, although it is true that it is our own ego. Remaining within the purity of the method applied, we first have to take the ego exclusively and purely in its function of being "the bearer

[13] Ms. C 3 III, p. 9.
[14] Cf. *Krisis*, pp. 182–90.

of the fact that the world is accepted as being" (*Geltungs-träger*) . . .[15]

Reduction is the going-back upon this ego in order to make explicit how it possesses the world, a going-back upon this all-encompassing life of consciousness which is our life, and which as world-experiencing we want to make explicit in all its purity. Through reduction we want to get acquainted with our Being and life through which world is world-for-us.[16]

Thus Husserl's phenomenological reduction must not be understood as a putting into action of a subjectivity that exists for itself, of a consciousness that looks upon itself and whose structures we want to examine while we "put into brackets" the world and the world's existence. Nor does the ego go back upon itself as a concrete individual human being who acts only in relation to his personal conscious life and who refrains from every "positing of Being" except that of his own consciousness; on the contrary, the ego goes back upon itself as ego-in-the-world, as world-experiencing life since it does *not* exist exclusively as subject. What is put between brackets is what is naïve and unproved, the world as it is usually taken by the ego, in contradistinction to the world which the ego now attempts to make explicit and which has been concealed until now by the natural world, although it was already implied and predelineated there. In both its aspects, as going-back-upon and as abstention (*epochē*), the reduction does not make the world disappear but, on the contrary, makes it come to the fore; it is the positive bringing-to-light of the original world.[17] Husserl explains it with perfect clarity:

"The world is and remains for me the one I always accept at face value—the reduction does not alter this fact in the least. It only prevents me from taking the real world in the way in which it always seems to be real, and continues to pass for ground, as pre-given

15 Ms. K III 6, p. 148.
16 *Cf.* Ms. C 7 1, p. 29; Ms. C 7 11, pp. 21–22.
17 *Cf.* A. De Waelhens, *"Phénoménologie et Métaphysique,"* *Revue Philosophique de Louvain,* 47 (1949), 366–76, pp. 368–70.

Being-horizon, from asking only what in a certain case, or even in any case, can be said in truth about the world. But when in reduction I deny myself the ground of all my questioning concerning the natural world and, therefore, also the goal of theoretically explaining that world, which always is already there, this does not alter the fact that it continues to seem what it was before, in all its foundations from which this Being took shape for me. But I take this new trend of questioning as an original and exclusive one: I conceive of the world as it has meaning for me purely as thus having meaning for me; in this context this "having-meaning-for-me" is to be understood in harmony with the meaning-content (with all its changes and its unity) which maintains itself in all these changes; all this to be taken just as it is operative in my conscious life. To consider the world, that is, this one which with its concrete meaning has value for me, in a purely subjective way, means indeed to go back upon my subjectivity, with which we are dealing here in the first place; but this does not mean that I consider only myself as being, assert myself as real, whereas the world is in no way to be considered as being just because I have decided to perform the *epochē* in regard to the Being of the world. One must not mistake the *epochē* in our sense—in which we refrain from affirming that the assumed reality of the pre-given world has the value of an absolute foundation, within the realm of which one need ask only how this world is constituted and how its Being can be determined in a methodical way through experience and science—for another kind of *epochē* that wants to refrain from every judgment concerning the world and from every acknowledgment of its Being, and in consequence also of its So-Being."[18]

What is put into brackets in the reduction is not the Being of the world, but only our natural, naïve notions of the world and its Being. We feel absolutely certain as far as the Being of the world is concerned; for all our questioning and

[18] Ms. B I 5 *ix*, pp. 27–28.

inquiry already refer to the world. Through the *epoché* we lose nothing; we gain the possibility of understanding the world of whose Being we are certain, in its true and genuine Being. [. . .]

Intentional Analysis

For Husserl, phenomenological reduction leads to the dimension in which philosophy must take its starting point—the discovery of the functioning intentionality as the last originality, which, consequently, tells us what is in question in phenomenology.

"I begin, therefore, by questioning that which has in me, under the heading 'world,' the character of the conscious, the experienced, and the intended, and which is accepted by me as being; I ask what it looks like in its being accepted thus; I ask how I become conscious of it, how I may describe it, how I can designate it, in terms valid for every occasion; how what is subjective in this way manifests itself in different modes, what it looks like in itself, as experienced or as intended as this or that, or what this experiencing itself as experience of the mundane looks like, how it is to be described, what kind of achievement it is that brings about in me a world of this typical existential character. I ask how all these manifold experiences of our consciousness of world meld into the unity of a common achievement by which, across multiple subjective [elements], a unity of one supposedly objective thing is found and by which, universally speaking, a unity of one objective universe continuously manifests itself. That is the general theme opened up by the reduction. . . ."[19]

In the reduction the functioning intentionality becomes uncovered, and here we find that we must begin by questioning the functioning of the functioning intentionality itself. If this is the object of our questioning, then it is already clear

[19] Ms. B I 5 *ix*, p. 31.

how we must go about our questioning: when we uncover
the functioning intentionality we already have a provisional
understanding of its functioning, insofar as it constitutes a
synthesis implied on many levels, living, and continuously
transcending itself. But if the functioning intentionality is a
living synthesis, then it can be analyzed; in other words one
can set going an analysis—the intentional analysis. We have
already seen how the apparently compact unities that are
given to us are the results of an anonymous, simplifying
achievement that is itself founded upon implications of manifold and various levels. If we want to meet a being just as it
is in itself, then the implications of the founding functioning
must be brought to light and described. By actually making
them explicit, we will find the "explication" of that being;
that is to say, intentional analysis explains to us what that
being is.

How does this take place, in concrete terms? How must
intentional analysis be set in motion? This, too, we already
know, at least roughly. For the analysis of the functioning
intentionality can be nothing but the systematic continuation
of its uncovering, which must have its starting point in the
radical distinction between what is given and what is co-
intended. [. . .]²⁰

Every given datum always "means" more than itself, [in
that it refers to something which transcends the effectively
given].²¹ Because it is a genuine datum only as it refers
from itself to the possibilities of its explicitation as opened
up by the ego, intentional analysis begins when we explicate
the given, when we ask: what do we genuinely "mean" by
this given datum?—that is to say, when we try to clarify this
intending or intention.

"I already know how a meaning in general, how a being-
conscious-of is questioned and explicated: by eluci-
dating and clarifying it by turning toward the manifold
explanatory intentions, and finally by turning to the multi-

²⁰ Ms. K III 6, p. 180.
²¹ Cf. Cart. Med., pp. 83 ff.

plicities characteristic of the experience of our self-comprehension, in which I come into immediate contact with what is meant. The term "clarification," has its strictest meaning, when what is meant implies a multiplicity of positional intentions, which in a determinate order must have been unfolded and again realized in order that the clear meaning—that is, what is meant in its clearness—comes to the fore as a datum. When one intends toward a being as gradually founded upon other beings, there correlatively the intending act is in its own way founded explicitly and clearly; and what is clear is then a unity of foundational coherence, a unity of a conscious act in which what is meant is unfolded in regard to its meaning which in turn, precisely in an *a priori* way, implicitly contains these foundations in itself."[22]

What does the intentional analysis accomplish? Intentional analysis is "genetic" analysis. It considers a unity of knowledge that manifests itself, pursues that unity of knowledge in its horizons, questions it about its surplus-meaning, and unfolds its "genesis," or, as Husserl also says, its "history."

Here a misunderstanding is to be precluded. In Husserl's view intentional analysis does not mean taking one's starting point in a ready-made unity and bringing to light by means of a regressive procedure the layers and sedimentations contained therein. For Husserl argues:

"Locke once spoke of a 'history' of consciousness, and his main interest apparently was in such a genesis; but he, the Father of Empiricism, soon confused it with the psychological genesis, and, in that way he completely falsified it. Every unity of knowledge, especially every real unity, has its history, or, correlatively formulated, the consciousness of this real thing has its 'history,' its immanent teleology in the form of an ordered system of essentially corresponding, testifying, and documenting modes which one can ask of it and extract from it."[23]

[22] Ms. B I 5 *ix*, pp. 6–7; *Ideen*, Vol. III, pp. 139–43.
[23] *Ideen*, Vol. III, p. 129.

In Husserl's view history and immanent teleology refer not only to the "whence," but also, and even principally, to the "whither." When it manifests itself, every unity of knowledge always testifies and documents something more than itself, which is, in the first and in the last place, the world.

Intentional analysis is "constitutive" analysis. As it makes explicit the potentialities that are implicitly contained in the given and that determine its meaning;[24] as it clarifies how the being is in itself, and as it brings to light what was truly already there before, intentional analysis is description of the original and is at the same time its production. In a certain sense, intentional analysis is the paradox of a descriptive constitution. The "new" elements brought to light by the uncovering were nevertheless "old" implications already there—which paradox, properly speaking, is found in any reflection, because reflection brings to light "afterward" what yet was there "before" (Merleau-Ponty speaks of a "miracle of consciousness").[25]

"When I 'uncover' this perception in regard to its intentional components and just as my present experience and its present Being-intentions, then I meet new experiences; but I say, nevertheless, that what they show, now uncovered, is the same as that which was implicitly contained in the old experience and was intended by it."[26]

Here we find the reason why Husserl often calls the intentional analysis constitutive analysis also. By this term Husserl means to express two things. In the first place, it is synonymous with "genetic"; constitutive analysis uncovers the constitutions already anonymously achieved—that is, it shows how functioning intentionality has already constituted the compact unities that we always accept as ready-made. Secondly, it means that the uncovering of the analysis, precisely because it touches the being in its showing-itself-in-itself, brings to the fore something "new," something that was not yet there before, and, thus, in the uncovering enriches that being

[24] Cf. Cart. Med., pp. 83–84.
[25] M. Merleau-Ponty, Phenomenology of Perception, p. 30.
[26] Ms. C 12, p. 5.

—as it were, co-constitutes it. This co-constitution is never a production or a construction. For Husserl constitution does not mean construction—he wants to avoid that confusion by combining "constitutive" with "analysis"—but it means the uncovering, bringing-to-light, of intentions which were already there in that they were already co-intended, albeit hidden and implicit. The original being is in a certain sense "constituted" as original by the fact that we uncover it and see it. In this sense only does the intentional analysis have a constitutive function.

Every uncovering of a horizon, every genuine explication is at the same time constitution as genuine enrichment of meaning.

"Every genuine explication has the intentional character of fulfilling the intention that refers to the horizon (an intention which is to be taken here as empty anticipation), realizing it in determinate steps through which from the certain but unknown determinations the corresponding definite and, henceforth, known determinations originate —known in the sense that the determinations that were implied in an indefinite way in the horizon become clarified. Although clarity is always a fulfilling self-manifestation of what, in an empty way, was already intended, it is still never pure and merely self-giving; the predelineation never goes so far that the predelineated meaning was already intended in absolute determination and now only passes into the intuitive clarity of the "in itself." Even where the object is "completely known," this perfection does not completely correspond to its idea. What is pre-intended in an empty way has its "vague generality," its open indeterminateness, which becomes fulfilled only in the form of a further determination. Therefore it is always, instead of a fully determined meaning, an empty frame-of-meaning although it is not grasped as a fixed frame-of-meaning. Its width, which according to circumstances may vary considerably, uncovers itself only in the fulfillments. It is in this way that the simple fulfill-

ment achieves not only a clarification but also an enrichment of meaning."[27]

Intentional analysis is so unlike construction that Husserl
calls it a description. But just as constitution is not construction, neither is description depiction. This typical character of the analysis as description is emphasized by Professor
Fink:

> "The methodical peculiarity of the phenomenological
> analysis of intentionality—which manifests itself in a
> "bringing-forth" in the uncovering of what at first, as
> given, 'is' not yet in any way—is easily misunderstood, if
> Husserl's characterization of the intentional analysis, as
> remaining in the realm of theoretical statements (namely
> the title 'intentional description'), is interpreted in terms
> of our usual understanding of description instead of the
> other way round, here deriving the meaning of the de-
> scription from the peculiarity of intentionality. The gen-
> eral meaning of description—a procedure in which one
> faithfully renders what one sees and the way in which
> one sees it—and in fact before all theories that "explain"
> what description is—remains valid also for intentional
> analysis. However, through the so-called descriptive sci-
> ences of nature we are too easily fixed upon the concep-
> tion that description has to be faithful description of what
> is present-at-hand and given ready-made. Intentional de-
> scription, however, is not depiction of psychic 'things'
> which are present-at-hand in the 'space' of consciousness,
> called intentionalities; it is intentional in that it thema-
> tizes functioning intentionality, and it itself is a mode of
> functioning."[28]

Description is not something in itself but gets its determination from that which is to be described; and as description
it is determined in such a way that it keeps at a distance
everything that is not a determination showing what the thing
is.

[27] Erf. u. Urt., pp. 140–41.
[28] Eugen Fink, "Das Problem der Phänomenologie," p. 269.

Thus, in the description with which it uncovers functioning intentionality, intentional analysis is in its own way active and passive, receptive, descriptive, and constitutive at the same time.

Intentional analysis is explanation as clarification.

Phenomenological philosophy takes its starting point in its striving for original knowledge of original being as that being manifests itself in itself. Phenomenology searches for evidence as self-giving and definitive truth.

Intentional analysis is the questioning of evidence by going back upon the "how" of functioning intentionality. "Going-back-upon the 'how' means to bring about evidence, to thematize this evidence itself insofar as it genuinely is self-giving of what I have taken as supposedly real."[29]

Having arrived at this point in our investigation, we must note with Husserl that evidence as self-givenness of being is not clarity, not *clara et distincta perceptio,* but clarification, and that evidence as self-givenness of the world is apodictic— in the certainty of belief.

> "When he [the one who is asking] begins to bring about evident givenness, then, as he proceeds, he will see that he cannot stop, that this evidence has horizons, that the self-giving is not yet genuine self-giving of the mundane, but that instead it would presuppose that further self-giving would fulfill the anticipation of that evidence. —Neither the mundane and the world itself, nor I myself as man in the world, become self-given in a ready-made way, but only transcendental subjectivity [our world-experiencing life] becomes so, as it brings to light the world in presumptive evidences and as it continuously maintains the world in a relative validity. The world 'proves' itself in the form of an apodictic presumption that continuously verifies itself, but in continuous relativity."[30]

29 Ms. K III 6, p. 382.
30 Ms. K III 6, pp. 386–87.

If, however, definitive evidence cannot be found in the world, which itself is evidently never given intuitively, are we then not necessarily led to the destruction of the fundamental principle of the phenomenological quest: evidence as intuition of being in its itself-being-there?

In regard to this "intuition" as seeing, we cannot allow ourselves to be guided by the restrictive example of sense-perception. For have we not known for a long time that "to see" does not mean merely to "gape at" being? In intentional analysis, the intuition of a being in its itself-being-there becomes the understanding of this being in the direction of the whole; for only in that way is it there itself.

The world announces itself in every being. On the other hand, the absolute but unintuitable clarity of the world implies the possibility that being becomes clarified without ever becoming completely clear. But at the same time the clarifying of being opens the possibility that we may come closer to the world, penetrate into that "foreign domain," although we can never catch up with it, or bring it to intuitive clarity. Because the world is present in the individual, I have the world's itself-being-there in an evident way.

Intentional analysis is clarification and remains so continuously.

"The process of clarification therefore means two things: first, clarification of concepts by appealing to a fulfilling intuition, but secondly a process of clarification which comes about in the domain of intuition itself: the object meant . . . must be brought to ever greater clarity, ever closer, and in the process of clarification to complete self-givenness."[31]

We know already, however, that complete self-givenness is meaningless.

"On the other hand, there is for all objects a nearness and a distance in the realm of intuition, an emerging into full light that allows us in our analyzing to bring to the fore

[31] *Ideen*, Vol. III, p. 103.

an inner richness of determined moments, but also a backsliding into darkness in which everything becomes blurred."[32]

The analysis of functioning intentionality is a continual bringing close of being in its itself-being-there, which we, however, must always bring closer within the absolute nearness of the world.

[32] *Ibid.,* p. 104.

PART II

FROM PHENOMENOLOGY
TO EXISTENTIAL PHENOMENOLOGY

I. HUSSERL'S PHENOMENOLOGY AND "EXISTENTIALISM"

Husserl's Phenomenological Philosophy in the Light of Contemporary Criticism*

JOSEPH J. KOCKELMANS

Although not quite thirty years have passed since Husserl's death, we find today a widespread phenomenological movement enjoying strong support in many countries. But while all contemporary phenomenologists recognize Husserl as the founder of the movement, very few of them accept Husserl's view without major modifications. Most of the leading phenomenologists are deeply aware of the exceptional value of Husserl's ideas; they nonetheless believe that his view on phenomenology contains certain unacceptable presuppositions. In developing new ideas in regard to these presuppositions, the various authors have for the most part adopted different courses. But however great may be the differences among the views developed by such phenomenologists as Scheler, Heidegger, Jaspers, Sartre, Merleau-Ponty, and others, and whatever may be their precise reasons for changing and developing Husserl's original conception, there can be no doubt that the present somewhat confused situation within the phenomenological movement can be attributed at least in part to the fundamental ambiguity characteristic of Husserl's philosophical work as a whole.

Landgrebe has often discussed the many difficulties that must be overcome before one arrives at a genuine understanding of Husserl's transcendental phenomenology. First of all, it must be remembered that much of Husserl's writing is not yet published or has only recently become available,

* From Joseph J. Kockelmans, *Husserl's Phenomenological Psychology* (Pittsburgh, Pa.: Duquesne University Press, 1966), pp. 268–84. Reprinted by permission of the publishers.

and that the readily available publications generally concern themselves with elaborating an ideal program, rather than with patiently worked-out detailed analyses. It seems that Husserl, without being quite aware of it, has cut the ground from under this ideal program in his analyses. In *Ideen* and *Cartesianische Meditationen* Husserl understands his work as an attempt to radicalize the Cartesian demand for an absolutely certain basis for philosophy as a strict science. One finds, however, that many of his detailed and unpublished analyses are often quite at odds with this quest. In them the attempt radically to comprehend the modern subject-problem turns out to be forever in vain: the analyses reveal that the problem is a pseudo-problem.[1]

In his systematic treatment of phenomenological philosophy Husserl has in mind philosophy as a strict science. He envisions an all-encompassing rational knowledge of all that is, as the proper and characteristic intention of all philosophy since the days of the ancient Greeks. Husserl proposes phenomenological and transcendental reductions that will make it possible for us to take the decisive step in the direction of this old ideal. The reductions do not destroy the world in which we live, nor do they deny it: they only put this world between parentheses. What remains after the reduction is nothing but the transcendental ego with its transcendental life. Once we have gained access to the transcendental sphere with the help of the reductions we can start the task of clarifying the essence of what we find there by means of the intentional and constitutive analyses.[2] The phenomenological and transcendental reductions and the theory concerning constitution form the two pillars upon which the main part of Husserl's phenomenology rests.[3] The phenomenological reductions make it possible for the mind to discover its own nature; originally lost in the world, the mind can find itself again by means of these reductions. Only when that discovery opens

[1] Ludwig Landgrebe, *Philosophie der Gegenwart* (Bonn: Athenäum Verlag, 1952), pp. 31–32.

[2] Gaston Berger, *Le Cogito Dans la Philosophie de Husserl* (Paris: Aubier, 1941), pp. 67–74.

[3] *Ibid.*, pp. 16 and 94.

up the possibility of an entirely new task can the mind begin to interpret the world as a coherent system constituted as such by itself. The coherence and unity of the world are ultimately founded upon the unity of the ego, to which all elements of the world necessarily refer. The task of constitutive analyses is to clarify how the ego constitutes worldly Being and the world itself.[4]

In this context it is necessary to know what Husserl means by the word "constitution." He uses the word to indicate the original relationship between the I and the world, between the ego and any worldly structure whatsoever. We must not forget here that any worldly being as well as the world itself, when analyzed in terms of *meaning*, will necessarily refer to the transcendental ego. The explanation of the constitution of the world concerns itself with how the ego gives *meaning* to whatever is present to it; it also reveals how this ego grants certain aspects of the world an *existential meaning*. To understand fully Husserl's concept of constitution we must place ourselves on the level of sense and meaning. We must be mindful that "the whole Being of the world consists in a certain meaning which presupposes an absolute consciousness as the domain in which and by which all meaning is given."[5] Phenomenology does not deny the real existence of the world, but only tries radically to explain its meaning. The same is true for the ego itself. Ultimately the ego, too, is a certain meaning that needs to be explained. The constitution-problem thus includes the ego itself. Transcendental phenomenology tries to make explicit and to ground radically the meaning of any possible being.[6]

This original view can be further interpreted in different ways, and whether Husserl's vision is acceptable to us will depend upon the particular interpretation we consider. Husserl's own interpretation is rooted in the conviction that a consistent phenomenology must turn its back on every established theory, on all traditional, prejudiced, and "metaphysical" views in order to gain access to a pure and primordial

[4] *Ibid.*, p. 94.
[5] Edmund Husserl, *Ideen*, Vol. I, p. 135.
[6] Gaston Berger, *op. cit.*, pp. 94–95.

experience in which the "things themselves" appear to us in a genuinely original way. Now we must ask ourselves what might be the criteria for such an experience and what position we must assume in order to be able to judge the originality of such an experience. Experience is a manner of possessing something in a conscious way; only consciousness itself can therefore distinguish between an original and real experience and an improper one. But as adult and educated members of society we already have a number of views on a great many things. The question, then, is to work through these derivative views on things and problems, back toward the original experience in which any being whatsoever emerges originally as it itself.[7]

This is the task of the intentional analysis, in which we question each and every being concerning the conscious modes and the conscious achievements in which it made its original appearance. The phenomenological reduction is of the greatest importance here since it enables us to reach the data in their purity and in the original form in which they appear in consciousness, to the exclusion of every conception that transcends the original data. Consciousness itself cannot be described, nor is it possible to distinguish the separate acts of consciousness, without our first becoming aware of the distinction between consciousness and that of which we are conscious, and noticing the particular manner in which each act is oriented toward its object. The object of the analysis of consciousness, therefore, includes the different ways in which acts of consciousness are directed toward objects; thus the analysis pursues to their bases the different ways in which intentionality can manifest itself. All questions concerning the very essence of each being are referred back to questions concerning the different modes of consciousness and, therefore, to the experiences in which the being manifests itself in its originality as "this there." The essence of any being whatsoever can thus be revealed by means of an intentional analysis of the acts of consciousness in which the particular being is constituted as such. In this way Being and conscious-

[7] Ludwig Landgrebe, op. cit., pp. 32–34.

ness appear to be strongly interwoven: there exists no object nor any quality of any object that does not find its correlate in the constituting acts of consciousness, by which it is originally given as this or that thing or quality.

Intentional analysis uses the essential difference between all possible objects of consciousness as a guiding clue when it inquires into the modes of consciousness in which these objects are given originally. The phenomenological reduction, which had manifested itself up to this point as a mere suspension of all unfounded opinions concerning objects, now assumes a more radical form. The reduction now becomes the process that leads us to the ultimate and irreducible point to which all our knowing and speaking of the world, the things in it, and their essential structures, refer—namely, the point where one is certain of oneself as a being that is conscious of itself and of the world. This *ego cogito* does not serve as a point of departure for a deductive philosophical system; rather, the discovering of the *ego cogito* frees an *original* field of description. Thus the analyses of phenomenology are always moving in two different directions; on the one hand, they are noematic descriptions that take as a guiding clue the essential difference between species, regions, etc.; on the other hand, they are noetic descriptions of conscious acts that intend a being of this or that type.[8]

Originally the ego also understands itself as a mundane being over and against other egos. A more radical analysis reveals that that understanding is based on an already constituted world in which the ego appears over and against other egos. This analysis can be pursued one step further, by which we discover in ourselves a center of intentional acts; through them each being is what it is, and through them alone can it appear as the particular being it is. The analysis thus reveals an absolute consciousness through which all that which is, is what it actually is.[9]

In Husserl's view this methodic conviction implies a particular way of raising and answering the fundamental metaphysi-

[8] *Ibid.*, pp. 34–35.
[9] *Ibid.*, pp. 35–37.

cal questions concerning Being, the meaning of Being, and the different modes of Being. To Husserl, Being *a priori* is the correlate of consciousness. "Being" means "being an object for consciousness." Each object is originally revealed in consciousness according to its own essence. True, absolute constituting consciousness ultimately is a stream of constituting achievements which as stream forms itself, but it can understand itself and unveil itself according to its essence in the products of its own achievements, that is to say in the objective unities: the things. The process of uncovering implies again the disclosure of the essential correlation between any being whatsoever and the corresponding conscious achievements. Every factual being, including man himself, loses its real meaning in the analysis of the absolute constituting consciousness. Particular objects are seen in this perspective as mere examples of this or that class, as guiding clues in the question concerning the discovery of the universal and necessary conscious achievements associated with a certain class of beings. Idealism cannot be avoided here, however.[10]

The weak points in Husserl's position become clear when we compare him with Heidegger.[11] We have already seen that Husserl's method demands that we doubt every being. In that way we must ultimately arrive at the "unquestionable" that constitutes the ground of all beings. Husserl finds that root in the transcendental ego. If the transcendental ego be the ultimate ground for all that is, we must find that everything is ultimately constituted in it. Thus, all beings ultimately must be dissolved in the ego's consciousness of them; the transcendental ego becomes the only absolute and real being. The whole of Husserl's method is characterized by this transcendental reduction in which the whole realm of Being is placed between parentheses in order to yield the transcendental ego. But Heidegger makes no use of these reductions. The relationship between *Dasein* and other beings belongs to

---

10 *Ibid.*, pp. 37–38.
11 For the following discussion, see: Ludwig Landgrebe, *Phänomenologie und Metaphysik* (Hamburg: Schröder, 1949), pp. 83–100.

the essence of *Dasein* itself.[12] While Husserl tries to free the transcendental ego from the world by means of his reductions, Heidegger sees *Dasein* as the being that discloses the world. The relationship of *Dasein* and world is of such importance in Heidegger that he defines *Dasein* as Being-in-the-world. Husserl's "pure ego" is an abomination to Heidegger, a mere artificial abstraction which only hampers our understanding of man as concrete *ek-sistence*, that is to say of man as "standing out" toward things in the world and, in the final analysis, to the world itself.[13] It would be helpful to try to clarify this perhaps overstated difference between the two thinkers.

Both Husserl and Heidegger begin from the idea that each kind of Being gives and manifests itself in a way which is characteristic only of that kind of Being. Solely on the basis of its self-presentation are meaningful philosophical statements about any kind of Being possible.[14] Both Husserl and Heidegger link this basic principle with their demand for a reinstatement of a "natural world-concept." The function of such a concept is not the same in both philosophers. Husserl gives the following explanation. Intentional analysis, as the universal disclosure of conscious achievements, owes its guiding clue to objects—that is to say to the ever-changing ontological status of the objects which continuously require particular types of conscious achievements by which the objects can be presented. Therefore the true point of departure for any investigation into conscious achievements cannot be found without insight into the structure of objectivity itself. Only in that way can we gain insight into the original and genuine object of our experience; and only thus can we correlatively find the deepest and most primary achievements of our consciousness in which objects are originally given. Over the course of the centuries the exact sciences have imposed upon us certain prejudices concerning the original object of our ex-

---

[12] Walter Biemel, *"Husserls Encyclopaedia Britannica Artikel und Heideggers Anmerkungen dazu," Tijdschrift voor Philosophie*, 12 (1950), 246–89, pp. 273–76.

[13] *Ibid.*, pp. 276–80.

[14] Ludwig Landgrebe, *op. cit.*, p. 85.

perience. For they claim that the original Being consists in the object as it manifests itself in the exact determination of science. Actually, though, the objects that the sciences deal with are abstractions and are constructions in regard to the world of our immediate and original experience. We must, therefore, renounce the prejudices of science if we are to discover the real, original structure of the objects of the different realms of beings and their correlative conscious achievements. Instead, we must penetrate Being as it announces itself, prior to every scientific investigation, in the immediacy and primacy of our original experience. We must leave the cultural world of the sciences and try to find our way back to the original *Lebenswelt*. A special reduction is an essential condition without which this return never can be successful. However, the link between this reduction and the phenomenological-transcendental reduction is, according to Husserl, an essential one.[15]

This reduction from the scientific, cultural world toward the *Lebenswelt* is also found in Heidegger. His Being-in-the-world forms one of the basic structures of *Dasein*. Yet, to understand the world in its relationship to *Dasein* and to understand *Dasein* itself insofar as it originally *is* mundane and *has* world are the main themes of Heidegger's fundamental ontology, by which he hopes to bring to light what Husserl called "the natural world-concept."[16] Heidegger rejects the phenomenological reduction even though in many respects he is much more faithful to Husserl than most of the other important disciples. With Husserl, Heidegger protests against those who try to interpret phenomenology in the classical realistic sense and fail to see it as a "going back into the depths of subjectivity."[17]

Husserl and Heidegger are most notably different in their interpretations of what a phenomenon is. Heidegger defines phenomenon as "that which shows itself in itself" or "the Being of beings, its meaning, its modifications and deriva-

15 *Ibid.*, pp. 85–87.
16 *Ibid.*, p. 87; Martin Heidegger, *Sein und Zeit*, p. 52.
17 Ludwig Landgrebe, *op. cit.*, p. 87.

tives."[18] Heidegger arrived at this interpretation because, in contrast to Husserl, he chose to see intentionality as a relating to that which is, as a relation to the world. This is directly evident from his description of *Dasein* as Being-in-the-world.[19] With this in mind we can easily understand that Heidegger's intentional analysis can never take the form of a constitutive analysis as we find it in Husserl. This is also the reason why Heidegger will have nothing to do with a phenomenological or transcendental reduction, with a transcendental subjectivity, with a theory of the ego as a "disinterested observer," or with a complete and universal reflection.[20]

In sum we may say that Heidegger rejects Husserl's method because it did not take sufficient note of *Dasein's* original experience of itself as Being-in-the-world. Husserl's method cannot fully penetrate *Dasein* in the originality of its ek-sistence. It can lead only to an idealized subject, never to *Dasein's* essence, to its ek-sistence. The subjectivity in its most essential meaning is thus bypassed.[21] Once the true meaning of subjectivity is revealed, we immediately become convinced of the impossibility of a statement that equates Being with object. With that insight the possibility of Husserl's transcendental idealism comes to an end.[22]

Ricoeur forcefully summarizes all this in his study of Husserl's *Cartesianische Meditationen*.[23] He takes as his starting point Husserl's statement:

> Since the monadically concrete ego includes also the whole of actual and potential conscious life, it is clear that the problem of explicating this monadic ego phenomenologically (the problem of his constitution for himself) must include all constitutional problems without

[18] Martin Heidegger, *op. cit.*, pp. 28 and 35.
[19] *Ibid.*, pp. 52–62.
[20] Ludwig Landgrebe, *op. cit.*, pp. 87–94.
[21] *Ibid.*, p. 94.
[22] *Ibid.*, pp. 99–100.
[23] Paul Ricoeur, *"Etude sur les 'Méditations Cartésiennes' de Husserl,"* Revue Philosophique de Louvain, 52 (1954), 75–109.

exception. Consequently the phenomenology of the self-constitution coincides with phenomenology as a whole.[24]

Ricoeur explains Husserl's final view as follows. If the whole of transcendental reality is limited to that of the ego, the problem of the constitution of reality coincides with the problem of the self-constitution of the ego. Phenomenology becomes a self-explanation of the ego, even there where the original interest was in the constitution of the object, the realm of the psychical or the cultural. The ego is here no longer the subject-pole placed opposite an object-pole; it instead becomes that which encompasses everything. Everything now becomes *constructum* of and for transcendental subjectivity; the whole world of reality becomes a mere product of the transcendental ego's activity. Phenomenology as a whole becomes a "self-explanation of one's own ego taken as subject of all possible knowledge."[25] Husserl's definitive view on the ego links phenomenology inseparably with idealism, a conclusion fully accepted by Husserl himself.[26]

The thing Husserl's phenomenology speaks about, therefore, is not Being itself; it rather is a being which is essentially an object. Husserl maintains that the question which asks about the link between Being and Being-object is a pseudo-question. In this manner he dodges the problems connected with this question primarily because he *a priori* refuses to make use of speculation. He decrees without further explanation that Being is phenomenon and that phenomenon is Being. The basic mistake that Husserl makes in this *a priori* decision is that he understands the appearance of the object *only* as an appearing before a *knowing* subject, whereas this appearing of the object must originally be grasped in its metaphysical dimensions as an ontological relationship between two beings. Husserl does not realize that the self-presentation of a being encompasses more than the presentation of that same being in and through man's theoretical knowledge. As far as its ontological possibility is concerned, man's knowledge

24 Edmund Husserl, *Cart. Med.*, pp. 102–3.
25 *Ibid.*, p. 118.
26 Paul Ricoeur, *l.c.*, pp. 107–9.

is grounded in the general Being of things for other things.[27] Husserl's phenomenology sees intentionality purely as relationship of knowledge. This ties in with the fact that he practically always interprets substance as subject, as has generally been done in the metaphysical tradition since Descartes and Leibnitz. This view sees the phenomenon as indeed identical to a represented object for a representing ego. Without explicitly subscribing to this view, and even without being fully aware of it, Husserl places himself on the same foundation as modern metaphysics.

Heidegger tries to overcome the difficulties inherent in Husserl's vision by replacing the idealized and abstract subject of modern philosophy with the concretely human ek-sistence. He feels that we can bypass certain pitfalls in Husserl's theory only when we understand man's Being as Being-in-the-world. At the same time this vision does not basically conflict with the rest of Husserl's insights.

In this connection we must mention another important factor. More than once commentators have found in Husserl's one-sided interest in analysis an important source of errors and prejudices. Heidegger was one of the first to notice this. Jaspers, Marcel, Merleau-Ponty, De Waelhens, and Strasser, too, have shown a great deal of interest in this aspect of phenomenology.[28] And we must also mention Gadamer's *Wahrheit und Methode,* in which Heidegger's view of the matter is put into a larger historical context.[29]

In his *Phenomenology and the Human Sciences,*[30] Strasser arrived at a particularly fortunate synthesis of the most important aspects of this point. Strasser characterizes contem-

[27] Eugen Fink, *"L'analyse intentionnelle et le problème de la pensée spéculative,"* in *Problèmes actuels de la phénoménologie.* Ed. H. L. Van Breda (Paris: Desclée de Brouwer, 1952), 53–87, p. 70.

[28] Joseph J. Kockelmans, *"Over de methode der wijsbegeerte,"* *Algemeen Nederlands Tijdschrift voor Wijsbegeerte en Psychologie* 54 (1962), 201–18, pp. 208–15.

[29] H.-G. Gadamer, *Wahrheit und Methode. Grundzüge einer philosophischen Hermeneutik* (Tübingen: Niemeyer, 1960).

[30] Stephan Strasser, *Phenomenology and the Human Sciences* (Pittsburgh, Pa.: Duquesne University Press, 1963), pp. 245–76.

porary phenomenological philosophy as hermeneutic, intuitive, and dialectical.[31] The hermeneutical attitude can be negatively described as that attitude in which the philosopher no longer maintains the pretense of being an a-cosmic, a-historical, and a-social consciousness. The attitude can be positively defined as one in which the philosopher must consider his own ek-sistence and all its essential characteristics as previously given. He then must try to clarify the essential structures of his ek-sistence and to understand their ontological meaning. The hermeneutic postulate arose when the phenomenology of the postwar period rejected the Cartesian ideal of an absolute beginning, which Husserl always maintained. Contemporary phenomenologists have turned their backs on the ideal because it implies a *regressus in infinitum*. It is felt also that such an ideal runs counter to the phenomenological situation. A philosopher's thought is always situated; in particular, his thought always presupposes his concrete ek-sistence. Ultimately our thinking is a thinking together with others, including the great philosophers of the past; so philosophy must be conceived of as an hermeneutic interpretation of man's concrete ek-sistence in which his social and historical situation is fully recognized. Heidegger's research in this matter is now generally recognized as correct, at least in principle.[32]

An explanation of the intuitive character of phenomenology must choose as its point of departure a description of the concept of "phenomenon." A physicist uses this concept to indicate a "merely subjective appearance"; the physicist is likely to forget here that all mediate and experimental evidences necessarily presuppose an immediate evidence based on original phenomena. These original and immediate phenomena are characterized by Heidegger as "that which manifests itself in itself, the manifest."[33] Such a phenomenon places us in an immediate contact with the thing itself. Since Husserl, we speak of "evidence" to designate such an immediate contact with things. In addition to describing things as

[31] *Ibid.*, p. 249.
[32] *Ibid.*, pp. 249–51.
[33] Martin Heidegger, *op. cit.*, p. 28.

self-given, Husserl distinguishes things as merely intended (*bloss Vermeintes*); in the latter case things are not self-given, not intuited nor seen. Only that which is immediately intuited is evident and this Being-evident of its object is the ultimate goal of every cognitive act.

Intuition thus is that act of knowledge which corresponds to the Being-evident of real things. And since the self-givenness upon which the Being-evident of things depends does not occur only within the realm of sense-perception, intuition is not identical with sense-perception, although it remains true that all intuitive grasping and understanding of things reaches back to a perceptual intuition. Thus emerges a very important methodological insight: that all that presents itself to us in obvious evidence cannot and need not be subjected to proof. The philosopher's task is to bring evidence to light and to incorporate all his other insights into it.[84]

This evidence-principle has certain typical limitations, though, which arise primarily from the perspectivity to which every perception and all subsequent derivative acts are subjected. A further limitation is that one object can be covered by another. We must finally remember in this context that the horizon-structure makes all "seeing" into a "conceiving as";[35] here is the main reason why most contemporary phenomenologists maintain a hermeneutic attitude in addition to the intuitive character of phenomenology, as we have seen.

Phenomenologists usually are least explicit when it comes to the dialectic aspect of phenomenology. Yet it is clear from what has been said above that the principle of intuition is incomplete without a dialectic principle. The fact that there is nothing *behind* phenomena does not exclude the possibility that a phenomenon may be partly hidden. It is even true that phenomena do not originally present themselves in their entirety in intuition. It is precisely because phenomena are clear as well as obscure (*verdeckt*) that we are in need of a phenomenology.[36] The dialectical method now plays an essential part in the process of uncovering phenomena. By dialectic

84 Stephan Strasser, *op. cit.*, pp. 251–54.
35 *Ibid.*, pp. 254–56.
36 Martin Heidegger, *op. cit.*, p. 36.

we understand here: any orderly change in perspective that enables man in search of meaning to overcome in a systematic manner, the limitations of the one-sided perspectives and limited horizons. Mute experiences and the "incarnated" dialectic are further in need of a language that has an intersubjectively valid meaning. Besides the pre-predicative dialectic, we are, therefore, in need of a predicative dialectic which in a community of human beings necessarily takes the form of a dialogue. The word "dialogue" points here to the mutual effort of the "we" in which truth, goodness, and beauty are brought to light by means of language and other means of "expression." This dialectical-dialogical effort is and forever remains an attempt to rescue things from their original darkness and to bring them to light.[37]

Husserl at first overestimated the value of the evidence principle. In the years following the Second World War some of the limitations of this principle were revealed, particularly through the influence of Merleau-Ponty's contention that philosophical evidence is valid only within a certain sphere of thinking. Philosophical evidences in particular are determined by social, historical, and cultural horizons. These evidences do not make themselves come true, but rather *we* must make them come true from the perspectives of our own social and cultural situations.

To understand these statements correctly one must make a distinction between the formal evidences of logic and mathematics and the material evidences of pre-scientific and scientific life. It is then easy to see that formal evidences arise out of material evidences of an intuitive nature, by means of "abstraction" and "idealization." Intuitive evidences arise out of immediate experiences. These experiences are not to be understood as the "sensory perceptions" of empiricism but rather as the original, existential orientations of man toward beings, insofar as they include insight and lead to knowledge. Experience, then, is the origin of all forms of consciousness; thinking in concepts or categories is the continuation of the same orientation toward beings on an essentially higher level.

[37] Stephan Strasser, *op. cit.*, pp. 256–59.

We can state, therefore, that every evidence corresponds to the result of a certain experience. But just what are we to think of this intuitive evidence itself?

We should note first of all that not every experience leads to evidence. Only after all the different intentionalities that are included in one particular experience are fulfilled can we speak of genuine evidence. A further requirement is that we express in language the complete concordance that exists between that which we see and that which is given in intention.

It is possible, however, for a situation to arise in which something is held to be evident when in fact it is not. When that happens, it may be due either to mistakes made in observation, to gaps in the process of fulfillment, or to mistakes made in the process of verbalization. This does not detract from the fact that there are evidences which are unshakable. Strasser speaks here of primordial evidences.[38] These refer to obvious aspects which make the concrete dialectical process itself possible, regardless of whether it elicits a truth or a mistake in a particular instance. These aspects include my ek-sistence, your ek-sistence, our Being-in-the-world, our "openness," the world itself, etc. Primordial evidences are relatively small in number.

Even if we accept this view in its general outline, we nevertheless run into a difficult problem: how to differentiate between primordial evidences and other evidences, especially the naïve ones that we encounter on the level of the existential dialectic itself. Most phenomenologists, including Husserl, have underestimated this problem. It seems that we will need a special method in order to keep these evidences apart. In our search for such a method we would probably do well to start with the following questions: What are the methods used by the philosopher that permit him to discover "universality" and "necessity"? and How are these two categories related? It seems clear that necessity cannot simply be derived from universality on the basis of empirical observations. Universality is the consequence of necessity and not the other way round. Existential necessity can be discovered only by dialectic, by which we mean the systematic choosing and discarding of determinate horizons. The desired method, then, is found to consist in postponing our judgment concerning a particular experiential fact, to formulate an antithesis from this fact, and to see then whether the thesis can be "destroyed" by the antithesis. If that does not happen, we are facing a primordial evidence. If the antithesis turns out to be not only thinkable but also livable and capable of forming part of our ek-sistence, we are faced not with a primordial evidence, but instead with a limited evidence.

Phenomenology, then, is a philosophy concerned with man's ek-sistence in its dialectical interwovenness with other beings. The philosopher gives an analytic and a hermeneutics of his ek-sistence and of his original interwovenness with other ek-sistences. His existential orientation toward and his dealing with other people and with things form the starting point of his philosophical work. The evidences that relate to this orientation are spontaneous, naïve, and experiential. The philosopher is required to point out their universal and essential structures, and to that end he employs the dialectic method. A methodical and critical sifting of all the natural evidences results, then, in primordial evidences.

When we view phenomenology from this perspective, we see it as a methodically developed "wisdom" of man's ek-sistence, as a strict philosophy rather than a strict science. Starting from such a "philosophical anthropology," the philosopher must try to rise above the world while remaining in it, in his search for a genuine understanding of Being.[39]

[39] *Ibid.*, pp. 260–76 (passim).

Transcendental Phenomenology
and Existentialism*

JAMES M. EDIE

The great drama of the phenomenological movement, particularly since the Second World War, has been the development and enlarging of the perspectives of Husserl's original transcendental phenomenology into an existential phenomenology. André de Muralt has described this development accurately, if negatively, as the "ultimate form of the refusal to platonize"[1] on the part of Husserl's progeny—a refusal which is, no doubt, characteristic of the general spirit of contemporary philosophy as a whole and which justifies those who find in phenomenology a method and a spirit of search capable of renewing and deepening the realistic and pragmatic approach to philosophy characteristic of American thought. Husserl, during his middle period, characterized phenomenology as a "transcendental idealism," and a large number of his followers have consistently remained faithful to an idealistic interpretation of his works.[2] They have resisted the "existentialist" interpretation of his thought which is associated with the early Heidegger, with Sartre and with Merleau-Ponty and his followers in particular. We cannot hope to solve the historical question as to which of these divergent interpretations (the "idealist" or the "existential") has the greater claim to Husserlian legitimacy

* From James M. Edie, "Transcendental Phenomenology and Existentialism," *Philosophy and Phenomenological Research*, 25 (1964–65), pp. 52–63. Reprinted with permission of the author and the editors.

[1] André de Muralt, *L'idée de la phénoménologie*, Paris, 1958, p. 361.

[2] This is true not only of many of the older generation of phenomenologists who were close to Husserl himself but also of such post-existentialist writers as André de Muralt and Suzanne Bachelard.

in the space of this short paper. We will, therefore, limit ourselves to pointing out some of the themes, particularly in Husserl's later writings, which lend support to the existential interpretation of his thought and, in a positive way, attempt to
show how existential phenomenology is a genuine and authentic phenomenology.[3]

We will center the discussion around the meaning which
has been given to the term "transcendental" in recent phenomenology. In the history of Western philosophy we find three
major conceptions of *the transcendental:* that of Greek
philosophy, that of Kantian idealism, and that of phenomenology. Before distinguishing them, we can note that they
share in common a view of philosophy as a search for the
radical, ultimate, foundational structures of experience,
thought and reality. A transcendental philosophy is always a
"metaphysics of experience" in the sense that it means to go
beyond and beneath the ordinary, common-sense, taken-for-
granted evidences of daily life and "natural" thought to the
foundations of these evidences. Such an enterprise involves a
conception of philosophy as an attempt to come to grips with
experience and to *com-prehend* it by disclosing its fundamental structures. The transcendental "categories" recognized
by ancient philosophy were always categories of *objective being,* the transcendent object of experience, as it is in itself
independent of human consciousness. Hence the essentialism
and "objectivism" of Greek thought which nevertheless can be
approached as a rich, yet naive, noematic analysis of experienced *being*—in which *being* is understood not as the exercise
of an activity which the philosopher *is* but as the *object of his
experience.*

This early conception of *the transcendental* as the objective
structure of a transcendent reality was replaced by that of

---

[3] It is necessary to distinguish, of course, the nonphenomenologi-
cal or "ontic" existentialism of writers such as Kierkegaard, Nietzsche, Jaspers, Marcel and Camus from the phenomenological or
"ontological" existentialism represented by the early Heidegger,
Sartre, Merleau-Ponty and their followers. What is characteristic
of the latter group is its concern for transcendental analysis as
defined in this paper.

idealistic philosophy. Descartes reversed the traditional meta-physical standpoint by turning to the radical subjectivity of the thinking subject as the only *accessible* foundation and source of truth. Descartes saw that all "objective evidence" is given *in* and *to* consciousness. The only possible basis for a truly radical philosophy, said Descartes, lay in the *reflexive analysis* of those elements and acts of consciousness in the very exercise of which consciousness coincides with itself. On the basis of the apodictic certitude of the coincidence of self with self in self-consciousness it is possible to build a "scientific," *i.e.* a certain and valid, philosophy.

This project was further developed by Kant when he attempted to transform the objectified, transcendental categories of traditional philosophy into structural elements of human reason and thus establish a *metaphysics of subjectivity*. For Kant *the transcendental* is no longer the *object* of knowledge but the immanent structure of knowledge.[4] *The transcendental* is no longer *transcendent* but *immanent* to consciousness.[5] It is the *a priori* condition of the possibility, not of being, but of the knowledge of being. The object of reflexion is no longer the eternal, necessary, unchanging order of transcendent being, but the transcendental conditions, the foundations, of our experience of transcendent being.

The transcendental categories of Kantian philosophy are not *innate ideas* but structures of judgment; they are not the *content* but the *form* of knowledge, and they represent in a schematic way all the *essential* functions of thought.[6] They are deduced in a rigorous and symmetrical manner from the nature of judgment; for there to be a judging consciousness, says Kant, these categories must necessarily constitute the complete and unified logical structure which is the *a priori* condition of the possibility of such a consciousness. This structure of consciousness is not itself experienced; it is inferred or deduced; it gives us the *rules* of knowledge.[7] Transcendental conscious-

---

[4] Immanuel Kant, *Critique of Pure Reason,* tr. Norman Kemp Smith, London, 1958, p. 299.

[5] *Ibid.,* pp. 118–119.

[6] *Ibid.,* pp. 97–98.

[7] *Ibid.,* p. 100.

ness is not given in direct, lived experience but as the apperception of the necessity of a principle of unification by means
of which the multiple, diverse sensations and feelings of experience are identified as the experience of a unique and identical subject.[8]

Underlying Kant's deduction of the twelve transcendental
categories of understanding is the notion, which he never made
fully explicit, of a consciousness which is *nothing but* an act or
a series of acts of judging. For Kant the *I think* is a fully reflexive, fully awakened judging consciousness; it is an *intellect,*
so to speak, inserted in a sense-world to which it must *by
nature* give a sense or a meaning without ever experiencing
this world *in itself, in person.* For this reason Kant never
seriously considers any kind of experience other than fully
reflexive, fully explicit intellectual judgment. Even when he
goes on to treat of ethical and aesthetic experience, it is always
in terms of the necessary structures of intellectual judgment
that he does so. His only concern is to guarantee the validity
and determine the limits of necessary and universally valid
structures of thought. The subject, for Kant, is not ultimately
an "experiencer" but a pure "thinker."

Finally, Kant accepted, from Hume, a notion of sense-
experience as an intrinsically undifferentiated, chaotic, disor-
dered mass of impressions. In itself it has no meaning, no
structure; all structure comes from *a priori thought.* The transcendental categories which unify experience are *a priori* concepts completely independent of and prior to experience.
Sense-experience, says Kant, is only a blind *indication* or *sign*
(*Anzeige*) of reality, and the ego, conscious of its unity
through the transcendental unity of the categories of understanding, can know nothing about the world as it is in itself.[9]
Though the subject *needs* experience to discover itself as the
source of the *order* and *differentiation* of the experienced

[8] *Ibid.,* pp. 136–137.
[9] See the important and, in my view, sound study by Ludwig
Landgrebe, "La phénoménologie de Husserl est-elle une philosophie transcendentale?" *Les Etudes Philosophiques,* 1954, pp. 315–
323.

world, experience itself does not enter in any way into this differentiating (*i.e.* judging) function of consciousness.

In attempting to define the sense in which Husserl's phenomenology is a transcendental philosophy we cannot avoid Husserl's relation to Descartes and Kant. With Descartes (and against Kant) he is concerned not only with the problem of the validity of knowledge but with the *actual experience* of the thinking subject. Unlike Kant, Husserl poses questions of fact. The "fundamental fact" (*Urtatsache*) is the experienced I-am, the experience of subjectivity which is not only "mine" but "me."[10] Descartes had freed philosophy from its fascination with the external transcendent world and turned it towards an analysis of *experience* of the world. In this Husserl was his disciple. His philosophy is not a philosophy of "the beyond" but of "the beneath"[11] a return to the *foundations,* to the "things themselves" as they are presented to consciousness in immediate intuition. Husserl called his philosophy an *archeology*[12] of human experience, a search for the ultimate, constitutive foundations of experience of the world as the world of human consciousness. However, whereas the method of Descartes is a *reflexive* analysis of the very acts in which the thinking subject coincides with its own being, enclosed within itself, the method of Husserl is a *reflective* analysis directed towards the *transcendental field of pure experience.*

Whereas in Descartes and Kant the subject is enclosed within itself and possesses itself in untroubled, immanent peace and clarity, the subject, for Husserl, *intends* a world. The transcendental field of experience revealed by phenomenological reflection is neither strictly transcendent to the subject (as in Greek philosophy) nor strictly immanent to the subject

[10] *Formale und transzendentale Logik,* no. 95. *Cf.* Herbert Spiegelberg, *The Phenomenological Movement,* Volume I, The Hague, 1960, p. 87.

[11] Husserl contrasted his method with that of Kantianism by stating that his point of departure was "from below" (the concrete phenomena) whereas the starting point of the Kantians was "from above" (abstract forms of thought). *Cf.* Spiegelberg, *op. cit.,* p. 111.

[12] Eugen Fink, "Das Problem der Phänomenologie E. Husserls," *Revue internationale de philosophie,* I, 1938–1939, p. 246.

(as in Cartesianism and Kantianism); it is both immanent and transcendent. In Husserl's terms it consists of those bipolar noetic-noematic structures which are constituted by *experience of*. The subject does not *coincide* with being as in the *cogito-sum* of Descartes; the subject is intentionally directed towards a world which it *is not* but *of which* it is the *lived experience*.

The Phenomenological Conception of the Phenomenon

Husserl's writings reveal two deep-seated and probably incompatible aims: (1) to establish the method of a phenomenology which would escape phenomenalism (and all other philosophical standpoints) and, as he puts it, bring us "to the things themselves," as they are given in immediate experience, and (2) to establish a complete rationalization of experience. These two themes run through his writings and have given rise to the conflicting idealistic and existential interpretations of his thought. Let us take the second one first. Husserl frequently states his will to make philosophy "a completely rational science."[13] In his attempt to reconcile reason and experience he is led in the Kantian direction of attempting to discover the laws which are intrinsic to both. This will be possible to the extent that consciousness is conceived of as the *constitutive* source of its objects and all objectivity is inclosed within the immanent cycle of subjectivity. On this reading of Husserl, which seems fully justified by many passages in his writings, the phenomenon appears as a wholly ideal reality, as an "essence" immanent to consciousness, detached from the real world.[14] The whole project of "phenomenological reduction" can thus be understood as a process of *ideation*, and intentional analysis moves from the noetic act to its noematic correlate—the ideal essence—as it is actualized and constituted within the wholly immanent sphere of subjectivity. It is necessary that both noesis and noema be wholly immanent to subjectivity if we are to speak of the "necessity" and the "univer-

[13] *Logische Untersuchungen, Prolegomena,* chapter 11. *Cf.* J. Q. Lauer, *The Triumph of Subjectivity,* New York, 1958, pp. 120 ff.
[14] *Cf.* Aron Gurwitsch, *Théorie du champ de la conscience,* Paris, 1957, pp. 143 ff.

sal validity" of the essences intuited by the phenomenologist. Phenomenology, in this view, requires a consciousness which can achieve a complete awareness of its own acts and their objects *within* consciousness. Such a consciousness would be an active power, the constitutive source of all meaning, whose necessary laws could be discovered by the analysis of its operations.

But this view runs counter to other passages in which Husserl explains intentional analysis as a progressive "clarification" of the phenomena which must be, in principle, unending. Neither the ego nor the world, he says, is ever known with full rational clarity. To suppose otherwise would be to suppose either that (1) the world could be experienced as a totality from all aspects at once, or (2) that consciousness is independent of and prior to experience, that it can achieve a total, rational clarification by a reflexive turning-in on itself. Both of these suppositions are incompatible with the new sense given to the word "phenomenon" by Husserl. The *phenomena* and *noemata* which it is the task of phenomenology to clarify are not creations of the ego; they are given in direct intuition. They are the "things themselves" *as experienced*. The phenomenon does not cut consciousness off from the world because the phenomenon *is* the world as experienced, from a certain point of view, under a certain aspect.

This is the phenomenological conception of the *phenomenon* which has been elaborated by Sartre and Merleau-Ponty[15] but on the basis of Husserl's own writings on intentionality and intentional analysis. For example, Husserl shows that in the perception of physical objects the aspect (*Abschattung*, perceptual noema) which is immediately and directly presented to consciousness is surrounded by and *given with* a ground of interlocking "horizons" which constitute the "sense" or structure of the perceptual experience. The internal and external horizons of the perceptual noema *are perceived* as implicated in and by the noema itself. It is in this concentration on the structure (or "sense") of *the perceived* (figure-ground;

---

15 *Cf.* Maurice Merleau-Ponty, *Phénoménologie de la perception*, Paris, 1945, "Le Champ Phénoménal," pp. 64 ff.

noema-horizons) that phenomenology escapes phenomenalism from the start. The phenomenon does not block one's contact with the "thing itself." It is *that which* is experienced—the very contact with the "thing itself"—and not an intellectual or conceptual construction. The structure of the phenomenon (noema-horizons) can be analyzed and this is the role of reflection in phenomenology, but its structure is constituted (in a "passive synthesis" says Husserl) prior to any contribution of thought.

The Transcendental Field: the Lebenswelt

The transcendental field of phenomena (experience-of-the-world-as-such) is the noematic field of phenomenological investigations. In the idealistic interpretation of Husserl the phenomenal field is interpreted as the field of pure transcendental subjectivity—the field of the "world-as-meaning" which is effortlessly constituted by an active meaning-giving operation (*Sinngebung*) which is the very definition of "pure consciousness."[16] This transcendental field of consciousness is not "mine" or "yours" or "ours." The problem of intersubjectivity is solved by a "transcendental reduction" thanks to which we reach a pure, anonymous, impersonal consciousness beneath the empirical and historical level of individual experience. This is the realm of transcendental subjectivity which contains within itself the laws of intentional constitution.

But Merleau-Ponty has rightly pointed out that this is not Husserl's final word on the "transcendental field" since he finally recognized the "genetic" or "historical" character of all experience and, secondly, because he recognized intersubjectivity as a problem which was not solved by the "transcendental reduction." In the *Krisis* Husserl wrote that "the transcendental" is the "object of a direct experience of myself and of my conscious life *with the world of which I am conscious*."[17] In his turn to *experience as experience* Husserl found that the two poles, myself and the world, are given

[16] *Ibid.*, pp. v–vi, 61–63.
[17] *Krisis*, nos. 26–27. "Mein Bewusstseinsleben zur Welt deren ich bewusst bin."

correlatively at the outset and are never lost; consciousness is always *consciousness of* something. The "transcendental reduction" and the "transcendental attitude" describe a method of philosophical (attentive, meditative, direct) reflection to put us in the presence of *experience as experience,* independent of any of our "natural" expectations or prejudices.

In his later writings Husserl calls the transcendental field of consciousness the *Lebenswelt* and he defines phenomenology as a *Rückgang auf die Lebenswelt,*[18] a going-back to the prepredicative or prethematic region of experience which is prior to any thought about experience. The *Lebenswelt* is the object of an *immediate experience* (intuition) which is the necessary point of departure of phenomenological research. It is by a return to the experienced *Lebenswelt* as such, he says, that we will overcome the dogmatic positions of *Standpunktsphilosophien,* like empiricism, realism, naturalism, idealism, *etc.,* which are "prejudiced" by an interpretation of experience antecedent to experience itself.[19]

This "return to the things themselves" is possible because of the necessary and apodictic correlativity of consciousness and the world. For Husserl consciousness is a *Welterfahrendesleben,* life-experiencing-the-world, and the sense of this definition includes not only the intentional, world-directed nature of consciousness but also the sense that, thanks to the strict correlativity of subject and object in experience, the subject is constituted as subject only through its active involvement with the world. The ego and the world are given in *any* experience as the constituent subject-object poles of this experience.

On the other hand, phenomenology is clearly not a realism or an empiricism if by that one means that meaning and value are to be found in "things" independently of any reference to human consciousness. It is true to say that phenomenology is not a description of the "real world," but it is a description of the *experience* of the perceived world as the primary reality. If by "real world" one understands the world *minus* subjectivity or the world as a totality independent of

18 *Cf.* note 26 below.
19 *Ideen I,* no. 26, Gibson tr. pp. 95–96.

and prior to any relationship to consciousness, it would be
nonsensical to speak of a phenomenological elucidation of the
"real world." On the other hand consciousness does not create
the world since it is *experience of* the world. What consciousness adds to the "real world" is a relationship to itself, and it
is in terms of the directional, intentional structure of consciousness that we can speak of the *a priority* of consciousness:
it is the subject which experiences the world and not vice versa.
The world has no meaning *in itself* because meaning always
involves consciousness. But the constitutive intentionality of
consciousness should not be understood as the creation of
meaning and value *ex nihilo,* or out of itself alone, or, much
less, the creation of the world as such. Consciousness is constitutive of the world in the sense that it objectifies the world,
differentiates and "constitutes" objects within the world, and
that it is in and through this essential objectifying activity of
consciousness that it experiences itself as *subject.*

Thus, for Husserl, the world as the noematic correlate of
experience is as apodictically certain as the ego; those who
place all apodicticity on the side of the *cogito* have a non-
Husserlian, *i.e.* a nonintentional, notion of consciousness.[20]
But to say that the ego and the world are apodictically certain
and always given together, with the same evidence, in expe-

[20] *Cf.* Ludwig Landgrebe, *loc. cit.,* p. 322. Aron Gurwitsch, *op.
cit.,* pp. 182–185, and pp. 232 ff., argues on the basis of "principles
established by Husserl" that we have only "presumptive evidence"
of the existence of "real things" and of the "perceptual world" in
general. Gurwitsch adopts this position because of a generalization
of Husserl's theory of signification in which the "perceptual noema"
holds the same relationship to the signifying acts of consciousness
as, for instance, the spoken word to its meaning. It is not in any
sense, says Gurwitsch, a constituent of its own meaning. This notion
of the "perceptual noema" appears to me unfaithful to Husserl's
most profound intentions and it erases the essential distinction between "evident" (*Selbstgebung*) consciousness and nonevident consciousness, between presentive (intuitive) acts of consciousness and
nonevident (symbolic) acts. If followed consistently, this interpretation of Husserl would nullify the specifically phenomenological
notion of intentionality as well as the new phenomenological notion of the "phenomenon" as the perceived thing *itself* under one of
its aspects. Gurwitsch's notion of the perceptual noema as a completely idealized phenomenon is more Kantian than Husserlian.

rience, is not to say that either is ever known adequately or completely. In the words of Merleau-Ponty: we can have absolute certitude of the world in general but only relative certitude about any particular thing in the world.[21] The world, in short, is given in *any* experience as the ultimate horizon or ground of experience, as the ultimate meaning-structure in which any given phenomenon is inserted and in which it is understood.

The Primacy of Perception

One of Husserl's major contributions to philosophy is his "pure logic of significations," and the study of the purely formal structures of consciousness, what he called "formal ontology." It was in this search for the structures of pure thought that Husserl's philosophy most closely resembled Kantianism. However, this must not blind us to the absolutely fundamental differences between Husserl and Kant. There is no "transcendental deduction" of categories or forms of judgment in Husserl. He is more concerned with "material" logic than with "formal" logic. The eidetic structures of even purely formal thought are not acquired by deduction but by a method of "free variation" based on *what is given*.[22] Secondly, even those purely formal structures of thought are the objects of experience; the experienced world (*Lebenswelt*) contains "ideal entities" which can be the objects of *categorial intuition*.[23]

Let us try to be clear. Men do not live only in the "real" world of perception but also in the worlds of imagination, of artistic creation, of social institutions, and in the ideal worlds of mathematics and purely formal thought.[24] But it is the

21 Maurice Merleau-Ponty, *op. cit.,* p. 344.
22 *Cf.* Ludwig Landgrebe, *loc. cit.,* p. 322.
23 *Formale und transzendentale Logik,* no. 11.
24 For Husserl the "real" world of perceptual experience is the domain of "passive" or prereflexive syntheses; the other domains of experience are founded on this one and they involve "active" as well as "passive" syntheses. Aron Gurwitsch in his article on "La conception de la conscience chez Kant et chez Husserl," *Bulletin de la Société française de philosophie,* 1960, pp. 65–96, has shown

constant doctrine of Husserl that all imaginative and categorial intuitions (and all "higher-order" intuitions) are *founded on* perceptual intuitions. This is what Merleau-Ponty calls the *primacy of perception* in phenomenology.[25] Here we touch on the sense in which phenomenology is an "empiricism" of a new kind even when it is still called a "logic of experience" or a "rational science." Perceptual intuition does not give us the "confused ideas" of Descartes; it is not the blind *Anzeige* of Kant. Perception is, rather, the area of "transcendental" experience and ultimately all structures of consciousness are founded on the primary perceptual contact of consciousness with the world.[26]

As we descend from the categorial or "predicative" structures of fully conscious thought to their experiential foundations, we discover, says Husserl, the underlying substructures of "prepredicative" experience. This is the area of what he calls "passive syntheses" or the "hidden achievements" of intentional consciousness. This is the foundational, prereflexive field of pure experience in which the world is constituted as a world *for consciousness*. The primary task of phenomenology is to return to this world as the matrix of all the derived constructions of thought. Experience precedes any thought about

how radically Husserl's theory of consciousness differs from Kant's and the importance of his notion of passive syntheses.

[25] Maurice Merleau-Ponty, "Le primat de la perception et ses conséquences philosophiques," *Bulletin de la société française de philosophie*, 1947, pp. 119–153. In the *Phénoménologie de la perception* he even speaks of a "phenomenological positivism," p. xii.

[26] *Logische Untersuchungen*, 6th Investigation, chapters 5 and 6. Cf. *Erfahrung und Urteil*, no. 10: "Auf die Evidenzen der Erfahrung sollen sich letzlich alle prädikativen Evidenzen gründen. Die Aufgabe der Ursprungsklärung des prädikativen Urteils, dieses Fundierungsverhältnis nachzuweisen und das Entspringen der vorprädikativen Evidenzen aus denen der Erfahrung zu verfolgen, erweist sich nach der nunmehrigen Aufklärung des Wesens der Erfahrung als Aufgabe des *Rückgangs auf die Welt*, wie sie als universaler Boden aller einzelnen Erfahrungen, *als Welt der Erfahrung vorgegeben ist, unmittelbar und vor allen logischen Leistungen*. Der Rückgang auf die Welt der Erfahrung is Rückgang auf die 'Lebenswelt,' d. i. die Welt, in der wir immer schon leben, und die den Boden für alle Erkenntnisleistung abgibt und für alle wissenschaftliche Bestimmung." Italics mine.

experience. When we begin to reflect on experience and "attend to" it, we discover that consciousness has already been at work ahead of us. We discover an intersubjectively constituted world of meaning and value to whose constitution we have already contributed without *knowing* it. We discover ourselves as fatally immersed in a world which is already ours. At this point the work of phenomenology truly becomes an archaeology of consciousness: a digging-down-to and an uncovering of the prepredicative and preconscious structures of experience which are the "essences" of experience. Such structures are the *transcendentals* of phenomenology in the most radical sense. They are the primary structures of *experience as experience*. They possess an "eidetic" necessity and a transcendental validity of a special kind: not as closed, fixed, innate ideas (since an intentional consciousness cannot be a "container of forms"), but as open, historical, asymptotic meaning-structures of lived human existence. They are neither categories of objects (as in Greek philosophy) nor categories of the subject (as in Kantianism) but categories of bipolar, noetic-noematic experience itself. Through the disclosure of the perceived world as the transcendental field of phenomenology in the primary sense of the term, we discover the new meaning given to *the transcendental* in phenomenology. The transcendental structures of phenomenology are rooted in perceptual experience, and because this experience is essentially temporal or historical they can have only a provisional validity. They are not the structures of a "pure" consciousness but of an intentional existence. They can be defined as the "meanings" of experience in the most fundamental sense of the word: the structures which constitute the world as the world of human consciousness. These structures clearly do not have the "formal" necessity of formal logic or geometry but rather the "objective" or "material" necessity inherent in the objects of *transcendental logic* (in Husserl's sense). They have the "essential" or "eidetic" necessity of experienced meaning-structures which cannot be experienced otherwise than according to their "essence."

The want of time prohibits us from giving detailed examples of transcendental structures in the sense in which we have attempted to define them.[27] Suffice it to say that phenomenology recognizes no such thing as an absolutely chaotic mass of primary sensations or "impressions" which, as in Kant for instance, have to be organized and structured according to the *a priori* categories of reason. Experience of the world is always structured, *i.e.* meaningful, experience. Its structures are autochthonous to experience itself and as such are neither wholly objective nor wholly subjective. Nor are they ever wholly fixed. Moreover, these structures are all interrelated and the analysis of any one necessarily leads to others with which it is related by a mutual implication. The ultimate horizon of this interlocking system of structures is the historical *Lebenswelt*—the transcendental field of all experience.

Conclusion

If we were now to assess the contribution of existential phenomenology to the original perspectives of Husserl in this view of the nature and goal of phenomenology, we would find two developments of exceptional importance—both of which nevertheless appear to be entirely faithful to Husserl's most profound intentions. First of all, Heidegger showed that phenomenology could not limit itself to an investigation of "pure" consciousness but must necessarily involve an analysis of human existence as a unitary whole. With Heidegger any tendency to consider transcendental subjectivity as a disembodied "thinker" is definitively overcome; man as presence-to-the-world is the only possible point of departure for phenomenological analysis. This discovery marks the continuity between the transcendental analysis of Husserl and the existential-analytics of later existential phenomenology. The second point concerns the extremely important phenomenolog-

[27] By way of example and to indicate what we have in mind: Heidegger's *Dasein*-analytics, Sartre's discussions of being-and-doing, being-and-having, doing-and-having, Merleau-Ponty's analyses of spatiality, sexuality, temporality in their perceptual grounding, Gurwitsch's analysis of the structure of the phenomenal field, Schutz's analyses of the "typifications" of life-world experience, all furnish sound and well-developed analyses of what we are here calling transcendental structures of experience.

ical distinction between (1) operating intentionality or "perceptual consciousness" and (2) the intentionality of "intellectual" or fully reflexive consciousness, which has been emphasized by Sartre and Merleau-Ponty.[28] This distinction was explicitly made by Husserl himself, as we have seen, but it was left to the French phenomenologists to draw out the fuller phenomenological consequences of this distinction. This is not a distinction between two distinct intentionalities or consciousnesses, but the distinction between two moments of the same intentional consciousness. Fully reflexive consciousness, the realm of the "idea" and of the constructions of thought, flows from a reflection on the prereflexive understanding (*verstehen*) of the meaning-structures of lived experience. It is the realm of prepredicative experience which is the primary field of phenomenology, and phenomenology itself is possible because this original field of experience (*Lebenswelt*) is already "pregnant with meaning." Its meaning-structures can be brought to the level of thematic awareness by a "radical" phenomenological reflection[29]—of which they are the source and the guarantee.

It is by further developing these briefly sketched directions of phenomenology that it will become clear to what extent an existential and "ontological" interpretation of phenomenology is justified.

28 *Cf.* Merleau-Ponty, "Le primat de la perception . . ." *loc. cit.*, pp. 123, 127, ff.

29 The term "radical reflection" is usual in Merleau-Ponty; Sartre prefers to speak of "existential psychoanalysis" in his own specific sense; Heidegger speaks in his early (phenomenological) works of *Dasein*-analytics or ontological analysis. What is important is that the projects designated by these terms share in common a fundamental phenomenological intention of disclosing and thematizing those foundational noetic-noematic structures which are given in experience as the constitutive conditions of the possibility of experience as such.

Husserl's Phenomenology
and Sartre's Existentialism

HERBERT SPIEGELBERG

There is good reason for believing that Husserl's fame in the Anglo-American world shines today largely with a reflected light. Its source is the more fashionable interest in the offspring of the strange alliance between Kierkegaard's "unscientific" existential thinking and Husserl's new phenomenological science that goes by the name of existentialism. In very much the same way as happened in France in the thirties, when Heidegger was the center of interest, it is now Sartre's glamor that has aroused a retroactive interest in Husserl as his supposed teacher. This circumstance suggests the need for a fresh examination of the entire relationship between Husserl's phenomenology and today's existentialism.[1]

I propose to broach the subject by first bringing out some facts, not always duly noticed, about the historical connections between the two movements. Then I shall discuss in a more systematic frame the essential relations between them.

But this program presupposes at least some preliminary agreements about the Protean terms "phenomenology" and "existentialism." To make them sufficiently precise will require cutting off some marginal types. In this context there will be

[1] This paper was read in a Symposium on Phenomenology and Existentialism arranged by the Western Division of the American Philosophical Association for its Annual Meeting at the University of Wisconsin in Madison on April 30, 1959. Two papers on the same subject by William Earle (Northwestern University) and Maurice Natanson (University of North Carolina) followed it. It is reprinted here from Herbert Spiegelberg, "Husserl's Phenomenology and Existentialism," *The Journal of Philosophy*, 57 (1960), pp. 62–74, by permission of the author and the editors. The opening paragraphs of the article have been revised by the author expressly for this edition.

no time to justify the eliminations. So I shall have to be rather dogmatic, keeping my reasons in reserve.

In the case of phenomenology it would be improper to advocate here a wider conception which would include more than Husserl's version of it, as I have tried to do elsewhere.[2] Not only out of respect for Husserl, but for the purpose of sharpening the issue, it seems fitting to consider here phenomenology in its most rigorous form. To be sure, even then one has to take account of the development of Husserl's conception from a merely descriptive phenomenology to transcendental phenomenology. Yet for the sake of the present confrontation it seems defensible to condense the most important constants of his phenomenology in the following minimum list of propositions:

1. Phenomenology is a rigorous science in the sense of a coherent system of propositions; it goes even beyond positive science by aiming at absolute certainty for its foundations and at freedom from presuppositions that have not passed phenomenological scrutiny.

2. Its subject-matter is the general essences of the phenomena of consciousness; among these phenomena, the phenomenologist distinguishes between the intending acts and the intended objects in strict parallel; he pays special attention to the modes of appearance in which the intended referents present themselves; he does not impose any limitations as to the content of these phenomena.

3. Phenomenology is based on the intuitive exploration and faithful description of the phenomena within the context of the world of our lived experience (Lebenswelt), anxious to avoid reductionist oversimplifications and overcomplications by preconceived theoretical patterns.

4. In order to secure the fullest possible range of phenomena and at the same time doubt-proof foundations it uses a special method of reductions which suspends the beliefs associated with our naive or natural attitude and shared even by science;

2 The Phenomenological Movement: A Historical Introduction (Phaenomenologica 6) (The Hague: Martinus Nijhoff, 1960).

it also traces back the phenomena to the constituting acts in a pure subject, which itself proves to be irreducible.

5. Its ultimate objective is the examination and justification of all our beliefs, both ordinary and scientific, by the test of intuitive perception.

To perform the same kind of surgery on the much more amorphous body of beliefs and attitudes that sail under the flag of existentialism may appear as an even more foolhardy enterprise. In attempting it one does well to remember that self-confessed existentialism does not date earlier than 1944 when Sartre, having already published his major philosophical works, took the word "existentialism" out of the hands of his hostile critics and applied it retroactively to his own writings and to those of his predecessors. Any attempt to define such a sprawling phenomenon has to make incisions which may seem arbitrary. I submit, however, that there is something like a hard core of present-day existentialism based on affinities in interest and approach. It includes not only the self-confessed phenomenological existentialists such as Sartre and Merleau-Ponty but also Gabriel Marcel, however repentant as to the term "Christian existentialism," and such unrepentant existentialists as Nicolai Berdyaev or Nicolò Abbagnano. Besides, according to their major concerns and themes, Jaspers' deliberately non-phenomenological elucidation of existence and Heidegger's phenomenological analytics of existence are inseparable from full-fledged existentialism, their vigorous protests notwithstanding. Even if their own objectives were different and ulterior, the existentialism of the forties would never have been possible without them.

Sartre has attempted to condense the cloudy essence of these existentialisms into the neat though mystifying formula that in existentialism "existence precedes essence." But this formula has been repudiated, with good reasons, by everyone but himself. For the present purposes it may be more helpful to match the preceding propositions about phenomenology by a similar set that is meant to apply to hard-core existentialism only:

1. Existentialism, unlike phenomenology, does not aspire to be scientific, though it is not essentially anti-scientific or even anti-systematic. Systematic structures and absolute certainty are simply none of its primary objectives.

2. Its subject-matter is human existence or "human reality," not consciousness, as in phenomenology. It studies existence in its involvement in a situation within a world. Consciousness, however, reflective as well as pre-reflective, is part of the encompassing structure of existence.

3. Existentialism is not restricted to any particular method; Kierkegaard's existential dialectics and Jaspers' elucidation of existence have historical priority over phenomenological existentialism.

4. Phenomenological existentialism goes beyond the phenomenological description of certain highly selective phenomena by a special kind of interpretation, the so-called hermeneutic method, which aspires to decipher their meaning for existence. Phenomenological reduction as practiced by Husserl, if it is mentioned at all, is rejected; so is Husserl's concern for transcendental subjectivity as the absolute foundation of all being.

5. The ultimate objective of existentialism is not theoretical justification, but the awakening to a special way of life, usually called "authentic existence."

We are now in a position to approach the question of the historical relations between the two movements. Husserl himself during his lifetime faced only the predecessors of self-confessed existentialism: Karl Jaspers' *Existenzphilosophie* and Martin Heidegger's existential analysis of human *Dasein*. Jaspers, although he had used phenomenological description in his psychopathology, had rejected phenomenology at the very outset of his independent philosophizing because of its claim to scientific rigor. Heidegger, however, publishing his magnum opus *Sein und Zeit* in Husserl's *Yearbook for Philosophy and Phenomenological Research*, gave every indication of adhering to the phenomenological method, although he claimed at the same time the right to develop it further and, implicitly at least, to omit some of it. One example of such a tacit omission was that of Husserl's cherished phenomenological reduction.

Three years later Husserl's only printed pronouncement about *Existenzphilosophie* appeared, notably in a Postscript to his *Ideen,* at the very end of the last volume of his Yearbook. It came two years after Heidegger had been appointed the successor to his chair at the University of Freiburg, an appointment which, as a matter of fact, had resulted from Husserl's own recommendation. Although this pronouncement did not mention either Jaspers or Heidegger by name, it left no doubt about the identity of the addressees. This statement rejected summarily the actual or suspected charges against Husserl's own philosophizing. It also declared *Existenzphilosophie* a relapse into the deadly sins of anthropologism and psychologism, hence not acceptable even as a specimen of genuine philosophy. Other expressions, such as lectures, letters, and especially marginal comments to his readings in Heidegger, leave no doubt about the fact that Husserl saw especially in the latter's analytics of existence a corruption of the phenomenological enterprise. These indictments led soon to a cooling off and a final ceasing of the once cordial relations between Husserl and his erstwhile assistant. From then on Heidegger practically stopped using the term "phenomenology" in his own philosophizing. As a result, phenomenology and the philosophy of existence remained two completely separate movements, as far as Germany was concerned.

It would, however, be premature to infer from this that Husserl had no appreciation for the questions raised by the philosophers of existence. Even the Postscript to the *Ideen,* while rejecting the charges that phenomenology was unable to cope with the problems of "so-called 'existence,'" implied that such problems do exist. What Husserl objected to was merely the claim to priority of the existential analytics over his own transcendental phenomenology, which Heidegger had implied. It is therefore not surprising to find Husserl himself in his last decade repeatedly resorting to existential phraseology.[3] How far the conception of the *Lebenswelt* (the world of our immediate life experience), which plays such an important part in Husserl's last work, can be traced to indirect stimulation by Heidegger's conception of *Dasein* as being-in-the-world need not be decided here. Hence there is no reason to deny the possibility of an existential philosophy within the framework of Husserl's phenomenology. There are even indications that Husserl himself conceived of his transcendental phenomenology as a distinctive existential possibility, and that in particular the transcendental reduction included for him a liberating conversion of human existence.

By contrast the French philosophers never seem to have questioned the identity of phenomenology and existentialism. One even wonders whether, when in the early thirties Sartre took up the study of phenomenology and existential philosophy, he was at all aware of the seriousness of the break between Husserl and Heidegger. Part of the explanation for this oversight may be in the fact that Heidegger impressed the young Frenchmen interested in German philosophy much more than Husserl, and that in his writings Heidegger, ostensibly Husserl's appointed heir, gave no clear indication of serious friction between him and the master.

However, mere factual statements about the historical connection between phenomenology and existentialism, pertinent

[3] Thus his last publication, the introduction to transcendental phenomenology entitled *The Crisis of the European Sciences and Transcendental Phenomenology*, speaks of the crisis of European *"Existenz"* which has arisen from the loss of meaning brought on by modern positivistic science, of the "existential conflict" (*existenzieller Widerspruch*) which this entails for the contemporary philosopher committed to the cause of scientific rigor, and of the responsibility of philosophers, as agents of humanity, which determines their "existential being" (*Husserliana*, Vol. VI, pp. 10, 15, ff.). Also, in the Vienna lecture of 1935 Husserl had hinted that the new radical "rationalism" of his transcendental phenomenology would have room even for the question of "so-called existence" (*Ibid.*, p. 346). How deeply, if not "existentially," Husserl himself was involved in his philosophic enterprise can be seen from some of his private diary notes ("Persönliche Aufzeichnungen," published by Walter Biemel in *Philosophy and Phenomenological Research*, Vol. XVI (1956), pp. 293 ff.).

though they may be, cannot resolve the problem of their essential relation. What is required is a systematic consideration of the following questions:

1. Are the two movements compatible?
2. If compatible, are they necessarily connected?
3. If not necessarily connected, have they at least an affinity?
4. Can today's phenomenological existentialism be considered sound phenomenology?

1. With regard to the first question I maintain: Phenomenology and existentialism are compatible in principle. The opposite view may be argued on grounds like the following:

a. Phenomenology is outspokenly rationalistic; existential philosophy is opposed to all forms of rationalism. Now it is true that Husserl's phenomenology professes rationalism in the sense of a concerted effort to justify all human claims by rational evidence, although he opposes the uncritical rationalism of pure a priori metaphysics. But this does not mean that phenomenology rejects insights based on non-theoretical, notably on emotive experience. On the other hand, it is a fateful error to identify existentialism with the advocacy of "irrational man." Existentialism stresses, indeed, the practical part of human nature as expressed in choice and commitment. But "thought," though not logical thought in the technical sense, is an essential feature of Heidegger's philosophizing, and Sartre stresses the Cartesian cogito to the extent of seeing in the emotions primarily magic attempts to evade our situation, instead of facing it rationally.

b. It is also argued that phenomenology "brackets" all questions of existence, hence that it is essentially a philosophy of detachment in contrast to existentialism's philosophy of commitment (engagement). But it is a misunderstanding of the phenomenological reduction to think that bracketing our beliefs in the existence of the phenomena eliminates the phenomenon of human existence. This misunderstanding is based on an unfortunate equivocation in the meaning of the word "existence." For the existence-character in the phenomena which we bracket is something quite different from Existenz or *Dasein* as the structure of being-in-the-world, which is found only in human beings. As far as the latter is concerned, bracketing may well affect the belief in the reality of the world and even of the human being who is in such a world. But even this does not mean that being-in-the-world and its believed reality is totally ignored. It may be described *qua* phenomenon like any other reduced phenomenon. One may consider Husserl's treatment of this phenomenon inadequate. It may also be true that the phenomenologist's detachment implies a temporary retreat from the involvement and active participation in concrete existence. But this does not mean total neglect of the phenomena of existence. Nor must it be overlooked that the immanent residuum of consciousness which survives the ordeal of the phenomenological reduction has the character of absolute existence—an existence that can certainly rival in poignancy the existence which the existentialists attribute to the human being incarnated in the world.

c. Finally, it is alleged that phenomenology deals with universal essences, whereas existentialism is concerned with the concrete single individual. However, even though it is correct that Husserl's phenomenology is restricted to universal essences, it is an oversimplification to say that existentialism deals only with concrete individuals. Even existentialism describes its findings in universal terms and claims that its universal statements are valid for more than one single individual. Heidegger's much quoted pronouncement that "the essence of *Dasein* is existence" grants to human existence an essence. How else could this statement about an essence be substantiated except by an essential insight, a *Wesenseinsicht* in the phenomenological sense?

2. If then phenomenology and existentialism are compatible, are they dependent upon each other? My answer to this question is an unqualified "no."

That existentialism does not depend on phenomenology can be shown by the obvious examples of Kierkegaard and Jaspers. Quite apart from Jaspers' own disclaimers, the methods which they applied differ basically from those used by Husserl and even by Heidegger.

That phenomenology in turn does not depend on existentialism seems equally obvious. Yet it has been held that phenomenology entails existentialism as an essential, if not a necessary, consequence. At least implicitly this is asserted by Gilbert Varet,[4] and he is followed in this point by Wilfrid Desan in his Harvard dissertation.[5] To be sure, these assertions are based on grave misconceptions of German phenomenology. It is therefore more serious that so keen an expert as Alphonse de Waelhens tries to show an essential trend from Husserl's phenomenology to existentialism.[6] De Waelhens bases his case on the fact that the emphasis in phenomenology on the importance of perspectives necessitated a consideration of the concrete existences that occupy these perspectives. But this does not seem to me compelling. Thus in the analogous case of Einstein's theory of relativity the need of considering the standpoint of the observer did not necessitate a study of the observer's personality. And even a consideration of the concrete existence of the subject at the source of a perspective does not justify the abandonment of the phenomenological attitude of suspension of belief. I can therefore see no valid reason for asserting a logical necessity in the historical procession from Husserlian phenomenology to Heideggerian or Sartrian existentialism.

This denial has important consequences. It cuts the ground from under Varet's and Desan's case against phenomenology based on the failure of existentialism in Sartre's supposed tragic finale. Since Sartre's existentialism is not the necessary consequent of phenomenology, denying the consequent does not affect the right of the antecedent, phenomenology.

Besides, it must not be overlooked that Husserl's phenomenology has inspired a considerable number of phenomenological enterprises other than existentialism. Specifically I have in mind the so-called Older Phenomenological Movement, as represented by such researchers as Alexander Pfänder, Moritz Geiger, or Roman Ingarden. The descriptive investigation of

[4] *L'Ontologie de Sartre,* Paris, 1947.
[5] *The Tragic Finale,* Cambridge, 1954.
[6] "Les constants de l'existentialisme," *Revue internationale de philosophie,* Vol. 9 (1949), pp. 255–269.

psychological, logical, ethical, esthetic, and religious phenomena constitutes at least equally legitimate expressions of original phenomenology. And there seems to be good reason to assert that what has been achieved in these areas does not reflect too unfavorably on Husserl's initiating enterprise.

3. While phenomenology and existentialism are essentially independent enterprises, have they at least enough affinity for fruitful coöperation? This question I shall answer affirmatively.

This answer hardly needs much substantiation. While phenomenology as such has no preference for the phenomena of human existence, it stands to gain in significance by turning its powers to a field of such vital interest. On the other hand, the pre-phenomenological insights of existentialism by means of Kierkegaard's dialectics and Jaspers' non-objectifying elucidation of existence have been provocative, but highly elusive. Once existentialism comes to grips with the epistemological problem, which it will not be able to shrug off indefinitely, it has little hope of support from the more empirical and positivist philosophies or psychologies. Its best chance is an approach which stresses and develops the faithful description of the phenomena as they present themselves, regardless of whether they fit into the framework of our more traditional methodologies. Besides, if for the existentialist, as Kierkegaard puts it, "subjectivity is the truth," a phenomenology aimed at finding the source of all consciousness in subjectivity is at least a congenial approach. Yet, before existentialism can expect substantial benefit from invoking the aid of phenomenology, it will have to accept it in its own right and undergo its discipline, instead of trying to convert it into its handmaiden.

4. How far, then, can today's existentialism be considered phenomenologically sound? Here, I am afraid, I have to make grave reservations.

Phenomenology has never been foolproof. But some of the fooling that has invoked its name need not be laid at its doorsteps. I do not want to deny that the phenomenological existentialists have made suggestive and at times even striking contributions to the fund of phenomenological insights. But most of these have to be gone over more cautiously and more critically. Thus, I submit that such brilliant pieces as Sartre's phenomenology of the social gaze are vitiated by a selective emphasis on isolated aspects of a more comprehensive phenomenon, by inadequate description, and by a hasty interpretation which ignores alternative meanings that would have deserved consideration.

However, instead of taking such sweeping exceptions I would like to present a concrete example from the very beginning of Sartre's phenomenological career which can at the same time demonstrate Husserl's still unsurpassed descriptive powers. I have in mind his discussion of the ego or the "I."

There is something strange about the relative lack of interest in the "ego" in a philosophy which professes its prime concern in personal existence. This is true particularly of Heidegger's analysis of *Dasein*. Sartre, a vigorous advocate of Husserl's descriptive phenomenology, went even farther. In his first major article, "The Transcendence of the Ego,"[7] published in 1936, he launched a frontal attack on Husserl's doctrine of the pure ego. In so doing he tried to show that this ego was not, as Husserl had maintained, the immanent source of all consciousness, but its transcendent and constituted object.

This is not the place to discuss the considerable merits and the weaknesses of Sartre's first "sketch of a phenomenological description" and its ulterior objectives. I shall focus merely on the reasoning which made Sartre repudiate one of Husserl's central tenets. For it throws light on Sartre's entire approach to phenomenology.

Sartre's primary objection to Husserl's pure ego is its superfluousness for the description of consciousness. Should such an argument carry any weight in matters of phenomenological description? It smacks more of Occam's razor, which may

---

[7] "La transcendance de l'égo, Esquisse d'une description phénoménologique," *Recherches philosophiques,* Vol. VI (1936), pp. 85–123. English translation, with the misleading subtitle "An Existentialist Theory of Consciousness," by Forrest Williams and Robert Kirkpatrick (New York, Noonday Press, 1957).

have its place in keeping down the number of explanatory hypotheses, but certainly not in describing the phenomena.

Phenomenologically more significant is Sartre's attempt to show that the "I" is not part of our ordinary unreflective consciousness: thus, to him, we are not aware of the "I" in reading a book or listening to a paper, but only when we reflect upon our reading or listening. Whence he infers that it is reflective consciousness which constitutes the "I" or "me" as transcendent to the immanent stream of consciousness.

Is this sound phenomenology? In what sense may reflection be said to constitute the object on which it reflects? This raises, of course, the whole question of the meaning of constitution in Husserl's phenomenology. But there is certainly no good reason for assuming *a priori* that reflection brings its object into being rather than that it merely uncovers or discovers it. In fact, when it comes to other acts of consciousness, including Sartre's original pre-reflective consciousness, Sartre himself seems to think that reflection simply illumines, but does not bring into being a consciousness which has been there all the time in pre-reflective twilight, as it were. What is more, there seems to be very good evidence for thinking that the "constitution" of the ego in reflection consists simply in its emergence from the background of consciousness rather than in its formation on its outskirts. What is constituted is its phenomenal character, not its being.

I conclude that Sartre's critique of Husserl's conception of the ego is anything but convincing, and particularly that its phenomenological basis is inadequate.[8]

How, then, does Sartre's pseudo-phenomenology of the ego compare with Husserl's research on the subject? Sartre was well aware of the fact that Husserl's views on the ego had changed between the first edition of his *Logische Unter-*

[8] It seems worth mentioning that in *L'Être et le néant* (Part III, Chapter I, iii, pp. 290 f.) Sartre modified his position, not to be sure as far as the "transcendence of the ego" is concerned, since he continues to consider Husserl's ego as a useless and nefarious (*néfaste*) hypothesis. But he no longer asserts that the stream of consciousness is impersonal. Instead he ascribes to it the character of "ipseity," without however making it sufficiently clear what this quality involves.

suchungen of 1901 and the *Ideen* of 1913. But he took it for granted that this change was a change for the worse and meant nothing but Husserl's return to the transcendental ego of Kant or rather the Neokantians. What Sartre and other critics of Husserl's shift seem to discount is the fact that when, in a foot-note to the second edition of his *Logische Untersuchungen*, he frankly admitted this reversal, he stated: "Since then (i.e., my earlier failure to discover the ego) I have learned to find it, or more precisely, I have learned not to be diverted from the pure grasp of the given by the excesses of the metaphysics of the ego"[9]; and in his *Ideen* he declared that he had found his earlier scepticism with regard to the ego untenable.[10] I suggest that Husserl's explanation of the reasons for his shift should be taken seriously. There must have been phenomeno-logical evidence behind his seeming about-face. In fact, some of this evidence has become available through the recent publication of Volume II of the *Ideen*, edited by Marly Biemel.[11] For it contains the chapter on the pure ego which Husserl had promised in the first volume. It deserves the closest attention of those who think they can dispose of the pure ego as a remnant from the pre-phenomenological past. Specifically, Husserl's phenomenology of the ego makes the following points:

1. It is of the essence of the pure ego that it can be seized firsthand (*originäre Selbsterfassung*) by what Husserl calls self-perception (*Selbstwahrnehmung*) (§23). It is neither ca-pable nor in need of a special constitution (§26). It forms an immanent phenomenon which does not present itself by differ-ent perspectives (*Abschattungen*).

2. This original perception of the self is subject to reflective modifications, for instance by recall. In these reflective modi-fications the identity of the persistent ego is given with self-

[9] *Logische Untersuchungen*, 2nd edition (Halle, Max Niemeyer, 1913), Vol. II, 1, p. 361.
[10] *Ideen I* (Halle, Max Niemeyer, 1913), §57 footnote. English translation by W. R. Boyce Gibson, p. 173.
[11] *Husserliana*, Vol. IV (1952), Zweiter Abschnitt, Erstes Kapi-tel: Das reine Ich.

evidence. Only its modes of appearance differ. Reflective modifications presuppose original perception to which they refer back in their very structure.

Nevertheless, Husserl denies that this intuitively self-given ego has any similarity with a Cartesian substance, much as he subscribes to the indubitableness of Descartes' "ego cogito." To him, the ego cannot occur in abstraction from his acts, just as little as the acts can be given in abstraction from the ego. Both are dependent on each other. But this does not affect their distinct existence.

The chapter on the pure ego makes other important points. Thus, it distinguishes between the pure ego as the focus of all our experiences and the empirical or "real" human ego with its factual properties, its character, its aptitudes, etc. Like Sartre, Husserl treats the latter ego as a "transcendent object" constituted by the transcendental consciousness with its focal ego.

All this does not mean that Husserl's phenomenology of the ego had reached its final form. Husserl saw well enough that, since the pure ego lives in immanent time, it is affected by the problems of constitution which are posed by the consciousness of inner time. Moreover, it cannot and must not be overlooked that, during Husserl's last period, in which he collaborated closely with Eugen Fink, his doctrine of the ego proliferated into a bewildering multiplicity of at least three egos.[12] This proliferation may well have been the cause for the increasing scepticism even among Husserl's close followers, and finally for Sartre's drastic cure. But this scepticism sacrificed the legitimate core along with the questionable outer shells.

This is not the place to pursue further the problems of Husserl's phenomenology of the ego. I introduced it merely as an instance of a case where Husserl's patient search may be shown to be more penetrating than, and still unsurpassed by, the more spectacular assertions of the existentialists who supposedly use his method. Besides, I do not mean to suggest

---

[12] Eugen Fink, "Die phänomenologische Philosophie Edmund Husserl's in der gegenwärtigen Kritik," *Kantstudien,* Vol. 38 (1933), 381 ff.

that Husserl's claims concerning the direct perception of the ego and concerning the reflective modifications of this act are to be taken at face value. Nor should it be overlooked that Husserl withheld the volume of the *Ideen* with the chapter on the pure ego during his lifetime. All his findings will have to be examined, re-examined, and developed. But in the meantime it remains a remarkable fact that Husserl, after his initial scepticism, came out with such definitive and positive suggestions for a phenomenology of the ego. Moreover, I submit that Husserl's defense of the ego as the center of our conscious existence may be closer to the original existential conception of Kierkegaard, with his insistence on inwardness and subjectivity as the truth, than Sartre's denial of the pure ego and his ejection of the empirical ego into the outside transcendent world. Sartre's attack on the pure ego, which he replaces by a stream of impersonal consciousness, actually volatilizes existence. By denying it a center and the dimension of inwardness he deprives it at the same time of its existential weight.

Existentialism may be on the trail of more vital, more fruitful insights than pure phenomenology. But it has still to learn a few lessons from the older phenomenology, particularly from Husserl. One of these is the injunction which I heard him address to an informal group of students when he criticized Max Scheler's much more rapid but not equally solid production: "One needs bright ideas, but one must not publish them." Another lesson is his insistence on the need of making sure of the epistemological groundwork: "One must not consider oneself too good to work on the foundations." It is such lessons, lessons of philosophical solidity, integrity, and humility, which both phenomenologists and existentialists still have to learn or to relearn.

II. MARTIN HEIDEGGER

Introduction

1. Biographical Note

Martin Heidegger, born in Messkirch (Baden) on September 26, 1889, was the eldest son of Friedrich Heidegger and Johanna Kempf. His father was the sexton of St. Martin's church in Messkirch. By the age of twelve Heidegger had finished his elementary education and gone to the Gymnasium at Constance. Subsequently he completed his secondary education in Freiburg im Breisgau, in 1909. From that year until 1914 Heidegger was at the University of Freiburg, studying first philosophy and theology, then mathematics and physics, and finally deciding to become a philosopher. He wrote his doctoral thesis, *Die Lehre vom Urteil im Psychologismus* (The Theory of Judgment in Psychologism) (1914) under the supervision of Schneider. While he was still working on his thesis, Heidegger published a critical survey on certain logical studies of that time (1912). Husserl's name is repeatedly mentioned in this study, and so it is clear that quite early in his development Heidegger was thoroughly familiar with the content of Husserl's *Logische Untersuchungen* (Logical Investigations). In the same year Heidegger published an article on modern epistemology entitled *"Das Realitätsproblem in der modernen Philosophie"* (The Problem of Reality in Modern Philosophy), in which he was not attempting to express a personal point of view, but rather trying to defend the realism of Geyser and Külpe against all forms of psychologism. Heidegger's doctoral thesis itself was written in a Neo-Kantian style that clearly reflected the influence of Rickert's thought; the study contains an analysis and critique of the theory of judgment defended in psychologism and deals in particular with the points of view developed by Wundt, Lipps, and Brentano. Here Husserl's criticism of psychologism is mentioned only in passing.

Heidegger's poor health exempted him (at least for a time) from military service during World War I. He was able during this period to prepare his *Habilitationsschrift*. By 1916 he had written a probationary thesis on Duns Scotus' doctrine of categories and meanings, *Die Kategorien- und Bedeutungslehre des Duns Scotus*, which deals for the most part with the *Grammatica Speculativa* (at that time still attributed to Duns Scotus, but probably written by Johannes of Ehrfurt). In this book, the appearance of which entitled Heidegger to teach philosophy as *Privatdozent*, it becomes apparent that at some time between 1912 and 1916 he had outgrown his original Scholasticism and Rickert's Neo-Kantianism, and also that he must have made a thorough study of Husserl's *Ideen*.

Husserl came to Freiburg in 1916 and from the first day exerted a deep influence on Heidegger. In 1920 Heidegger became Husserl's assistant, working in close cooperation with him until 1923. In that year Heidegger received an invitation to the University of Marburg and also, through the help of Nicolaï Hartmann, an appointment as *professor ordinarius* in philosophy. Heidegger's friendship with Husserl continued during this time, and certainly both worked together on various projects, but gradually Heidegger's way of thinking departed from Husserl's characteristic ideas to the extent that Heidegger began to develop his own philosophy. He met Bultmann at Marburg and the two became close friends. Bultmann introduced him to the theology of Karl Barth, whose publications, in turn, propelled Heidegger toward the works of Luther and Kierkegaard. During the Marburg years Heidegger also devoted himself to the works of Pascal and Dostoevsky. Finally, and importantly, he made friends with Scheler and Jaspers during this period.

Heidegger wrote his main work, *Sein und Zeit* (Being and Time), in Marburg between 1923 and 1927. A large part of it is the fruit of his lectures at the University. The first volume appeared in 1927, but the second volume, although partly ready at that time, never appeared at all, because Heidegger did not think it adequately expressed his most fundamental ideas. In fact he felt that it somehow seemed to develop ideas that were in contradiction to the basic insights of his philo-

sophical view. However, the first volume, despite the great linguistic difficulties it presents and the new way of thinking it
calls for, was extremely well received. Its publication made
Heidegger an overnight success as a philosopher.

In 1928 he received an invitation to return to Freiburg as
professor ordinarius. He had not been there long before Husserl went officially into retirement with a request that his
former assistant be made his successor, although he realized
that Heidegger rejected many important ideas of his own phenomenology and had developed completely new insights which
in many aspects were contradictory to the fundamental principles of the Husserlian philosophy. On the occasion of his
retirement, Husserl's best-known former students presented
him a memorial volume in tribute; Heidegger contributed his
outstanding essay *Vom Wesen des Grundes* (On the Essence
of Ground) to this work. Later that year Heidegger published
the famous Kant study, *Kant und das Problem der Metaphysik* (Kant and the Problem of Metaphysics), a portion of
which, in all probability, was part of the second volume of
Being and Time. His inaugural address, *Was ist Metaphysik?*
(What Is Metaphysics?) was also written in 1928.

In 1933 Heidegger was appointed *Rector Magnificus* of
the University of Freiburg. In his inaugural address of March
27, 1933, entitled *Die Selbstbehauptung der deutschen Universität* (The Self-Preservation of the German University), he
spoke in favor of the National Socialistic movement, which
had come to power earlier that year. It was to be some years
before Heidegger found his way through the great political
turmoil and came to understand the regime's real meaning.
By the late thirties he had drawn away from the movement, a
fact that, in the forties, led to an order forbidding him to publish. In the ten years from 1933 on Heidegger published very
little. In 1937 his book on Hölderlin appeared, *Hölderlin und
das Wesen der Dichting* (Hölderlin and the Essence of Poetry), followed in 1942 by *Platons Lehre von der Wahrheit*
(Plato's Doctrine of Truth), and in 1943 by his remarkable
essay *Vom Wesen der Wahrheit* (On the Essence of Truth).

Since the end of World War II Heidegger has lived in
Todtnauberg near Freiburg. He lectured and gave various

addresses with relative frequency until 1957, but since then
has done very little in the line of public exposure. In 1947 he
published his well-known *Brief über den "Humanismus"* (Letter on "Humanism"); from 1950 on he published several important books containing lectures given at Freiburg after 1929,
addresses and other essays. A complete list of these publications appears in the accompanying bibliography.

It is a well-known fact that there is a significant difference
in content, method, and style between the works of Heidegger
written between 1923 and 1930 and published between 1927
and 1943, and those which have appeared since 1943. The
difference is so great that Richardson refers to a Heidegger I
and Heidegger II.[1] No one can deny that the shift of focus
from *Dasein* to Being itself implies a genuine transformation
of thought,[2] nor that from a methodical point of view the
earlier Heidegger uses a phenomenological procedure whereas
the method of the later Heidegger consists in a process of
"thought."[3] Nevertheless it is my opinion that this is not sufficient evidence to warrant an explicit distinction between
"two" Heideggers. I could adopt such a way of referring to
Heidegger only if it could be shown that it is impossible to
bring the content of the later works into harmony with that
of the works written between 1923 and 1930, and, even more
importantly, if it can be proved that the later publications can
be understood without the earlier writings. Undeniably there
is development in Heidegger's thought, not only insofar as his
method of thinking is concerned, but also and primarily in the
content of his philosophy. It is true also that Heidegger's development has a bearing on essential points of his philosophy,
and it is certain that in later publications problems are brought
up and dealt with which had not manifested themselves in his
first publications. Therefore, I do not deny a shift in Heidegger's philosophy, nor do I underestimate the depth of the
famous "Kehre"; in fact I will go so far as to say that Heidegger's later philosophy is neither a necessary nor a "logical"

[1] William J. Richardson, *Heidegger: Through Phenomenology to
Thought* (The Hague: Martinus Nijhoff, 1963), p. 22 and *passim*.
[2] *Ibid.*, p. 207 and *passim*.
[3] *Ibid.*, pp. 623–24.

development of *Being and Time*. But in my view one has to maintain at least that Heidegger's later philosophy is a possible development of his earlier thinking, and that alone it would not be understandable, nor have meaning. Therefore, although I wholeheartedly agree with the fundamental themes of Richardson's book and think that this work is one of the best studies on Heidegger's philosophy as a whole, I believe one should not project a Heidegger I and II. Rather I am in favor of pointing to the differences while stressing equally the demonstrable continuity in Heidegger's philosophy.

Heidegger is most frequently thought of as a philosopher belonging to the group of existentialist thinkers. However, such a label cannot be acceptable in view of the unique place he holds in contemporary continental philosophy, a place certainly beyond classification. Heidegger himself has on several occasions explicitly warned against any attempts to oversimplify his philosophical position by placing him in the existentialist category. In his *Letter on Humanism,* for example, he took a clear stand against Sartre's existentialism. However, even though it is true that Heidegger belongs to no one group, and that in fact he stands apart from all other philosophers, he nonetheless occupies an important place within the phenomenological movement. Section 7 of *Being and Time* is a landmark within that movement as a whole, and as such has deeply influenced the reinterpretation of Husserl's phenomenology by the later French phenomenologists. Some readers may be inclined to remark that after 1930 Heidegger explicitly rejected his attachment to Husserl's phenomenology, that his later process of "thought" excludes any phenomenological attitude, and thus that Heidegger ought to be seen as an opponent rather than as a promoter of the phenomenological movement. Admittedly there is truth in this remark, insofar as in Heidegger's later works the phenomenological method is neither mentioned, dealt with, nor much applied. Nevertheless I believe that these facts alone create a wrong impression. For as I see it, even today Heidegger believes that a hermeneutic phenomenology is the obvious method for an analytics of *Dasein*'s Being and that such an analytics, although insufficient in itself to cope with the "fundamental" problem of philosophy, is and remains a necessary condition for authentic thought.

Generally speaking, Heidegger seems at first contact to take a rather negative stance in regard to traditional philosophy; any positive relationship seems to be only in the direction of certain Pre-Socratic philosophers such as Anaximander, Heraclitus, and Parmenides, and of the meditating poet Hölderlin. Upon closer investigation, however, one realizes that Heidegger's negative attitude toward traditional metaphysics after Plato and Aristotle did not preclude a great interest in the outstanding philosophers of all eras. The list of courses that he gave over the years at the Universities of Marburg and Freiburg attests to that.

There are other ambiguities about Heidegger's work. It is often said, for instance, that his earlier philosophy was inspired in particular by the works of Kierkegaard, Nietzsche, Dilthey, and Husserl. Yet, though no one can deny the influence of these authors on his thinking in *Being and Time,* the statement does not give a real picture of the situation, for a careful reader of *Being and Time* will discover a lively dialogue with Plato and Aristotle and their commentators on the one hand, and Kant and Hegel on the other. From a certain point of view one could even say that Heidegger's earlier philosophy is an attempt to transcend the opposition between classical and modern philosophy, as found especially in Aristotle and Kant. In my opinion this holds for the later Heidegger also, although it is true that in the second period the influences of Pre-Socratic philosophy and of Hegel's thinking are clearly in evidence.

2. *Heidegger and Husserl*

We noted earlier that there was no personal contact between Husserl and Heidegger before 1916. Nevertheless Heidegger must have been familiar with Husserl's *Logische Untersuchungen* as early as 1912, and he evidently made a profound study of his *Ideen* between 1912 and 1916. During these years before the completion of his studies at the University of Freiburg, he maintained a strong interest in Husserl's phenomenology, and would have studied under Husserl in Göttingen had it not been for financial difficulties. By the time Husserl arrived in Freiburg, Heidegger had already been admitted to the faculty as *Privatdozent*. It was in 1919, after Heidegger had returned to Freiburg following his brief military service at the end of World War I, that something of a closer contact between the two men was established. In 1920 Heidegger became Husserl's assistant and from then until 1923 they worked in close cooperation. This cooperation continued even after Heidegger left Freiburg in 1923 to go to Marburg, undoubtedly because his interest in Husserl's version of phenomenology continued unchanged at that time. The two cooperated in the preparation of an article on phenomenology for the *Encyclopædia Britannica;* in addition Heidegger prepared for publication the Husserl lectures on inner time consciousness, *Vorlesungen zur Phänomenologie des inneren Zeitbewusstseins,* which Husserl had given between 1905 and 1910.

In each of the above instances, however, it was becoming evident that although Heidegger had great admiration for Husserl's *Logische Untersuchungen* and for the "first phase" of his phenomenology, he could not accept the fundamental theses of Husserl's transcendental phenomenology as it was developed in *Ideen* and later publications. Heidegger clearly maintained this attitude in *Sein und Zeit* and *Kant und das Problem der Metaphysik;* in each it was evident that his criticism was directed at Husserl's theory of the phenomenological reduction and at his view of the transcendental ego.

When Heidegger took over Husserl's chair in the fall of 1928, their contacts became less and less frequent, finally ending completely although there was no formal break. The situation had been quite difficult for Heidegger between 1927 and 1929. On the one hand it is apparent that he respected Husserl highly not only as a man but as a philosopher. But it is equally clear that Heidegger could not follow Husserl in his transcendentalism and that he must have felt Husserl's deep disappointment in gradually realizing how little of the transcendental philosophy was acceptable to him. Heidegger must also have known that in 1928 Husserl still hoped to win him

over to his "transcendental idealism"; but the positions Heidegger took in *Sein und Zeit* had made it clear that this would
never be the case. When the situation became untenable, Heidegger decided to drop all references to phenomenology in
his lectures and writings, fully respecting Husserl's prior claim
to the term. We know from the notes written in his copy of
Sein und Zeit that Husserl seriously studied Heidegger's philosophy. Husserl apparently came to the conclusion that since
Heidegger rejected the phenomenological reduction, he never
transcended the realm of the natural and naïve attitude, and
that by substituting human ek-sistence for the pure and transcendental ego Heidegger transformed phenomenology into a
"philosophical anthropology" which suffered from the same
weakness as older, well-known forms of psychologism. For his
part Heidegger made it clear that for him the stumbling
blocks in Husserl's philosophy consisted in the transcendental
reduction as "bracketing of Being," in the "reduction" of man
to pure consciousness, and, finally, in the "reduction" of Being into Being-object-for.

The relationship between Husserl and Heidegger from 1930
to 1938 was deeply influenced by political events. But however tragic the situation may have been, particularly from
Husserl's point of view, it would seem that dwelling upon it
serves no purpose in clarifying the relationship between their
philosophies. In my opinion a perpetuation of this irretrievable
aspect of the relationship between the two great philosophers
lends more to sensationalism than to the quest for wisdom.

In view of what has been said in the introduction to the
second part of this anthology, I think that the two selections
which follow give a good idea of Heidegger's position within
the phenomenological movement. I have put Schrag's article
before Heidegger's essay on phenomenology because the former will help the reader substantially toward an understanding
of the deeper meaning of Section 7 of *Sein und Zeit*.

3. Selective Bibliography

MAJOR WORKS OF MARTIN HEIDEGGER

Die Lehre vom Urteil im Psychologismus. Ein kritisch-positiver Beitrag zur Logik (Leipzig: Johann Ambrosius Barth, 1914).

Die Kategorien–und Bedeutungslehre des Duns Scotus (Tübingen: J. C. B. Mohr Verlag, 1916).

Sein und Zeit (Halle: Max Niemeyer Verlag, 1927).

Being and Time. Trans. John Macquarrie and Edward Robinson (London: SCM, 1962).

Kant und das Problem der Metaphysik (Bonn: Fred. Cohen, 1929).

Kant and the Problem of Metaphysics. Trans. James Churchill (Bloomington: Indiana University Press, 1962).

Vom Wesen des Grundes (Halle: Max Niemeyer, 1929). Foreword added to third edition (Frankfurt a.M.: Vittorio Klostermann, 1949).

Was ist Metaphysik? (Bonn: Fred. Cohen, 1930). Postscript added to fourth edition and Introduction added to fifth edition (Frankfurt a.M.: Vittorio Klostermann, 1949).

What Is Metaphysics? Trans. R. F. C. Hull and Alan Crick, in *Existence and Being,* ed. Werner Brock (Chicago: Regnery, 1949), pp. 353–92.

Die Selbstbehauptung der deutschen Universität (Breslau: Korn, 1933).

Hölderlin und das Wesen der Dichtung (München: Albert Langen, 1937).

Hölderlin and the Essence of Poetry. Trans. Douglas Scott, in *Existence and Being* (Chicago: Regnery, 1949), pp. 291–315 and 251–90.

Vom Wesen der Wahrheit (Frankfurt a.M.: Vittorio Klostermann, 1943).

On the Essence of Truth. Trans. R. F. C. Hull and Alan Crick, in *Existence and Being* (Chicago: Regnery, 1949), pp. 317–51.

Erläuterungen zur Hölderlins Dichtung (Frankfurt a.M.: Vittorio Klostermann, 1944).

Platons Lehre von der Wahrheit. Mit einem Brief über den "Humanismus" (Bern: Francke Verlag, 1947).

Holzwege (Frankfurt a.M.: Vittorio Klostermann, 1950).

Der Feldweg (Frankfurt a.M.: Vittorio Klostermann, 1953).

Einführung in die Metaphysik (Tübingen: Niemeyer Verlag, 1953).

Introduction to Metaphysics. Trans. Ralph Manheim (New Haven: Yale University Press, 1958).

Was heisst Denken? (Tübingen: Niemeyer Verlag, 1954).

Aus der Erfahrung des Denkens (Pfullingen: Neske, 1954).

Vorträge und Aufsätze (Pfullingen: Neske, 1954).

Hebel—Der Hausfreund (Pfullingen: Neske, 1956).

Was ist das—die Philosophie? (Pfullingen: Neske, 1956).

　What Is Philosophy? Trans. W. Kluback and J. T. Wilde (New York: Twayne, 1958).

Zur Seinsfrage (Frankfurt: Vittorio Klostermann, 1956).

　The Question of Being. Trans. W. Kluback and J. T. Wilde (New York: Twayne, 1959).

Der Satz vom Grund (Pfullingen: Neske, 1957).

Identität und Differenz (Pfullingen: Neske, 1957).

Unterwegs zur Sprache (Pfullingen: Neske, 1958).

Gelassenheit (Pfullingen: Neske, 1959).

　Discourse on Thinking. Trans. John M. Anderson and E. Hans Freund (New York: Harper & Row, 1966).

Nietzsche. 2 vols. (Pfullingen: Neske, 1960).

La fin de la philosophie et la tâche de la pensée. Trans. Jean Beaufret and François Fédier, in *Kierkegaard Vivant* (Paris: Gallimard, 1966), pp. 167–204.

STUDIES IN ENGLISH

Joseph J. Kockelmans, *Martin Heidegger. A First Introduction to his Philosophy* (Pittsburgh: Duquesne University Press, 1965).

Thomas Langan, *The Meaning of Heidegger: A Critical Study of an Existentialist Phenomenology* (New York: Columbia University Press, 1959).

William J. Richardson, *Heidegger: Through Phenomenology to Thought* (The Hague: Martinus Nijhoff, 1963).

Herbert Spiegelberg, *The Phenomenological Movement, A Historical Introduction,* 2 vols. (The Hague, Martinus Nijhoff, 1960), Vol. I, pp. 271–357.

Vincent Vycinas, *Earth and Gods: An Introduction to the Philosophy of Martin Heidegger* (The Hague: Martinus Nijhoff, 1961).

Phenomenology, Ontology,
and History in the Philosophy of Heidegger*

CALVIN O. SCHRAG

In his major philosophical work, *Sein und Zeit*, Heidegger defines philosophy as universal phenomenological ontology which takes its point of departure from the hermeneutics of human being (*Dasein*). This hermeneutics of *Dasein*, as an historical analytics of existence, provides the guiding thread of all philosophical enquiry, constituting the whence of its origination and the whither of its return.[1] It is in this passage that the nature and task of Heidegger's philosophy has its most explicit formulation. The primary consideration which defines the philosophical task is the problem of Being; the proper method of a philosophical analysis which seeks to delineate the structures and explicate the meaning of Being is phenomenology; the point of departure of such an ontological analysis which employs the phenomenological method is hermeneutics or the historical interpretation of existence.

The philosopher as ontologist seeks to delineate the character and the universal structures of Being as they manifest themselves in the phenomena. "The discernment of the Being (*Sein*) in that which is (*Seiendes*) and the explication of this Being is the task of ontology" (*SZ*, 27). From the period of the pre-Socratics to the advent of Hegel's *Logic*, the question

* From Calvin O. Schrag, "Phenomenology, Ontology, and History in the Philosophy of Martin Heidegger," *Revue Internationale de Philosophie*, 12 (1958), pp. 117–132. Reprinted by permission of the author and the editors.

[1] "Philosophie ist universale phänomenologische Ontologie, ausgehend von der Hermeneutik des Daseins, die als Analytik der *Existenz* das Ende des Leitfadens alles philosophischen Fragens dort festgemacht bat, woraus es *entspringt* und wohin es *zurückschlägt*." *Sein und Zeit*, 7th ed. (Tübingen: Max Niemeyer Verlag, 1953), p. 38. Subsequent references to this edition will appear in the text as *SZ*.

of Being has defined the nature of the philosophical enterprise. Heidegger is indissoluably linked with this tradition, and with its representatives he engages in a continuing conversation. His conversation with the great metaphysicians of western thought is a *critical* conversation, for he sees much in this tradition which has contributed to the oblivion of the ontological quest in contemporary thinking. But with Anaximander and Parmenides, with Plato and Aristotle, with Augustine and Scotus, with Spinoza and Hegel, he shares a common question—*What is the nature of Being?* The "essence of truth", he writes in one of his later essays, is the "disclosing (*Entbergung*) of the meaning of that which we call Being".[2]

The proper method of an ontological analysis which seeks to explicate the meaning of Being is the method of descriptive phenomenology. Hence, philosophy must properly be understood as *phenomenological* ontology. This phenomenological method has for its guiding principle the maxim: to the data themselves (*Zu den Sachen selbst!*). Only by strict adherence to this phenomenological formula, argues Heidegger, are we able to preclude "all abstract constructions and formulations, accidental findings, acceptance of only apparently demonstrated concepts, and adoption of pseudo-questions which often present themselves as real problems" (*SZ*, 27–28). The task of the phenomenologist is to describe, analyze, and interpret the data of immediate experience. An ontological analysis, which remains true to the phenomenological method, can never cut itself off from the original data. Heidegger rejects without qualification any rationalist metaphysical speculation and a priori epistemological construction which focuses upon mental and cognitive processes to the neglect of the phenomena themselves. On this point Heidegger is a radical and consistent empiricist—in the broadest sense of the term. The goal of his phenomenological ontology is to return to the original data of man's experience, and to provide a conceptual clarification of these data by delineating the constitutive structures which make them what they are. This phenomenological pro-

---

[2] Heidegger, "Vom Wesen der Wahrheit", 3rd ed. (Frankfurt: Vittorio Klostermann, 1954), p. 27.

cedure involves an emancipation from any possible epistemological prejudgments and a priori limitations which can only distort the original phenomena in question, or indeed prevent their manifestation. The data or the phenomena are always prior to man's logical and epistemological theories concerning them. The task of the phenomenologist is to give full attention to the immediately given data and seek to describe, analyze, and interpret them.

In his explication of the meaning of phenomenology Heidegger appeals to the Greek language—a language which is intrinsically philosophical. A proper understanding of the phenomenological method, he argues, can be achieved only when the constitutive elements which comprise the term, *phenomenology,* are examined and the meaning of their juxtaposition is clarified. The Greek etymological elements of the term are φαινόμενον (*phainomenon*) and λόγος (*logos*), on the basis of which *phenomenology* can be understood in its most general sense as simply the logos or science of the phenomena (*Wissenschaft von den Phänomenen*) (*SZ,* 28). The Greek *phainomenon* is itself derived from the Greek verb, φαίνεσθαι (*phainesthai*), which means: that which shows itself. Accordingly, *phenomenon* means that which shows itself (*das Sichzeigende*) or that which manifests itself (*das Offenbare*). *Phenomenon* is that which is manifest and can be brought to light. In the original Greek the term was simply identified with τὰ ὄντα (*das Seiende*)—that which is. *Phenomenon* is that which shows itself in the manner in which it is. Understood in this sense the term must clearly be distinguished from the term, *appearance* (*Erscheinung*). Phenomena are not simply appearances, but rather *that which* appears or *that which* shows itself. Appearances are always referential to some phenomenon. Appearances are appearances *of something*—of that which shows itself.[3]

The concept of the *logos* had already been used by Plato and Aristotle in the fundamental sense of discourse (*Rede*). Discourse is here understood in terms of its root meaning of

[3] "Phänomene sind demnach *nie* Erscheinungen, wohl aber ist jede Erscheinung angewiesen auf Phänomene." *SZ,* p. 30.

δηλοῦν (*deloun*)—making manifest that which the discourse is about or that on which the discourse turns. Aristotle, Heidegger reminds us, had explained this function of discourse more precisely in his use of the term ἀποφαίνεσθαι (*apophainesthai*). The *logos* as discourse "opens to sight" or "lets something be seen" (*apo*). And that which discourse "opens to sight" is precisely phenomenon or that which shows itself (*phaines-thai*). Phenomenology must thus properly be understood as *apophainesthai ta phainomena*—to disclose or "open to sight" that which shows itself in the manner in which it shows itself. The main objective of the phenomenological method is to return to the primary data as they show themselves. It is intent upon examining the phenomena as they are given. Thus it takes as its cardinal principle, *Zu den Sachen selbst!*

Phenomenology, thus understood, provides the appropriate mode of access to that which constitutes the subject matter of ontological investigation—Being. With the use of the phenomenological method Heidegger intends to submit an accurate "reading" of the structures of Being as they manifest themselves in the phenomena. Ontology is therefore properly understood as phenomenological ontology. *"Ontology is possible only as phenomenology*. The phenomenological concept of phenomenon means the showing of the Being of that which is, its meaning, its modifications, and its derivation" (*SZ*, 35).

Inextricably bound up with Heidegger's phenomenological method we find a radical and emphatic doctrine of intentionality. Brentano and Husserl are clearly in the background of this doctrine, but its roots can already be found in ancient and mediaeval philosophy. Heidegger is at one with Brentano and Husserl in his view that intentionality is the presupposition of the phenomenological method. In his *Ideen* Husserl made the notion of intentionality a fundamental theme of his philosophy. "To the essence of every actual cogito there always belongs a consciousness *of* something."[4] Every experience is a consciousness *of* something, and is thus properly said to be "intentionally related" to this something. Intentionality, for

4 Husserl, *Ideen zu einer reinen Phänomenologie und phänomenologischen Philosophie*, Vol. I, p. 79 (*Husserliana*, Vol. III, Haag: Martinus Nijhoff, 1950).

Husserl, is the basic structure of consciousness. The act of consciousness (*noesis*) is always directed toward its intentional object (*noema*).[5] Heidegger follows Husserl in his accentuation of the theme of intentionality, but he regards as more inclusive the framework in which intentionality properly functions. For Husserl the intentional relation of the act of knowing and the thing-as-known is primarily a cognitive or theoretical operation which he calls "pure consciousness". His point of departure is still the Cartesian *cogito*.[6] For Heidegger, on the other hand, the intentional structure is present not only in the realm of consciousness, understood in terms of man's cognitive and theoretical relation to his world, but already in the whole of man's pre-cognitive awareness. Man "intends" his world not only in perceiving and judging, but also in the use of tools or utensils (*Zeug*) in his daily practical concerns (*Besorgen*), and in his encounter and response to other selves who share his world, which Heidegger calls personal concern (*Fürsorge*). Prior to any cognitive reflection there is a primordial pre-conceptual awareness through which man already understands himself as fundamentally related to his world. Human being or *Dasein* has what Heidegger calls a "pre-conceptual understanding of Being" (*vorbegriffliches Seinsverständnis*) in which the intentional structure of experience is already operative.[7] This pre-conceptual awareness,

---

[5] *Ibid.*, pp. 223–228. In his study on the doctrine of the categories in Duns Scotus Heidegger points out that Husserl's notion of intentionality was already present in Scotus' doctrine of the *modi significandi activi*. For Scotus each *modus significandi* has an active or subjective side which corresponds to Husserl's *noesis*, and a passive or objective side which corresponds to the *noema*. Every mode of signification signifies an object or an essence with which it is in an intentional relation. *Die Kategorien- und Bedeutungslehre des Duns Scotus* (Tübingen: J. C. B. Mohr, 1916), pp. 129–130.

[6] "Als Ausgang nehmen wir das Bewusstsein in einem prägnanten und sich zunächst darbietenden Sinne, den wir am einfachsten bezeichnen durch das Cartesianische *cogito*, das 'Ich denke'." Husserl, *Ideen*, Vol. I, p. 75.

[7] *SZ*, pp. 5, 197. A similar attempt to reach a pre-cognitive level of experience is made by Sartre in the development of his notion of the "*cogito préréflexif*" which is itself the condition for the reflective ego. In the "*cogito préréflexif*" the primacy of cognitive

which forms the original link of the *Dasein*-world correlation, is commonly known as mood (*Stimmung*). Mood, in its various modifications of melancholy, boredom, fear, anxiety, and despair, discloses possible modes of *Dasein*'s being-in-the-world (In-der-Welt-sein).[8] Mood is here understood not as a psychological state, but as an *intentional determinant*. Mood discloses and reveals. Heidegger deems it significant that Aristotle, for example, treated the phenomenon of fear in his Rhetoric (B5 1382 a21) rather than in his Psychology. Fear discloses a manner or mode of man's relation to his natural and social environment. Mood in its various modifications performs a revealing function. It discloses dimensions of man's existence in his world.

Heidegger's accentuation of the "pre-conceptual understanding of Being" constitutes an explicit rejection of the isolation of the epistemological subject or the *res cogitans* as formulated in the Cartesian tradition. There is never an isolated "I" given without a world, which is then confronted with the task of formulating a theory of knowledge to account both

---

knowledge is abandoned; the world is initially disclosed through man's pre-reflective acts. Sartre, *L'Etre et le Néant* (Paris: Gallimard, 1943), pp. 16–23.

[8] The concept of "being-in-the-world" in Heidegger's analysis is not to be understood as a spatial "being-in" which might obtain between two substances or two objects. The world is not a spatial container into which *Dasein* is placed. The relationship of *Dasein* to the world is the relationship of practical preoccupation and personal involvement. To say that *Dasein* is in the world is to say that he lives, dwells and sojourns in the world. "Das In-sein meint so wenig ein räumliches 'Ineinander' Vorhandener, als 'in' ursprünglich gar nicht eine räumliche Beziehung der genannten Art bedeutet; 'in' stammt von innan-, wohnen, habitare, sich aufhalten . . ." (SZ, p. 54). Walter Biemel has aptly characterized Heidegger's concept of "being-in-the-world" as an attitude of intimacy or familiarity—as "being-with" in distinction from purely spatial relationship of "being-besides". "Le *dans* de l'être-dans-le-monde se réfère à une attitude de familiarité. Il signifie 'être familier avec . . .', *être-auprès* (*Sein-bei*) . . . La différence qui existe entre la proximité purement spatiale et la proximité au sens de familiarité s'exprime en français par la différence qu'il y a entre les termes *près* et *auprès*." Biemel, *Le Concept de Monde chez Heidegger* (Paris: J. Vrin, 1950), p. 12.

for its own existence as well as the existence of an "external" world. Prior to the rise of the epistemological question there is already a pre-conceptual disclosure of man's relation to his world. The mistake of Descartes, contends Heidegger, was that he never accounted for the understanding of the *sum* which is presupposed by the *cogito*. "With the *cogito sum* Descartes claimed to provide philosophy with a new and certain foundation. But what he leaves undetermined with this 'radical' departure is the kind of being characterizing the *res cogitans,* or more precisely stated, the ontological *meaning of the 'sum'* " (*SZ,* 24). Heidegger's marked affinity to the existential thinking of Kierkegaard becomes evident at this point. The continuing argument of Kierkegaard in his doctrine of truth as subjectivity is that the real self is not the cognitive self but the ethically existing self. In the Concluding Unscientific Postscript he writes: "That the knowing spirit is an existing individual spirit, and that every human being is such an entity existing for himself, is a truth I cannot too often repeat; for the fantastic neglect of this is responsible for much confusion." (p. 169). Heidegger is at one with Kierkegaard in his criticism of Descartes. The primary datum is not the thinking subject or the Cartesian *cogito,* but the *sum* or the act of existing, and this in the sense of an already being-in-a-world.[9] In thus granting priority to the act of existence and man's pre-conceptual awareness of this existence, the subject-object dichotomy, with its objectivization of reality, is undercut. There is a level of experience or encounter which precedes the split between subject and object. The latter is a noetic or theoretical distinction which arises later in man's experience and is itself grounded in man's primordial awareness of being-with and having a world. There is a *Dasein*-world correlation, or more precisely, a relational complex of *Dasein* being-in-the-world which constitutes the ontological prius of any analysis and enquiry into the nature of knowledge. *Dasein* is not an epistemological Archimedian point, but is a being who is intentionally related to his world in his pre-theoretical preoccupations and con-

[9] "Die erste Aussage ist dann: 'sum' und zwar in dem Sinne: ich-bin-in-einer-Welt." *SZ,* p. 211.

cerns. In all of man's practical and personal concerns a world
is presupposed. To exist is to find oneself in a world to which
one is related in one or several of the manifestations of care
(*Sorge*)—in one's construction and use of tools, in one's undertaking and ordering of projects, or in one's encounter and
dealings with other selves.

The distinctive character of Heidegger's phenomenological
ontology is that it is an ontology of *Dasein* or human existence.
As such one can properly speak of it as an *existentialist* ontology. The point of departure of this existentialist ontology is
a hermeneutics of the concrete experience of the historically
existing self. This does not mean that Heidegger's ontology is
simply an elucidation of a "standpoint" or a private "point of
view".[10] His philosophical intention is to delineate the universal structures of human being as they show themselves in the
actualization of existence. Unlike his contemporary, Karl Jaspers, who denies the possibility of an *ontology* of existence,
Heidegger develops a systematic and unified perspective of
existential reality.[11] *Dasein,* the focal point in this existentialist
ontology, is described by Heidegger as that "special ontolog-
ical-ontic being" who is to bring to light the question as to
the meaning of Being itself (*SZ,* 37). Man himself, in his concrete historical existence, provides the gateway to the understanding of Being.[12]

[10] "Damit verschreibt sich diese Abhandlung weder einem 'Standpunkt', noch einer 'Richtung', weil Phänomenologie keines von
beiden ist und nie werden kann, solange sie sich selbst versteht."
SZ, p. 27.

[11] Jaspers insists that his "elucidation of existence" (*Existenzer-
hellung*) not be construed as an ontology. He argues that because
of man's inevitable "shipwreck" (*scheitern*) in passing from one
situation to another, a unifying perspective of existence is impossible. "Existenz gewinnt *keine Rundung* als Bild, weder für andere
noch für sich selbst; denn der Mensch muss in der Welt *scheitern.*"
Jaspers, *Philosophie,* Vol. II (Heidelberg: Springer-Verlag, 1948),
p. 647.

[12] Paul Tillich expresses a basically similar approach when in his
Systematic Theology I he writes: "Whenever man has looked at his
world, he has found himself in it as a part of it. But he also has
realized that he is a stranger in the world of objects, unable to
penetrate it beyond a certain level of scientific analysis. And then

Historical existence itself becomes the subject of a hermeneutic interpretation and phenomenological description. Man is indelibly historical. History is a fundamental determinant of his "nature"—indeed, history *is* his "nature". "This being (*Dasein*) is in himself historical; thus, the unique ontological illumination of this being necessarily becomes an 'historical' interpretation" (*SZ*, 39).[13] For Heidegger phenomenological description becomes indissolubly linked with hermeneutics or "historical" interpretation. The datum, existence, which is to be described and analyzed has an intrinsically historical character, ultimately grounded in the modes of temporality. Man as an historical being is always arriving out of the past, anticipating the future, and deciding in the present. In his existence he is "stretched out" (*erstreckt*) over the past, present, and future. Historicity and temporality constitute the kernel or the core of his Being.[14]

In this recognition of and emphasis on the historical Heidegger seems to stand directly in line with the *Geistesphilosophie* of Dilthey and the historical consciousness which it inaugurated. Indeed, some interpreters have understood Heidegger's philosophy as essentially a development of Dilthey's historical thinking to its logical conclusion.[15] Heidegger's interest, as was that of Dilthey, centers in the concrete historical. Ontological analysis is rooted in the historicity of *Dasein* which constitutes "the whence of its *origination* and the whither of its *return*" (*SZ*, 38). Truth emerges from history. The truth of Being, he writes in his essay, "Vom Wesen der Wahrheit",

---

he has become aware of the fact that he himself is the door to the deeper levels of reality, that in his own existence he has the only possible approach to existence itself." (University of Chicago Press, 1951), p. 62.

[13] Cf. *Die Kategorien- und Bedeutungslehre des Duns Scotus:* "Der lebendige Geist ist als solcher wesenmässig historischer Geist im weitesten Sinne des Wortes," p. 238.

[14] See particularly *SZ*, part II, chap. v: "Zeitlichkeit und Geschichtlichkeit". For a discussion of Heidegger's view of time the reader is referred to John Wild's article, "The New Empiricism and Human Time", *Review of Metaphysics*, Vol. VII, 1954.

[15] See Karl Löwith, *Heidegger: Denker in Durftiger Zeit* (Frankfurt: S. Fischer Verlag, 1953), p. 46.

always "unconceals (*ent-birgt*) itself from the state of 'concealedness' (*Verborgenheit*) in the process of historical becoming" (p. 16). The question concerning the truth of Being is always asked from within man's history. Kierkegaard had already suggested this in his penetrating analysis of the human condition when he affirmed that every individual begins in an historical nexus and seeks to understand himself in the historicity in which he is involved.[16] Heidegger develops this theme suggested by Kierkegaard and focuses upon the historical character of existence with an attempt to set forth the truth which discloses itself in this history. This endeavor to "grasp" the truths from historical existence proceeds by way of a delineation of the ontological structures present in this historical existence which provide its formal condition and make possible its conceptual clarification.

Now what are these ontological structures and what is their quality and status? The primary structures or universal determinants of existence in Heidegger's philosophy are care (*Sorge*), anxiety (*Angst*), being-unto-death (*Sein-zum-Tode*), estrangement (*Entfremdung*), guilt (*Schuld*), and resolve (*Entschlossenheit*). These structures of existence define man's radical finitude. And whatever other classification one may give to Heidegger's philosophy it must be understood as a consistent and thoroughgoing philosophy of human finitude. Already in Kant, with his emphasis on the finite character of human reason, Heidegger sees the birth of an ontology understood in terms of finite structures.[17] Heidegger refers to these structures of existence as *existentialia* (*Existenzialen*). The term, *existentialia*, arises from his fundamental distinction between the "existential" (*das Existenzielle*) and the "existentialist" (*das Existenzial*). The German word, *Existenzielle*, has the specific denotation of the *concrete act of existing*. It refers to man's understanding of himself in his concrete-historical and ontic situation. The word, *Existenzial*, on the other hand, refers to the *universal conditions* present in the concrete act of

[16] Kierkegaard, *The Concept of Dread*, trans. Walter Lowrie (Princeton University Press, 1946), p. 65.

[17] Heidegger, *Kant und das Problem der Metaphysik*, 2nd ed. (Frankfurt: Vittorio Klostermann, 1951), pp. 69–74.

existing. It denotes the universal and the ontological as over against the concrete and the ontic. An *existentialist* analysis is thus geared to a "theoretical penetration of the ontological structures of existence" (*SZ*, 12). The elements which comprise this ontological structure are known as *existentialia*. *Existentialia* are the elements of the structure of existence which are implied in the concrete act of existing itself. Heidegger is explicit in his assertion that ontological analysis must never cut itself off from the ontic and the concrete. "The existentialist analysis is finally rooted in the existential, i.e. the ontic" (*SZ*, 13).[18] *Existentialia* are universals which are "read off" or "read out" of man's concrete experience, and are understood as the ontological elements of the structure which makes this concrete experience what it is. As Walter Biemel rightly says, for Heidegger *"l'ontologique est précisément ce qui rend possible le 'concret' "* (*op. cit.* p. 90). *Existentialia* are the universal conditions of the concrete.

These *existentialia,* Heidegger argues, must clearly and consistently be distinguished from the traditional cosmological categories (i.e. substance, quality, quantity, relation, etc.). The historical character of *Dasein* prohibits an application of cosmological categories, drawn from an interpretation of nature, to human existence. The historical *Dasein* must be understood in and through its history rather than as an instance or expression of nature. *Existentialia* are thus not to be confused with categories. Categories apply properly to the mode of non-human being (*nichtdaseinsmässiges Seiende*), but only to this mode. "All explications arising from the analysis of *Dasein* are derived with reference to the structure of existence. Since they are determined with reference to existence, we call these characterizations of *Dasein* '*existentialia*'. They are to be sharply distinguished from the characterizations of non-human being which we call categories" (*SZ*, 44). Heidegger's philosophy is a consistent protest against any naturalistic reductionism of the historical *Dasein*. Man is never the object

---

[18] Cf. p. 295: "Gleichwohl erschliesst die existenzial ursprünglichere Interpretation auch Möglichkeiten ursprünglicheren existenziellen Verstehens, solange ontologisches Begreifen sich nicht von der ontischen Erfahrung abschnüren lässt."

of a categorial analysis. According to Heidegger, classical
metaphysics in its failure to distinguish *existentialia* from categories interpreted man simply as an expression of nature or
an instance of finite substance in general. In such a categorial
interpretation man is reduced to the mode of "on-handness"
(*Vorhandensein*), and becomes a thing among other things,
a substance among other substances, or an object among other
objects. And precisely that which makes man "human"—his
personal freedom, his irreplaceable uniqueness, his memory
and his futurity; in short, his historicity—is lost. A phenomenological description of existence will therefore demand historical concepts rather than cosmological categories. Man is not a
substance or an entity which stands-in-itself, but rather an "ek-
sisting" being—a being who "stands-out" or is projected into
his possibilities of historical becoming.[19] Hence, existential
concepts fulfill what Paul Tillich has appropriately described
as a double demand. They are "non-objectivating" (they do
not transform men into things), but at the same time they
are not simply "subjective". They have a psychological character but carry an ontological signification.[20]

Existentialia, as distinct from categories, are thus seen as
the ontological elements which provide the necessary condition for *human* existence. In this sense they can properly be
understood as a priori and transcendental elements.[21] Heidegger states clearly that a priori in no way designates an a priori
construction of the mind.[22] Nor are *existentialia* a priori in
the sense of being known prior to man's concrete historical
experience, but are a priori in that they are constituents presupposed in the reality of existence itself. In this sense one can

---

[19] Heidegger uses the terms, *"Ek-sistenz"*, *"Ecstasis"*, and *"Entwurf"* (project) to denote the distinctive character of human existence. Human existence is ecstatic and projective. To exist means
to "stand out" from non-being and to be projected into one's possibilities of actualization.

[20] Tillich, "Existential Philosophy", *Journal of the History of
Ideas*, Vol. I (1944), p. 57.

[21] *SZ*, 44, 50, 53, 199; "Phänomenologische Wahrheit (Erschlos-
senheit von Sein) ist *veritas transcendentalis*," p. 38.

[22] "Erschliessung des Apriori ist nicht 'aprioristische' Konstruk-
tion." *SZ*, p. 50.

also properly speak of them as transcendental. They are present in the concrete existent, providing its very condition for being, but at the same time they lie beyond every particular instance of concrete existence.[23] All knowledge of the structures of human being is therefore transcendental knowledge.[24] Here we see Heidegger's relation to the central tradition of *transzendentale Philosophie,* as represented by Kant and Husserl in particular. Phenomenology, for Heidegger, is both descriptive and transcendental, as it already had been for Husserl. Whereas Husserl, however, in his eidetic reduction was interested solely in a science of essential being, and in his transcendental reduction suspended the world of facts by placing it into brackets[25]; Heidegger insists that it is precisely this bracketed "factual" world of existence which is to be described and subjected to a fundamental ontological analysis. Husserl's phenomenology is directed toward a "science of essences" (*Wesenswissenschaft*); Heidegger's phenomenology is consistently geared to a fundamental ontology of existence (*Existenzialontologie*). Yet we have seen that Heidegger's task is to delineate the ontological elements present in the structure of existence—elements which are universal and transcendental. How then do these ontological elements or *existentialia* differ from the universal essences of Husserl's *Wesenswissenschaft* and from essentialist philosophy in general? First of all it must be said that they differ from the essences of essentialist philosophy in that they are peculiar determinants of *human* existence, applicable to this mode of being and *only* to this mode of being. But they are distinct from essences in another sense. Like essences they are universals, but they are universals which are *present in the process of actualization itself.* Whereas es-

[23] "Sein und Seinsstruktur liegen über jedes Seiende und jede mögliche seiende Bestimmtheit eines Seienden hinaus. *Sein ist das transcendens schlechthin.*" *SZ,* p. 38.

[24] "Jede Erschliessung von Sein als des transcendens ist *transzendentale Erkenntnis.*" *SZ,* p. 38.

[25] "Demgegenüber wird die *reine oder transzendentale Phänomenologie nicht als Tatsachenwissenschaft, sondern als Wesenswissenschaft (als 'eidetische' Wissenschaft) begründet werden;* als eine Wissenschaft, die ausschliesslich 'Wesenerkenntnisse' feststellen will und *durchaus keine 'Tatsachen'.*" Husserl, p. 6.

sences are potential, i.e. universal structures which may or may
not become actual, *existentialia* share in the concrete actuality
of existence and are realized in this actuality. The *existen-
tiale*, care (*Sorge*), for example, is an element present in the
actualization which constitutes man's concrete experience.
Man understands himself ontically and in his concrete existence as that being who is concerned with or *cares* for his
Being.[26] In his use of tools and utensils he finds himself related to his environmental world (*Umwelt*) in the mode of
practical care (*Besorgen*), and to his communal world (*Mitwelt*) in the mode of personal care (*Fürsorge*). In this analysis
and description of man's concrete experience the care-
structure emerges as a fundamental ontological determinant
of human existence. Care is the universal and transcendental
element present in the structure of actualization, understood
as that which makes this actualization what it is and which
provides its conceptual clarification.[27]

Heidegger's phenomenological ontology must therefore be
understood as a delineation of the universal structures present
in the actualization of existence. This existence is indelibly
historical, grounded in the modes of temporality. Phenomenological description thus proceeds from hermeneutics or
"historical" interpretation. It can be said that in his accentuation of the historical, Heidegger has cast his lot with the historical thinking of Dilthey, but has provided Dilthey's historical
Erlebnis with an ontological structure and has thus proceeded
beyond the historical relativism which Dilthey never succeeded

[26] "Das Dasein ist ein Seiendes, das nicht nur unter anderem
Seiendem vorkommt. Es ist vielmehr dadurch ontisch ausgezeichnet,
dass es diesem Seienden in seinem Sein *um* dieses Sein selbst geht."
SZ, p. 12; cf. pp. 41, 52, 143, 191, 333.
[27] The care-structure in Heidegger's ontology is itself a complex
of the three structural moments of facticity (*Faktizität*), existentiality (*Existenzialität*), and fallenness (*Verfallenheit*)—three moments rooted respectively in the temporal modes of past, future,
and present. Facticity defines man's situationality—his "given" character of being thrown into a world (*Geworfenheit*), already shaped
by his past decisions and influences. Existentiality characterizes
man as projected into his future possibilities and existing in advance-
of-himself. Fallenness describes man's loss of himself in his present
preoccupations.

in overcoming.[28] The point which needs to be underscored here is that Heidegger has sought to overcome historical relativism through an analysis and description of the *historical itself*, rather than through an appeal to cosmological categories and structures which could overcome relativism only at the expense of a reduction of the historical to the natural. The historical *Dasein*, for Heidegger, is understood *through* history rather than *through* nature. Historical relativism is overcome by way of a delineation of the universal conditions which underlie man's concrete, historical, lived experience. In the same way it could be said that Heidegger has provided Kierkegaard's human subjectivity with ontological feet on which to walk. Such an ontology of subjectivity was already implied in Kierkegaard's ethico-religious concepts. His primary intent had to do with an elucidation of human subjectivity in its concrete ethical and religious encounters, but in describing these concrete encounters he already pointed to the structural determinants which underlie this subjectivity. The descriptions in the voluminous writings of Kierkegaard are hardly descriptions of the private and adventitious details of his personal life. They already suggest a method and approach to an elucidation of the human situation in which the question of what it means to exist can be systematically pursued. It has been the task of Heidegger's philosophy to set forth an explicit phenomenological method through which a systematic delineation of the structural determinants of existence can be achieved. He has attempted to show that human existence is not simply an unknowable and discontinuous succession of lived experiences, but that in its radical historicity it is grounded in ontological structures which provide the condition for its historical freedom.

Has Heidegger succeeded in this strenuous philosophical en-

---

[28] See particularly Dilthey's work, *Die geistige Welt: Einleitung in die Philosophie des Lebens* (*Gesammelte Schriften*, Vol. V; Leipzig: Verlag von B. G. Teubner, 1924). "Die Endlichkeit jeder geschichtlichen Erscheinung, sei sie eine Religion oder ein Ideal oder philosophisches System, sonach die Relativität jeder Art von menschlicher Auffassung ist das letzte Wort der historischen Weltanschauung, alles in einem Prozess fliessend, nichts bleibend" (p. 9).

deavor? That Heidegger's philosophy offers a most searching analysis of human existence can hardly be doubted. Yet, there are a few major points in his existentialist "system" which demand further clarification and evaluation. There are at least two critical questions which the author feels must be put to Heidegger. The one concerns the respective roles of phenomenological description and hermeneutical understanding in his philosophical method, and the other has to do with his tendency to reduce history to a mode of personal existence.

Has Heidegger succeeded in successfully combining the method of a scientifically oriented phenomenological description with hermeneutics or the historical interpretation of existence? What, in the final analysis, are their respective roles in his philosophy? Where do they meet—if indeed they do meet at all? One possibility would be to maintain that it is hermeneutics which provides the "material" for phenomenological description. The philosopher as phenomenologist describes what is given to him in his historical self-understanding. And this, it would seem, is what Heidegger is saying. But this raises more questions than it solves. If there is a self-understanding which precedes any phenomenological description does not this self-understanding preclude any simple "reading off" of the structures of the phenomena *as they are given?* Now Heidegger may not wish to maintain that there is ever a "pure" description of a phenomenon without some implicit understanding, but the point which is not clear in his philosophy is the specific role which this understanding plays in his phenomenological method. Understanding, by virtue of its historical character, is never a strictly theoretical or rational operation which simply "grasps" its intentional object. It is always in some sense practical and projective, "shaping" its object in the process of knowing it. Hence, it would seem that in spite of his insistence on the rejection of any apriori construction in the knowing process, he remains within a Kantian mold of thought in which the categories of the understanding shape the data given in experience. But the consequences of such a view would be most unwelcome by the Fribourg philosopher. This would mean that the *existentialia* or universal structures of *Dasein* are "projected into" rather than "read out of" the phenomena;

and Heidegger is explicit and unambiguous in his contention that the task of the phenomenologist has to do with the "lifting off" (*Abhebung*) of the structures of existence as they disclose themselves in the phenomena. Here then we see Heidegger's phenomenological side with its insistence on scientific description. But this phenomenological side is never successfully coupled with his method of hermeneutical interpretation which arises from his deeply entrenched historical mode of thinking.

The second question which must be raised concerns Heidegger's analysis and interpretation of the historical itself. Although he has not yet written a comprehensive philosophy of history—and probably never will—his discussion in *Sein und Zeit* places an unwarranted restriction on the reach of the historical. History, in the final analysis, becomes for Heidegger a mode of human existence itself. His interest resides with the historical *Dasein* who remembers a past, anticipates a future, and decides in the present. History is understood as this personal "stretchedness" (*Erstrecktheit*) over the modes of temporality. But is history not also the context of social or *inter*personal relations—past, present, and future—*in which* the personal, historical *Dasein* defines himself and searches for his meaning? Heidegger neglects, as do most existentialist thinkers, the community of selves with their common social memory which is the very stuff out of which history is made. To be sure, for Heidegger, being-in-the-world is always being-with-others, but it is the radically isolated *Dasein* who determines the significance of this communal world for his personal existence. The context of historical meaning arises not from the interdependent experiences and reflections of a community of selves, but from the individual projects of a solitary *Dasein* who is concerned for his authentic existence. Heidegger has indeed taken the phenomenon of personal history seriously and has shown that history, properly understood, must be understood through the historical itself. But in restricting history to a mode of personal existence he has sacrificed the historical community of remembering selves, which alone can provide the contextual structure for an ontology of *Dasein* which makes the claim of proceeding from the data themselves.

Phenomenology and Fundamental Ontology*

MARTIN HEIDEGGER

In provisionally characterizing the object which serves as the theme of our investigation (the Being of entities, or the meaning of Being in general), it seems that we have also delineated the method to be employed. The task of ontology is to explain Being itself and to make the Being of entities stand out in full relief. And the method of ontology remains questionable in the highest degree as long as we merely consult those ontologies which have come down to us historically, or other essays of that character. Since the term "ontology" is used in this investigation in a sense which is formally broad, any attempt to clarify the method of ontology by tracing its history is automatically ruled out.

When, moreover, we use the term "ontology", we are not talking about some definite philosophical discipline standing in interconnection with the others. Here one does not have to measure up to the tasks of some discipline that has been presented beforehand; on the contrary, only in terms of the objective necessities of definite questions and the kind of treatment which the 'things themselves' require, can one develop such a discipline.

With the question of the meaning of Being, our investigation comes up against the fundamental question of philosophy. This is one that must be treated *phenomenologically*. Thus our treatise does not subscribe to a 'standpoint' or represent any special 'direction'; for phenomenology is nothing of either sort, nor can it become so as long as it understands itself. The expression 'phenomenology' signifies primarily a *method-*

* From *Being and Time* by Martin Heidegger, translated by John Macquarrie and Edward Robinson, pp. 46–63. Copyright © 1962 by S.C.M. Press Ltd. Reprinted by permission of Harper & Row, Publishers.

ological conception. This expression does not characterize the what of the objects of philosophical research as subject-matter, but rather the *how* of that research. The more genuinely a methodological concept is worked out and the more comprehensively it determines the principles on which a science is to be conducted, all the more primordially is it rooted in the way we come to terms with the things themselves,[1] and the farther is it removed from what we call "technical devices", though there are many such devices even in the theoretical disciplines.

Thus the term 'phenomenology' expresses a maxim which can be formulated as 'To the things themselves!' It is opposed to all free-floating constructions and accidental findings; it is opposed to taking over any conceptions which only seem to have been demonstrated; it is opposed to those pseudo-questions which parade themselves as 'problems', often for generations at a time. Yet this maxim, one may rejoin, is abundantly self-evident, and it expresses, moreover, the underlying principle of any scientific knowledge whatsoever. Why should anything so self-evident be taken up explicitly in giving a title to a branch of research? In point of fact, the issue here is a kind of 'self-evidence' which we should like to bring closer to us, so far as it is important to do so in casting light upon the procedure of our treatise. We shall expound only the preliminary conception [Vorbegriff] of phenomenology.

This expression has two components: "phenomenon" and "logos". Both of these go back to terms from the Greek: φαινόμενον and λόγος. Taken superficially, the term "phenomenology" is formed like "theology", "biology", "sociology"—names which may be translated as "science of God",

---

[1] The appeal to the 'Sachen selbst', which Heidegger presents as virtually a slogan for Husserl's phenomenology, is not easy to translate without giving misleading impressions. What Husserl has in mind is the 'things' that words may be found to signify when their significations are correctly intuited by the right kind of *Anschauung*. (Cf. his *Logische Untersuchungen*, vol. 2, part 1, second edition, Halle, 1913, p. 6.) We have followed Marvin Farber in adopting 'the things themselves'. (Cf. his *The Foundation of Phenomenology*, Cambridge, Mass., 1943, pp. 202–3.) The word 'Sache' will, of course, be translated in other ways also.

"science of life", "science of society". This would make phenomenology the *science of phenomena*. We shall set forth the
preliminary conception of phenomenology by characterizing
what one has in mind in the term's two components, 'phenomenon' and 'logos', and by establishing the meaning of
the name in which these are *put together*. The history of the
word itself, which presumably arose in the Wolffian school,
is here of no significance.

A. The Concept of Phenomenon

The Greek expression φαινόμενον, to which the term 'phenomenon' goes back, is derived from the verb φαίνεσθαι, which
signifies "to show itself". Thus φαινόμενον means that which
shows itself, the manifest [das, was sich zeigt, das Sichzeigende, das Offenbare]. Φαίνεσθαι itself is a *middle-voiced* form
which comes from φαίνω—to bring to the light of day, to put
in the light. Φαίνω comes from the stem φα–, like φῶς, the
light, that which is bright—in other words, that wherein something can become manifest, visible in itself. Thus we must
keep in mind that the expression '*phenomenon*' signifies *that
which shows itself in itself,* the manifest. Accordingly the
φαινόμενα or 'phenomena' are the totality of what lies in the
light of day or can be brought to the light—what the Greeks
sometimes identified simply with τὰ ὄντα (entities). Now an
entity can show itself from itself [von ihm selbst her] in many
ways, depending in each case on the kind of access we have
to it. Indeed it is even possible for an entity to show itself as
something which in itself it is *not*. When it shows itself in this
way, it 'looks like something or other' ["sieht" . . . "so aus
wie . . ."]. This kind of showing-itself is what we call "*seeming*" [*Scheinen*]. Thus in Greek too the expression φαινόμενον
("phenomenon") signifies that which looks like something,
that which is 'semblant', 'semblance' [das "Scheinbare", der
"Schein"]. Φαινόμενον ἀγαθόν means something good which
looks like, but 'in actuality' is not, what it gives itself out to
be. If we are to have any further understanding of the concept
of phenomenon, everything depends on our seeing how what
is designated in the first signification of φαινόμενον ('phenome-

non' as that which shows itself) and what is designated in the second ('phenomenon' as semblance) are structurally inter-connected. Only when the meaning of something is such that it makes a pretension of showing itself—that is, of being a phenomenon—*can* it show itself *as* something which it is *not;* only then *can* it 'merely look like so-and-so'. When φαινόμενον signifies 'semblance', the primordial signification (the phenom-enon as the manifest) is already included as that upon which the second signification is founded. We shall allot the term 'phenomenon' to this positive and primordial signification of φαινόμενον, and distinguish "phenomenon" from "semblance", which is the privative modification of "phenomenon" as thus defined. But what *both* these terms express has proximally nothing at all to do with what is called an 'appearance', or still less a 'mere appearance'.[2]

2 '. . . was man "Erscheinung" oder gar "blosse Erscheinung" nennt.' Though the noun 'Erscheinung' and the verb 'erscheinen' behave so much like the English 'appearance' and 'appear' that the ensuing discussion presents relatively few difficulties in this respect for the translator, the passage shows some signs of hasty construc-tion, and a few comments may be helpful. We are told several times that 'appearance' and 'phenomenon' are to be sharply distinguished; yet we are also reminded that there is a sense in which they coin-cide, and even this sense seems to be twofold, though it is not clear that Heidegger is fully aware of this. The whole discussion is based upon two further distinctions: the distinction between 'showing' ('zeigen') and 'announcing' ('melden') and 'bringing forth' ('hervor-bringen'), and the distinction between ('x') that which 'shows it-self' ('das Sichzeigende') or which 'does the announcing' ('das Meldende') or which 'gets brought forth' ('das Hervorgebrachte'), and ('y') that which 'announces itself' ('das Sichmeldende') or which does the bringing-forth. Heidegger is thus able to introduce the following senses of 'Erscheinung' or 'appearance':

1a. an observable event y, such as a symptom which announces a disease x by showing itself, and in or through which x an-nounces itself without showing itself;
1b. y's showing-itself;
2. x's announcing-itself in or through y;
3a. the 'mere appearance' y which x may *bring forth* when x is of such a kind that its real nature can *never* be made manifest;
3b. the 'mere appearance' which is the *bringing-forth* of a 'mere appearance' in sense 3a.

Heidegger makes abundantly clear that sense 2 is the proper sense of 'appearance' and that senses 3a and 3b are the proper senses of

This is what one is talking about when one speaks of the 'symptoms of a disease' ["Krankheitserscheinungen"]. Here one has in mind certain occurrences in the body which show themselves and which, in showing themselves as thus showing themselves, 'indicate' ["indizieren"] something which does *not* show itself. The emergence [Auftreten] of such occurrences, their showing-themselves, goes together with the Being-present-at-hand of disturbances which do not show themselves. Thus appearance, as the appearance 'of something', does *not* mean showing-itself; it means rather the announcing-itself by [von] something which does not show itself, but which announces itself through something which does show itself. Appearing is a *not-showing-itself*. But the 'not' we find here is by no means to be confused with the privative "not" which we used in defining the structure of semblance.[3] What appears does *not* show itself; and anything which thus fails to show itself, is also something which can never seem.[4] All indications, presentations, symptoms, and symbols have this basic formal structure of appearing, even though they differ among themselves.

In spite of the fact that 'appearing' is never a showing-itself in the sense of "phenomenon", appearing is possible only *by reason of a showing-itself* of something. But this showing-itself, which helps to make possible the appearing, is not the

_____

'mere appearance'. On H. 30 and 31 he concedes that sense 1b corresponds to the primordial sense of 'phenomenon'; but his discussion on H. 28 suggests that 1a corresponds to this more accurately, and he reverts to this position towards the end of H. 30.

[3] '. . . als welches es die Struktur des Scheins bestimmt.' (The older editions omit the 'es'.)

[4] 'Was sich in *der* Weise *nicht* zeigt, wie das Erscheinende, kann auch nie scheinen.' This passage is ambiguous, but presumably 'das Erscheinende' is to be interpreted as the *x* of our note 2, not our *y*. The reader should notice that our standardized translation of 'scheinen' as 'seem' is one which here becomes rather misleading, even though these words correspond fairly well in ordinary usage. In distinguishing between 'scheinen' and 'erscheinen', Heidegger seems to be insisting that 'scheinen' can be done only by the *y* which 'shows itself' or 'does the announcing', not by the *x* which 'announces itself' in or through *y*, even though German usage does not differentiate these verbs quite so sharply.

appearing itself. Appearing is an *announcing*-itself [das Sich-*melden*] through something that shows itself. If one then says that with the word 'appearance' we allude to something wherein something appears without being itself an appearance, one has not thereby defined the concept of phenomenon: one has rather *presupposed* it. This presupposition, however, remains concealed; for when one says this sort of thing about 'appearance', the expression 'appear' gets used in two ways. "That wherein something 'appears'" means that wherein something announces itself, and therefore does not show itself; and in the words [Rede] 'without being itself an "appearance"', "appearance" signifies the *showing-itself*. But this showing-itself belongs essentially to the 'wherein' in which something announces itself. According to this, phenomena are *never* appearances, though on the other hand every appearance is dependent on phenomena. If one defines "phenomenon" with the aid of a conception of 'appearance' which is still unclear, then everything is stood on its head, and a 'critique' of phenomenology on this basis is surely a remarkable undertaking.

So again the expression 'appearance' itself can have a double signification: first, *appearing,* in the sense of announcing-itself, as not-showing-itself; and next, that which does the announcing [das Meldende selbst]—that which in its showing-itself indicates something which does not show itself. And finally one can use "appearing" as a term for the genuine sense of "phenomenon" as showing-itself. If one designates these three different things as 'appearance', bewilderment is unavoidable.

But this bewilderment is essentially increased by the fact that 'appearance' can take on still another signification. That which does the announcing—that which, in its showing-itself, indicates something non-manifest—may be taken as that which emerges in what is itself non-manifest, and which emanates [ausstrahlt] from it in such a way indeed that the non-manifest gets thought of as something that is essentially *never* manifest. When that which does the announcing is taken this way, "appearance" is tantamount to a "bringing forth" or "something brought forth", but something which does not make up the real Being of what brings it forth: here we have an appearance in the sense of 'mere appearance'. That which does the announcing and is brought forth does, of course, show itself, and in such a way that, as an emanation of what it announces, it keeps this very thing constantly veiled in itself. On the other hand, this not-showing which veils is not a semblance. Kant uses the term "appearance" in this twofold way. According to him "appearances" are, in the first place, the 'objects of empirical intuition': they are what shows itself in such intuition. But what thus shows itself (the "phenomenon" in the genuine primordial sense) is at the same time an 'appearance' as an emanation of something which *hides* itself in that appearance —an emanation which announces.

In so far as a phenomenon is constitutive for 'appearance' in the signification of announcing itself through something which shows itself, though such a phenomenon can privatively take the variant form of semblance, appearance too can become mere semblance. In a certain kind of lighting someone can look as if his cheeks were flushed with red; and the redness which shows itself can be taken as an announcement of the Being-present-at-hand of a fever, which in turn indicates some disturbance in the organism.

"Phenomenon", the showing-itself-in-itself, signifies a distinctive way in which something can be encountered.[5] *"Appearance"*, on the other hand, means a reference-relationship which is in an entity itself,[6] and which is such that what *does the referring* (or the announcing) can fulfil its possible function only if it shows itself in itself and is thus a 'phenomenon'. Both appearance and semblance are founded upon the phenomenon, though in different ways. The bewildering multiplicity of 'phenomena' designated by the words "phenomenon", "semblance", "appearance", "mere appearance", can-

[5] '. . . eine ausgezeichnete Begegnisart von etwas.' The noun 'Begegnis' is derived from the verb 'begegnen', which is discussed in note 2, p. 70, H. 44 [in *Being and Time*].

[6] '. . . einen seienden Verweisungsbezug im Seienden selbst . . .' The verb 'verweisen', which we shall translate as 'refer' or 'assign', depending upon the context, will receive further attention in Section 17. See also our note 2, p. 97, H. 68 [in *Being and Time*].

not be disentangled unless the concept of the phenomenon is understood from the beginning as that which shows itself in itself.

If in taking the concept of "phenomenon" this way, we leave indefinite which entities we consider as "phenomena", and leave it open whether what shows itself is an entity or rather some characteristic which an entity may have in its Being, then we have merely arrived at the *formal* conception of "phenomenon". If by "that which shows itself" we understand those entities which are accessible through the empirical "intuition" in, let us say, Kant's sense, then the formal conception of "phenomenon" will indeed be legitimately employed. In this usage "phenomenon" has the signification of the *ordinary* conception of phenomenon. But this ordinary conception is not the phenomenological conception. If we keep within the horizon of the Kantian problematic, we can give an illustration of what is conceived phenomenologically as a "phenomenon", with reservations as to other differences; for we may then say that that which already shows itself in the appearance as prior to the "phenomenon" as ordinarily understood and as accompanying it in every case, can, even though it thus shows itself unthematically, be brought thematically to show itself; and what thus shows itself in itself (the 'forms of the intuition') will be the "phenomena" of phenomenology. For manifestly space and time must be able to show themselves in this way—they must be able to become phenomena—if Kant is claiming to make a transcendental assertion grounded in the facts when he says that space is the *a priori* "inside-which" of an ordering.[7]

If, however, the phenomenological conception of phenomenon is to be understood at all, regardless of how much closer we may come to determining the nature of that which shows itself, this presupposes inevitably that we must have an insight into the meaning of the formal conception of phenomenon and its legitimate employment in an ordinary signification.—But before setting up our preliminary conception of

[7] Cf. *Critique of Pure Reason*, 'Transcendental Aesthetic', Section 1, p. 34.

phenomenology, we must also define the signification of λόγος so as to make clear in what sense phenomenology can be a 'science of' phenomena at all.

B. The Concept of the Logos

In Plato and Aristotle the concept of the λόγος has many competing significations, with no basic signification positively taking the lead. In fact, however, this is only a semblance, which will maintain itself as long as our Interpretation is unable to grasp the basic signification properly in its primary content. If we say that the basic signification of λόγος is "discourse", then this word-for-word translation will not be validated until we have determined what is meant by "discourse" itself. The real signification of "discourse", which is obvious enough, gets constantly covered up by the later history of the word λόγος, and especially by the numerous and arbitrary Interpretations which subsequent philosophy has provided. Λόγος gets 'translated' (and this means that it is always getting interpreted) as "reason", "judgment", "concept", "definition", "ground", or "relationship".[8] But how can 'discourse' be so susceptible of modification that λόγος can signify all the things we have listed, and in good scholarly usage? Even if λόγος is understood in the sense of "assertion", but of "assertion" as 'judgment', this seemingly legitimate translation may still miss the fundamental signification, especially if "judgment" is conceived in a sense taken over from some contemporary 'theory of judgment'. Λόγος does not mean "judgment", and it certainly does not mean this primarily—if one understands by "judgment" a way of 'binding' something with something else, or the 'taking of a stand' (whether by acceptance or by rejection).

Λόγος as "discourse" means rather the same as δηλοῦν: to make manifest what one is 'talking about' in one's discourse. Aristotle has explicated this function of discourse more precisely as ἀποφαίνεσθαι.[9] The λόγος lets something be seen

---

[8] '. . . Vernunft, Urteil, Begriff, Definition, Grund, Verhältnis.'
[9] '. . . offenbar machen das, wovon in der Rede "die Rede" ist.' [De Interpr., cap. 1–6; Met., Z, 4; and Ethic. Nic., Z.]

(φαίνεσθαι), namely, what the discourse is about; and it does so either *for* the one who is doing the talking (the *medium*) or for persons who are talking with one another, as the case may be. Discourse 'lets something be seen' ἀπό . . .: that is, it lets us see something from the very thing which the discourse is about.[10] In discourse (ἀπόφανσις), so far as it is genuine, *what* is said [*was* geredet ist] is drawn *from* what the talk is about, so that discursive communication, in what it says [in ihrem Gesagten], makes manifest what it is talking about, and thus makes this accessible to the other party. This is the structure of the λόγος as ἀπόφανσις. This mode of making manifest in the sense of letting something be seen by pointing it out, does not go with all kinds of 'discourse'. Requesting (εὐχή), for instance, also makes manifest, but in a different way.

When fully concrete, discoursing (letting something be seen) has the character of speaking [Sprechens]—vocal proclamation in words. The λόγος is φωνή, and indeed, φωνή μετὰ φαντασίας—an utterance in which something is sighted in each case.

And only *because* the function of the λόγος as ἀπόφανσις lies in letting something be seen by pointing it out, can the λόγος have the structural form of σύνθεσις. Here "synthesis" does not mean a binding and linking together of representations, a manipulation of psychical occurrences where the 'problem' arises of how these bindings, as something inside, agree with something physical outside. Here the συν has a purely apophantical signification and means letting something be seen in its *togetherness* [*Beisammen*] with something—letting it be seen *as* something.

Furthermore, because the λόγος is a letting-something-be-seen, it can *therefore* be true or false. But here everything depends on our steering clear of any conception of truth which is construed in the sense of 'agreement'. This idea is by no means the primary one in the concept of ἀλήθεια. The 'Being-true' of the λόγος as ἀληθεύειν means that in λέγειν as ἀποφαίνεσθαι the entities *of which* one is talking must be

10 '. . . von dem selbst her, wovon die Rede ist.'

taken out of their hiddenness; one must let them be seen as something unhidden (ἀληθές); that is, they must be *dis-covered*.[11] Similarly, 'Being false' (ψεύδεσθαι) amounts to deceiving in the sense of *covering up* [*verdecken*]: putting something in front of something (in such a way as to let it be seen) and thereby passing it off *as* something which it is *not*.

But because 'truth' has this meaning, and because the λόγος is a definite mode of letting something be seen, the λόγος is just *not* the kind of thing that can be considered as the primary 'locus' of truth. If, as has become quite customary nowadays, one defines "truth" as something that 'really' pertains to judgment,[12] and if one then invokes the support of Aristotle with this thesis, not only is this unjustified, but, above all, the Greek conception of truth has been misunderstood. Αἴσθησις, the sheer sensory perception of something, is 'true' in the Greek sense, and indeed more primordially than the λόγος which we have been discussing. Just as seeing aims at colours, any αἴσθησις aims at its ἴδια (those entities which are genuinely accessible only *through* it and *for* it); and to that extent this perception is always true. This means that seeing always discovers colours, and hearing always discovers sounds. Pure νοεῖν is the perception of the simplest determinate ways of Being which entities as such may possess, and it perceives them just by looking at them.[13] This νοεῖν is what is 'true' in the purest and most primordial sense; that is to say, it merely discovers, and it does so in such a way that it can never cover up. This νοεῖν can never cover up; it can never be false; it can at worst remain a *non-perceiving*, ἀγνοεῖν, not sufficing for straightforward and appropriate access.

---

[11] The Greek words for 'truth' (ἡ ἀλήθεια, τὸ ἀληθές) are compounded of the privative prefix ἀ- ('not') and the verbal stem -λαθ- ('to escape notice', 'to be concealed'). The truth may thus be looked upon as that which is un-concealed, that which gets discovered or uncovered ('entdeckt').

[12] 'Wenn man . . . Wahrheit als das bestimmt, was "eigentlich" dem Urteil zukommt . . .'

[13] '. . . das schlicht hinsehende Vernehmen der einfachsten Seinsbestimmungen des Seienden als solchen.'

When something no longer takes the form of just letting something be seen, but is always harking back to something else to which it points, so that it lets something be seen *as* something, it thus acquires a synthesis-structure, and with this it takes over the possibility of covering up.[14] The 'truth of judgments', however, is merely the opposite of this covering-up, a secondary phenomenon of truth, *with more than one kind of foundation*.[15] Both realism and idealism have—with equal thoroughness—missed the meaning of the Greek conception of truth, in terms of which only the possibility of something like a 'doctrine of ideas' can be understood as philosophical *knowledge*.

And because the function of the λόγος lies in merely letting something be seen, in *letting* entities be *perceived* [im *Vernehmenlassen* des Seienden], λόγος can signify the *reason* [*Vernunft*]. And because, moreover, λόγος is used not only with the signification of λέγειν but also with that of λεγόμενον (that which is exhibited, as such), and because the latter is nothing else than the ὑποκείμενον which, as present-at-hand, already lies at the *bottom* [zum *Grunde*] of any procedure of addressing oneself to it or discussing it, λόγος *qua* λεγόμενον means the ground, the *ratio*. And finally, because λόγος as λεγόμενον can also signify that which, as something to which one addresses oneself, becomes visible in its relation to something in its 'relatedness', λόγος acquires the signification of *relation* and *relationship*.[16]

---

[14] 'Was nicht mehr die Vollzugsform des reinen Sehenlassens hat, sondern je im Aufweisen auf ein anderes rekurriert und so je etwas *als* etwas sehen lässt, das übernimmt mit dieser Synthesisstruktur die Möglichkeit des Verdeckens.'

[15] '. . . ein *mehrfach fundiertes* Phänomen von Wahrheit.' A 'secondary' or 'founded' phenomenon is one which is based upon something else. The notion of 'Fundierung' is one which Heidegger has taken over from Husserl. See our note 1, p. 86, on H. 59 [in *Being and Time*].

[16] Heidegger is here pointing out that the word λόγος is etymologically akin to the verb λέγειν, which has among its numerous meanings those of *laying out, exhibiting, setting forth, recounting, telling a tale, making a statement*. Thus λόγος as λέγειν can be thought of as the faculty of 'reason' ('Vernunft') which makes such activities possible. But λόγος can also mean τὸ λεγόμενον (*that*

This Interpretation of 'apophantical discourse' may suffice to clarify the primary function of the λόγος.

C. The Preliminary Conception of Phenomenology

When we envisage concretely what we have set forth in our Interpretation of 'phenomenon' and 'logos', we are struck by an inner relationship between the things meant by these terms. The expression "phenomenology" may be formulated in Greek as λέγειν τὰ φαινόμενα, where λέγειν means ἀποφαίνεσθαι. Thus "phenomenology" means ἀποφαίνεσθαι τὰ φαινόμενα—to let that which shows itself be seen from itself in the very way in which it shows itself from itself. This is the formal meaning of that branch of research which calls itself "phenomenology". But here we are expressing nothing else than the maxim formulated above: 'To the things themselves!'

Thus the term "phenomenology" is quite different in its meaning from expressions such as "theology" and the like. Those terms designate the objects of their respective sciences according to the subject-matter which they comprise at the time [in ihrer jeweiligen Sachhaltigkeit]. 'Phenomenology' neither designates the object of its researches, nor charac-

---

which is laid out, exhibited, set forth, told); in this sense it is the underlying subject matter (τὸ ὑποκείμενον) to which one addresses oneself and which one discusses ('Ansprechen und Besprechen'); as such it lies 'at the bottom' ('zum Grunde') of what is exhibited or told, and is thus the 'ground' or 'reason' ('Grund') for telling it. But when something is exhibited or told, it is exhibited in its *relatedness* ('in seiner Bezogenheit'); and in this way λόγος as λεγόμενον comes to stand for just such a relation or relationship ('Beziehung und Verhältnis'). The three senses here distinguished correspond to three senses of the Latin *'ratio'*, by which λόγος was traditionally translated, though Heidegger explicitly calls attention to only one of these. Notice that 'Beziehung' (which we translate as 'relation') can also be used in some contexts where 'Ansprechen' (our 'addressing oneself') would be equally appropriate. Notice further that 'Verhältnis' (our 'relationship'), which is ordinarily a synonym for 'Beziehung', can, like λόγος and *'ratio'*, also refer to the special kind of relationship which one finds in a mathematical proportion. The etymological connection between 'Vernehmen' and 'Vernunft' should also be noted.

terizes the subject-matter thus comprised. The word merely informs us of the *"how"* with which *what* is to be treated in this science gets exhibited and handled. To have a science 'of' phenomena means to grasp its objects *in such a way* that everything about them which is up for discussion must be treated by exhibiting it directly and demonstrating it directly.[17] The expression 'descriptive phenomenology', which is at bottom tautological, has the same meaning. Here "description" does not signify such a procedure as we find, let us say, in botanical morphology; the term has rather the sense of a prohibition—the avoidance of characterizing anything without such demonstration. The character of this description itself, the specific meaning of the λόγος, can be established first of all in terms of the 'thinghood' ["Sachheit"] of what is to be 'described'—that is to say, of what is to be given scientific definiteness as we encounter it phenomenally. The signification of "phenomenon", as conceived both formally and in the ordinary manner, is such that any exhibiting of an entity as it shows itself in itself, may be called "phenomenology" with formal justification.

Now what must be taken into account if the formal conception of phenomenon is to be deformalized into the phenomenological one, and how is this latter to be distinguished from the ordinary conception? What is it that phenomenology is to 'let us see'? What is it that must be called a 'phenomenon' in a distinctive sense? What is it that by its very essence is *necessarily* the theme whenever we exhibit something *explicitly*? Manifestly, it is something that proximally and for the most part does *not* show itself at all: it is something that lies *hidden*, in contrast to that which proximally and for the most part does show itself; but at the same time it is something that belongs to what thus shows itself, and it belongs to it so essentially as to constitute its meaning and its ground.

Yet that which remains *hidden* in an egregious sense, or which relapses and gets *covered up* again, or which shows itself only *'in disguise'*, is not just this entity or that, but rather

17 . . . in direkter Aufweisung und direkter Ausweisung . . .'

the *Being* of entities, as our previous observations have shown.
This Being can be covered up so extensively that it becomes
forgotten and no question arises about it or about its meaning.
Thus that which demands that it become a phenomenon, and
which demands this in a distinctive sense and in terms of its
ownmost content as a thing, is what phenomenology has taken
into its grasp thematically as its object.

Phenomenology is our way of access to what is to be the
theme of ontology, and it is our way of giving it demonstra-
tive precision. *Only as phenomenology, is ontology possible.*
In the phenomenological conception of "phenomenon" what
one has in mind as that which shows itself is the Being of entities, its meaning, its modifications and derivatives.[18] And
this showing-itself is not just any showing-itself, nor is it some
such thing as appearing. Least of all can the Being of entities
ever be anything such that 'behind it' stands something else
'which does not appear'.

'Behind' the phenomena of phenomenology there is essentially nothing else; on the other hand, what is to become a
phenomenon can be hidden. And just because the phenomena
are proximally and for the most part *not* given, there is need
for phenomenology. Covered-up-ness is the counter-concept
to 'phenomenon'.

There are various ways in which phenomena can be covered up. In the first place, a phenomenon can be covered up
in the sense that it is still quite *undiscovered*. It is neither
known nor unknown.[19] Moreover, a phenomenon can be
buried over [*verschüttet*]. This means that it has at some time
been discovered but has deteriorated [*verfiel*] to the point
of getting covered up again. This covering-up can become

---

[18] 'Der phänomenologische Begriff von Phänomen meint als das
Sichzeigende das Sein des Seienden, seinen Sinn, seine Modifika-
tionen und Derivate.'
[19] 'Über seinen Bestand gibt es weder Kenntnis noch Unkenntnis.'
The earlier editions have 'Erkenntnis' where the latter ones have
'Unkenntnis'. The word 'Bestand' always presents difficulties in
Heidegger; here it permits either of two interpretations, which we
have deliberately steered between: 'Whether there *is* any such thing,
is neither known nor unknown', and 'What it comprises is something of which we have neither knowledge nor ignorance.'

complete; or rather—and as a rule—what has been discovered earlier may still be visible, though only as a semblance. Yet so much semblance, so much 'Being'.[20] This covering-up as a 'disguising' is both the most frequent and the most dangerous, for here the possibilities of deceiving and misleading are especially stubborn. Within a 'system', perhaps, those structures of Being—and their concepts—which are still available but veiled in their indigenous character, may claim their rights. For when they have been bound together constructively in a system, they present themselves as something 'clear', requiring no further justification, and thus can serve as the point of departure for a process of deduction.

The covering-up itself, whether in the sense of hiddenness, burying-over, or disguise, has in turn two possibilities. There are coverings-up which are accidental; there are also some which are necessary, grounded in what the thing discovered consists in [der Bestandart des Entdeckten]. Whenever a phenomenological concept is drawn from primordial sources, there is a possibility that it may degenerate if communicated in the form of an assertion. It gets understood in an empty way and is thus passed on, losing its indigenous character, and becoming a free-floating thesis. Even in the concrete work of phenomenology itself there lurks the possibility that what has been primordially 'within our grasp' may become hardened so that we can no longer grasp it. And the difficulty of this kind of research lies in making it self-critical in a positive sense.

The way in which Being and its structures are encountered in the mode of phenomenon is one which must first of all be *wrested* from the objects of phenomenology. Thus the very *point of departure* [*Ausgang*] for our analysis requires that it be secured by the proper method, just as much as does our *access* [*Zugang*] to the phenomenon, or our *passage* [*Durchgang*] through whatever is prevalently covering it up. The idea of grasping and explicating phenomena in a way which is 'original' and 'intuitive' ["originären" und "intuitiven"] is directly opposed to the *naïveté* of a haphazard, 'immediate', and unreflective 'beholding' ["Schauen"].

[20] 'Wieviel Schein jedoch, soviel "Sein".'

Now that we have delimited our preliminary conception of phenomenology, the terms 'phenomenal' and 'phenomenological' can also be fixed in their signification. That which is given and explicable in the way the phenomenon is encountered is called 'phenomenal'; this is what we have in mind when we talk about "phenomenal structures". Everything which belongs to the species of exhibiting and explicating and which goes to make up the way of conceiving demanded by this research, is called 'phenomenological'.

Because phenomena, as understood phenomenologically, are never anything but what goes to make up Being, while Being is in every case the Being of some entity, we must first bring forward the entities themselves if it is our aim that Being should be laid bare; and we must do this in the right way. These entities must likewise show themselves with the kind of access which genuinely belongs to them. And in this way the ordinary conception of phenomenon becomes phenomenologically relevant. If our analysis is to be authentic, its aim is such that the prior task of assuring ourselves 'phenomenologically' of that entity which is to serve as our example, has already been prescribed as our point of departure.

With regard to its subject-matter, phenomenology is the science of the Being of entities—ontology. In explaining the tasks of ontology we found it necessary that there should be a fundamental ontology taking as its theme that entity which is ontologico-ontically distinctive, Dasein, in order to confront the cardinal problem—the question of the meaning of Being in general. Our investigation itself will show that the meaning of phenomenological description as a method lies in *interpretation*. The λόγος of the phenomenology of Dasein has the character of a ἑρμηνεύειν, through which the authentic meaning of Being, and also those basic structures of Being which Dasein itself possesses, are *made known* to Dasein's understanding of Being. The phenomenology of Dasein is a *hermeneutic* in the primordial signification of this word, where it designates this business of interpreting. But to the extent that by uncovering the meaning of Being and the basic structures of Dasein in general we may exhibit the horizon for any further ontological study of those entities which do not have the character of Dasein, this hermeneutic also becomes a 'hermeneutic' in the sense of working out the conditions on which the possibility of any ontological investigation depends. And finally, to the extent that Dasein, as an entity with the possibility of existence, has ontological priority over every other entity, "hermeneutic", as an interpretation of Dasein's Being, has the third and specific sense of an analytic of the existentiality of existence; and this is the sense which is philosophically *primary*. Then so far as this hermeneutic works out Dasein's historicality ontologically as the ontical condition for the possibility of historiology, it contains the roots of what can be called 'hermeneutic' only in a derivative sense: the methodology of those humane sciences which are historiological in character.

Being, as the basic theme of philosophy, is no class or genus of entities; yet it pertains to every entity. Its 'universality' is to be sought higher up. Being and the structure of Being lie beyond every entity and every possible character which an entity may possess. *Being is the transcendens pure and simple.*[21] And the transcendence of Dasein's Being is distinctive in that it implies the possibility and the necessity of the most radical *individuation*. Every disclosure of Being as the *transcendens* is *transcendental* knowledge. *Phenomenological truth* (*the disclosedness of Being*) *is veritas transcendentalis*.

Ontology and phenomenology are not two distinct philosophical disciplines among others. These terms characterize philosophy itself with regard to its object and its way of treating that object. Philosophy is universal phenomenological ontology, and takes its departure from the hermeneutic of Dasein, which, as an analytic of *existence*, has made fast the guiding-line for all philosophical inquiry at the point where it *arises* and to which it *returns*.

The following investigation would not have been possible if the ground had not been prepared by Edmund Husserl, with whose *Logische Untersuchungen* phenomenology first

---

[21] 'Sein und Seinsstruktur liegen über jedes Seiende und jede mögliche seiende Bestimmtheit eines Seienden hinaus. *Sein ist das transcendens schlechthin.*'

emerged. Our comments on the preliminary conception of phenomenology have shown that what is essential in it does not lie in its *actuality* as a philosophical 'movement' ["Richtung"]. Higher than actuality stands *possibility*. We can understand phenomenology only by seizing upon it as a possibility.[22]

With regard to the awkwardness and 'inelegance' of expression in the analyses to come, we may remark that it is one thing to give a report in which we tell about *entities*, but another to grasp entities in their *Being*. For the latter task we lack not only most of the words but, above all, the 'grammar'. If we may allude to some earlier researches on the analysis of Being, incomparable on their own level, we may compare the ontological sections of Plato's *Parmenides* or the fourth chapter of the seventh book of Aristotle's *Metaphysics* with a narrative section from Thucydides; we can then see the altogether unprecedented character of those formulations which were imposed upon the Greeks by their philosophers. And where our powers are essentially weaker, and where moreover the area of Being to be disclosed is ontologically far more difficult than that which was presented to the Greeks, the harshness of our expression will be enhanced, and so will the minuteness of detail with which our concepts are formed.

[22] If the following investigation has taken any steps forward in disclosing the "things themselves," the author must first of all thank E. Husserl, who, by providing his own incisive personal guidance and by freely turning over his unpublished investigations, familiarized the author with the most diverse areas of phenomenological research during his student years in Freiburg. [Heidegger's note.]

III. JEAN-PAUL SARTRE

Introduction

1. Biographical Note[1]

Jean-Paul Sartre was born in Paris on June 21, 1905. One of the events of his early boyhood which was to have far-reaching effects on the shaping of his life was the untimely death of his father. Shortly after this tragedy Sartre's mother returned with her young son to live in her father's house. When Sartre completed his elementary and high school education he went on to the École Normale Supérieure at Paris (1924) where for several years he devoted himself to literature and philosophy. During this time he was able, also, to take some courses in philosophy at the Sorbonne. He failed his finals on the first trial, but on a successive attempt passed and was graduated from the École Normale Supérieure with a doctorate in philosophy in 1929. For the next ten years he taught philosophy and literature in various lycées at Le Havre, Laon, and Paris. During this time he also traveled quite extensively in Europe and the Near East; between 1932 and 1934 he spent an academic year in Berlin, followed by a semester in Freiburg, where he studied German phenomenology. It was a subject that generated a great deal of enthusiasm in Sartre, for he saw in this new philosophical movement the possibility of freeing himself from the French philosophical tradition so deeply influenced by the Cartesian and Kantian

[1] See for the following: Robert Denoon Cumming, *The Philosophy of Jean-Paul Sartre* (New York: Random House, 1965), pp. 3–47; Wilfrid Desan, *The Tragic Finale: An Essay on the Philosophy of Jean-Paul Sartre* (New York: Harper & Brothers, 1960), pp. *xiii–xix,* and pp. 7–14; Herbert Spiegelberg, *The Phenomenological Movement* (The Hague: Martinus Nijhoff, 1960), Vol. II, pp. 445–97 (passim); Jean-Paul Sartre, *The Transcendence of the Ego.* Trans. Forrest Williams and Robert Kirkpatrick (New York: The Noonday Press, 1965). Translators' Introduction, pp. 11–27; Francis Jeanson, *Sartre par lui-même* (Paris: Gallimard, 1955).

philosophies. Initially Sartre was interested mainly in Husserl's original version of phenomenology, both in its pure form as philosophy and in its application to the sciences of man, but later he became convinced that Heidegger's "reinterpretation" of Husserl's view as presented in *Being and Time* was of greater importance. It was for this reason that during the late thirties and early forties Sartre devoted much time to a careful study of the main ideas Heidegger was then advancing in his major publications.

Sartre returned from his studies in Germany to take up teaching again at Le Havre (1934–36). From there he went to Laon (1936–37) and, finally, back to Paris where he taught at the Lycée Pasteur (1937–39). In 1939 he was drafted for World War II. Shortly after the invasion of France in May 1940, he was taken prisoner—ironically enough, in Lorraine on his birthday, June 21. Because he had not had an important position in the French army the Germans liberated him in 1941, allowing him to return to Paris and teach again at the Lycée Pasteur. He remained there for a year and then went to teach at the Lycée Condorcet for two years (1942–44). At the war's end he gave up teaching completely and has since that time lived in Paris and devoted himself entirely to his scientific, literary, and political career.

Sartre's first "novels" were produced when he was only ten years old. At eighteen he published his first short story, which was entitled *L'ange du morbide.* Later a collection of literary essays, which neither Gallimard nor Aubier was willing to publish, appeared in part in the periodical *Bifur* (June 1931) under the title *"Légende de la vérité."* Then in the early thirties Sartre became interested in the contemporary American novel, which he later evaluated as having created a technical revolution in the art of story telling, and as having greatly influenced his own style. But in the beginning at least, Sartre had greater success with his philosophical publications than with any others. His book *L'imagination* was published by the Presses Universitaires de France in 1936, and his long article *"La transcendence de l'égo"* was accepted by *Recherches philosophiques* in the same year. In 1938, however, Gallimard accepted his first great novel, *La nausée.*

The book was a best seller from the outset and established Sartre as a novelist of first rank. In 1939 Gallimard brought out his collection of short stories, *Le Mur*, and his psychological study *Esquisse d'une théorie des émotions*, followed in 1940 by *L'imaginaire: Psychologie phénoménologique de l'imagination*.

During the German occupation Sartre produced three of his most widely recognized and best publications: his own version of the Orestian legend in the play, *Les Mouches* (1943), a very long one-act play, *Huis clos* (1944), and his most important philosophical study, *L'être et le néant* (1943).

There is no doubt that from the very beginning of his career Sartre's ambitions were chiefly literary. Even in the mid-thirties, when his attention shifted toward philosophy, he continued with his literary work. After World War II Sartre became more and more involved with his interest in politics, which had been aroused when he was for a time a member of the French underground (1941). His ideas about the most important political events and situations can be found in the review, *Les Temps Modernes*, and in his series of studies called *Situations*, which appeared in six volumes between 1947 and 1965. But as vitally interested as he was in politics, he nevertheless continued to devote a substantial part of his time to literature and to philosophy in the strict sense of the term. In 1946 he published *L'existentialisme est un humanisme*, which was followed by *Baudelaire* in 1947, and *Saint Genet: comédien et martyr* in 1952. His latest contribution to philosophy appeared in 1960 with the title *Critique de la raison dialectique*. In addition to the works mentioned Sartre has written numerous plays, novels, and a few film scripts. Among them are *Les chemins de la liberté*, *Morts sans sépuluture*, and the plays *Les mains sales* and *Le diable et le bon Dieu*. A complete list of his publications appears in the accompanying bibliography.

2. Sartre's Position
within the Phenomenological Movement

It is helpful to reconsider certain historical data when attempting briefly to determine Sartre's position within the phenomenological movement as a whole. His involvement began "officially" in 1932 when he received a grant to study phenomenology in Germany. For reasons never fully explained Sartre first installed himself in Berlin, where as *pensionnaire de l'Institut français* he mapped out his own study program for the works of Husserl, Jaspers, Scheler, and Heidegger. During the winter semester of the second year of his stay in Germany he went to Freiburg. Although it is most unlikely that while there Sartre had any personal contact of importance with either Husserl or Heidegger, nonetheless he was thoroughly introduced to the main themes of phenomenology and certainly, as was to be seen later, profoundly affected by them.

When Sartre returned to France he again took up his teaching post in Le Havre. Evidently this assignment afforded him free hours for study and writing, for, as previously noted, between 1934 and 1939 he wrote not only two of his best novels, but three important psychological studies as well. It was also during this period that he wrote two articles presenting his personal view on Husserl's phenomenology as found in *Ideen I*. In the first article, "La transcendence de l'égo" (1936), Sartre clearly showed that at that time he was in substantial agreement with Husserl's phenomenological philosophy in general and in particular with Husserl's view that phenomenology entails important consequences for the sciences of man. The article was primarily concerned with whether it makes sense, after the phenomenological reduction, to speak of a "transcendental ego" which precedes consciousness. Although Sartre agreed with the essential components of Husserl's phenomenology, he denied the existence of a transcendental ego in addition to consciousness and that manifests itself *in* it. In Sartre's view there is no ego *in* consciousness, but only an ego *for* consciousness. The original datum that manifests itself after the phenomenological reduction as the ultimate source of all meaning is not a transcendental ego "having" consciousness, but a pure transcendental field of consciousness. Consciousness itself contains neither a transcendental ego nor any "hyletic datum." It is simply pure spontaneity, a mere activity transcending itself toward mundane things. In the manner of all phenomena, the ego, too, is not a content *in* consciousness, but an object *for* consciousness whose constitution by consciousness is to be described by phenomenology.

Sartre's view becomes more understandable when one bears in mind that Husserl had not only admitted an ego as part of the indubitable field of consciousness, but, beginning with *Ideen I*, had also developed a complete "egology" in which he tried to show how the ego as transcendental constitutes the transcendental field. Sartre denies just such a transcendental ego; the ego is not transcendental, but transcendent like all mundane things. As such the ego is not part of the original structure of consciousness, but something that is constituted by the pure stream of conscious acts. For Sartre consciousness itself is mere lucidity whereas the ego is opaqueness. According to him, therefore, liberating consciousness as transcendental field from the ego means liberating consciousness of all thingness and letting it appear in its genuine no-thing-ness as pure and free spontaneity. In defense of these views Sartre appeals primarily to our immediate experiences: in the unreflected experience we do not find an ego; it manifests itself only in reflection upon direct experiences. The passages of *"La transcendence de l'égo"* that are reprinted in this anthology have just this point as their main theme.

In the second article, *"Une idée fondamentale de la phénoménologie husserlienne: l'intentionnalité"* (1939), Sartre gives his attention to what he considers the most important characteristic of consciousness. To Sartre's way of thinking Husserl's concept of intentionality surpasses any idea of immanence, since consciousness as consciousness-of refers necessarily to something beyond itself and thus, as such, expels all things from it. Although it is true that within the realm of meaning intending consciousness and the intended things are necessarily connected and interrelated and thus, in a certain sense, one, yet both consciousness and object are nevertheless real things. Consciousness is congenitally oriented toward being-other-than-itself; it does not constitute, but it reveals being.[2] In addition to being phenomena in the realm of meaning, they are transphenomenal if one looks upon them from an ontological point of view. In explaining his view Sartre assumes a starting point in the fact that things, indeed, appear; they are perceived, and they are phenomena. This does not mean, however, that we perceive things adequately just as soon as they appear. Because of the perspectivism essential to our way of perceiving, the in-itself transcends its own appearance. Thus a thing can always be perceived more adequately, and this process of "fulfillment," as Husserl calls it, can go on even to infinity. Thus, infinity is implicitly contained in actual perception and, in the last analysis, constitutes the massiveness of real things. All this means that things indeed appear, but that they also have some kind of transphenomenality. The transphenomenality of things, however, is not something hidden; phenomena are not signs of entities that are unable to manifest themselves: there is no Kantian noumenon and no "inside of things" concealed somewhere beneath the surface. On the other hand, consciousness is always consciousness of something, of something which itself is not consciousness. Thus it implies the existence of the in-itself. For if consciousness is necessarily consciousness of that which is not consciousness, then either it must constitute that which itself is not consciousness, or it is merely facing a transcendent real thing. In Sartre's view the first hypothesis involves a contradiction and therefore one is required to admit that consciousness itself and that which is not consciousness must be real things in the world.

Sartre returns to the most important of these ideas in his major philosophical work, *L'être et le néant*. Here he also turns his attention again to some fundamental ideas from the philosophies of Hegel and Heidegger with which he dealt for the first time in the psychological studies, *L'imaginaire* and

---

[2] Jean-Paul Sartre, *Being and Nothingness*. Trans. Hazel E. Barnes (New York: Philosophical Library, 1956), p. *lxiii*.

L'imagination. Even in these earlier publications it had been clear that in Sartre's view Bergson had been wrong to reject the problems connected with "nothingness" and the "negativity" of consciousness as possible metaphysical themes, and in fact that the problem of nothingness asks for new ontological investigations into the very essence of consciousness. In addition to consciousness' intentionality, consciousness' "freedom" to produce something "non-real" is also to be stressed. It appears that Sartre wishes to determine the meaning of nothingness (taken in the Hegelian sense of the term) in function of the negativity characteristic of consciousness. This negativity of consciousness is, in turn, to be considered in relation to that which consciousness itself has posited within the realm of consciousness' intentionality (taken in the Husserlian sense of the term). Undoubtedly one of Sartre's greatest contributions was made here; in setting out to determine the meaning of nothingness, he brought back to the realm of our concrete psychological experience the dialectical scheme characteristic of any form of philosophy influenced by Hegel. Through the positing and nullifying function of consciousness, the no-thing-ness can be given only as the substructure of something else.

In his novels and plays Sartre has tried to show concretely that the world is deeply contaminated by this immanent "naughting" (*néantisation*), which he sees as the characteristic and distinctive trait of man's presence in the world (*Le mur, La nausée*). Man is that being through which nothingness (*le néant*) comes into the world. These themes constitute the main themes of *L'être et le néant.*

In the *Introduction* to *L'être et le néant* Sartre makes an immediate distinction in the realm of Being between the for-itself and the in-itself. The latter bears a strong resemblance to Descartes' *res extensa:* it is the global system of brute reality, the totality of the immediate which cannot be isolated, which is irreducible, inert, and deprived of any possibility of rational justification; it is. The for-itself is consciousness that "moves" within this "reality" and takes distance from it by putting between itself and the in-itself an infinite texture of relations (phenomena of Being), which must not be understood as faces behind which reality hides itself, but as constituting the very Being of consciousness as the eternal flight from the in-itself. It is along these lines that Sartre tries to account for the transcendence of consciousness that in his view is the central idea of Husserl's phenomenology of intentionality. "Consciousness is consciousness of something. This means that transcendence is the constitutive structure of consciousness; that is, that consciousness is born supported by a being which is not itself. That is what we call the ontological proof."[3] There can be no doubt that Sartre's further development of these ideas was very much influenced by Heidegger, in particular by the latter's view on man as ek-sistence and Being-in-the-world. "Certainly we could apply to consciousness the definition which Heidegger reserves for *Dasein* and say that it is a being such that in its Being, its Being is in question. But it would be necessary to complete the definition and formulate it more like this: consciousness is a being such that in its Being, its Being is in question insofar as this Being implies a being other than itself. . . . It is . . . the Being of the world which is implied in consciousness."[4]

Finally, it is from the indissoluble link between the radically incommunicable in-itself and the for-itself that Sartre derives the two fundamental aspects of subjectivity, namely its negativity and its freedom. Consciousness grasps itself as that which is not what it encounters in the world by negating the in-itself as its own Being. Freedom then is the necessary correlate of the negativity of consciousness as the complete negation of the in-itself. Thus man is not a thing; in fact as nothingness in the realm of Being man is not yet determined; he is free; freedom is even his essence. Man must "make" himself in freedom and complete responsibility.

In considering Sartre's work, it is important to note that whereas in his first article he makes no criticism of Husserl's view on reduction (*epochē*) and constitution, in his article on intentionality there is at least an implicit denial of the possibility of a reduction; in assuming this position Sartre simultaneously discards Husserl's conception of constitution. It is

[3] Jean-Paul Sartre, *op. cit.*, p. *lxi*.
[4] *Ibid.*, p. *lxii*.

this view which he steadfastly maintains in *L'être et le néant*. In Sartre's opinion, if there is no transcendental ego *in* consciousness, and if consciousness has no hyletic data whatsoever, then the Being of objects cannot be constituted by a transcendental ego with the help of contents of consciousness. The Being of objects is either dis-covered, as Heidegger puts it, or it can never be found by any act of consciousness. Since the latter alternative denies the intentionality of consciousness, one must admit that consciousness which experiences itself as genuinely being, dis-covers real being. But if consciousness is nothing but a "revealing intuition"[5] of things, the Being of which is different from the Being of consciousness, then a phenomenological reduction as a suspension of all affirmation of real being becomes meaningless. In trying to isolate consciousness from that toward which it is *essentially* oriented, such a reduction necessarily would annihilate consciousness. The world cannot be in consciousness, as Husserl would have it, but consciousness is in the world, as Heidegger has shown. It is this problem which forms the subject of the critical study by Natanson.

3. *Selective Bibliography*

SARTRE'S PHILOSOPHICAL PUBLICATIONS

"*La transcendence de l'égo,*" *Recherches philosophiques* 6 (1936), 85–123.

    The Transcendence of the Ego. Trans. Forrest Williams and Robert Kirkpatrick (New York: The Noonday Press, 1957).

L'imagination (Paris: Alcan, 1936).

    Imagination. Trans. Forrest Williams. (Ann Arbor: University of Michigan Press, 1962).

"*Une idée fondamentale de la phénoménologie de Husserl: l'intentionnalité,*" in *Nouvelle Revue Française,* January 1939; reprinted in *Situations,* Vol. I, pp. 31–35 (see below).

Esquisse d'une théorie des émotions. (Paris: Hermann, 1939).

    The Emotions: Outline of a Theory. Trans. Bernard Frechtman (New York: Philosophical Library, 1948).

L'imaginaire: Psychologie phénoménologique de l'imagination (Paris: Gallimard, 1940).

[5] *Ibid.,* p. lxii.

Psychology of the Imagination. Trans. Bernard Frechtman (New York: Philosophical Library, 1948).

L'être et le néant: Essay d'ontologie phénoménologique (Paris: Gallimard, 1943).

Being and Nothingness. Trans. Hazel Barnes (New York: Philosophical Library, 1956).

L'existentialisme est un humanisme (Paris: Nagel, 1946).

Existentialism. Trans. Bernard Frechtman (New York: Philosophical Library, 1947).

Situations. 6 vols. (Paris: Gallimard, 1947–65).

Partly translated in:

Literary and Philosophical Essays. Trans. Annette Michelson (New York: Criterion Books, 1959).

What Is Literature? Trans. Bernard Frechtman (New York: Philosophical Library, 1949).

Essays in Aesthetics. Trans. Wade Baskin (New York: Philosophical Library, 1963).

Réflexions sur la question juive (Paris: Mortihien, 1946).

Anti-Semite and Jew. Trans. George J. Becker (New York: Schocken Books, 1948).

Baudelaire (Paris: Gallimard, 1947).

Baudelaire. Trans. Martin Turnet (New York: New Directions, 1950).

Saint Genet: comédien et martyr. (Paris: Gallimard, 1952).

Saint Genet: Actor and Martyr. Trans. Bernard Frechtman (New York: Braziller, 1963).

Critique de la raison dialectique (Paris: Gallimard, 1960).

Partly translated in:

Search for a Method. Trans. Hazel Barnes (New York: Knopf, 1963).

SARTRE'S NOVELS AND PLAYS

La Nausée (Paris: Gallimard, 1938).

Nausea. Trans. Lloyd Alexander (New York: New Directions, 1949).

Le Mur (Paris: Gallimard, 1939).

Intimacy and Other Stories. Trans. Lloyd Alexander (New York: New Directions, 1948).

Les Mouches (Paris: Gallimard, 1943).

The Flies. Trans. Stuart Gilbert (New York: Knopf, 1948).

Les Chemins de la Liberté:

I. *L'âge de raison* (Paris: Gallimard, 1945).

The Age of Reason. Trans. Eric Sutton (New York: Knopf, 1947).

II. *Le sursis* (Paris: Gallimard, 1945).

The Reprieve. Trans. Eric Sutton (New York: Knopf, 1947).

III. *La mort dans l'âme* (Paris: Gallimard, 1947).

Troubled Sleep. Trans. Gerard Hopkins (New York: Knopf, 1950).

Les jeux sont faits (Paris: Nagel, 1946).

The Chips Are Down. Trans. Louise Varèse (New York: Lear, 1948).

Huis Clos (Paris: Gallimard, 1947).

No Exit. Trans. Stuart Gilbert (New York: Knopf, 1948).

Morts sans sépulture (Paris: Gallimard, 1947).

The Victors. Trans. Lionel Abel (New York: Knopf, 1949).

La putain respectueuse (Paris: Gallimard, 1947).

The Respectful Prostitute. Trans. Lionel Abel (New York: Knopf, 1949).

Les mains sales (Paris: Gallimard, 1948).

Dirty Hands. Trans. Lionel Abel (New York: Knopf, 1949).

L'engrenage (Paris: Nagel, 1949).

In the Mesh. Trans. Mervyn Savill (London: Dakers, 1954).

Le diable et le bon dieu (Paris: Gallimard, 1951).

The Devil and the Good Lord. Trans. Kitty Black (New York: Knopf, 1960).

Kean, ou désordre et génie (Paris: Gallimard, 1954).

Kean, or Disorder and Genius. Trans. Kitty Black (New York: Knopf, 1960).

Nekrassov (Paris: Gallimard, 1960).

Nekrassov. Trans. Sylvia and George Leeson (New York: Knopf, 1960).

Les séquestrés d'Altone (Paris: Gallimard, 1960).

The Condemned of Altona. Trans. Sylvia and George Leeson (New York: Knopf, 1961).

Les Mots (Paris: Gallimard, 1964).

The Words. Trans. Bernard Frechtman (New York: Braziller, 1964).

STUDIES IN ENGLISH

Wilfrid Desan, *The Tragic Finale. An Essay on the Philosophy of Jean-Paul Sartre* (New York: Harper & Brothers, 1960).

Iris Murdoch, *Sartre, Romantic Rationalist* (New Haven: Yale University Press, 1953).

Maurice Natanson, *A Critique of Jean-Paul Sartre's Ontology* (Lincoln: University of Nebraska Press, 1951).

R. J. Champigny, *Stages on Sartre's Way: 1938–1952* (Bloomington: Indiana University Press, 1959).

Herbert Spiegelberg, *The Phenomenological Movement*, 2 vols. (The Hague: Martinus Nijhoff, 1960), Vol. II, pp. 445–515.

Maurice Cranston, *Jean-Paul Sartre* (New York: Grove Press, 1962).

Joseph Fell, *Sartre's Theory of the Passions* (New York: Columbia University Press, 1962).

Alfred Stern, *Sartre, His Philosophy and Psychoanalysis* (New York: Liberal Arts Press, 1953).

The Transcendence of the Ego*

JEAN-PAUL SARTRE

A. The Theory of the Formal Presence of the I

If we reject all the more or less forced interpretations of the *I Think* offered by the post-Kantians, and nevertheless wish to solve the problem of the existence *in fact* of the *I* in consciousness,[1] we meet on our path the phenomenology of Husserl. Phenomenology is a scientific, not a critical, study of consciousness. Its essential way of proceeding is by intuition.[2]

---

* Reprinted from *The Transcendence of the Ego* by Jean-Paul Sartre, pp. 35–54, by permission of Farrar, Straus & Giroux, Inc. Copyright © 1957 by the Noonday Press, Inc.

[1] I shall use here the term "consciousness" ["*conscience*"] to translate the German word *Bewusstsein*, which signifies both the whole of consciousness—the monad—and each moment of this consciousness. The expression "state of consciousness" seems to me inaccurate owing to the passivity which it introduces into consciousness. [AUTHOR.]

[2] No single term is more central to phenomenology and more alien to current trends in British and American philosophy than the term "intuition." Its exposition would merit an essay longer than

Intuition, according to Husserl, puts us in the presence of *the thing*. We must recognize, therefore, that phenomenology is a science of *fact*, and that the problems it poses are problems

---

this translation. The interested reader is referred to the classic discussions by Edmund Husserl in *Ideen zu einer reinen Phänomenologie und phänomenologischen Philosophie*—Volume I, published in *Jahrbuch für Philosophie und phänomenologische Forschung*, I (1922), pp. 1–323 (henceforth abbreviated *Ideen I*). An English translation to which the reader may refer by Section numbers is published under the title *Ideas* (New York: Macmillan, 1931). The most relevant passages are in Secs. 1–4, 7, and 18–24.

Perhaps the essential point to be retained in connection with this phenomenologically oriented essay by Sartre is that for the phenomenologist the primary mode of evidence is intuitive. An intuition (summarily explained) is an act of consciousness by which the object under investigation is *confronted*, rather than merely indicated *in absentia*. Thus, it is one thing merely to indicate the Eiffel Tower (merely "to have it in mind," as we say), and another thing to confront the indicated object by an act of imagination or perception. The indicative act is "empty"; the intuitive act of imagination or perception is "filled out." Once this distinction has been made, it would seem difficult to disagree with the phenomenologist that every cognitive inquiry must ultimately base its claims upon acts of intuition, even if supplementary modes of evidence (e.g., inductive reasoning regarding the external world which is confronted by perceptual intuition) must be invoked to develop the inquiry. For an object must be present, confronted, to be investigated, however far from such original confrontation the investigation may wander as it proceeds. In the physical sciences, the reliance in the last analysis upon perceptual evidence is patent. In phenomenology, the subject matter under investigation is consciousness. The method is intuitive, then, in the sense that consciousness must regard itself to determine just what consciousness is, what consciousness does and does not include. In the present essay, of course, the issue is whether consciousness is or is not inhabited by an "I" or ego operating within or behind consciousness. When Sartre writes in the present passage, therefore, that phenomenology is a "scientific" rather than a "critical" study of consciousness because phenomenology proceeds by "intuition," he means that as in any descriptive science the first requirement is to *look at* the subject matter, in contrast to Kantian philosophy, which might be said to begin with the nature of science and to construct subsequently an account of consciousness by inference.

Owing to the impracticality of a detailed account in this place of the phenomenological concept of intuition, it may be helpful to note briefly some familiar senses of "intuition" which would be

of fact,[3] which can be seen, moreover, from Husserl's designation of phenomenology as a *descriptive* science. Problems concerning the relations of the *I* to consciousness are therefore existential problems. Husserl, too, discovers the transcendental consciousness of Kant, and grasps it by the ἐποχή.[4] But

---

quite out of place. First, intuitive knowledge has no traffic with mystical insight. The "filling out" of a previously empty consciousness of an object represents a logically distinct kind of consciousness, not some flow of feeling. Second, intuitive knowledge is not an identification with the object in the Bergsonian sense. Third, intuitive knowledge is not limited to the familiar type of intuition of the external world which we call "sense-perception." Intuition may be directed to consciousness itself (i. e., introspectively). Intuition may be directed to a highly complex object, i. e., a "state of affairs," previously set forth for consciousness by a process of judgment. For example, I may confront by an act of intuition the state of affairs "that this knife is to the right of the plate." Fourth, as may be evident from the last example, intuition is possible at any level of abstraction (e.g., I may confront in intuition the genus Red). Fifth, almost invariably to intuit an object or state of affairs is not to know its existence (e.g., to imagine the Eiffel Tower and to perceive the Eiffel Tower are both intuitive confrontations of the object). The exception concerns reflective intuition of the specious present. Sixth, to intuit an object is not necessarily to know everything about it, viz., the inadequacy of sense-perception, which is always an apprehension of the object "in profile." (Cf. below, n. 17, on the alleged inadequacy of intuition of the ego.) Thus, the notion of intuition in phenomenology does not necessarily imply the notion of certain knowledge. Yet the primary mode of evidence in any cognitive inquiry must be intuitive, according to the phenomenologist, for to learn, one must at the very least confront some of the objects in question, e.g., physical things, psychological states, number, principles of logic. [TRS.]

[3] Husserl would say, "a science of essences." But, for the point of view we adopt, it amounts to the same. [AUTHOR.] In a study of consciousness by consciousness, *what* present consciousness is (its essence) and *that* it is (the fact that it exists) obviously make up only one question. Consequently, Sartre speaks indifferently of an "essential" and a "factual" inquiry. This would not appear to be orthodox Husserlian phenomenology (viz., *Ideen I,* Introduction). [TRS.]

[4] The *epochē* (ἐποχή) is an act of withdrawal from the usual assertiveness of consciousness regarding what does and does not exist in the world. The effect of this withdrawal is to reveal the world as a correlate of consciousness. The term "reduction" employed in the same paragraph has the same meaning. (Cf. *Ideen I,* Secs. 31–34.) [TRS.]

this consciousness is no longer a set of logical conditions. It is a fact which is absolute. Nor is this transcendental consciousness a hypostatization of validity, an unconscious which floats between the real and the ideal. It is a real consciousness accessible to each of us as soon as the "reduction" is performed. And it is indeed this transcendental consciousness which constitutes our empirical consciousness, our consciousness "in the world," our consciousness with its psychic and psycho-physical *me*.

For our part, we readily acknowledge the existence of a constituting consciousness. We find admirable all of Husserl's descriptions in which he shows transcendental consciousness constituting the world by imprisoning itself in empirical consciousness. Like Husserl, we are persuaded that our psychic and psycho-physical *me* is a transcendent object which must fall before the ἐποχή. But we raise the following question: is not this psychic and psycho-physical *me* enough? Need one double it with a transcendental *I*, a structure of absolute consciousness?

The consequences of a reply are obvious. If the reply is negative, the consequences are:

First, the transcendental field becomes impersonal; or, if you like, "pre-personal," *without an I*.

Second, the *I* appears only at the level of humanity and is only one aspect of the *me*, the active aspect.

Third, the *I Think* can accompany our representations because it appears on a foundation of unity which it did not help to create; rather, this prior unity makes the *I Think* possible.

Fourth, one may well ask if personality (even the abstract personality of an *I*) is a necessary accompaniment of a consciousness, and if one cannot conceive of absolutely impersonal consciousnesses.

To this question, Husserl has given his reply. After having determined (in *Logische Untersuchungen*[5]) that the *me* is a synthetic and transcendent production of consciousness, he

---

[5] Halle, 1900–1901 (5th Investigation, Sec. 4). See also, Marvin Farber, *The Foundation of Phenomenology* (Cambridge, 1943), pp. 337–338. [TRS.]

reverted in *Ideen zu einer reinen Phänomenologie und phänomenologischen Philosophie*[6] to the classic position of a transcendental *I*. This *I* would be, so to speak, behind each consciousness, a necessary structure of consciousnesses whose rays (*Ichstrahlen*) would light upon each phenomenon presenting itself in the field of attention. Thus transcendental consciousness becomes thoroughly personal. Was this notion necessary? Is it compatible with the definition of consciousness given by Husserl?[7]

It is ordinarily thought that the existence of a transcendental *I* may be justified by the need that consciousness has for unity and individuality. It is because all my perceptions and all my thoughts refer themselves back to this permanent seat that my consciousness is unified. It is because I can say *my* consciousness, and because Peter and Paul can also speak of *their* consciousnesses, that these consciousnesses distinguish themselves from each other. The *I* is the producer of inwardness.

Now, it is certain that phenomenology does not need to appeal to any such unifying and individualizing *I*. Indeed, consciousness is defined by intentionality. By intentionality consciousness transcends itself. It unifies itself by escaping from itself. The unity of a thousand active consciousnesses by which I have added, do add, and shall add two and two to make four, is the transcendent object "two and two make four." Without the permanence of this eternal truth a real unity would be impossible to conceive, and there would be irreducible operations as often as there were operative consciousnesses. It is possible that those believing "two and two make four" to be the *content* of my representation may be obliged to appeal to a transcendental and subjective principle of unification, which will then be the *I*. But it is precisely Husserl who has

[6] Cf. *Ideen I*, Sec. 57. [TRS.]

[7] Two paragraphs below Sartre asserts that "consciousness is defined by intentionality." Five paragraphs after that assertion, reference is made once more to "the fruitful definition cited earlier." Strictly speaking, Husserl never concerned himself with a final definition, but certainly he regarded intentionality as essential to consciousness, i.e., consciousness is necessarily consciousness *of something*. (Cf. *Ideen I*, Sec. 84.) [TRS.]

no need of such a principle. The object is transcendent to the consciousnesses which grasp it, and it is in the object that the unity of the consciousnesses is found.

It will be said that a principle of unity *within duration* is nonetheless needed if the continual flux of consciousness is to be capable of positing transcendent objects outside the flux. Consciousnesses must be perpetual syntheses of past consciousnesses and present consciousness. This is correct. But it is characteristic that Husserl, who studied this subjective unification of consciousnesses in *Vorlesungen zur Phänomenologie des inneren Zeitbewusstseins*,[8] never had recourse to a synthetic power of the *I*. It is consciousness which unfies itself, concretely, by a play of "transversal" intentionalities which are concrete and real retentions of past consciousnesses. Thus consciousness refers perpetually to itself. Whoever says "a consciousness" says "the whole of consciousness," and this singular property belongs to consciousness itself, aside from whatever relations it may have to the *I*. In *Cartesianische Meditationen*,[9] Husserl seems to have preserved intact this conception of consciousness unifying itself in time.

Furthermore, the individuality of consciousness evidently stems from the nature of consciousness. Consciousness (like Spinoza's substance) can be limited only by itself. Thus, it constitutes a synthetic and individual totality entirely isolated from other totalities of the same type, and the *I* can evidently be only an *expression* (rather than a condition) of this incommunicability and inwardness of consciousnesses. Consequently we may reply without hesitation: the phenomenological conception of consciousness renders the unifying and individualizing role of the *I* totally useless. It is consciousness, on the contrary, which makes possible the unity and the personality of my *I*. The transcendental *I*, therefore, has no *raison d'être*.

[8] Published in *Jahrbuch für Philosophie und phänomenologische Forschung,* IX (1928), pp. 367–498. [TRS.]

[9] Published in *Husserliana,* I (1950), pp. 1–183. A French translation by G. Peiffer & E. Levinas is published under the title *Méditations Cartésiennes* (Paris, J. Vrin, 1947). For the discussion of temporal unifications, see esp. Secs. 18 & 37. [TRS.]

But, in addition, this superfluous *I* would be a hindrance. If it existed it would tear consciousness from itself; it would divide consciousness; it would slide into every consciousness like an opaque blade. The transcendental *I* is the death of consciousness. Indeed, the existence of consciousness is an absolute because consciousness is consciousness of itself. This is to say that the type of existence of consciousness is to be consciousness of itself. And consciousness is aware of itself *in so far as it is consciousness of a transcendent object*. All is therefore clear and lucid in consciousness: the object with its characteristic opacity is before consciousness, but consciousness is purely and simply consciousness of being consciousness of that object. This is the law of its existence.

We should add that this consciousness of consciousness—except in the case of reflective consciousness which we shall dwell on later—is not *positional*, which is to say that consciousness is not for itself its own object. Its object is by nature outside of it, and that is why consciousness *posits* and *grasps* the object in the same act. Consciousness knows itself only as absolute inwardness. We shall call such a consciousness: consciousness in the first degree, or *unreflected* consciousness.

Now we ask: is there room for an *I* in such a consciousness? The reply is clear: evidently not. Indeed, such an *I* is not the object (since by hypothesis the *I* is inner); nor is it an *I of consciousness*, since it is something for consciousness. It is not a translucent quality of consciousness, but would be in some way an inhabitant. In fact, however formal, however abstract one may suppose it to be, the *I*, with its personality, would be a sort of center of opacity. It would be to the concrete and psycho-physical *me* what a point is to three dimensions: it would be an infinitely contracted *me*. Thus, if one introduces this opacity into consciousness, one thereby destroys the fruitful definition cited earlier. One congeals consciousness, one darkens it. Consciousness is then no longer a spontaneity; it bears within itself the germ of opaqueness. But in addition we would be forced to abandon that original and profound view which makes of consciousness a *non-substantial* absolute. A pure consciousness is an absolute quite simply because it is consciousness of itself. It remains there-

fore a "phenomenon" in the very special sense in which "to
be" and "to appear" are one. It is all lightness, all translu-
cence. This it is which differentiates the *Cogito* of Husserl
from the Cartesian *Cogito*. But if the *I* were a necessary structure of consciousness, this opaque *I* would at once be raised
to the rank of an absolute. We would then be in the presence
of a monad. And this, indeed, is unfortunately the orientation
of the new thought of Husserl (see *Cartesianische Meditationen*[10]). Consciousness is loaded down; consciousness has
lost that character which rendered it the absolute existent *by
virtue of non-existence*. It is heavy and *ponderable*. All the
results of phenomenology begin to crumble if the *I* is not, by
the same title as the world, a relative existent: that is to say,
an object *for* consciousness.

B. The Cogito *as Reflective Consciousness*

The Kantian *I Think* is a condition of possibility. The *Cogito*
of Descartes and of Husserl is an apprehension of fact. We
have heard of the "factual necessity"[11] of the *Cogito,* and
this phrase seems to me most apt. Also, it is undeniable that
the *Cogito* is personal. In the *I Think* there is an *I* who thinks.
We attain here the *I* in its purity, and it is indeed from the
Cogito that an "Egology" must take its point of departure.
The fact that can serve for a start is, then, this one: each
time we apprehend our thought, whether by an immediate
intuition or by an intuition based on memory, we apprehend
an *I* which is the *I* of the apprehended thought, and which is
given, in addition, as transcending this thought and all other
possible thoughts. If, for example, I want to remember a certain landscape perceived yesterday from the train, it is possible for me to bring back the memory of that landscape as
such. But I can also recollect that *I* was seeing that landscape.
This is what Husserl calls, in *Vorlesungen zur Phänomenologie des inneren Zeitbewusstseins,*[12] the possibility of *reflect-*

---

[10] Cf. *op. cit.,* "Meditation V." [TRS.]

[11] The phrase is quoted from *Ideen I,* Sec. 46. In the *Cogito,* the
fact that the *Cogito* is taking place is necessarily so. [TRS.]

[12] Cf. *op. cit.* [TRS.]

ing in memory. In other words, I can always perform any recollection whatsoever in the personal mode, and at once the *I* appears. Such is the *factual* guarantee of the Kantian claim *concerning validity.* Thus it seems that there is not one of my consciousnesses which I do not apprehend as provided with an *I*.

But it must be remembered that all the writers who have described the *Cogito* have dealt with it as a reflective operation, that is to say, as an operation of the second degree. Such a *Cogito* is performed by a consciousness *directed upon consciousness,* a consciousness which takes consciousness as an object. Let us agree: the certitude of the *Cogito* is absolute, for, as Husserl said, there is an indissoluble unity of the reflecting consciousness and the reflected consciousness (to the point that the reflecting consciousness could not exist without the reflected consciousness). But the fact remains that we are in the presence of a synthesis of two consciousnesses, one of which is consciousness *of* the other. Thus the essential principle of phenomenology, "all consciousness is consciousness *of* something,"[13] is preserved. Now, my reflecting consciousness does not take itself for an object when I effect the *Cogito.* What it affirms concerns the reflected consciousness. Insofar as my reflecting consciousness is consciousness of itself, it is *non-positional* consciousness. It becomes positional only by directing itself upon the reflected consciousness which itself was not a positional consciousness of itself before being reflected. Thus the consciousness which says *I Think* is precisely not the consciousness which thinks. Or rather it is not *its own* thought which it posits by this thetic act. We are then justified in asking ourselves if the *I* which thinks is common to the two superimposed consciousnesses, or if it is not rather the *I* of the reflected consciousness. All reflecting consciousness is, indeed, in itself unreflected, and a new act of the third degree is necessary in order to posit it. Moreover, there is no infinite regress here, since a consciousness has no need at all of a reflecting consciousness in order to be conscious of itself. It simply does not posit itself as an object.

13 Cf. *Ideen I,* Sec. 84. [TRS.]

But is it not precisely the reflective act which gives birth to the *me* in the reflected consciousness? Thus would be explained how every thought apprehended by intuition possesses an *I*, without falling into the difficulties noted in the preceding section. Husserl would be the first to acknowledge that an unreflected thought undergoes a radical modification in becoming reflected. But need one confine this modification to a loss of "naïveté"? Would not the appearance of the *I* be what is essential in this change?

One must evidently revert to a concrete experience, which may seem impossible, since by definition such an experience is reflective, that is to say, supplied with an *I*. But every unreflected consciousness, being non-thetic consciousness of itself, leaves a non-thetic memory that one can consult. To do so it suffices to try to reconstitute the complete moment in which this unreflected consciousness appeared (which by definition is always possible). For example, I was absorbed just now in my reading. I am going to try to remember the circumstances of my reading, my attitude, the lines that I was reading. I am thus going to revive not only these external details but a certain depth of unreflected consciousness, since the objects could only have been perceived *by* that consciousness and since they remain relative to it. That consciousness must not be posited as object of a reflection. On the contrary, I must direct my attention to the revived objects, but *without losing sight of the unreflected consciousness,* by joining in a sort of conspiracy with it and by drawing up an inventory of its content in a non-positional manner. There is no doubt about the result: while I was reading, there was consciousness *of* the book, *of* the heroes of the novel, but the *I* was not inhabiting this consciousness. It was only consciousness of the object and non-positional consciousness of itself. I can now make these a-thetically apprehended results the object of a thesis and declare: there was no *I* in the unreflected consciousness. It should not be thought that this operation is artificial or conceived for the needs of the case. Thanks to this operation, evidently, Titchener could say in his *Textbook of Psychology*[14]

---

[14] Cf. E. B. Titchener, *Textbook of Psychology* (New York: Macmillan, 1919), pp. 544–545. [TRS.]

that the *me* was very often absent from his consciousness. He went no further, however, and did not attempt to classify the states of consciousness lacking a *me*.

It is undoubtedly tempting to object that this operation, this non-reflective apprehension of one consciousness by another consciousness, can evidently take place only by memory, and that therefore it does not profit from the absolute certitude inherent in a reflective act. We would then find ourselves, *on the one hand,* with an absolutely certain act which permits the presence of the *I* in the reflected consciousness to be affirmed, and, *on the other hand,* with a questionable memory which would purport to show the absence of the *I* from the unreflected consciousness. It would seem that we have no right to oppose the latter to the former. But I must point out that the memory of the unreflected consciousness is not opposed to the data of the reflective consciousness. No one would deny for a moment that the *I* appears in a reflected consciousness. It is simply a question of opposing a reflective memory of my reading ("I was reading"), which is itself of a questionable nature, to a non-reflective memory. The validity of a present reflection, in fact, does not reach beyond the consciousness presently apprehended. And reflective memory, to which we are obliged to have recourse in order to reinstate elapsed consciousnesses, besides its questionable character owing to its nature as memory, remains suspect since, in the opinion of Husserl himself, reflection *modifies* the spontaneous consciousness. Since, in consequence, all the non-reflective memories of unreflected consciousness show me a consciousness *without a me,* and since, on the other hand, theoretical considerations concerning consciousness which are based on intuition of essence have constrained us to recognize[15] that the *I* cannot be a part of the internal structure of *Erlebnisse,* we must therefore conclude: there is no *I* on the unreflected level. When I run after a streetcar, when I look at the time, when I am absorbed in contemplating a portrait, there is no *I.* There is consciousness *of the streetcar-having-to-be-overtaken,* etc., and non-positional consciousness of consciousness.

[15] Cf. above, Part I, Sec. A. [TRS.]

In fact, I am then plunged into the world of objects; it is they which constitute the unity of my consciousnesses; it is they which present themselves with values, with attractive and repellent qualities—but *me,* I have disappeared; I have annihilated myself. There is no place for *me* on this level. And this is not a matter of chance, due to a momentary lapse of attention, but happens because of the very structure of consciousness.

This is what a description of the *Cogito* will make even more obvious to us. Can one say, indeed, that the reflective act apprehends the *I* and the thinking consciousness to the same degree and in the same way? Husserl insists on the fact that the certitude of the reflective act comes from apprehending consciousness without facets, without profiles, completely (without *Abschattungen*). This is evidently so. On the contrary, the spatio-temporal object always manifests itself through an infinity of aspects and is, at bottom, only the ideal unity of this infinity. As for meanings, or eternal truths, they affirm their transcendence in that the moment they appear they are given as independent of time, whereas the consciousness which apprehends them is, on the contrary, individuated through and through in duration. Now we ask: when a reflective consciousness apprehends the *I Think,* does it apprehend a full and concrete consciousness gathered into a real moment of concrete duration? The reply is clear: the *I* is not given as a concrete moment, a perishable structure of my actual consciousness. On the contrary, it affirms its permanence beyond this consciousness and all consciousnesses, and—although it scarcely resembles a mathematical truth—its type of existence comes much nearer to that of eternal truths than to that of consciousness.

Indeed, it is obvious that Descartes passed from the *Cogito* to the idea of thinking substance because he believed that *I* and *think* are on the same level. We have just seen that Husserl, although less obviously, is ultimately subject to the same reproach. I quite recognize that Husserl grants to the *I* a special transcendence which is not the transcendence of the object, and which one could call a transcendence "from above." But by what right? And how account for this privileged treatment of the *I* if not by metaphysical and critical preoccupations which have nothing to do with phenomenology? Let us be more radical and assert without fear that *all transcendence* must fall under the ἐποχή; thus, perhaps, we shall avoid writing such awkward chapters as Section Sixty-one of *Ideen zu einer reinen phänomenologischen Philosophie*.[16] If the *I* in the *I Think* affirms itself as transcendent, this is because the *I* is not of the same nature as transcendental consciousness.

Let us also note that the *I Think* does not appear to reflection as the reflected consciousness: it is given *through* reflected consciousness. To be sure, it is apprehended by intuition and is an object grasped with evidence. But we know what a service Husserl has rendered to philosophy by distinguishing diverse kinds of evidence. Well, it is only too certain that the *I* of the *I Think* is an object grasped with neither apodictic nor adequate evidence.[17] The evidence is not apodictic, since by saying *I* we affirm far more than we know. It is not adequate, for the *I* is presented as an opaque reality whose content would have to be unfolded. To be sure, the *I* manifests itself as the source of consciousness. But that alone should make us pause. Indeed, for this very reason the *I* appears veiled, indistinct through consciousness, like a pebble at the bottom of the water. For this very reason the *I* is deceptive from the start, since we know that nothing but consciousness can be the source of consciousness.

In addition, if the *I* is a part of consciousness, there would then be *two I*'s: the *I* of the reflective consciousness and the

[16] The awkwardness alluded to is presumably the attempt made by Husserl in Section 61 of *Ideen I* to distinguish essences into two types, "transcendent" and "immanent." A consciousness not inhabited by an ego would doubtless have no "immanent essences," thus obviating the necessity for such a distinction. [TRS.]

[17] The "I" is grasped "with evidence" in reflection in the sense that the "I" is intuitively apprehended (cf. above, n. 2). Evidence is "adequate" when the object in question is grasped in its entirety (e.g., perceptual intuition is always inadequate evidence). Evidence is "apodictic" when the object or state of affairs in question is apprehended as being necessarily thus-and-so (e.g., that color is extended may be known apodictically). Sartre points out that the "I" with which reflective intuition is confronted is grasped neither adequately nor apodictically. [TRS.]

I of the reflected consciousness. Fink, the disciple of Husserl, is even acquainted with a third *I*, disengaged by the ἐποχή, the *I* of transcendental consciousness. Hence the problem of the three *I*'s, whose difficulties Fink agreeably mentions.[18] For us, this problem is quite simply insoluble. For it is inadmissible that any communication could be established between the reflective *I* and the reflected *I* if they are real elements of consciousness; above all, it is inadmissible that they may finally achieve identity in one unique *I*.

By way of conclusion to this analysis, it seems to me that one can make the following statements:

First, the *I* is an *existent*. It has a concrete type of existence, undoubtedly different from the existence of mathematical truths, of meanings, or of spatio-temporal beings, but no less real. The *I* gives itself as transcendent.

Second, the *I* proffers itself to an intuition of a special kind[19] which apprehends it, always inadequately, behind the reflected consciousness.

Third, the *I* never appears except on the occasion of a reflective act. In this case, the complex structure of consciousness is as follows: there is an unreflected act of reflection, without an *I*, which is directed on a reflected consciousness. The latter becomes the object of the reflecting consciousness without ceasing to affirm its own object (a chair, a mathematical truth, etc.). At the same time, a new object appears which is the occasion for an affirmation by reflective consciousness, and which is consequently not on the same level as the unreflected consciousness (because the latter consciousness is an absolute which has no need of reflective consciousness in order to exist), nor on the same level as the object of

---

[18] Cf. Eugen Fink, "Die phänomenologische Philosophie Edmund Husserls in der gegenwartigen Kritik. Mit einem Vorwort von Edmund Husserl," *Kantstudien*, XXXVIII (1933), pp. 356 ff., 381 ff. [TRS.]

[19] It will be recalled (see above, n. 2 and n. 17) that there are no mystical or magical connotations to this "special kind" of "intuition." In reflection, consciousness can intuit the "I" in a "special" manner in the sense that confronting this transcendent object is not the same as, say, confronting a physical thing by an act of perceptual intuition. [TRS.]

the reflected consciousness (chair, etc.). This transcendent object of the reflective act is the *I*.

Fourth, the transcendent *I* must fall before the stroke of phenomenological reduction. The *Cogito* affirms too much. The certain content of the pseudo-"Cogito" is not "*I have* consciousness of this chair," but "There is consciousness of this chair." This content is sufficient to constitute an infinite and absolute field of investigation for phenomenology.

Phenomenology and Existentialism: Husserl and Sartre on Intentionality*

MAURICE NATANSON

Heraldry and genealogy are cognate disciplines; the former often leads to exciting emblems, the latter sometimes to family embarrassments. An exploration of some central roots of existentialism certainly leads back to phenomenology, and following the line of Sartrean thought brings us quickly to Husserl's philosophy. Whether the results are more embarrassing than exciting may be decided later. Right now the problem is the nature of the family relationship. I will begin by suggesting that this relationship has as its ground Husserl's doctrine of the intentionality of consciousness and that Sartre's existentialism derives from a problematic critique and transformation of that doctrine. I will end by suggesting that Sartre's inadequacies illuminate Husserl's achievements.

The prime character of consciousness, for Husserl, is its implicit directionality. All consciousness is consciousness *of* something; all acts of consciousness intend some object. The ontological status of the intended object is neutralized by phenomenological reduction, so that the question of whether the

* From Maurice Natanson, "Phenomenology and Existentialism," *The Modern Schoolman,* 37 (1959), pp. 1–10. Reprinted by permission of the author and the editors.

object intended is real, illusory, hallucinatory, imaginary, independent, subsistent, or transitory is set aside for purposes of
description. Whether the intended object is veridical has nothing to do with its status as intended. The task of the phenomenologist, then, is to investigate phenomena as correlates
of the acts which intend them. Just as phenomenological reduction neutralizes the ontological placement of the object, so
it sets in abeyance the belief in personal identity, history, and
empirical reality of the individual making phenomenological
descriptions. The central terms of the phenomenological enterprise are within the structure of intentionality; real object and
real person are no proper part of that structure. Instead, they
may appear only as intentional concerns; that is, they may be
considered as meant or intended objects of consciousness.

Some critics of phenomenology have taken this conception
of intentional consciousness as a paradigm case of subjectivism
or some kind of solipsism. They have suggested that Husserl
has abandoned the real world, that his procedure of phenomenological reduction leaves the phenomenologist in epi-
stemic isolation, and that, consequently, there is no way of
ever achieving objective confirmation of phenomenological re-
ports. An indirect but interesting answer to these complaints
is found in Sartre's interpretation of intentionality, for the
whole point of his positive reaction to phenomenology is that
he found in Husserl's early writings a deliverance from subjectivism, an escape from the egocentric predicament. The
overwhelming importance of intentionality for Sartre was
what he took to be Husserl's insistence on a view of consciousness which transcended the subject-object dualism, which
overcame the traditional debates of idealism and realism, and
which opened up for the first time a view of consciousness
which placed the self in the world, in the midst of life, in direct
confrontation with being. Through phenomenology a return
to "the things themselves" had taken place. What Quentin
Lauer has called phenomenology's "triumph of subjectivity"
was initially, for Sartre, a triumph over subjectivism. But
victor and vanquished must be examined more closely.

What impresses Sartre in the phenomenological theory of
intentionality is the nonegological conception of consciousness

developed in Husserl's *Logical Investigations*. Intentionality in this perspective does not derive from a subject pole which is the condition for its activity. At this stage there is no transcendental ego to serve as the dynamic matrix for intentional acts. The emphasis, then, is necessarily on the noematic side of the intentional stream. Consciousness brings us face to face with reality as the correlate of intentional acts. Instead of an ego building its world, constituting its experiential façade, consciousness is thrust into reality and locates its egological nature after the encounter. The ego arises with experience; it has no status prior to experience. It is at this point that Sartre seizes on the nonegological conception of consciousness and announces its existential possibilities. For if the ego is not an original resident of consciousness, consciousness reveals itself as translucent, as a nothingness which fulfills itself purely in its intentional activity. What for Husserl began as an emphasis on the noematic aspect of the phenomena is radically transposed by Sartre into a theory of consciousness in which the non-being of the ego is the prime phenomenological datum. Husserl's nonegological theory of consciousness becomes transformed into a philosophy of nihilation.

Although Sartre's essay "The Transcendence of the Ego" is the first major statement announcing his transformation of Husserl's doctrine, his fascination with the possibilities of the phenomenological doctrine of intentionality can be seen more dramatically perhaps in his note entitled "A Fundamental Idea of the Phenomenology of Husserl: Intentionality," published in 1939.[1] Here Sartre interprets Husserl as insisting on the co-givenness of object and consciousness. Consciousness and the world are given simultaneously. And consciousness is an irreducible fact which we can only characterize through metaphors that suggest its thrusting, volatile nature. Knowing is like exploding; mind is centrifugal; consciousness is a vortex; awareness is like combat. Here Sartre is struggling to rid epistemology of the metaphysical incubus of knowledge as possession. For Sartre, one does not *have* knowledge; one

---

[1] Originally published in *Nouvelle revue française*, January 1939; reprinted in Jean-Paul Sartre's *Situations I* (Paris: Gallimard, 1947), pp. 31–35. Our references are to the latter edition.

bursts out in the acts of knowing toward the object known. Consciousness fires itself toward its mark. These strange metaphors (some of which are Sartre's and some of which are mine) support each other in suggesting a conception of consciousness as a nonsubstantial presence to the world. Sartre writes:

> Knowledge cannot, without dishonesty, be compared to possession. . . . consciousness is purified, it is clear like a great wind, it no longer has anything in it, except a movement to avoid itself, a gliding beyond itself; if, against all impossibility, you were to enter "into" a consciousness, you would be seized by a vortex and thrown out . . . because consciousness has no "inside"; it is nothing but the outside of itself, and it is that absolute flight, that refusal to be substance which constitutes it as consciousness.[2]

Here, then, is the nexus between Sartre and Husserl, between existentialism and phenomenology. For Sartre the phenomenological doctrine of the intentionality of consciousness not only leads to but *is* an existential theory. Instead of the rather staid conception Husserl presented, Sartre sees in intentionality the full drama of the life of consciousness.

> Imagine [he writes] a linked series of explosions which wrench us from ourselves . . . which throw us on . . . the dry dust of the world, on the rough earth, among things; imagine that we are thus rejected, forsaken by our very nature in an indifferent, hostile and restive world; you would then know the profound meaning of the discovery that Husserl expresses in that famous phrase: "All consciousness is consciousness *of* something."[3]

On the basis of this existentialized conception of intentionality Sartre builds his world. All of the structures of man's being that he explores—the body, concrete relations with other

[2] *Ibid.,* pp. 32–33.
[3] *Ibid.,* p. 33.

selves, the emotions, imagination—are comprehensible only in terms of their intentional foundation. Perhaps one way of viewing this procedure is to suggest that perception, understood in the broad Cartesian sense, possesses a cognitive dimension. Feeling, sensory awareness, emotionality are meaning-laden aspects of human experience, for their nature is grounded in intentional consciousness. Meaning here is not designative or referential; it is precisely that which is presented as the correlate of intentional activity. This approach to meaning becomes clearer if we turn to a further point of connection between phenomenology and existentialism.

Husserl and Sartre agree in their rejection of a naturalistic or scientistic *Weltanschauung*. Physics and mathematics are not accepted as disciplines whose methodological form is paradigmatic for all other intellectual enterprises. Rooted and remaining in the natural attitude, science commits the sin of pride if it insists on projecting its naive realistic vision of the world on to the concrete and unique problems of philosophy and the social sciences. The rejection of scientism is not a rejection of natural science. Rather, phenomenology and existentialism hold to a common front in their insistence on facing phenomena in their givenness, quite apart from causal and genetic considerations. The liberation of logic from physics and psychology in the late nineteenth and early twentieth century must be matched by a liberation of epistemology from neurological and behavioristic grounds. This is the whole point of Husserl's refutation of psychologism. And implicit in Sartre's position is the same root dissatisfaction with psychologistic theories. Phenomenology and existentialism are thus bound to each other as much by negative as by positive agreements. The common denominator of intentionality is matched by a mutual disenchantment with the explanatory categories of naturalism.

Yet despite all sympathetic connecting bonds, there are still differences between Husserl and Sartre which are more than family quarrels. There are two points of basic conflict, and they center about Sartre's rejection of the phenomenological reduction and the transcendental ego. His radicalization of

Husserl's doctrine of intentionality appears to require the abandonment of the central instrument of phenomenological method as well as the whole grounding of conscious life in a transcendental subject. Sartre's reasons for moving in this direction are complex. In addition to an early invocation of Occam's razor against the transcendental ego in his essay "The Transcendence of the Ego," Sartre goes on later in *Being and Nothingness* to protest against Husserl's idealistic reduction of the phenomenon to the noema as an irrealized object. Sartre writes:

> It is futile to attempt, by a sleight of hand, to found the *reality* of the object on the subjective plenitude of impressions and its *objectivity* on non-being; the objective will never come out of the subjective nor the transcendent from immanence, nor being from non-being. But, we are told, Husserl defines consciousness precisely as a transcendence. In truth he does. This is what he posits. This is his essential discovery. But from the moment that he makes of the *noema* an *irreal*, a correlate of the *noesis*, a noema whose *esse* is *percipi*, he is totally unfaithful to his principle.[4]

Phenomenological reduction and the transcendental ego rob intentionality of its genius by relinquishing the immediate world seized through intentional consciousness. What Sartre calls the transphenomenality of being is lost in the reduction. Now, this criticism relates to, but is not synonymous with, the argument that Sartre rejects the reduction because it brackets out precisely what the existentialist is most concerned with: existence. It is a distortion of Husserl's theory of reductions to accuse the phenomenologist of disregarding or of being unable to regard concrete existence as a philosophical problem. But the misunderstanding appears to me to be compounded by those who suggest it, since neither Husserl nor Sartre, in my opinion, makes this claim or is necessarily in-

---

[4] *L'Etre et le néant* (Paris: Gallimard, 1943), p. 28. The present translation is my revision of Hazel E. Barnes's translation, *Being and Nothingness* (New York: Philosophical Lib., 1956), p. lxiii.

volved in such an interpretation. Sartre's attack against the reduction rests immediately on his conviction that the irrealized noema lacks transphenomenal being, that the whole purpose, therefore, of Husserl's doctrine of intentionality has been undermined. Instead of consciousness transcending itself toward the objects of reality, consciousness falls back upon itself. Sartre does not argue, however, that the phenomenologist's concept of existence is somehow a shadow of the real thing, that existence in its givenness as phenomenon is a surrogate for flesh and blood reality. Indeed, it might be suggested at this point that Sartre's rejection of the reduction is based partly on phenomenological considerations, upon a common refusal with Husserl to take what is called concrete existence at face value. Those who insist on a distinction between the object as intended or meant and the real honest-to-goodness object itself presuppose a theory of *action* in which the term "real" operates as a predicate of force, displacement, and material efficacy. One major consequence of the alignment between Sartre and Husserl, I submit, is the interpretation of action as an intentional category. The real honest-to-goodness thing is the thing interpreted as honest and good, and interpretation becomes the signal moment of action. Sartre's break with Husserl is not to be found along these lines. It is not a question of existence but of transcendence. Phenomenological reduction and the transcendental ego, according to Sartre, draw us away from the reality which intentionality not only promised but gave. The Husserlian *cogito* remains trapped in immanence. Sartre writes:

> If Husserl's *cogito* is first given as instantaneous, there is no way to get outside it . . . Husserl for the length of his philosophical career was haunted by the idea of transcendence . . . But the philosophical techniques at his disposal removed from him any way of accounting for that transcendence; his intentionality is only the caricature of it. Consciousness, as Husserl conceived it, can not in reality transcend itself either toward the world or toward the future or toward the past.[5]

[5] *Being and Nothingness*, p. 109.

Sartre believes that he has liberated the lonely ego and delivered Husserl's theory of intentionality from the essential misunderstanding of its creator. It is now time to examine Sartre's good works.

Although the radicalization of intentionality requires the rejection of the transcendental ego, what is gained carries with it the impact of what is lost. Sartre is now faced with the problem of accounting for the unity and continuing identity of the ego. If the ego is, as Sartre maintains, "a being of the world, like the ego of another," if it arises only through reflection, then how is it possible to account for the ego as being *mine?* How is it that I do not confuse my ego with that of the other? Sartre answers these questions by appealing to a certain intimacy which attends my ego, to transverse intentions which spontaneously bind together the ego as object of reflection. The result, he says, is that "my I, in effect, is *no more certain for consciousness than the I of other men.* It is only more intimate."[6] But this spontaneously personal ego constitutes itself as mysteriously as any transcendental ego. Moreover, a circle in explanation results. A phenomenology of intimacy is invoked to account for personal identity when the very recognition of the ego presupposes a recognizing agent. Recognizer and recognized are reconciled in the assertion that "my I . . . is no more certain for consciousness than the I of other men." And this, I am suggesting, is reconciliation at the price of circularity. Giving up the transcendental ego deprives Sartre of a constitutive ground for the unity and identity of the self.

Coeval with the rejection of the transcendental ego is the apparent though problematic repudiation of the phenomenological reduction. Sartre argues[7] that Husserl cannot account for the transposition from the mundane to the phenomenological attitude of the individual who begins, as we all do, in the natural attitude. He interprets the natural attitude itself as a kind of objectification of the ego, an instance of "bad faith"

---

[6] *The Transcendence of the Ego,* trans. Forrest Williams and Robert Kirkpatrick (New York: Noonday Press, 1957), p. 104.
[7] *Ibid.,* pp. 102 ff.

in which consciousness seeks to escape from itself. A miracle becomes necessary for the individual in the natural attitude to perform the *epochē*. On Sartrean grounds, however, consciousness is perpetually confronted with *epochē* not as an intellectual method but, in Sartre's words, as "an anxiety which is imposed on us and which we cannot avoid."[8] Phenomenological reduction, then, is really transposed by Sartre rather than simply repudiated. But in his efforts to avoid the idealistic implications of the reduction, Sartre fails to acknowledge his profound debt at this point to Husserl's method. It is, rather, Merleau-Ponty who makes explicit the indebtedness of existentialist philosophy to phenomenological reduction. He writes:

> The philosopher . . . is a perpetual beginner. This means that he holds nothing as established which the popular majority or the scientists believe they know. It also means that philosophy cannot consider itself as definitively established in any of the truths which it can utter, that it is a renewed experience of its own beginning, and that it consists entirely of a description of this beginning. It means, finally, that this radical reflection is consciousness of its own dependence upon a non-reflective life which is its initial, constant and final situation. Far from being, as one might think, the formula for an idealistic philosophy, the phenomenological reduction is that of an existentialist philosophy.[9]

Reduction, then, opens up for phenomenological appreciation the full drama of consciousness and its initial placement in the *Lebenswelt*. And rather than Sartre, it is Husserl who should be credited with seeing the full depth of his methodological creation. Here as elsewhere, Sartre's efforts to correct

[8] *Ibid.*, p. 103.
[9] Maurice Merleau-Ponty, *Phénoménologie de la perception* (Paris: Gallimard, 1945), p. lx. The present translation is my revision of John F. Bannan's translation of the "Avant-Propos" which appears in *Cross Currents* (VI [Winter 1956], 59–70) under the title "What Is Phenomenology?" The quotation cited appears on pp. 64–65.

Husserl's "mistakes" miscarry, and this miscarriage is our final theme.

Sartre sees in most of the major principles of phenomenology implicit clues to existential philosophy; he believes that he is carrying out the vital impulse of Husserl's discoveries. This attitude and its consequences are at once suggestive and misleading. More than anything else, Sartre's advances beyond Husserl illuminate the full range of insights achieved in traditional phenomenology. Husserl's original doctrine of the intentionality of consciousness is not "liberated" through Sartre's radicalization; it merely includes the existential dimension as one of its possibilities; phenomenological reduction is not positively transposed in Sartre's analysis, for the existential possibilities were there all along; and finally, Sartre's rejection of the transcendental ego ignores its existential implications.[10] Here Sartre's determination to rescue Husserl from himself blinds him to the very subjectivity existentialism seeks. It is in this sense that Sartre's inadequacies illuminate Husserl's achievements.

If Sartre's existentialism cannot be examined without some concern for Husserl's phenomenology, it is no less the case today that Husserl is being looked at suspiciously because of Sartre's exploits. Professor Herbert Spiegelberg in a recent paper[11] warns us that phenomenology should not sell its birthright for a mess of existentialist pottage. I would suggest instead that this warning should be the occasion for self-examination rather than embarrassment, and self-examination is the first principle of Husserl's philosophizing. Most, if not all, of the results of Sartre's technical contributions will have to be reexamined phenomenologically to separate the responsible from the purely spectacular, but there is no doubt in my mind that something responsible as well as original is there to be sifted. Talk of "existentialist pottage" may give comfort to those who have little patience with either existentialism or

10 *Ibid.*
11 "Husserl's Phenomenology and Existentialism," paper read as part of a symposium on phenomenology and existentialism held by the Western Division of the American Philosophical Association on April 30, 1959, at Madison, Wisconsin.

phenomenology but who are willing to admit that Husserl, at least, is respectable. If there is any conclusion to these considerations it is that Sartre stole much of his existential fire from Husserl. Or to put the same thing differently, the lesson to be learned from Husserl is that a responsible philosopher may also be a conceptual terrorist.

IV. MAURICE MERLEAU-PONTY

Introduction

1. *Biographical Note*

Maurice Merleau-Ponty is recognized as one of the greatest French philosophers of our era. But although his name and works are known throughout the world almost nothing of a personal nature is known about him. Accounts of his life appearing in various studies contain conflicting information even about major events. In order to avoid a repetition of error, we shall include here only the most pertinent facts of his life and career as a philosopher.

Maurice Merleau-Ponty was born in Rochefort-sur-Mer in the district of Clarente Maritime, in 1908. Both his primary and secondary education were received there, the latter apparently completed with great distinction because he was admitted immediately to the École Normale Supérieure in Paris (1926), a feat not easily accomplished. It was there that Merleau-Ponty first met Sartre (1927), an event that he later described in an article as follows: "I met him [Sartre] one day twenty years ago when the École Normale unleashed its fury against one of my schoolmates and myself for having hissed the traditional songs, too vulgar to suit us. He slipped between us and our persecutors and contrived a way for us to get out of our heroic and ridiculous situation without concessions or damages."[1] From that time forward the two seem to have enjoyed a rather close friendship which finally ended by amicable mutual agreement in 1953 because of basic differences of opinion about the Korean War and other political questions.

Merleau-Ponty earned his certificate in philosophy at the

[1] Maurice Merleau-Ponty, *Sense and Non-Sense*. Trans. Hubert L. Dreyfus and Patricia Allen Dreyfus (Evanston: Northwestern University Press, 1964), p. 41.

École Normale in 1931 and immediately became a private teacher in the same school. He remained in this capacity until 1935 when he was appointed professor of philosophy at the Lyceum of Chartres, later receiving an appointment to the Lycée Carnot in Paris where he was affiliated until 1944. It is known that between 1931 and 1936 he became increasingly critical of the traditional French philosophy in which he had been schooled, and much more drawn to Scheler's version of phenomenology as well as Marcel's philosophy of existence. Side by side with these new interests, he devoted considerable time to the study of empirical psychology.

No one could have had a more excellent opportunity to further his knowledge of the "sciences of man" and of phenomenology than Merleau-Ponty had between 1935 and 1938. As it happened, during these years the experts in biology and psychology lived and taught in Paris; there were also distinguished phenomenologists on hand who were willing and able to give him reliable, firsthand information about Husserl's philosophy. Nevertheless his first contact with Husserl's phenomenology came via Sartre, who upon his return from Germany in 1934 showed Merleau-Ponty a copy of Husserl's *Ideen* and urged him to make an immediate and thorough study of the book. Merleau-Ponty was extremely impressed with Husserl's views on the "natural attitude," the reductions, consciousness's intentionality, and the intentional analysis—so much so in fact that he began also to study the *Logische Untersuchungen* and the *Cartesianische Meditationen*, which had been available in French since 1931. Merleau-Ponty was especially captivated by Husserl's last publication, *Krisis,* the first part of which appeared in 1936 and wherein for the first time Husserl's view on the *Lebenswelt* as the ultimate foundation of science was very clearly outlined.

It was during this period that Merleau-Ponty was deeply influenced by new ideas being developed by Aron Gurwitsch and Alfred Schuetz, both then teaching in Paris. Stimulated from this side, as well as by his own studies, Merleau-Ponty was rapidly coming to the conclusion that the predominant trends in biology, psychology, and sociology were not equal to the task of accounting for the organic, psychological, and social relationships between consciousness and nature. He proposed as the source of their inadequacy the implicit "naturalistic" philosophy upon which the major trends in the sciences were based. In his opinion, solutions for the problems involved would be forthcoming neither from idealism nor from Brunschvicg's critical philosophy. It would be phenomenology, he felt, that would ultimately provide the answers. Eventually these thoughts led to the writing of his first book, *La structure du comportement*, which was completed in 1938 but not published until 1942.

In 1944 Merleau-Ponty received an appointment as professor of philosophy at the Lycée Condorcet in Paris. During the course of his teaching there he wrote his second major book, *Phénoménologie de la perception*, which has come to be considered his masterwork. Upon its publication his name became established among philosophers, and he was recognized as the leading figure of the phenomenological movement in France. A careful study of the book reveals that Merleau-Ponty was not only studying Husserl between 1938 and 1945 (including several weeks at the Husserl Archives in Louvain), but also that he must have given quite some time and study to Heidegger's *Sein und Zeit* as well as to the fundamental ideas of Hegel and Marx; their influence is clearly in evidence.

In a different vein, Sartre and Merleau-Ponty, just on the eve of the Liberation, decided to found a journal, which they hoped would give them an opportunity to express their ideas and versions of existential phenomenology in all modalities of man's experience. They called it *Les Temps Modernes*. In its various issues they were able, by employing their more systematic philosophies, to interpret cultural and political events without falling back on specialized vocabularies, or making it necessary for their readers to be sophisticated in the history of philosophy before they could understand the philosophical meaning of the events dealt with. Merleau-Ponty was editor-in-chief and political director of the review from 1945 to 1952. During those years he, Sartre, Simone de Beauvoir and others contributed many important essays and studies to it.

Merleau-Ponty wrote several important articles between 1945 and 1947, and in 1948 he published them in a new book entitled *Sens et Non-sens*. As a collection these essays present a good cross section of the main ideas of his philosophy as he developed it in *Phénoménologie de la perception*. They are in effect a summary of his most significant original insights, concretely applied in the realms of aesthetics, ethics, politics, the sciences of man, history, and religion.

Merleau-Ponty was active in teaching between 1944 and 1950, spending time at various schools and colleges. He went from the Lycée Condorcet to the Lycée Saint Quentin, and from there to Lyon to become professor of philosophy from 1949 to 1950, when he was invited to occupy the chair of child psychology at the Sorbonne. The lectures for two of the courses which Merleau-Ponty gave at the Sorbonne were published in the *Cours de Sorbonne* in 1953. The first deals with the relationship between phenomenology and the sciences of man, whereas the second studies the child's relations with others.

In 1952 Merleau-Ponty was appointed professor of philosophy at the renowned Collège de France. In this position he succeeded L. Lavel who, in turn, had succeeded E. Le Roy and Henri Bergson. Merleau-Ponty's inaugural address was given on January 15, 1953 and published shortly thereafter under the title *Eloge de la philosophie*. In this invaluable booklet he first relates his own way of thinking to those who had preceded him in the chair of philosophy, and then proceeds to describe his own conception of philosophy. In the final sections he compares his own "philosophy of ambiguity" with two forms of absolute knowledge, Christianity and Marxism.

In 1955 Merleau-Ponty published *Les aventures de la dialectique*. The book was an attempt to survey his philosophy of history, but as it turned out much of it is devoted to a penetrating analysis and criticism of Sartre's philosophy. Merleau-Ponty holds here that Sartre has destroyed dialectic reason in his uncritical borrowing of the absolute concepts, the "for-itself" and the "in-itself" from Descartes. He goes on to indict this "dualism" as being not only a plain contradiction of our primordial experiences, but also a position absolutely incompatible with a phenomenological approach to philosophical problems in that it contradicts both Husserl's basic idea of intentionality and Heidegger's conception of ek-sistence.

The most significant articles written by Merleau-Ponty between 1947 and 1959 appeared in a book entitled *Signes*, which was published in 1960. All these articles presuppose an understanding of his *Phénoménologie de la perception*, and in them Merleau-Ponty is interested in showing how our perception of the immediately given lived world is the proper starting point for philosophical investigations of such phenomena as language, science, culture, art, history, and politics.

In 1960, a few months before his untimely death, he completed an essay on art, focused particularly on painting, for the inaugural issue of *Art de France*. Both Sartre and De Waelhens consider this essay to be one of Merleau-Ponty's most important publications. According to Claude Lefort, *"L'oeil et l'esprit"* is to be recognized as a preliminary statement of ideas that Merleau-Ponty intended to develop in the second part of a book he was working on at the time of his death. The book, entitled *Le visible et l'invisible*, was meant to be a new synthesis of the fundamental ideas of his philosophy; with his unexpected demise on May 3, 1961, even the first part of the book was not quite completed. However, what he had finished gives clear evidence that Merleau-Ponty intended it as a new confrontation with scientism, idealism, rationalism, Sartre's philosophy, and the so-called "platonic" elements in Husserl's phenomenology—philosophical positions with which he could not agree. The posthumously published book contains the first introductory and critical part, and also the first chapter of the second part in which he had planned to work out the new philosophical position to which he had come between 1955 and 1961. Both chapter and text notes attest to the fact that by 1960 he had come to the conclusion that the dialectic relationship between man and world cannot be the *final* source of all meaning. This "book" also reveals that Merleau-Ponty, while adopting a more critical attitude toward Husserl's phenomenology, had simultaneously become more positively drawn to the ideas of Heidegger and Hegel, and that they were, in fact, coming to occupy a central place in his thought.

2. *Merleau-Ponty's Position within the Phenomenological Movement*

From 1935 on Merleau-Ponty was vitally interested in Husserl's phenomenology. In the ten years between 1935 and 1945 he was able to obtain a profound and thorough knowledge of Husserl's philosophy as a whole. Just before the publication of *Phénoménologie de la perception* he went to Louvain for the purpose of gaining better insight into the ideas that Husserl had developed toward the end of his life. Merleau-Ponty was well versed in Scheler's interpretation of phenomenology and completely acquainted with Heidegger's and Sartre's conceptions of Husserl's original view. From his many publications it is apparent that Merleau-Ponty's version of Husserl's phenomenology remains much closer to the original ideas of the founder of the phenomenological movement than does Scheler's, Heidegger's, or Sartre's. Notwithstanding, if the *Introduction* of *Phénoménologie de la perception* is studied very carefully, along with the notes that deal explicitly with Husserl's phenomenology, it will be seen that on several important issues Merleau-Ponty has transcended Husserl's point of view by incorporating certain ideas of either Hegel, Heidegger, Scheler, or Sartre. The well-informed reader finds it somewhat strange that in other sections of the book Merleau-Ponty attempts to give the impression that his version of phenomenology is in complete agreement with the ideas of Husserl, especially with those that appeared in the manuscripts written between 1930 and 1938. When questioned about this "inconsistency" in Royaumont in 1957, Merleau-Ponty answered that his own interpretation of Husserl's ideas, even those from the later manuscripts, was meant to be an "optimistic" interpretation, that is, more a description of what Husserl must have meant than what he had actually written down in his notes. It was only in his last, unfinished, posthumously published book that Merleau-Ponty undertook to make very explicit the difference between Husserl's conception of phenomenology and his own.

There is, of course, more to be said about Merleau-Ponty's

position in the phenomenological movement as a whole. As this question constitutes the subject matter of the two essays of Kwant which follow, our remarks here were purposely kept brief.

3. Selective Bibliography

MAJOR WORKS OF MAURICE MERLEAU-PONTY

La structure du comportement (Paris: Presses Universitaires de France, 1942).
  The Structure of Behavior. Trans. Alden L. Fisher (Boston: Beacon Press, 1963).
Phénoménologie de la perception (Paris: Gallimard, 1945).
  Phenomenology of Perception. Trans. Colin Smith (London: Routledge & Kegan Paul, 1962).
"Le primat de la perception et ses conséquences philosophiques," Bulletin de la Société française de philosophie, 4 (1947), 119–53.
  "The Primacy of Perception and Its Philosophical Consequences." Trans. James M. Edie, in *The Primacy of Perception and Other Essays.* Ed. James Edie (Evanston: Northwestern University Press, 1964).
Sens et Non-Sens (Paris: Nagel, 1948).
  Sense and Non-Sense. Trans. Hubert L. Dreyfus and Patricia Allen Dreyfus (Evanston: Northwestern University Press, 1964).
Humanisme et terreur (Paris: N.R.F., 1948).
Les sciences de l'homme et la phénoménologie (Paris: Les Cours de Sorbonne, 1953).
  Phenomenology and the Sciences of Man. Trans. John Wild, in *The Primacy of Perception and Other Essays,* pp. 43–95.
Les relations avec autrui chez l'enfant (Paris: Les Cours de Sorbonne, 1953).
  The Child's Relations with Others. Trans. William Cobb, in *The Primacy of Perception and Other Essays,* pp. 96–155.
Eloge de la philosophie (Paris: Gallimard, 1953).
  In Praise of Philosophy. Trans. John Wild and James M. Edie (Evanston: Northwestern University Press, 1963).
Les aventures de la dialectique (Paris: Gallimard, 1953).
Signes (Paris: Gallimard, 1960).
  Signs. Trans. Richard C. McCleary (Evanston: Northwestern University Press, 1964).
"L'oeil et l'esprit," Les Temps Modernes, 184–85 (1961), 193–227.

"Eye and Mind." Trans. Carleton Dallery, in *The Primacy of Perception and Other Essays*, pp. 159–90.

Le visible et l'invisible. Suivi de notes de travail par Maurice Merleau-Ponty. Ed. Claude Lefort (Paris: Gallimard, 1964).

STUDIES IN ENGLISH

Mary Rose Barral, *Merleau-Ponty: The Role of the Body-Subject in Interpersonal Relations* (Pittsburgh: Duquesne University Press, 1965).

Remy C. Kwant, *The Phenomenological Philosophy of Merleau-Ponty* (Pittsburgh: Duquesne University Press, 1963).

Remy C. Kwant, *From Phenomenology to Metaphysics*. An Inquiry into the Last Period of Merleau-Ponty's Philosophy (Pittsburgh: Duquesne University Press, 1966).

Thomas Langan, *Merleau-Ponty's Critique of Reason* (New Haven: Yale University Press, 1966).

Herbert Spiegelberg, *The Phenomenological Movement*, 2 vols. (The Hague: Martinus Nijhoff, 1960), Vol. II, pp. 516–62.

What Is Phenomenology?*

MAURICE MERLEAU-PONTY

What is phenomenology? It may seem strange that this question has still to be asked half a century after the first works of Husserl. The fact remains that it has by no means been answered. Phenomenology is the study of essences; and according to it, all problems amount to finding definitions of essences: the essence of perception, or the essence of consciousness, for example. But phenomenology is also a philosophy which puts essences back into existence, and does not expect to arrive at an understanding of man and the world from any starting point other than that of their 'facticity'. It is a transcendental

* From Maurice Merleau-Ponty, *Phenomenology of Perception*, translated by Colin Smith, Routledge & Kegan Paul Ltd., London, and The Humanities Press, New York, 1962, pp. vii–xxi. Reprinted by permission of the publishers.

philosophy which places in abeyance the assertions arising out of the natural attitude, the better to understand them; but it is also a philosophy for which the world is always 'already there' before reflection begins—as an inalienable presence; and all its efforts are concentrated upon re-achieving a direct and primitive contact with the world, and endowing that contact with a philosophical status. It is the search for a philosophy which shall be a 'rigorous science', but it also offers an account of space, time and the world as we 'live' them. It tries to give a direct description of our experience as it is, without taking account of its psychological origin and the causal explanations which the scientist, the historian, or the sociologist may be able to provide. Yet Husserl in his last works mentions a 'genetic phenomenology',[1] and even a 'constructive phenomenology'.[2] One may try to do away with these contradictions by making a distinction between Husserl's and Heidegger's phenomenologies; yet the whole of *Sein und Zeit* springs from an indication given by Husserl and amounts to no more than an explicit account of the 'natürlicher Weltbegriff' or the 'Lebenswelt' which Husserl, towards the end of his life, identified as the central theme of phenomenology, with the result that the contradiction reappears in Husserl's own philosophy. The reader pressed for time will be inclined to give up the idea of covering a doctrine which says everything, and will wonder whether a philosophy which cannot define its scope deserves all the discussion which has gone on around it, and whether he is not faced rather by a myth or a fashion.

Even if this were the case, there would still be a need to understand the prestige of the myth and the origin of the fashion, and the opinion of the responsible philosopher must be that *phenomenology can be practised and identified as a manner or style of thinking, that it existed as a movement before arriving at complete awareness of itself as a philosophy*. It has been long on the way, and its adherents have discovered it in every quarter, certainly in Hegel and Kierkegaard, but equally in Marx, Nietzsche and Freud. A purely linguistic examina-

---

[1] *Méditations cartésiennes*, pp. 120 ff.
[2] See the unpublished *6th Méditation cartésienne*, edited by Eugen Fink, to which G. Berger has kindly referred us.

tion of the texts in question would yield no proof; we find in texts only what we put into them, and if ever any kind of history has suggested the interpretations which should be put on it, it is the history of philosophy. We shall find in ourselves, and nowhere else, the unity and true meaning of phenomenology. It is less a question of counting up quotations than of determining and expressing in concrete form this *phenomenology for ourselves* which has given a number of present-day readers the impression, on reading Husserl or Heidegger, not so much of encountering a new philosophy as of recognizing what they had been waiting for. Phenomenology is accessible only through a phenomenological method. Let us, therefore, try systematically to bring together the celebrated phenomenological themes as they have grown spontaneously together in life. Perhaps we shall then understand why phenomenology has for so long remained at an initial stage, as a problem to be solved and a hope to be realized.

It is a matter of describing, not of explaining or analysing. Husserl's first directive to phenomenology, in its early stages, to be a 'descriptive psychology', or to return to the 'things themselves', is from the start a rejection of science. I am not the outcome or the meeting-point of numerous causal agencies which determine my bodily or psychological make-up. I cannot conceive myself as nothing but a bit of the world, a mere object of biological, psychological or sociological investigation. I cannot shut myself up within the realm of science. All my knowledge of the world, even my scientific knowledge, is gained from my own particular point of view, or from some experience of the world without which the symbols of science would be meaningless. The whole universe of science is built upon the world as directly experienced, and if we want to subject science itself to rigorous scrutiny and arrive at a precise assessment of its meaning and scope, we must begin by re-awakening the basic experience of the world of which science is the second-order expression. Science has not and never will have, by its nature, the same significance *qua* form of being as the world which we perceive, for the simple reason that it is a rationale or explanation of that world. I am, not a 'living creature' nor even a 'man', nor again even 'a consciousness' endowed with all the characteristics which zoology, social anatomy or inductive psychology recognize in these various products of the natural or historical process—I am the absolute source, my existence does not stem from my antecedents, from my physical and social environment; instead it moves out towards them and sustains them, for I alone bring into being for myself (and therefore into being in the only sense that the word can have for me) the tradition which I elect to carry on, or the horizon whose distance from me would be abolished—since that distance is not one of its properties—if I were not there to scan it with my gaze. Scientific points of view, according to which my existence is a moment of the world's, are always both naïve and at the same time dishonest, because they take for granted, without explicitly mentioning it, the other point of view, namely that of consciousness, through which from the outset a world forms itself round me and begins to exist for me. To return to things themselves is to return to that world which precedes knowledge, of which knowledge always *speaks,* and in relation to which every scientific schematization is an abstract and derivative sign-language, as is geography in relation to the countryside in which we have learnt beforehand what a forest, a prairie or a river is.

This move is absolutely distinct from the idealist return to consciousness, and the demand for a pure description excludes equally the procedure of analytical reflection on the one hand, and that of scientific explanation on the other. Descartes and particularly Kant *detached* the subject, or consciousness, by showing that I could not possibly apprehend anything as existing unless I first of all experienced myself as existing in the act of apprehending it. They presented consciousness, the absolute certainty of my existence for myself, as the condition of there being anything at all; and the act of relating as the basis of relatedness. It is true that the act of relating is nothing if divorced from the spectacle of the world in which relations are found; the unity of consciousness in Kant is achieved simultaneously with that of the world. And in Descartes methodical doubt does not deprive us of anything, since the whole world, at least in so far as we experience it, is reinstated in the *Cogito,* enjoying equal certainty, and simply labelled 'thought about . . .'. But the relations between subject and world are not strictly bilateral: if they were, the certainty of the world would, in Descartes, be immediately given with that of the *Cogito,* and Kant would not have talked about his 'Copernican revolution'. Analytical reflection starts from our experience of the world and goes back to the subject as to a condition of possibility distinct from that experience, revealing the all-embracing synthesis as that without which there would be no world. To this extent it ceases to remain part of our experience and offers, in place of an account, a reconstruction. It is understandable, in view of this, that Husserl, having accused Kant of adopting a 'faculty psychologism',[3] should have urged, in place of a noetic analysis which bases the world on the synthesizing activity of the subject, his own *'noematic reflection'* which remains within the object and, instead of begetting it, brings to light its fundamental unity.

The world is there before any possible analysis of mine, and it would be artificial to make it the outcome of a series of syntheses which link, in the first place sensations, then aspects of the object corresponding to different perspectives, when both are nothing but products of analysis, with no sort of prior reality. Analytical reflection believes that it can trace back the course followed by a prior constituting act and arrive, in the 'inner man'—to use Saint Augustine's expression—at a constituting power which has always been identical with that inner self. Thus reflection itself is carried away and transplanted in an impregnable subjectivity, as yet untouched by being and time. But this is very ingenuous, or at least it is an incomplete form of reflection which loses sight of its own beginning. When I begin to reflect my reflection bears upon an unreflective experience; moreover my reflection cannot be unaware of itself as an event, and so it appears to itself in the light of a truly creative act, of a changed structure of consciousness, and yet it has to recognize, as having priority over its own operations, the world which is given to the subject, because the sub-

---

[3] *Logische Untersuchungen, Prolegomena zur reinen Logik,* p. 93.

ject is given to himself. The real has to be described, not constructed or formed. Which means that I cannot put perception into the same category as the syntheses represented by judgements, acts or predications. My field of perception is constantly filled with a play of colours, noises and fleeting tactile sensations which I cannot relate precisely to the context of my clearly perceived world, yet which I nevertheless immediately 'place' in the world, without ever confusing them with my daydreams. Equally constantly I weave dreams round things. I imagine people and things whose presence is not incompatible with the context, yet who are not in fact involved in it: they are ahead of reality, in the realm of the imaginary. If the reality of my perception were based solely on the intrinsic coherence of 'representations', it ought to be for ever hesitant and, being wrapped up in my conjectures on probabilities, I ought to be ceaselessly taking apart misleading syntheses, and reinstating in reality stray phenomena which I had excluded in the first place. But this does not happen. The real is a closely woven fabric. It does not await our judgement before incorporating the most surprising phenomena, or before rejecting the most plausible figments of our imagination. Perception is not a science of the world, it is not even an act, a deliberate taking up of a position; it is the background from which all acts stand out, and is presupposed by them. The world is not an object such that I have in my possession the law of its making; it is the natural setting of, and field for, all my thoughts and all my explicit perceptions. Truth does not 'inhabit' only 'the inner man',[4] or more accurately, there is no inner man, man is in the world, and only in the world does he know himself. When I return to myself from an excursion into the realm of dogmatic common sense or of science, I find, not a source of intrinsic truth, but a subject destined to be in the world.

All of which reveals the true meaning of the famous phenomenological reduction. There is probably no question over which Husserl has spent more time—or to which he has more

[4] In te redi; in interiore homine habitat veritas (Saint Augustine).

often returned, since the 'problematic of reduction' occupies
an important place in his unpublished work. For a long time,
and even in recent texts, the reduction is presented as the return to a transcendental consciousness before which the world
is spread out and completely transparent, quickened through
and through by a series of apperceptions which it is the philosopher's task to reconstitute on the basis of their outcome.
Thus my sensation of redness is *perceived as* the manifestation
of a certain redness experienced, this in turn as the manifestation of a red surface, which is the manifestation of a piece
of red cardboard, and this finally is the manifestation or outline of a red thing, namely this book. We are to understand,
then, that it is the apprehension of a certain *hylè*, as indicating
a phenomenon of a higher degree, the *Sinngebung*, or active
meaning-giving operation which may be said to define consciousness, so that the world is nothing but 'world-as-meaning',
and the phenomenological reduction is idealistic, in the sense
that there is here a transcendental idealism which treats the
world as an indivisible unity of value shared by Peter and
Paul, in which their perspectives blend. 'Peter's consciousness'
and 'Paul's consciousness' are in communication, the perception of the world 'by Peter' is not Peter's doing any more than
its perception 'by Paul' is Paul's doing; in each case it is the
doing of pre-personal forms of consciousness, whose communication raises no problem, since it is demanded by the
very definition of consciousness, meaning or truth. In so far as
I am a consciousness, that is, in so far as something has meaning for me, I am neither here nor there, neither Peter nor
Paul; I am in no way distinguishable from an 'other' consciousness, since we are immediately in touch with the world
and since the world is, by definition, unique, being the system
in which all truths cohere. A logically consistent transcendental idealism rids the world of its opacity and its transcendence.
The world is precisely that thing of which we form a representation, not as men or as empirical subjects, but in so far as
we are all one light and participate in the One without de-
stroying its unity. Analytical reflection knows nothing of the
problem of other minds, or of that of the world, because it
insists that with the first glimmer of consciousness there ap-

pears in me theoretically the power of reaching some universal truth, and that the other person, being equally without thisness, location or body, the Alter and the Ego are one and the same in the true world which is the unifier of minds. There is no difficulty in understanding how *I* can conceive the Other, because the I and consequently the Other are not conceived as part of the woven stuff of phenomena; they have validity rather than existence. There is nothing hidden behind these faces and gestures, no domain to which I have no access, merely a little shadow which owes its very existence to the light. For Husserl, on the contrary, it is well known that there is a problem of other people, and the *alter ego* is a paradox. If the other is truly for himself alone, beyond his being for me, and if we are for each other and not both for God, we must necessarily have some appearance for each other. He must and I must have an outer appearance, and there must be, besides the perspective of the For Oneself—my view of myself and the other's of himself—a perspective of For Others —my view of others and theirs of me. Of course, these two perspectives, in each one of us, cannot be simply juxtaposed, *for in that case it is not I that the other would see, nor he that I should see.* I must be the exterior that I present to others, and the body of the other must be the other himself. This paradox and the dialectic of the Ego and the Alter are possible only provided that the Ego and the Alter Ego are defined by their situation and are not freed from all inherence; that is, provided that philosophy does not culminate in a return to the self, and that I discover by reflection not only my presence to myself, but also the possibility of an 'outside spectator'; that is, again, provided that at the very moment when I experience my existence—at the ultimate extremity of reflection—I fall short of the ultimate density which would place me outside time, and that I discover within myself a kind of internal weakness standing in the way of my being totally individualized: a weakness which exposes me to the gaze of others as a man among men or at least as a consciousness among consciousnesses. Hitherto the *Cogito* depreciated the perception of others, teaching me as it did that the I is accessible only to itself, since it defined *me* as the thought which I have of myself, and which clearly I am alone in having, at least in this ultimate sense. For the 'other' to be more than an empty word, it is necessary that my existence should never be reduced to my bare awareness of existing, but that it should take in also the awareness that *one* may have of it, and thus include my incarnation in some nature and the possibility, at least, of a historical situation. The *Cogito* must reveal me in a situation, and it is on this condition alone that transcendental subjectivity can, as Husserl puts it,[5] *be* an intersubjectivity. As a meditating Ego, I can clearly distinguish from myself the world and things, since I certainly do not exist in the way in which things exist. I must even set aside from myself my body understood as a thing among things, as a collection of physico-chemical processes. But even if the *cogitatio*, which I thus discover, is without location in objective time and space, it is not without place in the phenomenological world. The world, which I distinguished from myself as the totality of things or of processes linked by causal relationships, I rediscover 'in me' as the permanent horizon of all my *cogitationes* and as a dimension in relation to which I am constantly situating myself. The true *Cogito* does not define the subject's existence in terms of the thought he has of existing, and furthermore does not convert the indubitability of the world into the indubitability of thought about the world, nor finally does it replace the world itself by the world as meaning. On the contrary it recognizes my thought itself as an inalienable fact, and does away with any kind of idealism in revealing me as 'being-in-the-world'.

It is because we are through and through compounded of relationships with the world that for us the only way to become aware of the fact is to suspend the resultant activity, to refuse it our complicity (to look at it *ohne mitzumachen,* as Husserl often says), or yet again, to put it 'out of play'. Not because we reject the certainties of common sense and a natural attitude to things—they are, on the contrary, the constant theme of philosophy—but because, being the presupposed basis of any thought, they are taken for granted, and go un-

[5] *Die Krisis der europäischen Wissenschaften und die transzendentale Phänomenologie,* III (unpublished).

noticed, and because in order to arouse them and bring them
to view, we have to suspend for a moment our recognition of
them. The best formulation of the reduction is probably that
given by Eugen Fink, Husserl's assistant, when he spoke of
'wonder' in the face of the world.[6] Reflection does not withdraw from the world towards the unity of consciousness as the
world's basis; it steps back to watch the forms of transcendence fly up like sparks from a fire; it slackens the intentional
threads which attach us to the world and thus brings them to
our notice; it alone is consciousness of the world because it
reveals that world as strange and paradoxical. Husserl's transcendental is not Kant's and Husserl accuses Kant's philosophy
of being 'worldly', because it *makes use* of our relation to the
world, which is the motive force of the transcendental deduction, and makes the world immanent in the subject, instead of
being filled with wonder at it and conceiving the subject as a
process of transcendence towards the world. All the misunder-
standings with his interpreters, with the existentialist 'dissi-
dents' and finally with himself, have arisen from the fact that
in order to see the world and grasp it as paradoxical, we must
break with our familiar acceptance of it and, also, from the
fact that from this break we can learn nothing but the un-
motivated upsurge of the world. The most important lesson
which the reduction teaches us is the impossibility of a complete reduction. This is why Husserl is constantly re-examining
the possibility of the reduction. If we were absolute mind, the
reduction would present no problem. But since, on the contrary, we are in the world, since indeed our reflections are
carried out in the temporal flux on to which we are trying to
seize (since they *sich einströmen*, as Husserl says), there is no
thought which embraces all our thought. The philosopher, as
the unpublished works declare, is a perpetual beginner, which
means that he takes for granted nothing that men, learned or
otherwise, believe they know. It means also that philosophy
itself must not take itself for granted, in so far as it may have
managed to say something true; that it is an ever-renewed
experiment in making its own beginning; that it consists wholly

[6] *Die phänomenologische Philosophie Edmund Husserls in der
gegenwärtigen Kritik,* pp. 331 and ff.

in the description of this beginning, and finally, that radical
reflection amounts to a consciousness of its own dependence
on an unreflective life which is its initial situation, unchanging, given once and for all. Far from being, as has been
thought, a procedure of idealistic philosophy, phenomenological reduction belongs to existential philosophy: Heidegger's
'being-in-the-world' appears only against the background of
the phenomenological reduction.

A misunderstanding of a similar kind confuses the notion
of the 'essences' in Husserl. Every reduction, says Husserl, as
well as being transcendental is necessarily eidetic. That means
that we cannot subject our perception of the world to philosophical scrutiny without ceasing to be identified with that act
of positing the world, with that interest in it which delimits
us, without drawing back from our commitment which is itself thus made to appear as a spectacle, without passing from
the *fact* of our existence to its *nature,* from the Dasein to the
Wesen. But it is clear that the essence is here not the end, but
a means, that our effective involvement in the world is precisely what has to be understood and made amenable to con-
ceptualization, for it is what polarizes all our conceptual par-
ticularizations. The need to proceed by way of essences does
not mean that philosophy takes them as its object, but, on the
contrary, that our existence is too tightly held in the world to
be able to know itself as such at the moment of its involvement, and that it requires the field of ideality in order to become acquainted with and to prevail over its facticity. The
Vienna Circle, as is well known, lays it down categorically
that we can enter into relations only with meanings. For example, 'consciousness' is not for the Vienna Circle identifiable
with what we are. It is a complex meaning which has developed late in time, which should be handled with care, and
only after the many meanings which have contributed,
throughout the word's semantic development, to the formation of its present one have been made explicit. Logical positivism of this kind is the antithesis of Husserl's thought. Whatever the subtle changes of meaning which have ultimately
brought us, as a linguistic acquisition, the word and concept

of consciousness, we enjoy direct access to what it designates. For we have the experience of ourselves, of that consciousness which we are, and it is on the basis of this experience that all linguistic connotations are assessed, and precisely through it that language comes to have any meaning at all for us. 'It is that as yet dumb experience . . . which we are concerned to lead to the pure expression of its own meaning.'[7] Husserl's essences are destined to bring back all the living relationships of experience, as the fisherman's net draws up from the depths of the ocean quivering fish and seaweed. Jean Waehl is therefore wrong in saying that 'Husserl separates essences from existence'.[8] The separated essences are those of language. It is the office of language to cause essences to exist in a state of separation which is in fact merely apparent, since through language they still rest upon the ante-predicative life of consciousness. In the silence of primary consciousness can be seen appearing not only what words mean, but also what things mean: the core of primary meaning round which the acts of naming and expression take shape.

Seeking the essence of consciousness will therefore not consist in developing the *Wortbedeutung* of consciousness and escaping from existence into the universe of things said; it will consist in rediscovering my actual presence to myself, the fact of my consciousness which is in the last resort what the word and the concept of consciousness mean. Looking for the world's essence is not looking for what it is as an idea once it has been reduced to a theme of discourse; it is looking for what it is as a fact for us, before any thematization. Sensationalism 'reduces' the world by noticing that after all we never experience anything but states of ourselves. Transcendental idealism too 'reduces' the world since, in so far as it guarantees the world, it does so by regarding it as thought or consciousness of the world, and as the mere correlative of our knowledge, with the result that it becomes immanent in consciousness and the aseity of things is thereby done away with. The eidetic reduction is, on the other hand, the deter-

[7] *Méditations cartésiennes,* p. 33.
[8] *Réalisme, dialectique et mystère,* l'Arbalète, Autumn, 1942, unpaginated.

mination to bring the world to light as it is before any falling
back on ourselves has occurred, it is the ambition to make
reflection emulate the unreflective life of consciousness. I aim
at and perceive a world. If I said, as do the sensationalists,
that we have here only 'states of consciousness', and if I tried
to distinguish my perceptions from my dreams with the aid of
'criteria', I should overlook the phenomenon of the world. For
if I am able to talk about 'dreams' and 'reality', to bother my
head about the distinction between imaginary and real, and
cast doubt upon the 'real', it is because this distinction is already made by me before any analysis; it is because I have an
experience of the real as of the imaginary, and the problem
then becomes one not of asking how critical thought can provide for itself secondary equivalents of this distinction, but of
making explicit our primordial knowledge of the 'real', of describing our perception of the world as that upon which our
idea of truth is for ever based. We must not, therefore, wonder whether we really perceive a world, we must instead say:
the world is what we perceive. In more general terms we
must not wonder whether our self-evident truths are real
truths, or whether, through some perversity inherent in our
minds, that which is self-evident for us might not be illusory in
relation to some truth in itself. For in so far as we talk about
illusion, it is because we have identified illusions, and done so
solely in the light of some perception which at the same time
gave assurance of its own truth. It follows that doubt, or the
fear of being mistaken, testifies as soon as it arises to our
power of unmasking error, and that it could never finally tear
us away from truth. We are in the realm of truth and it is
'the experience of truth' which is self-evident.[9] To seek the
essence of perception is to declare that perception is, not pre-
sumed true, but defined as access to truth. So, if I now wanted,
according to idealistic principles, to base this *de facto* self-
evident truth, this irresistible belief, on some absolute self-
evident truth, that is, on the absolute clarity which my
thoughts have for me; if I tried to find in myself a creative
thought which bodied forth the framework of the world or

[9] *Das Erlebnis der Wahrheit* (*Logische Untersuchungen, Prolegomena zur reinen Logik*), p. 190.

illumined it through and through, I should once more prove unfaithful to my experience of the world, and should be looking for what makes that experience possible instead of looking for what it is. The self-evidence of perception is not adequate thought or apodeictic self-evidence.[10] The world is not what I think, but what I live through. I am open to the world, I have no doubt that I am in communication with it, but I do not possess it; it is inexhaustible. 'There is a world', or rather: 'There is the world'; I can never completely account for this ever-reiterated assertion in my life. This facticity of the world is what constitutes the *Weltlichkeit der Welt,* what causes the world to be the world; just as the facticity of the *cogito* is not an imperfection in itself, but rather what assures me of my existence. The eidetic method is the method of a phenomenological positivism which bases the possible on the real.

We can now consider the notion of intentionality, too often cited as the main discovery of phenomenology, whereas it is understandable only through the reduction. 'All consciousness is consciousness of something'; there is nothing new in that. Kant showed, in the *Refutation of Idealism,* that inner perception is impossible without outer perception, that the world, as a collection of connected phenomena, is anticipated in the consciousness of my unity, and is the means whereby I come into being as a consciousness. What distinguishes intentionality from the Kantian relation to a possible object is that the unity of the world, before being posited by knowledge in a specific act of identification, is 'lived' as ready-made or already there. Kant himself shows in the *Critique of Judgement* that there exists a unity of the imagination and the understanding and a unity of subjects *before the object,* and that, in experiencing the beautiful, for example, I am aware of a harmony between sensation and concept, between myself and others, which is itself without any concept. Here the subject is no longer the universal thinker of a system of objects rigorously interrelated, the positing power who subjects the manifold to the law of the understanding, in so far as he is to be able to put together a

---

[10] There is no apodeictic self-evidence, the *Formale und transzendentale Logik* (p. 142) says in effect.

world—he discovers and enjoys his own nature as spontaneously in harmony with the law of the understanding. But if the
subject has a nature, then the hidden art of the imagination
must condition the categorial activity. It is no longer merely
the aesthetic judgement, but knowledge too which rests upon
this art, an art which forms the basis of the unity of consciousness and of consciousnesses.

Husserl takes up again the *Critique of Judgement* when he
talks about a teleology of consciousness. It is not a matter of
duplicating human consciousness with some absolute thought
which, from outside, is imagined as assigning to it its aims. It
is a question of recognizing consciousness itself as a project
of the world, meant for a world which it neither embraces nor
possesses, but towards which it is perpetually directed—and
the world as this pre-objective individual whose imperious
unity decrees what knowledge shall take as its goal. This is
why Husserl distinguishes between intentionality of act, which
is that of our judgements and of those occasions when we
voluntarily take up a position—the only intentionality discussed
in the *Critique of Pure Reason*—and operative intentionality
(*fungierende Intentionalität*), or that which produces the natural and ante-predicative unity of the world and of our life,
being apparent in our desires, our evaluations and in the landscape we see, more clearly than in objective knowledge, and
furnishing the text which our knowledge tries to translate into
precise language. Our relationship to the world, as it is un-
tiringly enunciated within us, is not a thing which can be any
further clarified by analysis; philosophy can only place it once
more before our eyes and present it for our ratification.

Through this broadened notion of intentionality, phenomenological 'comprehension' is distinguished from traditional
'intellection', which is confined to 'true and immutable natures', and so phenomenology can become a phenomenology
of origins. Whether we are concerned with a thing perceived,
a historical event or a doctrine, to 'understand' is to take in the
total intention—not only what these things are for representation (the 'properties' of the thing perceived, the mass of 'historical facts', the 'ideas' introduced by the doctrine)—but the
unique mode of existing expressed in the properties of the

pebble, the glass or the piece of wax, in all the events of a revolution, in all the thoughts of a philosopher. It is a matter, in the case of each civilization, of finding the Idea in the Hegelian sense, that is, not a law of the physico-mathematical type, discoverable by objective thought, but that formula which sums up some unique manner of behaviour towards others, towards Nature, time and death: a certain way of patterning the world which the historian should be capable of seizing upon and making his own. These are the *dimensions* of history. In this context there is not a human word, not a gesture, even one which is the outcome of habit or absent-mindedness, which has not some meaning. For example, I may have been under the impression that I lapsed into silence through weariness, or some minister may have thought he had uttered merely an appropriate platitude, yet my silence or his words immediately take on a significance, because my fatigue or his falling back upon a ready-made formula are not accidental, for they express a certain lack of interest, and hence some degree of adoption of a definite position in relation to the situation.

When an event is considered at close quarters, at the moment when it is lived through, everything seems subject to chance: one man's ambition, some lucky encounter, some local circumstance or other appears to have been decisive. But chance happenings offset each other, and facts in their multiplicity coalesce and show up a certain way of taking a stand in relation to the human situation, reveal in fact an *event* which has its definite outline and about which we can talk. Should the starting-point for the understanding of history be ideology, or politics, or religion, or economics? Should we try to understand a doctrine from its overt content, or from the psychological make-up and the biography of its author? We must seek an understanding from all these angles simultaneously, everything has meaning, and we shall find this same structure of being underlying all relationships. All these views are true provided that they are not isolated, that we delve deeply into history and reach the unique core of existential meaning which emerges in each perspective. It is true, as Marx says, that history does not walk on its head, but it is also true

that it does not think with its feet. Or one should say rather
that it is neither its 'head' nor its 'feet' that we have to worry
about, but its body. All economic and psychological explanations of a doctrine are true, since the thinker never thinks
from any starting-point but the one constituted by what he is.
Reflection even on a doctrine will be complete only if it succeeds in linking up with the doctrine's history and the extra-
neous explanations of it, and in putting back the causes and
meaning of the doctrine in an existential structure. There is,
as Husserl says, a 'genesis of meaning' (*Sinngenesis*),[11] which
alone, in the last resort, teaches us what the doctrine 'means.'
Like understanding, criticism must be pursued at all levels,
and naturally, it will be insufficient, for the refutation of a
doctrine, to relate it to some accidental event in the author's
life: its significance goes beyond, and there is no pure accident in existence or in co-existence, since both absorb random
events and transmute them into the rational.

Finally, as it is indivisible in the present, history is equally
so in its sequences. Considered in the light of its fundamental
dimensions, all periods of history appear as manifestations
of a single existence, or as episodes in a single drama—without
our knowing whether it has an ending. Because we are in the
world, we are *condemned to meaning,* and we cannot do or
say anything without its acquiring a name in history.

Probably the chief gain from phenomenology is to have
united extreme subjectivism and extreme objectivism in its
notion of the world or of rationality. Rationality is precisely
measured by the experiences in which it is disclosed. To say
that there exists rationality is to say that perspectives blend,
perceptions confirm each other, a meaning emerges. But it
should not be set in a realm apart, transposed into absolute
Spirit, or into a world in the realist sense. The phenomenological world is not pure being, but the sense which is revealed
where the paths of my various experiences intersect, and also
where my own and other people's intersect and engage each

---

[11] The usual term in the unpublished writings. The idea is already
to be found in the *Formale und transzendentale Logik*, pp. 184
and ff.

other like gears. It is thus inseparable from subjectivity and
intersubjectivity, which find their unity when I either take up
my past experiences in those of the present, or other people's
in my own. For the first time the philosopher's thinking is
sufficiently conscious not to anticipate itself and endow its
own results with reified form in the world. The philosopher
tries to conceive the world, others and himself and their interrelations. But the meditating Ego, the 'impartial spectator'
(*uninteressierter Zuschauer*)[12] do not rediscover an already
given rationality, they 'establish themselves',[13] and establish
it, by an act of initiative which has no guarantee in being, its
justification resting entirely on the effective power which it
confers on us of taking our own history upon ourselves.

The phenomenological world is not the bringing to explicit
expression of a pre-existing being, but the laying down of being. Philosophy is not the reflection of a pre-existing truth,
but, like art, the act of bringing truth into being. One may
well ask how this creation is *possible,* and if it does not recap-
ture in things a pre-existing Reason. The answer is that the
only pre-existent Logos is the world itself, and that the philosophy which brings it into visible existence does not begin
by being *possible;* it is actual or real like the world of which
it is a part, and no explanatory hypothesis is clearer than the
act whereby we take up this unfinished world in an effort to
complete and conceive it. Rationality is not a *problem.* There
is behind it no unknown quantity which has to be determined
by deduction, or, beginning with it, demonstrated inductively.
We witness every minute the miracle of related experiences,
and yet nobody knows better than we do how this miracle is
worked, for we are ourselves this network of relationships.
The world and reason are not problematical. We may say, if
we wish, that they are mysterious, but their mystery defines
them: there can be no question of dispelling it by some 'solution', it is on the hither side of all solutions. True philosophy
consists in relearning to look at the world, and in this sense a
historical account can give meaning to the world quite as

'deeply' as a philosophical treatise. We take our fate in our hands, we become responsible for our history through reflection, but equally by a decision on which we stake our life, and in both cases what is involved is a violent act which is validated by being performed.

Phenomenology, as a disclosure of the world, rests on itself, or rather provides its own foundation.[14] All knowledge is sustained by a 'ground' of postulates and finally by our communication with the world as primary embodiment of rationality. Philosophy, as radical reflection, dispenses in principle with this resource. As, however, it too is in history, it too exploits the world and constituted reason. It must therefore put to itself the question which it puts to all branches of knowledge, and so duplicate itself infinitely, being, as Husserl says, a dialogue or infinite meditation, and, in so far as it remains faithful to its intention, never knowing where it is going. The unfinished nature of phenomenology and the inchoative atmosphere which has surrounded it are not to be taken as a sign of failure, they were inevitable because phenomenology's task was to reveal the mystery of the world and of reason.[15] If phenomenology was a movement before becoming a doctrine or a philosophical system, this was attributable neither to accident, nor to fraudulent intent. It is as painstaking as the works of Balzac, Proust, Valéry or Cézanne—by reason of the same kind of attentiveness and wonder, the same demand for awareness, the same will to seize the meaning of the world or of history as that meaning comes into being. In this way it merges into the general effort of modern thought.

[14] 'Rückbeziehung der Phänomenologie auf sich selbst,' say the unpublished writings.
[15] We are indebted for this last expression to G. Gusdorf, who may well have used it in another sense.

Merleau-Ponty and Phenomenology*

REMY C. KWANT

Intentionality

Generally speaking, Merleau-Ponty is considered to be one of the greatest phenomenologists of our time. Let us point out first that no doubt is possible about the fact that he belongs to this style of thinking. The *Avant-Propos* of *Phénoménologie de la perception* reads like a kind of "phenomenological act of faith." Secondly, Merleau-Ponty has developed phenomenology in a way that is characteristically his own.

Merleau-Ponty and Hegel. That Merleau-Ponty does not want to bind himself fully to the trend of thought stimulated by Husserl becomes evident from what he writes about Hegel on the occasion of a conference given by Jean Hyppolite at the institute for Germanic studies in Paris, on February 16, 1947. Hegel, says Merleau-Ponty,[1] lies at the source of everything outstanding in the realm of philosophy achieved in the last one hundred years. He is the origin, e.g., of Marxism, the philosophy of Nietzsche, phenomenology, German existentialism, and psychoanalysis. Hegel launched the first effort to investigate the realm of the irrational and to integrate it into reason, more broadly conceived; and the continuation of this attempt remains the main task of our century. Hegel is the inventor of that reason which is more encompassing than the intellect. This reason showed itself capable of respect for the variety of psychical attitudes of different human beings, for

---

* From Remy C. Kwant, *The Phenomenological Philosophy of Merleau-Ponty* (Pittsburgh: Duquesne University Press, 1963), pp. 153–168. Reprinted by permission of the publishers.

[1] "L'existentialisme chez Hegel," *Sens et non-sens*, pp. 125–139. These two paragraphs are a paraphrase of pp. 125–126.

the different civilizations, the different methods of thinking, and the contingency of history. Nevertheless, despite its reverence for these differences, this reason does not forsake its task of finding unity in plurality, of understanding everything and thus giving everything its own truth.[2]

However, the successors of Hegel place more emphasis on what they reject in his heritage than on what they owe to him. If we do not want to abandon hope for a truth which transcends the difference of positions, if, despite our lively feeling for subjectivity, we want to remain faithful to our desire for a new classicism and an organic culture, then our most urgent task is this: we have to reconnect the ungrateful theories with their Hegelian origin which they are trying to forget. For in Hegel we find a language common to all, and a crucial confrontation of the different theories can be made in this language. We do not mean that Hegel himself embodies the truth which we seek. Hegel's work lets us hear a variety of voices; nonetheless, all the oppositions encountered among us can be found in this one life and this work of a single man. To interpret Hegel means to assume a position with respect to all philosophical, political and religious problems of our century.

These words of Merleau-Ponty should make us prudent. He wrote them after the publication of his main work. True, later he expressed himself with more reserve about Hegel,[3] yet he retained his great respect for the German philosopher. Thus,

---

[2] See the penetrating formulation of this problem in Albert Dondeyne, "Reason and the Irrational in Contemporary Thought," *Contemporary European Thought and Christian Faith,* Pittsburgh, 1958, pp. 67–107.

[3] "L'histoire universelle de Hegel est le rêve de l'histoire. Comme dans les rêves, tout ce qui est pensé est réel, tout ce qui est réel est pensé. Il n'y a rien à faire pour les hommes qui ne soit déjà compris dans l'envers des choses, dans le système. Et le philosophe leur fait bien cette concession d'admettre qu'il ne peut rien penser qui n'ait été déjà fait par eux, il leur accorde ainsi le monopole de l'efficience. Mais, comme il se réserve celui du sens, c'est dans le philosophe, et en lui seul, que l'histoire rejoint son sens. C'est le philosophe qui pense et décrète l'identité de l'histoire et de philosophie, ce qui revient à dire qu'il n'y a pas identité." *Eloge de la philosophie,* pp. 67 f.

Husserl does not constitute an absolute beginning or even an absolute norm for Merleau-Ponty. He himself situates his work in a much broader historical perspective. In general, we may say that Merleau-Ponty uses the fundamental concepts of phenomenology, but interprets them in his own way. This personal interpretation can become so important that one may legitimately ask whether the core of his philosophy is fully indicated by calling Merleau-Ponty a phenomenologist. In the following pages we will show this point in relation to some of the fundamental ideas of phenomenology.

Husserl's Intentionality. The most important category of phenomenology is undoubtedly that of intentionality. Our consciousness, says Husserl, is always consciousness *of* something. For this reason there are in every conscious act two poles, often indicated by the terms "noesis" and "noema." The choice of these terms shows that Husserl's phenomenology devotes most of its attention to the cognitive acts, even though it does not in principle limit itself to these acts.

By means of his theory of intentionality Husserl wants to say that consciousness is not first something in itself and then enters also into relationship to something else. The relationship to the other enters into the very essence of the conscious act. Thus, it follows that consciousness is codetermined by the term to which it is related. We arrive at an understanding of a conscious act by analyzing the term to which it is directed: we understand the "noesis" through the analysis of the "noema." For this reason Husserl distinguishes different "realms" in the intentional correlate of our life, and by means of these realms he distinguishes our various conscious acts. When, against all forms of relativism, he wants to show the existence of something absolute, he does so by pointing to something absolute in the intentional correlate of our conscious acts. Accordingly, against all forms of subjectivistic thinking, Husserl emphasizes the importance of the object. This return to the objective explains in part the enthusiasm which greeted the phenomenology of Husserl.

Husserl, however, always held fast to the conscious character of human intentionality. The subject pole or "noesis" has

always remained a conscious act for him. No matter how
much this conscious act is overgrown with all kinds of conceptions, opinions and interpretations, no matter how much
we have forgotten what we originally are, man's original acts
always remain conscious acts.

Merleau-Ponty's Pre-conscious Intentionality. Taking over
Husserl's idea of intentionality, Merleau-Ponty follows him in
opposing the self-contained consciousness. Regardless of how
deeply we penetrate into ourselves we always find there the
reference to the other. However, for him, the orientation,
characterizing us in the depth of our essence, is no longer, at
least not first of all, a conscious directedness. As he writes,
"Unlike what classical idealism thought, the relationship of
subject and object is no longer that *cognitive relationship* in
which the object always appears as constructed by the subject, but is a *relationship of being,* through which, to use a
paradox, the subject *is* his body, his world, his situation, and
in a certain sense enters into *interaction* with it."[4] For
Merleau-Ponty, intentionality becomes an ontological relationship. At its deepest point intentionality is, as we have already seen, pre-conscious, and in its proper core it is not
self-experience.

Of course, Merleau-Ponty does not deny that at a certain
level human intentionality begins to have a conscious character. But it is striking that he has never made this conscious
intentionality the main theme of his philosophical thought. His
attention goes mainly to our pre-conscious intentionality and,
when he speaks of conscious intentionality, he does so as a
rule only to show that the conscious level is supported by the
pre-conscious level.

Moreover, Merleau-Ponty very sharply indicates how far
removed he is from Husserl—even though he does not explicitly mention him—when he says that consciousness originally is not an "I think" but an "I am able."[5] For Merleau-

[4] *Sens et non-sens,* pp. 143 f.
[5] "La conscience est originairement non pas un 'je pense que',
mais un 'je peux'." *Phénoménologie de la perception,* p. 160. Note
that he does not say: "consciousness is *rooted* in an 'I am able,'"
but in its innermost depth "consciousness *is* an 'I am able'."

Ponty, the original subject is a power to give meaning, and consciousness seems to become something marginal. We cannot quite say that it is something accidental, for Merleau-Ponty realizes very clearly that consciousness cannot develop from the wholly unconscious. For this reason he says that consciousness has to be present from the very beginning, for that which does not think of itself from its very inception can never attain to such thinking. Strictly speaking, however, in the depth of our intentional life consciousness sinks so deeply into darkness that it becomes imperceptible. We are unable to bring it to light through reflection. Merleau-Ponty hovers between the affirmation of the pre-conscious and the realization that consciousness itself has to be also original, without being able to arrive at clarity. He himself concedes that his formulas remain enigmatic.[6]

Difference Between Husserl and Merleau-Ponty. Accordingly, the original intentionality is not yet characterized by the distance between a subject and an object. Merleau-Ponty himself says that this distance is connected with expression and especially with the word. Distance arises only on the level of consciousness and freedom. Hence the original intentionality is pre-objective. In its innermost nucleus our existence is fused with the world. Husserl, on the other hand, has always affirmed the distance between "noesis" and "noema." "Insofar as every thought demands a thought object," he says, "and this object has a relationship to the pure 'I' in the cognitive act, we find a remarkable polarity in every act: on the one side, the 'I'-pole and, on the other, the object as counter-pole. Each of these two is an identity, but the character and origins of these two identities are radically different."[7] Husserl does not know a subject that is not at a distance from the world but fused with it. He even admits a distance between the pure 'I' and the body, for he says that the pure 'I' realizes that the objects of sense experience imply a relationship to the body.

[6] *Op. cit.,* p. 463.
[7] *Ideen zu einer reinen Phänomenologie und phänomenologischen Philosophie,* Zweites Buch, *Husserliana,* vol. 4, The Hague, 1952, p. 105.

In other words, the pure 'I' looks at the relationship between objects of experience and the body and consequently has to be to some extent outside this relationship.

Thus, we see that Merleau-Ponty's intentionality differs from that of Husserl. For him, intentionality is a dialectic relationship within which meaning originates. It is an interaction through which an organism makes its material surroundings its situation. It is a remarkable mean between the causal relationship existing between things and the subject-object relationship spoken of by Husserl. For this causal relationship lies hidden in the darkness of things, and Husserl's subject-object relationship lies in the light of consciousness. In this respect also Merleau-Ponty's philosophy is a philosophy of ambiguity. The above-mentioned term "mean" is not intended to indicate a kind of conciliatory attitude. What Merleau-Ponty hopes to do is to overcome the traditional opposition of subject and object by affirming a new mode of being.

Eidetic Reduction

Meaning of Reduction. Another important topic of phenomenology is so-called "reduction." For Husserl, to reduce means to bring the immediately given back to the essential, the original. This assertion should not be misunderstood. Husserl is a phenomenologist, i.e., someone who, as the very term indicates, wants to give expression to that which appears, the phenomenal. This implies that he cannot reduce the phenomenal to anything else than that which appears. However, Husserl is not a philosopher who is simply satisfied with the phenomenal as it appears to us here and now. Our consciousness is not purely passive with respect to the phenomenal, for we make things appear to us, so that the way in which they appear depends also on ourselves.

A very simple analysis, e.g., of a human act of looking at something, suffices to show this point. All looking takes place within a field of vision. However, the presence of a visual field is not enough to speak of real looking. To look requires that within this field something comes forward as a figure. What, then, is the "something" that stands out as a figure? The reply depends very much on the human being who is looking. When, for example, father, mother, and their boy walk through the streets, they look within the same visual field, but they see quite different things. The boy looks at the playing children, the toys and candy in the stores; the mother looks mostly at the shops and the dress of other women; the father sees what is connected with his usual occupation and field of interest. What we, modern men, see is connected also with our common history. Our looking is influenced by the sciences and technology. The analysis presented here of a single example applies to all our intentional acts. In other words, much is arbitrary in that which appears to us immediately.

Husserl's "Eidetic Reduction." For this reason Husserl is not satisfied with a consideration of the immediate phenomenal world. He wants to penetrate into that which is essential, necessary in the phenomenal field. He attempts to do so by means of the "eidetic reduction." "Eidetic" comes from the Greek, *eidos,* which means, especially in the Platonic tradition, "essence." In other words, the eidetic reduction is a reduction of the concrete and immediate phenomenon to its essential nucleus. Husserl is convinced that in the concrete phenomenon there is an essential core, consequently, an element of necessity, and it is to this element that he wants to penetrate. Especially in the first period of his philosophical life Husserl placed great emphasis on the eidetic reduction. We must look, he says, at the concrete phenomenon from all sides; we have to ask ourselves what in this concrete phenomenon could be omitted, leaving it nonetheless essentially the same. In this way we must attempt to disengage the essential core from the accidental. Note that both aspects, the essential and the accidental, belong to the phenomenon itself; the essence is not something lying behind the phenomenon. Husserl applies this procedure to mathematical figures, e.g., the triangle, to cultural things, such as a table, and also to man himself.

Husserl, then, is convinced that an essential nucleus is present in the phenomenal, and that this nucleus can be discovered through analysis. This nucleus lies in the sphere of the necessary, for the essential cannot be otherwise than it *de facto* is. It appears to us and therefore can be grasped. Our search for it should not be guided by current definitions, but we should see the phenomenal essence itself. Once this essence is seen, we have to express what we have seen. Husserl's works, including those of his later years, contain many examples of such a search for the essential core. He is convinced that this core is the same for all men. By virtue of the essential core present in the phenomenal, there exists for us necessary and intersubjective truth.

Merleau-Ponty on the Eidetic Reduction. From the preceding study of Merleau-Ponty's philosophy it should be sufficiently clear that his perspective leaves no room for a necessary and universal essential nucleus. Consequently, an eidetic reduction in the same sense as that of Husserl is out of place in his thought. True, in the *Avant-Propos* of his *Phénoménologie de la perception* Merleau-Ponty endeavors to assign a place to the eidetic reduction within his philosophical perspective.[8] He acknowledges that it is necessary to penetrate into our factual existence by way of essential description. Conceptual determinations (*fixations conceptuelles*) are strictly indispensable. We are able to reflect on our existence only by becoming provisionally to some extent detached from it, by making it the object of a philosophical inquiry, by making the fact of our existence an essence. In this way we arrive at a sphere of "separate essences." They arise especially through language, for linguistic expressions fix reality. This phase, however, says Merleau-Ponty, is merely transitional. The order of fixed essences has to be reconnected with the living stream of reality. The essence is not the goal but merely a means, for it is the living stream of existence itself that we want to understand. "The necessity of having recourse to essences," to quote him verbatim, "does not mean that philosophy makes them its object. On the contrary, this necessity arises from the fact that our existence is too much locked up in the world to know

8 *Op. cit.*, Avant-Propos, pp. IX–XII.

itself at the moment when it plunges into the world. It needs the realm of ideality to know and conquer its facticity."[9]

Our existence is too much a chiaroscuro to permit us to know ourselves by simply pursuing it. For this reason we have to pass through conceptual fixation. But this fixation is only a means, a transitional phase. Merleau-Ponty quotes Jean Waehl, who says that Husserl "separates the essences from existence." What Jean Waehl means is that Husserl sees the essences as absolute points in the fluid world of the phenomenal and that he separates these absolute points from the flowing stream. Merleau-Ponty combats this opinion,[10] for he views the entire order of essences merely as a provisional conceptual fixation, imposed on us by the character of language. It is our task to overcome this fixation.

The Difference Between Husserl and Merleau-Ponty. Accordingly, the determination of the essential core, which for Husserl is one of the goals of philosophical reflection, is for Merleau-Ponty merely a phase of thinking that has to be overcome by living thought. Thinking makes use of words; it exists in words, and by using words we fix the phenomenal. In this way Merleau-Ponty attempts to assign a place in his philosophy to the eidetic reduction. However, we may ask, does his attempt not amount to this that he strips this reduction of the importance and scope it had in Husserl's thinking? Merleau-Ponty says that to understand religion and to affirm it are not the same but almost exactly the opposite. Understood and interpreted religion is no longer affirmed religion. We would like to apply these words also to his interpretation of Husserl's eidetic reduction. He understands it, he situates it within his own style of philosophical thinking, but by doing this he strips it of the meaning it had in Husserl's thought.

The ultimate reason for Merleau-Ponty's position in this matter is not difficult to find. Husserl was convinced that there are necessary and absolute grounds within our field of thought. But, for Merleau-Ponty this field has no room for necessity and absoluteness. Because Husserl's eidetic reduction presup-

9 *Ibid.*, p. IX.
10 *Ibid.*, p. X.

poses necessity, Merleau-Ponty had to interpret it in such a way that necessity is no longer presupposed. For this reason he was forced to strip it of the meaning it had in Husserl's thinking.

It is easy to illustrate the point by means of an example. Husserl is convinced that there is a human essence. He knows also that this human essence has many aspects, such as corporeity and consciousness. He attempts to penetrate into the essence of man and the essential aspects of being-man. This attempt is made by means of the eidetic reduction. Philosophy would reach one of its goals, if through this reduction it could penetrate into the essential nucleus of man.

According to Merleau-Ponty, however, there can be no question of a human essence. True, in man everything is connected. It is not purely accidental that the same being walks erect and has a thumb that can be placed opposite the other fingers.[11] In both these aspects of man one and the same grip on the world reveals itself. In this sense there is nothing accidental in man, for everything in him is connected with everything. However, this coherence is not guaranteed by any essence, but is a Gestalt, in which everything is interconnected.[12] For this reason, despite all this connection, man is permeated with contingency. Man is an historic idea and not a species of nature.[13] Thus, Merleau-Ponty is unable to apply here the eidetic reduction wanted by Husserl, for there simply is no essence to be discovered through this reduction. All we can do is understand an existential interconnection, for which we need conceptual fixations. Our terms constantly threaten to fixate human existence; hence we should be careful always to connect the words we use with the object spoken about, which is of a dynamic character.

Accordingly, it goes without saying that the sphere of Husserl's thinking differs enormously from that of Merleau-Ponty's work. A considerable mental passage has to be made when, after reading Husserl, one takes up the writings of Merleau-Ponty. Husserl's works, e.g., his *Ideen zu einer reinen*

---

[11] *Op. cit.*, p. 198.
[12] *Sens et non-sens*, p. 309.
[13] *Phénoménologie de la perception*, p. 199.

Phänomenologie und phänomenologischen Philosophie, contain many well-developed eidetic reductions.[14] He attempts, for example, to determine the core of being-a-thing and being-a-body. He tends to come to clearly-defined concepts, although he remains the eternal seeker who is never satisfied with established determinations. It would be useless to look for such attempted eidetic reductions in Merleau-Ponty. On reading his work, one senses that for him things are in principle beyond conceptual fixation.

Placing Being "Between Brackets"

Husserl knows also another form of reduction, the so-called "transcendental reduction," which became important especially in the later period of his philosophical life. This new reduction has two aspects. It is, first of all, a placing of being "between brackets" (*Einklammerung des Seins*) and, secondly, an attempt to penetrate to that which is original in our intentional life. We will consider here successively these two forms of reduction and devote attention to the position which Merleau-Ponty takes with respect to them.

Husserl and Descartes' Starting-Point. Invited to deliver a series of lectures in France, Husserl made a new and intensive study of Descartes. The results of this study were laid down in his book, *Cartesian Meditations.*[15] By way of this famous methodic doubt, Descartes had arrived at the *Cogito* which abstracts from the reality of the world. Descartes wanted to find a certainty leaving no room at all for any possible doubt. This certainty, says Descartes, cannot be found in our sense perception, for the facts indicate that the senses deceive us sometimes; consequently, we are not certain that they do not always deceive us. Moreover, says Descartes, we sometimes confuse reality and dreams. How, then, can we be certain

[14] As we will see, at the time when Husserl wrote this book he knew already other forms of reductions, which gradually began to occupy a more important place in his philosophy than the eidetic reduction.

[15] English edition published by Nijhoff, The Hague, 1961.

that we do not always dream and, therefore, live permanently in a world of dreams? Thus, we are not absolutely certain of the reality of the world. Is there anything that remains unaffected by this doubt? Yes, says Descartes, for I am absolutely certain that I think and that I have ideas, even though I do not know whether anything corresponds to these ideas. In this way Descartes thought that he had discovered an absolute and indubitable starting-point.

This Cartesian starting-point profoundly impressed Husserl. He, too, wanted to think in this perspective albeit with a different aim from that of Descartes. We must analyze, so he says in his above-mentioned book, the phenomenal precisely as it appears to us. But in that case it is only of secondary importance whether the phenomenal has any real content. There are many essences in our mind which do not have any real content, e.g., mathematical and logical entities. Yet they, too, should be of interest to the phenomenologist. He has to analyze the phenomenal, whether or not it has any real content. For this reason it is useful to abstract from the real content of the phenomenal, to place its being between brackets.

Thus, Husserl does not deny being, but no longer directs his attention to it. In doing so, he reacts especially against the empiricist and positivistic trends, which far too easily see the phenomenal as the expression or mirroring of reality, and make the real content of our ideas the criterion of their value. For this reason Husserl abstracts from the question of reality and limits himself to the phenomenal precisely as phenomenal. Thus, the primary object of his phenomenological analysis is that which appears to our mind, regardless of its real content.

By taking this position, Husserl comes close to the starting-point of Descartes' philosophy, albeit in a different way and for a different purpose. Husserl's way is different, for he does not doubt reality, but merely limits himself methodically to the phenomenal precisely as phenomenal. His purpose also is different. Descartes withdrew into his absolute certainty in order to find there a valid starting-point leading to absolutely certain knowledge of real being. He withdrew, as it were, into the fortress of interiority with the intention of leaving it as soon as possible for real being. Such is not Husserl's intention. What he wants is to analyze the structure of the phenomenal, precisely as appearing, and to penetrate into the nature of our intentional acts to which the phenomenal corresponds.

After placing being between brackets, Husserl still has a whole field-of-presence of appearing "noemata." He brings order into this field, marks its different zones, establishes the proper character of each of these zones, etc. Briefly, it is here that he finds his work. Many of Husserl's analyses are concerned with this field of presence stripped of reality.

It is a well-known fact that many of Husserl's students, who had given an enthusiastic welcome to his phenomenological way of thinking, refused to follow him on this road. They feared the danger of idealism, and this fear was not altogether unfounded. For Husserl himself speaks sometimes of "transcendental idealism," by which he means a kind of methodic idealism. There is no, or hardly any, question of a theory of being in Husserl, i.e., of any interest in the real character of reality.

Merleau-Ponty and the Methodic Reduction. The above-described aspect of Husserl's philosophy is something which has always remained foreign to Merleau-Ponty. There is hardly a trace in his works of this methodic reduction of such a pronounced Cartesian inspiration. For Merleau-Ponty, the human subject, the body-subject, is simply real mutual compenetration with a real world. No matter how profoundly we penetrate into the subject, we always find the world, the real world in it. If we were to place the real content of the world between brackets, we would have to do the same for the subject, for the subject is nothing else than project of the world, mutual compenetration with the world.[16]

[16] "La première vérité est bien 'Je pense', mais à condition qu'on entende par là 'je suis à moi' en étant au monde. Quand nous voulons aller plus loin dans la subjectivité, si nous mettons en doute toutes choses et en suspens toutes nos croyances, nous ne réussissons à entrevoir le fond inhumain par où, selon le mot de Rimbaud, 'nous ne sommes pas au monde', que comme l'horizon de nos engagements particuliers et comme puissance de quelque chose en

The "Transcendental Subject." To this must be added that Husserl's thinking on this point is spiritualistic in a way which Merleau-Ponty cannot accept. For, after this reduction there remains for Husserl a subject to which a field of presence appears. This subject, which he calls a "transcendental subject," is a thinking subject, to be distinguished from the concrete, empirical subject living concretely in the concrete world. For the concrete subject which eats and drinks itself is an appearing phenomenon with respect to the transcendental subject. Because of the character of his philosophy, Merleau-Ponty cannot accept such a spiritualistic subject. For him, this subject is an abstracted illusion of a way of thinking that has lost sight of its roots. Admitting such a subject is an expression of uprooted thought.

The objection could be raised that Merleau-Ponty comes close to Husserl's thinking when he says that there is no other being than being-for-us. For, doesn't this expression mean that he withdraws within the phenomenal precisely as phenomenal? The reply is entirely in the negative. This expression of Merleau-Ponty merely means that being, reality, is accessible to us only by virtue of our unveiling presence. However, we are an unveiling of the world, of the real world. Merleau-Ponty has never doubted, placed between brackets, the reality of the world. The reality of the world is for him a fundamental certainty, given together with the character of our being. When he speaks about the perspectivistic character of our experience, and remarks that not a single concrete thing is fully given to us since it can always reveal itself in a different way, he makes the curious remark that a subsequent observation can falsify the preceding observations of the same object. Consequently, we are never absolutely certain concerning any particular thing. About the world in general, however, we are absolutely certain.[17]

---

général qui est le fantôme du monde. L'intérieur et l'extérieur sont inséparables. Le monde est tout au dedans et je suis tout hors de moi." *Phénoménologie de la perception,* pp. 466 f.

[17] *Op. cit.,* p. 344.

The Discovery of the Original Phenomena

Husserl's Reduction of the Constituted to the Constituent.
It is striking that the transcendental reduction discussed in the
preceding paragraphs has never found great favor among the
philosophers who seek their inspiration in Husserl. However,
as we have already pointed out, the phenomenological or transcendental reduction has still another aspect—namely, the return to the original—and this aspect is more important. Even
within the transcendental field not all phenomena are equally
important for Husserl. For we must distinguish constituted
and constituent phenomena, founded and founding phenomena. The constituted or founded phenomena are not original
but have arisen from other phenomena. They have an "intentional history," i.e., they have been constructed by intentional
consciousness. Examples of them may be found in all scientific
phenomena, for scientific phenomena are not original but constructed or constituted by the scientific attitude of mind. For
instance, Newton's absolute space, empty space devoid of anything but in which things can be located, is not an original
correlate of consciousness. This absolute space is a concept of
scientific consciousness.

As we have indicated, Husserl wants to bring clarity into the
realm of phenomena. He believes that this can be done only
by reducing the constituted or founded phenomena to constituent or founding phenomena. His ideal is to penetrate into
the most profound, most original phenomena and from there
to understand the field of the phenomenal. Thus, the scientific
phenomena have to be reduced to prescientific phenomena,
and among the latter we must seek to discover the fundamental phenomena. Husserl aims at the ultimate, the irreducible.
In many masterful analyses he endeavors to execute his self-
appointed task without, however, ever being satisfied with
himself. He constantly delves deeper, but his philosophical
endeavor never seems to reach bottom. He assigned the task
of realizing his ideal to phenomenology and seems to have
thought that this task was capable of being executed. Its execution, he hoped, would provide a permanent basis not only for

philosophy but also for the entire life of science. With genuine passion he labored his whole life at this task and he demanded of his students that they take it over.

The Terminus of the Reduction: Absolute Philosophy. What, we may ask, is the nature of these so-called "grounds," which Husserl endeavored to discover? They lie concealed under the constituted, the founded, yet they are phenomena, i.e., correlates of consciousness. Their phenomenal character should be evident even from the fact that Husserl, as we have pointed out, placed being between brackets and limited himself to the phenomenal field in order to penetrate into these fundamental phenomena. These phenomena, then, are supposed to lie in the ideal field in which the transcendental 'I' places itself. Thus, the terminus of the reduction is something that is a light to the mind, even though it is buried under superficial phenomena. For this reason Husserl always aimed at absolute evidence, absolute knowledge. He endeavored to find *the* philosophy, which would give definitive clarity to the searching mind. He could not be satisfied with subjectivism and relativism. Even at the very beginning of his philosophical career he wanted to refute all kinds of relativism by pointing to absolute moments in man's cognitive life. Despite all the subsequent modifications of his philosophical inquiries he never abandoned this ideal.

Merleau-Ponty's Rejection of Husserl's Ideal. Like Husserl, Merleau-Ponty accepts a kind of transcendental reduction and he also wants to reduce the constituted, the founded to the original. However, these Husserlian notions undergo an essential change in Merleau-Ponty's philosophy. For, according to him, the original lies buried in a dimension of darkness in such a way that it cannot be brought to light. Our existence is interwoven with the world, is a dialogue with the world. This dialogue reaches its most profound point there where the first and most original meaning arises, a meaning that is preconscious and pre-personal. Whatever is in our consciousness, whatever comes to light, becomes lucid, originates also in this darkness. As we have seen, man is able to obtain a measure of knowledge regarding this dark depth. He is able to divine something about the mysterious dialogue between the body-subject and the world. However, according to Merleau-Ponty, an absolute illumination of the phenomenal field is in principle impossible. All man can do is to erect some pointers in a darkness which resists full illumination.

Thus, Merleau-Ponty rejects the very ideal aimed at by Husserl. His fundamental philosophical aim itself differs radically from that of Husserl. Despite a certain similarity of terminology, these two philosophers differ essentially on this point. We have the impression that Merleau-Ponty is well aware of this, but tries to conceal the difference through his interpretation of Husserl. He quotes Husserl when it suits his interpretation, but omits numerous texts that do not permit his view.[18] The fundamental sphere of his philosophy differs from that of Husserl. The difference manifests itself very clearly when one reads the works of these two men. Merleau-Ponty does not and cannot believe in a definitive form of philosophical thought. He rejects absolute insights that would be valid for all. He does not admit any ultimate knowledge to which the entire history of philosophical thought would be tending. Husserl's tendency to an ideal of intelligibility is wholly foreign to Merleau-Ponty.

Merleau-Ponty and Phenomenology. By considering a few of the important topics of phenomenology we have shown that there is a deep-seated difference between Husserl and Merleau-Ponty. While Merleau-Ponty takes up the phenomenological themata and speaks the language of phenomenology, he has his own unique interpretation. Undoubtedly, phenomenology has exercised great influence on him, but the reverse is also true. Merleau-Ponty's fundamental discovery is, as we have said, his theory of the body-subject. It is in the light—or should we say, in the darkness?—of this discovery that he interprets all phenomenological data.

How, one may ask, should we characterize Merleau-Ponty, the philosopher? As the philosopher of the body-subject or as

[18] Sometimes, however, Merleau-Ponty admits that his philosophy differs from that of Husserl. See, e.g., *op. cit.,* p. 73, footnote 1.

phenomenologist? What is the crucial element of his philosophy, the discovery of the body-subject or his phenomenological inspiration? In reply let us quote a text of Merleau-Ponty. "Phenomenology," he says, "may be practised and can be recognized as a way of thinking, as a style. It exists as a movement before it becomes fully conscious of itself as a philosophy. It has been pursued for a long time already, and one may find its disciples everywhere, in Hegel and in Kierkegaard, of course, but also in Marx, Nietzsche and Freud."[19] If phenomenology as a way and style of thinking is present in all these philosophers, it evidently is a way of thinking that can be pursued in very divergent fashions. Merleau-Ponty himself has used it in a wholly personal way. He is and remains himself even when he speaks the language of phenomenology. He cannot be classified as belonging to any particular school of thought.

A man is a philosopher only, writes Merleau-Ponty, when he thinks and writes simply because there are things to see.[20] Because human beings are dependent on one another, we have to let those who have thought and written before us help us when we want to say what we see. Nevertheless, we must pursue philosophy, for we have our gaze fixed on the things that are to be seen. This is what Merleau-Ponty himself does. He is an original philosopher and, therefore, remains personal even when he lets himself be inspired by others. He is not satisfied with simply explaining one or the other trend of thinking. He is simply himself, even when he accepts the aid of others in being himself. Such a thing can be affirmed only of great and independent philosophers. Any generation has at most a few of these.

[19] *Op. cit.*, Avant-Propos, p. II.
[20] "Car philosopher, c'est chercher, c'est impliquer qu'il y a des choses à voir et à dire." *Eloge de la philosophie*, p. 57.

Merleau-Ponty's Criticism
of Husserl's Eidetic Reduction*

REMY C. KWANT

A. Introduction

During the last years of his life, Merleau-Ponty wrote two important texts on Husserl's philosophy. The first, entitled, "The Philosopher and His Shadow,"[1] was published in *Signs;* the second is the chapter from *The Visible and the Invisible* that we will now consider, viz., "Interrogation and Intuition."[2] The character of the two texts is quite different. The first is a positive criticism of Husserl's philosophy, while the second tends to be negative.

In "The Philosopher and His Shadow," Merleau-Ponty says that we should make a distinction between the explicit statements of a philosopher and the fundamental light which enabled him to advance those statements.[3] This fundamental light itself is usually not stated; yet it is somehow present in all the statements he makes. According to Merleau-Ponty, Husserl's explicit philosophy is rationalistic, and even idealistic. He brackets Being and seems to be looking for absolute concepts. There are, however, many signs that Husserl was never a complete rationalist and that he never denied the awareness which Merleau-Ponty expressed in the sentence,

---

* From Remy C. Kwant, *From Phenomenology to Metaphysics,* (Pittsburgh: Duquesne University Press, 1966), pp. 156-169. Reprinted by permission of the publishers.

[1] *Signs,* pp. 159-181.

[2] M. Merleau-Ponty, *Le visible et l'invisible* (Paris: Gallimard, 1964), pp. 142-171. This book is hereafter quoted as *V.I.*

[3] "We should like to try to evoke this unthought-of element in Husserl's thought in the margin of some old pages." *Signs,* p. 160.

"J'en suis."[4] Merleau-Ponty collects these indications and tries to demonstrate that the fundamental light in which Husserl thought is more acceptable than many of his explicit statements.

In "Interrogation and Intuition" Merleau-Ponty analyzes and rejects Husserl's eidetic reduction. While in this chapter Merleau-Ponty's judgment of Husserl is more negative than in "The Philosopher and His Shadow," the two texts do not contradict one another at all. In "Interrogation and Intuition" Merleau-Ponty criticizes the explicit statements of Husserl, which he also rejected earlier in "The Philosopher and His Shadow." In the later text Merleau-Ponty demonstrates that there is an implicit ground which is more acceptable than the explicit statements; this, of course, is not excluded in the first text. For our purpose, "Interrogation and Intuition" is more important.

Merleau-Ponty wrote about Husserl's eidetic reduction as early as the Preface of *Phenomenology of Perception.*[5] He denied then the ultimate value of the eidetic reduction, although he attributed a provisional value to it.[6] The phenomenologist tries to find the character, the structure of the experienced world, of the temporal stream of real life. There is no room here for conceptual idealization. But Merleau-Ponty admits that the conceptual idealization, the eidetic reduction, is useful and even necessary as a provisional phase which, however, must be surpassed.[7] We abstract some aspects from the integral unity of concrete experience and transform them into the content of our concepts. We try to define the content of

---

[4] "Originally a project to gain intellectual possession of the world, constitution becomes increasingly, as Husserl's thought matures, the means of unveiling a back side of things that we have not constituted." *Signs,* p. 180.

[5] *Phenomenology of Perception,* Preface, pp. XIV–XVII.

[6] "Husserl's essences are destined to bring back all the living relationships of experience, as the fisherman's net draws up from the depth of the ocean quivering fish and seaweed." *Phenomenology of Perception,* Preface, p. XV.

[7] "Jean Wahl is therefore wrong in saying that 'Husserl separates essences from existence'. The separated essences are those of language." *Ibid.*

such concepts in a rational manner. We are not allowed, however, to stop at this point. The conceptual fixation serves only to understand better the stream of real experience. The conceptual fixation, therefore, must be provisional and our concepts finally must be reduced to experience.[8]

It is evident that this interpretation of the eidetic reduction differs from Husserl's conception of it, because Husserl did not see his eidetic reduction as a provisional phase of thought. But in his first text Merleau-Ponty tried to leave room for this important element of Husserl's philosophy. In "Interrogation and Intuition," however, Merleau-Ponty radically rejects the eidetic reduction. Here he says that we must finally break with the myths of induction and eidetic reduction.[9] We will now summarize this chapter of Merleau-Ponty's book.

B. The Function of Eidetic Reduction in Husserl's Philosophy

In daily life we often ask questions which can easily be answered.[10] We ask where we are, what time it is. We can answer such questions because we have constructed systems which help us to indicate the time and the place in which we stand. These systems, however, have an artificial character. The answers themselves can be questioned again. We can make the questions themselves radical and so arrive at the question of what it means to be in space and to exist in a temporal manner. Philosophy seems to be a radical asking of the common questions of everyday.[11] But when we radically ask the common questions of everyday, they take on a different meaning.[12] When we simply ask what time it is, we suppose our fundamental awareness of existing in a temporal manner; but we do not question this fundamental awareness itself. Philosophy does so.

[8] Kwant, *The Phenomenological Philosophy of Merleau-Ponty*, pp. 157–161.
[9] *V.I.*, p. 155.
[10] *V.I.*, pp. 142–143.
[11] "La philosophie, à première vue, généralise seulement ce genre de questions." *V.I.*, p. 142.
[12] "En s'étendant à tout, la question commune change de sens." *V.I.*, p. 144.

No Escape from Perceptive Certainty. Our perceptive awareness teaches us that we live in space, in time, in a world, in a field of colors and sounds. But our perceptive awareness is a perceptive faith. Real perception and illusion are commingled. According to many philosophers our perceptive faith is not reliable; and the method of doubt must help us to arrive at real and undoubtable certainties.

However, the philosophers who say that our perceptive faith is unreliable and who look for another foundation of certainty are always to a certain extent "hypocritical." They deny on the one hand that our perception is reliable; but, on the other, they always select some data of exterior or interior perception and base their certainty on that data. They rely, e.g., on our perception of quantity and quantitative relations, on our perception of the appearance of things, sensations, representations or thought. If they want to avoid radical scepticism—and this attitude of mind ultimately is impossible because the sceptical philosopher is certain at least about his scepticism—they must base their certainty on some data of perceptive faith. Perceptive faith is our primordial contact with Being, and it is, therefore, our final basis of certainty.[13]

Descartes' methodic doubt does not escape this ambiguous attitude.[14] Descartes admits that our perception is certain, because his philosophical doubt is only methodic. But the certainty of perception, he maintains, is commingled with many ambiguous facts; and he wants to arrive at a certainty of pure reason that does not depend on any fact. This desire itself, however, finds its origin in his experience of perceptive certainty. He could not desire to have the certainty of pure reason if he were not living in his perceptive certainty. His experience of ambiguous certainty inspires his desire for absolute certainty.[15] He bases his so-called absolute certainty on

[13] "C'est au nom et au profit de ces réalités flottantes que la réalité solide est mise en doute. On ne sort pas du quelque chose, et le doute comme destruction des certitudes n'est pas doute." *V.I.,* p. 143.

[14] *V.I.,* pp. 143–144.

[15] "Ainsi le doute methodique, celui qui est conduit dans la zone volontaire de nous-mêmes, se réfère à l'Être, puisqu'il résiste à une

the cogito, but this cogito is also commingled with facts. It would not exist in the manner Descartes experiences it if man did not speak. We are certain because we are involved in Being. This involvement is a clarity which is essentially commingled with facts. We cannot arrive at a reasonable certainty that is completely free of all facts.

Husserl's Philosophy of Meaning. Husserl recognizes this. He therefore does not use the method of doubt, whether sceptical or methodic. He does not deny real Being nor does he doubt it; he simply puts the question of Being aside. He does not ask whether Being exists. Whether Being is real or unreal, whether it occasions certainty or doubt, there always remains one fundamental question, viz., *what is Being?* Being appears to us. What does appear to us? Husserl does not affirm that Being transcends us, nor does he say that Being is merely immanent. He simply asks what Being is. This is the fundamental question of Husserl. Being is the intentional object of our human activities. Husserl questions this intentional object without being concerned about its ontological status.[16]

Husserl's philosophy is a philosophy of meaning. However, he is not looking for the meaning which reveals itself as a matter of fact, but for absolute and necessary meaning. Our words always mean something. When we say "table" or "world," these words have a meaning. Husserl seeks the conditions which must be fulfilled so that we can speak of "table" and "world." He distinguishes between the accidental and the necessary aspects of meaning. He tries to remove all the accidental aspects in order to penetrate into the necessary ones. It is accidental that this table is brown and small. Which are the essential conditions of any table at all? Husserl looks for

évidence de fait, refoule une vérité involontaire dont il avoue qu'elle est déjà là et dont s'inspire le projet même d'une évidence qui soit absolue." *V.I.*, p. 144.

16 ". . . ne plus nier, ne plus douter même, reculer seulement pour voir le monde et l'Être, ou encore les mettre entre guillemets comme on fait des propos d'un autre, les laisser parler, se mettre à l'écoute.

"Alors, si la question ne peut plus être celle du *an sit,* elle devient celle du *quid sit.*" *Ibid.*

the essence of things. This essence is an ideal being. It is neither this nor that appearance. It is the essence which reveals itself in all the appearances.[17] The essences condition the appearance of meaningful things; they condition our language and all our logical operations as well.

Husserl looks for the philosophical grammar of our field of meaning. There must be nuclei of meaning, fundamental points of light which make the whole field of meaning possible. These nuclei of meaning determine the coherence of our whole field of meaning. What makes us say that beings are living, that they are material, that they are spiritual, that they are human? Which are the most fundamental meanings? How do the other meanings derive from them? These are Husserl's questions as he studies the composition of our field of meaning.[18]

Husserl views beings, but he views them solely as meaningful, and it does not interest him whether the meaningful beings do or do not really exist. He transforms Being into meaning. Science does so, but only to a certain extent.[19] As a matter of fact, science sets up many idealizations. Galileo's concept of nature is an idealization because he views only some aspects of appearing nature and abstracts from all others. But in science an interaction between the idealizations and the real experience of facts always remains. Science tries to verify its idealizations and hypotheses in a real contact with real facts.[20]

Husserl's phenomenology goes to the roots of science. His philosophy idealizes everything, reduces everything to meaning; it asks what nature, history, world and Being finally are. Science is often an unconscious idealization because it thinks its idealizations are reality. It confuses reality and meaning. Husserl reduces everything to meaning and looks for the essential, necessary laws of our field of meaning. The field of

[17] "Il sera *ce sans quoi* il n'y aurait ni monde, ni langage, ni quoi que ce soit, il sera l'essence." *V.I.*, p. 145.

[18] ". . . à ce qui fait que le monde est monde, à une grammaire impérieuse de l'Être, à des noyaux de sens indécomposables." *Ibid.*

[19] "Démarche qui est déjà celle de la science." *Ibid.*

[20] "Mais ce travail, elle (la science) ne le termine pas: ses essences, elle ne les dégage pas tout à fait du monde, elle les maintient sous la jurisdiction des faits." *V.I.*, pp. 145–146.

necessary meanings is the object of Husserl's research. The eidetic reduction is the method employed to reveal the nuclei of meaning.[21]

C. Philosophical Certainty Is Not Based on the Husserlian Essences

If the philosopher is caught in a realm of dubious facts, he will try to penetrate to a deeper realm where he might find certainty. But because philosophy is essentially reflective, the philosopher will have to investigate the character and the ontological status of that new realm. Is Husserl right when he says that the philosopher finds a base for certainty in the realm of essences? Is the essence the final answer to our philosophical questions?[22] The essence is not a real thing but an ideal object. An ideal object demands a subject. Accepting the order of essences, Husserl consequently accepts also an ideal subject which is related to the essences, or rather, to which the essences are related. Is man in his deepest being the contemplator of essences, and are the essences the most profound datum of philosophy?

Merleau-Ponty answers these questions negatively.[23] What is the Husserlian essence? It is the point at which our intellect rests when it searches out the conditions which enable reality to appear. Husserl poses the same kind of questions that we find in the works of Kant. Kant often says: If a world exists it has to fulfill the following conditions . . . ; or, If science exists it must be both synthetic and universal.[24] Husserl proceeds in the same way. He looks for the "conditions of possibility" for reality to appear.

[21] "La philosophie serait cette même lecture du sens menée à son terme, science exacte, la seule exacte, parce qu'elle seule va jusqu'au bout de l'effort pour savoir ce que *c'est* la Nature et l'Histoire et le Monde et l'Être." *V.I.,* p. 146.

[22] "La question de l'essence est-elle la question ultime?" *V.I.,* p. 147.

[23] "L'être de l'essence n'est pas premier, ne repose pas sur lui-même, ce n'est pas lui qui peut nous apprendre ce que c'est que l'Être, l'essence n'est pas *la* réponse à la question philosophique." *Ibid.*

[24] *Ibid.*

How do we arrive at this kind of questioning? There must first of all be some meaning which reveals itself in appearing reality. This meaning appeals to the intellect, but it has an ambiguous character. It has to say something to the intellect yet does not convince it. It happens, e.g., that the same meaning reveals itself in many appearing realities, but in such a way that the meaning differs somewhat in the different phenomena. It also happens that many things reveal themselves as a whole, but we do not immediately know how they belong together, how they constitute a whole. In such cases our intellect grasps the meaning without being satisfied. It tries to formulate what it sees. It constitutes an essence.

The essence, however, is not an original datum. Our experience precedes it. Kant could never have formulated the meaning of the term "world" if a real world had not appeared to him; he could not have formulated the conditions of science if his experience had not taught him that science existed. This also applies to all the essences of Husserl. They are a formulation, an idealization of preceding knowledge.[25]

The essence is not the primordial level of philosophical knowledge. It is not the final source of knowledge which teaches us what Being really is. We do not find there the final answer of our philosophical questions. Hence the subject which views essences is not the primordial subject. We constitute appearing reality as an essence; in the same way, we constitute ourselves as contemplators of essences. Husserl is wrong in considering the essence the primordial object of philosophical thought. It is a secondary expression of experience.[26]

Merleau-Ponty admits that there is some truth in the Husserlian idea of essence. It is true that our experiences are connected. Our field of experience is not a collection of accidental

---

[25] "Des essences que nous trouvons, nous n'avons pas le droit de dire qu'elles donnent le sens primitif de l'Être." *Ibid.*

[26] "Les possibilités d'essence peuvent bien envelopper et dominer *les faits,* elles dérivent elles-mêmes d'une autre possibilité, et plus fondamentale: celle qui travaille mon expérience, l'ouvre au monde et à l'Être, et qui, certes, ne les trouve pas devant elle comme *des faits,* mais anime et organise leur facticité." *V.I.,* p. 148.

relationships. The coherence of our field of experience, how-ever, is not due to essences; that something like an essence exists is due to the coherence of our field of experience. Es-sences do not underlie our experience, but our experience underlies essences.

Merleau-Ponty thus rejects the idea that essences comprise something more than our field of experience.[27] Such an idea is not new at all; Plato expressed it when he opposed the neces-sity of essence to the contingency of our field of perceptive experience. He then rightly concluded that the latter cannot be the cause of the former. The essence must exist, therefore, in another realm and it must have another source. This is why Plato said that the idea, the essence, is innate and that there is a separate world of ideas. Yet, according to Merleau-Ponty we are involved in Being; as "perceiving perceptibles" we are open to the world to which we belong. This original experience is the only source of our idealizations; thus they cannot con-tain more than their source. The essence is not the basis of knowledge since it is derived from a more original knowledge. If we find some necessity in essences, we must find this neces-sity in our original experience itself.[28]

It is quite possible that the essence expresses an aspect of original experience which was there only in a latent manner. Were our original experience completely clear, expression would be useless and philosophy superfluous. The idealization unfolds the original experience and manifests what that ex-perience is. But the expression does not open us to a more original realm of reality. It does not ground our experience.

[27] "(Les essences) sont prélevées par eux sur un être brut où il s'agit de retrouver à l'état sauvage les répondants de nos essences et de nos significations." *V.I.*, p. 149.

[28] "Les essences, les necessités d'essence, la possibilité interne ou logique, toutes solides et incontestables qu'elle soient sous le regard de l'esprit, n'ont finalement leur force et leur éloquence que parce que toutes mes pensées et les pensées des autres sont prises dans le tissu d'un seul Être." *V.I.*, p. 148.

D. The Pure Essence Does Not Exist

What Husserl calls "essence" is not the ground of our experience, but its expression. As a "perceiving perceptible," I am situated in the world. Many things reveal a common style of Being. It makes sense to use the word "nature," and I can speak of a "world." I can give abstract names to many things which reveal a common style of existence. From this experience, how did Husserl arrive at his "essences"?

He applied the method of eidetic variation, which is an active intervention of the human mind.[29] He analyzed the appearing phenomena and asked whether things would remain the same if this or that element were eliminated. In this way he tried to distinguish between the essential and the accidental aspects of things.

The result of this method he called "essence." But what did he really achieve? He discovered those elements which could not disappear without the thing itself disappearing, e.g., man would not be man if he did not have a human face. Husserl discovered the invariable style of existence which makes things what they are. His essences are the expression of the fundamental style of existence which constitutes the Being of things.[30]

This is not, however, another and radically different realm of reality.[31] It is an expression of real Being. This expression is always partial because our power of eidetic variation is partial. Our experience measures and limits our power of eidetic variation; and if we could survey all possible experience, our eidetic variation would be perfect and complete.[32] But this is impossible for an experiencing being because of its involvement in Being. Our experience extends over a realm of

[29] "La solidité, l'essentialité de l'essence est exactement mesurée par le pouvoir que nous avons de varier la chose." *V.I.*, p. 149.

[30] *V.I.*, pp. 149–150.

[31] "Elle (l'essence) n'est donc pas un être positif. Elle est un invariant." *V.I.*, p. 149.

[32] "Une essence pure qui ne fût pas du tout contaminée et brouillée par les faits ne pourrait résulter que d'un essai de variation totale." *Ibid.*

clarity enclosed in a vague horizon. All our idealizations are rooted in such an experience. In my idealizations I collect many experiences, but I can collect them only because they all belong to one and the same temporal life.[33] The unity of my ideas is supported by the temporal unity of my life and by the connection of my life with the life of the community of men to which I belong. The "flesh of the world," the "flesh of history," supports all our idealizations. Our idealizations can never transcend the density of Being, the density of temporal and spatial experience. If the essence is isolated from this density, it is nothing at all, a mere illusion.

The pure essence does not exist. We have only the provisional expressions of our coherent experience. There is no absolute vision of an essence transcending our experience. There is no absolute essence, no absolute vision of an essence.[34]

Merleau-Ponty also refuses to accept the pure essence as an ideal, a "limit-idea" at which we aim without ever attaining.[35] If we were to accept the absolute essence as an ideal, we would devaluate all our real experiences in the false light of an impossible goal. We would then fall into relativism. Such false ideals are an immense danger. They have often occurred in the history of human thought. Many values in human life always exist in an ambiguous manner, in an interchange with other values; moreover, real values can to a certain extent be opposed to one another. However, our intellect sometimes abstracts these values from their real context and transforms them into absolute, isolated ideals. The conclusion seems to be that man must aim at such absolute ideals, although they cannot be actualized. But, as a consequence, the real values which exist in actual life, in an interchange with other values, are emptied. The real values are considered shadows of what they should be. We make the real values relative, or even condemn them in the name of false ideal values. This happens

[33] "Toute idéation est portée par cet arbre de ma durée et des durées; cette sève ignorée nourrit la transparence de l'idée." V.I., p. 150.

[34] "Il n'y a pas de vision positive qui me donne définitivement l'essentialité de l'essence." V.I., p. 151.

[35] Ibid.

when we consider the absolute essence as the ideal of human knowledge. We will never arrive at any absolute essence. When we accept the absolute essence as an ideal, we devalue all our real knowledge in the name of an impossible goal.

The relationship of our knowledge to the order of facts, to the realm of real experience, to "savage Being," is not an imperfection, an impurity to be deplored.[36] I am not an exterior contemplator of Being, a "cosmotheoros," but am involved in Being. It is because of my involvement in Being that there is meaning, light, value. I cannot survey Being, precisely because I am involved in it. The total field of Being will never lie open before my surveying look. We must exclude this, not only as being something which we will never realize, but also as an ideal. God has been conceived as the Absolute Look surveying everything. Such a God emerges out of man's feelings of failure. God becomes the successful man. God is conceived as the actualization of an impossible human ideal.

The Husserlian concept of absolute essence is similarly a false and impossible ideal. It is extremely dangerous because it makes us blind to the light which we do have because of our involvement in Being. Merleau-Ponty does not at all deny that there is coherence in Being, that there are understandable connections, that we can even speak of necessity. He does not even refuse to speak of "essential aspects" of Being. But we find this real light in the Being in which we are involved, in the order of facts. He refuses to separate the "that" and the "what"; the "what" is the connection, the coherence, the interior intelligibility of the "that." Merleau-Ponty does not deny that there is room for idealization. We can abstract the aspect of "what" from the "that." But this abstraction does not allow us to penetrate into an order of absolute essences preceding in some manner the concrete, appearing reality.

The time has come, says Merleau-Ponty, for us to reject the myths of inductive knowledge and of the intuition of essences (*Wesensschau*).[37] Merleau-Ponty calls Husserl's *Wesensschau* a myth, and he compares it with the myth of induc-

---

[36] ". . . d'un impossible travail de l'expérience sur l'expérience qui la dépouillerait de sa facticité comme d'une impurité." *Ibid.*
[37] *V.I.*, p. 155.

tive knowledge. This comparison was alien to Merleau-Ponty when he wrote *Phenomenology of Perception*. At that time he already rejected the value of inductive knowledge, but he tried to save the Husserlian eidetic reduction. Now he rejects both of them and evidently sees some connection between them. The connection is rather obvious. Both the eidetic reduction and the inductive method start from the order of facts and intend to arrive at something different; the eidetic reduction aims at the necessary essence and induction aims at the necessary law. Both methods of thinking start from contingent facts and pretend to arrive at a realm of necessity. For Merleau-Ponty such a transition is a myth. If there is no necessity in the order of facts themselves, there will never be any necessity at all.

In *Sense and Non-Sense* Merleau-Ponty said that not a single induction has ever completely succeeded;[38] in "Interrogation and Intuition" he writes that in Husserl's works there is not one eidetic reduction, not one so-called *Wesensschau*, which Husserl always accepted without any change.[39] Even when Husserl thought he had revealed some essence (*Wesen*) by an eidetic reduction, he always returned to the question and spoke of the same essence in a different manner. This is a clear indication that there is no absolute essence in some mysterious realm, and that the so-called "essence" is the expression of the interior connection of the facts. Facts and essence are two indissoluble aspects of one and the same field of experience.[40]

E. *The Unity of Essences and Facts*

Merleau-Ponty denies the existence of absolute essences, but he does not deny the endeavor of science and philosophy to arrive at general knowledge. How, he asks, did psychology, ethnology and sociology advance? Their progress has not re-

[38] *Sense and Non-Sense,* p. 98.

[39] *V.I.,* p. 155.

[40] "il serait naïf de chercher la solidité dans un ciel des idées ou dans un *fond* du sens: elle n'est ni au-dessus, ni au-dessous des apparences, mais à leur jointure." *Ibid.*

sulted from induction nor from Husserl's eidetic speculation.[41]
We are involved in Being, and each of us has his own experience of psychic life, of social existence, and of the life of
the people to whom he belongs. If we ourselves were not involved in Being we would not have access to the experiences
which are expressed by science. Moreover, we can also contact
one another and exchange our experiences. We do so by
speaking with one another and also by reading and by penetrating into civilizations of the past. Involved in Being, we can
share the involvement of other people. In this way we can
enrich our own experience and see more coherence, more
connections of the Being in which we are involved.

We can use the term "eidetic variation" in this context. For
it is a fact that we compare our experiences with the experiences of others; we correct and amplify our own ideas.
We practice together the "eidetic variation" which Husserl
reserved for the solitary imagination and thought of the individual philosopher. He was wrong on this point. The real
"eidetic variation" takes place in the encounter of scientists
and philosophers.[42] The "cosmotheoros," the thinker who surveys the world, has no need for encounter, at least not in
principle. But the thinker who knows that his involvement in
Being is the source of his thought, who recognizes that he is
essentially a local and temporal involvement in Being, understands that he needs other people in order to think for himself,
understands that the enrichment of his own thought depends
on the encounter with other "involvements" in Being.
Merleau-Ponty calls science a "common opinion." He does
not mean, of course, that science has no real insight into Being but that this insight is conditioned by the mutual contact
between scientists and philosophers.

In this way there is an increasing objectivity of knowledge.

[41] "Nulle recherche féconde n'est inductivité pure, pur recense-
ment des constantes en soi." *V.I.*, p. 156.
[42] ". . . en organisant l'*Ineinander*, et, finalement, en pratiquant
cette variation eidétique que Husserl a eu le seul tort de réserver
d'abord à l'imagination et à la vision solitaires du philosophe, alors
qu'elle est le support et le lieu même de cette *opinio communis*
qu'on appelle la science." *Ibid.*

This must not be explained by some mysterious reflection of a "Being-in-itself," nor by an equally mysterious contact with absolute essences or ideas. It is simply explained by the enrichment of our access to Being which is the result of encounter with other people.[43] This encounter makes possible the "eidetic variation" which deepens our involvement in Being and helps us to correct and enrich our concepts.

It is in this way that we discover an authentic generality in the facts themselves. There is intelligibility in the facts and in their coherence; we can discover essences in the facts and in their interconnection. It is not necessary to appeal to some heaven of ideas in order to have access to essences. If we separate facts and essences we are confronted with two idle abstractions: the facts have become unintelligible since they are separated from their intelligibility, and essences have lost the density of reality since they are exterior to the real facts. The primary realm in which we are involved is the world which is a unity of essences and facts. In this world everything is related to everything else. Being placed in it is the same as being related to other things. Without relationships to other things and to the whole, nothing could be itself. This totality is not strange to us who live in it.[44] All the basic concepts of philosophy and science imply our experience of the total Being in which we are involved. Merleau-Ponty promises to analyze time, space, and the relationship between time and space, the bilaterality of our body—its visible and invisible aspects—in the light of this basic truth.[45] For the moment he stresses the fact that the intrinsic unity of Being transcends the classical distinction of essence and existence, of essence and fact.

Because we are involved in Being, Being reveals itself to us. It does not reveal itself as an object which is distinguished from us. Being penetrates us. Our body is a "perceiving per-

[43] "Il est bien sûr qu'on accède à l'objectivité. . . . en tant que nous sommes intérieurs à la vie, à l'être-humain et à l'Être, aussi bien que lui en nous." *Ibid.*

[44] "Ce milieu de l'existence et de l'essence brutes n'est pas mystérieux: nous n'en sortons pas, nous n'avons pas d'autre. Les faits et les essences sont des abstractions." *Ibid.*

[45] *V.I.*, p. 157.

ceptible." The reality it perceives is both in the body itself and
outside it. One and the same reality penetrates the body and
extends beyond it. Our experience of Being is the same. Being
penetrates us and extends beyond us, and yet it remains the
same Being. Being becomes aware of itself in us. All the aspects of our existence are an access to Being. We usually forget this fundamental unity which precedes and supports all
the distinctions. It is not useless to make distinctions. Merleau-
Ponty makes many distinctions himself. But it is dangerous to
forget that all the distinctions we make are distinctions within
a fundamental unity.[46] All authentic metaphysicians have
known this. Merleau-Ponty stresses here points which are
really metaphysical. Our existence itself *is* access to Being;
and it is, therefore, our "natural light." Being obtains an "interiority" in man. Man is the self-revelation of Being. In Being facts and essence are not at all opposed.

[46] "Il suffit de faire voir, pour le moment, que l'Être unique, la
dimensionnalité à laquelle appartiennent ces moments, ces feuillets
et ces dimensions, est par-delà l'essence et l'existence classiques et
rend compréhensible leur rapport." *Ibid.*

PART III

PHENOMENOLOGY
AND THE SCIENCES OF MAN

Introduction

Over the course of the last twenty-five years many studies have been devoted to the problem occasioned by the appearance on the scientific horizon of the so-called "phenomenological psychology."[1] It was not clear even at the outset, however, whether these various publications were attempting to deal with a new trend or school in contemporary psychology, or whether they were attempting to cope with the pros and cons of a completely new kind of discipline in addition to but in harmony with empirical psychology. When one studies the most important of the publications which address themselves to the relative merits and drawbacks of the situation, one is left with the impression that only a few seem to be really aware of "phenomenological" psychology's historical origin, and consequently of its original meaning and function. And it becomes quite clear, also, that what is defended so fervently by one group cannot possibly be the same thing which is so vehemently rejected by another. It is the conviction of some phenomenologists that in neither case can there be found what so many dedicated psychologists have been awaiting for such a long time, namely, the means to solve certain radical problems which still exist at the foundational level of empirical psychology. Therefore, a prime goal of the third part of this anthology is to attempt to burn off at least part of the haze which continues to becloud that typical contemporary phenomenon called "phenomenological psychology."

Although the meaning and function of phenomenology (taken either as a method or as a philosophy) in its relation to an empirical study of man was debated at first only in the realm of the psychological disciplines, it became clear almost immediately that analogous ideas could be developed for other

[1] For the most important literature on the subject see: Stephan Strasser, *Phenomenology and the Human Sciences. A Contribution to a New Scientific Ideal* (Pittsburgh: Duquesne University Press, 1963); Joseph J. Kockelmans, *Husserl's Phenomenological Psychology* (Pittsburgh: Duquesne University Press, 1967).

sciences of man, and for sociology and the political sciences in particular. Some authors have even seen advantages in putting the quite complex phenomenon "phenomenological psychology" from the very start in the much broader context of the problems characteristic of the sciences of man as a whole.

Since in my opinion the latter view is right, I shall first make some introductory remarks about the actual situation in which the sciences of man in general find themselves on the contemporary scene. Then I shall attempt to show how *phenomenological psychology* was born in the context of Husserl's investigations concerning his new *phenomenological philosophy,* how his ideas were further developed by other phenomenologists and how, finally, the results of these investigations were extended and applied to other empirical sciences of man. In these introductory remarks I shall limit myself to that which seems to be the necessary material for providing a frame of reference in which to read the following essays and selections to the best advantage.

The group of sciences which I have in mind when I refer to the "sciences of man" has for quite some time now been indicated by the term *"Geisteswissenschaften,"* "sciences of the mind." This term was acceptable as long as those who used it, philosophers as well as scientists, were willing either in the rationalistic tradition of Descartes to conceive of man as a "thinking substance," or in the empiricist tradition of Locke and Hume to make a distinction between the "external world" as the object of "perception" and the "mind" as the object of "reflection." However, when it became apparent that scientific research involving man must be directed to man's concrete behavior and self-realization, the term "behavioral sciences" suggested itself as a more accurate indication of the procedures. More recently these sciences have been called "human sciences" and even more aptly, "sciences of man."[2]

"Sciences of man" is to be understood as certain empirical sciences dealing with man, which share the common characteristic of pursuing a scientific investigation of *man as man* with the help of *empirical methods.* Man is not an agglomer-

[2] Stephan Strasser, *op. cit.,* pp. 4–5.

ate of molecules and cells for these sciences, nor is he considered by them according to certain aspects or "parts"; on the contrary, it is precisely man's specifically human character as such which they take into consideration.[3] The term "sciences of man," however, does not always have the same extension for the various authors who employ it in this context. For example, for Strasser the term implies history, the linguistic sciences, the empirical sciences of art, literature, culture, law, economics, and religion, as well as psychology and sociology.[4] Merleau-Ponty uses the term to indicate only psychology, sociology, and history.[5] For methodological reasons I shall use the term in its limited sense as Merleau-Ponty has done. Furthermore, as it is my opinion that the *"epistemological" problems concerning history* are of a completely different order, especially when taken in their historical context, from those attached to psychology and sociology, I shall restrict myself here to psychology, social psychology, sociology, and the political sciences.

The scholars who prefer here to use the term "empirical sciences of man" hold that from the start the psychological, social, and political sciences attempted to imitate the empirical sciences of nature—physics, chemistry, biochemistry, biology, and physiology. Gradually, however, it became evident that such a "physicalization" of the sciences of man leads to serious problems, not only in the delineation of the subject matter of the sciences in question, but also in the choice and circumscription of the logical and methodological tools. That this statement is not mere fabrication can be shown quite easily in a consideration of the historical development of these sciences from 1850 on.

In view of the fact that "physicalization" of the sciences of man creates extremely serious problems, the scholars in ques-

---

[3] *Ibid.*, pp. 3–4.

[4] *Ibid.*, p. 3.

[5] Maurice Merleau-Ponty, "Phenomenology and the Sciences of Man," in *The Primacy of Perception and Other Essays.* Ed. James M. Edie (Evanston: Northwestern University Press, 1963), p. 43; H.-G. Gadamer, *"Les problèmes épistémologiques des sciences humaines,"* in *Le Problème de la conscience historique* (Louvain: Nauwelaerts, 1963).

tion have maintained that one must draw the conclusion that
there is an essential difference between the sciences of nature
and the sciences of man. In elaboration of this viewpoint they
declare that it is not their intention to defend the thesis that
for this reason the sciences of man are to be excluded from the
application of all empirical methods. On the contrary, they
believe either that these methods must be adapted to the requirements imposed by the very nature of the subject matter
of the empirical sciences of man, or that it must be possible to
contrive a new set of empirical methods which both guarantee
intersubjectively valid conclusions, and safeguard and respect
the specifically human character of man as man: that he is
the originator and organizer of his own *Umwelt*.[6]

Acceptance of this point of view carries with it the following
crucial problem in connection with the empirical sciences of
man: How can man as man be made "object" of an empirical
investigation?[7] Upon closer consideration the question shows
itself to have different aspects. First of all the specialist in the
empirical sciences of man, he who is interested in individuals
and groups as originators and organizers of their respective
"worlds," obviously must include his own science in these
worlds, for it is evident that no one escapes the deep influence
of modern psychology, sociology, and the political sciences.
Such an inclusion, however, means that the man who studies
the human sciences changes his own subject matter while he
studies it and because he studies it to the extent that we must
ask the question: Where, then, is the firm foundation needed
for the pursuit of a supposedly "objective" empirical study?[8]

Moreover, the scholars involved here argue, is not the creation and organization of a world an expression of human
freedom? Although the life of an individual and the "culture"
of a group reveal definite styles, one must know whether there
is a possibility of empirically investigating free activities. If
"being free," for instance, should mean "to be able to do
whatever one wants," or even if it should mean "being able to
be unreasonable, immoral, unsocial, unjust, and inhuman,"

6 Stephan Strasser, *op. cit.*, pp. 5–7.
7 *Ibid.*, p. 7.
8 *Ibid.*, pp. 7–8.

how would it be possible to describe these changeable beings, to compare their behavior, to characterize their realizations, and to discover general laws applying to them?[9]

Finally, individual human beings as well as social groups are sensitive to values, they are attracted to purposes, and they make projects. But how is it possible to "measure" values? And even if we accept an "objective hierarchy of values," and believe that the appreciation of values gives rise to the motives which determine man's action, how do we know what an individual man or a group is going to decide and to choose? Are we not here fully in the realm of the purely subjective where no real science is possible?[10]

In summary, all these questions point to reasons why the empirical study of man as man is affected with very difficult problems: either we accept the fact that the only empirical method possible is that used in the empirical sciences of nature, which means that an empirical science of *man as man* is impossible, or we accept the possibility of an empirical science of *man as man,* expecting to prove the possibility of a second form of "objectivity" in the realm of empirical sciences and to delineate its fundamental characteristics.

If we adopt the first point of view and see physics as the model science, the example to be followed in all kinds of empirical research, we must demand that the conceptual framework, method, and scientific apparatus to be used in the different sciences do not deviate essentially from those associated with physics. We may admit, of course, that *accidental* modifications will be possible in the application of empirical methods to the various realms pertaining to the study of man, but must demand that in these accidental modifications attention be paid to the great line running from physics to chemistry, biochemistry, biology, physiology, and the behavioristic currents in the "sciences of man." The consequence of this point of view is, of necessity, that the empirical sciences of man cease to be "human" because it is clear that the methods used by the empirical sciences of nature cannot be applied to

[9] *Ibid.,* p. 8.
[10] *Ibid.,* pp. 8–9.

human behavior *as such,* as these methods abstract and must abstract from certain aspects which are essential for human behavior as such. For the method of the empirical sciences of nature is based on a complete abstraction from the human subjectivity. The goal of "objective" science is to achieve a systematic explanation which is universally valid and amenable to controlled verification by anyone at any time; such an explanation must be "causal" and, therefore, deal with a world of "facts" which in themselves are independent of the subjectivity of the observer. Finally, the rich and variegated world of life-world experiences must be reinterpreted in terms of experiments involving a limited and controllable number of variables which can be codified in abstract mathematical formulae or some similar symbolic construction.[11]

If we adopt the second point of view, however, we may admit that man as part of nature can be studied legitimately as a body among bodies, but on the other hand we must maintain simultaneously that in regard to a total and integral explanation of human behavior *as such* we are in need of more subtle and less abstract methods of investigation, because here we must deal above all with the experiencing subject himself, the world of meaning and value which depends on the free and personal interventions of the subject, and also on the not-yet-free and not-yet-conscious decisions of man taken on the level of his "bodily-ego," as it is called by Merleau-Ponty.

Faced with this dilemma, many "phenomenologists" do not find it difficult to make a choice between the two possibilities. If it is really true, they say, that empirical science must exclude from the competence of a strictly scientific method such considerations as the proper activity of the behaving subject as such, and consequently cannot explain why it is that my eksistence has sense and value for me, and if empirical science, furthermore, has to make abstraction from the intentionality, the purposiveness, and finally from my orientation toward the world as it is experienced by me, and ultimately also from the gestural and linguistic expressions of these purposes and

11 *Ibid.,* pp. 11–17 and pp. 25–26.

meanings, then we need a different method because these aspects are constitutive of human behavior as such.[12]

However, other phenomenologists are very well aware of the fact that modern science has found acceptable solutions for many aspects of the problems posited here, using both the precision instruments which contemporary empirical methods have at their disposal, and their logical and mathematical elaborations. But even these authors believe that despite these accomplishments there still remains the disturbing question whether *man as man* is a valid subject for empirical investigation.

In the following essays an attempt is made to show how phenomenological psychology was born in the context of Husserl's inquiries concerning his transcendental phenomenology. It will be shown there that Husserl did not come immediately to an admissible view on phenomenological psychology and its relation to empirical psychology and transcendental phenomenology, but that, rather, his final view emerged at the culmination of a penetrating investigation performed over the course of some thirty years. The most important phase in this long development will be described briefly.

The second essay of this part of the anthology shows how Schuetz has tried to adapt Husserl's view to other sciences of man, and to the social sciences in particular. Then the third, fourth, and fifth essays, respectively, describe Sartre's, Merleau-Ponty's, and Strasser's further development of Husserl's and Schuetz's ideas. The last essay attempts to deliver a "critical" appraisal of these various endeavors.

[12] *Ibid.*, pp. 56–62.

I. HUSSERL'S ORIGINAL VIEW
ON PHENOMENOLOGICAL PSYCHOLOGY*

JOSEPH J. KOCKELMANS

Some forty years ago Edmund Husserl spoke publicly for
the first time of a new phenomenological psychology. He saw
this new psychology as a discipline that was destined to play
an important role in the already established empirical psychology as well as in philosophy. Subsequently under the influence
of his ideas an extensive phenomenological psychological
movement began to spread through various European countries. When a careful analysis of this phenomenological movement is made, one becomes aware of a number of clearly
distinguishable currents and schools, all of which claim Husserl as their origin. The truth is, however, that only a very
few psychologists actually use Husserl's concepts without making major modifications. Furthermore, many psychologists talk
about phenomenology without stipulating precisely what is
meant by the term. To compound the difficulties there is no-
ticeable in phenomenological literature a frequent failure to
make a clear distinction between Husserl's thought and that
of other phenomenologists such as Scheler, Heidegger, Jaspers,
Merleau-Ponty, Sartre, and Binswanger.

The confusion becomes understandable when one realizes
that in psychology as well as in sociology and anthropology
different trends of thought did in fact develop in the absence
of clearly formulated philosophical premises. In addition, it
has been virtually impossible for most writers to see phenomenological problems in historical perspective. Also, and most
importantly, until very recently Husserl's thought has been
available only to a privileged few who had access to his
manuscripts. Knowledge about his ideas as communicated by

* This selection is a translation and expansion of Parts I and II
of a lecture given at Tilburg (The Netherlands) in 1964 and subsequently published in the *Tilliburgis* series ('s-Hertogenbosch:
Malmberg, 1964).

these secondary sources has shown considerable divergence on many points. All of these factors constitute difficulties when one tries to determine just what is to be understood by phenomenological psychology. It is apparent that a reasonable solution cannot be found by using some kind of largest common denominator of all the existing phenomenologies as a point of departure for a description of phenomenological psychology. A meaningful formulation can be reached only through a careful historical investigation into the essential differences underlying the different phenomenologies. It is, in fact, now possible to make a fresh start with important historical and critical investigations, for thanks to the indefatigable efforts of the Husserl-Archives we have access to the complete text of Husserl's last work *Krisis* and to all his other important contributions to phenomenological psychology from 1920 to 1938.[1]

However, the specific task with which we are presently concerned is not that of an historical and critical appraisal of Husserl's own development as a phenomenological psychologist between 1891 and 1938, for anyone who is interested in this issue may find several such studies at his disposal.[2] It is against the background of these historical studies, however, that certain questions shall be dealt with briefly here: How did Husserl arrive at his views regarding phenomenological psychology? What task did he envision for this new discipline? What are its essential aspects? How does this psychology relate to empirical psychology on one hand and to philosophy on the other? Only after these questions have been answered

[1] Edmund Husserl, *Die Krisis der europäischen Wissenschaften und die transzendentale Phänomenologie. Eine Einleitung in die phänomenologische Philosophie,* herausgegeben von Walter Biemel (Husserliana, Band VI) (The Hague: Martinus Nijhoff, 1954). For the foregoing remarks see: Stephan Strasser, *Phenomenology and the Human Sciences: A Contribution to a New Scientific Ideal* (Pittsburgh: Duquesne University Press, 1963), pp. 245–48.

[2] Hermann Drüe, *Edmund Husserls System der phänomenologischen Psychologie* (Berlin: Walter de Gruyter, 1963); Joseph J. Kockelmans, *Edmund Husserl's Phenomenological Psychology. A Historico-critical Study* (Pittsburgh: Duquesne University Press, 1967); Aron Gurwitsch, *Studies in Phenomenology and Psychology* (Evanston: Northwestern University Press, 1966).

will it be possible to evaluate Husserl's work in the light of the recent developments that have been proposed by various protagonists of phenomenological psychology. This approach, I believe, will clear up an embarrassing situation by disclosing the real perspectives that Husserl's thought has opened up for present-day psychology.

In order to explain the problems mentioned as clearly as possible I shall focus attention primarily on Husserl's final view as explained in *Phenomenological Psychology* and *Krisis*. However, a few remarks on Husserl's earlier view seem to be a necessary introduction to his final standpoint.

1. *The Genesis of the Idea of a Phenomenological Psychology*

PSYCHOLOGISM AND HUSSERL'S CRITICISM

It was in Leipzig in 1876 that Husserl first became acquainted with the psychology of his day. He had started his scientific career with a thorough study of mathematics and physics, but after only a few years of work he had come into contact with psychology under the influence of Wundt, Paulsen, Brentano, and Stumpf. Now Husserl's interest in philosophy, at first minimal, was eventually aroused by Brentano; and thus, under the influence of his psychological studies with Brentano and Stumpf and also through his contact with the works of Stuart Mill, Spencer, Locke, and Hume, he very soon became entangled in empiricism and psychologism. He would later have to shake off psychologism's tendency to found the objects of mathematics, logic, epistemology, theory of value, and so on, on subjective psychical experiences.

Initially Husserl's special interest in philosophy was focused on the philosophical foundation of mathematics and logic. In his first book, *Philosophy of Arithmetic* (1891),[3] he tried to derive the fundamental concepts of arithmetic from certain psychological acts. It was in this book that Husserl defended a kind of psychologism by advancing the thesis that

---

[3] Edmund Husserl, *Philosophie der Arithmetik. Psychologische und logische Untersuchungen*. Erster Band, Halle a.S. (1891).

the epistemological foundations of arithmetic must be given
ultimately by empirical psychology. Influenced by Frege's critique of this book and by a publication of Natorp, Husserl
very soon came to the conclusion that psychologism is inadmissible. In 1895 in his lectures at Halle, Husserl began to
present his own critique of psychologism which was later published in 1900 in the first volume of the *Logical Investigations*.[4] In the second part of this book Husserl explained that,
although the ideal objects studied by mathematics and logic
have a being of their own, there must be a typical correlation
between these ideal objects, belonging to the realm of logic
and pure mathematics, and our psychical, lived experiences
as the activities which constitute them. Although the fundamental ideas of a phenomenological philosophy are already
implicit in the second volume of the *Logical Investigations,*
it was not until 1907, in a series of lectures entitled *The
Idea of Phenomenology*,[5] that Husserl was able to formulate
these basic insights in a systematic way.

From 1907 on we find psychology as a constant pole of
comparison in Husserl's explanations of the meaning of his
phenomenological philosophy. Practically speaking, in every
work dealing with the foundations of phenomenological
philosophy, Husserl tries to explain his view on empirical psychology and to describe the difference and the relationship
between these two sciences.

PHENOMENOLOGICAL PSYCHOLOGY

Between 1911 and 1913 the problem concerning the relation between empirical psychology and phenomenological philosophy had Husserl's special attention again. Gradually it became clear to him that it is possible and even necessary to
bridge the gap between empirical psychology and transcendental phenomenology with the help of a completely new sci-

---

[4] *Logische Untersuchungen*, 2 vols., Halle a.S. (1900–1).

[5] Edmund Husserl, *Die Idee der Phänomenologie. Fünf Vorlesungen* (1907). Herausgegeben und eingeleitet von Walter Biemel
(Husserliana, Band II) (The Hague, 1950).

The Idea of Phenomenology. Trans. William P. Alston and
George Nakhnikian (The Hague, 1964).

ence which was called "rational psychology," or "eidetic psychology" first, and "phenomenological psychology" afterward. This view is explicitly expressed for the first time in *Ideas* (1913),[6] although the first traces of these insights are already found in his *Logos* article.[7]

It seems that between 1913 and 1923 Husserl was especially concerned with the so-called constitutional problems. As a result of these investigations it became apparent to him that his explicitation of the meaning of phenomenological psychology as presented in *Ideas* was not adequate, in that the distinction between phenomenological psychology and transcendental philosophy had not yet been founded in a radical way. It became apparent also that the new science, phenomenological psychology, was of such importance for the development of the empirical psychology of his time that a radical investigation of it seemed to be demanded. It was for this reason that he dealt with the topic in different lecture courses between 1923 and 1927. The results of these investigations were published posthumously in 1963 in a book entitled *Phenomenological Psychology*.[8] In this work phenomenological psychology is described as an aprioristic, eidetic, intuitive, purely descriptive, and intentional science of the psychical, which remains entirely within the realm of the natural attitude.[9] Here Husserl tries to found the necessity of such a new kind of psychology by pointing to the fact that

6 Edmund Husserl, *Ideen zu einer reinen Phänomenologie und phänomenologischen Philosophie. Erstes Buch: Allgemeine Einführung in die reine Phänomenologie.* Herausgegeben von Walter Biemel (Husserliana, Band III) (The Hague, 1950).

Ideas. General Introduction to Pure Phenomenology. Trans. W. R. Boyce Gibson (New York, 1962).

7 Edmund Husserl, *"Philosophie als strenge Wissenschaft,"* in *Logos,* 1 (1910–11), 289–341.

"Philosophy as Rigorous Science," in Quentin Lauer, *Edmund Husserl: Phenomenology and the Crisis of Philosophy* (New York, 1965), pp. 69–147. See also: *Cross Currents,* 6 (1956), pp. 228–46 and pp. 324–44.

8 Edmund Husserl, *Phänomenologische Psychologie* (1925). Herausgegeben von Walter Biemel (Husserliana, Band IX) (The Hague: Martinus Nijhoff, 1962).

9 *Ibid.,* pp. 46–51.

traditional empirical psychology still lacks a systematic framework of basic concepts grounded in the intuitive clarification of the psychical essences. Whatever psychology has accumulated and is still accumulating by way of measuring and experimentation concerning objective correlations is wasted as long as there is no clear grasp of what it is that is being measured and correlated. According to Husserl, phenomenological psychology is destined to supply the essential insights needed to give meaning and direction to the research presented under the title "empirical psychology."

Exactly the same ideas are found in Husserl's *Encyclopædia Britannica* article,[10] his *Amsterdam Lectures,*[11] and the *Cartesian Meditations.*[12] It is in these publications that Husserl mentions for the first time that a special reduction is essential and indispensable for a phenomenological psychology, too. In his last book, *Krisis,* Husserl returns to this point and in a detailed and minute inquiry tries to determine the very nature of this reduction and to found its necessity.[13] In these investigations he comes to very strange conclusions regarding the relation between psychology and phenomenology.[14]

2. *Husserl's View on Empirical Psychology.*
"Eidetic Psychology"

Spiegelberg has rightly pointed to the fact that Husserl never opposed psychology as a whole, but only certain types of psychology which he indicated with the epithets "naturalistic" and "objectivistic." With these expressions Husserl refers to

[10] "Phenomenology," in *Encyclopædia Britannica,* 14th ed. (London, 1927), Vol. 17, cols. 699–702.

[11] *"Amsterdamer Vorträge,"* in *Phänomenologische Psychologie,* pp. 302–49.

[12] Edmund Husserl, *Cartesianische Meditationen und Pariser Vorträge.* Herausgegeben und eingeleitet von Prof. St. Strasser (Husserliana, Band I) (The Hague, 1950).
Cartesian Meditations. An Introduction to Phenomenology. Trans. Dorion Cairns (The Hague, 1960).

[13] Edmund Husserl, *Krisis,* pp. 238–69.

[14] Joseph J. Kockelmans, *Husserl's Phenomenological Psychology,* Chapter VI and the literature quoted there.

psychologies which, in mistaken imitation of the physical sciences, tried to get rid of the essential features of psychological phenomena.

To understand Husserl's point of view in regard to empirical psychology, we must realize that the psychology of his day consisted of a combination of psychophysical and physiological investigations carried out to determine quantitatively and experimentally the relationship between objective stimuli and subjective responses. Brentano and James had evidently proposed several very important remarks to correct this fundamental misconception of psychology, but neither had materially altered the classical conception. The same holds true for Gestalt-psychology, which was also still trapped by the prejudices of objectivism and scientism. According to Husserl, Dilthey was the first scientist who clearly saw the fundamental mistakes in the leading psychological schools: naturalism and objectivism. But even Dilthey was not able to indicate a new and correct way to psychology.[15]

Husserl explained this view on empirical psychology for the first time in his article *Philosophy as a Strict Science*. Since it provided the basis for the preliminary description of the new phenomenological psychology that Husserl introduced in his *Ideas*, a short summary of the most important insights proposed in the *Logos* article is in order.

FIRST MISCONCEPTION OF TRADITIONAL PSYCHOLOGY: NO PURE ANALYSIS

In the first part of his *Logos* article Husserl attempted to explain the necessity of a phenomenological philosophy. There he described his phenomenology as a science of consciousness, but distinguished from psychology as a *natural* science about consciousness. Ultimately he concluded that there is an evident strong relationship between phenomenology and psychology since both are concerned with consciousness, though in a different way and according to different orientations. Psychology is concerned with empirical consciousness, that is, with

15 Edmund Husserl, *Phän. Psychol.*, pp. 4–13. See also: Herbert Spiegelberg, *The Phenomenological Movement. A Historical Introduction*, 2 vols. (The Hague, 1960), Vol. I, pp. 150–51.

consciousness as an empirical being in the real world, whereas phenomenology is concerned with pure consciousness.[16]

From this it will be clear that, in principle, psychology is more closely related to philosophy than the other sciences, which do not deal with consciousness at all. However, what has been said here of a necessary relationship between psychology and philosophy does not apply to modern empirical psychology. For the fundamental conviction of this psychology is that pure analysis and description of the data which immediately manifest themselves in immanent intuition are to be put aside in favor of certain indirect psychologically relevant facts brought to light by observation and experiment. Such a psychology does not see that without an essential analysis of conscious life these facts are deprived of their real meaning. In other words, although it is true that empirical psychology is able to bring to light valuable psychophysical facts and norms, it nevertheless remains deprived of a deeper understanding and a definitive scientific evaluation of these facts so long as it is not founded in a systematic science of conscious life which investigates the psychical as such with the help of "immanent" intuitive reflection. By the very fact, therefore, that experimental psychology considers itself as already methodologically perfect, it is actually unscientific wherever it wishes to penetrate to a *real* psychological understanding. On the other hand, it is equally unscientific in all those cases where the lack of clarified concepts of the psychical as such leads to an obscure formulation of problems and consequently to merely apparent solutions. The experimental method is indispensable, particularly where there is a question of fixing intersubjective connections of facts. But this does not alter the fact that it presupposes what no experiment can accomplish, namely, the analysis of conscious life itself.[17]

Some psychologists, such as Stumpf and Lipps, have recognized this defect of empirical psychology and, in the manner of Brentano, have tried to undertake thorough analytical-descriptive investigations of psychical experiences. The results

---

[16] Edmund Husserl, *Phil. str. W.*, pp. 299–322 (*Phil. Rig. Sc.*, 90–110).

[17] *Ibid.*, pp. 302–23 (pp. 92–94).

of these investigations were denied recognition by most of the experimental psychologists, who disdainfully called them "scholastic analyses." The only reason for this depreciation, however, was that Brentano, Stumpf, and Lipps took ordinary language as the starting point of their investigations. But if one reads these investigations it becomes clear immediately that Brentano, Stumpf, and Lipps do not derive any judgment at all from word-concepts, but rather penetrate to the phenomena themselves which immediately present themselves to man's intuitive reflection.

Be this as it may, it is evident that the fixation of scientific language presupposes a complete analysis of the original phenomena, and that as long as that has not been accomplished the progress of the investigations remains to a great extent in the realm of vagueness and ambiguity.[18]

SECOND MISCONCEPTION OF TRADITIONAL PSYCHOLOGY: IMITATION OF PHYSICS

In the reactions against this so-called Scholasticism it is very often brought out that "empty" word-analyses are meaningless and that one has to question the things themselves and to go back to experience, which alone can give sense and meaning to our words. The question is, however, what is to be understood here by "the things themselves," and what kind of experience is it to which we have to return in psychology. Are they perhaps the answers the psychologist gets from his "clients" or subjects of experimentation? Or is his interpretation of their answers the experience we must look for? Every experimental psychologist will say, evidently, that the primary experience lies in the subjects and that an interpretation of this experience presupposes certain self-perceptions of the psychologist which—whatever they may be—in any case are not "introspections."[19]

Despite some exaggeration, there is something in this view which is unquestionably right. But there is also a fundamental error in this psychology, for it puts analyses realized in empathetic understanding of others' experiences, and analyses

[18] *Ibid.*, pp. 303–5 (pp. 95–96).
[19] *Ibid.*, pp. 305–9 (pp. 96–98).

based on one's own formerly unnoticed experiences, on the same level with the analysis characteristic of natural science, in the belief that it is an experimental science of the psychical in fundamentally the same way as natural science is the experimental science of the physical. In so doing, however, it overlooks the specific character of consciousness and the psychical data.

Most psychologists believe they owe all their psychological knowledge to experience. Nevertheless the description of the naïve empirical data, along with an immanent analysis which goes hand in hand with this description, is effected with the help of psychological concepts whose scientific value will be decisive for all further methodological steps. These concepts, however, remain by the very nature of the experimental method constantly untouched, but nevertheless enter into the final empirical judgments which claim to be scientific. On the other hand, the scientific value of these concepts was not present from the beginning, nor can it originate from the experience of the subjects or of the psychologists themselves. Logically it can be obtained even from no empirical determinations whatsoever. And here is the place for phenomenological, eidetic analyses.[20]

What has been constantly muddled in empirical psychology since its beginnings in the eighteenth century is the deceptive idea of a scientific method modeled after that of the physico-chemical sciences. The British "associationists" as well as the German "experimentalists" were convinced implicitly that the method of all empirical sciences, considered in its universal principles, had to be one and the same; therefore, that it ought to be the same in psychology as in the natural sciences. Just as metaphysics suffered for a long time from an imitation of the geometrical and physical methods (in the work of Descartes and many others), so psychology in the same way has suffered from an unacceptable simulation of the physical sciences. It is not without significance that the fathers of experimental psychology (Fechner, von Helmholtz, and

20 *Ibid.,* pp. 309–12 (pp. 98–102).

Wundt) were physiologists and physicists. Be this as it may, it is clear that in following these lines the typical character- istics of the psychical phenomena must be denied. The true method has to follow that nature of the things to be investi- gated, not our prejudices and preconceptions.[21]

Since all psychological knowledge presupposes essential knowledge of the psychical, and since such knowledge can- not be obtained by means of physical procedures, it is evi- dent that only phenomenological analyses can give us a correct solution for the problems mentioned. It is the fundamental error of modern psychology that it has not recognized the necessity of a phenomenological method. For only a really radical and systematic phenomenology, carried out not inci- dentally and in isolated reflections, but in exclusive dedication to the extremely complex and confused problems of conscious- ness and executed in an attitude free from all naturalistic prej- udices, can give us a real understanding of the psychical. Only then will the plenitude of empirical facts and the interesting laws which have been gathered bear their real fruit as the result of a critical evaluation and psychological interpretation. Then, too, will it become clear in what sense psychology stands in close relationship to philosophy.[22]

3. *Phenomenological Psychology: Its Relation to Empirical Psychology and Phenomenological Philosophy*

INTRODUCTION

We have seen in the preceding discussion that according to Husserl we shall only be able to correct the fundamental mis- takes of traditional empirical psychology by means of a phe- nomenological psychology which will fill the gap between phi- losophy and empirical psychology. Hence we must try now to describe the nature of this phenomenological psychology as accurately as possible, and to indicate the relations between

---

21 *Ibid.*, pp. 312–14 (pp. 102–3).
22 *Ibid.*, pp. 314–22 (pp. 103–10).

this phenomenological psychology and empirical psychology, as well as its relation to phenomenological philosophy.

We have seen also that in the gradual process of attempting to determine the nature of phenomenological psychology as it is related to empirical psychology and transcendental phenomenology, Husserl's thinking was in a constant state of evolution toward what may be called its final phase, which (with the probable exception of his description of the phenomenological-psychological reduction) was reached about 1928. For this reason a short survey of the most significant ideas in Husserl's *Amsterdam Lectures,* which contained for the first time the explanation of this final view, will be presented now.[23]

At the start of these lectures Husserl states that around 1900, as philosophy and psychology struggled for a strictly scientific method, a new science was born, and, at the same time, a completely new method for philosophical and psychological inquiry came into being. This science was called phenomenology because its new method had its origin in a radicalization of the phenomenological method, the need for which had long been felt, and which had even been applied in some instances by physicists and psychologists such as Mach, Hering, Stumpf, and Brentano. The radicalization of these methodological conceptions, however, led not only to a completely new method in psychology and epistemology, but simultaneously to a new way of handling typically philosophical, foundational problems, so that a new kind of scientific pursuit emerged.

In the further development of this new phenomenology it became necessary to make a fundamental distinction between phenomenological psychology as the foundational science for all psychological disciplines, and transcendental phenomenology, which in the realm of philosophy was designed to take over the function of first philosophy and to subject the foundations of philosophy itself to a radical investigation.[24]

[23] Edmund Husserl, "*Amsterdamer Vorträge,*" in *Phän. Psychol.,* pp. 302–49.

[24] *Ibid.,* pp. 302–3.

PHENOMENOLOGICAL PSYCHOLOGY:
ITS SUBJECT MATTER, METHOD, AND FUNCTION

Present-day psychology is the science of the real psycholog-ical events which occur in the concrete domain of the spatio-temporal world. In this context "psychical" is to be under-stood as the ego and all that necessarily is connected with this ego, namely, all ego-centered experiences such as perceiving, thinking, willing, etc. The "psychical" manifests itself in im-mediate experience as a non-self-sufficient realm of being because it appears only in man and animals, which according to another more fundamental sphere of being are also physi-cal realities. This is why psychology may be considered a branch of the more concrete anthropology and zoology which deal also with the physical and psychophysical aspects of these living beings.[25]

It is an essential characteristic of the world of experience taken as a whole that it differentiate itself in an open infinity of concrete individual realities. Furthermore, it is also an es-sential trait of every individual reality that it, irrespective of all possible superstructures, possess bodily-physical reality. Ac-cordingly man always has the possibility of abstracting from everything that is non-physical in order to consider each real being and also the world as a whole merely as "physical na-ture." Already in the domain of the merely physical there is a determinate, essential, structural regularity and legality of the world of experience. Not only does each concrete, intra-mundane being possess its own nature, its bodily-physical real-ity, but all mundane bodies whatsoever co-constitute an har-monious unity governed by the universal, unifying form of spatio-temporality. By means of a consistently abstracting ex-perience one can focus attention only and exclusively on the physical in intramundane beings and the world of experience as a whole. Afterward it is possible to build upon this expe-rience a theoretical science which is complete in itself, namely, natural physical science, at once comprising chemistry, phys-ical zoology, and biology.[26]

[25] Ibid., p. 303.
[26] Ibid., pp. 303–4.

The question now is to what extent (in another one-sided orientation toward the psychical which as self-sufficient never occurs in the same world) a continuously consistent experience and a theoretical inquiry founded on it are possible which, proceeding from the psychical to the psychical, never take the physical as such into consideration. In other words, in addition to the pure empirical natural sciences, in how far is a pure psychology possible? Without further investigation it is clear that factually existing psychology as an empirical science of facts never will be able to become a pure science of merely psychical facts free from any physical datum. For, no matter how far the pure psychological experience and the theory founded on it could reach, it is certain that the merely psychical about which each intends to speak possesses its spatio-temporal determinations in the real world, and in its real factualness is determinable only by means of spatio-temporal determinations. Spatio-temporality, however, originally and essentially belongs to nature taken as physical nature. Everything non-physical, such as the psychical, possesses a spatio-temporal position only because of its foundation in the physical "bodiliness." Thus it becomes clear that it will be forever impossible within the realm of empirical psychology to delineate theoretically a pure psychological investigation from a psychophysical inquiry. In other words, within the domain of empirical psychology as an objective science of facts, it is absolutely impossible to constitute a pure empirical science of the mere psychical as a separate and independent discipline with a clear-cut task, because in empirical psychology which has to deal with concrete real beings, a reference to the psychophysical and the physical seems to be essential and necessary.[27]

However, a pure psychological inquiry is not completely impossible; and for an empirical psychology which strives for a really and strictly scientific character, such a psychology is in fact indispensable. For without a pure psychology it is impossible to obtain the strictly scientific concepts in which the very essence of the psychic phenomena can be expressed

[27] *Ibid.*, pp. 304–5.

truthfully. And since to these concepts belong also those which delineate the universal and necessary essential form of the psychical as such, the necessity of an aprioric science of the essence of the psychical as such makes itself felt. Such a science is not parallel to physics, but to a pure natural science which focuses attention on the necessary a priori of any imaginable "nature" as such, and in part is already materialized in a pure science of time, pure geometry, and pure mechanics.[28]

It is not easy to bring aprioric truths to the fore. As really essential truths they originate in apodictical insight only from the initial source of experience. How can these truths be faithfully brought to light and uncovered? They can be fruitfully considered only in a methodical study and by an accurate unveiling of their all-sided horizons. For only in this way is it possible to uncover the psychical as such in a truly original and concrete manner. In such a procedure, in which the psychical is held to manifest itself in its proper and essential selfhood, that which is concretely experienced functions only as an example. One has to focus attention here first and foremost on that which in the changing and varying examples manifests itself as invariable and abiding.

Above all, therefore, the exemplary, possible, and actual experiences are of importance; and for a scientific investigation of these experiences a determinate method is indispensable. We have to bear in mind here, however, that the psychical cannot be discovered in any experience except by reflection or "perversion" of the natural attitude. We are accustomed to concentrating upon the things, thoughts, and values of the moment, and not upon the psychical acts of experience and the psychical as such. The psychic life and all our psychical acts of experience, with all their different modalities, properties, and horizons, are revealed only by reflection; and such a reflection can be practiced on every concrete, actual, or possible experience. Furthermore we have to realize that everything which comes to light in reflection possesses the typical characteristic of being intentional. Intentionality manifests itself as the essential trait of psychic life in the

[28] *Ibid.*, p. 305.

strict sense of the term. Whenever we speak of appearances, we are referred to subjects to which something appears and to certain aspects of their psychic life according to which an appearance as an appearance-of-something occurs and, therefore, we are also and even necessarily referred to what appears in and through those appearances.[29]

In a certain sense we could say that in every psychic experience something appears to the subject in question insofar as this subject is conscious of it. From this perspective the phenomenality, as the proper trait of the appearances and of that which appears, manifests itself then as the fundamental characteristic of the psychical as such, so that from the same perspective pure psychology can be called "phenomenology," or even better, apriorric phenomenology. Such a psychology evidently must deal also with the ego-subjects in their individual and social aspects, but only insofar as they are subjects of such a phenomenality.[30]

PHENOMENOLOGIC-PSYCHOLOGICAL REDUCTION

But let us return now to our original problem: How can a pure phenomenological experience be brought to light truthfully? Here phenomenological experience is to be understood as only that reflection in which the psychical as such becomes accessible in the way briefly indicated above. In this context we must first ask how this experience can be performed methodically in such a way that by means of its purity it brings to the fore what is essentially characteristic of the psychical as such. The term "purity" has a double meaning here. In the first place, this experience must be *pure* in the sense of free from all the psychophysical and the physical with which it is essentially connected. All that a physical and psychophysical experience could teach us must here be thematically left out of consideration, so that we have to restrict ourselves to a pure phenomenological experience in order to try to explicitate only what in this experience is given immediately and as such. There are evidently many problems here. For how is a pure phenomenological experience to be performed, and how can

[29] *Idem.*
[30] *Ibid.,* pp. 307–8.

one proceed from such an experience to a uniform and purely psychical field of experience which even *ad infinitum* would not imply anything non-essential to the psychical as such? Moreover, this experience must be "pure" in a second sense in that it must be free from all prejudices which spring from other scientific spheres of experience and which could blind us to that which phenomenological reflection immediately offers us.[31]

The difficulties necessarily connected with these two requirements are so great that to this date an intentional analysis has never been performed properly in modern psychology. Even Brentano did not succeed in this task although he gave a central place to the concept of intentionality in psychology and tried to lay the foundations of psychology in a systematic and descriptive inquiry of consciousness.[32]

Traditional psychology's confused attempt to imitate the methods of the natural sciences[33] derives from the equalization of immanent temporality and objective real time. Objective time is the "extensional" form of all objective realities and, in particular, of their structural foundation, namely physical nature. The psychical experiences, taken individually and also in their totality, do not in themselves possess the unitary form of coexistence and succession which are characteristic of the spatio-temporal as such. Characteristic of the psychical experiences is the form of "flowing"; according to their very essence they are flowing in the unity of the stream of consciousness as a whole; and this is evidently not a parallel form of spatio-temporality. The intentional analysis of immanent temporality brings to the fore the strong as well as the weak side of the metaphor of the stream, and furthermore makes it perfectly clear that every real analogy between the analysis of consciousness and natural, physical, chemical, and biological analyses and, at the same time, every analogy between consciousness and nature are to be abandoned. "Naturallogical" concepts such as thing, property, whole, part, compound, separation, cause, effect, action, etc., are essentially founded in reality, nature, the *res extensa;* in the realm of

31 *Ibid.*, pp. 308–9.
32 *Ibid.*, p. 309.
33 *Ibid.*, pp. 309–10.

the psychical they lose their proper meaning. Taken as psychological terms, they are empty husks or shells because there are left over only formal-logical concepts such as object, quality, etc.[34]

However, there are other fundamental difficulties connected with the realization of a consequent and pure phenomenological experience. First of all we have to abandon all the prejudices of tradition as well as the most general self-evidences of logic which are already interpreted too much from the viewpoint of the physical. As a result we have to restrict ourselves to that which phenomenological reflection brings to light as consciousness and the conscious, and to that which manifests itself there in real self-evidence. So we must exclusively adhere in this situation to the phenomenological experience without paying any attention to the factual data which actually appear in it. This experience is first of all self-experience; only in this experience are consciousness and the consciousness-ego given in completely original selfhood. All other forms of experience of the psychical are founded in the immediacy of this self-experience; this holds good also for the pure experience of things, the others, and society. Thus from its first conception Husserl explained the method of pure self-experience as the method of a consistently performed phenomenological self-disclosure.[35]

Somehow we must omit from consideration what refers to external experience, which is the original source of every physical consideration. This is difficult to realize, particularly since the psychical belonging to the others is to be excluded also. For every experience is an experience of something, of the world, and every reflection presupposes an immediate experience of something other.[36]

If I as a phenomenologist am to realize a pure phenomenological experience in order to make consciousness, my own conscious life as regards its pure and proper essence, into a universal and consequent theme of investigation and, therefore, first into a domain of pure phenomenological experience, then

[34] *Ibid.*, pp. 310–11.
[35] *Ibid.*, pp. 311–12.
[36] *Ibid.*, p. 312.

I have to eliminate as non-psychic-being the real world as a whole (the being-value of which was already accepted a priori in my natural life) from the theme of investigation.[37]

On the other hand, it is evident that all consciousness is indeed consciousness of something, and that in direct experience what we are immediately conscious of is the natural world, the real spatio-temporal world. If that is true, then it is possible to describe a perception and an act of memory according to their very essences without mentioning the fact that they are perception and memory of this determinate object. The consequence is that reflection on consciousness as such does not yet bring to light the psychical in its own pure essence. We must, besides, refrain from our natural belief in the reality of the world. As phenomenologists we must as it were be the "disinterested onlookers" of our own conscious life which only in this way can become a theme of investigation given in experience. Instead of living "in" our own consciousness and being interested in the world given in it, we have only to look upon it just as consciousness of this or that and just as it is thus interested in itself; otherwise the non-psychic world rather than our own consciousness would be the object of our description. However, within the sphere of such an *epoché* consciousness remains as always consciousness of something, of this or that objectivity. That the conscious datum itself as such comes to the fore in every consciousness of something is essential for consciousness as psychic datum. Within the realm of the *epoché*, however, this conscious datum is taken only as such; that which is experienced in every conscious intentional act is—within the realm of the *epoché* —not a being in the real world; this being is taken here only as that toward which consciousness' intention is directed; as reality in the world this object is put between brackets. In this way the phenomenological reduction is, essentially speaking, delineated. It is, however, important to call attention again to the fact that in this reduction not only is the noetical preserved, but also the noematical as an endlessly fruitful theme of phenomenological description. It is precisely through phe-

[37] *Idem.*

nomenological reduction that for the first time intentional objectivities can be delivered as such, that is as essential constituents of intentional experiences.[38]

Phenomenological reduction also influences our attitude
with respect to the consciousness-ego, because here, too,
every *real* animal and *real* human aspect is put between
brackets. Just as nature is reduced by means of the reduction
to a noematic phenomenon only, so also is the real human
ego in the natural attitude reduced to pure psychic life. My
"being-a-man" in the real world and my mundane life is maintained only as "meant," that is, as that toward which the
intentional conscious acts of intentional life, reduced to the
pure psychical, are and continue to be oriented.[39]

The consistent disclosure of the noema can shift toward a
consideration and analysis of the correlative noeses. But in
addition to these conscious intentional acts the ego-center as
such manifests itself as something on and in itself, as the ego
of every *cogito,* as an ego which in all these acts is and continues to be phenomenologically identical, as the center of
radiation from which all the various and specific ego-acts
beam forth. The ego thus manifests itself here as the center
from which all acts emanate and toward which all affects flow
back. But in both these respects the phenomenological ego-
center is an important and extensive phenomenological theme
closely connected with every other phenomenological topic.

It is in these analyses concerning the pure life of the ego
that the fundamental and essential distinction between the
mode of being of consciousness in its phenomenological purity and nature as it is given in our natural attitude clearly
manifests itself; this distinction is clearest in the ideality according to which the noematic contents are included in every
conscious act. Therefore one can also say that this difference
consists in the typical synthesis which makes each consciousness-of into a unity and connects it with other conscious acts,
making a unity of *one* consciousness. All forms of synthesis

[38] *Ibid.,* pp. 312–14.
[39] *Ibid.,* pp. 312–15.

ultimately go back to identity syntheses.[40] Let me try to explain this briefly.

In every conscious act we are directed toward an object, we "intend" it; and reflection reveals this to be an immanent process characteristic of all experiences. To be conscious of something is not an empty having of such a something in consciousness. Each phenomenon has its own intentional structure, which analysis shows to be an ever-widening system of intentionally related, individual components. The perception of a house, for instance, reveals a multiple and synthesized intention: a continuous variety in the appearances of the house, according to differences in the points of view from which it is seen and corresponding differences in perspective, and all the differences between the front side actually seen at the moment and the back side which is not seen and which remains, therefore, relatively indeterminate, and yet is supposed to be equally existent. Observation of the stream of these noemata and of the manner of their synthesis, shows that every phase is already in itself a consciousness-of-something, yet in such a way that with the constant entry of new phases the total consciousness, at any moment, is a consciousness of one and the same house. In this it is implied that in every conscious act we are referred to an indeterminate number of similar experiences of the same house and, therefore, that in the noema of a certain individual act there are already implied references to other aspects of the same house which in this individual act are already predelineated as real or possible aspects of it. The same holds true for every conscious intentional act. Here the real essence of an intentional relation becomes manifest: that of which I am conscious in every intentional experience is a noematic pole which refers to an open infinity of always new intentional experiences in which this house would appear as identically the same. This means that the noematic pole is not really but only ideally contained in the different possible experiences.[41]

40 *Ibid.*, p. 316.
41 *Idem.*

PHENOMENOLOGICAL PSYCHOLOGY

In conclusion we may say that a systematic construction of a phenomenological psychology requires: 1) the description of all the characteristics belonging to the essence of an intentional lived experience and of the most general law of synthesis in particular; 2) the explanation of the characteristic features and forms of the different types of lived experiences which necessarily are found in every consciousness, and all their typical syntheses; 3) the explanation and essential description of the very essence of the universal stream of consciousness; 4) an inquiry into the ego as center of the lived experiences and as pole of all actualities and potentialities of consciousness. When this static description is drawn we must try to analyze and describe the genesis of the life of the personal ego with its universally eidetic laws; thus we must combine a genetic phenomenology with the static type previously described. Our genetic phenomenology must explain the different modes of active and passive genesis, and in regard to the latter, especially the phenomenological, new concept of association. The static and the genetic phenomenology of reason is a special, coherent field of inquiry of a higher level which is probably most important within the realm of transcendental phenomenology.

Finally we must remark again that the validity of all these investigations will obviously extend beyond the particularity of the psychologist's own consciousness. For psychical life may be revealed to us not only in self-consciousness but equally in our consciousness of other selves, and this latter source of experience offers us more than a reduplication of what we find in our self-consciousness, for it establishes the difference between "our own" and "the other" which we experience, and presents us also with the characteristics of the "social life." Hence the further task becomes a matter of psychology's revealing the intentions of which the social life consists.[42]

[42] *Ibid.*, pp. 315–21.

PHENOMENOLOGICAL AND EMPIRICAL PSYCHOLOGY

Let us suppose now that via the phenomenological reduction mentioned above we have put ourselves in the sphere of the pure psychological, and that with the help of intentional analyses and the method of free variation we have gained an insight into the essence of the psychical in its diverse modalities. The aprioric concepts which in this sphere are formed through eidetic reduction must then express an essentially necessary style to which every imaginable, factual, and real psychic life is tied. All empirical psychological concepts are governed by these aprioric concepts as well as by their logical "forms," just as analogically such is the case with physics and the general aprioric science of nature. It is self-evident, therefore, that the aprioric truths founded in these aprioric concepts possess an unconditional, normative validity in regard to the regions of being in question, and in this particular case, in regard to the empirical domain of the pure psychical.[43]

In comparing phenomenology with the much more embracing empirical psychology, it must be said that phenomenological psychology is the absolutely necessary fundament for the performance of an exact empirical psychology, a long-standing goal heretofore pursued in attempts to follow the example of the exact physical, natural sciences. It is now necessary that empirical psychology conform to the exactness required by *modern* natural science. Natural science, which was once also a vague, inductive, empirical science, owes its modern character to the a priori system of forms characteristic of nature as such; this system is constituted by pure geometry, pure mechanics, and the pure science of time. By theoretically referring the factual in experience to the a priori of these forms, the originally vague experience is able to participate in the essential necessity, which is the last root of the exactness of the physical sciences.[44]

The methods of natural science and psychology are admit-

[43] *Ibid.*, pp. 321–24.
[44] *Ibid.*, pp. 324–25.

tedly quite different, but the latter, like the former, can only reach exactness by means of a rationalization of the essential. This means that in empirical psychology the exactness must be founded in the very essence of the psychical as such. As we have seen, the essence of the psychical as such must be brought to light through the investigations of phenomenological psychology, so that phenomenological psychology has to provide us with the fundamental concepts which, describing the a priori structure of the psychical as such, must govern every possible psychological description.[45]

Here, however, a typical problem manifests itself. For the a priori of empirical psychology is more extensive than that which is explained by phenomenological psychology. Empirical psychology as a science of the physical which in the given world manifests itself as a real moment and thus belongs to nature as psychophysical datum is, therefore, also co-founded by the a priori of physical nature. The necessary consequence is that empirical psychology also is based on the empirical and aprioric sciences of nature. Ultimately it is even founded in its own a priori which belongs to the psychophysical as such. In other words, the a priori of empirical psychology is not exclusively phenomenological, for it depends not only on the essence of the psychical but also upon the essence of the physical, and more particularly upon the essence of the psychophysical of organic nature.[46]

PHENOMENOLOGICAL PSYCHOLOGY
AND TRANSCENDENTAL PHILOSOPHY

Finally we must try to describe the relation between phenomenological psychology and transcendental phenomenology. On the one hand, psychology, both as an eidetic and empirical discipline, is a "positive" science effected within the realm of the "natural attitude" and, therefore, accepting the world as the ground of all its statements, whereas transcendental phenomenology is completely "unworldly." On the other hand, however, there is a close relationship between phenomenological psychology and transcendental phenome-

[45] *Ibid.,* p. 325.
[46] *Ibid.,* pp. 326–28.

nology in that phenomenological psychology requires only a more stringent re-employment of the formal mechanisms of reduction and analysis to disclose the transcendental phenomena which form the subject matter of transcendental phenomenology. In order to explain this double relationship between phenomenological psychology and transcendental phenomenology we must take our starting point in Husserl's view of the meaning of the transcendental reduction.[47]

Man normally lives in the natural attitude in accordance with which the world around him is at all times known and accepted as a *real fact-world* that has its real being independent of man's consciousness. Phenomenological philosophy invites every philosopher to alter this standpoint radically. This change of attitude is to be performed by the "transcendental reduction." Although this alteration of attitude has a certain similarity with Descartes' methodical doubt, the transcendental reduction is itself completely different from such a doubt. For the attempt to doubt any object in regard to its actually being there necessarily demands a certain suspension of the general thesis of the natural attitude, while the transcendental reduction is not a transformation of the thesis of the natural attitude into its antithesis, nor a transformation of one's certain conviction into a presumption or a real doubt. We do not rule out the thesis; we take it out of the picture only in that we "bracket" it; it itself remains, however, like the bracketed in the brackets. In short, the general thesis of the natural attitude is still experienced as lived, but we choose to make no use of it within the realm of transcendental phenomenology.

It can be seen from this description that the transcendental reduction is responsible for putting the general thesis of the natural attitude out of action; whatever is included in this general thesis is placed in brackets with due respect for its nature as "being real." In so doing the real world is not denied; neither is it doubted; the transcendental reduction is used only in the sense of completely barring one from using any judgment that concerns the real spatio-temporal existence of the world out there. That is why all sciences which relate to

[47] *Ibid.*, p. 328.

this natural world are also disconnected in the transcendental reduction, although there is no intention here of objecting to them ultimately. No use is made of their methods and conclusions.

Such a procedure is required for philosophy because the transcendental reduction is the absolutely necessary condition for finding a realm of being that is *apodictically evident*. For what is left over after the reduction is pure consciousness with its pure correlates and its pure ego, insofar as they are not affected by the transcendental reduction. Transcendental reduction, therefore, is the necessary operation which renders pure consciousness and subsequently the whole phenomenological region accessible. It opens up the absolute, apodictically evident region of being—the region of absolute consciousness, of transcendental subjectivity, in which the totality of being, the whole actual and possible universe is contained. After the reduction there is neither a world that *really* exists for man, nor a science which he can accept. In this new attitude the whole world is for man only something *that claims being*. From this point on, the world as a whole and every intramundane being is for each one only a phenomenon instead of something that really exists out there.

By the transcendental reduction we gain possession of the whole stream of our conscious life as it is given in *apodictical evidence*, and of everything meant in its lived experiences, as meant in them purely: the universe of pure phenomena. The being of the pure ego and its pure cogitations, as a being that is necessarily prior in itself, is antecedent to the natural being of the world. The natural, real world is a realm of being whose existential status is secondary; it continually presupposes the realm of "transcendental" being: pure consciousness and its pure cogitata.[48]

Comparing this brief description of the transcendental reduction with the explanation of the reduction which is characteristic of phenomenological psychology, it becomes immediately clear that there is a great similarity between the two. At first consideration this resemblance is even so striking

[48] Edmund Husserl, *Cart. Med.*, pp. 48–63 (*C.M.*, pp. 7–23).

that one could believe the two to be completely identical. On closer investigation, however, it appears that notwithstanding this similarity there are also fundamental points of difference which come to the fore immediately when we focus attention on the fact that both transcendental phenomenology and phenomenological psychology adopt a completely different attitude in regard to the transcendental problem. Let us try to understand this.

We have seen that the world with its property of "being in and for itself" is as it is, whether or not I happen to be conscious of it. But as soon as this world makes its appearance in consciousness as "the" world, it appears to be related to consciousness. Then it becomes clear to me that whatever exists for me and is accepted by me, exists for me and is accepted in my own conscious life, which, in all consciousness of "the" world and even in all scientific investigation, adheres to itself. In other words, I begin to realize that every showing of truth and being goes on wholly within myself. According to traditional philosophy a great problem lies in this ascertainment. For it is quite understandable that I attain certainties and evidences *within* the domain of my own consciousness; but how can this showing process, going on completely within the immanency of my conscious life, acquire objective significance for "the" world out there? With the advent of phenomenological philosophy it became possible to show that this whole problem is nonsense, since it involves an inconsistency into which modern philosophy had to fall because it did not understand that a transcendental reduction is needed in order to attain that ego by which transcendental questions, that is to say, questions about the possibility of transcendent knowledge, can be asked. However, as soon as we carry out the transcendental reduction and attempt in a systematic self-investigation and as *pure* ego to uncover the ego's whole field of consciousness, it becomes clear that all that exists for the pure ego becomes constituted in itself and that every kind of being has its own form of constitution. This means that transcendence is an immanent characteristic, constituted within the ego, and that every imaginable being, whether immanent or transcendent, falls within the domain of transcendental subjectivity, as the subjectivity that finally constitutes all sense and being.[49]

Be this as it may, it is clear from the preceding discussion that phenomenological psychology is not interested in this transcendental problem and its possible solution and that at any rate it is powerless in the face of this problem. For the purpose of the phenomenological-psychological reduction is not to bring the transcendental subjectivity to light. Phenomenological psychology hopes to expose only the foundations of empirical psychology. It is true that it will never be able to explain these foundations if in its forward development it is interested only in the intramundane beings which manifest themselves in our lived experience. Phenomenological psychology is possible and meaningful only if one is able to perform a determinate reflection in which the lived experiences themselves come to the fore as intentional. This determinate reflection is made possible by a reduction—the phenomenological-psychological reduction—through which the "objective" human ways of behavior studied in empirical psychology are reduced to unities of sense as given in subjectivity as a real psychological entity in the real world. That is why phenomenological psychology remains within the realm of the natural attitude.

However, all this does not alter the fact that there still is a great similarity between the two kinds of reductions. For the transcendental reduction may be considered as a certain further purification of the psychological interest. The psychologist reduces the ordinary valid world to a subjectivity of "souls," which as such are a part of the world which they inhabit. The transcendental phenomenologist reduces the already psychologically purified to the transcendental, to that most general subjectivity which constitutes the world and its "souls." From this point of view it becomes clear that the phenomenological-psychological reduction in its attempt to separate the psychical in its purity from everything which is not psychical has a bearing only on the different modes of man's intentional orientation toward the world reducing them to unities of sense, but does

49 Edmund Husserl, *Phän. Psychol.*, pp. 331–42.

not touch the psychologist's subjectivity itself which, therefore, still is to be understood as a real psychological entity in the real world. Transcendental subjectivity, however, is not a part of this objective world, but that subjective conscious life itself, wherein the world and all its content are constituted for me. Within the realm of the transcendental reduction I, this man, "spiritually" and "bodily" existing in this world, am, therefore, only an appearance unto myself as transcendental ego, so that the "I" which I apprehend here, presupposes a hidden ego to whom the former is "present."

On the other hand, however, transcendental self-experience may at any moment, merely by a change of attitude, be turned back into psychological self-experience. Passing thus from the one to the other attitude we notice a certain "identity" about the ego. What I saw within the psychological reflection as "my" objectification, is within the realm of the transcendental reduction seen as self-objectifying, that is to say, as objectified by the transcendental ego. We have only to recognize that what makes the psychological and transcendental spheres of experience parallel is an "identity" in their significance, and what differentiates them is merely a change of attitude. Under the more stringent reduction the psychological subjectivity is transformed into the transcendental subjectivity, and, eventually, the psychological intersubjectivity into the transcendental intersubjectivity. It is this last which is the last concrete ground whence all that transcends consciousness, including all that is real in the world, and, therefore the phenomenological-psychological intersubjectivity, derives the sense of its being.[50]

CONCLUSION

On the basis of this explanation phenomenological psychology can be characterized as an aprioric, eidetic, intuitive, purely descriptive and intentional science of the psychical as such that remains entirely within the natural attitude.[51]

The expression "a priori" refers to the fact that this psychology is focused first of all on that without which the psychical as such cannot be thought of. Only secondarily does it

[50] *Ibid.*, pp. 343–44.
[51] *Ibid.*, p. 46.

strive to understand psychological facticity, to formulate theories or to find explanations, although our natural attitude makes us interested primarily in these latter aspects. Thus phenomenological psychology is interested primarily in the necessary a priori of every possible empirical psychology.

Intuition and description point to the source of this a priori. The inner intuition reveals generalities which are analyzed, and then what is seen is guided further by the intuition toward general necessities of the intuited situation by means of the eidetic reduction. This method reveals the general characteristic of intentionality in the realm of the psychical. Now the double polarity involved in the conscious act, which can be expressed as *ego cogito cogitata,* must be considered. Consciousness implies not only the object of conscious acts, but also the ego, the conscious person. Thus psychological investigations acquire typically a twofold aspect and a teleological orientation. From this arises the necessity to investigate descriptively in two directions the systematically interwoven multiplicities of conscious acts which belong essentially to the conscious revelation of the objects of knowledge.

The phenomenological psychologist, however, remains in the natural attitude during these investigations. The transcendental attitude seeks the philosophical, radical, and apodictically evident aspects of our conscious life and in so doing leads to a radically founded philosophy. A psychologist does not wish to leave the non-philosophical, natural, and dogmatic attitude. Yet phenomenological psychology can become a point of departure which will lead to philosophy ultimately, although it can never assume the character of a necessary and founding science. Sciences of the natural attitude are sciences of the world and therefore are sciences which presuppose the world. The eidetic sciences remain also sciences of the world insofar as they seek knowledge of the world.

The pure science of the essence of the psychical life of man and society is *eo ipso* a science of the world. It seeks the apodictic, necessary structure of psychological facts and laws within the realm of facticity. It is only by means of and together with an eidetic science that any empirical science can become a rigorously scientific discipline. In addition to the

eidetic psychology an empirical psychology must be maintained which will concern itself with the determinations of the
factual as such. The a priori as such provides only a formal
framework within which facts insofar as they are thinkable
can find a place.

Phenomenological psychology, as the eidetic and aprioric
study of the psychical, is distinguished from the traditional
empirical psychology in that phenomenological psychology is
interested only in the essence of the psychical phenomena and
not in facts purely as such, and in that it tries to explain these
essences as unities of sense within the realm uncovered by a
typical phenomenological-psychological reduction. Phenomenological psychology is distinguishable from transcendental
phenomenology since only in philosophy is a transcendental
reduction performed.[52]

In conclusion, one further remark is in order. It was noted
in the foregoing discussion that in the continuous process of
attempting to determine the very essence of phenomenological
psychology, especially insofar as it is related to transcendental
phenomenology, Husserl's thinking probably reached its final
phase about 1928. In his last work, *Krisis*, Husserl qualifies
his final description of the meaning of the phenomenological-
psychological reduction by stating that even though phenomenological psychology and transcendental philosophy are essentially distinct from each other because of their different
reductions, still phenomenological psychology necessarily
fades into transcendental philosophy, where it has its ultimate
foundation.[53] As Husserl explains it, the psychologist deals
with the world as an intersubjective communal product of an
indefinitely open community of subjects whose conscious lives
are interwoven with one another. But the logic of this development demands that the psychologist perform the transcendental reduction, so that it may become clear how he, as
a pure transcendental ego, apprehends other egos as similar
to him; and so that he may see how he enters into communication with them in order to constitute, by intersubjective cooper-

[52] *Ibid.*, pp. 46–51.
[53] Edmund Husserl, *Krisis*, pp. 238–60.

ation in its diverse forms, the one identical world common to all.

But even if it is true that phenomenological psychology, developed with absolute consistency, turns into transcendental phenomenology, this does not mean that these two sciences are completely identical.[54] The meaning of this statement seems to be only that phenomenological psychology as a theoretical science necessarily strives for and, therefore, also really debouches into transcendental phenomenology. Or to put it in another way, phenomenological psychology understood as separated from a transcendental phenomenological horizon is impossible. In short, there is no psychology that can always remain merely psychology. The endeavor for radicalization, characteristic of every science in one way or another, drives theoretical phenomenological psychology, as it deals with intentional consciousness, into the arms of transcendental phenomenology. In the psychological practice, however, every psychologist must return to the world of our immediate experience, applying there his insights to "real" men in mundane situations.[55]

[54] *Ibid.*, pp. 261–69.
[55] Joseph J. Kockelmans, *Husserl's Phenomenological Psychology,* Chapter VI.

II. PHENOMENOLOGY
AND THE SOCIAL SCIENCES*

ALFRED SCHUETZ

The significance of Husserl's Phenomenology for the foundation of the social sciences will presumably become fully known
only when the Husserl manuscripts which are relevant to this
problem have been published. To be sure, the published works
already contain the most important themes of thought pertaining to this subject. Husserl was constantly concerned with
them from the time of writing the sixth *Logical Investigation*.
But these important implicit themes remain scarcely noticed,
not only because the extensive discoveries of phenomenology
in the realm of pure logic and the general theory of knowledge
have taken first place in the public discussions, but also because only in the later writings of the master has the problem
of the social sciences been attacked systematically.

Even in these later writings Husserl proceeded with great
hesitation. As is known, he had completed a second volume
of the *Ideen* in 1913, as far as proof-reading. In this volume
the problems of personality, intersubjectivity, and culture were
to have been treated. Just before publication, misgivings concerning the result of his work befell this scholar, who was
always a model of conscientiousness. He recognized that the

AUTHOR'S NOTE.—I wish to express my gratitude to Professor
Richard H. Williams of the University of Buffalo for the great
interest and the untiring efforts which he has devoted to the translation of my essay. The task of reproducing faithfully Husserl's
language, which in the original German offers serious difficulties
even to German readers, is, I believe, really creative work. To
Professor Marvin Farber I am deeply indebted for his kind interest
and his careful supervision of the text. To Professor Fritz Machlup
I owe valuable suggestions concerning the English rendition.

* From Alfred Schuetz, "Phenomenology and the Social Sciences," in Marvin Farber, ed., *Philosophical Essays in Memory of
Edmund Husserl* (Cambridge, Mass.: Harvard University Press,
1940), pp. 164–86. Reprinted by permission of the publishers.

attack on these problems presupposed carrying out still further analyses, especially the clarification of the constitutive activities of consciousness.

It was first in the *Formal and Transcendental Logic* (1929) that an avenue of approach was opened to this new thematic field, but again it proceeded from the point of view of purely logical problems. In this work can also be found[1] the starting-points toward considerations which were carried further in the postscript to the English translation of the *Ideen* and in the fifth *Cartesian Meditation* (both in 1931), and which would have found their complete presentation in an extensive series of essays planned under the title "The Crisis of European Sciences and Transcendental Phenomenology." In the last conversations which the writer had the good fortune of having with Husserl, he repeatedly designated this series of essays as the summary and the crowning achievement of his life work. He was working continuously on them during the last three years of his life, but only the first essay appeared, in the journal *Philosophia* (Belgrade, 1936). Then death took the pen from Husserl's hand and only the penetrating fragment which appeared in the *Revue internationale de Philosophie*[2] on "The Question about the Origin of Geometry" gives an indication of the extent of the work which had been begun in this period.

In the following paragraphs of this essay an attempt will be made to trace in concise form the initial phases of a phenomenological foundation of the social sciences which are contained in the writings referred to above. Following this, in the second part of the essay, the question concerning the independence of the social sciences will be raised and, going beyond Husserl, an inquiry will be made concerning the contribution which phenomenology can make to their concrete methodological problems. It goes without saying that all this must be limited to inadequate intimations.

[1] See especially *Logik*, pars. 94 ff.
[2] Brussels, 1939, 1, 2.

I

All sciences, be they related to objects of nature or to so-called cultural phenomena, are, for Husserl, a totality of human activities, namely, those of scientists working together. The fact of science itself belongs to that realm of objects which must be clarified by the methods of the cultural sciences, which in German are referred to as *Geisteswissenschaften*. Furthermore, the basis of meaning (*Sinnfundament*) in every science is the pre-scientific life-world (*Lebenswelt*) which is the one and unitary life-world of myself, of you, and of us all. The insight into this foundational nexus can become lost in the course of the development of a science through the centuries. It must, however, be capable in principle of being brought back into clarity, through making evident the transformation of meaning which this life-world itself has undergone during the constant process of idealization and formalization which comprises the essence of scientific achievement. If this clarification fails to occur, or if it occurs to an insufficient degree, and if the idealities created by science are directly and naïvely substituted for the life-world, then in a later stage in the development of science those problems of foundation and those paradoxes appear from which all so-called positive sciences are suffering today; they ought to be remedied by an *ex post facto* critique of knowledge which comes too late.

Phenomenological philosophy claims to be a philosophy of man in his life-world and to be able to explain the meaning of this life-world in a rigorously scientific manner. Its theme is concerned with the demonstration and explanation of the activities of consciousness (*Bewusstseinsleistungen*) of the transcendental subjectivity within which this life-world is constituted. Since transcendental phenomenology accepts nothing as self-evident, but undertakes to bring everything to self-evidence, it escapes all naïve positivism and may expect to be the true science of mind (*Geist*) in true rationality, in the proper meaning of this term.

However, a whole series of difficult problems is already revealed by this point of departure. We shall select a few of the groups of problems treated by Husserl which are especially relevant to our topic.

(1) First of all, how can a transcendental philosophy, such as constitutive phenomenology, risk the assertion that the life-world as viewed with the natural attitude remains its basis of meaning while at the same time the troublesome effort of phenomenological reduction is needed in order to bracket this natural world? This reduction thus creates the prerequisite of the investigation of the contributive intentionalities in which the world is constituted for transcendental subjectivity.

(2) If the life-world as viewed with the natural attitude remains the basis of meaning of transcendental phenomenology, then not only I but also you and everyone belong to this life-world. My transcendental subjectivity, in the activities of which this world is constituted, must thus from the beginning be related to other subjectivities, in relation to the activities of which it authorizes and rectifies its own. And to this life-world, which is characterized as the single and unitary life-world of us all, belong indeed all the phenomena of social life from the simple Thou-relation to the most diverse types of social communities (including all the sciences as a sum total of the accomplishments of those who are engaged in science). In short, all that constitutes our own social world in its historical actuality, and all other social worlds concerning which history gives us knowledge, belongs to it. But must not the attempt to constitute the world from the activities of transcendental subjectivity necessarily lead to solipsism? Can it explain the problem of the *alter ego* and thereby of all social phenomena which are founded on the interaction of man with his fellows in the real life-world?

(3) Can the assertion be justified that positive sciences have naïvely substituted idealities for the life-world, and thus have lost the connection with their basis of meaning, namely the life-world, in view of the unquestionable success of the natural sciences and especially of mathematical physics in the control of this life-world? And is a special cultural science (*Geisteswissenschaft*) at all thinkable which would not necessarily refer to natural science, since the entire world of mind (*Geist*) seems to be based on things of the natural world and the

psychical appears only in psychophysical connections? Must not rather a single style be demanded for all sciences which claim to be exact, and is not this style of the unified science precisely that of the mathematical sciences, whose remarkable successes, even in their practical application, we must always gratefully admire?

(4) If in fact the phenomenological method is able to prove its legitimate claim to the establishment of the cultural sciences, and if in this way it succeeds in bringing to light a style of thought peculiar to these sciences by an analysis of the constitutive activities of the transcendental subjectivity, would such a proof yield any contribution at all to the solution of the methodological problems of the concrete sciences of cultural phenomena (law, the economic and social world, art, history, etc.), since all these sciences are related to that mundane sphere which transcendental phenomenology has bracketed? Can any help at all be expected from phenomenology for the solution of all these questions? Is it not rather an affair of a psychology oriented to everyday life to solve this problem?

In the following paragraphs we shall attempt to draw together the answers to these questions which Husserl has given in diverse places in the writings cited above.

Ad 1. It should be pointed out at once that there is widespread misunderstanding to the effect that transcendental phenomenology denies the actual existence of the real life-world, or that it explains it as mere illusion by which natural or positive scientific thought lets itself be deceived. Rather, for transcendental phenomenology also there is no doubt that the world exists and that it manifests itself in the continuity of harmonious experience as a universe. But this indubitability must be made intelligible and the manner of being of the real world must be explained. Such a radical explanation, however, is only possible by proving the relativity of this real life-world, and of any imaginable life-world, to the transcendental subjectivity which alone has the ontic sense of absolute being.[3]

In order to uncover this sphere of the transcendental sub-

---

[3] Husserl, "Nachwort zu meinen *Ideen,*" *Jahrbuch,* XI, 562 ff.

jectivity at all, the philosopher, beginning his meditation with a natural attitude, must undertake that change in attitude which Husserl calls phenomenological epochē or transcendental phenomenological reduction. That is to say, he must deprive the world which formerly, with the natural attitude, was simply posited as being, of just this posited being, and he must return to the living stream of his experiences of the world. In this stream, however, the experienced world is kept exactly with the contents which actually belong to it. With the execution of the epochē, the world in no way vanishes from the field of experience of the philosophically reflecting ego. On the contrary, what is grasped in the epochē is the pure life of consciousness in which and through which the whole objective world exists for me, by virtue of the fact that I experience it, perceive it, remember it, etc. In the epochē, however, I abstain from belief in the being of this world, and I direct my view exclusively to my consciousness of the world.

In this universe of the experiencing life of the transcendental subjectivity I find my entire cogitations of the life-world which surrounds me, a life-world to which also belong my life with others and its pertinent community-forming processes, which actively and passively shape this life-world into a social world. In principle all of these experiences found in my conscious life, if they are not themselves originarily giving and primally founding experiences of this life-world, can be examined concerning the history of their sedimentation. In this way, I can return fundamentally to the originary experience of the life-world in which the facts themselves can be grasped directly.

To interpret all this by showing the intentional accomplishments of the transcendental subjectivity makes up the enormous area of work of constitutive phenomenology. It is thus a true science of mind (*Geist*), and claims to be a method, in fact the only method, which seriously means to be a radical explanation of the world through mind.

Ad 2. But this life-world, which has constantly been referred to above, and which may only be constituted by the activities of my transcendental subjectivity, is certainly not my private world. To be sure, others, fellow men, also belong to it, indeed not only as other bodies or as objects of my experience of this world but as *alter egos,* that is to say as subjectivities which are endowed with the same activities of consciousness as am I. The world which is experienced after the completion of the reduction to my pure life of consciousness is an intersubjective world, and that means that it is accessible to everyone. All cultural objects (books, tools, works of all sorts, etc.) point back, by their origin and meaning, to other subjects and to their active constitutive intentionalities, and thus it is true that they are experienced in the sense of "existing there for everybody." (Of course, this is only true "for everybody" who belongs to the corresponding community of culture—but that is a problem of a quite different character, which will be discussed later.)

Thus, for phenomenology the problem of the experience of others need not be a dark corner which, to use a beautiful expression of Husserl,[4] is feared only by children in philosophy because the specter of solipsism or psychologism and relativism haunts it. The true philosopher, however, must light up this dark corner rather than run away from it.

In the fifth *Cartesian Meditation* Husserl offered the following solution of the problem, which we shall attempt to render in its main outline, as far as possible in his own words.[5]

After the execution of the epoché I can first eliminate from the thematic field within the transcendental universal sphere all the constitutive activities which are immediately or mediately related to the subjectivity of Others. In this way I reduce the universe of my conscious life to my own transcendental sphere (*transzendentale Eigensphäre*), to my concrete being as a monad. What is left by the abstractive elimination of the sense of other subjectivity is a uniformly connected stratum of the phenomenon "world"—Husserl calls it the primordial sphere—which is no longer a world objectively existing for

[4] *Logik,* p. 210.

[5] For this purpose we have not used the French translation but the original unpublished German manuscript. A critique of the Husserlian establishment of the transcendental subjectivity, against which, in my opinion, certain important objections can be raised, must wait for another publication.

everybody, but is my world belonging peculiarly to me alone. And thus, in the truest sense, it is my private world.

Within this reduced world-phenomenon, one object is distinguished from all other objects of the likewise reduced nature. I call it my body, and it is distinguished by the fact that I can control it in action and that I attribute sensorial fields to it in conformity with my experience. If I reduce other human beings in a similar way I get peculiar corporealities; if I reduce myself as a human being, I get "my body" and "my mind" or me as a psychophysical unity, and in it my personal I which functions in my body, or which acts on and endures the exterior world by means of it. Now, in this reduced exterior world the "Other" also appears as a corporeality, but as a corporeality which I apprehend as a body, and indeed as a body of *another* by a process of appresentative pairing.[6]

The other corporeality, once experienced, continues indeed to manifest itself as a body through its changing, but always concordant gestures, which appresentatively indicate a psychical side. This psychical side, at first only indicated by appresentation, has to be fulfilled by original experience. In this way an Other is appresentatively constituted in my monad, as an ego that is not "I myself," but a second ego which mirrors itself in my monad. This second ego, however, is not simply there and given in and of itself, but is an *alter ego;* it is an Other which, in accordance with his constitutive sense, refers back to me, the ego of this *alter ego.* This "Other" is nevertheless not simply a duplicate of myself. The alien corporeality

[6] By *appresentation* Husserl understands a process of analogy, but this process is in no sense a conclusion by analogy. By it an actual experience refers back to another experience which is not given in actuality and will not be actualized. In other words the appresented does not attain an actual presence. For instance, by looking at the obverse of an object the reverse is appresented. *Pairing* ("accouplement" in the French translation) is a principal form of passive synthesis, which means of association. Its characteristic is that two data, distinguishable each from the other, are presented in the unity of consciousness; that means, that they constitute as a pair a phenomenological unity of similarity established by pure passivity, although they appear distinct and regardless of whether or not they are noticed. Cf. *Méditations Cartésiennes*, sec. 50 and 51.

that is apperceived as an "Other" appears in my monadic sphere above all in the mode of the "there" (*illic*), while my own body is in the mode of the absolute "here" (*hic*). That which becomes appresented in this way does not derive from my own sphere of peculiarity; it is a coexistent ego in the mode of the *illic* and therefore an *alter ego*.

The first communality which exists between me, the primordial psychophysical I, and the appresentatively experienced Other, and which forms the foundation of all other intersubjective communities of a higher order, is the community of Nature, which belongs not only to my primordial sphere but also to that of the Other. There is, however, the difference that the Other's world of Nature is seen as *illic* from my point of view, which is to say that the Other gets that aspect from it, which I should get if I myself were not *hic* but *illic*. In this way every natural thing which is experienced or which can be experienced in my primordial sphere obtains a new appresentative stratum, namely, as the same natural thing in the possible manners of its givenness for the Other.

Starting from myself as the original constitutive monad, I thus get other monads, that is, Others as psychophysical subjects. These Others are not merely related by means of associative pairing to my psychophysical being in their capacity as being bodily opposite me; rather it is a question of an objective equalization, a mutual interrelatedness of my existence and that of all Others. For as the body of the Other is appresented by me as an Other, so my body is experienced by the Other as his Other, and so forth. The same thing obtains for all subjects, that is for this open community of monads which Husserl has designated as transcendental intersubjectivity.

It should be stressed that this transcendental intersubjectivity exists purely in me, the meditating ego. It is constituted purely from the sources of my intentionality, but in such a manner that it is the *same* transcendental intersubjectivity in every single human being (only in other subjective manners of appearance) in his intentional experiences. In this constitution of the transcendental intersubjectivity that of the single and uniformly objective world is also executed, and along with it the constitution of those peculiarly mental objectivities, especially those types of social communities, which have the character of personalities of a higher order.

Of special importance for our topic is the constitution of the specifically human, and that means cultural, worlds in their peculiar manner of objectivity.[7] According to Husserl, accessibility for everyone belongs in essence to the constitutive sense of Nature, of corporeality and of the psychophysical human being. *But the world of culture is of a limited kind of objectivity,* and with this it should be borne in mind that the life-world is given to me, and to everyone who retains the natural attitude primarily as his cultural world, namely, as a world of signification which the human being in question historically takes a part in forming. The constitution of the world of culture, similar to the constitution of any "world," including the world of one's own stream of experience, has the lawful structure of a constitution, oriented with respect to a "null point" (*Nullglied*), i.e., to a personality. Here am I and my culture; it is accessible to me and to my cultural companions as a kind of experience of others. Other cultural humanity and other culture can become accessible only by a complicated process of understanding, namely, on the basic level of the common Nature, which, in its specific spatio-temporal structure, constitutes the horizon of being for the accessibility to all the manifold cultural phenomena. As Nature is thus concretely and uniformly constituted, so human existence itself is referred to an existent life-world as a realm of practical activity, which, from the first, is endowed with human significations. All this is in principle accessible to the explication of a phenomenological constitutive analysis which, proceeding from the apodictic ego, must finally reveal the transcendental meaning of the world in its full concretion, which is the continuous life-world of us all.

Ad 3. It was stated above that the natural sciences generally, and especially the natural sciences which use mathematics, have lost their relation to their basis of meaning, namely the life-world. How can this reproach be justified, when it has just been shown that it is precisely this universal Nature which

[7] In this connection see especially *Méd. Cart.*, sec. 58.

constitutes itself concretely and uniformly in intersubjectivity, and which must almost be considered as the form of access to the worlds of other culture, in their manner of oriented constitution? We may reply first of all that Nature as the object of the natural sciences does not mean precisely the same thing as Nature as a constitutive element of the life-world. That which the naïvely living human being takes for natural reality is not the objective world of our modern natural sciences; his conception of the world, as valid for him in its subjectivity, obtains with all its gods, demons, etc. *Nature in this sense, as an element of the life-world, is thus a concept which has its place exclusively in the mental* (geistig) *sphere.* It constitutes itself in our everyday meaningful experience as this experience develops in our historically determined being.

Let us take geometry as an example. When we, in our perceptual life-world, direct our view by abstraction to merely spatial and temporal figures we experience, it is true, "solids." However, they are not the ideal solids of geometry, but they are solids as we actually realize them, with the same content which is the true content of our experience.[8] To the world which is pre-given to our everyday experience belongs the spatio-temporal form, in which are included the corporeal figures ordered within it, and in which we ourselves live in conformity with our personal, bodily manner of being. But here we find nothing of geometrical idealities, of geometrical space or of mathematical time with all their forms.[9] Concretely empirical figures are given to us, in our life-world, merely as forms of a material, of a "sensory fullness"; thus they are given with that which is represented by the so-called specific sense-qualities (color, odor, etc.). But pure geometry deals with solids in the corporeal world only in pure abstraction; that is to say only with abstract figures in the spatio-temporal framework, which are, as Husserl recognizes, purely ideal "meaning figures," meaning-creations of the human mind. This is not to say that geometrical existence is psychological or personal existence in the personal sphere of consciousness. On the contrary, geometrical existence is of the

[8] Husserl, "Krisis," pp. 98 ff.
[9] *Ibid.,* pp. 125 ff.

same kind as the existence of meaning structures, and it is objective for everyone who is a geometer or understands geometry.

Geometrical figures, axioms, and propositions, just as most structures of the world of culture, have an *ideal objectivity;* they can always be *reactivated* as identically the same. That is to say, the meaning-producing activity which has led to their sedimentation can be reëxecuted. But reactivation in this sense is also explication of the meaning which lies implicated in the abbreviations of this sedimentation, by referring it back to the primal evidence. The possibility always remains open to examine into the primal evidence of a tradition, for example, of geometrical or of any other deductive science, which works on through the centuries. If this does not occur, then the original activities, which are found within the fundamental concepts of this deductive science, and their foundation in pre-scientific materials remain undisclosed. The tradition in which these sciences are handed down to us is then emptied of meaning, and the basis of meaning to which these sciences refer, namely the life-world, is forgotten.[10] But according to Husserl this is the situation in modern times not only in respect to geometry and mathematics, including all natural sciences using mathematics, but also in respect to traditional logic.[11]

The fundamental idea of modern physics is that nature is a *mathematical* universe. Its ideal is exactitude, which means an ability to recognize and determine the things of nature in absolute identity, as the substratum of an absolutely identical, methodically unequivocable and discernible character. In order to achieve this ideal, physics makes use of measurement and of the mathematical methods of calculation and formulae. In this way it seeks to create an entirely new kind of prediction for the corporeal world, and to be able to calculate the occurrences in this world in terms of a compelling necessity. But on the one hand the sensory fullness of solids in the life-world and the changes of this fullness are not capable of be-

[10] Husserl, "Geometrie," pp. 203–226, and especially pp. 209–217.

[11] In relation to this last point, about logic, cf. *Logik,* sec. 73–81, sec. 94 ff.

ing mathematized, and on the other hand the pre-scientific intuitable nature does not lack this predictability. In the world perceptible by our senses, changes in the spatio-temporal positions of solids, changes in their form and fullness, are not accidental and indifferent, but they are dependent on each other in sensuously *typical* ways. The basic style of our visible immediate world is empirical. This universal, and indeed causal, style makes possible hypotheses, inductions, and predictions, but in pre-scientific life they all have the character of the approximate and typical.[12] Only when the ideal objectivities become substituted for the empirical things of the corporeal world, only when one abstracts or co-idealizes the intuitable fullness, which is not capable of mathematization, does the *fundamental hypothesis* of the entire realm of mathematical natural science result, namely, that a universal inductivity might prevail in the intuitable world, an inductivity which suggests itself in everyday experience but which remains concealed in its infinity. Consequently this universal causality of the mathematical sciences is also an idealization. Now it is doubtless true, says Husserl, that in the remarkable structure of the natural sciences this hypothesis holds good in infinity, and precisely in its prediction of events in the life-world. But in spite of all verification it still remains a hypothesis and thus an unclarified supposition of mathematical natural science.

The natural scientist, in unquestioned tradition, accepts the inherited idealizations and unclarified suppositions as technics (τεχνή) without becoming conscious of the shift which the originally living meaning of the aim to get knowledge of the world itself has experienced.[13] In the process of mathematization of the natural sciences, says Husserl, we measure the life-world for a well-fitting garment of ideas. In just this way we get possibilities for a prediction which goes far beyond the accomplishments of everyday anticipation, concerning the occurrences in the intuitable life-world. But everything which represents the life-world to the natural scientists as "objectively actual and true nature" is clothed by this garment of symbols and disguised. The cloak of ideas has the effect that

12 Cf. "Krisis," pp. 101–105.
13 "Krisis," pp. 113–116 and pp. 132 ff.

we take a method to be true being, in order infinitely to improve upon the *raw* predictions which are the only ones possible within the actual experiences of the life-world. But the proper meaning of methods, formulae, and theories remains unintelligible so long as one does not reflect about the historical meaning belonging to their primordial establishment.

With the enormous success of the mathematical natural sciences has come the fact that modern philosophy and critique of knowledge generally perceive the prototype of scientific thought in their methods. The consequence is a dualistic cleavage into a real and self-contained corporeal world, and a mental world, which latter, however, remains dependent upon the natural world and is not brought to any independent status in its own right. The further consequence is that even this mental world ought to be explained *more geometrico* according to the unclarified rationalism of the mathematical natural sciences, or, as Husserl terms it, by means of physicalistic rationalism. Above all, psychology ought to be treated objectivistically, wherein objectivistic should mean that in the realm of the world which is self-evidently given through experience one will search for the "objective truths" without inquiring about the subjective activities of the mind, out of which alone the ontic sense of the pre-given life-world is constituted. For the life-world is a subjective formation resulting from the activities of the experiencing pre-scientific life. Inasmuch as the intuitable life-world, which is purely subjective, has been forgotten in the thematic interest of natural science, and also of objectivistic psychology, the working subject, namely the human being himself who is pursuing his science, has in no way become thematic. It is only in purely cultural scientific knowledge that the scientist does not become confounded by the objection of the self-disguise of his activity. It is consequently erroneous if the social sciences contend with the natural sciences for an equal warrant. As soon as they grant to the natural sciences their objectivity as their own independent attribute, the social sciences themselves fall into objectivism, for only mind (*Geist*) has being in itself and is independent. To regard nature as something in itself alien to mind and then to found the cultural sciences on the natural sciences, and thus supposedly to make them exact, is an absurdity. The cultural scientists, blinded by naturalism, have completely neglected even to raise the problem of a universal and true cultural science.

Ad 4. But is it an affair of the cultural sciences at all, in the sense of that term as used today, to make inquiries concerning the problem of a universal science of the mind in Husserl's sense? Is this task not specifically a philosophical, or more properly a phenomenological, problem that becomes visible only in the transcendental sphere, and thus only after that mundane world, which alone is the topic and ought to be the topic of all efforts of the concrete sciences of culture, has been bracketed? The ideal of history to recount "as it then actually was" (von Ranke) is also, with certain modifications, the ideal of all other sciences of culture, namely, to determine what society, the state, language, art, economy, law, etc., actually is in this our mundane life-world and its historicity, and how the meaning of each can be made intelligible in the sphere of our mundane experience. And should not an appeal be made to psychology in this sphere for a solution of the problem of a universal cultural science?

For Husserl there is also no doubt that all the hitherto existing cultural and social sciences are related in principle to phenomena of mundane intersubjectivity. Hence the transcendental constitutive phenomena, which only become visible in the phenomenologically reduced spheres, scarcely come within the view of the cultural sciences. However, a psychology from which a solution of the problems of the cultural sciences might be expected must become aware of the fact that it is not a science which deals with empirical facts. It has to be a science of essences, investigating the correlates of those transcendental constitutional phenomena which are related to the natural attitude. Consequently, it has to examine the invariant, peculiar, and essential structures of the mind; but that is to say it examines their *a priori*.[14] The concrete description of the spheres of consciousness as it has to be undertaken by a true descriptive psychology with the natural attitude remains, how-

[14] "Nachwort," p. 553; cf. p. 14 of Boyce Gibson's translation.

ever, the description of a closed sphere of the intentionalities. That is to say it requires not only a concrete description of the experiences of consciousness, as in the Lockean tradition, but also necessarily the description of the conscious (intentional) "objects in their objective sense"[15] found in active inner experiences. But such a true *psychology of intentionality* is, according to Husserl's words, nothing other than a *constitutive phenomenology of the natural attitude*.[16]

In this eidetic mundane science (thus in the psychological apperception of the natural attitude), which stands at the beginning of all methodological and theoretical scientific problems of all the cultural and social sciences, all analyses carried through in phenomenological reduction essentially retain their validation. It is precisely here that the tremendous significance of the results achieved by Husserl for all the cultural sciences lies. This will now be briefly carried further.

II

In the above résumé of some of the most important lines of thought of the later philosophy of Husserl, the concept of the life-world is revealed in its entire and central significance as the basis of meaning of all sciences, including natural sciences and including also philosophy in so far as it wishes to appear as exact science. Thus every reflection finds its evidence only in the process of recurring to its originally founding experience within this life-world, and it remains the endless task of thought to make intelligible the intentional constitution of the contributive subjectivity in reference to this as its basis of meaning. We, however, who live naïvely in this life-world, encounter it as already constituted. We are, so to speak, born into it. We live in and endure it, and the living intentionality of our stream of consciousness supports our thinking, by which we orient ourselves practically in this life-world, and our action, by which we intervene in it.

Our everyday world is, from the outset, an intersubjective

15 *Ibid.*, p. 565.
16 *Ibid.*, p. 567.

world of culture. It is intersubjective because we live in it as
men among other men, bound to them through common influence and work, understanding others and being an object
of understanding for others. It is a world of culture because,
from the outset, the life-world is a universe of significations
to us, i.e., a framework of meaning (*Sinnzusammenhang*)
which we have to interpret, and of interrelations of meaning
which we institute only through our action in this life-world.
It is a world of culture also because we are always conscious
of its *historicity*, which we encounter in tradition and habituality, and which is capable of being examined because the
"already-given" refers back to one's own activity or to the
activity of others, of which it is the sediment. I, the human
being born into this world and naïvely living in it, am the
center of this world in the historical situation of my actual
"Now and Thus"; I am the "null point toward which its constitution is oriented."[17] That is to say, this world has significance and meaning first of all by me and for me.

In the following we intend to try to clarify this topic by
drawing from Husserl's course of ideas some fundamental
consequences not found in his own writings, for the knowledge of the structure of the social sciences.

This world, built around my own I, presents itself for interpretation to me, a being living naïvely within it. From this
standpoint everything has reference to my actual historical
situation, or as we can also say, to my pragmatic interests
which belong to the situation in which I find myself now and
thus. The place in which I am living has not significance for
me as a geographical concept, but as my home. The objects
of my daily use have significance as my implements, and the
men to whom I stand in relationships are my kin, my friends,
or strangers. Language is not a substratum of philosophical
or grammatical considerations for me, but a means to express
my intentions or to understand the intentions of others, etc.
Only in reference to me does that relation to others obtain its
specific meaning which I designate with the word "We." In
reference to Us whose center I am, others stand out as "You,"

[17] Cf. above, p. 459 [of this anthology].

and in reference to You, who refer back to me, third parties stand out as "They." My social world with the *alter egos* in it is arranged, around me as the center, into associates (*Umwelt*), contemporaries (*Mitwelt*), predecessors (*Vorwelt*), and successors (*Folgewelt*),[18] whereby I and my different attitudes to others institute these manifold relationships. All this is done in various degrees of *intimacy* and *anonymity*.

Furthermore, the life-world is arranged into fields (*Zentren*) of different relevance according to my current state of interest, each one of which has its own peculiar center of density and fullness, and its open but interpretable horizons. In this connection the categories of *familiarity* and *strangeness* and the very important category of *accessibility* enter into consideration. This last category refers to the grouping of my environments according to (1) that which actually lies within the extent of my reach, seeing and hearing, or has once lain there and might at will be brought back into actual accessibility; (2) that which is or was accessible to others and might thus potentially be accessible to me if I were not here (*hic*) but there (*illic*);[19] (3) the open horizons of that which in free variation can be thought of as attainable.

To this it should be added that I assume everything which has meaning for me also has meaning for the Other or Others with whom I share this, my life-world, as an associate, contemporary, predecessor, or follower. This life-world presents itself also to them for interpretation. I know about their perspectives of relevance and their horizons of familiarity or

[18] The translation of these terms follows the usage in an article by Alfred Stonier and Karl Bode concerning Dr. Schuetz's work, "A New Approach to the Methodology of the Social Sciences," *Economica*, IV (November 1937), 406–424. These terms are developed at length in Dr. Schuetz's *Der sinnhafte Aufbau der sozialen Welt* (Vienna, 1932). The *Umwelt* is the immediate world within which direct and relatively intimate experience of others is possible. The *Mitwelt* is a world of mediate, but contemporary, experience within which indirect and relatively anonymous experience of others can be obtained. The *Vorwelt* refers to experiences of the historical past. The *Folgewelt* refers to the future, of which no experience is possible, but toward which an orientation may exist. —TRANSLATOR'S NOTE.

[19] Cf. above, p. 458 [of this anthology].

strangeness; indeed I also know that with segments of my meaningful life I belong to the life-world of Others as Others belong to my life-world, etc. All this is a manifold orientation for me, the naïve human being. I posit meaningful acts in the expectation that Others will interpret them meaningfully, and my schema of positing is oriented with respect to the Others' schema of interpretation. On the other hand, I can examine everything which, as a product of Others, presents itself to me for meaningful interpretation as to the meaning which the Other who has produced it may have connected with it. Thus, in these reciprocal acts of positing meaning, and of interpretation of meaning, my social world of mundane intersubjectivity is built; it is also the social world of Others, and all other social and cultural phenomena are founded upon it.

All this is self-evident to me in my naïve life just as it is self-evident to me that the world actually exists and that it is actually *thus*, as I experience it (apart from deceptions which subsequently in the course of experience prove to be mere appearances). No motive exists for the naïve person to raise the transcendental question concerning the actuality of the world or concerning the reality of the *alter ego*, or to make the jump into the reduced sphere. Rather, he posits this world in a *general thesis* as meaningfully valid for him, with all that he finds in it, with all natural things, with all living beings (especially with human beings), and with meaningful products of all sorts (tools, symbols, language systems, works of art, etc.). Hence, the naïvely living person (we are always speaking of healthy, grown-up, and wide-awake human beings) automatically has in hand, so to speak, the meaningful complexes which are valid for him. From things inherited and learned, from the manifold sedimentations of tradition, habituality, and his own previous constitutions of meaning, which can be retained and reactivated, his *store of experience* of his life-world is built up as a closed meaningful complex. This complex is normally unproblematical for him, and it remains controllable by him in such a way that his momentary interest selects from this store of experience those things which are relevant to the demand of the situation. The experience of the life-world has its special style of verification. This style results from the process of the harmonization of all single experiences. It is co-constituted, last but not least, by the perspectives of relevance and by the horizons of interest which are to be explicated.

All that has been said so far, however, is no more than chapter-headings for an extensive exploration. For the present, it will suffice to keep firmly in mind that a special motivation is needed in order to induce the naïve person to pose the question at all concerning the meaningful structure of his life-world, even *within the general thesis*. This motivation can be very heterogeneous; for example, a newly appearing phenomenon of meaning resists being organized within the store of experience, or a special condition of interest demands a transition from a naïve attitude to a reflection of a higher order. So-called rational action can be given as an example of the latter. Rational action is given when all the ends of action and all the means which will lead to it are clearly and distinctly presented, as, for example, in the case of economic action. If such a motivation to leave the natural attitude is given, then by a process of reflection the question concerning the structure of meaning can always be raised. One can always reactivate the process which has built up the sediments of meaning, and one can explain the intentionalities of the perspectives of relevance and the horizons of interest. Then all these phenomena of meaning, which obtain quite simply for the naïve person, might be in principle exactly described and analyzed even *within the general thesis*. To accomplish this on the level of mundane intersubjectivity is the task of the mundane cultural sciences, and to clarify their specific methods is precisely a part of that constitutive phenomenology of the natural attitude of which we have been speaking (and concerning which this section of the essay mentions only a few topics as programmatic examples). Whether one will call this science Intentional Psychology or, better, General Sociology, since it must always be referred back to mundane intersubjectivity, is a quite secondary question.

All science presumes a special attitude of the person carrying on science; it is the attitude of the disinterested observer. In this manner it is distinguished above all from the attitude of the person who lives naïvely in his life-world and who has an eminently practical interest in it. With the transition to this attitude, however, all categories of experience of the life-world undergo a fundamental modification. As a disinterested observer, not as a private person, which certainly he also is, the scientist does not participate in the life-world as an actor, and in his doing he is no longer carried along by the living stream of intentionalities. The person living naïvely in the life-world can become, as we have said, motivated so as to raise the question concerning the structure of its meaning. But, although he reflects in this manner, he in no way loses his practical interest in it, and he still remains the center, the "null point," of this his world, which is oriented with regard to him. *But to make up his mind to observe scientifically this life-world means to determine no longer to place himself and his own condition of interest as the center of this world, but to substitute another null point for the orientation of the phenomena of the life-world.* What this null point is and how it comes to be constituted as a type (economic man, subject of law, etc.) depends upon the particular problem-situation which the scientist has chosen. Predominantly the life-world, as an object of scientific investigation, will be for the investigator *qua* scientist, the life-world of Others, the observed. This does not alter the fact that the scientist, who is *also* a human being among human beings in this single and uniform life-world and whose scientific work is in itself a working-together with Others in it, constantly refers and is obliged to refer in his scientific work to his own experience of the life-world. But it must always be clearly borne in mind that the disinterested observer has to a certain extent departed from the living stream of intentionalities. *Together with the substitution of another null point for the framework of orientation, every meaning reference which was self-evident to the naïve person, in reference to his own I, has now experienced a fundamental specific modification.*[20] It remains for each social and cultural

[20] For example, the social scientist does not study the concrete action (*Handeln*) of human beings, like you and me and everyone in our daily lives, with our hopes and fears, mistakes and hates, happiness and misery. He analyzes only certain definite sequences

science to develop the type of such modification proper to it; that means nothing other than *to work out its particular methods*. In other words, each of these sciences must give the equation of transformation according to which the phenomena of the life-world become transformed by a process of idealization.

For idealization and formalization have just the same role for the social sciences as the one which Husserl has stated for the natural sciences, except that it is not a question of *mathematizing the forms* but of developing a *typology of "fullnesses"* (*Füllen*). Also in the social sciences the eminent danger exists that their idealizations, in this case typologies, will not be considered as methods but as true being. Indeed this danger is even greater in the sciences which deal with the human being and his life-world, because they are always obliged to work with a highly complex material involving types of a higher order. This material does not refer back immediately to the subjective activity of individuals, which is always the chief problem if it is in the sphere of mundane apperception.

In relation to these problems it is the great contribution of Max Weber[21] in his "verstehende Soziologie" to have given the principles of a method which attempts to explain all social phenomena in the broadest sense (thus all objects of the cultural sciences) in relation to the "intended meaning" which the actor connects with his action. At the same time he has given the main characteristics of the style of method of these sciences in his theory of the ideal type and its laws of formation. But, it seems to me, these methods can only become fully intelligible by means of the far-reaching investigations of a constitutive phenomenology of the natural attitude.

Such a science will find more than a guide in Husserl's investigations in the area of transcendental phenomenology, for,

---

of activity (*Handlungsabläufe*) as types, with their means-end relations and their chains of motivation; and he constructs (obviously, according to quite definite structural laws) the pertinent ideal personality types with which he peoples the segment of the social world he has selected as an object of his scientific research.

[21] An excellent presentation of his theory is to be found in English in Talcott Parsons, *The Structure of Social Action* (New York, 1937).

as we have already said, in essence all analyses carried out in phenomenological reduction must retain their validation in the correlates of the phenomena investigated within the natural sphere. Therefore it is to be the task of this science to apply the whole treasure of knowledge opened up by Husserl to its own area. We mention only Husserl's analysis of time, his theory of signs and symbols, of ideal objects, of occasional judgments, and finally his teleological interpretation of history. To develop the program of such a science, even in its main characteristics, beyond the mere suggestion given above, would go far beyond the limits placed on this essay.[22]

[22] I have presented several of the main principles in *Der sinnhafte Aufbau der sozialen Welt.*

III. PSYCHOLOGY, PHENOMENOLOGY, AND PHENOMENOLOGICAL PSYCHOLOGY*

JEAN-PAUL SARTRE

Psychology is a discipline which aspires to be positive; that is, it tries to draw its resources exclusively from experience. The age of associationists is certainly gone, and contemporary psychologists are no longer prohibited from *asking* and *interpreting*. But like the doctor they want to face their object. When one speaks of contemporary psychology it is still necessary to limit the concept of experience, for, in effect, there can be a host of diverse experiences; for example, one may have to decide whether or not there is an experience of essences or values or a religious experience. The psychologist intends to use only two types of well defined experiences, that which gives us the spatial-temporal perception of organized bodies, and the intuitive knowledge of ourselves that is called reflexive experience. If there are any disputes among the psychologists as to method, they can bear almost solely on the following problem: are these two types of information complementary, should one be subordinated to the other, or should one of them be boldly discarded? But they are in agreement on one essential principle: the inquiry should start, before everything else, with *facts*.

If we ask ourselves what a fact is, we see that it is defined by that which one should *meet* in the course of an investigation and that it always presents itself as an unexpected enrichment and a novelty in relation to anterior facts. It is therefore not necessary to count on the facts to organize themselves in a synthetic totality which by itself might yield its meaning. In other words, if one calls anthropology a disci-

* From Jean-Paul Sartre, *The Emotions: Outline of a Theory*, translated by Bernard Frechtman (New York: The Philosophical Library, 1948), pp. 1–21, 93–94. Reprinted by permission of the publishers.

pline which claims to define the essence of man and the human condition, psychology—even the psychology of man—is not and never will be anthropology. It does not intend to define and limit *a priori* the object of its inquiry. The idea of man which it accepts is quite empirical: throughout the world are a number of creatures who present analogous natures to experience. Moreover, other sciences, sociology and psychology, proceed to inform us that there are certain objective connections between these creatures.

No more is needed for the psychologist, in the name of a working hypothesis, to accept prudently to limit his investigations provisionally to this group of creatures. The available sources about them are indeed more easily accessible since they live in society, speak a language, and leave traces of their activity. But the psychologist does not commit himself; he does not know whether the notion of man may not be arbitrary. It may be *too vast;* we do not have to put the Australian primitive into the same psychological class as the American workman of 1939. It may be *too narrow;* nothing says that an abyss separates the higher apes from the human beings. In any case, the psychologist rigorously guards against considering the men about him as *his fellow-creatures.* This notion of similitude, on the basis of which one might be able to build an anthropology, seems to him ridiculous and dangerous. He will readily admit, with the reservations made above, that he is a man, that is, that he is a part of the class which has been isolated provisionally. But he will take into consideration that this human character should be conferred upon him *a posteriori* and that he can not, insofar as he is a member of that class, be a privileged object of study, except for the sake of experiments. He will therefore learn *from others* that he is man and his nature as a man will not be revealed to him in a particular way by the pretext that he *is* himself what he studies. Like "objective" experimentation, introspection will furnish only facts.

If it is necessary that there be later a rigorous concept of *man*—and even that is doubtful—this concept can be envisaged only as the crown of a finished science, that is, one which is done with forever. It would be still only a unifying hypothesis, invented to co-ordinate and grade the infinite collection of facts which have been brought to light. This is to say that the idea of man, if ever it takes on a positive meaning, will be only a conjecture aiming to establish connections between disparate materials and will attain verisimilitude only by its success. Peirce defined hypothesis as the sum of the experimental results which it allows us to foresee. Thus, the idea of man can be only the sum of the established facts which it allows us to unite. However, if some psychologists were to use a certain conception of man *before* this ultimate synthesis were possible, it would be a strictly personal act, a conducting wire as it were or, better, like an idea in the Kantian sense, and their first duty would be never to lose sight of the fact that it was a regulating concept.

It follows from so many precautions that psychology, insofar as it claims to be a science, can furnish only a sum of miscellaneous facts, most of which have no connection with the others. What can be more different, for example, than the study of the stroboscopic illusion and the inferiority complex? This confusion is not due to chance but to the very principles of the science of psychology. To expect the *fact* is, by definition, to expect the isolated, to prefer, because of positivism, the accidental to the essential, the contingent to the necessary, disorder to order; it is, on principle, to cast what is essential into the future: "That will do for later, when we shall have assembled enough facts." In short, psychologists do not realize that it is just as impossible to get to essence by accumulating accidents as to reach 1 by adding figures to the right of 0.99.

If their only aim is to accumulate details of knowledge there is nothing to be said; one simply does not see what interest there is in these labors of a collector. But if they are animated, in their modesty, by the hope, in itself praiseworthy, that later on, on the basis of their monographs, an anthropological synthesis will be realized, they are in full contradiction with themselves. It will be said that this is precisely the method and ambition of the natural sciences. The answer to that is that the natural sciences do not aim at knowing *the world,* but the possible conditions of certain general phenomena. This notion of *world* has long since vanished beneath the criticism of methodologists, and precisely because one could not both apply the methods of the positive sciences and hope that they would one day lead to discovering the meaning of the synthetic totality which one calls *world*. But *man* is a being of the same type as *the world*. It is even possible, as Heidegger believes, that the notions of world and of "human reality" (*Dasein*) are inseparable. Psychology should resign itself to doing without human reality for precisely that reason, supposing at least that this human reality does exist.

Applied to a particular example, the study of the emotions, for example, what will the principles and the methods of the psychologist give us? First of all, our knowledge of the emotion will be added *from without* to other knowledge about the psychical being. The emotion will present itself as an irreducible novelty in relation to the phenomena of attention, memory, perception, etc. You can, indeed, inspect these phenomena and the empirical notion of them we build following the psychologists; you can turn them about again and again as you please and you will not discover the slightest essential connection with emotion. All the same, the psychologist grants that man has emotions because experience teaches him so.

Thus, emotion is first of all and in principle an *accident*. In textbooks of psychology it is a chapter which follows other chapters, as calcium follows hydrogen or sulphur in textbooks of chemistry. As for studying the possible conditions of an emotion, that is, wondering whether the very structure of human reality makes emotions possible and *how* it makes them possible, that would appear useless and absurd to a psychologist: what good is it to ask whether emotion is possible precisely because it is.

The psychologist will likewise turn to experience to establish the limits and definition of emotive phenomena. In fact, he would be able to observe there that he already has an *idea* of emotion, since, after inspecting the facts, he will draw a line of demarcation between the facts of emotion and those which are not such; indeed, how could experience furnish him with a principle of demarcation if he did not already have it? But the psychologist prefers to hold to the belief that the facts group themselves before his eyes by themselves. At present it is a matter of *studying* the emotions one has just isolated. To do that we shall agree to realize affecting situations or to turn to those particularly emotive subjects which pathology offers us. We shall then apply ourselves to determining the factors of this complex state; we shall isolate the *bodily reactions* (which, moreover, we shall be able to establish with the greatest precision), the *behavior,* and the *state of consciousness,* properly so called. Following this we shall be able to formulate our laws and offer our explanations; that is, we shall try to unite these three types of factors in an irreversible order. If I am a partisan of the intellectualist theory, for example, I shall set up a constant and irreversible succession between the inner state considered as antecedent and the physiological disturbances considered as consequents.

If, on the contrary, I think with the partisans of the peripheric theory that "a mother is sad because she weeps," I shall, at bottom, limit myself to reversing the order of the factors. In any case, what is certain is that I shall not seek the explanation or the laws of emotion in the general and essential structures of human reality, but *in the processes of the emotion itself,* with the result that even when it has been duly described and explained it will never be anything but one fact among others, a fact closed in on itself which will never permit either of understanding a thing other than itself or of grasping by means of it the essential reality of man.

It was in reaction against the inadequacies of psychology and psychologism that about thirty years ago a new discipline was constituted called phenomenology. Its founder, Husserl, was struck by this truth: essences and facts are incommensurable, and one who begins his inquiry with facts will never arrive at essences. If I seek the psychic facts which are at the basis of the arithmetic attitude of the man who counts and calculates, I shall never arrive at the reconstitution of the arithmetic essences of unity, number, and operation. However, without giving up the idea of experience (the principle of phenomenology is to go to "things themselves" and the basis of these methods is eidetic intuition), it must be made flexible and must take into account the experience of essences and values; it must even recognize that essences alone permit us to classify and inspect the facts.

If we did not have implicit recourse to the essence of emotion, it would be impossible for us to distinguish the particular group of facts of emotivity among the mass of psychic facts. Since one has had implicit recourse to the essence of emotion as well, phenomenology will therefore prescribe that we have explicit recourse to it and, by concepts, that we set up the content of this essence once and for all. One understands well enough that the idea of man can no longer be an empirical concept, the product of historical generalizations, but that, on the contrary, we have to use, without mentioning it, the *"a priori"* essence of *human being* in order to give a somewhat solid basis to the generalizations of the psychologist. But besides, psychology, considered as a science of certain human facts, could not be a beginning because the psychic facts we meet are never the first ones. They are, in their essential structure, man's reactions against the world. Therefore, they assume man and the world and can only take on their true meaning if one has first elucidated these two notions. If we wish to found a psychology, we shall have to go beyond the psychic, beyond man's situation in the world, to the very source of man, the world, and the psychic: the transcendental and the constitutive consciousness which we attain by "phenomenological reduction" or "putting the world in parentheses."

It is this consciousness which must be interrogated, and what gives value to its responses is precisely that it is *mine.* Thus Husserl knows how to take advantage of this absolute proximity of consciousness in relation to itself from which the psychologist had not wished to profit. He takes advantage knowingly and with full security, since every consciousness exists to the exact extent to which it is conscious of existing. But there, as above, he refuses to interrogate consciousness about *facts;* on the transcendental level we should again find the confusion of psychology. What he is going to try to describe and fix by concepts is precisely the essences which preside as the transcendental field unrolls. Therefore, there will be, for example, a phenomenology of emotion which, after having "put the world in parentheses," will study emotion as a pure transcendental phenomenon—and will do so not by turning to particular emotions but by seeking to attain and elucidate the transcendental essence of emotion as an organized type of consciousness.

Heidegger, another phenomenologist, likewise took as his point of departure this absolute proximity of the investigator and the thing investigated. The thing which differentiates every inquiry about man from other types of rigorous questions is precisely the privileged fact that human reality is *ourselves*. "The existant which we must analyze," writes Heidegger, "is our self. The being of this existant is *mine*."[1] Now it is not a matter of indifference that this human reality is *I* precisely because, for human reality, to exist is always to *assume* its being, that is, to be responsible for it instead of receiving it from the outside like a stone. "And as 'human reality' is essentially its own possibility, this existant can 'choose' itself in its being; it can win itself and can lose itself."[2] This "assumption" of self which characterizes human reality implies an understanding of human reality itself, however obscure this understanding may be. "In the being of this existant, the latter relates itself to its being."[3] In effect, understanding is not a quality coming to human reality from the outside; it is its characteristic way of existing. Thus, the human reality which is *I* assumes its own being by understanding it. This understanding is mine. I am, therefore, first, a being who more or less obscurely understands his reality as man, which signifies that I make myself man in understanding myself as such. I may therefore interrogate myself and on the basis of this interrogation lead an analysis of the "human reality" to a successful conclusion which can be used as a foundation for an anthropology. Here, of course, it is no longer a question of introspection, first because introspection meets only the fact, then because my understanding of human reality is obscure and not authentic. It must be cleared up and explained.

In any case, the hermeneutic of existence will be able to

[1] *Sein und Zeit*, p. 41.
[2] *Ibid.*, p. 42.
[3] *Ibid.*, p. 43.

found an anthropology, and that anthropology will serve as a basis for any psychology. We are, therefore, in a situation which is the reverse of that of the psychologists, since we *start* from the synthetic totality that is man and establish the essence of man *before* making a start in psychology.

At any rate, phenomenology is the study of phenomena—not facts. And by phenomenon must be understood "that which manifests itself," that whose reality is precisely appearance. "And this 'self-manifestation' is not any sort of manifestation . . . the being of the existant is not something 'behind which' there is still something 'which does not appear.' "[4] In effect, for human reality, to *exist* is, according to Heidegger, to assume its own being in an existential mode of understanding; for consciousness, to *exist* is to *appear*, in Husserl's sense of the word. Since appearance is here the absolute, it is appearance which must be described and interrogated. From this point of view, Heidegger thinks that in every human attitude—for example in emotion, since we were speaking of it a little while ago—we shall find the whole of human reality, since emotion is the human reality which assumes itself and which, "aroused," "directs" itself toward the world. As for Husserl, he thinks that a phenomenological description of emotion will bring to light the essential structure of consciousness, since an emotion is precisely a consciousness. And conversely, a problem arises which the psychologist does not even suspect; can types of consciousness be conceived which would not include emotion among their possibilities, or must we see in it an indispensable structure of consciousness? Therefore, the phenomenologist will interrogate emotion *about consciousness* or *about man*. He will ask it not only what it is but what it has to teach us about a being, one of whose characteristics is exactly that he is capable of being moved. And inversely he will interrogate consciousness, human reality, about emotion: what must a consciousness be for emotion to be possible, perhaps even to be necessary?

We can understand, at the present time, the reasons for the psychologist's mistrust of phenomenology. The psycholo-

---

[4] *Sein und Zeit*, pp. 35–36.

gist's first precaution consists, in effect, of considering the psychic state in such a way that it removes from it all *significa-tion*. The psychic state is for him always a *fact* and, as such, always accidental. And this accidental character is just what the psychologist holds to most. If one should ask a scientist, "Why do bodies attract each other in accordance with New-ton's Law?" he will reply, "I know nothing about that; because it happens to be so." And if one should ask him, "What does this attraction *signify?*" he will reply, "It signifies nothing. It is." In like manner, the psychologist, when questioned about emotion, is quite proud of answering, "It is. Why? I know nothing about that. I simply state it. I know nothing about its signification." For the phenomenologist, on the contrary, every human fact is, in essence, significative. If you remove its signification, you remove its nature as human fact. The task of a phenomenologist, therefore, will be to study the signification of emotion. What are we to understand by that?

To signify is to indicate another thing; and to indicate it in such a way that in developing the signification one will find precisely the thing signified. For the psychologist emotion signifies nothing because he studies it as a fact, that is, by cutting it away from everything else. Therefore, it will be non-significative from its beginning; but if every human fact is really significative, the emotion studied by the psychologist is, by its nature, dead, non-psychic, inhuman. If, in the manner of the phenomenologist, we wish to make of emotion a true phenomenon of consciousness, it will, on the contrary, be nec-essary to consider it as significative from the first. That is, we shall affirm that it *is* strictly to the extent that it signifies. We shall not first lose ourselves in the study of physiological facts, precisely because, taken by themselves and in isolation, they signify *almost* nothing. They are—that's all. But on the con-trary, we shall try, by developing the signification of behavior and of the affected consciousness, to make explicit the thing which is signified. We know what the thing signified is from its origin: the emotion signifies, *in its own way*, the whole of consciousness or, if we put ourselves on the existential level, of human reality. It is not an accident because human reality is not an accumulation of facts. It expresses from a definite point of view the human synthetic totality in its entirety. And we need not understand by that that it is the *effect* of human reality. It is the human reality itself in the form of "emotion." That being so, it is impossible to consider emotion as a psycho-physiological disorder. It has its essence, its particular structures, its laws of appearing, and its signification. It cannot come to human reality *from the outside.* On the contrary, it is man who *assumes* his emotion, and consequently emotion is an organized form of human existence.

We have no intention of entering here upon a phenomenological study of emotion. Such a study, if one had to sum it up very briefly, would deal with affectivity as an existential mode of human reality. But our ambitions are more limited. We should like to see in a study of emotion as a precise and concrete case, if pure psychology can reasonably extract a method and some lessons from phenomenology. We agree that psychology does not put man into question or the world in parentheses. It takes man in the world as he presents himself through a multitude of situations, in the café, with his family, at war. Generally speaking, what interests it is *man in situations.* As such, it is, as we have seen, subordinate to phenomenology, since a really positive study of man in situations should first have elucidated the notions of man, world, being-in-the-world, and situation. But, after all, phenomenology has scarcely been born and all these notions are quite far from their definitive elucidation. Should psychology wait until phenomenology reaches maturity? We do not think so. But if it does not wait for the definitive establishment of an anthropology, it ought not lose sight of the fact that this anthropology is realizable, and that if one day it is realized, the psychological disciplines will have to have their source there. For the time being, it should not aim so much at gathering facts as at interrogating *phenomena,* that is, to put it exactly, psychic events, insofar as they are significations and not insofar as they are pure facts. For example, it will recognize that emotion *does not exist* as a corporeal phenomenon, since a body cannot be affected, for want of power to confer a meaning on its own manifestations. It will immediately seek something beyond vascular or respiratory disturbances, this something being the *feeling* of joy or sadness. But as this feeling is not exactly a quality imposed on joy or sadness from the outside, as it exists only to the extent to which it appears, that is, to which it is "assumed" by the human reality, it is consciousness itself which it will interrogate, since joy is joy only insofar as it appears as such.

And precisely because it seeks not facts but significations, it will abandon the methods of inductive introspection or external empirical observation to seek only to grasp and fix the essence of phenomena. It will, therefore, also proclaim itself an eidetic science. However, through the psychic phenomenon it will not aim at the *thing signified* as such, that is, the human totality. It does not have sufficient means at its disposal to attempt this study. What will interest it solely is the phenomenon *insofar as it is significative*. In the same way I can try to grasp the essence of the "proletariat" through the word "proletariat." In that case, I will be practising sociology. But the linguist studies the word proletariat *insofar as it signifies proletariat* and he will be uneasy about the vicissitudes of the word as a carrier of signification. Such a science is perfectly possible.

What does it lack to be real? To have shown proofs. We have shown that if human reality appears to the psychologist as a collection of miscellaneous data, it is because the psychologist has readily taken a point of view from which its reality had to appear to him as such. But that does not necessarily imply that human reality is anything other than a collection. What we have proved is only that it *can*not appear otherwise to the psychologist. It remains to know whether it can bear a phenomenological investigation at its roots, that is, whether emotion, for example, is truly a significative phenomenon. The following pages should be regarded as an *experiment* in phenomenological psychology. We shall try to place ourselves on the grounds of signification and to treat emotion as a *phenomenon*.

We have said in our introduction that the signification of a fact of consciousness comes down to this: that it always indicates the total human-reality which *becomes* moved, attentive, perceiving, willing, etc. The study of emotions has quite verified this principle: an emotion refers back to what it signifies. And, in effect, what it signifies is the totality of the relationships of the human reality to the world. The passage to emotion is a total modification of "being-in-the-world" according to the very particular laws of magic. But at once we see the limits of such a description; the psychological theory of emotion supposes a preliminary description of affectivity insofar as the latter constitutes the being of the human reality; that is, insofar as it is constitutive for *our* human-reality of being affective human-reality. In this case, instead of starting from a study of the emotion or the inclinations which might indicate a human reality not yet elucidated as the ultimate term of all research, an ideal term, moreover, and in all likelihood, beyond the reach of anyone who begins with the empirical, the description of affect would take place *on the basis* of the human reality described and fixed by an *a priori* intuition. The various disciplines of phenomenological psychology are *regressive*, and yet the term of their regression is *for them* a pure ideal. Those of pure phenomenology are, on the contrary, progressive. It will doubtless be asked why it is expedient in these conditions to use these two disciplines simultaneously. It seems that pure phenomenology would be sufficient. But if phenomenology can prove that emotion is in essence a realization of human-reality insofar as it is *affection*, it will be impossible for it to show that human-reality must necessarily manifest itself in *such* emotions. That there are such and such emotions, and only these, manifests without any doubt the *factitiousness* of human existence. It is this factitiousness which makes necessary a regular recourse to the empirical; it is this which, in all likelihood, will prevent psychological regression and phenomenological progression from ever coming together.

IV. THE INTERCONNECTIONS
OF PSYCHOLOGY AND PHENOMENOLOGY

Difficulties Involved in a
*Subordination of Psychology**

MAURICE MERLEAU-PONTY

To [the] conception of an eidetic psychology two kinds of objection can be made and, as a matter of fact, have been made. First, we may easily go astray, since this kind of psychology rests on a misunderstanding. The second objection goes much further. It was seen by Husserl himself, and led him to alter his ideas and to develop his doctrines beyond the stage of the *Ideas.*

The first objection maintains that an eidetic psychology would be merely a return to introspection and would therefore lead to all the difficulties from which psychology attempted to escape when it decided to become a science.

On this point no confusion is possible. For Husserl the discovery of the essence, or the meaning, of a process certainly involves a power of reflection, the ability to find the sense of what is lived through by oneself or by another. At the period of the *Ideas* he thought that reflective consciousness can arrive at an evidence concerning itself which is absolutely final and that in it what appears and what is are not distinct. In this sense Husserl held that consciousness, or *cogito,* is incomparable with external things. These external things appear in successive experiences through different perspectives, or *Abschattungen.* If consciousness were eternal to itself there would be no certitude nor science concerning it. In this sense, it is true to say that for Husserl, as for all the Cartesians, the existence

* From Maurice Merleau-Ponty, *The Primacy of Perception and Other Essays,* edited with an introduction by James M. Edie (Evanston, Ill.: Northwestern University Press, 1964), pp. 64–78. Reprinted by permission of the publishers. Copyright © 1964 by Northwestern University Press. © Editions Gallimard 1955.

of consciousness is inseparable from the consciousness of existing and that consequently the consciousness I need to know is
the subject that I am. It is also clear, finally, that Husserl
wishes to use this proximity of myself to myself, and more generally of man to man, in defining the *cogito* and reflection. In
order that knowledge may be possible, I must not be cut off
from myself and from the other.

But this does not mean that the internal relation of myself to
myself and to the other is already scientific knowledge and
that reflective psychology is introspective. This introspection
is supposed to consist in the presence of data internal to the
subject, which he observes and which are revealed to him by
the mere fact that they are "in him." This is an internal perception, the noting of an event with which I coincide. But
reflection is not at all the noting of a fact. It is, rather, an
attempt to understand. It is not the passive attitude of a subject
who watches himself live but rather the active effort of a subject who grasps the meaning of his experience. Husserl was so
far from making internal perception into a principle that he
granted a greater certitude, in certain respects, to external perception than to internal observation. *Reflection on the meaning or the essence of what we live through is neutral to the distinction between internal and external experience.*

It is rather a question of explaining what these phrases
mean. In particular, nothing prevents my phenomenological
reflection from having a bearing, for example, on another
person, since I perceive him and his modes of behavior. Nothing prevents the clarification of the intentions or meanings or
ways of acting from referring not only to my own conduct but
to that of another whom I witness. Nothing prevents me from
explaining the meaning of the lived experience of another person, in so far as I have access to it, by perception. According
to Husserl, "Pure internal psychology, the authentic psychology of intentionality, is, in the last analysis, a psychology of
pure intersubjectivity." This pure internal psychology is not
restricted to the subject in himself. It grasps just as well the
relations of different subjects to each other—i.e., intersubjectivity.

Internal observation is related to the empirical self. But

Husserlian reflection is related to a transcendental subject which is pre-personal, and neutral with respect to the distinction between the empirical self and the other. In fact, in the *Cartesian Meditations,* he uses the notion of conduct, *Gebaren,* to introduce his discussion of the perceiving of another. Behavioristic psychology, therefore, offers no difficulties for an eidetic method. Eidetic insight applies just as well to the experience of another, because my experience and his are interrelated in my dealings with him (by "intentional transgression," as the *Cartesian Meditations* say). In a very early article of 1910 Husserl also said that the intersubjective determination of individual psychisms is possible.

Of this first objection, then, let us retain only the notions which Husserl left unclarified, at the time of the *Ideas,* concerning the relation between radical reflection—founded on the fact that I am no stranger to myself (Heidegger would say that I am not hidden from myself)—and that other awareness of myself which is not immediate and is capable of error as well as truth. This leads us now to the second objection, which is more interesting, since it penetrates to the heart of the matter. It will lead us to complete what we have said up to this point, just as it led Husserl himself to deepen his thought. Is it not true that an eidetic psychology, reflectively determining the basic categories of psychic life by reflecting on my experience of myself and the other, reduces psychology, in the narrower sense, to a very restricted role? Is it not, then, limited to a mere study of details?

In his earlier works Husserl went so far as to say at certain points that the relation of psychology to philosophy is almost that of content to form. It is philosophy that knows what space is. It is from psychology, on the other hand, that I gain some information concerning the perception of space through certain visual and tactual contents of experience. If one clings to formulae of this kind, everything essential seems to be furnished by phenomenology, or philosophic insight. Nothing more is left to psychology than to study certain empirical curiosities within the frames that are furnished by phenomenology.

In other texts Husserl wrote as if psychology ought to con-

cern itself with causal relations, laws of fact through which
the phenomena actually belonging to the province of philosophy are manifested. Psychology studies a consciousness which
is introduced into the body and naturalized. It should concern
itself only with those conditions of existence, or of the temporal order, in which certain aspects of the phenomenon, or
essence, appear. But the description and comprehension of the
phenomenon itself fall to phenomenology. Since the order of
essences has its own certainties, these transcendental relations
can never be denied by the order of psychological genesis
which is concerned only with a special application. Is this
really all that Husserl thought about the question? After all,
the notion of *Wesensschau* was developed to found an activity
of consciousness which would be concrete as well as philosophical, both linked to my experience as well as capable of universality. Does the conception of noetic insight, such as Husserl
had developed it up to this point, correspond to these two
conditions?

This question was not resolved in a satisfactory manner at
the period of the *Ideas*, the work on which I have been so far
commenting. But in the later works we can see a further effort
to resolve it.

At the beginning of his career Husserl considered all questions concerning psychological genesis as secondary. They
could in no case prevail against the philosophical problems
concerning essence. But as his thought matured, he gave a
meaning to genesis which was very different and much more
positive—to such a degree, indeed, that in the *Cartesian Meditations* he speaks of a phenomenology of genesis.

If in Husserl's view the knowledge of facts is impossible
without some insight into essence and is always helped by this,
it follows that all sound knowledge of facts must include, at
least implicitly, some insight into essences, and that Husserl
must admit, as he does in effect, that those psychologists who
have been preoccupied with facts have nevertheless been able
to find out something concerning essences. The division of
labor between eidetic and empirical psychology turns out to be
extremely difficult, since as soon as one engages in even the
most experimental type of psychological research, in so far as

he says anything sound and true, some insight into essence is implied by his work.

Husserl himself pointed out an analogy between what has happened in physics and what has happened in psychology. The physicists who created physics, in the modern sense of the word, had an insight into what a physical thing is. Galileo, for example, of whom Husserl often spoke, was certainly not a phenomenologist. He was not even a philosopher in any strict sense of the word. Nevertheless when he decided to study falling bodies, a certain intuition of what a physical body is was implied in this experimental investigation. Spatial determination, for example, was regarded as altogether fundamental. And when, after Galileo, other physicists added to our knowledge of nature, one can say that each of them contributed to the development of *an eidetic of physical things*. Husserl was not interested in making the knowledge of essences an exclusive privilege of phenomenologists. These are implied in all experimental research, and they appear there whether one is looking for them or not and whether one wants them or not.

But more needs to be said. It is not only true that a knowledge of facts always implies a knowledge of essences, but in addition to the factual link between the two psychologies, we are going to see that there is a much closer connection. In order to make this more precise, let us turn for a moment to the nature of the *Wesensschau*. We must remember that for Husserl this has the nature of a finding (constatation). He often speaks of an "eidetic constatation." We must also remember that he never envisaged an *a priori*, in the sense of a deductive psychology. He says in the *Ideas* that there is no "mathematics of phenomena," no "geometry of the lived."[1] Why not? Because eidetic, or phenomenological, psychology, in distinction from mathematics, is a science which is essentially descriptive. The multiplicities with which geometry is concerned are "mathematical multiplicities," which can be exhaustively defined—that is, by a system of axioms. But in phenomenology there is no question of defining the objects of

[1] Edmund Husserl, *Ideen,* Vol. I, secs. 71 and 72.

psychology by any system of axioms which would enable us
to construct these different psychical realities.

This is because the essences we may discover, when we
force ourselves to think about lived experience, are not, in
Husserl's terms, "exact essences" capable of an univocal determination. They are, rather, "morphological essences,"
which are inexact by nature. Husserl says in the *Ideas* that if
one were to dream of a phenomenological psychology which
would be deductive, he would fall into the same sort of difficulty as a geometer who, for example, might dream of giving
a rigorous geometrical definition of terms such as "jagged,"
"notched like a lentil," or "like a sunshade."[2]

There is no geometric definition of these forms, and it is
equally impossible to give any constructive definition of the
different realities with which psychology is concerned. It is
through experience alone that they can be known, and not
otherwise. From the very beginning, therefore, it has been
necessary to maintain a close relation between eidetic intuition
and that which we do, in fact, experience.

Husserl often says that to see an essence one must begin by
having a perception, which serves as the base, or point of departure, for a *Wesensschau* but not as the source of its validity. The relation between perception and *Wesensschau* is one
of founding [*Fundierung*]; perception, that is, serves as the
ground, or pedestal, on which an insight into essence is formed.
Thus insight into essence is an intellectual taking over, a making explicit and clarifying of something concretely experienced, and a recognition that it comes after something else,
from which it starts, is essential to its nature. It also knows
itself to be retrospective. The idea that it succeeds a more
direct contact with the thing itself is enclosed within its very
meaning.

One sees already in Husserl the idea of a double envelopment. It is true that reflective thought, which determines the
meaning or essence, ends by possessing its object and envelop-
ing it. But it is also true that essential insight always understands the concrete perception of experience as something here

[2] *Ibid.*, sec. 74.

and now which precedes and therefore envelops it. In Husserl's words, the essence presupposes "an important part of intuition" bearing on the individual. It presupposes that an individual has appeared and that one has had a view of it. It also presupposes the *Sichtlichkeit*, the visibility of this individual. Or, to put it in another way, it is no insight into an essence if one's reflection cannot turn to a corresponding individual, if one cannot work out "a sense of examples" to illustrate his insight.

What, then, exactly is the relation between this sense of examples and what is called induction? It is in working out an answer to this question that we may be able to understand the relation between phenomenological and empirical, or inductive, psychology.

We must here recall the profound remarks of Husserl on induction in general. These were basically opposed to the theory of induction which held sway at the end of the nineteenth century, essentially that of Mill. According to this theory induction is a process by which, in considering a group of facts, we discover a common character and set it apart by abstraction, regarding it as essential to the group of facts from which we started. Or again, induction is an operation which enables us to find the cause of a phenomenon among its various antecedents, by discarding those which are neither constant nor unconditioned. According to Husserl, induction is not, and never has been, this. His remarks here anticipate those of Brunschwicg in his *l'Expérience humaine et la causalité physique*.

Let us return to the example of Galileo and the fundamental induction which, we may say, created modern physics. How does Galileo proceed? Does he consider different examples of falling bodies and then, by a method of agreement, following the theory of John Stuart Mill, abstract what is common to these examples? As a matter of fact, he proceeds in a totally different manner. The conception of the fall of bodies which guides his experiment is not found in the facts. He forms it actively; he constructs it. He freely conceives the pure case of a freely falling body, of which there is no given example in our human experience. Then, having constructed this idea, he verifies it by showing how the confused empirical facts, which never represent the free fall in its pure state, can then be understood through the introduction of additional conditions (friction, resistance, etc. . . . .), which explain the difference between the facts and the pure concept. On the basis of the free fall, therefore, one constructs the fall of a body on an inclined plane.

Husserl says in the first volume of the *Logical Investigations* that the physicists proceed by *"idealisierende Fiktionen cum fundamento in re"*—that is, by idealizing fictions which are nevertheless founded on the facts. Let it be, he says, the law of Newton. Basically it makes no assertion about the existence of gravitating masses. It is another one of those idealizing fictions by which one purely conceives of what a gravitating mass would be. Then one determines what properties it would have, on the supposition that it exists. According to Husserl, Newton's law says nothing at all about existence. It refers only to what would belong to a gravitating mass as such.[3]

The method actually used by physicists, therefore, is not the chimerical induction of Mill, which is never practiced in the sciences. It is rather *a reading of the essence*. Through certain impure and imperfect phenomena, such as the fall of a body on an inclined plane, I read off the free fall of the body, which is theoretically conceived, or forged, by the intellect. That which gives its probable value to the induction and which finally shows that it is truly founded on things is not the number of facts invoked to justify it. No! It is rather the intrinsic clarity which these ideas shed on the phenomena we seek to understand. Just as Brunschwicg will show, in his *l'Expérience humaine et la causalité physique*, that one experiment will suffice to establish a law—that Davy, for example, established the existence of potassium by only one experiment of electrolysis—so Husserl maintained that induction is not founded on the collection of a vast number of cases. It is, rather, a process of intellectual analysis whose verification consists in the total, or at least sufficient, clarity which the group of concepts worked out in this way bring to the given phenomena. Thus laws are

[3] "Prolegomena zur reinen Logik," *Logische Untersuchungen,* I, p. 150.

not basically live realities which would have a *force* and could rule over the facts. One should say, rather, in the language of Malebranche, that they are a light and not a force.

Let us now compare induction, understood in this way, with the phenomenological *Wesensschau*. This intuition of essences, like induction, as we have seen, is based on facts. The difference is that *Wesensschau* is based on the *imaginary "free variation" of certain facts.* In order to grasp an essence, we consider a concrete experience, and then we make it change in our thought, trying to imagine it as effectively modified in all respects. *That which remains invariable* through these changes is the essence of the phenomena in question.

For example, if we are seeking to form an idea of, or to understand the essence of, a spatial figure, such as this lamp, we must first perceive it. Then we will imagine all the aspects contained in this figure as changed. That which cannot be varied without the object itself disappearing is the essence. Suppose that we wish to form the idea of melody. We recall a tune which we have learned to sing, and suppose that all the notes and all the relations between the notes are changed. That which remains invariable and without which there would be no more melody is the essence we are seeking. In the same way, if we are trying to conceive the essence of a "social process," we will represent to ourselves a social process in which we have participated or concerning which we have some historical understanding. That which does not vary through all conceivable variations will be the essence. Even when one thinks in terms of the pure essence, one always thinks of the visible—the fact. But in the case of *Wesensschau,* the individual fact is neither grasped nor assumed as a reality, which is shown by the fact that we subject it to an imaginary variation.

We are thus led to the following conclusion: If eidetic psychology is a reading of the invariable structure of our experience based on examples, the empirical psychology which uses induction is also a reading of the essential structure of a multiplicity of cases. But the cases here are real and not imaginary. After closer examination, the only difference which we find between inductive procedure—so far as it is justifiable and moves toward what is truly essential—and the procedure of eidetic psychology is that the latter applies imaginary variation to its examples, while the former refers to effective variations in considering the different cases that are *actually realized.*

If we reflect further, we may see that the relation between the two is even closer. For when you make an induction on the basis of facts which are very large in number, you do not examine every possible, individual case. For example, when you establish the law of a physical phenomenon, you are not going to verify the law by every possible value of each variable. You will limit yourself to a finite number of experiments, and you will then single out one relation that you consider to be always true, even for the intermediate values between those that you have verified. This is called "interpolating," and it requires the use of that free variation of which Husserl spoke—at least in the intervals between the values effectively verified. In a certain number of decisive experiments you perceive certain relations, and you imagine the rest in function of these relations which are actually perceived in a finite number of cases. You link together the different examples effectively perceived by an imaginary variation which will lead from one to the other.

Let us now turn to an example from psychology, not physics: the important and interesting notion, now widely used, of behavioral lability or instability. How does one arrive at a notion of this sort? One says that a type of behavior is labile either when it is reproduced without any change under very different conditions—that is, when it is not flexible—or when it changes or disappears in a way that is wholly unpredictable. One calls an attitude labile both when it is too rigid and when it is not rigid enough. In using this notion, one therefore identifies the two extreme cases—excessive fixity on the one hand and too frequent change on the other. How is this possible? How does one arrive inductively at such a psychological notion? It is certainly not by any comparison of the given characters of psychological facts. One could compare the relevant psychological facts as much as one wishes without finding anything held in common. What is there in common between a stereotyped mode of conduct and one that is ever ready to disappear? Nothing, certainly, that is given with the facts. The notion of lability is constructed.

Goldstein introduced it with reference to what he called centered or non-centered behavior. The common element in extremely automatic behavior, on the one hand, and ephemeral behavior, on the other, is that neither of them is centered in the whole conduct of the individual. The lack of centering is the meaning held in common by modes of behavior which are absolutely episodic and others which are invariable and monotonous. In both of them we see that the connection between the situation and the response is wholly external, so that the situation does not guide the response. The construction of a concept of this kind is very close to Husserl's *Wesensschau*. This is doubtless why he says so often that everyone performs the *Wesensschau*. "The intuition of essences does not involve any more difficulties or 'mystical' secrets than perception."[4]

This *Wesensschau* is not the exclusive possession of the phenomenologists. As a matter of fact, Husserl says in the *Ideas*[5] that "everyone is constantly seeing ideas or essences and that everyone uses them in the operations of thought, in spite of the widespread opposition put forth in the name of points of view in the theory of knowledge." The empiricist theory of induction is one of these points of view (in the pejorative sense of this phrase), a vague opinion without rigor, which prevents us from seeing ourselves when we practice the *Wesensschau*, especially in making inductions.

In presenting the matter as I have, I am pushing Husserl further than he wished to go himself. He never expressly recognized the fundamental homogeneity of these two modes of knowledge, the inductive and the essential. He never admitted that in the last analysis they were indiscernible and simply differed in degree. Nevertheless his notion of an experienced essence, or an eidetic experience, contains in germ the consequence that I have just drawn from it. But it is a question here not so much of a consequence as of an inevitable dialectic of the concept of essence. It follows on prin-

---

4 "Die Philosophie als strenge Wissenschaft," *Logos* I (1910), pp. 289 ff.

5 *Op. cit.*, sec. 23.

ciple from Husserl's point of departure and from what he proposed to do—namely, to show that this knowledge of essences is altogether experiential, that it does not involve any kind of supersensible faculty, and that in the last analysis the essence is just as contingent as the fact. It also follows inversely, from Husserl's point of departure and from the problem we have formulated in the preceding lectures, that any knowledge of fact always involves an *a priori* understanding of essence.

Instead of clearly recognizing the homogeneity of the two modes of knowledge, Husserl was content to insist, as he did very often, on the parallelism between psychology and phenomenology. "As a matter of principle," he said, psychology in its whole development is parallel to phenomenology. Of course, one might just as well say that phenomenology is always parallel to psychology and that every significant proposition of empirical psychology anticipates a phenomenological truth. As a matter of fact, Husserl did say that "every empirical discovery as well as every eidetic discovery made on the one side must correspond to a parallel discovery on the other."[6] This means that for every assertion of experimental psychology a corresponding eidetic assertion can be found.

We are here very far from the idea of an eidetic psychology which by reflection alone would give us the principles of any possible psychological process and which would pass from the particular case of a real mental activity to that of other men as well. We are far from the idea of a philosophical psychology which would determine not the real but the whole range of the possibly human. It is human reality which now emerges as *the locus of the Wesensschau.* It is in becoming conscious of myself as I am that I am able to see essences, and in this context the real and the possible are not distinct.

Husserl even comes to say that "intentional psychology already carries the transcendent within itself."[7] This really means that there cannot be any basic discord between the point of view of psychology and that of phenomenology. It is always the same subject, man, that is being approached in one way or the other. Our image of man may be acquired

[6] *Nachwort zu meinen Ideen.*
[7] Edmund Husserl, *Cart. Med.,* p. 174 (trans. p. 147).

with all the presuppositions of an empirical psychology, which takes him as situated within the chains of worldly causality. But this empirical psychology, if it really pays attention to what it is describing, will always end by making room for a different perspective which sees man not as a mere part of the world but as the bearer of reflection. Thus the interpenetration of psychology and phenomenology—their reciprocal envelopment—is clearly indicated in these texts as well as in those I have previously cited.

Certain formulae of Sartre, therefore, in the last chapter of his small book on *Imagination,* where he tries to define the thought of Husserl, definitely stand in need of correction. Sartre writes here as if phenomenological, or eidetic, psychology ought to come *first* and ought to rule over all the fundamental questions. Then after we have learned something about all possible psychic processes in general, experience may show us the actual facts. But in the basic intention of Husserl, the relation of these two approaches is not merely one of simple succession, as if one could see essences without any factual experience or could come to the facts without implying, in his very approach, a certain vision of essence. Sartre writes: "After one has determined the various conditions that a psychic state must necessarily possess if it is to be an image, then only may we pass from the certain to the probable, and ask of experience what it can teach us about the images which are actually present in a contemporary human consciousness." What is perhaps the most important aspect of Husserl's whole project is lacking in this statement.

As a matter of fact, Sartre himself does not follow the rule that he here lays down. Although he presents empirical psychology as the servant of phenomenology, he says, nevertheless, that he embarks on the study of emotion "without waiting for the phenomenology of emotion to be completed."[8] This means that basically experimental studies, like those of Janet, Lewin, and the psychoanalysts, must already reveal to us, at least in a confused way, the essence of that

[8] *Esquisse d'une théorie des émotions* (Paris, 1939) (trans. pp. 18–19).

with which they are concerned. However it may be with his formulations, Sartre actually understands the relation between psychology and phenomenology in the way which I have just now tried to explain.

When he departs from this, he is led to artificial distinctions. For example, his book, *L'Imaginaire,* follows this simple plan: Part I, "The Certain"; Part II, "The Probable." In the first part he gives a phenomenological analysis of the essence of the image. In the second, he turns to the data of experience with the understanding that what has been acquired in the first part is unshakable and certain, while what is now coming is only probable. But when one reads the work carefully, one finds that certain results of the first part are actually called in question in the second. At the beginning of his book, for example, Sartre shows that the image is defined by its deception and by the fact that it is unobservable and empty. When I try to imagine the Pantheon, I believe that I see it. But if I try to count the pillars, I find that I cannot do so, which means that basically I do not see anything at all. The initial phenomenological analysis determines the essence of the image as a false presence, as a nothing which tries to present itself as a something.

But in the second part of the book this fundamental definition of the image is placed in question when the author analyzes certain states where a clear distinction between the perceived and the imaginary cannot be made. If the image were nothing but what was first said—empty and absent—we would never confuse it with a perception, and illusions would be hard to understand. Thus in so far as Sartre raises the question of illusions in the second part, he necessarily suggests the possibility of a situation anterior to the clear distinction between perception and imagination which was made at the start. He does this, and with good reason. But this means that it is impossible to understand the image by an examination of the pure possibility of an image in general and by a definition which we would then merely apply to the analogous empirical examples.

These remarks have a certain importance because they will enable us to reply to a certain objection often made against phenomenologists—namely, that they represent a new type of scholasticism. This means that phenomenological research remains purely verbal. In this view, eidetic intuition would consist in reflecting on the meaning of certain words in use, like the word "image" or the word "emotion," and then in developing this meaning with the firm conviction of reaching the things themselves. This complaint is not well founded if one refers to what Husserl actually intended. But there are certain formulae of Max Scheler which merit this reproach. For example, Scheler says that the intuition of essences is absolutely indubitable for a rather simple reason: because, by definition, experience can never contradict such an intuition. If experience should show me an image which does not correspond to what I have determined to be the essence, then of course, by definition, this is not an image. In the same way I may lay down a certain idea of social process. Then if I find a so-called social process in everyday history or in the past, which does not possess the essential characteristics I have focused, I have the right to say that it is not a social process. Here we are certainly close to scholasticism. If one had followed this principle in practice, the whole of phenomenology would be an instrument for developing the definitions of words.

But Husserl never thought in this way, and he was fully aware of the danger. Since his early article on "Philosophie als strenge Wissenschaft,"[9] he maintained that there was nothing in common between intuition, as he understood it, and a scholastic process which "pretends to draw a real knowledge of things from the analytic judgment that one can make on the meanings of words." Husserl was, therefore, well aware of the danger of self-deception in proceeding by "eidetic intuition." It is possible for me to believe that I am seeing an essence when, in fact, it is not an essence at all but merely a concept rooted in language, a prejudice whose apparent coherence reduces merely to the fact that I have become used to it through habit. The best way of guarding against this danger would be to admit that, though a knowledge of facts is never sufficient for grasping an essence and though the con-

[9] *Op. cit.*, p. 305.

struction of "idealizing fictions" is always necessary, I can never be sure that my vision of an essence is anything more than a prejudice rooted in language—if it does not enable me to hold together all the facts which are known and which may be brought into relation with it. Failing this, it may not be an essence at all but only a prejudice. I believe that the logic of things ought to have led Husserl to admit a very close relation between induction, as he understood it, and *Wesensschau* and consequently a final homogeneity among the different psychologies, whether they be inductive or phenomenological. I have already said that Husserl never explicitly stated this. But at least he was well aware of the necessity of defending phenomenology against verbalism. Also, after he renounced the dogmatic solution of an "apodictic evidence" which would enable us from the very start to transcend language, he was obliged, as we shall see, to reconsider the imaginary "variation" of anthropological experience as the way toward eidetic intuition.

Husserl consistently rejected the different psychologies which developed in his time, including Gestalt psychology, which had been created by writers familiar with his teaching and influenced by him. In his *Nachwort zu meinen Ideen,* Husserl declared that it makes no difference in principle whether one conceives of consciousness as a totality or as a sum of psychic atoms, since even this totality of the Gestaltists is just another thing and therefore not a consciousness.

In his *Principles of Gestalt Psychology,* Koffka replied to this criticism in an interesting way. "A theory like mine," he said, "seems to imply an extreme psychologism, the idea that all logical relations and subsistents can be explained by existing relations in the domain of psychology or physiology." Gestalt theory admits that all structures of consciousness finally depend on physiological processes of the same form ("isomorphic") as their causal foundation. This would seem to imply a position of extreme psychologism, since the whole order of meanings would seem to rest on the order of natural events. But Koffka is saying here that in a psychology like his there is a new way of describing consciousness which avoids the opposed difficulties of both psychologism and logicism. The description of "psychic process" in terms of structure should give basic satisfaction to philosophy in vindicating the order of meanings.

Koffka developed this idea in the following words: "This conception [of psychologism], which had gained ground at the end of the last century, was violently attacked by some of our best philosophers, and in particular by Edmund Husserl, who claimed to have refuted it once and for all. But Husserl's argument rests on the explicit or implicit assumption that every psychological theory reduces psychological relations to external relations of pure fact. Husserl, and also other philosophers, have certainly refuted a psychologism of this kind. But this refutation does not affect our psychologism, if, indeed, this term truly applies to our conception, for according to it, psychological and physiological processes, or rather, psycho-physical processes, are organized by relations that are wholly intrinsic. This means that according to our view, psychology and logic, existence and subsistence, and in certain respects even reality and truth, do not belong to two domains or two universes of discourse so basically different that no intelligible relation can exist between them. Here lies the opportunity for psychology to play the integrating role which we have assigned to it at the beginning of our work."[10]

These remarks of Koffka go very far. Husserl's constant objection to Gestalt theory, as to all psychology, is that it fails to understand the radical and absolute originality of consciousness, which it reduces either to psychological atoms, as the older psychologists did, or to "total" structures which are nevertheless dependent on the natural order of events. But following certain suggestions of Husserl which we have cited above, we may give the following reply: If the notion of Gestalt helps us to understand many facts and is fruitful in the empirical order, it must have some phenomenological truth and must have something to contribute to phenomenology. We do not have to take over the physiological hypotheses of the Gestaltists, their cerebral explanations of conscious structures. We should directly consider what they say of con-

[10] Koffka, *Principles of Gestalt Psychology* (London, 1935), pp. 570–71.

sciousness and of the patterns of conduct. We may then see that they are calling our attention at this level, not to events that are completely external to each other, but to an internal organization which makes the notions of value and meaning come to life. This is enough to show that the Gestalt theory is not merely a new variety of psychologism. It is rather a way of showing that conscious phenomena are both temporal (for they happen in time and occur at a definite moment) and yet at the same time internally significant, so that they can support a certain kind of knowledge and truth.

In other words, I believe that to give weight to his eidetic intuition and to distinguish it sharply from verbal concepts, Husserl was really seeking, largely unknown to himself, a notion like that of the Gestaltists—the notion of an order of meaning which does not result from the application of spiritual activity to an external matter. It is, rather, a spontaneous organization beyond the distinction between activity and passivity, of which the visible patterns of experience are the symbol. In Gestalt psychology everything bears a meaning. There is no psychic phenomenon which is not oriented toward a certain significance. It is really a psychology founded on the idea of intentionality. But this sense, which inhabits all psychic phenomena, is not produced by a pure activity of the spirit. It is, rather, an earthy and aboriginal sense, which constitutes itself by an organization of the so-called elements.

This, perhaps, might have been the occasion for Husserl to recognize a certain truth in the "integrating psychology" of Koffka. By entering into the region of facts and clarifying some of them, it has at the same time glimpsed certain essential, philosophical truths without knowing or willing this— just as Galileo, who had no intention of working out an eidetic of the *res extensa*, actually did, in his experimental work, lay the foundations for this eidetic.

V. PHENOMENOLOGY
AND THE HUMAN SCIENCES*

STEPHAN STRASSER

*On the Boundary of Philosophical Anthropology
and Empirical Human Science*

PHENOMENOLOGY'S CONTRIBUTION TO EMPIRICAL HUMAN
SCIENCE. The preceding considerations suggest in what way
the phenomenological philosopher can contribute to empirical
human science. The phenomenologist starts with the idea that
human experience contains a meaningful structure. He tries
to disclose and describe this structure in the wealth and manifold forms of man's experiences. For this purpose he disposes
of an analytic-explicitating method, which differs essentially
from scientific induction. In dialectics he possesses a means to
show the universal validity and necessity proper to his descriptions of essences. By laying bare a fundamental structure of
human experience, he provides the framework for empirical
research. He contributes to its comprehensibility. The phenomenological philosopher is able to say, albeit only in general terms, to which dimension of intelligibility the phenomena
belong. For this reason he can be a suitable partner in the
dialog with those who pursue empirical human science, such
as, historians in general and the historians of culture and of
religion in particular, anthropologists, sociologists, psychologists and psychiatrists. It is not *in spite of*, but precisely *because of* his independence as a thinker that he is able to play
a complementary, orientating and interpretative role.

The principle which he follows in this has a negative as
well as a positive aspect. The negative aspect may be formulated in this way. The phenomenological philosopher will not

* From Stephan Strasser, *Phenomenology and the Human Sciences* (Pittsburgh: Duquesne University Press, 1963), pp. 277–
94, 303–13. Reprinted by permission of the publishers.

attempt to explain man and the world on the basis of the
results obtained by scientific induction, for all scientific theories
implicitly presuppose man and his world. On the positive side,
the phenomenological philosopher will endeavor *philosophically to interpret all human forms of existence, including that
of pursuing science, on the basis of man's being-in-the-world.*
In this respect his attitude differs considerably from that of the
representatives of most other philosophical trends.

CONTRIBUTION OF EMPIRICAL HUMAN SCIENCE TO PHE-
NOMENOLOGY. These remarks are far from exhausting the
question of the relationship between phenomenology and empirical human science. As we have pointed out, because of his
phenomenological methods, the phenomenologist is able to
provide a framework for the empirical student of man who
wants to know what it is that his facts point to. However,
when we study the works of prominent phenomenologists,
they do not at all impress us as describing merely frame-
works. On the contrary, they discuss living groups and types
as well as theoretical, ethical and artistic realities produced
by human beings in certain situations. If the phenomenologist
were really to limit himself to uncover primarily evident structures of experience, he would produce an extremely abstract
philosophy which could hardly aspire to the title "philosophical anthropology."

As a matter of fact, none of the great phenomenologists
can be reproached for limiting himself to such structures. This
statement is obviously true with respect to Scheler, Merleau-
Ponty, Buytendijk, Plessner or Ricoeur. Let us consider however, the case of the relatively abstract thinker Husserl. In
his well-known Vienna lecture, *Die Krisis des europäischen
Menschentums und die Philosophie,*[1] Husserl compares *inter
alia* the spiritual ethos of Europe with that of India. One may
ask how this is possible if phenomenology is *nothing else*
than the discovery of the fundamental structures of intentionality. How does the philosopher Husserl even know about
the existence of such a thing as an old Indian culture? By

[1] *Die Krisis der europäischen Wissenschaften* . . . pp. 314 ff.,
see p. 320.

what right does he, the rigorously methodical philosopher, introduce such a notion in his philosophical discourse? Yet, on the other hand, it is obvious that these and other historical considerations give character and liveliness to Husserl's lecture.

One thing at least is certain—Husserl borrows the concept "old Indian culture" from the science of history, and he does so without the slightest hesitation. Without giving it a second thought, he makes use of established empirical data. Since Husserl is known for his conscientiousness, bordering on scrupulosity in methodological issues, there must be good reason for his seeming carelessness. This reason is not hard to find. Husserl gratefully uses the results of empirical research after he has scrutinized the essence of experience in a philosophical way. For Husserl, the historical data are not "ultimate data," as Sartre could polemically remark,[2] but noemata of certain noetic achievements which he has analyzed elsewhere. They are not a starting point for him, not a basis or a presupposition, but serve only to differentiate, enrich and clarify his argument.

This point is not without importance even in the philosophical perspective. The primarily evident insight into the structures of experience would remain fruitless for the philosopher if he were not able to apply it to the data of history, sociology or anthropology, even though these data themselves are not primarily evident.

The objection can be made, of course, that such a procedure is dangerous. It may happen that the empirical datum, to which the philosopher applies his principles, may be shown to be incomplete and uncertain as a consequence of subsequent research. Yet we should not be too seriously concerned about this objection. The implied risk has been taken by all great thinkers from Aristotle to Bergson. The fact that we know how incomplete Aristotle's psychological insights were and how defective Bergson's biological insights does not diminish our esteem for their philosophical achievements. The philosopher is undoubtedly justified in applying his principles

---

[2] Stephan Strasser, *Phenomenology and the Human Sciences*, p. 35. Hereafter referred to by Cf. only.

to the results of empirical research which he in his time could and had to consider firmly established.

Accordingly, the insight into the primarily evident structures of experience is a *starting point* for the phenomenological philosopher. Nevertheless, it is obvious that, when he takes part in a dialog with other searchers for truth, he will have to address himself to those who pursue empirical science. It would be misjudging the laws of dialectics to think that the philosopher is immune to the consequences of this dialog. It is impossible for him not to go beyond his starting point. And it is only then that it will appear whether or not his fundamental insights are fruitful; only then his principles will be tested for their usefulness; only then a philosophical anthropology can be born in which living human beings and groups of men recognize themselves as in a mirror.

What conclusion must be drawn from all this? A first conclusion presents itself in a very simple way. The philosopher cannot make use of the results obtained by the empirical sciences and at the same time ridicule scientific experience. Sartre, for example, who in his study of Baudelaire appeals to the objective data of the history of literature, has no right to declare war on "objective thought."[3] On the contrary, he should candidly admit that he makes generous use of the data supplied by the "second objectivity."

AN OBJECTION FROM THE VIEWPOINT OF EXISTENTIAL PHILOSOPHY. The same argument could easily be brought to bear against other antiscientistic writers. Like all other such arguments, however, this "appeal to the speaker" lacks the required philosophical scope. It does not clarify anything philosophically. For this reason it seems necessary to us to examine the further consequences of our view, especially because this view is exposed to fundamental criticism. Radical philosophers of existence will not fail to raise the following objection.

The fact as fact is not open to insight. It does not tell us anything about the existential orientation of a person or group. Man's exercise of freedom lies concealed *behind* the

[3] Cf. pp. 47 f.

fact but, as we ourselves have admitted, does not reveal itself *in* the fact.[4] It follows, therefore, that we would have to admit that man cannot be described in the language of facts, for man is not a thing, not an object.[5] With respect to man, the empirical scientist cannot predicate anything, for man has already transcended all "data" while they are being established. This is connected with his free existence. Freedom is essentially transcendence of everything factual, observable. Consequently, a philosopher who appeals to the data of empirical human science implicitly denies human freedom.

Moreover, the objector continues, this statement applies not only to man himself but also to everything human, to the deeds, the surrounding world, the situation of man. The situation also is nothing without man's free intention. Let us think, for example, of the typical situation arising from the fact that I encounter an obstacle. A huge rock lies across my path. Considered in itself, the rock is what it is. It receives the meaning of "obstacle" only from my intention to pass along this path. Only in this way does the situation arise which we call "path blocked by an obstacle."

The surrounding world likewise is a realization arising from man's free praxis. Despite Hyppolite Taine's stubborn defense, it is not true that every surrounding world is the product of a concurrence of conditions.[6] A totally different culture could have arisen on French soil if the intentions of its inhabitants had been orientated differently. The empirical scientist also either implicitly or explicitly presupposes in his descriptions that determining factors are at work, which he calls, e.g., "milieu," "race," "historic moment," "social structure," or "neurosis-creating situation." He makes use at least of a deterministic working hypothesis. He considers man, at least provisionally, as the result of endocrine secretions, drive mecha-

---

[4] Cf. p. 8.

[5] "Anthropology studies only objects," says Sartre in his recent work, *Critique de la raison dialectique*, Part I, Paris, 1960, p. 107. What he means by "anthropology" is exactly the same as what we call "empirical human science."

[6] Taine, *Les origines de la France contemporaine*, 25–27th impr., 12 vols., Paris, 1906–1909.

nism or economic processes. This implicit determinism cannot be reconciled with a philosophy that recognizes the freedom of human existence. Consequently, the philosopher, and especially the phenomenological philosopher, will in principle have to remain aloof from any form of empirical human science. Such is the objection raised by certain existentialistic philosophers.

THE FINITE ASPECT OF MAN'S EXERCISE OF FREEDOM. This objection makes us return to the problematics raised by "surrounding world" and "situation." A few critical remarks concerning this matter have already been made,[7] but they led to results that were mainly negative. We pointed out that for a creative freedom there is no situation, and that human freedom is not creative. Human freedom is finite, and this finiteness manifests itself negatively in its lack of absolute creativity and positively in its dependence on others. Consequently, it is just as incorrect to claim that man creates the situation as it is to assert that he is determined by the situation. To admit that he is determined would indeed amount to a denial of human freedom.

This critique may now be supplemented in a constructive fashion. We know now that the dependence implied in the dynamic unfolding of human existence assumes a dialectic form. It may be compared with a dialog in which the questioner and the questioned constantly appear to each other in a different light. This comparison applies equally to man's theorizing and his praxis. Thus it is an obvious procedure *to apply the dialectic principle to man's relationship with his situation*. A concrete analysis may serve to clarify the point.

In 1084 Saint Bruno went to establish himself as a hermit in a savage region of the French Alps. The term "environment" seems eminently suitable to indicate this inhospitable massif, which can be described only in terms borrowed from physical geography.[8] By the very fact, however, that Saint

[7] Cf. pp. 42–55.

[8] As we have seen, Sartre makes a distinction between the "environment" (*milieu*), which is what it is, and "situation," which is meaningful because of a human intention. Cf. p. 43.

Bruno seeks a place where he and his companions can devote themselves undisturbed to their pious meditations, the environment ceases to be environment. The saint asks the mountains and valleys a question: "Where can I establish myself as a hermit?" The mountains and valleys reply, albeit wordlessly. They reply by what they are. Thus there begins a dialectics, in which the things are involved negatively and positively. They are opposed to, or in favor of a certain human intention. They are "useful," "safe," "harmful," "unsuitable," "dangerous." Precisely because things arrange themselves, as it were, around an intention, a situation is born.

What, then, is the meaning of "environment"? It means that man addresses his question to *something*, that he speaks with *someone*, or negatively, that he does not call the situation into being from nothing. Thus the concept "environment" indicates a boundary of human freedom, it tells us that this freedom has to depend on other beings, which it is able to produce, elevate and ennoble but cannot create in the absolute sense. From this it follows also that what is called the "environment" cannot be wholly meaningless.

However, there is more. Let us revert to the year 1084 in the French Alps and assume that Saint Bruno has found a place where he and his companions can establish themselves. Their first question has now been answered. The landscape of the Chartreuse massif has become again "environment," i.e., surrounding reality without explicit meaning. But it does not remain such very long. The first reply has affected the questioner. From a man looking for a place where he can establish himself he has now become one looking for building materials. From the first reply there arises the second question: "Where do we find the materials for our cabins?" Thus the "environment" that had become situation Number One changes into situation Number Two. The Chartreuse landscape is no longer the same landscape, it is no longer a peaceful valley, suitable for hermits, but a landscape rich or poor in wood, it contains "useless" and "useful" wood, construction lumber or firewood.

In this way we could reconstruct the dialectic course of history from the year 1084 to the present time, in which an important intention of Saint Bruno's followers is to get rid of troublesome tourists. This intention, of course, gives rise to an entirely new situation. However, it is not necessary to reconstruct history in this way, for every part of it would merely reconfirm our above-expressed conviction. The possibility to "proceed in freedom from projected meaning to projected meaning" (Buytendijk) is not based on an absolute creative power but on a productive dialectics, which is typical of a finite existence.

The epistemological question to be raised in this connection is, *How can such a concrete dialectics be described?* A pointer to the reply may be found in our own analyses. Typical phases and stages have to be discovered in the dialectic communication of man with things and persons. In addition, for every phase one has to indicate the realities on which man or the group of men depend. In other words, the participants in his dialog have to be discovered, identified and characterized. They are the persons, things, conditions and relations which are indispensable for the actual pursuit of man's freedom. Thus, *the boundaries of his freedom have to be indicated,* and this task may very well be done by means of empirical science.

Such a groping search for and outlining of the limits pertaining to the concrete exercise of freedom does not mean a denial, not even an implicit denial, of freedom. Freedom is always presupposed, even though it cannot be described as freedom in the language of empirical science. Yet something is nonetheless said about this finite freedom—namely, what it is *not.* Thus the empirical scientist resembles the artist who makes a woodcut. Apparently he does nothing else than cut away parts of the wood. But it is precisely because of his cutting that something becomes visible on the wood—namely, a figure. The figure is that part of the surface which the artist's chisel does not touch. In an analogous way we may say that human freedom is that about which the empirical student of man says nothing but which he has always in mind and which he can concretely delineate by determining its boundary.

The remarks made here with respect to the situation apply also to the bodily and psychical "I" of man. Or more correctly expressed, the dialog with the situation contains also always a dialog with man's own bodily-psychical "I." A child, for instance, who learns to write asks certain questions of the pencil and paper, but in doing so, also questions his own motor mechanism ("How should I hold the pencil?") and memory ("How was that again?"). When the process of learning has reached a certain stage, the child is changed. The question of how the pencil is to be held is no longer in question, but there is now a dialog with recalcitrant muscles to produce a smooth motion of writing. The entire process of development can be described only through cross cuts, called "phases." The use of this term is not deceptive so long as the empirical student of man keeps in mind that *the "phase" is his own methodic idea.* Objectifications, likewise, are not harmful provided the psychologist knows that they are methodic auxiliary means. He may not forget here that "the" muscles, "the" motor mechanism, and "the" memory are also the child. They are the child insofar as in learning the child struggles with himself. They indicate a limit of his freedom, which lies within the child himself.

In the sociological realm the relationships are similar. If a sociologist, walking through a crowded quarter of a city, thinks that he can predict with a certain degree of accuracy the future social status of the children playing there,[9] his opinion does not necessarily include any determinism in the sense of Taine. All the sociologist claims is that he can determine with great probability the social conditions required for the exercise of freedom by human groups. This claim does not exclude that in principle there is a possibility for a Corsican lawyer's son to become a dictator or for an American newspaper boy to become a multimillionaire. The sociologist limits himself to observing the obstacles opposed to such a spectacular change of status. As George Gurwitsch emphasizes, "Sociology is the science of human freedom and of all the obstacles which this freedom encounters and overcomes in part. The other human sciences, whether they be called economics, law, moral sciences, anthropology, human geog-

9 Cf. E. J. Leemans, *Op de drempel van de sociologie,* Nijmegen, 1960.

raphy, or demography etc., are distinct from sociology only through the limitation of the direction taken by the effort [to overcome the obstacles] and by the selection of the obstacle to overcome. The reality studied by all these sciences is the same—namely, the human condition, viewed in the particular light thrown upon it by a specific method."[10]

A few conclusions may be drawn from all this.

1. *The reality of human freedom can neither be disproved nor proved by empirical methods, for this freedom is the basis of all human activities,* including that of pursuing science. The freedom of the researcher is primarily evident, and the validity of this primary evidence is always implicitly presupposed.

2. Even though *empirical human science* works with exact, statistical methods, it *does not imply a deterministic philosophy.*

3. Man's freedom is presupposed in all human sciences. This freedom makes the scientific discourse in question possible; consequently, it cannot be a term of this discourse. In other words, freedom is not a "factor" in the empirical sense.

4. *Empirical human science is a complex of sciences, all of which throw light on the finite aspect of human existence.* They determine the boundaries and the condition of the concrete exercise of human freedom. Thus they tell us, albeit indirectly, in what concretely the freedom of individuals and groups consists.

THE ORIENTATION OF HUMAN SCIENCE TO ITSELF. We are now sufficiently prepared to meet an especially difficult problem—namely, the fact that human science refers back to itself. The fact of this orientation to itself cannot be denied. A few examples will suffice to illustrate this.

As we have seen, archaic man lived in a "periodic time."[11] For his primitive mind the great events of primordial time kept repeating themselves. Thus the object of experience, for

[10] "Réflexions sur les rapports entre philosophie et sociologie," *Cahiers internationaux de sociologie,* vol. 22 (1957), p. 10.
[11] Cf. pp. 94 f.

the individual as well as the group, was a fixed datum. This archaic mentality, however, did not last. Sometime, somewhere mankind began to think historically. The result was that time was no longer a circle but a line; history no longer repeated itself but became travelling along a road, which is inevitably supposed to lead somewhere.[12] Once man no longer believed that the same events come back again, he began to transmit what happened first orally and then by way of writing. Briefly put, mankind began actively to pay attention to history. Inevitably this pursuit exercised influence on the course of history itself. The fact that certain human groups knew about their own, real or imagined, past and that they knew or thought they knew the purpose of history has caused the greatest historical developments. In other words, *knowledge of history has made history.*

Similar remarks apply to other human sciences. Archaic mankind lived in the conviction that the social structure was the expression of the cosmic order. It made no distinction between nature and culture. According as this archaic mentality began to disappear, man began to make a distinction between the immutable cosmos and changeable society. The laws governing society now became an object in themselves. By assuming control of society, mankind began to pay attention to sociology, in the broad sense of the term. The awareness, however, of the fact that human society is perfectible exercises influence on the course of history. For, realizing the imperfect character of his society, man looks at his social destiny quite differently from the way in which he would consider it if he were not aware of its imperfectness. In other words, *sociological ideas have codetermined social development.*

Psychology provides us with a final example. It is a well-known fact that modern man has psychology on his mind. We mean that he is aware of the existence of psychological laws. A well-known phenomenon may serve to illustrate this. While the Middle Ages did not sufficiently distinguish between "unable to believe" and "unwilling to believe," this distinction is very much present in the mind of modern western man. For

12 Cf. G. van der Leeuw, *De primitieve mens en de religie*, p. 107.

this reason religious tolerance is easier to achieve now, and man's behavior in this respect has become different. In other words, a *certain knowledge of psychology has modified the object of psychology*.[13]

The question now is *how this state of affairs has to be evaluated from the epistemological viewpoint*. How can the researcher as subject study himself as object? Has it not been stated quite clearly that we can establish facts only when we stand apart from and facing the whole in which facts are to be distinguished? Have we not claimed that this *standing-opposite-to*, at-a-distance-from is a condition required for the making of statements about facts? Where, then, is this inner distance needed for the attainment of the "second objectivity"?

Our reply to these objections is a simple denial of a presupposition contained in them. The well-known catch phrases, according to which the knowing subject cannot be at the same time the known object or the eye is unable to see itself, do not at all agree with the phenomenology of the pursuit of science. As soon as we reflect on the situation of encounter or on dialog as the fundamental situation of research about man as man,[14] important characteristics reveal themselves and make it clear that the way in which empirical human science refers back to itself is wholly different from a reflection in the sense in which this term is used in speculative philosophy. These distinguishing characteristics may be briefly indicated in the following way.

1. Man asks himself a question, but he does not ask himself as total existence. He interrogates himself in a certain respect, e.g., the historical, sociological or psychological respect.

2. Man asks himself a question, but he does not ask himself as he is but as he was. For, by raising the scientific question, man's existence has entered a new phase. All his preceding phases have now become past phases.

3. Man questions himself not as an acosmic, unhistorical, non-social spirit. The question, "Why was I who I was?" implies other persons, things, conditions and social relationships.

[13] Cf. pp. 123 ff.
[14] Cf. pp. 156 f.

Accordingly, the questioning man is not simply identical with questioned man. There is a certain distance between the two, a certain standing-opposite-to, limited though it be, and this distance suffices to give rise to the fundamental situation of a genuine encounter or an authentic dialog. In this way all the safeguards required by the "second objectivity" are present.

An analysis may serve to illustrate the point. A sociologist writing about the social conflict knows, of course, what a conflict is. He relies in this on a prescientific intuition, even though, as a sociologist, he never appeals to it in explicit fashion. Nevertheless, it is evident that without this prescientific experience he would never have thought of studying the problematics of the social conflict and of reporting about it in an understanding way.[15]

The evidence concerning the existence of human conflicts is merely the prescientific foundation. It permits the sociologist to consider reality from a formal viewpoint—viz., the viewpoint of conflict. The original choice of a formal object produces at the same time a first distance between man as questioning and man as questioned.

Secondly, the sociologist speaks about conflicts which, at the time of his research, are no longer his conflicts. For in his research he assumes the theoretical and not the practical attitude; otherwise he would not be pursuing science. Even if he has ever been personally involved in a certain social opposition, this fact pertains to a past phase of his life while he is trying to arrive at truth. The new, truth-seeking phase of his existence situates his former ardent aims, born from the conflict, in a new and scientific context and thus eliminates them.

Thirdly, empirical research is not a meditation on ideas. Our sociologist will not look, as it were, in a mental mirror to see the image of man in a conflict situation. The conflict situation cannot be described without taking into account social, economic, ethnical and juridical relations, political, cultural and religious conditions, geographical, demographic and technical data. Here, too, one will have to admit that the conflict

15 Cf. pp. 156 f.

of the free individual existence can be delineated and made concrete by empirically determining what in this conflict the free individual existence is *not*. In doing this, the empirical researcher simply presupposes the dynamism of free existence.

Accordingly, the problem of objectivity, as raised by positivists and behaviorists is a pseudo-problem. The essential orientation of the human sciences to themselves is not an invincible obstacle for their pursuit in the spirit of the "second objectivity." One restriction, however, has to be made. The student of man as man has to be resigned to an immediate consequence of this reference to itself of human science—namely, the fact that *a human science is never finished*. This incompleteness is a result of its dialectic nature. Just as, e.g., Sigmund Freud could not foresee what character western culture would assume, as co-influenced by the dissemination and popularization of psychoanalysis, so likewise is the contemporary psychologist or sociologist unable to predict what effect his own theory will produce. The only thing certain is that every human deed—and to conceive an anthropological vision is a deed —opens a new phase in the dialectic course of history, so that every subsequent pursuer of the human science in question will have to take this phase into account.

RELATIVE UNIVERSAL VALIDITY AND NECESSITY. If the phenomenological philosopher is entitled to introduce the results of scientific experience in his considerations, this right will have far-reaching consequences for his discourse. On the one hand, his descriptions will become richer, more differentiated, better attuned to concrete reality, and closer to life. On the other hand, the entire theory of primary evidences, as developed above, will need to be complemented on an important point.

While it is true that phenomenological philosophy is primarily a systematic discovery of the dialectics of existence and has to rely primarily on the corresponding primary evidences, the phenomenologist cannot be satisfied with this. He will want to apply his insights here and now to reality. But this desire implies that he has to complement the evidences of universal and necessary validity with evidences that possess only a more restricted validity.

As we have indicated, there exist structures of experience which are characteristic of man as man. But human beings are either male or female. The question of how these structures vary within the framework of male or female existence is a legitimate question even from the philosophical point of view. At least since the time of Plato there has been a philosophy of the sexes. How, for instance, does the woman experience her body, her orientation to the other, her existence in a cultural world, etc.? Such questions have to be answered, starting with general existential insights, yet in such a way that one does not rigidly cling to their universality. Buytendijk's well-known book about the woman begins with the words, "The starting point of this study has been that the woman is a human being," and he quotes with approval Paul Häberlin's saying that "the particular features of man cannot be investigated without a 'general concept' of man."[16] He then applies this methodic principle to the woman. To characterize the woman's specific mode of existence, he analyzes human intentionality. Intentionality, so it appears, reveals itself in two forms, as breaking resistance and as being-together. Starting with these two variants of intentionality, Buytendijk builds up a phenomenology of the male and female modes of existence. No phenomenological philosopher will deny that these analyses have philosophical importance. Nevertheless, Buytendijk does not formulate any absolute "a priori." There is question of universality and necessity, but only of the kind that is typical of male or female existence.

A second example may be borrowed from our own analyses. It is characteristic of man's mode of existing that the beings can be conceived as mutually connected. The whole of all meaningful connections gives rise, as we have seen, to the phenomenon of the world.[17] However, within the framework of this primary evidence it is possible to introduce a further

[16] Buytendijk, *De vrouw*, Utrecht, 1952, pp. 9 and 19. Published in German as *Die Frau*, Köln, 1953; in French as *La femme*, Bruges, 1954.

[17] Cf. p. 199.

differentiation. The mutual interconnection of the beings, which is always and of necessity presupposed, may be seen as a magic bond, as is typically done in the mythical world view of the archaic cultures. It may happen also that exclusively causal relations are recognized as real, which view would correspond with a postulate of the scientific illumination or at least of one of its phases. The formulation of such a typology of world views is not possible without data borrowed from positive anthropology, general history and history of culture. But such empirical data enable the philosopher to give a richer content to a general and rather abstract primary evidence.

These two brief analyses should suffice. We think that they have sufficiently shown that *relative universality and relative necessity also may be meaningful* for the philosopher and especially for the philosophical anthropologist. Mikel Dufrenne formulates this insight very clearly when he says: "Briefly put, certain a priori's are more universal than others."[18] The relativity of this universality does not diminish its philosophical value so long as it remains related to something non-relative. This non-relative element, we may repeat it, is found in the primarily evident insights as they flow from existence itself. The phenomenologist may, as is done, e.g., by Scheler and Merleau-Ponty, enliven and enrich his descriptions by using empirical data without giving in to empiricism. The philosopher may take this course without exposing himself to the reproach of ambiguity, provided that he knows what he is doing.

THE BOUNDARY REGION. In the preceding pages we have marked a boundary between the form of objectivity proper to the sciences of experience and that proper to philosophy and metaphysics. Attempting to stress the contrast, we endeavored to describe as distinctly as possible the essence of certain attitudes of mind. The differences, characterized in this fashion, are indeed essential. However, this statement does not

[18] *La notion d' 'a priori,'* Paris, 1959, p. 37. This shows how far the phenomenological *a priori* is removed from that of Kant. The many meanings attached to this technical term made us abstain from using it.

mean that the philosopher and the pursuer of a human science are concretely separated by a sharp boundary line. The very idea of relative universality, spoken of above, points in the opposite direction.

However, this is not all. As we have seen, the student of man as man is compelled to interpret the facts which he discovers. This interpretation, we said, will ultimately have to reach a supra-empirical level, and thus always requires an hermeneutic horizon.[19] Consequently, the empirical scientist will either have to make use of someone else's philosophical vision that is known to him or propose his own philosophical interpretation of his findings. This philosophical or also-philosophical interpretation may be prudent and modest, but it can also assume the form of a full-fledged philosophical meditation, for which the empirical data in question merely provided a suitable occasion.

On the other hand, philosophical investigations are possible which concentrate on a certain realm of human experience. Numerous examples to the point are provided by the philosophy of the sexes, of history, language, law and politics. As a rule, the philosophical insights acquired through these investigations have a less universal validity because the experiences in question are not universal. They are in fact limited, and this limitation is established by way of experience. For this reason we have given the philosopher the right to make use of those empirical data which he expertly can consider reliable.

When these conditions are taken into account, it becomes obvious that the study of man as man can be pursued also in these two forms: first, in the form of an empirical inquiry whose philosophical bearing is explicitly formulated, and secondly, in the form of a philosophical inquiry which is empirically enlightened and enriched. Concretely speaking, it may happen that the difference between the two types of anthropological studies will be very small. While such studies would actually be borderline cases, they are by no means rare. The value of such studies, likewise, should not be underestimated. There is no justification for denying that certain publications

[19] Cf. pp. 237 ff.

in the realm of the positive human sciences contain insights of great value for the philosophical anthropologist. On the other hand, there is no doubt that philosophical studies have been directly fruitful for the sciences of experience.

Accordingly, strictly speaking, there is no question of a boundary line separating philosophy from empirical human science. We come closer to the truth when we speak of a *boundary region*. By using this term, we convey the idea that, on the one hand, some pursuers of the empirical sciences, reflecting on the contents of their experience with man, have arrived at insights of philosophical importance, and on the other hand, that there are philosophers who have thrown light on the concrete existence of man in a way that has proved illuminating for the man of empirical research. Despite Comte's prophecies, there has been an encounter in this realm between the philosopher-metaphysician and the man of positive research.

Many prominent men of learning become somewhat nervous when they come within sight of the "boundary region." They would like to know "what they are supposed to be dealing with here," and ask themselves whether what is offered here is philosophy or empirical research. This dilemma is likely to lose some of its importance when it is approached from the standpoint of an hermeneutic concept of philosophy. The philosopher wants to interpret the riddle of human existence, and the student of a human science wants to make a contribution to this interpretation. The fact that the latter moves on an essentially different level and uses essentially different methods from the former does not jeopardize the identical orientation of their intentions. If the two methods are independent of each other, what is there to prevent a thinker from using both? If a philosopher throws light on the achievements of man as pursuer of science, why should he not make use of these achievements? Briefly, in itself, the external resemblance which may occur between empirical research that pays attention to philosophy and philosophical investigations that are empirically documented does not give rise to any alarm.

No *essential* objection can be raised against the close connection between philosophical anthropology and positive human science. However, this does not exclude that life in the "boundary region" has *de facto* to face certain dangers. It could even very well happen that an imperfect understanding of the nature of phenomenological philosophy would make these dangers even greater. Whether or not this is actually the case is a question that needs to be examined now explicitly.

The Possibility of Empirical Human Science

As Edmund Husserl has pointed out, the question of how science in general or any particular science is possible cannot be the first question of one who philosophizes in a radical way. Philosophy is more fundamental than science, philosophical insights are based on a special type of evidences, and philosophical objectivity cannot be simply compared with scientific objectivity. Thus it cannot be the principal task of the philosopher to conceive a theory of science. Nonetheless, it may be one of his undertakings. We have undertaken this task here with respect to a special pursuit of science, whose character is still under discussion.

One of the results of this extended and many-sided investigation may be expressed in these words: *empirical human science is possible*. It is possible not because it is actually pursued but because it *can* be pursued in a meaningful way. More specifically it can be pursued in such a way that it is empirically justified and at the same time remains human science. In other words, the terms "empirical" and "human" science do not constitute together a contradictory concept.

All the objections, raised against empirical human science from the standpoint of objectivism or from that of certain forms of existentialism, appeared to be ineffective. By way of conclusion, we may summarize here the three main objections.

THE ANTHROPOLOGICAL DILEMMA. There would really be a dilemma here if the situation were such as described by the imaginary objector.[20] True, one who pursues a human science considers human individuals and groups as founders and

[20] Cf. pp. 7 f.

workers of their surrounding world. It is true also that the culture known as "science" is a part of this surrounding world. Thus it may happen, indeed, that the scientific study of the human condition results in a change in this condition itself.

This description, however, of anthropological inquiry does not take into account the laws of dialectics. The act of theoretical wonder itself constitutes a new phase in the dialectics of human existence.[21] The very act of asking a question creates a certain distance between the new phase and the preceding phases of the individual or collective existence. Thus *enough* distance is present to give rise to the situation of an encounter. *Too much* distance between the questioner and the questioned subject would deprive the anthropological inquiry of its human character. For encounter and dialog demand a situation that is meaningful for all the persons taking part in it.[22] And *absolute* distance between two finite beings would make a cognitive act impossible in principle. Accordingly, no argument against the possibility of human science can be based on the fact that this science refers back to itself.

MAN'S FREEDOM. The difficulty drawn from man's freedom would be invincible if the description of freedom, presented by the objector, could pass as a phenomenological description. In reality, however, this description corresponds to the fancy image of freedom as ascribed by man to purely spiritual beings. With reference to these fanciful images we would like to make the following remarks. Let us assume that to be free means to be able to do whatever one wants. Since, however, human existence is a finite existence, it follows that *man cannot will everything*. He may will *this* or *that*, but he cannot will both if the one excludes the other. "To will this," moreover, means that he is willing to proceed in a certain way and to overcome an obstacle by making use of a certain means, so that he can attain *this*. In other words, willing a meaningful goal makes it appear to him as meaningful also to proceed in a certain way, to overcome a certain obstacle and to use a

[21] Cf. pp. 288 f.
[22] Cf. pp. 144 f.

certain means, for otherwise he cannot will the goal.[23] Thus free man is not as changeable as Proteus in the ancient Greek myth. On the contrary, his freedom is embedded in a whole of socially, economically and culturally determined ways, obstacles and means, which together constitute his *situation*. Thus it appears that *what free man tends to is that which is meaningful in a concrete situation.* Consequently, it is possible for one who knows the situation to construct a typology of his tendencies, of the typical obstacles he meets in his tendencies, and of the typical means he uses to overcome them. This typology may be constructed in an empirical way. By laying bare this aspect of unfreedom of the human situation, the pursuer of empirical human science makes a contribution to our knowledge of the concrete forms in which man exercises his freedom.

The objection could be raised that this aspect of unfreedom can be determined with great probability as soon as there is question of human *groups*. But what about the study of individual existences? Is it not true that here the most surprising value judgments and purposes play a role? Are not these purposes sometimes emotional and irrational? Are they not wholly unpredictable? Is not human existence capable of making true what is most improbable? These questions lead us to the third difficulty.

PURPOSE AS A PROBLEM. With respect to this difficulty, formulated at the beginning of this work,[24] we would like to make two remarks.

First of all, the individual existence cannot be compared with the existence of an acosmic, asocial and suprahistorical consciousness. Even the most eccentric individual person is involved in a concrete historical, social and cultural situation. He chooses, decides and acts within the framework of this situation. No matter how much his value judgments, purposes and projects deviate from those of the group, they are not entirely divorced from them. Even if a "revolutionary" indi-

---

[23] Cf. the concept of "necessity of the end" in Thomas Aquinas, *Summa theol.*, p. I, q. 82, a. 1 c.
[24] Cf. pp. 8 f.

vidual would deliberately go counter to the norms of the group, his behavior could still be understood as a protest against the group. In this way knowledge of the historical, cultural and social situation as well as of the group contributes to our understanding of the individual purposes and value judgments. And this knowledge is knowledge of facts, gathered by way of experience.[25]

Secondly, and this is even more important, we have pointed out that it is necessary to arrange the mass of facts meaningfully, and we have emphasized that *Verstehen* may play a very definite role in this arrangement. We have studied it in its three forms, as *prescientific intuition*,[26] as *hypothesis* or respectively *interpretation*,[27] and as *vision*.[28] With respect to the first two forms of intuitive understanding, it has been pointed out that their results may not simply be considered as true. Prescientific understanding of elementary behavior and expressions does not absolutely safeguard the correctness of this understanding; hence it is merely a starting point and not the substance of research concerning man as man. As to an hypothesis or interpretation, its correctness has to be confirmed by confronting it with the facts. Thus, these two forms of intuitive understanding simply fall under the principle of verifiability as we have re-interpreted and formulated it.[29]

The vision also is exposed to the critique of the research society. But in this case the critique will not assume the form of a verification in the narrow sense of the term. There is no question here of being factually true or false—for by definition "vision" implies knowledge of and familiarity with the entire realm of facts—but of the usefulness, scientific fruitfulness and adequacy of a certain way of viewing the facts. If this critique functions in a normal way, then every attempt of a fanciful author to say in the "language of facts" something that goes counter to the spirit of this language will be rejected as unscientific.

[25] Cf. pp. 45 f. and 48 ff.
[26] Cf. pp. 152 f.
[27] Cf. pp. 170 ff.
[28] Cf. pp. 178 ff.
[29] Cf. p. 136.

In none of these three cases does man's intuitive under-standing of man have the character of an illumination, a mystic inspiration, or an infallible revelation. On the contrary, in the discourse of the experts all insights into man as man, even those that have been gained intuitively, are communicated in humble awareness of the fact that they are subject to completion and correction. They are exposed to that form of critique which safeguards the continuity, discipline and self-control of any pursuit of science. It is in this sense that we consider ourselves entitled to conclude that human science can be pursued as an empirical science.

The Possibility of Empirical Human Science on a Phenomenological Foundation

PURIFICATION OF EXPERIENCE. If a genuinely human science can be pursued on an empirical basis, then this possibility has to be used. In this case there is no reason to substitute for the integrity of empirical research the dishonesty of a pseudo-empirical attitude, and all that really matters is to keep the pursuit of the human sciences free from all kinds of philosophical prejudices which do not flow from the very essence of the empirical sciences themselves. These philosophical prejudices may be compared with weeds. The superficial watcher of the garden does not recognize them, but the expert will distinguish them immediately from the useful plants. We have mentioned three types of these prejudices—*empiricism*, which is based on a faulty conception of the essence of experience;[30] *objectivism*, which flows from a misconception concerning the partners playing a role in experience;[31] and *scientism*, which results from a metaphysical overvaluation of empirical insights.[32]

It is greatly desirable that the research concerned with man as man be purified from all distracting pseudo-philosophical accretions, for these accretions are irrelevant to the nature of

[30] Cf. pp. 263 f.
[31] Cf. pp. 18 f., 75 f.
[32] Cf. pp. 269 f.

the empirical sciences. This statement, it should be noted, is made in reference to the nature of these intellectual realities known as the "empirical sciences," it does not express a wish to have those who pursue these sciences perform this purification. Psychologically speaking, it would be very naive to assume that the empirical scientist himself would undertake this task. For the possibilities and difficulties contained in his research situation lead very easily to the birth of the above-mentioned prejudices. It is very tempting for the man of research to conceive experience as a stream of stimuli from which knowledge arises automatically. For the formation of his theory it is very easy to suppose that the object of his study does not "act" but merely "reacts" in function of a situation known to him in all details. And being justly proud of his discoveries, he is readily tempted to attribute to his discovery an incorrect metaphysical value.

The obvious conclusion, then, is that the purification of experience from empiricist, objectivistic and scientistic prejudices cannot be the task of the empirical scientist alone.

On the other hand, there cannot be any question of giving up the empirical approach. It is simply impossible for mankind to disregard the "second objectivity" and to return to the "first objectivity" of the archaic cultures. The reasons why such a return cannot come under serious discussion have already been indicated: a deliberate primitivity is not primitive; a deliberate naiveness is not naive; a deliberate non-critique is a critique that has been artificially silenced. More generally expressed, there is no turning back on the road of dialectic experience. Mankind, which thanks to the scientific illumination has reached the level of the "second objectivity" is unable and even less willing to forget this achievement. The imposing experience of the "second objectivity," gathered over the centuries, can be eliminated only through another experience, the experience of a new intellectual reality. As Hegel says, "This new object, which entails the voiding of the former object, is the experience gained from it," i.e., gained from the former object.[33] This new "object," discovered by mankind's

[33] *Phänomenologie des Geistes*, p. 61.

dialectic experience in the course of the twentieth century, is *phenomenological philosophy.*

The purification of the human sciences from empiricist, objectivistic and scientistic prejudices is possible only through the close collaboration of those who pursue these human sciences with the phenomenological philosopher.

LIMITATION OF EXPERIENCE. In his philosophy Hegel often uses the technical term *"aufheben."* What is the meaning of this term and in what way is it connected with the problems discussed here? According to an interpretation based on Hegel himself,[34] three phases or moments should be distinguished in the act of *"aufheben,"* which may be characterized as "denial," "preservation," and "elevation." This means that the result of the former experience is, first, denied by the new experience and that its validity is corroded; that, secondly, this result is taken over and preserved; and that, thirdly, it is raised to a higher level through the new experience. When we demand here that phenomenological philosophy perform the act of *aufheben* with respect to empirical human science, we are thinking of these three "Hegelian" phases, albeit in a very special sense.

To begin with the first, what is the meaning of "denial" in connection with the problematics of this book? The "denial of the first [object is not its] destruction." The phenomenological philosopher will not destroy or eliminate the result of empirical experience, but he will draw attention to the limitation of this "first" experience. He will limit its value. He is eminently qualified to do so, for he knows the essentially different forms of intentional acts and the corresponding noemata. He is capable also of analyzing the achievements of scientific intentionality and of evaluating their scope. In doing so, he will ask himself especially what really has been experienced in the course of an empirical inquiry and what has been introduced merely as an hypothetical concept. Concretely speaking,

---

[34] See, e.g., *Die Wissenschaft der Logik,* ed. by G. Lasson, Leipzig, 2nd ed., 1932–1934, vol. I, pp. 93–95, vol. II, pp. 494–500; *Phänomenologie des Geistes,* pp. 57 f., 76 f., 121 f., 123 f.; *Enzyclopädie,* par. 82.

such a limiting critique will be concerned with two phases of the anthropological inquiry—namely, its *starting point* and the *development* of that which is contained in this starting point.

The *starting point* of the inquiry has to be a real experience concerning man and things human, even though the realm of possible experiences is conventionally limited within the framework of the human science in question. Moreover, this experience must have led to an evidence, to a first and provisional expression in words of that which was experienced. Again, this first natural evidence is not "infallible." In the course of the inquiry it may become clear that the experience is incomplete, based on a misunderstanding, or incorrectly expressed. Nevertheless, it constitutes the indispensable starting point of further inquiry. From the negative viewpoint, theories, hypotheses, models, philosophical, social or political conceptions cannot form the basis of a human science. They belong to what Husserl calls "opinions unrelated to the matter" (*sachferne Meinen*). Such "opinions" are not suitable starting points from which the pursuer of a human science can undertake his explorations.

The *further development of the inquiry* has to contain all the time the explicitation of that which is contained in the experience. This explicitation may be performed by means of interpretations, hypotheses, models and theories. However, care must be taken lest the known is "explained" through the unknown, the familiar through the hypothetical, human reality through a model of human reality. For the danger is not at all imaginary that the explaining assumes the character of a forced interpretation. As J. Lindschoten points out, "Every reconstruction of the person by way of a *model* precedes the original givenness of the person."[35] We may point here to the behavioristic explanations of the phenomena "behavior," "living being" and "situation," which, as we have seen, do violence to these phenomena.[36] Briefly, what is experienced or known may never be submitted to the Procrustean torture of a theory "unrelated to the matter."

[35] *Das Experiment in der phänomenologischen Psychologie,* lecture delivered in Bonn, July, 1955, Ms. 1955, p. 13.
[36] See above, pp. 23 f.

If the phenomenological principles regarding the choice of the starting point and the explicitation of the experiences are observed, no prejudices, such as empiricism, objectivism or scientism, will be able to exercise their confusing influence on the course of the research. In that case we can be certain that the above-demanded purification of empirical knowledge will be accomplished.

PRESERVATION OF EXPERIENCE. If the validity of something is subject to corrosion and limitation, it has to be, and if it is, it has to be recognized as being. As soon as something is recognized as being, its validity is "made true" and therefore preserved.[37]

What does this statement mean in connection with the problems facing us? It means that empirical knowledge has to be preserved as empirical, that the scientific apparatus has to be kept as scientific. This preservation is fully justified also from the phenomenological standpoint because this empirical knowledge and its apparatus, *considered in themselves,* are neither antiphenomenological nor phenomenological.

Accordingly, the experiment remains experiment, the inquiry inquiry, the medical examination medical examination, and the study of documents remains the study of documents. All the technical rules that apply to the respective methods remain in force; for instance, the rules governing statistics, medical differential diagnosis, paleography, and the historical critique of sources.

The scientific apparatus likewise remains what it is. Yet there is something that changes—namely, the attitude of the researcher with respect to the human being which he investigates. For it makes a difference whether the psychologist proceeds according to the schema of a "rat in a maze" or according to the fundamental thought of encounter. It is not irrelevant whether the sociologist, in interviewing someone, thinks that by means of sounds he has to provoke reactions from a strange organism or believes that he should have a conversa-

---

[37] ". . . das dies Aufheben sei, musz es dies Andere sein." Hegel, *Phänomenologie des Geistes,* p. 121.

tion which is meaningful both for him and for the interviewed person.

These critical remarks belong to what we have called "the purification of the human sciences from empiricist prejudices." Once more, however, considered in itself, the empirical apparatus has to remain empirical, i.e., changes and corrections in it may be demanded only on empirical grounds.

ELEVATION OF EXPERIENCE. The thesis which through the antithesis is affected in its validity but nonetheless preserved corresponds to what Hegel calls "the negation of the negation." It leads of necessity to a new unity on a higher level, i.e., to the elevation of the thesis and the antithesis to a level of higher intelligibility.

Within the scope of our inquiry the "elevation" in question refers to the last phase of research concerning man as man— the phase of *vision*.[38] It goes without saying that not every research project in the realm of human science has to culminate in a vision and even less in a relatively independent vision. What will usually happen is that most research projects are based on an *implicit* vision. This, however, does not take away from the fact that the value of a human science stands or falls with *the possibility of arriving at a justified vision*. If this possibility does not exist, then the pursuer of a human science will have to limit himself, as it were, to collecting little stones for a mosaic without ever being able to arrange them into a picture. The result would be that his study does not reach the level of a human science.[39]

As we have indicated, in the vision objectification is eliminated. The pursuit of human freedom, the free choice of purposes, the free value judgments, which were, so to speak, "frozen" in the climate of the "second objectivity," thaw under the rays of the vision. Human individuals and groups appear again as human.[40] The question is how this result can be attained in a responsible way.

[38] Cf. pp. 183 f. and 207 f.
[39] Cf. p. 210.
[40] Cf. pp. 184 f. See also Hegel, *Die Wissenschaft der Logik*, vol. II, p. 499: "Dieses Resultat hat nun als das in sich gegangene . . . Ganze sich die Form der *Unmittelbarkeit* wieder gegeben."

One thing is certain here. The formulation of a vision requires an hermeneutic horizon, an horizon which is always also of a philosophical metaphysical nature.[41] It is our contention that the hermeneutic horizon which phenomenological philosophy offers to the researcher concerned with man as man manifests itself as *essentially superior*. This contention admits that human science can be pursued also in a different philosophical perspective. For instance, it is possible to conceive a general psychological theory on the basis of a neo-Kantian,[42] neo-Hegelian[43] or personalistic[44] vision. Nevertheless, we insist that the hermeneutic horizon provided by phenomenology deserves preference. The reason why has already been indicated. It lies in the fact that *phenomenological philosophy*, and only phenomenological philosophy, *is a fundamental philosophy of human existence* and that this philosophy possesses a rigorous character. It contains in principle everything which in a universal and necessary way is valid for human existence, whether individually or collectively. The phenomenological philosopher tells us what the essential character will be of man's seeking of meaning, his aiming at purposes and his value judgments. He tells us this, albeit in very general terms, with reference to all realms of specifically human activity. By doing so, he offers the researcher of human science guidance in his understanding of the human element as such. This guidance may be compared with a skeleton, offering support to a body. It is the task of those who pursue human science to cover this skeleton with the flesh of empirical data. In this way the phenomenologist sees to it that the empirical study of human science is raised to the level of the "third objectivity." He enables the empirical student of man as man to formulate a vision which can pass scrutiny from the standpoint of "wisdom."

[41] Cf. p. 186 and pp. 237 f.

[42] Cf., e.g., Paul Natorp, *Allgemeine Psychologie nach kritischer Methode*, I Buch, Tübingen, 1912.

[43] Cf., e.g., Eduard Spranger, *Psychologie des Jugendalters*, Heidelberg, 23rd ed., 1953.

[44] Cf., e.g., William Stern, *Allgemeine Psychologie auf personalistischer Grundlage*, The Hague, 2nd ed., 1950.

TOWARD A NEW IDEAL OF SCIENCE. The light in which the phenomenological philosopher sees the phenomenon "science" differs from that of the nineteenth century scientistic thinkers. For him, scientific thinking is merely a phase in the process of mankind's growing consciousness. This thinking, moreover, is not essentially immutable, but develops dialectically and reveals alongside continuity also the discontinuity of typical phases.

It is possible that this dialectic-phenomenological view may exercise a fruitful influence at a turning point in the history of science. The turning point in question is historically characterized by this that a group of men of science more or less deliberately endeavors not to do violence to the human element when they try to determine and describe it empirically. For this endeavor implies that these pursuers of human science have de facto conceived a new norm governing the scientific character of human research. Meanwhile the theoretical justification of their new ideal of knowledge causes them great difficulties. These difficulties, however, cannot be overcome within the framework of the special human sciences. The phenomenological philosopher, who disposes of essential insights into human existence, may perhaps be able to make a contribution to the theoretical justification of the new form assumed by their scientific knowledge. Perhaps it is his role to act as "midwife" at the birth of *a new ideal of science*.

VI. SUMMARY AND CONCLUSION

Toward a Descriptive Science of Man*

JOSEPH J. KOCKELMANS

I. *Husserl's View on Phenomenological Psychology.*
Criticism and Further Development

HUSSERL'S ORIGINAL VIEW[1]

Some forty years ago Husserl spoke publicly for the first time of a new phenomenological psychology. He envisioned this new psychology as a discipline that was destined to play an important role in the already established empirical psychology as well as in philosophy. We have seen that Husserl characterizes phenomenological psychology as an aprioristic, eidetic, intuitive, purely descriptive, and intentional science of the psychical which science remains entirely within the natural attitude.[2] From this characterization it is immediately clear that phenomenological psychology, as the aprioric and eidetic study of the psychical, is distinguished from traditional empirical psychology in that phenomenological psychology is interested only in the essences of the psychical phenomena and not in facts purely as such, *and* insofar as it tries to explain these essences as unities of sense (*Sinn*) within the realm uncovered by a typical psychological-phenomenological

---

* This selection is a translation and expansion of Part III of a lecture given in Tilburg (The Netherlands) in 1964 and subsequently published in the *Tilliburgis* series ('s-Hertogenbosch: Malmberg, 1964).

[1] See for the following section: Edmund Husserl, *Phänomenologische Psychologie*. Ed. Walter Biemel (The Hague: Martinus Nijhoff, 1963); Max Drüe, *Das System der phänomenologischen Psychologie Edmund Husserls* (Berlin: Walter de Gruyter, 1963); Joseph J. Kockelmans, *Husserl's Phenomenological Psychology* (Pittsburgh: Duquesne University Press, 1967).

[2] Edmund Husserl, *op. cit.*, pp. 49–52.

reduction. Phenomenological psychology is distinguished from transcendental phenomenology because only in philosophy is a *transcendental* reduction performed.

Under the influence of Husserl's ideas about phenomenological psychology, an extensive psychological movement took place in many countries. There are, however, very few psychologists who use Husserl's insights without major modification. But the major difficulties experienced by the psychologists who read Husserl's explanations are not rooted in his view of empirical and phenomenological psychology as such, but are traceable to the transcendental phenomenology in which that view is founded. Most psychologists cannot understand and cannot accept Husserl's view on the transcendental reduction. That is why most of the psychologists who are interested in the phenomenological movement associate themselves with the existential interpretation of Husserl's phenomenology as it was given by Heidegger for the first time in 1927. Some explanation is in order.

In his discussion of the reduction as a "bracketing of Being,"[3] Husserl states that an attempt to practice the transcendental reduction, the systematic self-investigation which is made possible by it, and the uncovering of the ego's whole life of consciousness reveal that all that exists for the pure ego is constituted in itself, and that every kind of Being has its own way of constituting. After such a reduction it becomes clear that every imaginable entity, whether immanent or transcendent, falls *within* the domain of transcendental subjectivity which constitutes all sense and Being.

It is nonsense to conceive of the universe of apodictically true *Being* as something lying outside the universe of *consciousness* and related to it merely externally. Both belong together essentially, and belonging together essentially they are *concretely one,* in the absolute concretion of transcendental subjectivity. If transcendental subjectivity *is* the universe of possible sense (*Sinn*), then an outside of consciousness must be nonsense (*Unsinn*). Thus, if carried out with systematic concreteness, phenomenology is eo ipso *transcendental ideal-*

---

[3] Edmund Husserl, *Cart. Med.,* pp. 83–88.

ism. This is neither a psychological idealism which would derive a meaningful world from senseless, sensuous data (Berkeley); nor is it a Kantian idealism which believes somehow in the possibility of the world of things-in-themselves; it is a transcendental idealism as a consequently executed self-explication in the form of a systematic egological science. This is not a form of solipsism, ultimately, because in such a phenomenology it is possible to explain how the problems of intersubjectivity and the intersubjective world can be solved in a radical sense.

Be that as it may, it is not surprising that Heidegger explicitly dismisses the transcendental reduction. What he wants is to make the Being of the beings and Being itself the explicit object of the completely new ontology he wishes to create through Husserl's phenomenological method. What Husserl regarded as a necessary condition for philosophy as a rigorous science is for Heidegger the negation of an authentic philosophical attitude. In addition it does not make sense, in Heidegger's view, to reduce a human being to pure consciousness and Being to being-object. No one experiences himself as pure consciousness, but rather as a Being-in-the-world who ek-sists toward the intramundane beings.

For the moment it is sufficient to remark that according to Heidegger any phenomenon represents a suitable starting point for a phenomenological reflection. This does not mean, however, that *certain* phenomena are not *especially* suitable for such a reflection. Heidegger does not pursue phenomenology for its own sake, but wants to use it only to support an ontology. Therefore, his phenomenology is interested only in those phenomena which have a special meaning from his standpoint, that is, those which are able to enlighten us about the Being of beings. This Being, however, and Being itself in particular, usually remain hidden; it does not appear immediately. That is why it has to be disclosed and unconcealed. In Heidegger's opinion such is the primary task of phenomenology. For Husserl phenomenology is not only a complete, autonomous science, but also the only science which can absolutely and radically found all its statements independently of any other science and scientific method. For this reason phenomenology is for Husserl *the* philosophy; ontology is either phenomenology itself, or it is a system of conclusions which necessarily result from phenomenology. For Heidegger, however, the relation between ontology and phenomenology is entirely different. Heidegger is quite skeptical about the value which Husserl ascribes to pure analysis and description. He sees phenomenology not as the root and source of the whole of philosophy, but only as *the instrument of a pre-existing but still implicit doctrine.*[4]

It is evident that anyone who wants to accept a phenomenological psychology and at the same time to follow Heidegger, in one way or another, in his criticism of Husserl's transcendental phenomenology must try to find another way to explain the radical distinction between philosophy and phenomenological psychology, since "transcendental reduction" does not have any meaning for this point of view. It might be said, however, that within the context of Heidegger's explication of Husserl's phenomenology a phenomenological psychology does not make sense, because in Heidegger's fundamental ontology Husserl's transcendental phenomenology and his phenomenological psychology grow together. Since these observations are of some importance for an accurate insight into the development of contemporary phenomenological psychology, some attention must be given to them for a moment.

The careful reader will have observed that in *Phenomenology and the Human Sciences* Strasser never says that there is *a determinate discipline* called "phenomenological psychology" which should be distinguished somehow from empirical psychology in the classical sense of the term, and from philosophical phenomenology. Instead he speaks always of *an empirical psychology on the basis of philosophical phenomenology.* If I understand him properly, Strasser seems to mean that he accepts only a determinate *current or school* within the realm of empirical psychology as a whole, which insofar as

[4] Herbert Spiegelberg, *The Phenomenological Movement,* vol. I, pp. 275–83 and 283–91.

its philosophical foundations are concerned, leans on phenomenological philosophy.[5]

Sartre, on the contrary, explicitly maintains that phenomenological psychology is to be conceived of as a special discipline and not as a particular trend in contemporary psychology. He explains the difference between empirical psychology and phenomenological psychology by stating that the meaning of phenomenological psychology is to furnish empirical psychology with the necessary foundations for its empirical investigations by explaining the *human sense* (*sens*) of the phenomena with which empirical psychology deals in its observations, experiments, tests, correlations, and so forth. In reference to the relationship between phenomenological psychology and philosophy, Sartre says that phenomenological psychology is regressive in that phenomenological psychology necessarily has to take into consideration the factitiousness of man's ek-sistence, which necessitates a regular recourse to the empirical. Philosophy, on the other hand, is progressive in that the study of the very essence of man cannot be verified by a recourse to the empirical facts.[6]

To Sartre's justification of this distinction may be added Heidegger's viewpoint—that any philosophical "anthropology" is oriented ultimately toward the question of the meaning of Being, while phenomenological psychology is oriented toward an understanding of concrete human phenomena themselves. But distinguishing the two sciences does not entail that both are to be separated. On the contrary, all phenomenological psychology is and must be oriented essentially toward a philosophical anthropology in which it finds its ultimate foundation. It is apparent also that one could call phenomenological psychology, thus interpreted, "existential psychology," because philosophical anthropology, in which phenomenological psychology finds its ultimate foundation, is an analytic of human ek-sistence in Heidegger's sense.[7]

[5] Stephan Strasser, *Phenomenology and the Human Sciences*, pp. 245–48, 307–13.

[6] Jean-Paul Sartre, *The Emotions: Outline of a Theory*, pp. 18–21, 42, 92–94.

[7] Martin Heidegger, *Being and Time*, pp. 71–75.

COMPARISON. INTERIM CONCLUSION

In our comparison of these two points of view, we must first attend to some important consequences that are implicit in them. For instance, it is clear that Strasser's thesis implies a severe critique of all the psychological schools which developed between 1850 and 1940, with the exception of so-called "existential psychology." For if empirical psychology is held to be a science which must necessarily develop on the basis of and against the horizon of a philosophical phenomenology as it is interpreted by Heidegger and Merleau-Ponty, then any empirical psychology is and must be, at least implicitly, founded in a philosophical view of man and of science; and furthermore, this philosophical view of man and science is to be taken in the sense of existential phenomenology. In Sartre's view, however, phenomenological or existential psychology is a special discipline, distinguished from philosophical anthropology and empirical psychology. The insights developed in this special discipline will have a strong influence on the manner in which results of empirical investigations are interpreted, but they allow a certain freedom to empirical psychology to develop in accordance with the requirements proper to the empirical methods to be used as such, and proper to the logic and methodology in which these methods are explained and "founded."

In addition, Strasser defends the thesis that existential psychology, and only existential psychology, in contradistinction to all older schools and trends in empirical psychology, will be able to account for the *human* sense of the phenomena considered in psychology and *really* deal with *man as man*. And because it is clear, for Strasser, that the empirical methods of the sciences of nature, those formerly adopted by empirical psychology without further ado, are able neither to render an account of the human sense of the phenomena in question, nor to deal *scientifically* with *man as man*, we must search for a second type of "objectivity," for new methods of investigation, and for a completely new conceptual framework. This is contrary to Sartre's opinion that only existential psychology *as a special discipline* is to deal with *man as man* and explain the *human* sense of the phenomena brought to light by empirical psychology. He, too, would maintain that we must look for a new kind of "objectivity," a new conceptual framework, and new methods of investigation, but for him this task does not refer immediately to empirical psychology as such, nor does it affect its scientific status. Whether or not Sartre intends it explicitly, his point of view implies that the problems concerning the *methods* to be used in empirical psychology may be left to the skill of the psychologists themselves and to the scientists dealing with the logic and methodology of the different sciences; Sartre would concentrate his attention on the philosophical and methodological problems created by his *new* discipline, asking only that the psychologists, in the traditional sense of this term, respect the limits posited by the methods they have chosen. Once an existential psychology, in the sense of a special discipline, is built up, its role will be to reinterpret the results of the psychologists' empirical investigations in order to bring to the fore the *human* sense of the phenomena, and in this way to shed more light on *man as man* as already described and "understood" in existential psychological terms.

These and other consequences of Strasser's and Sartre's proposed points of view present a vital problem for which it will not be easy to find an acceptable solution. But it is a worthwhile pursuit to dwell on the subject and to try, if not concretely to solve the problem, at least to further elucidate the question itself and in the process prepare indirectly a possible solution. Such an attempt is my intention for the following section. First I shall propose a few fundamental insights into a philosophy of science conceived of in an existential phenomenological context, for I believe that only in this way, by making certain implicitly accepted insights explicit, can the problem be formulated properly. Finally, I shall make some general remarks indicating the direction in which I personally am looking for a possible solution.

II. *Psychology. Toward a Solution of Its Fundamental Problem*

1. EXISTENTIAL PHENOMENOLOGY AND SCIENCE[8]

Existential phenomenology posits an essential difference between science and philosophy, one of the most striking points of which is that science never comes to radical "thinking," while in philosophy a radical and presuppositionless comprehending is precisely what is characteristic. This fundamental difference in ways of thinking, which implies concomitantly a profound difference in method, forms an unbridgeable gap between philosophy and science. Any gradual transition from one form of knowledge to the other encounters insurmountable difficulties since there is no possibility to bridge the gap. If one wishes, nevertheless, to cross the cleft between the two, such a journey is possible only by means of a leap, an abrupt transition by means of an alteration of attitude.[9]

The sciences for the most part understand this contention of philosophy as a depreciation; and yet this is not and never has been philosophy's intention. Philosophy has no wish to speak against science, but intends just the opposite, that is, to take up the cudgels for science as part of its own search for a clear insight into the proper essence of science, since the sciences themselves are perforce unable to provide it. For a second characteristic of science, which comes to the fore immediately in any philosophical investigation of science, is precisely that it is not able to direct itself toward the essence of its own domain of inquiry. For an historian is not able as historian to unveil what the "historical" is in its very essence as long as he only and exclusively uses historical means. In like fashion a mathematician never will be able to explain the essence of the "mathematical" only and exclusively using purely mathe-

8 See for the following: Joseph J. Kockelmans, *Phenomenology and Physical Science* (Pittsburgh: Duquesne University Press, 1966), Part I, pp. 29–91; and *"L'objectivité des sciences positives d'après le point de vue de la phénoménologie," Archives de Philosophie*, 41 (1965), 171–88.

9 Martin Heidegger, *Was heisst Denken?* (Tübingen: Niemeyer, 1954), pp. 4–5.

matical expedients. The very essence of its own domain of investigation is destined to remain ever concealed for every science as such; it is the task of philosophy to ask the relevant questions and to attempt to find the answers. It is just because science does not have access to the essence of its own domain of investigation that one must say science cannot "think" in a really radical way. This statement may again make it appear that philosophy overrates itself in comparison with science. Philosophy is, however, mindful of the fact that until now it still has not succeeded in penetrating the essence of the "mathematical," of "nature," of the "historical," and so forth, and that consequently in this respect it actually knows less than science itself, which has distinguished itself for many centuries, and which, within the limits imposed on it by its methods, has already produced extremely important results. But notwithstanding all of this, it is and continues to be true that science is one-sided in the sense that it is not able to ponder the essence of the objects about which it speaks, as long at least as it remains faithful to its own character as a science. The fact that science has made such important strides in its own domain of investigation is precisely the reason that it sometimes forgets its own one-sidedness. Its history of successes has sometimes made science think it could arrogate the rights of philosophy to itself. But this "positivism" or "scientism" is completely unacceptable since it is, in fact, impossible to put philosophy and science on the same level.[10]

A third point that comes to light when one investigates seriously the essence of science is the fact that science always takes its starting point in certain presuppositions which it itself is not able to found, at least not in a really radical way. Philosophy, on the other hand, does not wish to found itself on the insights of science or on other presuppositions.

A final characteristic of contemporary science is found in the fact that for science, all-that-is appears only in the objectivity which is constituted and maintained in and by the objectivations of the various sciences themselves. This characteristic calls for further explanation; such an explanation

[10] *Ibid.*, p. 49, and pp. 56–58.

will be undertaken forthwith where we hope also to have an opportunity to elucidate the first three contentions concerning the essence of science and for founding them in a more convincing way than has been possible thus far.[11]

First we must point out that existential phenomenology attempts to explain the very essence of our human condition by means of the notion "ek-sistence." This term signifies (as we have seen) that man is an ek-sisting "subject" which places itself outside of itself in the world, which stands out (ek-sists) toward the intramundane beings and toward the world itself. Thus man is essentially, and is nothing else than, a project of the world. There is nothing in man which escapes from his Being-in-the-world.[12] Every mode of our ek-sistence is a manner of our living-the-world. Heidegger indicates the *original mode* of our ek-sistence by the term "concern"; originally man is fascinated by the world with which he is concerned.[13] Then in theoretical knowledge man achieves a new status-of-being toward the world. This new possibility can develop itself autonomously; it can become a task to be accomplished and as scientific knowledge it can even take over the role of guiding our Being-in-the-world. But even then, the "commercium" of the "subject" with the world is not created for the first time by theoretical knowledge: knowing is a mode of man's ek-sistence which is founded upon his Being-in-the-world itself.[14]

Thus theoretical knowledge is only a special mode of our Being-in-the-world. The characteristic proper to this mode of Being-in-the-world is that man confines himself to observing the world in a way that leaves him no longer completely engaged in it. In this "contemplation" there is already a certain stand of man in regard to the intramundane beings; and cor-

[11] See for the following: Martin Heidegger, *Holzwege* (Frankfurt a.M.: Klostermann, 1950), pp. 69–104 (passim).

[12] Martin Heidegger, *Being and Time*, pp. 67–68, 78–86; Maurice Merleau-Ponty, *Sens et Non-Sens* (Paris: Nagel, 1948), pp. 142–43; *Phénoménologie de la perception* (Paris: Gallimard, 1945), p. *xiii*, 466; W. Luypen, *Existential Phenomenology*. Trans. H. J. Koren (Pittsburgh: Duquesne University Press, 1960), pp. 15–19.

[13] Martin Heidegger, *Being and Time*, pp. 225–44.

[14] *Ibid.*, pp. 86–90.

relatively the intramundane beings which are encountered in this way are always considered from a certain point of view. The aspect of the intramundane beings which uncovers itself to man in his theoretical attitude depends on the original attitude of man toward those beings. The moment a man in his theoretical knowledge takes such an aspect as the object of his critical and methodical investigation, he lays the foundation of a determinate science.

Every scientist, by his attitude toward the given reality, begins to delimitate a certain region of the intramundane as his proper object of investigation and research.[15] The delimitation and the exact fixation of a well-defined domain of investigation is effectively the beginning of all scientific research. This delimitation of a definite region of beings is materialized in and by a *thematization* by means of which in a primordial way a certain aspect of those beings is taken as the theme of investigation, and as such is constituted and projected. It is by such a project (*Entwurf*) that the access to the proper domain of a science acquires its methodic directives, that the structure of the conceptual and discursive explanation acquires its first orientation, and that, finally, a proper language is progressively constituted. Thematization, therefore, comprises: the original project of the object of investigation as such, the delimitation of the domain of research, the determination of the methods to be used, the first orientation of the conceptual and discursive structure, and the linguistic means of expression.

Whoever applies himself to an empirical science begins first by adopting a *theoretical* attitude. He disengages himself from his primordial orientation toward the world in which he lived as long as he had not yet applied himself to science, and in which he was totally engaged in the surrounding world (*Umwelt*) of his everyday concern. But now he wants to "observe" and to "contemplate," and when he assumes this new attitude toward the world, the world itself changes from the world in which he had been living into an "objective world." Science must therefore be defined as a "theory of the real,"

15 *Ibid.*, pp. 408–15.

on the condition, however, that we understand clearly and correctly the present meaning of the words "theory" and "real." The term "real" signifies everything which makes something to be, which constitutes it; but it means also that which has been constituted and is now present. In each case the word "real" expresses that, that which it indicates has as its proper characteristic, that it accedes to full light, abides there, and "is." It is essential to all that to which man gives birth that it reveal itself and that it remain in full light. Characteristic of contemporary science is its bringing to light of intramundane beings in such a way that "reality" appears as "objectivity": for contemporary science, reality is identical with being-object-for. In Greek philosophy the word "theory" placed the stress, at first, on the passive element in the contemplative gaze of man's dealing with intramundane beings in a theoretical way. Nowadays the emphasis is on the active element involved. Whoever considers something in a theoretical way begins by "elaborating" that which he will later contemplate: thus, by constituting it in a state of objectivity, he isolates it from everything else.

Next we must consider in detail the *thematization* by means of which a certain aspect of the intramundane beings or a certain group of them is taken, in a primordial way, as the theme of investigation, and as such is constituted and projected. Such a thematization comprises different steps, the first of which is known as the demarcation of the domain or region of intramundane beings which are to be the subject matter of the science in question, and the determination of the formal aspect under which they will be investigated. This must go hand-in-hand with so-called formalization, functionalization, and quantification. *Formalization* is to be understood here as the description of beings or events in regard to their formal properties, so that formalization necessarily implies a certain abstraction of some "material" or "content-like" moments in preference to a group of formal characteristics. *Functionalization* refers to the consideration of formalized phenomena in function of other formalized phenomena according to the general scheme "if p then q," a scheme which is already employed in the realm of our everyday concern in a non-formalized manner.[16] Formalization and functionalization give the scientist the possibility of describing phenomena with the help of rules and laws within the general perspective of the scheme "if—then."

It is evident that the accuracy of our knowledge of the phenomena in question will depend on the precision with which their conditions are known. The degree of exactness attainable in all empirical science is determined by the subject matter and the thematizing project, that is to say by the type of formalization which this subject matter allows and permits within the realm of a determinate thematizing project. *Quantification* by means of which these conditions are described with the help of numbers, becomes one special mode of formalizing functionalization. Such a quantification, by means of which a very high degree of exactness can be attained, is, within certain limits imposed by the character of the subject matter and the thematizing project in question, possible in every empirical science in an analogous way. In this way the original phenomena are reduced to a so-called *reductive model* which is more or less abstract in comparison to the original, given phenomena.[17]

The scientific attitude is thus rooted in a certain thematization. This thematization opens many possibilities to the theoretician. The region of intramundane beings that forms the subject matter of a certain science, and also the formal aspect that will be envisioned, depend on the proper character of the thematizing project. But whoever dedicates himself to empirical science wants to question a certain region of intramundane beings under a determinate *comparable* aspect within the general perspective prescribed by the scheme "if—then." By this decision he thematizes these beings in such a manner, and constitutes them as objects in such a way that they can no longer be interrogated, except in a manner already determined in principle by the thematizing project.

By this new human attitude, which consists in *not* wanting to interrogate intramundane beings except under their com-

[16] *Ibid.*, pp. 410–12.
[17] Jan Linschoten, *Idolen van de psycholoog* (Utrecht: Bijleveld, 1964), pp. 33–37.

parable and even "measurable" aspects, the scientist projects a field or domain of sense (*Sinnfeld*) within which only beings of a well-defined kind can figure, that is to say, beings which have either countable or measurable aspects. "To be count-able" and "to be measurable" are the formal aspects of all intramundane beings, insofar as they are the objects of the attitude toward the world proper to empirical science. These characteristics of being countable and measurable are not "objective" properties of "objective" things which as such must exist independently of the counting and measuring man in a world, "by and in itself," for there is not such a world. They are but invitations which are addressed to man, modalities in which man can encounter those beings. Now the intra-mundane beings *insofar as* they are immediately or mediately countable and measurable constitute for empirical science the "region" of scientific investigation. If the scientist restricts himself only to the necessary demand of considering these beings and their events solely and exclusively in the light of this fundamental conception, his demonstrations will possess a solid form and will attain the exactitude so characteristic of empirical science.

The original project determines also the orientation which research must take in reference to the question of the concrete methods to be used, that is to say in reference to the formaliza-tion and functionalization to be employed. For if the domain of investigation must be objectivated in its entirety, then it will be necessary to bring this domain to light, down through all its layers and ramifications. As it so happens, the intramundane beings are in a constant state of change and evolution or de-velopment. The necessity is, therefore, that the scientist keep abreast of this development and never lose sight of it. For it is only in the perspective of the becoming of the changeable beings that the plenitude of their facticity becomes manifest. And it is precisely these "facts" that ought to be objectivated. Empirical science, therefore, in all its scientific procedures, will have to represent the changing beings in their development and evolution. The characteristic of remaining identical to themselves that these "facts" possess, notwithstanding the con-tinuity of their evolution, constitutes what we call *"regularity,"* while the continuity of the change in its inexorable evolution constitutes what we call *"law."* It is, therefore, only in the perspective of regularity and law that "facts" are intelligible. The analysis of "facts" always implies the elaboration and verification of rules and laws. But neither the laws, nor the experiences founding them, furnish a scientific comprehension of those "facts." Scientific comprehension requires further that the necessary relations between "facts" and "laws" be made evident. But since the "facts"—because of the quantification necessarily implied in formalizing functionalization—can speak only by means of the "measuring instruments," and since the laws can furnish only relations between numbers yielded by those "measuring instruments," it is mathematics alone which, in virtue of this original attitude of empirical science toward intramundane beings, can give access to the comprehension of the objects thus constituted. In its turn the mathematical procedure must take its starting point from experiences and laws in order to return ultimately to other experiences or experiments which either confirm or invalidate the ultimate findings. Experiences, experiments and mathematical procedures are therefore essential to the method of all empirical science. It is evident from the foregoing that expressions such as "quantification," "measurement" and "measuring instruments" have very broad and analogous meanings; the term "measuring instrument," for instance, can comprise the weighing with a pair of scales as well as a mental test.

In sum we may say that in interrogating the intramundane beings, man always assumes a well-determined attitude which is completely different from that of his spontaneous life wherein he is totally engaged in the intramundane beings of his surrounding world (*Umwelt*). But even in the original contact between man and the different intramundane beings, they impose themselves on him as beings which possess "quantitative aspects" of some kind or other. This being "quantitative," in its different modalities, invites us to make comparisons. In the horizon of a formalizing functionalization the comparison becomes immediately counting and measuring from the moment man ties this comparison to certain norms. Counting and measuring, which are but special forms of questioning the world, provide us with numbers which again invite man to compare. And this leads to laws which are mathematical relations between numbers yielded by counting or measuring. In turn a great number of laws invites man to order them with the help of mathematics; and in this process theories are formed which can be controlled through checks on their validity as to the facts in question by having recourse to representations or models of a different order from that of pure mathematics. But in this procedure as a whole it is man who, interrogating the intramundane beings, looks for relations and establishes them wherever the beings invite him to discover them. This is why numbers, laws, and theories do not furnish an "objective" description of "objective" qualities of things in a world "in itself"; numbers, laws, and theories arise only through the scientist's intentional "involvement" in the world. This is the reason, also, why the results of measurements, laws, and theories are valid only within the realm of the domain-of-sense constituted by the typical mode of intentionality which constitutes fundamentally the various empirical sciences.

It can be seen that this method also imposes on the empirical sciences an appropriate *language* and symbolism without which the objects which are to be investigated cannot be represented in their proper physiognomy. In the final analysis, however, all this is already determined by the original thematizing project, as has been pointed out previously.

Similarly the ideas of *truth* and *certitude* are already determined in their very roots by the original thematization. Existential phenomenology situates the truth of science neither in an internal relation between a series of concepts and statements, nor in a faithful reflection of a pre-given order of "facts" belonging to a world "in itself"; nor is this truth to be described as an agreement between knowledge and reality, with "reality" understood as something which is "in itself." An assertion of empirical science is true as long as the scientist interrogates the intramundane beings in the way in which these beings, within the framework of the typical intentional mode in question, are to be interrogated. As long as the intramundane beings continue to give fully meaningful answers to the questions which the scientist poses to them, the questions and answers of science remain true. An assertion of science is true, therefore, as long as an experience or an experiment confirms its presumptions born in function of a certain theory. All subsequent experiences or experiments may confirm this truth; but they may also demonstrate in a convincing way that the intramundane beings are alien to this form of interrogation.

It is in the constraining character of the answers furnished by the intramundane beings that existential phenomenology sees one of the essential arguments in favor of the *certitude* and exactness so typical of the empirical sciences. Beyond this the certitude seems to be the necessary consequence of the schematization and idealizing abstraction proper to the formalizing functionalization as practiced in the empirical sciences, which, in turn, renders possible the utilization of mathematics, the exact science *par excellence,* for a further consideration of the objects of investigation thus constituted. It is of course presupposed here that in all of these operations the scientist remains within the horizon of the domain-of-sense which is constituted by the original thematizing project.

Although in this way "reality" manifests itself to man exclusively by means of the original thematizing project within the horizon of the domain-of-sense proper to each particular science, science is objective because it keeps to the "facts," because it abstains from all "subjective" prejudices, and because it does not appeal to any uncontrollable a priori. It is objective also insofar as its statements possess an intersubjectively valid signification, on the condition that it adheres to the demands of the method determined by the thematization in question.

2. EMPIRICAL PSYCHOLOGY AND DESCRIPTIVE PHENOMENOLOGY OF MAN

In the preceding section the existential-phenomenological view on science was discussed with the help of terms and expressions customarily associated with those sciences which have attained a relatively high degree of excellence for quite some time, namely the empirical sciences of nature. What was said, however, holds true in an analogous way for all empirical sciences. In every individual science the terms "theory," "reality," and "objective" have their own specific significations, but each science endeavors to bring to light, faithfully and objectively, an isolated and well-defined aspect of intramundane beings. Each science projects its scientific "world" in its own way. All the "worlds" constituted in this way are different, and one is not more true than the other, at least in principle. But there is a bond which unites them despite their differences. This bond must not be conceived of as the kind which exists, for instance, between the pieces of a puzzle, as if the reassembly of those "worlds" would yield the total and "real world." The bond among those "worlds" consists in their all having been born from the world immediately lived by the community of men. Thus, despite their relative independence it is very difficult and sometimes impossible to clearly demarcate the frontier between adjacent sciences such as physics and chemistry, biochemistry and biology, physiology and psychology, psychology and sociology, and so on. The domains of investigation overlap, as all scientists admit, because in each instance the domains of sense are constituted with the help of an essentially identical method.[18]

Existential phenomenology, following Husserl, Heidegger, Jaspers, and Sartre, defends the point of view that the empirical sciences of man try to explain certain, at least in principle exactly demarcated, aspects of man's life taken individually or socially, by reducing them to legitimacies which are universally valid and intersubjectively acceptable as such. This necessarily presupposes formalization, functionalization, and quantification, which as forms of reduction lead to reductive models objectively describing certain aspects of man's life.[19]

If we accept this point of view, then as a necessary consequence we must also defend the thesis that an empirical science of *man as man*, or an empirical study of *man as person*, is impossible. An empirical science of man, because of the restrictions necessarily imposed by the methods to be used, has

18 *Ibid.*, p. 403.
19 *Ibid.*, pp. 24–38.

to restrict itself to the *quantifiable* aspects of man's existential orientation toward the world, in which expression the term "quantifiable" has a very broad and analogous meaning.

It is often said that such a point of view would also imply necessarily that every empirical science of man must leave outside the competence of a strictly scientific method considerations such as those dealing with the existential orientation of man toward the world *as such*, and cannot explain why it is that our ek-sistence has sense and value. For according to this point of view empirical science has to treat abstractly the fact that every concrete orientation toward the world is intentional, purposeful, and of a typical finality; and even if such an empirical science were somehow able to take those aspects of human behavior into account, it would never be able to describe them in the way they are experienced by us. Furthermore, according to the present argument, any empirical science of man has to set aside as imponderable our gestures and our linguistic behavior in their function as expressions of our emotions and meanings.[20]

Every phenomenologist defending the point of view outlined above is aware that an objectifying thematization, necessarily including formalization, functionalization, and quantification, will lead to a reductive model which is relatively poor in comparison with the concrete existential orientation toward the world and the immediately lived experience as such. But here we must realize that *every possible* kind of theoretical knowledge is unable to describe and to explain the *concrete as concrete*. Furthermore, in representing man's existential orientation toward the world with the help of reductive models, we must, indeed, set aside certain aspects of man's life which seen concretely are of the greatest importance; but we must realize, too, that in this way we gain the possibility of defining unambiguously certain aspects of man's "behavior" and of describing it in connection with other quantified phenomena. Finally, it certainly is not true that an empirical investigation has to set aside completely human phenomena such as meaning, intentionality, purpose, finality, and gestures and linguis-

[20] Stephan Strasser, *op. cit.*, pp. 11–17, 25–28, 56–62.

tic behavior as expressions of emotions and meanings, as can be shown easily with the help of modern literature (for instance in the studies on personality measurements, character tests, etc.) in which it is apparent that under certain conditions these aspects of man's orientation toward the world can be quantified in an indirect way.[21]

All of this, however, does not mean that an existential phenomenologist defending this point of view is insensitive to the problems and dangers to which the opponents of this view *really* intend to point: if the point of view defended here necessarily implied that we must return to what Husserl called "physicalization" of the sciences of man and to "naturalism,"[22] I would not refrain from adopting another point of view. But I do not see that this is the case. Obviously the meaning of the thesis defended here is not to reduce all science of experience to one single empirical science, all objectivity to the objectivity of the physical sciences, and all forms of verification to the criterion of an essentially univocal empirical verifiability, of all possible scientific languages to one identical language. I certainly agree with the statement that language, method, and system of concepts are not neutral technical means that can be used to express everything, nor is it my intention to defend the thesis that in psychology, for instance, we should return to a "stimulus-response behaviorism," forgetting all else. I can agree with the statement that physics is not the model science par excellence to be followed in empirical research in general, but I do not see in what sense the conceptual framework, method, and scientific apparatus of psychology should be *essentially* different from those of physics, and that the consequences of the point of view defended would consist in the sacrifice of psychology to the empirical method and that the goal of that science would be given up for the approach.[23]

Indeed, in a certain sense "physicalism," "objectivism," "naturalism" in psychology are unacceptable. The terms

---

[21] Jan Linschoten, *op. cit.*, pp. 24–38.

[22] Edmund Husserl, *"Philosophie als strenge Wissenschaft,"* *Logos* 1 (1910–11), 289–314, pp. 319–22 and 298–302.

[23] Stephan Strasser, *op. cit.*, pp. 21–26.

"methodical" and "logical" are not identical with "physical," and the term "scientific" is not identical with "being in accordance with the laws of methodology and logic *insofar* as these laws are factually applied in physics." But this does not mean that psychology could be an empirical science in a way which is *essentially* different from that which has developed in the physical sciences. Though we reject "naturalism," we nevertheless defend the possibility of a really *scientific* empirical psychology in which the laws of logic and methodology will be strictly observed and in which mathematics, provided it is not too one-sidedly conceived of as a scientific study of the quantitative in a limited sense, will play an important role. We require only that the methods to be used be adapted to the essential demands of the subject matter which is to be investigated. If this condition is fulfilled, the methods used in empirical psychology will not be identical with the methods used in physics, but they will not be essentially different either.[24]

However, we want to defend with Husserl and Sartre the necessity of a descriptive phenomenological study of man, which as a not yet philosophical discipline has to occupy a place and to play an important role in the realm between empirical psychology and philosophical anthropology. The desirability and even necessity of such a new discipline was earlier defended by Mach, Brentano, Stumpf, and others, and it would not be too difficult to adapt their demands to the point of view defended in the preceding paragraphs. Although it is the opinion of many phenomenologists that the function ascribed by Husserl and Sartre to this new discipline could be fulfilled by a philosophical anthropology in the style proposed by Heidegger in his existential analytic, and by Merleau-Ponty, it is my opinion that it is preferable not to reduce this descriptive phenomenology to philosophical anthropology. First of all, I think that the function of the new discipline does not presuppose an explicit orientation toward the question of Be-

---

[24] F. J. Buytendijk, *"Die Bedeutung der Phänomenologie Husserls für die Psychologie der Gegenwart," Husserl et la pensée moderne.* Ed. H. L. Van Breda et J. Taminiaux (The Hague: Martinus Nijhoff, 1956), 78–98, pp. 78–82.

ing, which, provided it is understood in the right way, is in my estimation the only fundamental philosophical question.[25] Furthermore, it is evident that the desirability and necessity of such a discipline was defended in the foregoing paragraphs only on methodological grounds. For my part I do not see any reason to draw conclusions from these considerations which would imply that every scientist should adopt an existential phenomenological point of view in philosophy. For if it were really true that empirical psychology necessarily requires on purely methodological grounds a phenomenology of man, understood as a philosophical discipline, then empirical investigation as such would be possible and legitimate only within the horizon of an existential phenomenological philosophy; and that is clearly nonsense. But whatever philosophical standpoint a scientist implicitly or explicitly adopts in addition to his empirical investigations as such, he still needs a descriptive phenomenology, especially in the realm of the sciences of man. For first of all, the scientist dealing with the sciences of man must be able to demarcate exactly the requirements of his empirical methods in order to be really able to investigate man's existential orientation toward the world as regards its essential structure and its typically human modifications. Furthermore, in summarizing the conclusions to which his investigations lead him, the scientist must try to reinterpret the results of his empirical investigation in terms of the immediately lived world in order to restore human sense to those results.

The method of such a new discipline cannot consist exclusively of what Husserl called the method of free variation[26] because this method in itself is not suitable for the purposes for which it is to be employed. I believe that in this science we must go in the direction of Merleau-Ponty's "existential analyses," or probably even more to the point, in the direction of Heidegger's *hermeneutical interpretation,* precisely because

[25] Martin Heidegger, *Was ist das—die Philosophie?* (Pfullingen: Neske, 1956); Joseph J. Kockelmans, *Over de zin der wijsbegeerte* (The Hague: Lannoo, 1964).

[26] Edmund Husserl, *Phil. str. W.,* pp. 315–19; *Ideas,* pp. 48–51, 180–84; *Cart. Med.,* pp. 103–6; *Phän. Psych.,* pp. 72–87.

of the temporal and historical aspects necessarily inherent in human behavior as such.[27]

Finally I wish to call attention to the fact that existential phenomenology does not defend the necessity of a descriptive phenomenology as a new science between empirical psychology and philosophical anthropology because there is a gap to be filled up between empirical psychology and the psychological praxis in which the results of empirical investigation are supposed to be applied to practical situations and problems and to concrete "cases." There are many younger psychologists who do not know how they are to apply the results of their scientific investigation in the realm of man's orientation toward the world to the situations and problems they meet in their everyday work in their respective areas. I think the gap they talk about really exists, but I do not believe it is the task of a descriptive phenomenology to fill it. In my opinion this is the task of a certain "art," and not one of a scientific, theoretical discipline.

[27] Martin Heidegger, *Being and Time*, pp. 58–63, 178–79, 188–95; Maurice Merleau-Ponty, *Phénoménologie de la perception*, pp. 158–60. See also: H.-G. Gadamer, *Wahrheit und Methode. Grundzüge einer philosophischen Hermeneutik* (Tübingen: Niemeyer, 1960); Stephan Strasser, *op. cit.*, pp. 231–40, 249–51.

I

ANCHOR BOOKS

PHILOSOPHY

Philosophy (continued)

ANCHOR BOOKS

RELIGION

ANCHOR BOOKS

SCIENCE AND MATHEMATICS